INSIDERS' GUIDE® TO

BRANSON
AND THE OZARK MOUNTAINS

HELP US KEEP THIS GUIDE UP TO DATE

We would love to hear from you concerning your experiences with this guide and how you feel it could be improved and kept up to date. Please send your comments and suggestions to:

editorial@GlobePequot.com

Thanks for your input, and happy travels!

INSIDERS' GUIDE® TO

BRANSON
AND THE OZARK MOUNTAINS

SEVENTH EDITION

FRED PFISTER

All the information in this guidebook is subject to change. We recommend that you call ahead to obtain current information before traveling.

INSIDERS' GUIDE®

Copyright © 2002, 2004, 2006, 2009 by Morris Book Publishing, LLC
Previous editions of this book were published by Falcon Publishing, Inc. in 1997, 1999, and 2000.

Interior Design: Sheryl Kober
Maps: XNR Productions, Inc. © Morris Book Publishing, LLC
Layout Artist: Maggie Peterson

ISSN 1539-3550
ISBN 978-0-7627-5028-3

Printed in the United States of America
10 9 8 7 6 5 4 3 2 1

CONTENTS

Directory of Maps

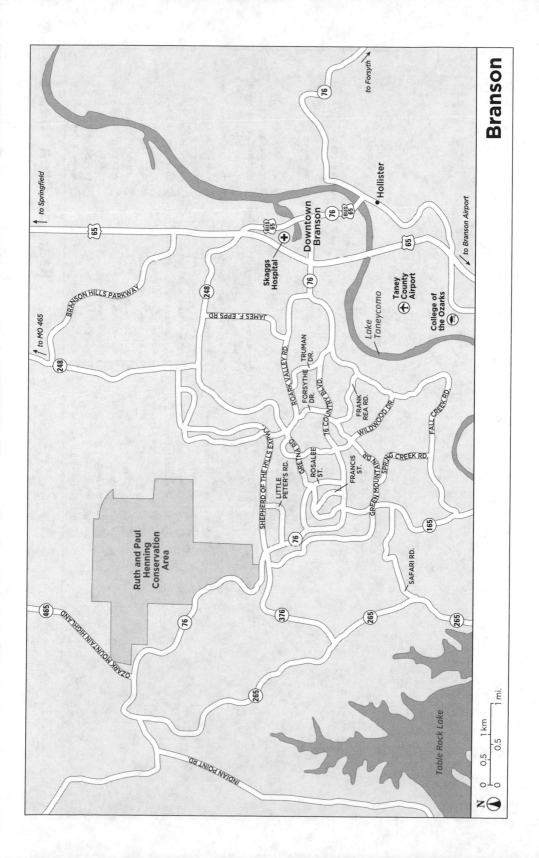

Branson

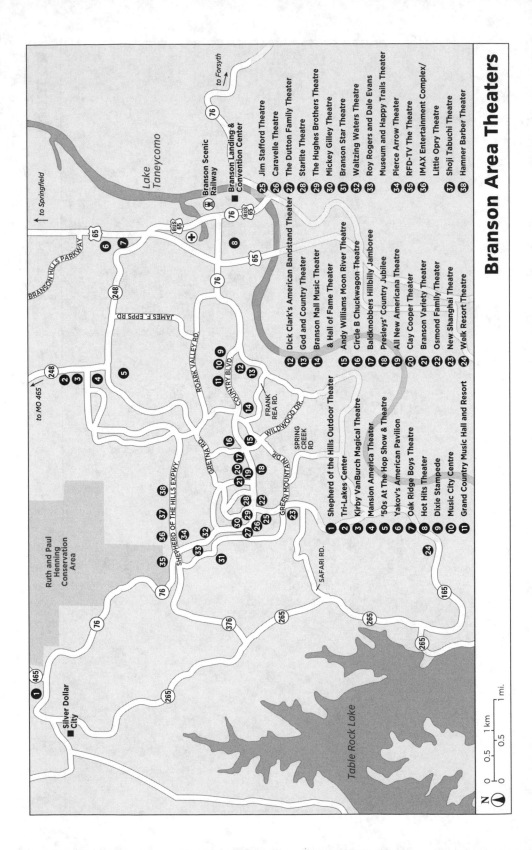

Branson Area Theaters

1. Shepherd of the Hills Outdoor Theater
2. Tri-Lakes Center
3. Kirby VanBurch Magical Theatre
4. Mansion America Theater
5. '50s At The Hop Show & Theatre
6. Yakov's American Pavilion
7. Oak Ridge Boys Theatre
8. Hot Hits Theater
9. Dixie Stampede
10. Music City Centre
11. Grand Country Music Hall and Resort
12. Dick Clark's American Bandstand Theater
13. God and Country Theater
14. Branson Mall Music Theater & Hall of Fame Theater
15. Andy Williams Moon River Theatre
16. Circle B Chuckwagon Theatre
17. Baldknobbers Hillbilly Jamboree
18. Presleys' Country Jubilee
19. All New Americana Theatre
20. Clay Cooper Theater
21. Branson Variety Theater
22. Osmond Family Theater
23. New Shanghai Theatre
24. Welk Resort Theatre
25. Jim Stafford Theatre
26. Caravelle Theatre
27. The Dutton Family Theater
28. Starlite Theatre
29. The Hughes Brothers Theatre
30. Mickey Gilley Theatre
31. Branson Star Theatre
32. Waltzing Waters Theatre
33. Roy Rogers and Dale Evans Museum and Happy Trails Theater
34. Pierce Arrow Theater
35. RFD-TV The Theatre
36. IMAX Entertainment Complex/ Little Opry Theatre
37. Shoji Tabuchi Theatre
38. Hamner Barber Theater

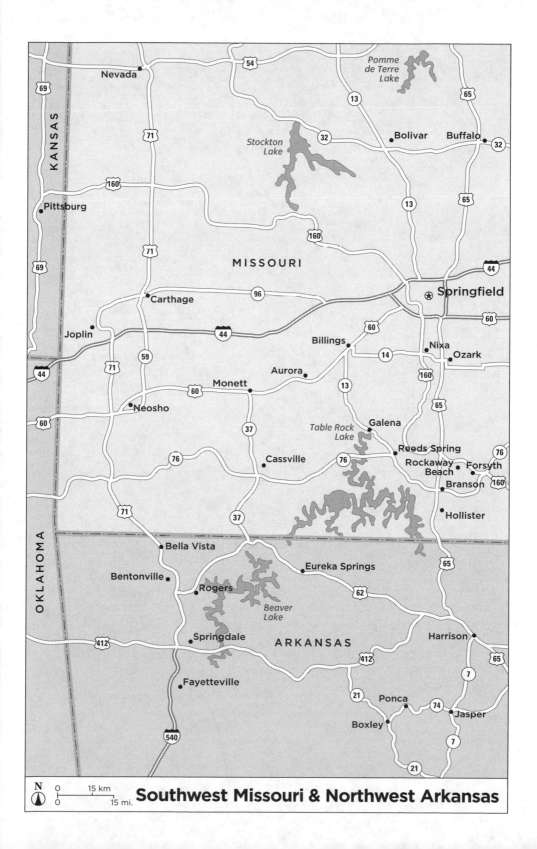

Southwest Missouri & Northwest Arkansas

PREFACE

Chances are that if you've picked up this book you have one of two questions. If you've never heard of Branson, you're probably wondering where it is. If you have heard of it but have never been here, you probably want to know what it is. Then again, if you have been here before or already live here, congratulations! You can skip the formalities and get right to the meat of the book.

The answer to the first question is easy. Branson is within a day's drive of half the country's population. For some folks with a fear of flying, that's important. More specifically, Branson is in south-central Missouri, about 12 miles north of the Arkansas state line and 39 miles south of the state's third-largest city, Springfield. Now, the answer to the second question is a little more complicated. Some call Branson the "live music capital of the world," and others think of it as a small rural town. Ironically, both descriptions apply to Branson and Ozark Mountain Country. We have 35 live-performance theaters and an annual visitor count of about eight million, yet our city population is just over 7,000. Nationally known performers such as Andy Williams, Jim Stafford, Les Brown, Mickey Gilley, the Lennon Sisters, Sons of the Pioneers, and Mel Tillis all call this place home. When Branson hosted the Miss USA Pageant, the town had a worldwide audience. And yet when you pick up a copy of our local newspapers, the *Branson Tri-Lakes Daily News* or the *Taney County Times*, you'll find out real fast that the small-town mentality is alive and well in Branson. With front-page headlines like "Flowers are planted for city," "Flood washes out low water bridge," and "Operation Shoebox comes to Branson," it's easy to see that Branson is nothing like other major tourist destinations around the country. It truly is a place where music stars, hillbillies, and everyone in between sit down at the same dinner table.

In the pages that follow, we attempt to provide you with the answers to the question "what is Branson?" We'll tell you about the music stars and their constant game of musical theaters. We'll tell you how to land a trout on Lake Taneycomo, one of the premier trout-fishing spots in the country. We'll explore the history of the Bald Knobbers and share some not-so-flattering stories about the area's notorious outlaws. If we've stumped you with the word *hillbilly*, we'll clear that up in the History chapter. We've got information on how to maneuver your way through traffic on The Strip, the Red Route, the Blue Route, and the Yellow Route. We'll tell you about our new airport and how you may now fly to Branson. We'll introduce you to the nearby towns of Reeds Spring, Forsyth, Hollister, and Springfield in Missouri and Eureka Springs and Mountain View in Arkansas.

If you're thinking about moving to Branson, we have information on the current real-estate climate. We've got listings for many of the area's schools and child-care centers. Retirees will find information on housing, health care, and social organizations. You'll find out everything from which hotels let kids stay free to how Table Rock Lake was formed to which of our championship golf courses the locals like best.

We will tell you about the people, both past and present, who have become icons for the Ozarks. You'll get to know Harold Bell Wright, author of *The Shepherd of the Hills*; artist Rose O'Neill, creator of the famous Kewpie doll; and entrepreneur Mary Herschend, who opened Silver Dollar City some 50 years ago, to name just a few.

When you visit Branson, you'll come face-to-face with the people who keep the wheels turning every day. It's the front-desk clerks, restaurant servers, theater ushers, fishing guides, and Duck captains who embody the true spirit of Ozark Mountain hospitality. One of the things visitors comment on is the friendly attitude of the folks who live and work here. We even have a hospitality training program for area employees, sponsored by a company called Branson Hospitality, Inc. It provides incentives for employees who go out of their way to make guests feel welcome and appreciated. Don't think that the big music stars are above this kind of service either. Most of them sign autographs and pose for pictures after the shows. They even board motor coaches to chat with visitors, and they routinely host charity events.

If you get lost in our maze of side streets or break down on US 65, a local will come along soon enough, or another visitor will most likely lend a hand. It seems as if Branson attracts the kind of person who knows and practices the golden rule. People who come to hear the smooth sounds of the Les Brown Band or the sweet gospel music of Barbara Fairchild are hardly the kind of people to pass by someone in need.

The "powers that be" have done everything possible to ensure that Branson remains the kind of place where veterans are honored, where kids can play in the parks without having to be fingerprinted first, and where crimes are so rare that you seldom hear about burglaries or other violent acts. Local businesspeople, church leaders, and politicians have opposed the introduction of gambling at every turn and have been successful, for the most part, in keeping out adult-oriented book and video stores. It's highly unlikely that you'll hear a single off-color remark on any stage in Branson—but you might hear some "outhouse jokes" that poke fun at ourselves. Many of the theaters host free Sunday morning gospel services where local singers and musicians provide the entertainment while a touring minister or speaker leads the program.

Branson is not just a place for golden girls and guys. While we do have our share of entertainers who know the better side of 60 and who primarily appeal to folks of the same age, we have plenty of attractions for young adults and children. Silver Dollar City's National Children's Festival is a real draw in the summertime, as are White Water theme park and a plethora of go-kart tracks and miniature golf courses. In the chapter on Kidstuff, you'll find everything from go-kart tracks to wild-animal parks to museums. We'll also tell you which of our more than 100 music shows appeal to young audiences.

Water sports are a perennial favorite for the young and young at heart. With three area lakes, you can do everything from snorkel to water ski to parasail. Canoe or kayak our area rivers and streams. Rent a houseboat and spend your entire vacation on the water if you're so inclined. Dozens of resorts line the shores of Table Rock Lake and Lake Taneycomo. We've got everything from your basic cabin with little more than four walls and a roof to deluxe condos with Jacuzzis and cable TV to quiet bed-and-breakfast inns that will cater to your every whim. Camping, hiking, and biking are very popular in the Ozarks as well.

Now that Branson has become one of the top outlet-shopping destinations in the United States, families on a budget or scrunched by a slowing economy can find great bargains on brand-name clothing, housewares, books, electronics, music, and more. We've got a huge selection of souvenir shops with supercheap T-shirts and such, but for a one-of-a-kind souvenir there are places such as Branson Craft Mall and Silver Dollar City, where you can take home the work of more than 100 resident craftspeople who make everything from pottery to furniture. The students at College of the Ozarks will weave a rug or make a fruitcake while you watch. There are a number of extremely talented craftspeople in the Branson area whose works are on display in boutiques and galleries.

We've tried to leave no stone unturned and no appetite unsatisfied. Speaking of appetites, if you've got one, our restaurants feature everything from Mexican to Chinese to Cajun to Greek. Our specialty, of course, is old-fashioned, traditional American. And yes, it's mostly fried. You can get a salad here, but we like to put fried chicken on top. It's so much better that way. Branson is not totally oblivious to the perils of those with special dietary needs. You can get sugar-free candy and fudge and low-cal salad dressing, but we still have a way to go in this department.

All in all, there's something for everyone to see and do in Branson all year long. We have even added a fifth season to the year to provide more variety for visitors. We call our seasons spring, summer, fall, Ozark Mountain Christmas, and Hot Winter Fun. During each season there are dozens of special events and festivals, such as Branson Fest, Veterans Homecoming, Plumb Nellie Days, Kewpiesta, and the list goes on.

Keep in mind that Branson is a dynamic town and things change often and rapidly. The entertainers like to hop from theater to theater during the off-season, and new restaurants and retail shops are opening all the time. Hotels change names and businesses come and go. The maps of Branson today don't look anything like they did a few years ago. The sleepy Branson lakefront of several years ago is now a dynamic convention center and retail complex called Branson Landing. Branson always has pockets of perpetual construction. The Branson/Lakes Area Chamber of Commerce (417-334-4136) is a great source of information on what's new in town. Give them a call or visit their Web site (www .explorebranson.com), and they'll be happy to mail you a package containing brochures, coupons, and lots of other useful information.

We hope your journey through the pages of this book will lead you to Branson and Ozark Mountain Country. If you've made it this far, then you're well on your way to arriving at a truly unforgettable destination. Howdy! And welcome to Branson!

ACKNOWLEDGMENTS

In doing any book, writers feel that the Beatles' "I get by with a little help from my friends" describes precisely their situation. There are many close friends who gave advice, recommendations, and reviews of shows, attractions, accommodations, and restaurants. Their two cents' worth totaled up to a large amount of help and a big debt of gratitude! Add to them the tourists I pumped for insights, recognizing that being an Insider is not always conducive to accurate observations or fresh outlooks, and I have a sizable crowd of Branson visitors to thank.

Specifically, I'd like to thank Milton Rafferty for his geographical and historical information, and former teacher, writer, and photographer Townsend Godsey for helping me appreciate my hillbilly heritage.

All the writers who have written about the Ozarks over the years for the *Ozarks Mountaineer* and who provided insights, observations, and information are to be thanked.

Others who need a big pat on the back are Chris Cooper of Cooper Appraisals for his insight and facts and figures relating to the real estate scene; Cindy Shook and Paula Grant of the Branson Parks and Recreation Department; Kurt Moore, who reviews the show scene in the town, and Dan Lennon of the Branson/Lakes Area Chamber of Commerce and Convention and Visitors Bureau, for information, releases, facts, and figures. Karen Nelson deserves credit for lots of the legwork and phone work necessary in checking facts. There are certainly others in and around Branson who need to be thanked, and omission of them is because of their request, lack of room, or pure and simple oversight.

And thanks to Globe Pequot editor Amy Lyons who had a streamlined and efficient system for the revision process.

Finally, in the "last shall be first category," a big thanks goes to my wife, Faye, who endured the clutter of books and clippings and brochures in the study and around the house.

HOW TO USE THIS BOOK

We Ozarkers are practical people, and this book reflects that practicality. It gives you quick and easy access to useful information whether you are a visitor and tourist, a "comehere" (someone who plans to move here and join our community), or even a current resident or native. It's a book designed to be used—not displayed on your coffee table. If you're visiting the area, don't leave the book in your hotel room. Keep it in your car or backpack or carry it with you. Dog-ear a page to mark a favorite restaurant or attraction. Forget the schoolmarm admonition about never ever writing in a book. Make your own notes and observations. Write in the margins: you'll be making the book more useful.

The book also reflects the Ozarks in another way: like our meandering streams and roads, you can meander in this book. The chapters are independent of each other and can be read in any order. Meandering doesn't mean disorganized. Far from it! We've organized our information to make it easy for you to explore areas that interest you and breeze through those that don't. However, we encourage you to explore those chapters that may not immediately catch your eye. You may not be buying a home here, but the assessment of the area real estate situation will help you understand the Branson phenomenon. And you don't have to be a history buff to appreciate the story of the Ozarks or how the geology of the area affects development. You may have come to Branson just for a couple of the shows, but you might want to check out the Recreation and the Outdoors chapter and Lakes and Rivers chapter to see what else the area has to offer. If you need lots of information about the area fast, the Branson/Lakes Area Chamber of Commerce (417-334-4136) is a great source of information on what's new in town. It's at 269 MO 248, north of town.

The *Insiders' Guide to Branson and the Ozark Mountains* covers a rather small town in detail but a fairly large area in general. Branson, that small town on the old White River that has become the number-two vacation destination in the United States, has a population of just more than 7,000. But the book is also about the greater Ozarks, a 55,000-square-mile area of steep and rugged terrain in southwestern Missouri and northern Arkansas, even reaching into southeastern Oklahoma.

The title explains the book. We figure Branson is your primary reason for coming to the Ozarks. After all, more than eight million people a year visit our town. There must be something that attracts them, and we explain what those attractions are. Therefore, the focus is on our town. But we also want to introduce what you can explore in the Ozarks using Branson as your base. We've included a general history of the Ozarks, major annual events in area towns, and suggested day trips. Information about fishing, canoeing, and water activities can be found in the Lakes and Rivers chapter. Hunting, hiking, and all land-based outdoor activities can be found in the Recreation and the Outdoors chapter. We even have an entire chapter devoted to shopping in the area. When you get here, we suggest places to stay. We have an entire chapter devoted to bed-and-breakfast inns, and the lakeside resorts and hotels and motels are covered in the Accommodations chapter. Camping and RV accommodations have a chapter to themselves. The table of contents is a good place for you to start with this book. It should give you an idea of what you want to look at first. The very end of the book is also handy, so don't ignore the index. To find information quickly, scan the index. Shows, attractions, and activities are also indexed.

Our "Close-ups" are short features scattered throughout the book. They give interesting history and background or focus on a local artist, craftsperson, personality, or phenomenon, providing depth and

(Q) Close-up

Ozark-speak

- Test this Ozarks weather predictor for its validity: When the grass is dry at morning light, look for rain before the night. When the dew is on the grass, rain will never come to pass.

- "These roads is so damn crooked that a feller can't tell if he's goin' somewheres or comin' back home." A White River fishing guide speaking of Ozark roads in the 1920s. The saying still holds true today, especially if you get off the beaten track.

- An Ozark newspaper reporting a turn-of-the-20th-century "Friday night literary" debate, Resolved: That Life is Not Worth Living, mentioned that the audience decided in favor of the affirmative and "made us feel so bad we wasn't able to eat but seven biscuits for breakfast."

- Something with a smooth surface is often described as being smooth as a schoolmarm's leg or smooth as a baby's bottom.

- If something is a time-saver, it is described as "handy as a hog with handles." Hogs are notorious for being stubborn. Free-range hogs, fattened on fallen acorns, could be driven to market or a railhead easily only when they had their eyelids stitched together—except for the single lead hog.

- Someone who is addle-brained is described as being "a half bubble off plumb" or "six sticks short of a cord."

- That road has more twists and turns than a bushel of snakes!

insight on our area. They are great magazine-type snippits that can be read quickly and easily during your busy vacation schedule. They give you background information and insight or clues for some new activities you may want to investigate. We've also scattered tips and tidbits throughout the book. Insiders' tips are those special little details only the locals are likely to know and are found in boxes on various pages. They can be of great help. Ozark-speak might give you an insight to the local mind and help you with the local lingo—or at least give you an appreciation of it. It won't make you a bona fide hillbilly, but it can help you talk like one, if you can get the accent right.

We've tried to keep everything simple but complete. We've given you the area codes for all phone numbers. (Though we cover a fairly large area, you'll be dealing with only four different area codes.) Everything in Missouri in the immediate Branson area is in the 417 area code. Only well east of Branson in the Big Springs area of the state will you be getting into the 573 area code. Arkansas, less than a dozen miles away, will have area codes of 501 or 870. (We're unlucky enough to live close to the dividing line between those two area codes, but if that's the biggest problem to complicate our lives, we're thankful!)

Branson is in Taney County, and every person and business has an official 911 address, and we've provided those official street addresses, though some spots could hardly be classified as streets. Though it has been some time since we've adopted street and road names with numbered addresses, we are still getting used to it ourselves. We're used to giving directions in relationship to landmarks: "where the old Wal-Mart used to be" or "just a jag down the road from Mr. Thornton's

- A devil's lane is the space between two fences built separately by landowners who cannot agree on their mutual property line.
- A heavy rain in the Ozarks is a gully-washer, frog-strangler, fence-lifter, or goose-drowner.
- A genuine hillbilly is a person who is shrewd enough and lazy enough to do it right the first time.
- Food or drink that's spicy is described as being "strong enough to raise a blister on a rawhide boot."
- A nervous person is described as being as "jumpy as a man with a pacemaker at a microwave cookoff" or "as nervous as a long-tailed cat in a room full of rocking chairs."
- During the spring rains, bottomland gets so muddy it will bog down a buzzard's shadow.
- At those Branson buffets, one Ozarker commented, "a fellow can eat so much it keeps him skinny just carryin' the weight around."
- Thriftiness is a great virtue in the Ozarks, but an overly thrifty person is described as "tight as the bark on a tree," "so tight he skins fleas for their hides and the tallow," or "so tight he squeezes a nickel until the buffalo burps."
- When someone obtains something more by luck or chance than skill or intelligence, an Ozarker is likely to remark, "Even a blind hog gets a good acorn once in a while."
- Something in short supply or rare is "scarce as hen's teeth" or "rare as rocking horse manure."

white, two-story frame house that burned down last year" or "just after that patch of sassafras that was so colorful last fall." Well, you get the drift. Nearby Stone County, which has been part of the Branson boom area, also has newly assigned 911 street addresses, but signs and numbers may not be up, and folks are in the process of getting used to them. We've given you the best we can; and we've provided directions. If you get lost looking for something, stop and ask. A friendly Ozarker will be glad to set your feet or your wheels on the right path. Be aware that not all names are on maps—some are too small or insignificant to mapmakers, but not to those who live there! Also, be aware that some places or communities have official names and the more common names that we all use. (One of our favorites is Mount Pleasant, officially, which everyone knows locally as Seed-tick.) MO 76 West in the city limits of Branson is known officially as "76 Country Music Boulevard," but the highway signs refer to it as Country Boulevard, and everyone calls that section "The Strip." All the names are the same place, so don't get confused! Another point of possible confusion could be old US 65, which goes through Branson and Hollister and is referred to as US Business 65. It has been renamed Veterans Boulevard, but all the signs aren't up yet.

Since we in the Ozarks abhor a straight line, the twisting and turning of the roads can get flat-landers right confused, so that they don't know which direction they're going! We suggest you read the Getting Here, Getting Around chapter carefully, provide yourself with a good local map, have an official Missouri highway map when you venture out on day trips, and never be reluctant to stop and ask for directions. If you get lost, that can be part of the fun!

GETTING HERE, GETTING AROUND

The maps of Branson today don't look anything like the maps of a few years ago. As the number of residents and visitors continues to climb, so do the miles of roads. The main arteries leading to town have been widened and improved to ease the flow of traffic into Branson. Visitors who came to town a decade ago endured major traffic jams on MO 76, the main east-west route through town. Now, with all of the side streets and major improvements in the roads, traffic jams are a thing of the past. The new four lanes of US 65 between Branson and Springfield opened in 2001, and US 65 is now four-laned all the way to the Arkansas line. You'll find some of the hairpin curves straightened out on some of the routes that parallel The Strip. The major roadway improvement is the opening of the first third of MO 465, the Ozark Mountain Highroad, north of Branson. This gives folks coming in from the north a bypass of the downtown and The Strip. The Highroad offers a scenic drive (no billboards!), and you'll hit MO 76 just west of the Shepherd of the Hills Homestead. It allows quick access to Silver Dollar City, the Shepherd of the Hills, and those attractions on the west side of town. When finished, MO 465 will cross Lake Taneycomo and join US 65 south of Hollister, providing a loop around Branson.

One service notably lacking in Branson has always been a commercial airport. The nearest facility had always been in Springfield, a good hour's drive away. Many area politicians and business leaders explored the possibility of building an airport in Stone County, just west of Branson, but nothing ever materialized. However, in early 2009 a new, $155 million commercial-aviation airport built entirely with private funds opened with great fanfare.

Branson used to be serviced by Greyhound Bus Lines, which brought passengers to and from Springfield, but that service has been discontinued. A number of trolley operators have tried their hand at providing public transportation in town, but none has lasted very long.

Your best bet when it comes to getting here by road is to drive your own vehicle or purchase a package from a motor-coach operator. After you finally make it to town, stop by one of the many area visitor information centers or the Branson/Lakes Area Chamber of Commerce at the corner of US 65 and MO 248. They will give you a city map, or you can have them send you one by calling (417) 334-4136. You can also obtain information online at www.explorebranson.com.

Before you leave home, choose a lodging facility near the particular theater or attraction you plan to visit. This can save you a lot of time in trying to get from one end of town to the other. Two of the most important factors to consider when you figure out how much time to allow for driving through town are the time of day you will be traveling and the location of your destination. The biggest traffic snarl in town usually occurs in the eastbound lane of MO 76 between 6 and 7 p.m., when many people leave Silver Dollar City for the day. If you are traveling to a 7 p.m. show, be sure to allow at least an hour if you have to go more than a few miles. Although you may be interested in seeing the famous Strip, be sure to check out Shepherd of the Hills Expressway and MO 165. These two roads will lead you to numerous restaurants, theaters, shopping centers, and attractions. Traffic usually flows much faster on these two roads.

One thing we'd like to warn you about is asking for directions. Because the roads have sprung up so fast around here, it's hard for locals to keep up with the best routes. Our advice is to rely on a map—a new one, that is.

GETTING TO BRANSON

By Car

If you come to Branson by car (unless you go out of your way to take the back roads), chances are you'll travel a portion of US 65, the north-south thoroughfare connecting Springfield on the north to Harrison, Arkansas, on the south. The section from Springfield to Branson is four lanes, and the stretch from Branson to the Arkansas state line now has four lanes as well and a new interchange at Hollister. As you wind through the majestic Ozark Mountains on your trip to Branson, you'll understand the amazing amount of rock blasting that has to be done to complete highway projects. What took Mother Nature millions of years to build up and carve out, road crews can blast away in a matter of months. When you look at it like that, the usual few years doesn't seem like much of a wait.

i Want to keep the kids amused on the trip to Branson? Ozarker Josh Young's *Missouri Curiosities* (The Globe Pequot Press, 2006) gives details about the Show Me State's exotic and unusual attractions, some of which you may just stop at on your road trip to inspect, from the world's largest goose to the world's smallest cathedral.

If you're coming from St. Louis or other points east, or from Tulsa, Oklahoma, northeast Texas, or other points west, you'll take I-44 to Springfield, where it connects to US 65 just 35 miles north of Branson. If you're coming from Kansas City or other points north, you have your choice. Either take four-lane US 71, which takes you through Carthage and on to I-44 just east of Joplin, or take the quicker, but busier, mostly two-lane MO 13 to I-44 just a few miles north of Springfield. The MO 13 route will save you the hour's drive from Carthage to Springfield, if you don't mind the two-way traffic and road construction on sections being rebuilt.

i For road conditions call the Missouri State Highway Patrol (800-222-6400). You can check road conditions online at www.modot.org.

US 60 runs parallel to I-44 through southern Missouri and connects to US 65 just south of Springfield's city limits. From the east, US 60 connects to US 63 at Cabool and continues on to I-55 just west of Memphis. If you're traveling from the south or east of Memphis, you can take the mostly two-lane US 63, or you can hop on I-40, head west to Little Rock, Arkansas, and then enter Branson from the south on US 65. Much of US 65 in Arkansas has now been four-laned, and many sections of the road straightened.

If you're coming from Texas via Oklahoma City and want a more scenic route than the I-44 path, take I-40 east to US 71 North. You'll travel alongside the Arkansas River on I-40, then on US 71 you'll pass through the Arkansas cities of Fayetteville and Springdale. US 71 winds through the hills to meet US 62 just west of Beaver Lake and Eureka Springs, Arkansas. (Check out exciting sightseeing opportunities in Eureka Springs in the Day Trips chapter.) Continue east on US 62 to US 65, and from there you're just 30 miles south of Branson.

Now that we've covered the major arteries leading to Branson, it's time to tell you about the back roads. For the truly adventurous driver, try US 160 South, which leads you out of Springfield through Nixa and Highlandville. The passage takes well over an hour and can be quite treacherous in wet or snowy weather. Once you come to the Reeds Spring Junction, you can continue on US 160 to MO 248, or you can go west to MO 13 until you come to Branson West. From there you can turn east on MO 76 and travel to Silver Dollar City, Inspiration Tower, and the Shepherd of the Hills Homestead. (See the Attractions chapter for more information about these sites.)

If you continue south on MO 13 at Branson West, you'll come to Kimberling City, known for its many marinas and resorts on Table Rock Lake. If you decide to stay on US 160 at the Reeds Spring

🔍 Close-up

Taking the Highroad

Veteran visitors to Branson will find some road changes. The biggest one is MO 465, the Ozark Mountain Highroad, which connects US 65 north of Branson with MO 76 just east of Silver Dollar City. In the works since 1992, the first third of the proposed "loop around Branson" opened in the summer of 2003.

If you're going to points west of The Strip, it allows for a rapid connection and avoids the clutter and traffic of Branson's "main drag." The Ozark Mountain Highroad eases congestion and showcases the area's beauty. And with a 55 mph speed limit, you can enjoy the beauty of nature's scenery!

The landscape is dotted with chicory, pink coneflowers, black-eyed Susans, and daisy-dotted fields. Rocky outcroppings hint at the caves, crevices, and clay seams of filled caves the builders encountered.

MoDOT engineers took other steps to create a scenic drive. The girders are done in a rusty brown to blend with the scenery rather than the usual green. Cement at the base of the bridges is textured to look less like a block of concrete.

A spectacular design choice is the bridge supports of its nine bridges. Most Missouri bridges have girders supported by a pair of simple, round columns. Highroad girders are supported with single, graceful columns that widen to a massive hammerhead top. The tallest column stands 120 feet above a streambed.

MoDOT bought easements extending 660 feet on either side of the road in an effort to discourage billboards and development. Access to the road is at only three intersections: US 65, MO 248, and MO 76. If you know where you're going, the Highroad can save you time and the frustrations of slow traffic.

OZARK MOUNTAIN HIGHROAD FACTS

- Construction cost: $53 million
- Cost of right-of-way: $8.5 million
- 5.8 million cubic yards of dirt and rock moved
- 250,000 tons of asphalt equal to 16,667 15-ton dump truck loads

Junction, this route will take you back across US 65 East to the Taney County seat of Forsyth. MO 248 leads south to the Ozark Mountain Highroad and then to the Shepherd of the Hills Expressway, known as The Other Strip. Shepherd of the Hills Expressway runs from MO 248 to the western end of MO 76, or what locals call The Strip, where it runs into MO 376 at the RFD Theatre. The Shoji Tabuchi Theatre, IMAX Entertainment Complex, Sight & Sound Theatre, and dozens of motels and restaurants line Shepherd of the Hills Expressway. The entire portion of Shepherd of the Hills Expressway from MO 248 to MO 76 is three and four lane.

The expressway was built to connect traffic from MO 248 to the western end of MO 76, so visitors to the Shepherd of the Hills Homestead could avoid congestion on The Strip. The Ozark Mountain Highroad (MO 465) allows you to bypass The Strip entirely if you arrive via US 65 from the north.

ℹ️ As you wind through the Ozark Mountains, you may be a little confused about which direction you are going. North-south roads are always odd numbered, and east-west roads are always even numbered.

GETTING AROUND BRANSON

In Town

In Branson, MO 76, or The Strip, runs from the intersection of MO 376 east into downtown Branson, where it intersects US Business 65, which has been renamed Veterans Boulevard. Many businesses along the route continue to use the old name. We will note the exceptions. Branson developer Jim Thomas was one of the first to build commercial property on The Strip. When he originally purchased the land where the Lodge of the Ozarks resort and theater complex now sits, it was a dirt airstrip, Branson's first airport. Today, you can't come to Branson without taking at least one pass down the famous road. Few building sites are left on the 5-mile stretch.

A few years ago locals did everything they could to avoid The Strip because of the tremendous traffic jams, especially before shows. But traffic moves along much faster now that a number of side roads carry cars on and off The Strip every few hundred yards or so. The rush before and after shows can still be a little nerve-wracking, especially in late fall when visitor numbers are highest. If you're taking The Strip just to see the sights, try it before 10 a.m. or between 7 and 9:30 p.m. Most people either haven't gotten around by 10 a.m. or are parked for a show after 7 p.m.

If you need to get from one end of town to the other and want to avoid The Strip, we suggest trying Gretna Road. Gretna Road runs parallel to The Strip on the north, beginning at MO 248 just south of where Shepherd of the Hills Expressway meets MO 248. Gretna Road winds through the Branson Meadows development past the Factory Shoppes of America outlet mall to the intersection of Roark Valley Road and then on past the White House Theatre. From Gretna Road you can see the backs of numerous buildings facing The Strip. A number of short roads connect Gretna Road to The Strip, including Wildwood Drive, Rosalee Street, and Frances Street. Gretna Road stops at The Strip next to the Titanic Museum Attraction. On the south side of The Strip, Gretna Road becomes MO 165.

The Many Aliases of Missouri Highway

The stretch of MO 76 between downtown Branson and the RFD Theatre is known locally as The Strip. The city of Branson renamed the famous section 76 Country Music Boulevard. You won't hear locals refer to it as 76 Country Music Boulevard very often, though. We prefer to say "The Strip" or just "76." Even though the official name includes the word *country*, many locals have dropped this in an attempt to broaden the public's perception that Branson is more than just a country-music town. Road signs leading to Branson, however, have the word *music* dropped and read 76 Country Boulevard. Many of the businesses located on The Strip list their addresses as 76 Country Boulevard. While this name game may be a little confusing, remember that The Strip, 76 Country Music Boulevard, and 76 Country Boulevard are all the same stretch of blacktop.

Roark Valley Road, which breaks off the north side of The Strip just east of the US 65 exit, runs parallel between The Strip and MO 248 and intersects Gretna Road a half mile from Shepherd of the Hills Expressway. James F. Epps Road connects Roark Valley Road to the eastern half of MO 248. Forsythe Street and Truman Drive connect Roark Valley Road to The Strip. With a little creative

ℹ **We like for you to drive our country roads, but low water crossings can be dangerous. Don't drive into flowing water. It doesn't take much force to push your vehicle off the road and wash it and you downstream.**

maneuvering you can get from MO 248 to The Strip to MO 165 in no time flat. Now, if you want to travel the side streets south of The Strip, start with Fall Creek Road, where it breaks off from The Strip at the light just before Dick Clark's American Bandstand Theatre. Fall Creek Road takes you to Wildwood Drive, where you can jump off and head on over to Green Mountain Drive, the road that runs behind the Grand Palace and past numerous hotels and restaurants. Green Mountain Drive eventually connects with MO 165 near the Stone Hill Winery. If you continue on Fall Creek Road, you will eventually wind through to MO 165. A turn north will take you back to The Strip, and a turn south will lead you to the Welk Resort, as well as the Shepherd of the Hills Fish Hatchery. Green Mountain Drive continues on across MO 165 to White River Drive, which runs behind many theaters and hotels on the west end of The Strip.

Also on the west end of The Strip is MO 376, linking Shepherd of the Hills Expressway with MO 265. MO 265 takes you south to MO 165, across Table Rock Dam, and then to US 65 just south of Hollister.

Downtown Branson

The old part of town, as it is called, is home to dozens of mom-and-pop ice-cream parlors, restaurants, and gift shops covering 4 or 5 blocks. It is also the home of the new $300 million Branson Landing development, a collection of shops, stores, restaurants, hotel and condos, and a convention center. Parking is limited downtown, but you may find a space in the lot between Commercial Street and US Business 65 (Veterans Boulevard) or in the parking garage just off Sycamore Street east of Commercial Street. Branson Landing offers several parking options. Free parking is located on both ends of the Promenade

i Many of the parking spaces in downtown Branson have a two-hour limit—and they are checked. Each space is clearly marked with a sign.

Red Route, Blue Route, Yellow Route

Have you wondered what the red, blue, and yellow road signs that look like a capital *B* standing on a guitar neck are for? They are road markers for time-saving routes. The red route is Shepherd of the Hills Expressway; the blue route is Gretna Road and Roark Valley Road; and the yellow route is Fall Creek Road, Green Mountain Drive, and Wildwood Drive (but only the portion of Wildwood south of The Strip). These roads also contain red, blue, and yellow markers painted on the pavement every few hundred yards or so that sometimes look like roadkill spots, and there are road signs marking the color routes. The Branson area map printed by the Branson/Lakes Area Chamber of Commerce has these passages color coded and suggests using them as alternates to The Strip. If you really want an education on these routes, tune in to the Vacation Channel (for more information on the Vacation Channel, see the Media chapter). It devotes an entire program to decoding the color codes, maps, and getting around Branson.

---

outside of Belk Department Store (north end) and Bass Pro Shops (south end). Covered parking is available in the large Branson Landing Parking Garage. If you follow The Strip east from US 65, it turns into Main Street and takes you right down to Branson Landing. You'll see the parking garage at the stoplight at Branson Landing Boulevard. Turning either left or right will take you to the free-area parking lots.

GETTING TO BRANSON

By Air

BRANSON AIRPORT
4000 Branson Airport Blvd., Hollister
(417) 334-7813
www.flybranson.com
You can now fly directly to Branson! The new, $155 million commercial-aviation airport was built entirely with private funds and opened in early 2009 with a spectacular air show. It is a single 7,140-foot-long, 150-foot-wide runway with partial taxiway and is approximately 8 miles south of the center of Branson. It has a 58,000-square-foot terminal with taxi and limousine service and car rentals. Commercial airlines serving the airport include Sun Country Airlines (www.suncountry.com) with three flights per week to Minneapolis and Dallas and AirTran Airways (www.airtran.com) with daily nonstop service to Milwaukee and Atlanta. Check the Branson Airport Web site for additional carriers. The airport also offers hangar and tie-down space for private aircraft and 24-hour fueling.

Those flying into Branson have the opportunity of joining GateONE, free of charge, and have their Branson experience customized for them. During registration, members are asked to identify interests and activities that would comprise their ideal vacation. GateONE matches those interests with participating sponsors and recommends additional Branson attractions. Further benefits include special offers and an online magazine packed with information and updates about Branson attractions and focused ideas that match your interests.

To get to the Branson Airport from US 65 North, turn right/east approximately 4 miles north of the Highway 86 intersection into the Communities at Branson Creek and follow Branson Creek Boulevard about 2.5 miles until it turns into Branson Airport Boulevard, continue another 2 miles to the Branson Airport. From US 65 South, turn left/east approximately 1 mile south of the Hollister exchange into the Communities at Branson Creek and follow Branson Creek Boulevard about 2.5 miles until it turns into Branson Airport Boulevard, continue another 2 miles to the Branson Airport.

BOONE COUNTY REGIONAL AIRPORT
2524 Airport Rd.
Harrison, AR
(870) 741-6954
www.boonecountyairport.com
A mere 30 minutes from Branson, the Boone County Regional Airport has a 6,150-foot paved and lighted runway open 24 hours a day. There is no landing fee. Regional Jet Center, (870) 741-4510, provides self-serve aviation gasoline 24 hours a day, and its staff is on call around the clock for maintenance and other needs. They will also help you make transportation arrangements to Branson, or you can check out the Hertz counter at the terminal (870-743-1432). Regional Jet Center does not charge a daily tie-down fee if you purchase gasoline. The airport's only commercial carrier, Great Lakes Airlines, (800) 237-7788, provides service to Dallas and Kansas City. Visit its Web site at www.greatlakesav.com.

> **i** There's no doubt about it—tourism's the biggest draw for Branson. In fact, this "big city with a small-town feel" generates a yearly average of more than $1.5 billion through its tourism industry alone.

SPRINGFIELD/BRANSON NATIONAL AIRPORT
5000 West Kearney St., Springfield
(417) 869-0300
www.sgf-branson-airport.com
The Springfield/Branson National is a 40- to 50-minute drive from downtown Branson. Servicing 65 flights each day, the airport is owned by the city of Springfield and features one-stop service to 360 domestic and 16 international cities. The new, $117 million, 275,000-square-foot terminal features modern architecture which is a kind of "ode to the Ozarks" and has 10 gates (expandable to 60), a full-service travel agency,

complete airline ticketing facilities, sky cap service, automated baggage handling, an on-site restaurant, a chapel, a gift shop, a lounge, and a visitor information center.

Four carriers provide flights to major cities. American Eagle, (800) 433-7300, flies to Dallas–Fort Worth, St. Louis, and Chicago. Northwest (www.nwa.com) provides service to Memphis and Minneapolis. Delta, recently merged with Northwest, (www.delta.com) has connections with several Midwest cities. Allegiant (www.allegiantair.com) flies to points on the east and west coasts. The airport also offers hangar and tie-down space for private aircraft and twenty-four-hour fueling. Tie-down fees for single-engine planes are $3 a day or $30 per month. Twin-engine rates are $4 a day and $40 per month. Small jet rates are $5 a day and $60 per month.

The airport provides a full range of aircraft repair and maintenance services along with aircraft sales, flight school, and air taxi and charter services of all types, including jet. Five rental car companies are located in the main terminal of the airport next to the baggage claim area. They are: Alamo, (417) 865-5311; Avis, (417) 865-6226; Budget, (417) 831-2662; Hertz, (417) 865-1681; and National, (417) 865-5311. A few hundred yards from the main terminal are Enterprise, (417) 866-0300, and Thrifty, (417) 866-8777. Both offer shuttle service to and from the terminal. There are 209 short-term parking spaces and 724 spaces in the long-term lot at the airport. All parking is open air. Short-term parking is $10 per day. Long-term parking is $7 a day, $35 a week.

TANEY COUNTY AIRPORT
College of the Ozarks, Hangar One
Point Lookout
(417) 332-1848
www.taneycountyairport.com
Located just 2 miles south of Branson on MO V, the Taney County Airport accommodates private aircraft and charter planes with a 3,600-foot lighted runway at an elevation of 940 feet, a parallel taxiway, a rotating beacon, and two approved instrument approaches. The airport provides aviation gasoline and jet fuel. The air-

port is open from 7 a.m. to 7 p.m. year-round. Tie-downs and hangar space are also available. The 16,000-square-foot terminal has restrooms, phones, and vending machines. Avis-Rent-A-Car, (417) 334-4945, is located on the premises.

IF YOU NEED TRANSPORTATION

Many hotels and motels provide transportation for their guests in Branson for a fee. A few of them will pick you up at the airport in Springfield. If you need transportation from the airport in Springfield to Branson and plan to use one of the shuttle services listed in this section, be sure to make your reservations well in advance.

If you want your own set of wheels, you can contact one of the rental car companies in Springfield or the following companies in Branson: A-1 Auto Rental, (417) 338-4446; Avis, (417) 334-4945; and Enterprise, (417) 338-2280 or (417) 336-2000. Depending on where you are staying and what activities you have planned, you might be able to see much of The Strip on foot. Just remember that you're in hill country.

A-1 Airport Shuttle, (417) 335-6001, has two cars and one van available to take individuals and families from Springfield to Branson and motor coaches for groups of 15 or more. One-way trips start at $70 for one or two persons. Group rates are available. For an extra charge they will take you to Kimberling City. Call at least three days in advance. Jerry's Shuttle Service, (417) 334-5678, charges $75 for one or two persons, and $95 for three or four. Shuttle around Branson is $9 for one person, $5 per person for two to four people. They operate 24 hours a day, seven days a week, year-round. You must call for service.

J. Howard Fisk Limousines, (417) 862-2900, one of the area's oldest and biggest limo services, provides transportation to Branson from Springfield for up to three people for $125, and $175 for up to eight people. Groups of 14 or more pay $187 for a shuttle bus. Individuals in Branson pay $60 per hour for transportation, and groups can call for package quotes. Many of the J. Howard Fisk Limousines vehicles are equipped with TVs, DVD players, beverages, and other amenities.

At Your Service-Limousines, (417) 230-3602 or (800) 218-4490, provides Springfield-Branson service. Price varies with vehicle and number of people. Call for rates.

Yellow Cab, (417) 862-5511, is the Springfield-based cab company to call if you need a ride to Branson. You can expect to pay $112.50 for one person, with 50 cents per person for additional passengers. You can usually find a Yellow Cab waiting at the airport if you land during the day, but if you arrive after dark, you should call from the courtesy phone at baggage claim as soon as you land.

MOTOR-COACH TOURS

One of the best ways to get to Branson and get around while you are here is via a chartered motor coach. Many tour companies in Branson provide complete travel package planning for groups of 20 or more. They will make your transportation arrangements from your home city to Branson and then see to it that you get to all the shows, restaurants, gift shops, and other neat attractions you so desire without having to look for a parking place. Most of the time you'll be dropped off at the front door. As with any destination, there are advantages to seeing Branson with a group. If you don't come on a motor coach but still want to get the royal tour by an experienced guide, hop aboard Ride the Ducks (417-334-3825) for a trip down The Strip and into Table Rock Lake. Not only is the ride a blast, but the driver will point out all the sights along the way and throw in some Ozark humor as well. Taking a trip on a Duck will help familiarize you with The Strip. (For more information about the Ducks, see the Attractions chapter.)

i If you want to avoid the rush for 7 and 8 p.m. shows, take in a morning or afternoon show instead. You'll miss the traffic jams, and you'll probably get better seats, too.

HISTORY

As Ozark novelist Donald Harington pointed out, everything in the Ozarks meanders. Perhaps that is a statement of the obvious, but it bears examination, for like the obvious, it is frequently missed for being under our very noses.

Rivers meander in their babbling journey to either the Missouri or the Mississippi. Roads meander as they follow ridgelines or make their sinuous *S* curves around hillsides. Snakes meander in their crawling toward wherever it is their serpentine mind and method are taking them. Grapevines meander snakelike among sycamore limbs, which in turn meander, making shade over Ozark streams. Butterflies meander from flower to flower like a hillbilly meanders from still to home after tasting its nectar. Good stories meander in their telling, and any devotee of Mark Twain knows they are the better for it.

Though this book is largely the story of Branson, that small town on the old White River that has become the number-two vacation destination in the United States (according to the American Tour Association in 2005), it is also about the greater Ozarks.

The name for this 55,000-square-mile area of steep and rugged terrain between the nation's two great mountain ranges, the Rockies and Appalachians, is fairly recent, though the area is old. An explorer in 1815, S. H. Long, is credited as being the first to use the term "Ozark Mountains." The 19th-century explorer Henry Rowe Schoolcraft ventured into the area in 1818 and 1819, three years before statehood, to explore part of Thomas Jefferson's bargain land purchase of the Louisiana Territory in 1803. Though he explored much of the Ozarks, including the Branson area, Schoolcraft never used the term "Ozarks" for it in his voluminous journals. Another explorer some 75 years later, the legendary one-armed explorer of the Grand Canyon, John Wesley Powell, who was a noted geologist and the second director of the U.S. Geological Survey, called the region "the Ozark Mountains" in his writings. Somewhere in a period of 75 years, the term Ozarks became the accepted name for the region. Most etymologists believe the word is an abbreviation of the French phrase "aux Arcs" (pronounced like the Ozarks of today), meaning "to the Arkansas," referring to the French territory on the outposts of that river named after the American Indian tribe, or meaning "to the arcs"—the bows (arcs) of the area's meandering rivers and creeks in general. This meandering makes possible a 20-mile float on the Gasconade River, with the takeout point being only a mile's walk from put-in point, and floaters often marvel at the meandering miles of Ozark streams. Missouri's tourism slogan, "Where the rivers run" (1998), doesn't take into account their roundabout method of doing so.

Today Branson and the Ozarks are almost a unit. You can't say one without thinking of the other. And so we meander in the History chapter among other nearby areas of the Ozarks the way the great White River meanders among the Ozark hills. Branson's history is intertwined with the story of the Ozarks. Enjoy the meandering. The shortest point between "A" and "B" may be a straight line, but it's not usually the most interesting.

THE LAND

You can't know and understand the Ozarks today unless you know something about the region's yesterdays. Development issues, environmental concerns—every problem or situation we face—actually have roots that go down as deep as the 500-million-year-old limestone beneath us.

So how do we tell so long a story? We follow Alice's (of Wonderland fame) advice: "We start at the beginning, proceed to the middle, and continue until we come to the end." And our beginning is 500 million years ago, when the Ozark Mountains weren't mountains at all, but a shallow sea. During that period, large quantities of shelled creatures died, and the accumulation of their calcium exoskeletons became the thick layers of limestone and dolomite we see today, so neatly exposed for reading in recent road cuts. Several thick areas of sandstone indicate that the area was also desert in climate after the seas retreated, and later layers of limestone indicate other undersea development. Gradually, there was a general uplift of that area we now call the Ozarks highlands, roughly south of the Missouri River and north of the Arkansas River, with Oklahoma and Kansas on the western border and the Mississippi River on the eastern border. It takes in a region that is the largest area of steep relief between the Appalachians on the east and the Rockies on the west. It encompasses more than 50,000 square miles, and were the Ozarks a state, it would rank 23rd in size. Milton D. Rafferty in *The Ozarks: Land and Life* remarked that "the Ozarks is one of America's great regions, set apart physically by rugged terrain and sociologically by inhabitants who profess political conservatism, religious fundamentalism and sectarianism, and a strong belief in the values of rural living."

The Ozark upland varies in altitude from 400 to 2,500 feet above sea level, and the plains area of Springfield running east toward Cabool and Willow Springs forms a major dividing ridge. Many of our major local rivers start within miles of each other in that area and flow their different directions: The Jacks Fork and the Eleven Point flow east; the Big Piney flows northeast; the Gasconade flows north; and the north fork of the White River and Bryant Creek flow southwest. All the oldest rivers of the Ozarks show a peculiar meandering trait, characteristic of rivers in lowlands and plains areas. They began their life probably before the uplift, laying down a basic channel that became more entrenched during the slow uprising of the area and over time, an uplift so slow and gradual and widespread that seldom were the layers of rock buckled and broken. Gradually, these rivers cut their paths deeper and deeper into the layers of limestone and sandstone laid down during the Paleozoic era. It doesn't take a trained geologist to see that most of the peaks in the Ozarks are about the same height. One can see an exposed layer of rock on one side of a river and find the same layer at the same altitude, sometimes miles away, on the other hillside across the river.

Outsiders coming into Branson from the north on US 65 often think they are driving "into the mountains"—*mountains* is rather a grandiose term for them; *hills* would be more accurate—when actually they are coming *down* from the Springfield plateau. Highlandville, between Springfield and Branson, is the line of demarcation, as its name suggests. Coming from Branson and going north, it is the "high land" before the general leveling of the plateau. Though it may not feel or look like you are going down when you drive south toward Branson, your reason confirms it when you look at the map and see that the James River, which starts north of Springfield, flows southwest into the White River (now Table Rock Lake). Springfield has an altitude of 1,267 feet, while Branson is 330 feet lower at 937.

ℹ️ **Be a rock watcher. The geology of the Ozarks can be read especially well in some of the recent road cuts. It gives a "clean page," and you can see the layers that were put down when seas covered the area. The rocks may be inviting to climb, especially for kids, but a word of caution is in order: some layers are shale and crumble easily.**

The highest point in the Missouri Ozarks, Taum Sauk Mountain, is only 1,772 feet, and the highest point in the Arkansas Ozarks, in the Boston Mountains, rises to 2,578 feet.

The Ouachita Mountains, south of the Arkansas River, are generally higher in elevation than the Ozarks and are considered part of the ancient highlands development. The two regions are similar: steep hillsides carved by water with modern economies dependent on tourism and before that mining, timbering, grazing, and subsistence agriculture. Westerners may sneer at the "peaks" in the Ouachitas, the Boston, and the Ozark chains as hardly being mountains at all compared to those of the Rockies. If the Ozarks are less than mountains, they are certainly more than hills. However, at 500 million years compared to the Rockies' babyish 200 million, the Ozarks region has been uplifted and weathered longer than any area of the country. When we use the metaphor "as old as the hills" in the Ozarks, it has real meaning! Like the wrinkled forehead of an old man, the furrows of the hollows and valleys on the face of the Ozarks are indicative of age.

The Ozarks' surface landscape of rugged bluffs and hillsides, clear rivers and streams that are still cutting into the solid rock, and gushing springs early attracted nature lovers, hunters, floaters, and anglers. Hunters came for the game in the forests, and the White River and its tributaries attracted floaters and anglers from the time that outsiders were first able to venture easily into the Ozarks. Caves, such as Marvel Cave (earlier called Marble Cave) beneath today's Silver Dollar City and Talking Rocks (once known as Fairy Cave), attracted their share of early adventurous tourists. Missouri could be known as "the Cave State," for it has more caves than any state in the Union. Caves give a glimpse of an equally important landscape of the Ozarks, that beneath the feet of the tourists who are admiring the surface landscape.

The entire Ozarks can be compared to a landscape of guacamole dip spread on the surface of a giant Swiss cheese. The green guacamole is the shallow soil supporting the grass and trees. The Swiss cheese is the limestone base. Geologists call such subsurface karst, land characterized by fissures and caving, formed as limestone dissolves over time because of contact with slightly acidic water. That which doesn't run off into streams and creeks flows into the "Swiss cheese" and becomes part of the water table or emerges at lower altitudes as springs. The surface of the land is characterized by wet-weather streams, disappearing streams (with water going underground), springs (at which an underground conduit surfaces), and sinkholes, which appear when the roof of a cave falls in. The underground conduits become caves when the surface rivers cut deep enough to intersect the underground streams and drain them. This is why you see cave entrances in the bluffs as you float Missouri streams. Some are rather small, but others, such as Jam Up Cave on the Jacks Fork River, have entrances so large that you would be able to stack a dozen buses in the opening. Sinkholes are part of the natural drainage system and should not be filled or have garbage and rubbish thrown in them, for it will pollute the water table and springs. Some sinkholes are modest, but others are quite large. Marvel Cave at Silver Dollar City was discovered by someone investigating a sinkhole. Beneath it was a room, dissolved out of the solid rock over eons, that is large enough to float a hot-air balloon. (Ask the cave guide there about the world's underground balloon altitude record!) Grand Gulf, near Thayer, is part of the Missouri state park system. The spectacular gorge, a miniature Missouri "Grand Canyon," was formed when the roof of a gigantic cave gave way. The remaining portions are natural bridges over the huge furrow in the stone. After a heavy rain, the gorge fills with water 75 to 90 feet deep—which rapidly drains away into a system farther underground. Bales of straw thrown in the gorge have emerged 7 miles away at Mammoth Springs, Arkansas, a spring so large that it is the source of Spring River.

Some springs are "wet-weather springs" and run only after a rain or when the ground is saturated. Others are "all-weather springs" that flow all year. Some are small and have a tiny flow, but others, such as Mammoth Springs or Big Springs,

i **Big Spring near Van Buren is the largest single-outlet spring in the United States. It supplies the Current River with 276 million gallons of water a day, more than twice what the population of Kansas City uses in one day.**

are veritable behemoths, springs the size of rivers, with entire trainloads of dissolved limestone being removed by the springs each year. The cave-forming process is always at work.

Like caves, springs are constant in temperature, and early settlers relied on springs for family water sources. Even during the dog days of August, you will feel a blast of air-conditioned air as you near a spring. The air is often misty, as the cool waters meet hot summer air. Cool- and wet-weather plants abound around springs: ferns, columbines, and mosses. Springwater often contains watercress, whose pungent, radishlike taste and greenery add zest to salads and which can even be picked in the dead of winter, growing in the constant-temperature water. On cold days in winter, springs often exhale "steam" as the warmer water of the spring meets the frigid winter air.

Springs were a source of cool, pure water for early settlers and allowed them to avoid the laborious job of digging wells. Some settlers built below a spring and took advantage of the force of gravity, with running water piped into their cabins. Some pioneers took advantage of nearby caves for "natural air-conditioning." Larger springs were often used by early settlers to power mills for grinding grain or even sawing lumber, and mills still remain at nearby Zanoni, Sycamore, and Dawt, much like the re-created Edward's Mill and Museum at College of the Ozarks.

Many of the big springs in the White River are now under the lakes, but east of Branson on the north fork of the White, Current, and Eleven Point Rivers are a number of impressive springs, and though the 100 to 150 miles from Branson make for a long day trip, it is worth it. The area can serve as an interesting stopping-off point if you are coming to Branson from the east (see the Recreation and Lakes and Rivers chapters). Branson visitors who choose to do so can stop and rubberneck at some of the most spectacular springs in the world.

Big Spring is aptly named. Once a state park, it is now part of the Ozark National Scenic Riverways. Located in Carter County near Van Buren, it is the largest spring in the Ozarks and one of the largest in the world. From under a bluff a turbulent river issues, flowing around mossy boulders. A popular picture point in the springtime, the bluff, with its dogwood, redbud, and serviceberry trees, makes an interesting mixture of colors among the blue and black of the water and the green of the mosses, watercress, and ferns. The spring gushes forth an average flow of 276 million gallons a day and a maximum of 840 million gallons. Even during the extended drought years of the 1950s, the minimum flow measured 152 million gallons per day. These figures can be put in perspective when one considers that Springfield's population of 151,000 may use 30 million gallons on a "big water day."

The springs of the Ozarks are its cave factories. According to studies by hydrologists, Big Spring removes about 175 tons of dissolved limestone a day, based on its average flow. Thus, in a year's time, enough limestone bedrock is removed to form a cave passage 30 feet high by 50 feet wide and a mile long. This erosion is, of course, spread out over all the solution channels of the many square miles of its drainage system, but the spring's cavern system grows bigger each day. Divers who have entered the spring via a small pit cave from above the bluff were not able to penetrate the system because of the turbulent current but report a tantalizing glimpse of "an immense cavern." Someday, when the spring is undercut and the water table drops, it too, like so many of Missouri's cave marvels, will be exposed to human sight.

Alley Spring, in Shannon County, with its red pioneer mill, is one of the most photographed points in Missouri. The mill was used to grind meal, flour, and cattle feed; operate a sawmill; and furnish electrical power for nearby houses. The powder-blue water issues forth at an average

🔍 Close-up

State Symbols and the Ozarks

Want to impress the natives? Both Missouri and Arkansas have lots of "official symbols," many of them known to locals who don't know they are "officially" recognized. You can show off your knowledge from our list.

ARKANSAS

Beverage: Milk, 1985 (not moonshine!)

Bird: Mockingbird, 1929

Flower: Apple blossom, 1901

Folk Dance: Square dance, 1991

Fruit: Arkansas Vine Ripe Pink Tomato, 1987

Gem: Diamond, 1967 (You can "mine" them at a state park.)

Historical Song: "The Arkansas Traveler," 1987

Historic Cooking Vessel: Dutch oven, 2001

Insect: Honeybee, 1973 (Missouri and a dozen other states also claim this nonnative insect.)

Mammal: White-tailed deer, 1993

Mineral: Quartz crystal, 1967

Musical Instrument: Fiddle, 1985 (also claimed by Missouri—two years later)

Song: "Arkansas" by Mrs. Eva Ware Barnett, 1987

MISSOURI

American Folk Dance: Square dance, 1995

Animal: Mule, 1995

Aquatic Animal: Paddlefish or spoonbill, 1997

Bird: Bluebird, 1927

Day: Missouri Day, third Wednesday in October, 1915

Fish: Channel catfish, 1997

Floral Emblem: Hawthorn blossom (of tree commonly called the "red haw" or "wild haw"), 1923

Fossil: Crinoidea (*Delocrinus missouriensis*), 1989

Horse: Missouri Fox Trotting, 2002

Insect: Honeybee, 1985

Mineral: Galena (lead ore), 1967 (Stone County's seat is named after ore deposits nearby.)

Musical Instrument: Fiddle, 1987

Nut: Fruit of Black Walnut tree, 1990

Rock: Mozarkite, 1967

Song: "Missouri Waltz," 1949 (Because it was frequently played during Harry S. Truman's 1948 campaign. *NOTE:* He hated the song!)

Tree: Flowering dogwood, 1955

---

flow of 81 million gallons per day, forming a large stream that meets the Jacks Fork a half mile away. Alley Spring was once a state park but is now part of the Ozark National Scenic Riverways.

Also part of the Ozark National Scenic Riverways is the former state park at Round Spring. The spring's average flow of 26 million gallons a day rises quietly in a circular basin formed when an ancient cavern roof collapsed. Part of the roof remains intact as a natural bridge, beneath which the waters of the spring flow toward the nearby Current River.

Less accessible, except to floaters, are Cave Spring and Blue Spring on the Current River. There are many Blue Springs in Missouri (there's one on the Jacks Fork at Jam Up Cave), but the one near Owls Bend is the deepest blue, so blue it was known by Native Americans as "the spring of the Summer Sky." It is also the deepest known spring in Missouri, at 256 feet. It ranks sixth in size in the state with an average daily flow of 90 million gallons.

Cave Spring issues forth from a cave and is big enough for canoeists to paddle back into it, and most floating the Current River can't resist the quick cave excursion without leaving their canoes. In the winter when the river water is cold, bass and sculpins by the hundreds take shelter in the warmer spring waters. During the spring mating season, the cave is shelter to many hellbenders (large river salamanders). The spring has a drainage connection to the nearby Devils Well, a large sink that can be entered only by a 100-foot descent in a bosun's chair and winch. The 400-foot-long underground lake, impounding more than 20 million gallons of water, is one of the largest in the nation.

Greer Spring, the second largest spring in Missouri, is on the Eleven Point River and retains much of its wilderness character. One can see little change today from photographs taken more than a hundred years ago. It is not as easily accessible as Big Spring. Visitors must travel a steep path that begins next to the 1899 mill that made use of the spring's constant flow by a turbine far below. You can feel the air temperature change as you descend to the spring, and the mosses and ferns in the micro-environment are green all year because the spring keeps the air cool in summer and warm in winter. A portion of the spring issues from a cave in a bluff, but most of the spring issues from a large pool that bubbles up like a huge boiling kettle. The spring's average daily flow is 187 million gallons, enough to double the flow of the Eleven Point River where it meets the river. Because the spring is now part of the Eleven Point National Scenic Riverway and within the Mark Twain National Forest, its pristine wilderness character is likely to be preserved, and signs posting rules remind visitors to make minimum impact when visiting.

If you are coming to Branson from the east, you may want to check out the area on your drive across the state. If you are already in Branson, to reach our "big spring region," head north on US 65, then east on US 60 to the Mark Twain National Forest. The locations of the springs are marked by highway signs.

THE PEOPLE

The Ozarks region has greeted many visitors over the past 10,000 years, and the area, like all of Missouri, shows the influence in its place-names and culture of the peoples that controlled the area: Native Americans, the Spanish, the French, and, after the Louisiana Purchase in 1803, the Americans. The area has a long tradition with Native Americans, though not many Native American place-names. The first evidence of inhabitation comes from the Paleo-Indian bluff dwellers, who left bone and stone tools, clothing, corncobs, and even dog collars in well-preserved cave finds. It is a regrettable price of progress that many of the best sites of the early bluff-dwelling inhabitants had their ancient archaeological record buried beneath the waters behind the dams built on the White River.

Following these first inhabitants, early Hopewell-Mississippian people were active as traders, often trading obsidian, seashells, and other commodities. They were the people Hernando DeSoto found when he plundered villages in southeast Missouri and northeast Arkansas in 1540, but in just more than a century, when the French explorers Marquette and Joliet arrived in 1673, these peoples were gone, replaced by the powerful local tribe known as the Osage. They expanded their domain quickly over much of Missouri, and by 1690 there were seventeen Osage villages in the Ozarks. American Indians valued the Ozarks for the game and later as a place of refuge. Because the Ozarks did not have rich farming land, the area was less desirable to the advancing white settlers, and the westward migration for a time went around the Ozarks. As a result, the Ozarks was an area much more slowly settled and developed than the rest of the state. Though the Osage ceded the Ozarks area to the federal government in 1808, they continued to use the area as a hunting ground, claiming they had only given up the land, not the game on it. As eastern tribes were pushed westward, the area had contact with the Cherokee, Shawnee, Peoria, Kickapoo, and Delaware. The infamous "Trail of Tears" went through the Ozarks when the Eastern Cherokee nation was shattered in 1838. The removal by Presidents Jackson and Van Buren of all Native Americans east of the Mississippi resulted in the mass migration, and roughly a third of the 20,000 Cherokees died on the trail. The displaced tribes traveled through the Ozarks to the new Indian Territory or sought shelter in the remote hills and hollows. They were viewed as outsiders by the Osage tribe. The Osage were a tall, well-built people, heavily armed because of trade contacts with both the French and the Americans, and superb horsemen, and the displaced eastern tribes were often at their mercy. The Osage tribe dominated the Ozarks until they too were relocated in Indian Territory. A good many of the Cherokee and other members of displaced eastern tribes stayed in the Ozark hills or intermarried with the white settlers, and today many Ozarkians have "Indian blood." After all, Taney County is only 90 miles from Oklahoma, which used to be known as Indian Territory until statehood in 1907, and the Ozark Mountain area extends into southeastern Oklahoma.

The occupation of the immigrant tribes and the Osage posed no real friction in the early waves of pioneer settlement. There were clashes, but full-fledged warfare was not part of the history of settlement of the Ozarks. The French, and later the Americans who lived in the Ozarks, dressed much like the Native Americans, in buckskin and, when they could get it, calico. They ate the same foods, hunted and trapped the same game. Both groups liked tobacco and whiskey and used them as trading commodities. The local tribes loved to gamble, betting deer hides and beaver pelts, moccasins, robes, and other valuables, and early settlers visited villages to play

the native game called chuckaluck. The similarity of the two groups frequently saw the settlers and the natives forming joint enterprises in hunting and trapping. Area towns with names such as Osceola, Wappapello, Tecumseh, Sarcoxie, and Ginger Blue show the respect Missourians had for Native American leaders, and a few place-names such as the Missouri and Niangua Rivers and Neosho are of American Indian origin. Largely, the Native American influence on place-names is not great, for those people had been pushed into Indian Territory when the great wave of settlers flowed into Missouri. The Ozarks today was a silent witness to a history and culture that lingers with a few place-names and the occasional arrowhead or other relic turned up during spring plowing or by the developer's bulldozer.

Missouri was under Spanish political control from 1763 to 1800, but Spain did not take much interest in the area, and certainly not the Ozarks. Place-name influence is largely on the Mississippi River side of the state. Three of the state's original counties were organized and named by the Spanish: St. Charles; Nuevo Madrid (1788), which became translated and corrupted to New Madrid (with the accent on the Mad); and Cape Girardeau—which obtained the name of a French ensign stationed at Kaskasia. The land picked up a De Soto (1893) after the discoverer of the Mississippi, and Stone County has Ponce de Leon, a spa town that wanted the Fountain of Youth connection the name gave. The Spanish also named a river, Rio Corriente, which was simply translated to the Current River.

i **The Missouri state insect is the honeybee, an oddity of choice because like many people now living in Ozark Mountain Country, it is not a native but a "come-here," having been introduced to North America by the early colonists. In 1839 Missouri had to expend $30,000, the cost of calling out the state militia, for the Honey War, fought with the Territory of Iowa. The war started when a Missouri resident cut a bee tree in territory claimed by Iowa.**

The French were more adventurous than the Spanish and traveled up the rivers, hunting and trapping game and exploring, trading with the Native Americans, and frequently intermarrying with them. They named rivers and streams and other geographical features and made a larger linguistic impression with place-names. When the area came under American influence with Jefferson's purchase of the Louisiana Territory, the French gradually became assimilated in the expanding American culture. The French influence can be seen in the faces and features of early pioneers in the paintings of George Caleb Bingham, and French names linger over the landscape, though the early French might not recognize the pronunciation today. Bois D'Arc is pronounced "Bow Dark"; Versailles is pronounced like it looks, not like the French city and palace; Pomme de Terre (the river and lake, French for "potato") comes out of our mouths something like "Pom le Tar"; and Tour de Loup (wolf track) was corrupted to "Toad a Loop." Names that didn't change pronunciation were translated, and la Riviere Blanche, named by the French for its white-water shoals and rapids, became the White River.

Branson is becoming more of an international tourist destination, now that Europe is discovering that the United States has a Midwest and does not just consist of East and West Coasts, and now that Missouri and Arkansas actively court foreign tourists.

Missouri's tourism industry generated more than $20 billion in 2005, and an increasing number of those spending money are not from the United States. The Spanish and French visitors who come can smile at the changes in the names their countrymen placed on the land, but there can be no doubt of their influence on the language and culture of those who live in Missouri and the Ozarks.

OZARK HILL FOLK

Henry Rowe Schoolcraft described the lifestyle and character of early pioneers in the Ozarks in his journals of his travels, remarking that "Corn and wild meats, chiefly bear's meat, are the staple of food. In manners, morals, customs, dress, contempt of labor and hospitality, the state of society is not essentially different from that which exists among the savages. Schools, religion, and learning are alike unknown. Hunting is the principal, the most honourable, and the most profitable employment. . . . They are consequently a hardy, brave, independent people, rude in appearance, frank and generous, travel without baggage, and can subsist anywhere in the woods."

He thus first records an account that was to become a type. The stereotypical, cartoon version of the Ozarker, the hillbilly, with bare feet, long beard, flop hat, and single-galImused trousers and the accoutrements of a stone jug of moonshine and a rifle, perhaps owes something to Schoolcraft. Certainly such stereotypes are abundant in Branson—in the motifs of restaurants, in yard ornaments, postcards, and the myriad of crafts and tasteless T-shirts and gewgaws found in gift shops that sprawl alongside the highways and byways of Branson—and in the humor of some of the music shows.

As with any stereotype, there is some truth behind the cartoon cutout. The Ozarks were the moonshine capital of the nation, if one is to base that title on the number of stills per capita, because whiskey was value added to corn and was cheaper and easier to store than the grain. It was an easy way to make "cash money," and after Prohibition it was an easy operation to hide in the maze of hollows and caves and forests. The Ozarks produced its share of sharpshooters because hunting was necessary to put meat on the table, and it was a rare family that didn't possess at least several guns. Having a sharp "shooter's eye" was something to be proud of and thankful for. The hardscrabble hill existence led to a poor lifestyle that put low emphasis on clothes and style and a high priority of getting the true value out of long wear. Furthermore, the ancestry on the hill folk was often of the eyebrow-raising type, according to Susan Klopfer's *How Branson Got Started*.

"It was not uncommon for early settlers to be criminals and black sheep of their families.

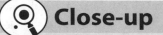 **Close-up**

A Look at the Ozarks Hillbilly

Hillbilly is a fightin' word for some hill folks in the Ozarks. Nobody enjoys being called slovenly, ignorant, and uncouth. *Hillbilly* is taken by a lot of people to mean those very things. For some, it is a politically incorrect word. For others, *hillbilly* is simply a term for a person who lives in the hills. It has no derogatory meaning at all, no more than flatlander does with respect to people who aren't lucky enough to live in hill country.

What the term conjures up in the mind for some is the cartoon stereotype of a shiftless, barefoot, single-gallused, rifle-totin', corncob-pipe smokin', moonshine-drinkin', long-bearded man who is slow in mind and speech. The women, if they're past middle age, are considered much the same, but without the beard. If they're young, they're curvaceous Daisy Maes. They're all stereotypes that you still find in some of the shows on The Strip in Branson.

A factor in helping define the stereotype is the dialect and accent we use here in the Ozarks. There is something about the language of the Ozarks that is different from standard English that marks us: dead-on bull's-eye metaphors but also convoluted euphemisms, a grammar and diction that are more Elizabethan than modern, and a sound that has the softness of the Old South and the twang of Texas but with a pushing together of words or a contraction of them found nowhere else. ("C'mere. Letsqueet" for "Come here. Let's go eat" or *opry* for *opera*.)

Hillbilly is a word that isn't as old as the Ozark Mountains. The earliest reference in print according to the *Dictionary of American English* appeared in 1902, and, as for its etymology, it's simply labeled as "unknown." May Kennedy McCord, longtime columnist for the Springfield paper and pioneer radio columnist with her *Hillbilly Heartbeats* on Springfield's KWTO years ago and an indefatigable collector of Ozarks folklore, said that the term was "sort of a smart-alec nickname that got attached to the hillmen of any hilly country" in the early years of this century. She figured that its source was the billy goat "because he roams the hills."

For some it is a term of contempt and derision, applied to people of rural origin in general—not just hill people. It is a term whose dim meaning has been gleaned from old *Ma and Pa Kettle* movies, the *Green Acres* and *Beverly Hillbillies* TV series, and James Dickey's novel *Deliverance*, with much of that being drawn from the movie version of the novel.

For those hill people who recognize that many use it as a term of disparagement, there are feelings of anger, resentment, and shame. Others from the Ozarks, like the Shakers, Quakers, Baptists, and Methodists of earlier days, who took a term of derision and turned it into a perfectly-acceptable-in-polite-company noun, take what other people consider as a badge of contempt and wear it with honor. The change came, according to Otto Rayburn, author of the *Ozark Encyclopedia*, after the Ozarks began developing as a playground and tourist area; "the term was cleaned up and accepted in the best of society." Some of the older businesses of that period of development in the Ozarks used the term *hillbilly* in their name and the hillbilly stereotype in their advertising.

People with something to hide often stopped off here. A lot of the natives, as a result, don't have the backgrounds of their families because relatives have kept the information a secret," said native Jerry Coffelt. It was easy for a person with a past to hide it, or find a future, in the Ozark hills. Wright's novel, *The Shepherd of the Hills*, has that idea as a major motif.

Most Ozarkers are of a Scotch-Irish ancestry, the descendants of Scottish Presbyterians who settled in Northern Ireland during the 17th century under the plantation system instituted earlier by Elizabeth I to "pacify the wild Irish." Though both the Scots and the Irish are of Celtic ancestry, the plantation scheme involved giving to the Protestant Scots large areas of land that had been

Bob Corbin says a hillbilly is someone who is practical and down to earth—"a person who can repair anything with baling wire and duct tape, a person who can eke out an existence on hard scrabble land where others would starve to death." A sixth-generation hillbilly, with tongue planted firmly in his cheek, he says that he "dislikes the term" and "prefers the more formal hill-william." The term of derision has gradually changed to a term of acceptance, sometimes with a feeling akin to pride.

The stereotype of the hillbilly existed before the word. No work of art had greater influence in picturing the typical hillbilly in the American mind than did a painting, *The Arkansas Traveler*. Painted in 1858 by a Vermonter named Edward Payson Washburn, the work was reproduced and widely distributed. The painting, combined with the story and the famous fiddle tune both attributed to Col. "Sandy" Faulkner, did much to establish the stereotype of the Ozark hillbilly.

The stereotype lingers on and was frequently played upon for the tourists. Ozark entrepreneurs made postcards of "hillbilly" scenes, carefully posed and costumed with the appropriate props: rickety outhouses, bonneted women, and lazy, whiskey-drinking, corncob-pipe-puffing, sleepy men wearing floppy straw hats.

The music shows in Branson get a lot of comedy mileage out of the hillbilly stereotype. Hargis in the Moe Bandy Show, Gary Presley's Herkimer in the Presleys' Jubilee Theatre, and Droopy Drawers Jr. in the Baldknobbers Hillbilly Jamboree Show (see The Shows chapter) are characters that draw on the Ozark hillbilly stereotype, but their creators, some who are real hill folk, would be the first to admit that they are characters not so much to be laughed at but laughed with. Other folks, however, put such comedy in the same class as that of the blackface minstrel shows at the turn of the 20th century. But the Presleys and the Baldknobbers, the oldest shows in Branson, must be doing something right to have survived the competition when big C&W names came in, and yuckin' it up by their comic artists has been a factor in the groups' popularity.

Many of the folk artists and craftspeople in the area and the theme parks are taken by tourists to be real hillbillies but are actually comeheres. They were attracted to the more laid-back lifestyle they found in the Ozarks, learned the craft from others, and delight in teaching and demonstrating it. They have taken to heart the words of a Stone County lawyer who defended his client in a divorce case after his wife called him a hillbilly. "An 'Ozark hillbilly' is an individual who has learned the real luxury of doing without the entangling complications of things that the dependent and over-pressured city dweller is required to consider as necessities, and who forgoes the hard grandeur of high buildings and canyon streets in exchange for wooded hills and verdant valleys."

The observation is probably true, and there even may be some truth to what early tour operator Pearl Spurlock used to tell tourists: "God has to keep people chained up in heaven for fear they'll come to the Ozarks and become hillbillies."

inhabited for centuries by the Catholic Irish. The religious and political problems in Ireland stem from this 400-year-old endeavor.

Continual fighting with the Catholic Irish and new, higher taxation by the English produced a Scotch-Irish exodus to the New World. Even before the American Revolution, some 250,000 of them had crossed the Atlantic for a better life in the wilderness of America. They were a breed of people who were an equal match to the hardships of a new land. They became the quintessential frontiersmen and the sharpshooters in Washington's army; they were the scouts who led the settlers farther westward. Most of these immigrants landed in Boston and Philadelphia, and they sought out landscapes that reminded them of their hilly home country, frequently settling in the Appalachian Mountains area. Some moved south to the frontier opportunities in the Great Smoky Mountains of the Carolinas or west through the Cumberland Gap, settling in Kentucky and Tennessee. Later, they or their children moved farther west into Missouri and Arkansas. They frequently married Native Americans or other immigrants of Welsh, Irish, English, or German background. Perhaps the best exponents of these people were the Boone family, who had already settled on Missouri's frontiers when Lewis and Clark began their famous voyage of exploration up the Missouri in 1806.

In the isolation of the Ozarks, aspects of the older Scotch-Irish culture persisted and continued, long after it was abandoned by those who settled in other areas. Characteristic of that culture was a deep sense of independence and a suspicion of government and outsiders. Residents preferred simple but lively music performed on the familiar instruments they brought with them: fiddles and dulcimers. They created crafts from materials at hand, weaving baskets or building homes and furniture from the wood and stone they found in their immediate environment. The crafts and the folk music of the Ozark Folk Center in Mountain View, Arkansas (see the Day Trips chapter), and the more modern versions found on The Strip are based on the older models, older traditions. Anyone who has traveled in Ireland will notice connections to the Ozarks, and perhaps those connections account for the pleasant surprise that Irish and Scottish tourists have when confronting the familiar as they visit the Ozarks, and why country artists such as the late Boxcar Willie have a large following in Ireland, Scotland, and Wales. Similarities can be found in subtle connections of grammar and metaphor in the language of Ozark hill folk with that of an older, archaic English language. The Scottish-Irish settlers were more interested in storytelling and storytelling music such as ballads than in books and abstract music. Thus the inherent suspicion of "book larnin'" by the Ozarker, the belief that everyone must be able to tell a good story, and the existence of ballad variations that have been

traced to similar versions in Scotland and Ireland. These people, like their Celtic ancestors, preferred herding to dirt farming and favored hunting and fishing to any agricultural endeavor. They were less interested than most in the trappings of material wealth, seeing it as a snare that took away independence. Often clannish and more concerned with family and the nearby community than the far-off government of the state and nation, they were proud of their isolation and independence. They could be passionate about love, politics, and religion, and they could be deeply stirred by the natural beauty of the hills or be emotionally responsive to music and the spoken word.

Today's country music and crafts and culture draw on this history, and they have evolved and adapted to the American experience of the early Scotch-Irish settlers. As another great wave of migration has come into the Ozarks with the advent of the modern tourist industry and the building of roads and dams, the Ozarker retains many of those early traits and again adapts to a changing time—but is always proud to be a hillbilly.

THE CIVIL WAR IN THE OZARKS

Missouri was a border state in two ways, north and south the most obvious, but also east and west, with the Mississippi River being the dividing line. Looking back at the perspective after the war, battles fought in Missouri as part of the Transmississippi War had little influence concerning the outcome, and because of the sparse population of the area, battles in this border state pale to mere skirmishes compared to the large-scale slaughter in eastern battles. In spite of having little impact on the Civil War's outcome, the Civil War had a tremendous impact on the Ozarks, and Missouri had a higher percentage of participants in the war than any other state—109,000 Union solders and 30,000 Confederate soldiers, 60 percent of all men old enough to be mustered.

At the outbreak of the war, the Ozarks was still sparsely populated, and in that sense was of little importance. It did not contain strategic materials needed by either the Confederacy or Union, but events in Missouri were harbingers of what was to happen back east later. Carthage, in Jasper County, was the site of the first land battle of the Civil War, July 5, 1861, preceding the first Battle of Bull Run by 16 days and Missouri's biggest battle at Wilson's Creek by more than a month.

The Ozarks area was marked by two large-scale battles. The first, Missouri's biggest, was the Battle of Wilson's Creek, occurring southwest of Springfield on August 10, 1861. Lasting for six hours, this brief but savage encounter of Gen. Sterling Price's Confederate forces with those of the Union's Gen. Nathaniel Lyon produced 2,330 casualties. One of the battle's dead was General Lyon himself, the first Union general to be killed in the Civil War. Wilson's Creek was a Confederate victory, but the Union regained control of southwest Missouri by the winter of 1862 (see Wilson's Creek National Battlefield in the Day Trips chapter).

The second major battle in the Ozarks was about 50 miles southwest of Branson at Pea Ridge, Arkansas, March 6–8, 1862. It was the turning point of the war in the Ozarks. After the victory at Wilson's Creek, the Confederate forces expected another victory, especially since they outnumbered their Union foes two to one. Included in the Confederacy's forces were a thousand Native Americans from the Five Civilized Tribes who had been moved to the Indian Territory some 30 years before. This band of Cherokees, Seminoles, Chicasaws, Choctaws, and Creeks was under the leadership of Cherokee Stand Watie, the only Native American to achieve the rank of general and the last Confederate general to surrender after the war. The tribes were divided on Civil War issues, but it was politically expedient to back the Confederacy, especially after the Union defeat at Wilson's Creek. But the outnumbered Union forces prevailed at Pea Ridge; as a result, the Ozarks area was ostensibly under Union control, and many Native Americans reversed their loyalty.

The compelling issue of the Civil War, slavery, was not a burning issue in the Ozarks. It did not develop a slave economy. The hilly, rocky Ozarks did not support the kinds of crops, largely cotton and tobacco, grown on the southern plantations that demanded a large labor force. Land use in the Ozarks consisted of small farms, worked by the landowner and his family within large areas of wilderness forest. The only farmers who had large holdings of slaves were those in the "Little Dixie" area along the fertile Missouri River, north of the Ozarks, and those in the bottomlands of the rivers south of the Ozarks, the Arkansas, and the lower end of the White. Some Ozark families had slaves, but not many. The 1860 census in Taney County showed a holding of 84 slaves spread over 24 families, with the largest owner having 10. There were five free blacks. Compare that to the better farmland area of Greene County, which had nine free blacks and 1,668 slaves. Douglas County (named after Stephen B. Douglas) recorded no African Americans, slave or free. In fact, many Ozarkers, even into the 20th century, never laid eyes on an African American. Most Ozarkers in Taney County were indifferent to the slavery issue or were generally supporters of the Confederacy. As one resident said, "Our sympathies are with the South but our interests are with the Union." This pro-Southern leaning is evidenced by the name of the county seat (after John Forsyth of Georgia) and the names of the county and the nearby village of Taneyville, after Roger Brooke Taney, the U.S. Supreme Court chief justice in the Dred Scott Decision of 1857. Though the county had been named for him 20 years earlier, there was no outcry to change the county name.

In a region that today is staunchly conservative and in which most residents are registered with "the party of Lincoln" as voters, one finds it difficult to conceive that 150 years ago, voters looked with disfavor on Abraham Lincoln, his policies, and the new Republican Party. In fact, residents of Greene County were shocked when Lincoln polled 42 votes in the 1860 election. In the counties of Taney, Stone, Christian, Ozark, and Douglas, not a single vote was cast for Lincoln. The next election produced equally lopsided results for Lincoln, largely because the Federals controlled the area, many Southern sympathizers were in the army or had been driven away, and Union soldiers voted in local elections.

The hostilities that resulted with the election of Lincoln produced, as pointed out, not large-scale battles; instead, hostilities were in the form of innumerable and interminable raids, forays, and skirmishes by roaming bands of bushwhackers. The use of small, mobile bands of marauding irregulars was introduced by the Confederacy. Such raiders could harass the stronger Union enemy and tie up resources and men that could be more effectively used in the more important and bigger battles east of the Mississippi.

The Missouri Ozarks, with few slaves, an indifference to the issue of slavery, and an independent people who just wanted to be left alone to hunt, trap, and till their gardens and farms, were caught between two radical and passionate elements. Not far from Taney and Stone Counties is Kansas, where radical abolitionist feelings predominated. Arkansas, to the south just a few miles, was a strong pro-Confederacy state, dominated by numerous plantation owners of the big river valleys. Geography and the independent temperament of the Scotch-Irish who settled here had both served to isolate the Ozarks. Now, as the result of politics, these people and their region were caught squarely in the middle of the conflict. The Ozarks were at the mercy of roving marauders from both sides—and those who believed in neither faction but used the excuse of war to raid, rape, rob, and pillage. To compound the bad situation of being caught between two

ℹ The gunplay on the square in Springfield on July 20, 1865, in which James Butler "Wild Bill" Hickok shot and killed Dave Tutt for wearing Hickok's watch in public—which Tutt had won at poker—became the prototype of the "Main Street showdown meeting" found so often in Westerns. According to the transcript of the trial, each shot one time, with Tutt firing first. Wild Bill's revolver shot struck Tutt in the heart from a distance of 75 yards, a feat that caused the encounter to be written up afterward in *Harper's Weekly* and dime novels.

forces, Indian Territory, just west in what is now Oklahoma, was just an easy ride's distance. It was a refuge for outlaws, vagabonds, and desperadoes of every ilk, and the no-man's-land law that prevailed there allowed gangs to make hit-and-run attacks on helpless Ozark homesteads whose men had enlisted and were off to war for one side or the other. Bands of guerrillas and bushwhackers terrorized the surrounding countryside. Those who weren't killed fled in terror. As an example of the decimation of the area's population, consider that the 1860 census counted 6,883 residents in Jasper County, but by the end of the war only 30 were left.

Names of desperadoes whose careers may have begun during the war but frequently continued after it are legion, and some became well known beyond the region of local history: Frank Dalton and gang, Cole Younger, Jesse and Frank James, "Bloody Bill" Anderson. A name less known is John R. Kelso, one of many leaders who were respected citizens in peacetime but when exposed to the rigors of war became psychopathic fanatics. Kelso was known as a scholar of languages and philosophy who became a schoolteacher at Ozark, but one who became an ardent Unionist and held all Confederates to be traitors, guilty of treason, and deserving death. It was said of Kelso that he could lie at the side of a road in ambush, with a Latin grammar in one hand and a cocked pistol in the other, waiting for his intended Confederate sympathizer victim. One of his reported exploits was creeping alone one night into a camp of three Confederate bushwhackers who were asleep and dispatching them silently with his knife. He was said to be a man of exceptional self-control; he believed in a spartan diet and did not smoke or drink, and he believed in the benefits of exercise, physical and mental. He was considered modern and liberal and forced his wife and daughter to adopt the freedom-giving dress advocated by Amelia Bloomer. After the war, he was elected to Congress as a Radical Republican and did all he could to thwart the president's efforts toward a rational plan of reunification and reconstruction.

Alfred Cook might be considered a pacifist bushwhacker. At the beginning of the war, Cook and his wife, Rebecca, and their seven children were living on a farm north of Taneyville. Both Alfred and Rebecca were descendants of slave-holding families, and their parents with the family slaves had come to Taney County in the 1830s and settled along Beaver and Swan Creeks. Though probably sympathetic to the Southern cause, Cook tried to remain neutral, but foraging parties from both sides raided area farms, taking what they pleased and displeasing those from whom it was taken. Men who stayed at home might be called to the door and shot down by some fanatic of one side or another. Confederate sympathizers, or those whose loyalties were unknown, were plagued by the "Mountain Feds" scattered through the area, who served as informants for the Unionists. Cook and his family, caught in the vortex of the rebellion, faced starvation. Driven by desperation and criminal acts committed against them and their families, Cook and 13 or more others banded together for mutual protection. They adopted the tactics of their despoilers, and Cook and his followers made retaliatory raids against those persons who had robbed them. Cook and his band may have saved themselves from starvation, but their vindictive and deadly activities came to the attention of the Federals, who began scouring the middle border from Ozark to the lower North Fork River for them.

Cook and his band took refuge in a cave high on a bluff. It had a natural stone wall at its entrance, so it could be easily defended, and a spring that provided freshwater. It did not, however, have any other opening. In January 1865, Lt. Willis Kissee and 25 men on a scouting trip, with orders to capture or exterminate Cook's band, learned of the hideout from an informer. Kissee located Cook's small son and forced him to act as a guide to the gang's cave, where he surrounded the entrance. Kissee demanded that the raiders surrender. It was a demand that if complied with, would have meant death. No one emerged. Kissee called out that the raiders would be treated as prisoners of war and not harmed if they surrendered, and he gave them four hours to decide. When the time expired, 11 of the men emerged from the cave. Cook and two others refused to surrender. Not wishing to risk lives in an effort to take the remaining raiders, Kissee built a huge fire on the ledge above the entrance and pushed it over the cliff into the mouth of the cave. Wind blew smoke inside. Blinded and nearly suffocated by the smoke, Cook and his companions emerged from their lair. They were gunned down and left where they fell. The bodies were later retrieved by two neighborhood girls, a 13-year-old boy, and an old man, then were buried in a common grave overlooking the stream that flowed from the spring at Cook's cave.

Another homegrown variety of bushwhacker was Stone County's Alf Bolin, who instituted a reign of terror during the war that is almost unequaled. Bolin, a large, wiry man with a long, chest-length red beard, was a bushwhacker with no allegiance to either North or South. He bragged of having killed more than 40 men. One of those was Calvin Cloud, his surrogate father. Bolin and his gang, at the height of his career, sought refuge one day at the home of Calvin and Mary Jane Cloud, near McCall Bridge in Stone County. Alf, wearing a mask, demanded that Calvin supply him with food and guns. Calvin denied the request, and Bolin drew his gun and shot him in the head. He then threatened to kill Mary Jane, who was pregnant, and her four children. Mrs. Cloud, who recognized the voice behind the mask, would later play another role in Bolin's career.

Bolin and his band of renegades, numbering several dozen at times, preyed on defenseless homesteaders, though Bolin was bold enough to bushwhack small units of Union soldiers. His motives behind his various crimes were seldom clear. One of his victims, 16-year-old Dave Tittsworth, was killed near his home near Walnut Shade, north of Branson. Some nearby women took Bolin to task for killing such a young boy. He is said to have replied, "Get in the house and shut your mouths if you want to save your scalps. That makes 19 I've killed."

Another victim was Bill Willis, who lived along Roark Creek just north of the White River. Bolin shot the 12-year-old boy off a rail fence. Other known victims of Bolin's gun were James Johnson, killed on Camp Creek in Christian County, and Bob Edwards, slain near the community of Bluff on Bull Creek, 9 miles north of Branson. Once Bolin forced an 80-year-old man from his wagon just after he had crossed the White River on Hensley's ferry, made him wade into the river, shot him, and left his body to float downriver.

Bolin raped, robbed, and murdered people from Union families over a wide area between Ozark, Missouri, and Crooked Creek, Arkansas. Many of his crimes occurred at Murder Rocks, sometimes referred to as Bolin Rocks, a castlelike geological formation on the Carrollton-Forsyth road just south of present-day Kirbyville on MO JJ. The fortified position that wagons had to pass by allowed Bolin to ambush his victims with ease. Today, the site is near the Branson Airport and the new Murder Rock Golf Course and Country Club.

So numerous and monstrous were Bolin's crimes that a $5,000 reward was offered by the federal government for his capture, dead or alive, as the Union militia fruitlessly pursued him and his band. One man who attempted to gain the reward pretended to join up with Bolin's gang and got the drop on the renegade by putting his Bowie knife to the sleeping Bolin's throat. A kick by Bolin disabled the bounty hunter, and he was stripped and branded on his chest with a hot poker—"I found Alf Bolin"—and sent packing. Others trying to cash in on the reward were found dead, brazenly displayed on trees, hanging by their own belts.

The outlaw's bloody reign was finally ended by Robert Foster and his wife, who were, ironically, Confederate sympathizers. Foster was a Rebel prisoner being held in the stockade at Springfield. Foster, who lived close by Murder Rocks, was uneasy at the thought of his wife alone in their cabin, though the Fosters had never done anything to antagonize Bolin and his band. So Foster struck a deal: He would betray Bolin if the Union would parole him. He then convinced his wife to cooperate with a twenty-two-year-old corporal from the Iowa Volunteer Cavalry, Zachariah E. Thomas. Zach Thomas was sent to the Foster farm, while Robert Foster remained in the stockade.

Thomas, dressed in a Rebel uniform, hid in the loft of the Foster cabin, his Colt revolver under his jacket. Bolin had been invited to the cabin by Mrs. Foster on the pretext of having Bolin buy their household goods, as her husband was to be released and they were going to leave the area. On the morning of February 2, 1863, Bolin came to the log cabin. He was not suspicious, as he had regular dealings with the Fosters, but the hidden Thomas accidentally made a noise in the loft. Improvising, Mrs. Foster told Bolin she was hiding a lone Rebel soldier, and Corporal Thomas was asked to come down from the loft. Thomas and Bolin talked and even shared a meal, and the suspicious Bolin gradually relaxed. They both examined and discussed a coulter from a plow that was lying by the fireplace. Bolin turned his back when he bent down to the fireplace for a coal to light his pipe, and Thomas dealt him a blow to his head with the heavy coulter. Why he didn't use his revolver, no one knows—perhaps just to save ammunition. Foster bashed Bolin's head three more times for good measure.

He and Mrs. Foster dragged the body outside to a log barn, but Bolin revived as she was cleaning up the blood on the hearthstone in the cabin. Thomas, who was saddling his horse, used the army Colt that he had never drawn in the cabin to finish off Bolin before leaving. When he returned at dawn the next day, Foster was with twenty-five cavalry troops, led by a major and two mule-drawn wagons. Bolin was placed in one wagon and all of the Fosters' meager belongings in the other, and the troop headed toward Forsyth.

In the county seat, news of Bolin's death attracted hundreds of locals, who came to view the corpse. An Iowa soldier wrote of seeing the dead Bolin: "He was a long, sinewy man and must have been of great strength and endurance. His hair was matted with blood and it was clotted over his face, rendering him an object of disgust and horror." When the caravan headed north toward Ozark, a bitter local, Colbert Hays, whose relatives had suffered during Bolin's reign of terror, stopped the procession just north of Forsyth and asked to identify the bushwhacker. He did so, and before the amazed group could stop him, he beheaded the dead Bolin with an ax. The headless body was unceremoniously buried, and with Bolin's bloody head in a gunny sack, the troops continued toward Ozark, the county seat of Christian County. It was Mary Jane Cloud, widow of Calvin Cloud and surrogate mother of Alf Bolin, who was ordered to Ozark to make a positive identification of Bolin's head. According to the story, she rode the 30 miles on horseback through a February snowstorm to confirm the identification. At Ozark the head was impaled on a pole and displayed. It is said that children threw rocks at it and that people cut locks of Bolin's hair and long red beard off for souvenirs. The grim trophy finally reached Springfield, was reduced to a skull, and was sent to Jefferson City, where it disappeared. To this day, no one knows what happened to Alf Bolin's head.

In a recent footnote to history, Mary Jane Cloud's grave was discovered in the spring of 1998. She had died in 1906 and was buried beside her husband in the family cemetery near her cabin, but the graves had become forgotten and overgrown. Their discovery in the gloomy, dark hollow in Stone County sparked renewed interest in Bolin's bloody history.

And what of the $5,000 bounty on Bolin's head? The full bounty, a tremendous sum of money in those days, was awarded to Corp. Zachariah Thomas, who was further rewarded by being commissioned a second lieutenant on March 24, 1863. Robert Foster was released from the stockade as agreed and reunited with his wife, and Thomas, remembering the bravery and quick thinking of Mrs. Foster that had saved his life, gave the Fosters $3,000 of the bounty in a generous gesture.

Though the Civil War ended two years later, peace did not come easily to the Ozarks. Today, few people know of the gruesome Ozark bushwhacker episode of Alf Bolin, and certainly not many of the seven million visitors to the area. At Silver Dollar City during the mock train robbery,

when a scruffy bushwhacker bandit announces, "I'm Alf Bolin, and I'm takin' yer valuables," be aware that the mock robbery has historical roots in the Ozark past, and for the robbed, a much happier ending than the victims of the real Alf Bolin.

THE BALD KNOBBERS

The guerrilla warfare carried on by the borderland Rebels against the Union forces during the last two years of the war was difficult to shut off when surrender was ordered and the war was over. During the war, Ozarks towns had been decimated. Of the 51 structures that comprised Berryville, Arkansas, in 1860, only Hubbert's Hotel and two small residences remained when peace was declared. The hotel was spared the torch, it is said, because Masonic records and regalia were stored in the upper story. Yellville, Arkansas, was destroyed by Union forces and bushwhackers, and before the fighting ceased, 32 buildings had been burned. Dubuque, Arkansas, on the White River, had been a busy steamboat landing with a thriving community, but the community and landing were totally destroyed by Union forces because the area had a lead smelter that furnished shot for Confederate forces. It was never rebuilt.

In Missouri, six of the border counties with Arkansas had their county seats destroyed by fire. Rockbridge, the first county seat of Ozark County, was burned and never rebuilt. Today only foundations remain, plus a postwar mill; the spring, which offers excellent trout fishing; and a rebuilt restaurant that is justly famous for its trout dinners. Vera Cruz, the pre–Civil War county seat of Douglas County, met a similar fate. After the war the county government was reestablished at Arno on Beaver Creek and later moved to Ava. On April 22, 1863, Union troops burned Forsyth, county seat of Taney County. All that remained of the town when settlers returned to rebuild were the scorched walls of the three-story brick courthouse. The county seat towns of Galena in Stone County and Ozark in Christian County had incendiary fires but escaped total destruction. The courthouse in Ozark, however, burned soon after hostilities ceased. Farms and homesteads suffered even more, and few remained standing at the end of the war, the inhabitants having fled.

The end of the war did not see the end of the factional hatred. Each survivor, each returning refugee, had cause to hate someone. This animosity was nurtured and kept alive in the hearts and minds of many as they began the arduous task of rebuilding homes and lives. It destroyed rational thought. It poisoned the souls of those who were afflicted by it. The lawless period of the war encouraged a general lawlessness, and hatred often flared up in acts of revenge. In the period from 1832 to 1860, only three murders had been reported in Taney County. In the postwar period of 1865 to 1885, there were 40 murders—and not a single conviction.

To combat the lawlessness, vigilance committee organizations were formed. There was the Anti–Horse Thief Association; another was simply called the Citizens' Committee. Greene County had its Honest Men's League—which soon became a part of the problem it attempted to resolve. In Taney County, the Law-and-Order League came into existence April 5, 1885, in an outdoor organizational meeting on Snapp Bald. Because its members met on the treeless top of a mountain, known locally as a bald, enemies dubbed the organization "the Bald Knobbers." The vantage point of the bald offered a wide view of the surrounding countryside. Its barren top prevented spies from sneaking up and spying on the secret organization, which discussed the crimes of lawless neighbors and decided what kind of vigilante justice should be dispensed. Their story and the organization's impact on the area is the interesting study of *Bald Knobbers: Vigilantes on the Ozarks Frontier*, by Mary Hartman and Elmo Ingenthron, found in many local bookstores.

The Bald Knobbers' desire to promote peace and prosperity was the stated motive for the organization's existence. Improved roads and the return of steamboat traffic on the White River after the war were now bringing more people into the Ozarks and allowing those who lived here a way to transport goods and produce to outside markets. Crossroads stores and post offices were coming into existence to service

drovers and freighters along new roads, and the new settlers moving into the Ozarks. The budding community of Branson was one such new town. Reuben Branson had given his name to the post office of his country store in 1882. However, darker reasons also existed—motives of revenge on the part of some who still harbored grudges from the past.

One of the newcomers to the area was Nathaniel "Nat" Kinney. He bought 267 acres of White River bottomland in 1883, just downriver from Branson along what is now Lakeshore Drive. His money came from the operation of a successful Springfield saloon. Kinney was a big man—6 feet, 6 inches and 300 pounds. He was a bare-knuckles prizefighter and a veteran of the Union army. Known as Captain Kinney (more for alliteration than accuracy, for army records show him as only a private), he appears in a photograph by the back bar in his saloon as a huge man with massive, folded arms and a large handlebar mustache. With a grim, unsmiling countenance and a close-cropped head, he looks like he could easily serve as his own bouncer—and delight in the job.

Kinney was also a religious man and founded a Sunday school at Oak Grove School near Snapp Bald (out on the current MO T). He was disgusted with the lawlessness he found in Taney County. As a successful businessman, he wanted order so that his farmland venture would prosper. When he assembled the group of nearly 200 on Snapp Bald that April night, Kinney saw the ordered elements of society: lawyers, mill and store owners, county officials. Seven were preachers—two Baptist, three Methodist, and two Disciples of God—and a great many were Masons. All would have been considered solid citizens of the community, taxpayers and churchgoers, but that did not mask darker motives. There was also a political twist to the situation. The Bald Knobbers were strongly Union and Republican. Their opposition were largely ex-Confederates and Democratic in politics.

The night after that April organizational meeting, a hundred armed and masked Bald Knobbers rode into Forsyth and placed a hangman's noose on the jail door of Newton Herrell, who was awaiting trial for the killing of Amus Ring, his mother's lover. They also left a noose draped over the judge's bench as a symbolic reminder that should the court not punish Herrell, the Bald Knobbers would.

Within a week, the Bald Knobbers' actions moved from the symbolic to the active. Action stemmed from the troublesome Taylor brothers, Frank and Tubal, two hellions who had gotten into a ruckus with J. T. Dickenson. Dickenson was an outsider and an Englishman who had come to Taney County and started a socialist commune. When it failed, he became a capitalist and operated a general store. The two Taylors, angry that Dickenson would not give them credit for a pair of boots, shot him in the mouth with a .32 caliber revolver. The bullet knocked out four of his teeth, but its energy was spent and deflected. The bullet exited his neck. After shooting him again, the Taylors fired five times at his wife. She was hit in the neck, and a finger was shot off. Thinking them dead, the Taylors left, but both survived.

It was such lawlessness that had spawned the Bald Knobbers. They now combed the rugged hills in search of the Taylors. A $1,000 reward was offered, and it was the reward that introduced a bizarre twist to events. The two brothers concocted a scheme with friends to turn them in. The friends would collect the reward, use part of it to bail them out, and then would split the remaining reward money. So Frank and Tubal and their buddies rode into Forsyth, April 14, 1885, and surrendered, joking with locals and the arresting lawmen. For the boys it was an adventure and a joke, a profitable one: they'd reap the money for their own reward, and they would be acquitted. They were, after all, longtime residents, and the English storekeeper was an outsider. Such had been the pattern of justice in the past.

That pattern changed that night when Kinney and his band of Bald Knobbers broke down the jail door, dragged the two pleading boys to a large black oak by Chadwick Road, and lynched them. Was the hanging preplanned, or did an attempt to shock the two Taylor brothers just get out of hand? No one knows. Ozark poet Mary

Elizabeth Mahnkey, who was eight years old when the event took place, later wrote about the lynching tree in "The Tree Accurst":

"Whene'er I pass that grim old oak I felt a sense of dread. / It spread its arms so wildly—It tossed its blighted head. / The shade it cast was black and still, / The earth was bleak and bare; / No flowers, no birds, no nestlings, / No sweet winds lingered there. / Then someone told the story / Of this piteous cursed tree / And then I went another way / For fear that I might see / The helpless wretches dying, / Swinging from that oak, / Victims of the savage mob / In sable hood and cloak."

The double lynching made news even beyond the Ozarks. The *New York Sun* carried the story of 100 masked men breaking into a jail in order to provide a necktie party for two people who were not African Americans. It also made some members of the Bald Knobbers ashamed, disgusted, and revolted by their own lawlessness, and a number refused to participate further in revenge justice.

The Bald Knobbers became a vortex of activity. For every one who had quit, there were a dozen to take his place, and they were often less high-minded than the original organizers. Soon the membership was at 1,000 in the vigilante force. Infractions that could bring a warning or a flogging were expanded. No longer only horse thieves and murderers received midnight, masked visitors. Gamblers, drunkards, "loose women," those "living in sin" or accused of marital infidelity merited a flogging. Debtors, especially those who owed money to Bald Knobbers, might expect a midnight visit. Before the vigilante justice ran its course, 30 men and 4 women died at the hands of the Bald Knobbers. Many others were forced to flee their homes, and the Taney County night riders made national news.

The Bald Knobbers were in control, and many believed they were corrupt. A planned audit of the county's books by an impartial, outside auditor never took place because on the night of December 19, 1885, someone broke into the brick, three-story Taney County courthouse, rebuilt within the walls of the structure gutted during the Civil

i Artist and historian Scottie Snider has painted the Bald Knobber past in a mural on the wall of the Ozark City Hall.

War, and saturated its floors and stairways with kerosene and started a fire under the stairs. Many people blamed the Bald Knobbers.

Several events caused a reaction against the Bald Knobbers. One was Kinney's murder of Andrew Coggburn (which Kinney declared to be self-defense) just after the Bald Knobber leader had preached a sermon at the Oak Grove church. Another was the later murder of Sam Snapp, the only witness (but one who refused to testify) to Coggburn's shooting. The Anti–Bald Knobbers organized and formed a local militia. Some of their more neutral neighbors finally appealed to John S. Marmaduke, the Missouri governor. Marmaduke sent his adjutant general to the area in April 1886. J. C. Jamison was ordered to make the Bald Knobbers, and the local militia that opposed them, disband; if they didn't, they'd face the consequences. The Missouri adjutant general had been a gold miner in California during the 1849 rush, had been a captain in William Walker's attempt to gain control of Nicaragua in 1855, and had served under Gen. Sterling Price in the Civil War. (Jamison's Confederate background was viewed with suspicion by the Bald Knobbers.) He was a seasoned soldier, and his demands could be backed up with state militia if need be.

On April 10, 1886, Jamison met with both sides of the conflict in Forsyth and informed each that they and their organizations were illegal. Jamison gave Nat Kinney 24 hours to disband, or he'd bring in the state militia to restore peace and order. Kinney asked for 48 hours, and Jamison agreed. A resolution was drawn up, signed, and forwarded to the governor. With the Bald Knobbers disbanded (though only on paper), the ill feelings by many toward Kinney did not disappear. Of course he'd been a target for killing from the beginning, but he was a formidable foe. Now, he never went anywhere without several armed bodyguards. When he preached now, Kinney would lay two Colt .45s—"Short Tom," a snub-barreled pistol, and "Long Tom," a long-barreled pistol—on the pulpit before he began his sermon. Anti–Bald Knobbers were known to offer prayers to God to strike Kinney dead; more practical ones offered to buy out his land holdings at a good price on the condition he leave Taney County forever. Kinney, however, had other ideas for his future. Since the Bald Knobbers controlled local elections, Kinney had his sights on becoming the area's next state representative.

The energy that had fueled the Bald Knobbers spawned similar enclaves in nearby counties. Christian County had its own version of the Bald Knobbers, though the territory toward the highland north lacked the balds of the White River country and forced the vigilantes to meet in caves. Dave "Bull Creek" Walker was the touchy fellow who was the driving force for that Bald Knobber franchise. The group was more inclined than the Taney County version to punish neighbors for smaller indiscretions, slights, and even jokes. The Christian County group used the "bull from Hell" mask now associated with the Bald Knobbers from murals by Steve Miller and by its use in *The Shepherd of the Hills* outdoor play (see the Attractions chapter). The mask was a cotton corn sack whose corners were tied up with corks inside to form horns and whose eyeholes were stitched or painted with red or black. Some members even spent the two bits that could buy a custom-designed mask.

It was the Christian County Bald Knobbers who became involved in the episode that effectively ended the reign of the vigilante group. Bill Edens had compared a Bald Knobber to a sheep-killing dog. He had already been flogged once for his Anti–Bald Knobber comments. The new insult was reported on the eve of the Bald Knobbers' disbanding, and it was decided by the hot-tempered, hard-drinking young son of Dave Walker, Bill, and his impressionable cronies to obtain revenge, in spite of Gen. J. C. Jamison's threat.

At 10:30 at night, the band surprised the sleeping Edens and his wife in their cabin. With them were his elderly parents, James and Elizabeth Edens, and another couple, Charles and Melvina Green, and the Greens' two small children. Threats were made, and gunfire erupted, leaving Bill Edens and Charles Green dead. James Edens had been shot and his head bashed with an ax, but he was alive. The two young widows were left screaming as the children, unhurt in the spray of bullets, crawled through the blood toward the fireplace.

By now, there was an anti-vigilante feeling, and local law enforcement authorities were not intimidated. Those responsible for the murders were hunted down, but some escaped. Those who were caught cooperated under pressure to bring their former cronies to justice. The four Bald Knobbers deemed most responsible for the outrage were sentenced to hang, including Dave Walker and his 16-year-old son, Billy—dubbed "the Baby Bald Knobber" by the press. Others, including a Baptist minister (who conducted the funeral service for Edens and Green after the murders), were sentenced to prison terms. Before the hanging, the two Matthews brothers put their woodcarving skills to use and escaped by whittling a key, but James was recaptured. The successful escapee, his brother Wiley, it is said, made his way to the frontier of Indian Territory in Oklahoma and lived out his life as a woodcutter, dying in 1937. His brother and other two compatriots weren't so lucky.

They were executed on the Ozark courthouse square, May 10, 1889, at 9:55 a.m. behind a stockade fence designed to provide some privacy and to keep at a respectable distance the thousands who had gathered—and to prevent a possible Bald Knobber rescue attempt. The trio had refused to have the hangings done by a professional hangman from Kansas City, and they left the duty to the sheriff, who had been a friend. Sheriff Johnson, it would be hoped, was a better sheriff than a hangman. He did not know how to calculate the proscribed drop based on the weight and build of the victims. Matthews was lucky, and his neck was broken when the trapdoor was sprung. Dave Walker, his feet barely dragging the ground, was allowed to slowly strangle. The third, young Billy, escaped hanging during the first attempt when his head slipped out of the noose during the fall, only to be dragged back up the stairs of the scaffold and quickly rehanged. The professional hangman, a Daniel Binkley, commented to the *Kansas City Star* about the Ozark effort, calling it "a horrible botch, crude and inartistic."

Meanwhile, in Taney County, between the sentencing and hangings in Ozark County, Nat Kinney was gunned down in a store. As the story goes, five Anti–Bald Knobbers rode to Springfield to consult Almus "Babe" Harrington, a prominent lawyer who lived on the James River. Asked what constituted a valid defense against first-degree murder, Harrington replied, "self-defense." The visitors paid the lawyer a $500 retainer in case one of them might be charged with murder, then retired to Harrington's barn and played a bizarre game of poker. The loser would have to kill Nat Kinney. A young farmer from Taney City (now Taneyville), Billy Miles, threw away enough good cards to lose the game.

The opportunity came soon enough. An Anti–Bald Knobber businessman, J. S. B. Berry, had to declare bankruptcy. Kinney was named as the receiver in Berry's bankruptcy filing. Berry had hired Billy Miles and his brother Jim as bodyguards because of a feud with a business friend of Kinney's that had taken a nasty turn. Kinney was in the store, taking stock of the inventory for the bankruptcy sale, when the two brothers entered. Kinney threatened them and reached for his revolver, but Billy drew his own .44 double-action Smith & Wesson. His first shot entered Kinney's left arm, breaking both bones, and traveled up into his body. A second shot hit his heart. A total of five shots were fired, but none by Kinney. He dropped dead behind the store's counter. Reloading his gun, Billy stepped outside. "I have just killed Cap'n Kinney in self-defense," he told the gathering crowd of townspeople.

Billy and Jim Miles later shot it out with a Bald Knobber sheriff, Galba Branson (brother of Reuben, who named Branson), and his deputized gunfighter at an Independence Day picnic at Kirbyville, killing both. The fact that Billy and Jim Miles were acquitted of all three killings was evidence that the people and the judicial system were fed up with the Bald Knobbers. Years later, in 1912, Jim Miles—described as "always trigger happy"—shot and killed a Branson merchant in his store and was convicted of second-degree murder and sentenced to 10 years in prison.

It was years before things settled down, and gunfire was not an unusual sound in the Ozark hills. Old scores were often settled violently, and Taney County gained an international reputation with its flirtation with vigilante justice, with accounts appearing in papers from coast to coast, as well as in Paris, London, and Berlin. The coming of the railroad in 1906 and Harold Bell Wright's novel about the Ozarks the next year, *The Shepherd of the Hills*, in which the Bald Knobbers have a role, brought tourists to the area and opened a market for timbering and fruit crops. When the *Ozark Weekly News* remarked in an editorial that "Bald Knobberism is buried in oblivion, never to be resurrected again," the editorial writer was only half right. Today on The Strip, music lovers are attracted to the first music show to open in Branson, the Baldknobbers (one word for the music group), and they witness the vigilante group's terrorism in the outdoor dramatization of Wright's novel. The Mabe family, which makes up the Baldknobbers (see The Shows chapter), is an old Ozark family who have no night riders in their ancestry, but those visitors who see the entertainment resurrection of the Bald Knobbers should be aware that what now passes for amusement has roots in the not-too-distant Ozark past.

RIVERS, RAILROADS, AND ROADS

The Ozarks, like a rugged butte sticking up in a flat landscape, saw most of the great wave of western migration pass around it, much the way a stampeding herd of buffalo parts and goes around an object, or the way the water of a river separates and flows around a boulder. The growth and development of the Ozarks can only be understood in context of the development of transportation that could take people into (and products out of) the Ozarks. In a sense, the story of the Ozarks is a story of the evolution and development of transportation, a story of rivers, railroads, and roads.

Travel had always been a challenge in the area, and the earliest settlers followed old Indian trails along the James and White Rivers, or they used the rivers themselves, the area's first "roads." These early Native American trails either followed rivers or ridgelines; either way, it always made for meandering routes, and the roads developed from them were equally winding, and travel was not easy. River travel was no easier and always a tricky proposition because of danger of upset in shoals and rapids, and travel was largely limited to going downstream. As the population in the Ozarks grew and commerce increased, wagon roads became necessary. By the mid-1830s, a road was developed between Springfield, then the seat of most of southwestern Missouri, and the junction of Swan Creek at the White River, the eventual town site of Forsyth, so that Springfield could have access to the White River. Reflecting the confidence placed in the promise offered by steamboat navigation, the official seal of Taney County (formed in 1837) bore a steamboat in its center, and steamboat traffic became a major topic of conversation among those living in southwestern Missouri and northwestern Arkansas. There were high hopes that farmers would be able to send products to markets downriver as well as take advantage of cheaper prices of products being brought in. The problem was two large shoals: Buffalo Shoals and Elbow Shoals. The *Eureka* finally conquered Buffalo Shoals in June 1851 but was turned back at Elbow. In June the next year, the *Yohogony* finally conquered Elbow Shoals, but only after laboring a full day and unloading 300 sacks of salt below the shoals. It was the first steamer to make it to Forsyth, and designers of the Taney County seal had proved prophetic. Steamboat design and technology were improving, and with the development of high-pressure boilers, these small, light paddle wheelers could make it up sometimes as far as the mouth of the James, but only during high water in the spring, and only by using both paddle wheel and a steam winch, hooking a cable to large trees above the shoal and pulling themselves over the rapid water and rock ledges. After the first steamboat made it as far as Forsyth, steamboat traffic on the upper White increased dramatically, but the Civil War brought river commerce to a halt. (An interesting and dramatic account of the White River steamer era can be found in *Steamboats and Ferries on the White River*, by Duane Huddleston, Sammie Rose, and Pat Wood.)

In 1858 the Butterfield Overland Mail began operation as a result of an authorization bill introduced by Senator William Gwinn of California and Congressman John S. Phelps of Missouri and passed the year before. It started at Tipton in central Missouri and ran southwest through Stone County into Arkansas, and then westward to California. By the time of the Civil War, the segment of this route in the Ozarks was called the Wire Road because of the telegraph wire strung along its route from Jefferson Barracks at St. Louis to Fort Smith, Arkansas. The road was used by both sides in the Civil War, but little used for commercial purposes during the war because of danger of guerrillas and bushwhackers. Today's I-44, which bisects the Ozarks, incorporates lengthy portions of the Wire Road.

When commerce began to grow again, the 1870s north-south roads were cleared and widened for use by large freight wagons. The major freighting route in Stone County followed a well-established Native American trail called the Wilderness Road. From Springfield it more or less followed today's US 160 and MO 13 south through Spokane, Reeds Spring, and Blue Eye to Berryville, Arkansas. In Taney County three freight roads connected outlying communities as far south of the White River as Harrison and Berryville to the Springfield railhead (Springfield had rail service by 1869) and the Chadwick railhead—as far south as a railroad could easily be built. Ponderous freight wagons traveled to market loaded with tobacco, cotton, animal pelts, and railroad ties and returned with merchandise to be sold in small stores along the route. The round-trip could take as long as two weeks, with nights spent in campgrounds along the way or boardinghouses in small towns. Roads wound back and forth, climbing steep hills and meandering along ridgetops; today's paved highways frequently follow these same routes, widened, upgraded, and paved. By the 1880s this road network required constant maintenance, and counties were divided into road districts. Men older than 21 were scheduled to work two to four days in lieu of certain taxes. Those who did not work had to pay the tax. The roadwork involved keeping trees and brush out of the roadways, pulling out and sometimes blasting out rocks, filling mud holes, and establishing safe fords across creeks. Work was done with axes, shovels, crowbars, and mule-drawn scrapers called slips. To slice through roots that clogged drain ditches or humped roads, a "rooter" was used, a plow with two guide handles and a single, sharp vertical cutting blade, pulled by a team of four mules.

While roads were being developed, efforts continued to expand the railroad into the hilly Ozarks. By 1858, a railroad had been built from St. Louis to Sullivan, Missouri, and by 1861 tracks had been laid to Rolla. The outbreak of the war delayed farther extension, but on April 21, 1870, citizens of Springfield greeted the Cuba, the first locomotive to steam into town on track laid only hours earlier. A line was extended to Chadwick in 1883, but the major problems of the hills to the south were still to be conquered. Plans and various routes had long been considered and debated but had been opposed by steamboat

ℹ️ **The sassafras tree was valued by Ozarkers for the tea made from its roots dug in the spring, said to "thin the blood" and serve as a spring tonic. Tender green branches and leaves were used to beat a chicken roost as their oils and pungent aroma helped to keep the chickens free of lice. Green wood was used with hickory to smoke meats. The wood, half as light as the next lightest wood, was often used for featherweight but strong boat paddles.**

interests. In addition, the building of the necessary trestles and tunnels was considered too expensive. But the gradual increase in commerce made the second argument less plausible. Debate continued, but actual work did not begin until spring 1903, when the Iron Mountain Railway Company began to extend the line up the White River valley. But it was not until January 21, 1906, that the first puffing, noisy locomotive hauled a few cars down the Turkey Creek valley into the town of Hollister, whose population had grown to 250. The trains' steam whistles could be heard as far as 9 miles north of Branson, and they so disturbed a relative of artist Rose O'Neill at Bonniebrook that he packed up and moved down to Hemmed-in Holler, a box canyon off the Buffalo River, so he could have "some peace and quiet." The shrill whistles of the new locomotives had finally replaced the dying echoes of the steamboats' whistles on the river. With the coming of the railroad, steamboat traffic dwindled, and a new era dawned. Depots in Branson, Hollister, and Reeds Spring were soon stacked high with departing goods: tons of mussel shells from the White River to be made into buttons; railroad ties, lumber, and cordwood; cotton from gins at Kirbyville, Mincy, and Kissee Mills; tobacco; fruit; and livestock. Coming in the area were cheaper staples, new luxuries—and tourists.

The coming of the railroad in 1906 actually spurred growth in road building. In 1914 citizens of Reeds Spring and Branson formed two cooperative road districts to build a road between the two towns. The road crossed the slope of Dewey Bald and ran past the Shepherd of the Hills farm and Marble Cave. Sometimes the roadbed eroded into steep, rocky stair steps, but the tree-lined road was often like a country lane. Certainly it

i **Branson's first signs of industrial independence asserted themselves in the form of a pencil factory, an ice plant, a candy factory, and a soft-drink bottling company soon after its incorporation as a city in 1912.**

made travel much easier between the two towns. In 1936 that route was reconstructed and later paved, becoming MO 76. In days before the Table Rock Dam, the rocky goat pastures filled with trees and sprouts that sloped down to the creeks on each side of MO 76 could be had for less than a hundred dollars an acre—the price depending on whether the land came with or without the goats. Now that the land has developed into the famous Strip in Branson, those prices are dream deals of the past. The road made the scrubland valuable (see the Relocation chapter).

In building roads, the many creeks and rivers posed problems. Most creeks could be forded except during high water, but to cross the bigger White River, ferries were used, and there were more than two dozen ferry crossings on the White and the James Rivers. Today only the Peel Ferry, which takes cars across Bull Shoals Lake at MO 125 south of Protem, is still operating. Ferries began disappearing in 1914 after four bridges were built across the White River. Arriving motorists voiced complaints about the general lack of bridges and the unpaved streets and roads, and in the mid-1920s, when local businessmen and residents began buying cars, funds for road improvement became available, and in 1929 from local property taxes and state and federal sources. Bridges (often low-water bridges) were built over the many creeks, and all streets and secondary roads were "paved" with gravel.

Upgrading of US 65 to concrete or asphalt from Springfield to the Arkansas border began in 1929, but work faltered during the Depression. It was completed eight years later as a WPA project to provide jobs for the unemployed. Rather than a two-day trip by wagon from Branson to Springfield, the journey over the new asphalt road could be completed by automobile in just less than two hours. In the process of upgrading US 65, both Branson's and Hollister's downtown areas were bypassed, with the highway (now US Business 65) going a block west of Commercial Street and Main Street and east of Hollister's Downing Street. Merchants howled and predicted the death of both towns. The old steel bridge at the foot of Branson's Main Street was bypassed, and a new bridge was built across Taneycomo. New concrete bridges were also constructed over Roark and Turkey Creeks and over the railroad in Hollister.

Recognizing that adequate roads would be necessary for the area to develop, Jack and Peter Herschend, developers of Silver Dollar City, lobbied hard for improvements to US 65. In a continuing series of engineering feats begun in the mid-1960s and finished in the mid-1970s, a new US 65 was cut through the mountains from Springfield to the Arkansas border, with new bridges being built over Roark Creek and Lake Taneycomo. The new, straighter US 65 bypassed downtown Branson, again with the prediction that the town would die, but more tourist traffic allowed Branson to grow west along The Strip. The new US 65 made the area more accessible and increased the numbers of people who annually discover the Ozarks, and it allowed many Ozarkers to discover the rest of the country. Driving time to Branson from Springfield was cut to 30 minutes. Now, the entire drive is four lanes, and the driving time is 25 minutes. Branson has again been bypassed with the completion of the Ozark Mountain Highroad. Again, extensive lobbying by the Herschends for the project, especially Peter, caused local wags to dub the proposed bypass "Pete's Pike" because the loop west around Branson has exits near Silver Dollar City, along with exits at MO 248 (the old US 65), Shepherd of the Hills, and The Strip.

Better roads brought more tourists. More tourists brought more development. More development made necessary more roads, and since 1992 the city of Branson has spent millions developing parallel and improved routes to provide shortcuts and alternatives to the often crowded MO 76. One of the alternative routes was the Shepherd of the Hills Expressway, developed not by the government but by developer and owner of the Shepherd of the Hills Homestead, Gary Snadon.

In the film The Visionaries, Snadon remarked: "Back in the late seventies, the State Highway Department laid out this road, and the gas shortage ruined funding for it. I happened to see the plans and started acquiring the land in '82 or '83 and started construction in '85. MO 76 was carrying 27 or 28,000 cars a day in 1985. The capacity of the highway was reached. Traffic would back up and simply stop. I had just purchased the Shepherd of the Hills Homestead, and we couldn't get people out to the farm to get their tickets." The expressway has since been taken over and rebuilt by the state, and development along it is almost equal to that of The Strip.

Visitors buy postcards that say, "All Roads Lead to Branson." That's not true, of course, but the ones that do are less meandering and are much wider and straighter than they were just several decades ago. Many people resent roads so straight that people can drive like Hell through God's country, and they believe that something has been lost with the meandering. New and better roads have brought more people to see what the Ozarks and Branson have to offer, but they have also set off another round of development and improvement. It's been that way since the first settlements; only the pace has quickened. Folks can fly directly to Branson commercially now that the Branson Airport has opened (2009), and a high-speed rail link with the Springfield/Branson National Airport is being looked into. Many decry the changes that have changed the culture as well as the landscape. Others consider them progress.

When does the Ozarks' story of rivers, railroads, and roads end? Probably never. There will just be another chapter.

HIGH DAMS, HIGH HOPES: BRANSON GROWS

Just as important as roads to the development of the Branson area were dams. Substantial rainfall could bring the creeks up quickly, and they poured their flow into the White River, resulting in floods of devastating destruction to homes, towns, and livestock, as well as a disruption of travel and transportation. It would be impossible for months at a time to cross the White, resulting in today's oddity of two schools just across the river from each other, Branson and Hollister Public Schools. There had been plans since the middle of the 19th century to build locks or to dam the White River. In fact, it was a series of locks authorized by Congress on the middle section of the White that spurred railroad interests to build the railroad up the White River valley.

Such projects were opposed by farmers (who would see the area's most fertile land inundated) and the developing float trip industry, headed up by successful entrepreneur Jim Owen and others, who would see business and a way of life dependent on shoals, rapids, gravel bars, and bluffs disappear under a lake.

The first dam was Powersite Dam in 1913, which created Lake Taneycomo (named for Taney County). Authorized in 1911, it was the largest power dam in the country at the time: 50 feet high and 1,200 feet long. Though small by today's measures, its impact was large. It brought electricity to the Ozarks and made a river without rapids, backing up water for 22 miles to what is now the base of Table Rock Dam. It created the area's newest scenic view, and it caused the development of resort town Rockaway Beach, modeled and named for the Adirondack resort town. It catered to people who came for a taste of the Ozarks and to fish, boat, swim, and ski its warm waters. The dam changed the tourist industry, but it did nothing to hinder the devastating floods that periodically swept the Ozarks. When the White went on a rampage, 600,000 acres of cotton, tobacco, corn, and beans were flooded. In the 1930s, farmers had only one year of every three in which their crops weren't wiped out by high water. Low-lying areas of Branson and Hollister were frequently inundated by high water of the White.

Through the efforts of U.S. Representative Dewey Short, a series of flood control dams were authorized. The first flood dam, in Arkansas, completed in 1951, was Bull Shoals Dam, which backed up water to the base of the earlier Powersite Dam in Missouri. Most of Forsyth was relocated from beside the White River, where it

had existed for more than 100 years, to the top of Shadow Rock Bluff. Next was Table Rock Dam, completed in 1958. Gone was the threat of floods to Branson and Hollister, but the tourist industry developed over a half a century based on Taneycomo's warm waters also was gone. Water entering Taneycomo came from the bottom of the impounded lake, and it was a chilly 50 degrees—too cold for swimming, too cold for skiing, and too cold for the many species that had led to a thriving sportfishing industry. But it was just right for trout, and Taneycomo became a major trout attraction, with a large trout hatchery at the base of Table Rock Dam. (See the Recreation and the Outdoors chapter.)

The fourth dam, number three of the flood dams, was Beaver Dam, again in Arkansas, completed in 1965. The White River, beginning in Arkansas and making a huge oxbow in Missouri before again flowing back into Arkansas, no longer existed as a river in Missouri. It was now a series of lakes. The dam prevented the devastating floods that ravaged the upper White River valley, but it destroyed a meandering river, and it changed forever the makeup, character, and development of the Ozarks.

No longer did people come to the area for float fishing, but other types of fishing attracted even more fisher-tourists. In the '50s and '60s, these anglers brought their wives and children, in part because of the 1960 opening of the tiny theme park in Silver Dollar City by Mary Herschend and her sons, Jack and Peter. The musical, entrepreneurial Mabe family filled a need by providing evening entertainment in an old building in downtown Branson. The Presley family opened its family music show in 1967 on what was to develop into The Strip. Their success brought others, including Roy Clark, the first nationally known artist to hang up a shingle on a Branson theater. Other stars found that having a permanent theater as a home was attractive; rather than being on the road going to audiences, it was easier to have the audiences come to them, and it allowed entertainers to have some home life instead of a series of motel rooms on the road. Soon such stars as Conway Twitty, Boxcar

Willie, Kenny Rogers, Merle Haggard, Moe Bandy, and Mel Tillis were making Branson a rival of Nashville. They were joined by pop singers such as Andy Williams, Wayne Newton, the Platters, and Bobby Vinton. The fact that Branson was a country-music mecca inspired *60 Minutes* to do a feature on the boomtown atmosphere, and the resulting national publicity produced what we call the Branson Boom and opened the way for other venues of entertainment, spawning the huge entertainment industry that now dominates Branson. The primary industry of sportfishing, though still an important reason for folks coming to Branson, is now secondary.

The growth and the publicity of the Branson Boom of the early 1990s produced another attraction: shopping. Now, as many people come to Branson to shop as come for the live music, and they frequently indulge in a little of both. And, increasingly, out-of-doors sports and natural beauty bring in hikers, bikers, and canoeists.

Branson has always been changing or developing in odd and unexpected ways. Cotton and tobacco growing are no longer important, and the gins and mills on the rivers are historic relics. The tie and lumber industry is of little importance. The mussel shell industry has come and gone. The canneries spawned by growing beans and tomatoes are vacant or have already disappeared. The old industries would boom, and then there would be a bust—until replaced by a different industry. At the core since the publication of Wright's *The Shepherd of the Hills* in 1907, however, has been the ever-growing, ever-developing, and ever-changing tourist industry. That primary industry is bigger than ever and much more diversified.

The changing Branson tourist industry might best be exemplified by changes on the Branson lakefront. Gone now are WPA-project Mang Field and the lakefront stone bleachers, the White River Hotel, the Sammy Lane Resort, the huge cottonwoods, and the 200-year-old Burr Oak Liberty Tree. So much of Branson's historic past disappeared to make room for the new $300-million, 96-acre Branson Landing development, with its convention center and hotel, condos, and upscale and trendy shops. The historic lakefront places, a wealth of memories to tourists past, are replaced by development that hopes to create more growth and wealth for the area and wonderful memories for future tourists.

What does the future hold for Branson? Will it go the way of Eureka Springs after the spa boom of the 1890s or the tourist-attracting English village of Hollister at the turn of the last century or the Adirondacks-style Rockaway Beach and enter a long bust phase before another big boom? Who knows, but it will be a long and meandering path, much like the creeks and rivers that characterize the Ozarks.

Come and visit and observe. Come and stay—and meander with us.

ACCOMMODATIONS

The tri-lakes area now has more than 23,000 hotel and motel rooms, more than Kansas City with 17,000 and St. Louis with 15,000. A few years ago it was tough to find a room on the spur of the moment during peak season in the summer and fall. With an annual visitor count of more than 3.5 million in 1990 and fewer than 10,000 rooms, you had to make reservations well in advance in order to ensure space. Between 1990 and 2000 however, the number of rooms grew by 150 percent, but the number of visitors had gone up only 87 percent. An equilibrium has been reached. Only rarely do visitors now have trouble finding a place to stay. The facilities on The Strip usually fill up first, but motels just a couple of blocks away may have plenty of rooms available even during our busiest months, October through December.

Many of the condominium resorts are still adding units. In fact, so many units have been built, it's a buyer's and renter's market. But other than that there has been relatively little new motel construction since 1995. One of the newer facilities is the 304-room, upscale Chateau on the Lake, which opened in 1997. You can still find plenty of mom-and-pop places, most of them with fewer than 30 units. The owners are usually retired couples who came to the area 20 years ago from some place up north and decided to live out their years making friends with their overnight guests. Their places may not have a list of amenities as long as the major chains, but they take your business seriously and will go out of their way to see that you leave with a good impression of our town.

Visitors today also have a variety of national chains to choose from, including Howard Johnson's, Sleep Inn, Holiday Inn, Comfort Inn, Travelodge, Best Western, Quality Inn, Residence Inn, Days Inn, Hampton Inn, Econo Lodge, and Super 8. We have profiled a few of them here, but you know what to generally expect.

Since they are located in the Live Music Capital of the World, many accommodations offer to set you up with show tickets. They find out what shows you want to see, then they call the theater box office to make your reservations. They hand you a voucher and charge the tickets to your room. You present the voucher at the box office and—voilà—you've got your seats. A few of the hotels charge a $2 to $3 fee per ticket for this service.

If you came to town years ago in January or February, trying to avoid peak season rates, you may not have found a soul in sight. That's all changed now with the efforts of a group of local businesses and the Branson/Lakes Area Chamber of Commerce. Their Hot Winter Fun promotion has really taken off in the last few years. Now more than 25 shows and dozens of attractions and major shopping centers stay open during the winter months, as do plenty of hotels. For a complete list of all Hot Winter Fun business members, log on to www.hotwinterfun.com. Unless otherwise noted, the ones we have listed here stay open year-round.

The room rates are very affordable in the winter months, with some properties slashing their prices by as much as 40 percent. There's no such thing as a traffic jam in January, but you'd better come now before the whole world finds out.

Branson motel owners are setting their sights

on families with children these days and have constructed playgrounds, miniature golf courses, volleyball courts, and basketball facilities, as well as video arcades and small water parks, as enticements. The biggest enticement of all is the kids-stay-free plan. A few places let children up to the age of 12 stay free in their parents' room. We have noted those that do. You can get baby cribs for free at some places and for as little as $5 at others. Little junior may have to leave Fluffy at home, though, since most places do not allow pets. Some charge extra for pets. Call first if you're thinking about bringing an animal friend.

Because many of the newer establishments were constructed after the Americans with Disabilities Act was implemented, you should be able to find wheelchair-accessible facilities. Ask if such rooms are available. Unless otherwise noted, all the structures in this section with more than one floor have elevators.

All of the establishments listed here have both smoking and nonsmoking rooms unless otherwise noted. Many are entirely smoke-free. Most have high-speed Internet access and Wi-Fi.

This chapter offers a representation of the full range of facilities available in the tri-lakes area. We can't tell you about them all, so if you need a little more help in deciding where to stay, we suggest you call the **Branson/Lakes Area Chamber of Commerce Welcome Center** at (800) 214-3661 or (417) 334-4136. Their computerized locator system allows them to pull up a list of all available lodging facilities with current vacancies. The system makes immediate reservations and prints driving directions to the facility. The system can also be used to make same-day attraction and show reservations. The one drawback to the system is that it is not an advance reservation system. If you need a room or ticket on a same-day basis, it is a good system to use. After 5 p.m. call (417) 336-4466 for access to the Lodging Locator system. For advance reservations you may call the **Branson/Lakes Area Lodging Association's Centralized Reservation System** toll-free at (888) 238-6782. They have a comprehensive list of all the association's members, with information on each establishment's rates, amenities, and policies.

You can make same-day and advance reservations via the Branson/Lakes Area Lodging Association's reservation system online at www.bransonarealodging.com or via www.hotels-rates.com/Branson/MO/USA.

RATES

The average rate for a room in Branson is a little more than $60, depending on whom you ask. You can find sites with "$25 for two" signs, however. Rates at individual properties can vary as much as 100 percent, depending on what kind of room you choose. If you're looking for a package deal, many of the motels, resorts, and nightly condo rentals offer lodging, show tickets, and meals for one price. Some of them will even throw in show tickets if you stay a minimum number of nights.

In addition to offering a reduced rate for children, many of the places offer a senior citizen discount, an AARP discount, or a AAA discount. Be sure to ask when you make your reservations. When you get in town, stop at a brochure rack to pick up brochures for motels. Some of them contain coupons.

Checkout time for most of the hotels and motels is 11 a.m. or noon. The resorts ask that you be out a little earlier, at 10 a.m.

A free continental breakfast is more the norm than the exception, but the fixings do vary, from your standard cold cereal to homemade breads and muffins. Unless otherwise noted, all continental breakfasts in this chapter are free. You can find a swimming pool at most every location, and some of the suites come with Jacuzzis. One nice thing about Branson motels is that the majority of them don't charge for local calls.

If you want to compare amenities at a glance, you can request the free *Slip Away* magazine from the Branson/Lakes Area Chamber of Commerce at (417) 334-4136. It contains a chart with all member properties listed.

Price Code

Our price code is based on the average rate for a double-occupancy room in peak season. You can expect to pay these rates September through December at hotels and motels. The resorts charge in-season rates June through August.

$.................. **Less than $50**
$$ .... **$51 to $85**
$$$ .... **$86 to $110**
$$$$ ....**$111 and higher**

LOCATION

We have divided this chapter into two categories: Hotels and Motels, then Resorts and Condominiums. Within each category the facilities are arranged by location. The location subcategories in the Hotels and Motels section are Shepherd of the Hills Expressway, East Half of The Strip, West Half of The Strip, Green Mountain Drive, and Just off The Strip. The east-west dividing line we used is Wildwood Drive, which runs north and south and crosses The Strip beside the Branson Variety Theater and the Grand Palace.

If you know you'll be spending a lot of time at Silver Dollar City or Shepherd of the Hills Homestead, it makes sense to stay on the west end of The Strip. Green Mountain Drive runs parallel to The Strip on the south. The properties in the Just off The Strip category are mostly located near the west end of The Strip on Ketter Street, Schaefer Drive, and Arlene Drive.

There are three categories for Resorts and Condominiums: Lake Taneycomo, Table Rock Lake, and Other Areas, which covers those that are not associated with one of the lakes. Some lodgings are pet friendly, others prohibit pets. Check to see what the policy is before packing Fido.

We've put all the bed-and-breakfast facilities in their own chapter, and campers will have to turn to the Campgrounds and RV Parks chapter for a list of places to stay.

HOTELS AND MOTELS

Shepherd of the Hills Expressway

BARRINGTON HOTEL $$
263 Shepherd of the Hills Expressway
(417) 334-8866, (800) 760-8866
www.barringtonhotel.com
Situated just west of the intersection of Shepherd of the Hills Expressway and MO 248, the Barrington Hotel is easy to miss if you're not looking. It's easier to see if you're coming from MO 248. Just look for the large pink letters on the brick four-story building. It's convenient to the Branson Landing, Sight and Sound Theatre, and the Mansion Theatre. The lobby looks more like that of a winter lodge than a hotel with its stone fireplace, plank wood floor, green marble tile, and hanging tapestries. The rooms are decorated in burgundy and turquoise; each comes with a queen-size bed, cable TV, and free local calls. There is an outdoor pool and hot tub, and some rooms come with Jacuzzis. Children younger than 17 stay free. Coffee is served all day, and you can get a deluxe continental breakfast in the morning.

CASCADES INN $$
3226 Shepherd of the Hills Expressway
(417) 335-8424, (800) 588-8424
www.cascadesinn.com
Located near the Shoji Tabuchi Theatre, Cascades Inn is a four-story, 160-room complex with an indoor pool and whirlpool, sauna, gift shop, game room, exercise room, and conference room for up to 100 people. The spacious rooms are outfitted in pastel decor, matching the general tropical theme. Each comes with two queen-size beds or one king-size bed. Each morning you can enjoy the inn's extended continental breakfast in the hospitality room. Children stay free.

CLASSIC MOTOR INN $$
2384 Shepherd of the Hills Expressway
(417) 334-6991, (800) 334-6991
www.classicmotorinn.com
What would you expect to find at the Classic

Motor Inn? Classic cars perhaps? You can usually find some kind of '50s model on display in the lobby and occasionally even a few parked outside. That's basically where the theme ends. A room at the Classic Motor Inn has either two queen-size beds or one king-size bed. The inn has an outdoor pool, gift shop, coin laundry, and continental breakfast. Children 16 and under stay for free. All three outlet malls are no more than a five-minute drive away, with the Shoji Tabuchi and Pierce-Arrow Theatres close by. Closed January.

FOXBOROUGH INN $$
235 Expressway Lane
(417) 335-4369, (800) 335-4369
www.bransonfoxborough.com

Located just off the east end of Shepherd of the Hills Expressway, the Foxborough Inn's 75 rooms have spectacular views of an as-yet-undeveloped wooded hillside. Because it's off the main road, you may miss the inn if you're not watching carefully. From MO 248, turn left at the second stoplight onto Shepherd of the Hills Expressway. It's on the left just past the Mansion Theatre.

The Foxborough has an Old English–fox hunting motif for decor. It's close to the Branson Meadows Mall and conveniently located between Branson Landing and the Strip. There is a coin-operated laundry and an outdoor swimming pool. A restaurant in the hotel serves snacks and light meals. A room comes with two queen-size beds or one king-size bed, cable TV (close-captioned), and phone. Some rooms have Jacuzzis.

HONEYSUCKLE INN AND
CONFERENCE CENTER $$
3598 Shepherd of the Hills Expressway
(417) 335-2030, (800) 942-3553
www.honeysuckleinn.com

The Honeysuckle Inn is conveniently located on Shepherd of the Hills Expressway next to the IMAX complex, with easy access to Branson's best attractions on The Strip. The 210 immaculate and comfortable rooms, legendary Ozark hospitality, and four acres of landscaping give guests the

best each season of the year. The Honeysuckle boasts one of the largest pools in Branson.

An added bonus is that it is the closest lodging to all of Branson's theme parks, including Silver Dollar City, White Water, and Shepherd of the Hills Homestead and Outdoor Theatre. A number of restaurants are within walking distance. Kids under 11 stay free, and a complimentary continental breakfast is served, with a full breakfast buffet available.

Rooms have king, queen, or double beds, and 24-hour guest laundry is available. Ticket services are available.

ORANGE BLOSSOM INN $$
3355 Shepherd of the Hills Expressway
(417) 336-6600, (800) 753-3711
www.bransonorangeblossominn.com

If you're coming to see the man with the fiddle, Shoji Tabuchi that is, you can stay right across the street from his theater at the seventy-seven-unit Orange Blossom Inn. It's closed January through March, but so is Shoji's theater. A number of restaurants are within walking distance: Golden Corral, Red Lobster, and McFarlain's in the IMAX complex. Each room has two queen-size beds or one king-size bed, a color TV, and phone. Some rooms have two-person Jacuzzis. There is an outdoor pool and hot tub. Coffee is served in the lobby along with a free continental breakfast. If there's a long line at the Shoji Tabuchi Theatre, you can ask the front desk to help you make reservations for his show and many others. The level parking lot has a dump station for motor coaches.

THE SAVANNAH HOUSE HOTEL $$
165 Expressway Lane
(417) 336-3132, (800) 383-3132
www.savannahhousebranson.com

The Savannah House Hotel is conveniently located near the Mansion Theatre and the Branson Meadows Mall. Sight and Sound Theatre is within walking distance. The first thing you'll notice when you step inside is the detailed fox-hunting scene painted on the wall behind the front desk. The lobby has a massive fireplace and beautiful wood bookshelves reaching to the ceiling. The decor throughout the 98 rooms is equally impressive. The color scheme includes rich hunter green and cranberry. A standard room comes with one king-size bed or two queen-size beds, cable TV, and phone. Some suites have Jacuzzis. Each of the furnished apartments has two bedrooms, two baths, a kitchen, a Jacuzzi, and a washer and dryer. Ask about long-term rates. There is an outdoor swimming pool and hot tub. The hotel serves a continental breakfast in the breakfast room, as well as ice cream and cobbler as a bedtime snack.

SAVANNAH HOUSE II   **$$**
245 Shepherd of the Hills Expressway
(417) 334-8272, (800) 525-8272
www.savannahhousebranson.com
If you can get to the Barrington Hotel, you can find the Savannah House II. It's located right next door. Since it's off the beaten path, there is very little drive-by traffic. The rooms are tastefully decorated with deep purples and greens. The four-poster bed in the king suites even has a satin bedspread. Dried flower arrangements are scattered about the dark cherry furniture. All king suites come with Jacuzzis and dark wood-beamed ceilings. The king suites have honeymoon appeal, and families fit nicely into their two-room suites, featuring a living area with large windows and French doors opening to the outdoor swimming pool area. A standard double room has a color TV, a sitting area, and phone. The inn serves a deluxe continental breakfast each morning. Closed January and February.

East Half of The Strip

BRANSON CLARION HOTEL AND
CONFERENCE CENTER   **$$**
2820 76 Country Blvd.
(417) 334-7666, (800) 725-2236
www.clarionhotelbranson.com
One of Branson's tallest hotels on the Strip, with five stories, the pink and white Branson Clarion Hotel and Conference Center is quite an impressive sight. From your private balcony overlooking

The Strip, you can conduct your own study of Branson traffic numbers.

The two-story lobby gets an award for its flower-patterned wallpaper. Those pink flowers will really catch your eye. They caught the eye of President George H. Bush when he stayed there in 1992, and the late presidential hopeful Pat Paulsen even announced his candidacy from the lobby during a press conference in 1996.

The 101 hotel rooms have king- or queen-size beds, cable TV, phones, coffee machines, and very high ceilings. Some rooms have Jacuzzis. The 65 less-expensive motel units in the South Tower all have refrigerators. The Branson Clarion Hotel and Conference Center has a penthouse, a two-bedroom family suite that sleeps eight, and a honeymoon suite. There is an indoor pool with a whirlpool and an outdoor pool with a whirlpool and sundeck. You can order from room service, visit the cocktail lounge, and enjoy a continental breakfast. They also have coin-operated laundry facilities, a beauty shop, and a massage therapist on staff.

When you're ready for a fine casual dining experience, check out Buckingham's Restaurant and Oasis Lounge, which is in the hotel. (For more information about Buckingham's and the Oasis Lounge, check the Restaurants and Nightlife chapters.) Even if you're not hungry, you've got to see the safari-themed decor.

i While the summers don't generally get too hot in the tri-lakes area (a few days hover around 95 degrees in August), all of the listings in this chapter have air-conditioning.

GAZEBO INN   **$$**
2424 76 Country Blvd.
(417) 335-3860, (800) 873-7990
www.bransongazeboinn.com
The Gazebo Inn looks more like a quaint little bed-and-breakfast than a hotel. The pale pink and green Victorian decor is carried throughout all 73 rooms. The honeymoon suites feature mar-

ble Jacuzzis with separate showers, sitting areas, and balconies overlooking The Strip and the outdoor swimming pool. The family suite has two bedrooms and a kitchenette. The standard room comes with two queen-size beds, a writing desk, cable TV, and a phone. All rooms are nonsmoking. For shoppers, it's close to the Tanger Mall.

GRAND COUNTRY INN $$
1945 76 Country Blvd.
(417) 335-3535, (800) 828-9068
www.grandcountry.com

Who needs to fight the traffic on The Strip when you can stay at the Grand Country Inn? You can do your shopping at the Grand Country Market (see the Shopping chapter), take in one of four live music shows at the Grand Country Music Hall (see The Shows chapter), eat at the Grand Country Buffet, and play a round of indoor miniature golf. The Splash Country Water Park, free to Grand Country Inn guests, features a huge wading pool, water slide, and lots of other neat water elements the kids will enjoy, plus shaded seating areas for Mom and Dad. You can do it all at Grand Country, adjacent to the 319-room Grand Country Inn. Each room comes with one king-size bed or two queen-size beds, cable TV, telephone, and a beautiful view of the hillside. Relax year-round in the indoor pool or cool off in the outdoor pool and spa in the summer. The staff will customize a vacation package including show tickets, meals, lodging, and attractions for one price.

HILTON PROMENADE AT
BRANSON LANDING $$$$
3 Branson Landing
(417) 336-5500, (800) HILTONS
www.hilton.com

This new hotel is about as east of The Strip as you can get. The new Hilton perches on the Branson Landing, overlooking Lake Taneycomo. The hotel is either the perfect beginning or end to your tour of The Strip (depending on which direction you're coming from!). Not only does the Hilton have easy access to several routes about town, many of the 242 rooms overlook the brick-

paved promenade and specialty shops of the Branson Landing. Inside, soothing colors inspire a residential feel. Rooms offer one king bed or two queen beds featuring the Hilton Serenity collection, which includes a pillowed topped mattress, down comforter, and 250 thread count triple sheets. Additional room amenities include an easy chair with ottoman, 32-inch flat panel television, large well-lit work desk with granite countertops, two (2) line phones with dataports and voice mail, high speed Internet access, minifridge, and much more. A fitness room and pool, concierge desk, and laundry/valet service round out the luxury experience. Don't forget to check out the Liberty Tavern, open for breakfast, lunch, and dinner, serving All-American cuisine in a contemporary casual atmosphere.

If you're with a group, the Hilton provides 800 square feet of meeting space, but if you need more, across the road is the Branson Convention Center. Totaling 220,000 square feet, the Convention Center has two exhibit halls, a ballroom, and five additional meeting rooms—all equipped with the latest in meeting technology. LCD screens, high-speed wireless Internet, video conference capabilities, soundproof rooms, and other audiovisual options are readily available. They can also handle all your catering requirements.

Room rates begin at just over $100 per night in the winter season, with full kitchen suites starting from $150. There is an additional charge for parking and valet service.

OUTBACK ROADHOUSE MOTEL
& SUITES $$
1910 76 Country Blvd.
(417) 334-7200, (800) 562-0622
www.outbackbranson.com

Can't afford a secluded lakeside resort? The Outback Roadhouse Motel & Suites is affordable and secluded. You'll have to settle for a heated outdoor pool, though. Located a good 500 yards off The Strip next to the Outback Steak and Oyster Bar (see the Restaurants chapter) and the Outback Pub (see the Nightlife chapter), the motel sits on 15 private acres. There are no hiking trails, but the motel encourages guests to explore the wooded terrain. The complex features Jacuzzi suites with two bedrooms and family suites with three beds, a kitchenette, whirlpool tub, wet bar, refrigerator, and microwave. The standard room comes with one or two queen-size beds, cable TV, and phone. They serve a hot continental breakfast. After your hike around the property, relax in their hot tub and sauna. Get 10 percent off your room if you make your reservations online through the motel's Web site. Also, check the coupons for the Outback Steak and Oyster Bar.

RAMADA INN AND CONFERENCE CENTER $$
1700 76 Country Blvd.
(417) 334-1000, (800) 641-4106
www.ramadabranson.com

Nestled on 22 wooded acres, Ramada Inn and Conference Center has 297 rooms, two swimming pools, a gift shop, coin-operated laundry, and an outdoor picnic area with a meeting room/reunion center for up to 75 people. It's next door to Dick Clark's American Bandstand Theatre and across the street from the Dixie Stampede. A deluxe room comes with two queen-size beds, a sofa bed, and a sitting area. If you need assistance with show tickets, meals, or attractions, Reception Services can put together a package vacation tailored to your specifications. You can ask the front-desk clerk for help or call (800) 641-4106. Closed January and February.

West Half of The Strip

COBBLESTONE INN $$
275 Tanger Blvd.
(417) 336-2152, (800) 641-5660
www.bransonwindmillinn.com

Step into a Dutch villa atmosphere at the Cobblestone Inn, right next to the Tanger Mall, Kids Kountry, the Track, and the Lost Silver Mine miniature golf course. While the kids are out entertaining themselves, Mom and Dad can relax in the honeymoon suite's two-person Jacuzzi or take a snooze in its king-size water bed. If togetherness is what your family is all about, you can stay in

the two-bedroom family loft suite. A standard room comes with two double beds or a king-size bed, cable TV, phones, and a sitting area. There is an outdoor swimming pool, and the Moon River Grill and Andy Williams Moon River Theatre are within walking distance. With 150 rooms and a windmill above the lobby, you can't help but notice this one.

DUTTON FAMILY INN $
3454 76 Country Blvd.
(417) 334-8873, (800) 942-4626
www.duttoninn.com

The Dutton Inn is right in the heart of Branson's theater district. You can walk to a number of shows, and the closest one is The Duttons! You can get a package deal of lodging and their show. Not far away is the Jim Stafford and Micky Gilley Theatres, and across the street is White Water. A room comes with two queen-size beds or one king-size bed, cable TV and phone, and a free hot breakfast buffet.

HOTEL GRAND VICTORIAN $$$
2325 76 Country Blvd.
(417) 336-2935, (800) 324-8751
www.hotelgrandvictorian.com

Just as the name implies, the Hotel Grand Victorian abounds with Victorian style, from the Italian marble in the two-story lobby to the four-poster bed in the Presidential Suite to the rich green and burgundy room decorations. Tasteful flower arrangements and green plants fill the lobby and sitting room. The Presidential Suite also has a marble Jacuzzi, couch, refrigerator, and microwave. Some of the 152 rooms have private balconies and Jacuzzis. There are indoor and outdoor swimming pools, an exercise room with video games, and a breakfast area where you will find muffins, bagels, donuts, fresh fruit, juice, and coffee each morning. There's even a fireplace in the gazebo pool house. The Tanger Outlet Center, the Grand Palace, Andy Williams Moon River Theatre, Branson Variety Theater, Ride the Ducks, and Wal-Mart are within a stone's throw.

LODGE OF THE OZARKS
ENTERTAINMENT COMPLEX $$$
3431 76 Country Blvd.
(417) 334-7535, (800) 213-2584
www.lodgeoftheozarks.com

Built more than two decades ago, the Lodge of the Ozarks has been called the "classiest hotel in Branson" by *People* magazine. When you step inside the two-story lobby, you are surrounded by elegance. Just down the corridor you'll find the hair salon, three gift shops, the Rafters Restaurant, and the Hughes Brothers Theatre. (See the and The Shows chapter.) The lodge has 190 rooms and a meeting facility that can hold up to 800 people. This is one of the largest convention sites in Branson, with three large meeting rooms and on-site catering.

The hotel rooms are spacious, and each has queen-size beds, cable TV, and a couch. Some rooms have Jacuzzis, refrigerators, wet bars, and extra vanities. You can look down on the indoor pool and hot tub from the second and third floors. During your stay you can enjoy room service and a continental breakfast, and you can make an appointment with their massage therapist. Bob and Elizabeth Dole stayed at the lodge on his first full day of presidential campaigning after resigning from the Senate in 1996.

MELODY LANE INN $$
2821 76 Country Blvd.
(417) 334-8598, (800) 338-8598
www.melodylanebranson.com

Right next door to the Baldknobbers Jamboree Theatre and across the street from the Branson Clarion Hotel and Conference Center, the Melody Lane Inn has 140 spacious rooms, each of which comes with either a king-size bed or two queen-size beds, cable TV, and a phone. There is a coin-operated laundry facility, and all rooms have a view of the outdoor swimming pool and Jacuzzi. Some rooms adjoin so you can keep an eye on the kids. The inn provides shuttle service to local attractions. The Melody Lane Coffee Shop serves a light breakfast each morning. Closed January and February.

QUEEN ANNE I AND II $$
3510 76 Country Blvd.
(417) 335-8100, (800) 229-3170

245 Schaefer Dr.
(417) 335-8101, (800) 229-3170
www.branson.com/branson/qanne/qanne.htm

Queen Anne I sits right on The Strip near the Dutton Family Theater across from White Water, and Queen Anne II is just 2 blocks south on Schaefer Drive. Number two offers a little more privacy but all the amenities of number one. During the Ozark Mountain Christmas season, both motels are decorated with white lights to show off their Victorian rooflines. Both motels have small but clean rooms with two double beds, two queen-size beds, or one king-size bed. Both also have cable television, outdoor swimming pools, and free coffee. The suites at both places have full kitchens. Guests at number two may park at number one and walk to the shows and attractions on The Strip. Children stay free.

SUPER 8 BRANSON CENTRAL $$
3460 76 Country Blvd.
(417) 334-3600, (800) 417-5253
www.super8branson.com

The Super 8 Branson Central has 78 spacious rooms, each with one or two beds, cable TV, and free local calls. The inn also has an outdoor swimming pool. Children stay free. You can get complimentary coffee in the lobby or hop on over to the Plantation Restaurant for an all-out breakfast feast. (See the Restaurants chapter for more information.) If you need assistance with your vacation plans, the Plantation will put together a package for one low price. Closed January and February.

Green Mountain Drive

ALPENROSE INN $
2875 Green Mountain Dr.
(417) 336-4600, (800) 324-9494
www.alpenroseinnbranson.com

An enchanting Bavarian setting is what you'll find at the Alpenrose Inn. In addition to the Alpine mural, you'll see a number of original pieces of art colorfully decorating the two-story lobby. Created by local artists, the works are all for sale. Each of the 50 rooms at the Alpenrose Inn comes with cable TV, phones, and a king-size bed or two queen-size beds. In the summer you can enjoy the outdoor pool and sundeck. Children 11 and younger stay free, and they'll be happy to know that the Pirate's Cove miniature golf course is right next door. (See the Kidstuff chapter for more on Pirate's Cove.) Closed January and February.

BRANSON'S BEST $
3150 Green Mountain Dr.
(417) 336-2378, (800) 404-5013
www.bransonsbest.com

For you late risers, Branson's Best has a 1 p.m. checkout time. You'll need it if you stayed up all night drinking the free coffee they serve 24 hours a day. Each of their 65 rooms comes with two queen-size beds or one king-size bed, cable TV, and phone. Baby cribs are no extra charge, and children younder than 18 stay free with a parent. The inn has an outdoor swimming pool and a 25-item continental breakfast, including donuts, bagels, juice, and cereal. Each evening you may enjoy free ice cream and hot cobbler. Branson's Best is located on Green Mountain Drive near the intersection of MO 165. Closed January and February.

GRAND OAKS HOTEL $$$
2315 Green Mountain Dr.
(417) 336-6423, (800) 553-6423
www.grandoakshotel.net

This 112-unit hotel is within walking distance of the 18-hole Thousand Hills Golf Course (see the Recreation and the Outdoors chapter). Situated on Green Mountain Drive just south of The Strip, the Grand Oaks Hotel is close to the Andy Williams Moon River Theatre, the Grand Village, Tanger Outlet Center, and dozens of restaurants. Choose one of two hotels, one with a French country motif, the other with a beachfront decor. A deluxe room comes with a king-size bed or two queen-size beds, two sink vanities, and a Jacuzzi.

The family suites sleep up to six. If you're waiting on your clothes to dry in the coin-operated laundry facility, you can check out the game room or burn off a little Ozark cookin' in the exercise room. The formal meeting room, with its audiovisual capabilities, makes the Grand Oaks Hotel a great corporate conference site.

HAMPTON INN $$
2350 Green Mountain Dr.
(417) 334-6500, (800) 443-6504
www.hamptoninn.com

Located behind the Grand Palace and the Andy Williams Moon River Theatre, the Hampton Inn is a two-story, 113-room motel with an impressive lobby featuring a crystal chandelier, huge windows, and rich green walls and floor tile. The rooms are quite large, and each comes with two queen-size beds or one king-size bed, cable IV, and phone. Some rooms connect, and the king suites have hot tubs. There is an indoor pool. The inn serves a continental breakfast and boasts a 100 percent satisfaction guarantee or you receive a free night's stay.

SETTLE INN RESORT AND
CONFERENCE CENTER $$$
3050 Green Mountain Dr.
(417) 335-4700, (800) 677-6906
www.bransonsettleinn.com

As you drive along Green Mountain Drive, just look for the white castle on the hill—it's hard to miss. Known for its 40 themed suites, the 300-room Settle Inn is an attraction all its own. If you're willing to pay a little more than the basic rate, around $100 or so, you can stay in the Safari Suite, complete with huge green plants, an African mural, and bamboo furniture. Or you can take a trip to New York in the Big Apple Suite with its Statue of Liberty mural. If you're looking for a period theme, try the Garden of Eden Suite. Adam and Eve would feel right at home. Or if you're into something a little more contemporary, try the Medieval Suite, complete with armored knight. If you haven't remodeled your home in the last 30 years, you'll feel at ease in the 1970s Saturday

Night Fever Suite. Each suite comes with a whirlpool, plenty of furniture, color TV (even though somewhat out of place in the Garden of Eden and Medieval Suites), and a phone. The regular rooms come with queen- or king-size beds and cherrywood furniture.

The list of amenities at Settle Inn runs the full range and includes a deluxe continental breakfast, 24-hour coffee service, two indoor pools and spas open 24 hours, tanning beds, video arcade, guest laundry and dry-cleaning service, and an outside gazebo and sundeck. You can get an evening snack in the Garden Cafe and Lounge, or if you're an early riser, you can catch the free morning musical variety show at 8 a.m. in the Stonehenge Banquet Room. Settle Inn's 7,000-square-foot conference center has meeting space for up to 500. They'll be happy to have your event catered.

Just off The Strip

BOXCAR WILLIE HOTEL   **$$**
360 Schaefer Dr.
(417) 337-7070
www.boxcarwilliehotel.com
Many people never realize that this quiet street exists just a guitar-lick off The Strip. The hotel is two streets west of The Strip, one street west of Green Mountain Drive, and about ¾ mile from Shepherd of the Hills Expressway. The new Boxcar Willie Hotel gives you the best of all Branson has to offer. The bright lights and bustle is a one-minute drive that puts you at the famous Strip with its shows, attractions, and restaurants. However, the location is birdsong and breezes. You can relax and recharge your batteries in a quiet, wooded setting——and yet be at the convenient midpoint between Silver Dollar City and the Branson Landing and Convention Center. It has loads of rooms, an indoor heated pool, and a state-of-the-art infrared sauna. And you get the complimentary Whistle Stop Breakfast.

DAYS INN BRANSON   **$$**
3524 Ketter St.
(417) 334-5544, (800) 334-7858
www.daysinnbranson.com
With 425 rooms conveniently located just off the west end of The Strip on Ketter Street, the Days Inn is one of the largest facilities in Branson. The inn's acreage is nicely landscaped, and the rooms all have a view of the south side of The Strip. Each room has two double beds or one king-size bed, cable TV, and phones. Some rooms connect. There is an outdoor swimming pool, wading pool, spa, and children's playground. There is a guest laundry facility, and you can get a room with a refrigerator and microwave if you desire. A continental breakfast is served in the lobby, or you can get a hot meal at Gambino's, which is located on the property. The cafe serves Italian and standard American fare for breakfast, lunch, and dinner. Children stay in the motel and eat at the cafe for free.

ECONO LODGE   **$$**
230 South Wildwood Dr.
(417) 336-4849, (800) 553-2666
www.econolodge.com
The Econo Lodge is just far enough off The Strip that you won't be bothered by the flashing neon theater marquees, but you'll be close enough to walk to Andy Williams Moon River Theatre and the Branson Variety Theater. If you get hungry, you can take an even shorter stroll to the Lone Star Steakhouse or the Pasta Grill. Each of the 67 rooms comes with two queen-size beds or one king-size bed, cable TV, and a phone. Some rooms have Jacuzzis. There is an outdoor swimming pool and spa as well as a guest laundry facility. The continental breakfast (18 different items) is served in the breakfast room each morning. Children younger than 18 stay free with their parents.

MOUNTAIN MUSIC INN   **$$**
300 Schaefer Dr.
(417) 335-6625, (800) 888-6933
www.mountainmusicinn.com
Located just 2 blocks off The Strip, the Mountain

Music Inn is a three-story, 140-room complex with large windows and a huge indoor pool. The 75-person meeting room and the coffee shop overlook the pool and Jacuzzi. The coffee shop stays open until midnight. The rooms feature a double vanity, two queen-size beds or one king-size bed, cable TV, and phones. Some rooms have Jacuzzis. There is an exercise room and an outdoor pool. The deluxe continental breakfast includes fresh homemade muffins, cinnamon rolls, bagels, toast, cereal, fruit, oatmeal, and juice. Children stay free with their parents. The parking lot is flat and tastefully landscaped. The concierge will reserve tickets to your favorite show.

RADISSON HOTEL $$$
120 South Wildwood Dr.
(417) 335-5767, (888) 566-5290
www.radisson.com

The Radisson Hotel towers above the Branson skyline with 10 stories and 500 rooms. Within easy walking distance are the Branson Variety Theater and the Andy Williams Moon River Theatre. The Veterans Cafe is located on the ground floor and provides room service. The R&R Bar is right next door and is a great place to go to have a drink and watch a little TV.

Each spacious room has a coffeemaker, dataport, hair dryer, ironing board, voice-mail telephone, and satellite television with in-room movies. The top floor houses the penthouse, presidential, and executive suites, which go for around $200 a night. Each suite has its own Jacuzzi. You also get a complimentary continental breakfast, evening cocktails, and hors d'oeuvres in the pricier suites.

The hotel has a swimming pool with half of it inside and half of it outside. Other upscale amenities include a hot tub, sauna, exercise room, gift shop, game room, salon, and boutique. If you're feeling tense after your trip, you can ask for a massage at the salon. The desk personnel will be happy to arrange show reservations for you, and you can also visit the concierge desk to find out what's going on in town during your visit.

The ground floor is designated as meeting space and can accommodate up to 600 people for catered banquets. The sunken lobby has a number of overstuffed chairs and couches as well as a piano.

SLEEP INN $$
210 South Wildwood Dr.
(417) 336-3770, (800) 221-2222
www.sleepinn.com

This 68-room facility is just 5 miles from Silver Dollar City. Each room comes with two double beds or one king-size bed, cable TV, phone, and oversized shower. There is an outdoor swimming pool and courtyard. You can get a hearty continental breakfast in the lobby each morning and then head on over to one of the nearby souvenir shops for some down and dirty shopping. If you're interested in shows, you can ask the front-desk staff to help make your reservations.

i Trying to decide which to pack—long sleeves or short sleeves? Call the WeatherFone at (417) 336-5000 anytime to get a current temperature in Branson and a forecast.

SPINNING WHEEL INN $
235 Schaefer Dr.
(417) 334-7746, (800) 215-7746
www.spinningwheelinn.com

The Spinning Wheel Inn has all the amenities a family on a budget might want. There is a large fenced-in outdoor swimming pool, a children's playground, and a shaded park with picnic tables. Some of the rooms even come with three beds. Plus, children younger than 16 get to stay in their parents' room for free. The rooms are a bit small but well kept. Each room has cable TV, a phone, and either two queen-size beds or one king-size bed. The inn provides a continental breakfast in the lobby consisting of donuts, coffee, and juice. The staff will help you make your show-ticket reservations. Be sure to pick up one of their brochures, which sometimes have coupons attached to the back, worth as much as $5 off. Or you can print one from their Web site. Closed January through March.

RESORTS AND CONDOMINIUMS

Resorts and condominiums in the Branson area cater to anglers, golfers, children, and show buffs alike. The amenities at these places run the full range. The only thing they don't offer is salt water. You can rent fishing boats, pontoon boats, Jet Skis, or canoes from the resorts with marinas. They have professional fishing guides who will go along to help you navigate unfamiliar territory while telling you stories about the good old days.

The rooms at these places range from your basic cabin to 1,000-square-foot deluxe condos with Jacuzzis, VCRs, and cherrywood furnishings. The outdoor activities range from sand volleyball to basketball to shuffleboard to horseback riding. Many of the places have exercise facilities for the truly disciplined and free deluxe continental breakfasts for the truly undisciplined. Whatever your taste, the Branson area's resorts and condominiums hit the spot.

Lake Taneycomo

LAKESHORE RESORT & REUNION CENTER $$
1773 Lakeshore Dr.
(417) 334-6262, (800) 583-6101
www.lakeshoreresortbranson.com

Lake Taneycomo has been ranked one of the top five trout lakes in the nation, and the popularity of the fishing resorts on Lakeshore Drive attest to that fact. Lakeshore Drive runs parallel along the bank of Lake Taneycomo just across from the Branson Landing. Follow US Business 65 (Veterans Boulevard) east across the Taneycomo Bridge and look for Lakeshore Drive immediately on your left. Lakeshore Resort, as it is appropriately called, is the place of choice among die-hard anglers. It has a marina with boats for rent, and it also provides guide service. The units can hold a family of up to 10 in their three-bedroom cottages. Some of the cottages have fireplaces, living rooms, kitchenettes, and Jacuzzis. They all come with cable TV. Outside there is a children's play area and a swimming pool. The picnic tables are just a stone's throw from the water.

SUNTERRA'S FALL CREEK RESORT $$$
1 Fall Creek Dr.
(417) 334-6404, (800) 562-6636
www.fallcreekresort.com

Follow MO 165 south from The Strip past the intersection of Fall Creek Road (notice that we have a Fall Creek Drive as well as a Fall Creek Road). Fall Creek Drive will be on your left before you get to the Welk Resort Center.

With 250 condominiums and motel rooms and a long list of lake amenities, Fall Creek Resort is one of the most popular in town. The Fall Creek Marina (417-336-3611 or 800-480-3611) rents all kinds of fishing boats and pontoon boats. They even provide fishing guides. Fall Creek Resort has an indoor and outdoor swimming pool, whirlpool, a fitness center, children's playground, miniature golf course, tennis court, shuffleboard, basketball court, and guest laundry facilities. A standard room comes with two beds, cable TV, and a phone. The more deluxe accommodations include Jacuzzis; one, two, or three bedrooms; fully equipped kitchens; and family-size living areas. Some units are two stories. You can get a deluxe continental breakfast in the clubhouse or hop on over to the Fall Creek Steak and Catfish House just down the road and catch a flying roll. (See the Restaurants chapter.)

TROUT HOLLOW LODGE $$
1458 Acacia Club Rd., Hollister
(417) 334-2332, (800) 328-1246
www.trouthollow.com

To get there from Branson, take US 65 south to MO V. Look for the signs directing you to College of the Ozarks. Go nearly 1 mile and make a right on Acacia Club Road. The lodge is 1 mile down the road on your right. Trout Hollow Lodge has remodeled its 26 one-, two-, and three-bedroom cabins. Each comes with a fully equipped kitchen, cable TV, and phones. All of the well-shaded cabins have a lake view and are within walking distance of the full-service Trout Hollow Marina. There is a swimming pool, picnic area with playground, 260-foot fishing dock, and a bait and tackle shop that also stocks people food. If you stay three nights, the fourth night is on the house.

Table Rock Lake

BIG CEDAR LODGE $$$
612 Devil's Pool Rd., Ridgedale
(417) 335-2777
www.big-cedar.com

The Bass Pro Shops of resorts is the 305-acre Big Cedar Lodge, located just 10 miles south of Branson on MO 86. With its Adirondack-style architecture and its wilderness-themed landscaping, Big Cedar is an attraction all its own. Developed by Bass Pro Shops owner Johnny L. Morris, Big Cedar has been attracting the attention of the rich and famous since its initial creation more than 70 years ago by two wealthy Missourians, Jude Simmons and Harry Worman, who incidentally now have buildings named after them. The two men built resort homes in what was then known as Big Cedar Hollow. In 1947 a real estate executive bought the property and added the Devil's Pool Ranch guest resort. Since that time, the White River was dammed to form Table Rock Lake. Morris later bought the property, and the rest is history.

With a list of amenities a mile long, a five-season rate card, and upwards of thirty different types of rooms, it is impossible for us to mention everything. We will tell you that the price for a basic room in peak season is around $189. That includes two beds, a phone, and cable TV. You can get the same room for around $80 in January. On the other end of the spectrum is the 2,500-square-foot Governor's Suite. It goes for approximately $1,500 a night in peak season and includes four bedrooms, four baths, private balconies, remote-controlled fireplaces, TVs, VCRs, a kitchen, bar, and boardroom.

The list of amenities includes riding stables, tennis courts, a swimming pool, Jacuzzis, private log cabin suites, a playground for children 4 through 12, three restaurants, and all the fish you can catch from their private marina on Table Rock Lake (you'll have to abide by Missouri fishing regulations, however). You can rent fully equipped Tracker bass boats, ski boats, pontoon boats, or canoes by the hour or by the day. If it's a guide you need, they'll supply that, too.

Their Top of the Rock executive nine-hole, par 3 golf course (now being expanded to an 18-hole course) was designed by Jack Nicklaus himself and is a member of the Audubon Signature Cooperative Sanctuary program for natural habitat conservation.

Just down the road 20 minutes is Dogwood Canyon, a 10,000-acre private wilderness refuge owned by the same folks. You can walk, rent a bicycle, or take the guided tram tour. Along the way you may spot Texas longhorns, American bison, white-tailed deer, and wild turkeys. For trout anglers who don't like much of a challenge, they even have well-stocked trout streams.

The restaurants at Big Cedar run the full gamut. You can get prime rib at the Devil's Pool Restaurant, a local favorite, and the Worman House Restaurant serves gourmet cuisine. (See the Restaurants chapter.)

If you're serious about visiting Big Cedar, call (800) 227-7776, and for $10 they'll send you a VHS videotape of the entire complex.

i Most of the area's motels receive Vacation Channel programming (see the Media chapter). It's on twenty-four hours a day and is a great source of information on the music shows, traffic routes, and local history of the area.

CHATEAU ON THE LAKE RESORT AND CONVENTION CENTER $$$$
415 MO 265 North
(417) 334-1161, (888) 333-5253
www.chateauonthelake.com

Local business owners long awaited the opening of the Chateau on the Lake's convention facilities. The one thing Branson had lacked was a facility large enough to accommodate large groups. With 40,000 square feet of meeting space, the Chateau can accommodate groups up to 4,000.

The most striking feature of the hotel, besides its imposing presence on a large mountain overlooking Table Rock Lake, is the ten-story atrium courtyard draped with a plethora of foliage, trees, and waterfalls. The glass elevators on either side of the atrium take visitors to their rooms on the third through tenth floors, which all have private balconies, some with a lake view. Each room is decorated in deep purples and mauves. The hallways are lined with cherry furniture, plants, and artwork. It is one of John Q. Hammon's best creations yet. He owns numerous resorts and hotels around the globe, including the Holiday Inn–University Plaza Hotel and the University Plaza Trade Center in Springfield.

The hotel has 302 rooms and two 1,000-square-foot Presidential Suites, which are located on the top floor. Besides the best view, these suites have just about every amenity you can think of: TVs, phones, Jacuzzis, king-size beds, and kitchenettes, to name just a few. Chateau on the Lake's new $6-million, 14,000-square-foot, full-service spa is a palace of pure indulgence, where signature treatments blend rich elements of the Ozarks with exotic European therapies.

The grounds of the resort are as impressive as the interior. They have a hiking and biking trail, tennis courts, indoor and outdoor swimming pools, a spa, fitness center, hair salon, full-service marina, and a supervised children's program called Crawdaddies Kid's Club, which is open daily and lets kids enjoy a place all their own. If you can't decide what to do, ask the full-time recreation coordinator to help you plan your day. After a hard day relaxing at the resort, you can pop into the Library for a cocktail and gawk at its massive stone fireplace. Or you can try out the Chateau Grille, a fine-dining restaurant. For dessert try the Sweet Shop, which is also a gift shop.

To get to Chateau on the Lake from The Strip, take MO 165 south until you come to MO 265. Turn left and look for the entry signs. Or, if you're coming from Silver Dollar City, turn right on MO 376 across from the RFD Theatre, follow it to MO 265, turn left, and wind around the two lanes until you see it on your right.

EAGLE'S VIEW COTTAGES $$
Indian Point Road
(417) 338-2227, (800) 888-1891
www.indianpoint.com

Eagle's View Cottages come in pink, green, or yellow. Take your pick. The basic cottage comes with two double beds or one queen-size bed, a full bath, a refrigerator, sink, cook top, and microwave. Cottages start at around $62 a night. Some cottages have ovens and dishwashers. The largest unit can accommodate 10 to 12 people. Eagle's View condo units have fireplaces and whirlpool tubs, but they start at around $90 a night for a studio and go up to $269 for a two-bedroom. You also get a view of Table Rock Lake, boat access, a swimming pool, and a picnic area.

INDIAN POINT LODGE $$
Indian Point Road
(417) 338-2250, (800) 888-1891
www.indianpoint.com

You can choose from two-bedroom condos, resort units with up to four bedrooms, or lakeside cabins at Indian Point Lodge on Table Rock Lake. The basic unit starts at $72 for two double beds and works its way up from there. Each room includes cable TV, a telephone, a kitchen, a fireplace, a lakeview patio, and a barbecue grill. A resort unit features wood-beamed ceilings, a sitting area, and a view of the outdoor swimming pool. The condos come fully furnished. There is a children's play area, a game room, and a full-service marina with bass boats and pontoon boats starting at $120 a day for a basic boat and motor. The lodge offers vacation packages, including show tickets, for around $295 for a three-night stay, and Angler's Adventure package trips.

STILL WATERS CONDOMINIUM RESORT $$
Indian Point Road
(417) 338-2323, (800) 777-2320
www.stillwatersresort.com

Except for a live music show, Still Waters has it all. If you're into water sports, you've come to the right place. Still Waters has its own full-service marina and boat launch. You can rent Jet Skis, fishing boats, and ski boats or take a leisurely tour of Table Rock Lake in one of their free paddleboats. If land activities are what you're after, the resort has a tennis court, sand volleyball court, bicycles, a hiking and jogging trail, horseshoe-throwing pit, and a covered pavilion with a huge barbecue grill. The kids can hang out in the video arcade, burn off some energy at the playground, or cool off in one of the three swimming pools. The resort has Zoom the Flume, a water slide free to guests of all ages. There's also a kiddy pool for the littlest ones—children younger than five stay free.

You can choose from basic motel units, cottages, and one-, two-, or three-bedroom luxury condos. Many of the units have two bathrooms, full kitchens, and Jacuzzis in the master bedroom. Each unit comes fully furnished and has cable TV and a phone. If there's nothing on to watch, you can rent a video. The units are decorated with modern furnishings and have large windows overlooking the swimming pools. If you want to go to town to see a show, Still Waters will make your reservations for you.

Other Areas

HOLIDAY HILLS RESORT & GOLF CLUB $$$
620 Rockford Dr.
(417) 334-4013, (800) 225-2422
www.holidayhills.com

Just 3 miles east of downtown Branson, just off MO 76, Holiday Hills is a golfer's paradise. The 18-hole golf course has bent-grass greens, shade trees, and plenty of Ozark Mountain twists and turns. If aliens beamed up your clubs, they'll rent you some. (We know you wouldn't forget to bring yours on vacation, now would you?) See the Recreation and the Outdoors chapter for more on the golf course. You can also try a little shuffleboard, tennis, or basketball. If fishing is more your speed, they will hook you up with a fishing guide.

The condos at Holiday Hills come with one, two, or three bedrooms and can sleep up to six adults. The basic unit has a private patio or balcony, cable TV, phone, fully furnished kitchenette, ceiling fans, plenty of comfortable furniture, and front-door parking. Some of the units feature Jacuzzis. Be sure to check out their restaurant, the Grille on the Greens, for a light lunch after a few

holes of golf. For those who want to use the kitchenette, Summer Fresh grocery in the Crossland Shopping Center nearby can provide provisions.

POINTE ROYALE CONDOMINIUM RESORT $$
158-A-SA Pointe Royale Dr.
(417) 334-5614, (800) 962-4710
www.pointeroyale.com

To get to Pointe Royale, take MO 165 south from The Strip. It's just across the street from the Welk Resort and only 2.5 miles from the Showboat Branson Belle. Many of the area's entertainers either have homes in the Pointe Royale residential community or rent condos on a long-term basis. You never know whom you may run into around there. Andy Williams often takes advantage of the resort's 18-hole championship golf course (see the Recreation and the Outdoors chapter).

Many of the 300 condos have a view of the fairway and rent for slightly higher than the units off the fairway. The basic unit comes fully furnished with linens, kitchen appliances and utensils, and patio furniture. The basic unit also has one queen-size bed in the bedroom and one queen-size sleeper sofa in the living room. Each unit has cable TV, a phone, and a private balcony. Other units come with two and three bedrooms, fireplaces, and washers and dryers. The outdoor amenities include a tennis court and swimming pool. Guests receive priority tee times and discounted rates for golf carts. Children younger than 12 stay for free. If you stay six nights, the seventh night is on the house.

THOUSAND HILLS GOLF AND CONFERENCE RESORT $$
245 South Wildwood Dr.
(417) 336-5873, (800) 864-4145
www.thousandhills.com

Thousand Hills is better known for its 150-acre, 18-hole, par 64 golf course than its condo rentals. (Golfers, see the Recreation and the Outdoors chapter.) Nevertheless, if you're going to play golf, it's best to be as close to the green as possible, right? It is located just off Green Mountain

Drive, the street that runs parallel to The Strip south of the Moon River Theatre. Thousand Hills has standard hotel units and one-, two-, and three-bedroom condos. The resort also has rooms with a bedroom, bath, and kitchenette that lock off from the living area. Some of the pricier units have private outdoor hot tubs overlooking the golf course. All the units come fully furnished with tasteful and subdued decor. Each unit features cable TV, phones, and a balcony with patio furniture. There is an indoor and outdoor swimming pool, hot tub, clubhouse, exercise center, tennis court, laundry facility, and meeting space for up to 200 people. Check-in is at the clubhouse on Wildwood Drive, but the 175 units are on Green Mountain Drive.

i **Need a place to sit down? Branson has more than 100,000 motel rooms, restaurant seats, and theater seats combined.**

WELK RESORT CENTER $$$
1984 MO 165
(417) 336-3575, (800) 505-9355
www.welkresort.com
Is it a resort with a theater or a theater with a resort? Turn to The Shows chapter if you're interested in performances at the Welk. Read on here if you're looking for a place to stay.

With 158 good-size rooms, an outdoor swimming pool, restaurant, gift shop, laundry facility, and hand-held video games for the kids, it is hardly just a place to catch some Zs. Throughout the year the resort hosts a number of special events. (For more on these events, see the Annual Events

chapter.) You can play horseshoes, croquet, and board games with the other guests at the resort, or you can lunch at the Stage Door Restaurant.

The basic room comes with two queen-size beds, cable TV, a phone, and country-style furnishings. Some units have Jacuzzis. Children stay free with their parents.

If you are interested in the shows there, you can buy a vacation package that includes lodging at the resort, tickets to the shows, and meals. They will even help you get tickets to other Branson shows as well. Closed January through March.

WESTGATE BRANSON WOODS RESORT $$
2201 Roark Valley Rd.
(417) 334-2324, (800) 935-2345
www.wgbransonwoods.com
The Woods has one of the best out-in-the-country-but-still-in-town locations in Branson. To get to it, look for the signs at the intersection of Roark Valley Road and Shepherd of the Hills Expressway. It's located high on a hill just north of the intersection. As you drive along the expressway, you may be able to catch a glimpse of the log cabins through the trees. Never fear, though, because the resort is as private as it is charming. You can choose from their 200 guest rooms or from their 25 one-, two-, or three-bedroom cabins. A standard motel room comes with two king-size or two queen-size beds, cable TV, and phones. Each private cabin has a fully equipped kitchen, fireplace, Jacuzzi, and deck.

Outside, there is a large swimming pool, a covered pavilion, shuffleboard, basketball, volleyball, and children's play area. You'll see a natural waterfall on the walking path. The resort serves a continental breakfast.

BED-AND-BREAKFAST INNS

Bed-and-breakfast inns, or B&Bs as they are called in the British Isles, where they are a time-honored option for travelers and sightseers, are beginning to catch on as an option in this country, even here in the Ozarks. One local inn owner estimates that 80 percent of her guests are first-time bed-and-breakfast visitors. The homey, often quaint accommodations with individually appointed and themed rooms offer a refreshing departure from what some would consider the cloned, cookie-cutter sameness of motels. You can expect bed-and-breakfast inns in the Ozarks to be sprinkled with romance, a sense of quiet retreat, local history, and splendor.

Often, large older homes in the British Isles are converted into bed-and-breakfast inns, but the Branson area does not have the lengthy history of the mother country nor a legacy of old, elegant architecture. Some of the area's old homes have made the bed-and-breakfast conversion, though most area bed-and-breakfast inns are newly built for that purpose. There are also quite a number of nice "regular" homes, owned by people who like people and whose kids have flown the nest. These folks use extra space in their homes as bed-and-breakfast inns "just for the fun of it," and they lavish attention on detail and their small number of guests.

Unlike their counterparts in the British Isles, Branson bed-and-breakfasts have private baths as the rule rather than the exception. Some inns are almost decadent in their luxury: fireplaces, private spas, libraries, king-size beds, and neat, one-of-a-kind appointments. Some of the inns are furnished with antiques. Many of the inns are off the beaten path, a plus for some visitors, and often feature a peaceful river valley or a mountain hillside with a panoramic view. They can be romantic and peaceful, and the personal service one gets transcends that of chain motels. Quite a number are built on Table Rock Lake and offer docks for fishing and swimming, and some can accommodate boats overnight, so you can arrive to your destination via water if you want!

And, of course, there are the famous breakfasts you expect, a meal so substantial that it should tide you over the entire day. The heart of the bed-and-breakfast inn is the personal care and attention for guests at reasonable rates, with breakfast. Many Ozark bed-and-breakfast innkeepers seem to believe that the way to your heart is through your stomach! While bed-and-breakfast inns may have smaller buildings than hotels and motels, they definitely have big hearts.

OVERVIEW

There is a good deal of variety within the realm of bed-and-breakfast inns in Branson. Some are new and some are old and historic. Some allow children but not pets—and vice versa. Some have showers; some don't. Some allow smoking; others are smoke-free. Most of them are wheelchair accessible. Whatever your individual concern, ask when you make your reservation.

There are so many inns in the Branson area now, space limitations preclude describing each, but we list the best, which offer good rooms, an interesting decor or location, and a friendly atmosphere. We've given you a price guide for a one-night stay for two with a double bed and breakfast, though some offer only a continental breakfast or a reduced rate for a continental breakfast. We've given directions for some inns; others said they don't take drop-ins and indicated they would give directions when reservations were made. Unless otherwise noted, all accept credit cards.

Price Code

$....................... $65 to $85
$$ .... $86 to $109
$$$ .... $110 to $160

AUNT SADIE'S GARDEN GLADE
BED & BREAKFAST $$$
163 Fountain St.
(417) 335-4063, (800) 944-4250
www.auntsadies.com

Just a few miles north of Branson, Aunt Sadie's country Victorian-style inn is on seven wooded acres overlooking Bee Creek Valley. Aunt Sadie's is obviously using *glade* to mean "a bright open space in the forest," which aptly describes her establishment, not the "rocky, barren, semidesert environment" that we typically mean here in the Ozarks. The inn, owned and operated by Linda and Dick Hovell, has four suites—three with private hot tubs, two with fireplaces—and four cottages with private bath and shower, hot tub, TV, microwave, refrigerator, and coffeemaker. The cottages sleep five adults comfortably and are perfect for two couples or guests traveling with kids.

Sadie's furnishes a hearty home-cooked breakfast: homemade biscuits and gravy, an egg dish, two meat dishes, fresh-baked pastries, and juice—a perfect way to start the sightseeing day. You're only minutes from MO 248. To get to Sadie's Garden Glade, take US 65 north of Branson and take the MO F exit. Turn left and go under US 65; then take the second left on the outer road, named West Outer Road South, and go 1.3 miles to the end and turn right onto Fountain Street.

BARN AGAIN BED-AND-BREAKFAST $$$
904 West Church St., Ozark
(417) 581-2276
www.ozarkusa.com

Located in Ozark, close to antiques stores yet within easy driving distance of both Branson and Springfield attractions, this five-unit bed-and-breakfast inn features 1910 "farmhouse suites," two in the barn and three in the original milking parlor, all near the swimming pool. Units are large (big as a barn!) and have private entrances and full baths (some units have a Jacuzzi), and all are within easy walking distance of the network of walking paths by the Finley River. Built in 1910 and restored by the Amish community, the inn, now listed on the Ozark Historical Register, has one unit named the Amish Room furnished with Amish antiques, furniture, and quilts. The inn has a full gourmet farm breakfast served in the main house, the original barn of this turn-of-the-20th-century homestead, operated by hosts Mark and Susan Bryant.

BRADFORD HOUSE BED &
BREAKFAST INN $$
296 Blue Meadows Rd.
(417) 334-4444, (888) 488-4445
www.bradfordhouse.com

Hosts Bob and Cristy Westfall offer you the serenity and peace of our mountains with the elegance of the finest hotel. They are away from the traffic of Branson but close to the thick of things, right off Fall Creek Road. You can pamper yourself in the exquisite Victorian interior graced with rich mahogany wood and glorious tapestries. The 14,000-square-foot inn provides 20 individually designed rooms. Each room is appointed with a king- or queen-size pillow-top mattress bed, private bath with two double pedestal sinks, cable television, VCR, and telephone. There is also a video library to check out movies. For those who have special needs, Bradford House has an ADA-approved guest room with a roll-in shower.

During the summer, you can cool off in "the pool with a view." They suggest you come hungry and enjoy the luscious home-cooked breakfasts.

The Bradford House, with its spiral staircase and balcony around three sides, is an ideal place for pictures and family gatherings, and the Westfalls specialize in small weddings and receptions.

Want the Bed-and-Breakfast Experience in the Ozarks?

You might first check out Bed-and-Breakfast Inns of Missouri, the state's only organization of inspected and approved inns, at www.bbim.org. Many bed-and-breakfasts in the Branson area will be listed and have a Web page with information.

There are also several free local reservation agencies you can call.

Show Me Hospitality books for 18 area bed-and-breakfast inns. Linda Hovell is familiar with all the inns and will match what you're looking for with the inn that has it. Call (800) 348-5210.

Ozark Mountain Bed & Breakfast Service can book you at any one of more than 100 inns, cottages, and suites in southern Missouri and northern Arkansas. Call (417) 334-4720 or (800) 695-1546. A descriptive list of all the bed-and-breakfast inns can be mailed to you in advance by calling the above number.

BRADFORD INN $

3590 MO 265
(417) 338-5555, (800) 357-1466
www.bradfordinn.net

The Bradford features decks with a spectacular view of the mountains, and it brings in the out-of-doors with more than 200 windows so you can enjoy the lake, mountains, sunrises, and sunsets, even inside! The Bradford is only a few miles from Silver Dollar City, the Shepherd of the Hills Homestead and Outdoor Theatre, and The Strip theaters. It has 32 individually themed units (Gothic Room, Golf Room, Rustic Room, Secret Garden Room with its own stone wall and gate), all with private bath, Jacuzzi, fireplace, cable TV, phone, king- or queen-size beds, writing desks, and deck or patio. There are two multi-bedroom units that sleep six and nine. Lucyanna and Bob Westfall, owners and operators of the Bradford, serve full breakfast: sausage and eggs, homemade Belgian waffles, fresh-baked breads, and fresh fruit. To get to the Bradford, take MO 76 west from Branson to MO 265 and turn left (south). You'll find the inn on your left after 2 miles.

CAMERON'S CRAG $$

738 Acacia Club Rd., Point Lookout
(417) 335-8134, (800) 933-8529
www.camerons-crag.com

This contemporary home, "voted most romantic, yet affordable B&B – 2008" by iLoveInns.com, is perched high on a bluff overlooking Lake Taneycomo and the Branson skyline. All four guest rooms have wonderful views, king-size beds, private baths, and hot tubs. The area is quiet and secluded but only minutes from Hollister, Branson, and the attractions on The Strip. School-age children are welcome. Kay Cameron provides a hearty breakfast with something different every day. Ask her about her cookbook! To find Cameron's Crag, take US 65 south from Branson. Turn right onto MO V, go past the College of the Ozarks entrance, and turn right on Acacia Club Road. You'll find the Crag about 1.5 miles down the road on your right.

i You can get a free *Missouri Travel Guide*, which contains a list of bed-and-breakfast inns for the entire state, as well as other interesting and helpful travel information for your Show Me State vacation, by calling the Missouri Division of Tourism, (573) 751-4133. A list of bed-and-breakfasts in the Arkansas Ozarks can be obtained by writing the Bed & Breakfast Association of Arkansas, P.O. Box 250261, Little Rock, AR 72225, or by requesting it at their Web site: www.bbonline.com/ar/bbaa.

EMORY CREEK VICTORIAN
BED & BREAKFAST $$
143 Arizona Dr.
(417) 334-3805, (800) 362-7404
www.emorycreekbnb.com
Located 3 miles north of Branson, this inn, built in 1993, overlooks Emory Creek where it joins Bull Creek. You can relax in a porch swing and perhaps see a deer as you walk down the wildlife trail to Emory Creek. The large, blue and white Victorian house has modern conveniences, including private Jacuzzi-tub baths in each of the six guest rooms, TVs, and good lighting. Forget your own robe and slippers? Owners Beverly and Sammy Pagma provide such luxuries for you. Rooms are not equipped with individual phones, but there is a dedicated line for guests, as well as free local calls and Wi-Fi. A grand staircase rises to the open second story from the main salon of the house. The decor is Victorian: old horse prints, a giant carousel rocking horse, cut-glass and stained-glass lamps, overstuffed chairs, carved beds with huge headboards, upright Chickering pianos, and a library of classics and best sellers. Rooms are named after writers and historical people of Missouri: Harry S. Truman, Laura Ingalls Wilder, Sammy Lane, and Rose O'Neill. Breakfasts are big, with piping-hot breads and muffins; pumpkin streusel; stuffed blueberry French toast; ham, potato, and cheese quiche; and creamed eggs in pastry puffs. Wash it down with Beverly's eye-opening Sunrise Surprise, a refreshing drink of freshly squeezed orange juice, lime juice, and local wildflower honey.

GAINES LANDING BED & BREAKFAST $$$
521 West Atlantic St.
(417) 334-2280, (800) 825-3145
www.gaineslanding.com
Gaines Landing is a spacious contemporary home featuring three separate poolside units with private entrances, baths, and enclosed patio with private hot tubs. All rooms have a TV and VCR/DVD, video library, wet bar, refrigerator, microwave, and comfortable chairs. Guests can enjoy the secluded swimming pool overlooking the

Nearby Eureka Springs, just over the line in Arkansas, has more bed-and-breakfast inns than any other city in the United States, according to *USA Today*. Eureka Springs has 125 bed-and-breakfasts, while San Francisco comes in second with 119.

natural landscape. A full breakfast is served in an elegant dining room. The inn is a smoke-free home and is in a quiet neighborhood of Branson, but only blocks from historic downtown Branson and minutes from The Strip's attractions.

JOSIE'S BED & BREAKFAST $$
508 Tablerock Circle
(417) 338-2978, (800) 289-4125
www.josiesbandb.com
Indian Point is the peninsula that juts out into Table Rock Lake south of Silver Dollar City, and Josie's, owned and operated by Bill and Josie Coats, is near the tip of the point right on the lake. It's a great place to stay if you're going to be doing lake activities or taking in Silver Dollar City, though it is only 8 miles back to The Strip. Josie's has three guest rooms and a suite, all with private baths. The inn is new, with Victorian decor, a hot tub, and fireplaces. Enjoy a walk along the lakeshore in the morning and come back to Josie's candlelight breakfast.

To get to Josie's from MO 76, take Indian Point Road to Coleman Junction (on your left). Turn left at Tablerock Circle. Then make an immediate right and go half a mile. You'll see Josie's sign and parking lot.

THE MARTINDALE BED & BREAKFAST $
164 Martinda Lane, Branson West
(417) 338-2588, (888) 338-6330
www.martindalebnb.com
Lucille and Ellis Martin provide good, old-fashioned Ozark hospitality in their lakeside home. The two units have private balconies and overlook the great room with its massive fireplace. Units have mirrored cherry armoires with TVs, scroll queen-size

beds, and private bathrooms. You can expect your native Ozarkian hosts to provide a full breakfast that is "sumpt'n special"—country omelette pie, savory sausage, biscuits and gravy, Amish bread, and fruit.

The Martindale is in the Kimberling City area, a perfect place to enjoy that area of Table Rock Lake and only 15 minutes from Silver Dollar City. To get there from Branson West, take MO 13 south toward Kimberling City. Turn left on MO DD and go 4.5 miles, turning left on Double Day Loop. Keep to the left, turning on Split Rail Pass, and you'll see the Martindale on your left. All lefts, right? Watch for the purple signs for the Martindale. No credit cards.

RED BUD COVE BED & BREAKFAST SUITES $$
162 Lakewood Dr., Hollister
(417) 334-7144, (800) 677-5525
www.redbudcove.com
Red Bud Cove is one of the quietest coves on Table Rock Lake. If you come in early April, you can see the pink mist of the redbuds in bloom on the hills, and you'll know how the cove got its name. Each suite has a private entrance and includes bedroom, living room, kitchenette, dining area, and private bath. Some come with a spa for two and some with a fireplace. You can expect a queen-size or king-size bed in each bedroom, as well as a sofa bed in the living room. You'll enjoy your hearty full breakfast served in the dining room in the main house overlooking the lake. Hosts Rick and Carol Carpenter will give you hints on how to best enjoy the Ozarks. There's an outdoor hot tub, and you can rent a fishing or

i Bed-and-breakfast operators are a friendly lot and often will greet you with homemade cookies and tea at your arrival. They are frequently area insiders and can be a valuable source of information about restaurants and area sights and attractions. Often they will have a library of local literature and sightseeing materials.

pontoon boat at the nearby marina. Swim, fish, or just watch the sun set at the lake's edge.

Red Bud Cove is at the end of Graham Clark Drive. Go south on US 65 past the MO 265 junction and look for the turnoff on Graham Clark Drive, which becomes Lakewood Drive, on your right.

3 OAKS BED & BREAKFAST $$
10205 Devore Dr.
Harrison, AR
(870) 743-4093, (866) 362-5722
www.3oaksbb.com
Innkeepers Larry and Kay McCully will make you feel in heaven in the four elegant guest rooms in this plantation farmhouse nestled in 23 acres atop Kirk Mountain.

The 3 Oaks is furnished with period antiques and reproductions. All rooms have a private bath and queen-size bed. There is a parlor on the main floor where guests can relax, read, listen to old 78s on the Victrola, or play the piano. There are two verandas and a screened-in back porch where guests can enjoy the clean Ozark air, or take a hike in the woods. At 3 Oaks guests will be treated to down-home hospitality, hearty breakfasts, and the peacefulness of country living. Just 30 miles south of Branson, it's close to the shows of Branson, the beauty of Eureka Springs, and the hiking, fishing, and canoeing on the White and Buffalo Rivers.

The 3 Oaks is just south of Harrison on AR 7. Call or check online for directions.

WHITE RIVER LODGE BED & BREAKFAST $$$
738 Ozark Hollow Rd., Blue Eye
(417) 779-1556, (800) 544-0257
www.whiteriverlodgebb.com
If you want Ozark mountain hospitality, rustic charm, and royal pampering—White River Lodge offers the best of all possible worlds. Innkeepers Bill and Becky Bablerare are waiting to show you the perfect vacation. Made of Colorado Engelmann Spruce logs, the lodge is a stunning tribute to country living at its best. The 10,000-square-foot log home features four

private guest rooms, as well as a two-bedroom suite—all with TV/VCR/DVD and Wi-FFi. Guests can revel in the handcrafted log beds, or survey the breathtaking lake views from the generous balconies. Of course, freshly ground coffee and a delicious breakfast are waiting to give you a perfect start to your day.

White River Lodge is south of Branson in the Table Rock Lake area, just minutes away from Dogwood Canyon, Silver Dollar City, the Show-boat Branson Belle, and all the live entertainment shows, shopping, and attractions that Branson has to offer. Don't miss out on the world-class trout fishing or lake recreation, too! Just go 8 miles south of Branson, on Highway 86, head west for 6.6 miles to UU. Turn right on UU for 1 mile to Ozark Hollow Road, then just another half mile or so to the entrance drive.

RESTAURANTS

I f you've come to Branson and are on a diet, put it on the back burner until you get back home. The selection of places to eat rivals the selection you have to make at the area's ubiquitous buffets. Because the competition for your food dollar is so fierce, food is relatively inexpensive—and it can be good.

A bit of history—it wasn't always like that. We can remember when there were only three cafes in town, and not a single stoplight. Now it seems like there are almost 3,000 eating establishments in the area, and we have stoplights now, too. Some of us joke about our eating habits and culinary tastes by saying, "If it ain't fried, it ain't food." And although Branson may be the cholesterol capital of the world, you can eat healthful, sensible, and enjoyable meals, too. We'll point out places that have health-conscious menus. But, as we've said, Branson is the place to backslide on that diet of yours.

OVERVIEW

Ozarkers, culinary-wise, could be divided into two types. The first is the basic meat and potatoes type, with a mind closed to outside food influences. The other type follows the philosophy, if it grows and God made it, it can be eaten. This type's table would be graced with scrambled eggs and squirrels' brains, barbecued 'coon, woodchuck ragout, venison, pawpaw and persimmon bread, fruit pies and cobblers, and jams and jellies from the cornucopia of local plants such as blackberry, pokeberry, mulberry, raspberry, gooseberry, wild grape, plum, and elderberry. In short, anything that could be picked and prepared. It was this type of Ozark eater who embraced, lovingly, the outside food influences that better transportation and tourism brought. You won't be fed this local fare in restaurants, but native fruit pies and cobblers are available and even featured in most area eating establishments. An influx of tourists and new residents brings various ethnic culinary possibilities, but the area is still pretty homogeneous when it comes to food. You'll also find the usual chain gang of fast-food establishments, from Applebee's and Blimpie's all the way to the end of the alphabet. We don't cover them in this

book, unless they have a unique local feature or you might not have yet experienced them in your neck of the woods. But don't allow yourself to be manacled to the sameness and security of fast food. Check out local eateries. If you don't like one, you can find a dozen others you do like.

This chapter will guide you to what we think are the best of the lot, and that includes some that you may have second thoughts about when you first drive up. One of the things we have learned over the years: never judge a book by its cover, people by their dress, or a restaurant by its facade. Some of the hole-in-the-wall and divey-looking joints serve the best food. You may find that the friendliness, food, or convenience of a particular place bring you back time after time during your stay, but we encourage you to experiment and spread your dollar more broadly. We locals think nothing of driving out to the boondocks toward Blue Eye to sample the fare at the Devil's Pool Restaurant at Big Cedar Lodge. The better roads and greater restaurant choices have broadened our diets and probably our girths. So follow our advice, and you'll leave Branson a better (and probably bigger) person for it!

One point to keep in mind: Many restaurants do not serve beer, wine, or mixed drinks. Some serve only beer, some only wine. There doesn't seem to be any rhyme or reason to the alcohol-serving situation. If drinks are in your dining plans, it might be wise to call and ask what the place serves. What about dress? We Ozarkers believe in being comfortable and making others feel comfortable. Dress in most establishments is country casual and typical tourist garb—just be clothed. A few of the more upscale spots might like you to wear slacks and even a tie and coat, but they aren't likely to refuse you service if you come in wearing shorts and a tank top. Common sense and the weather will dictate your choice of clothing.

As for when to eat, the rule seems to be: if you're hungry, they'll feed you. The schedules of those in the service industries and of the entertainers make for meals that are often on a catch-as-you-can basis. And there is no telling when a tourist will want to have the feed bag put on. Some restaurants are all-nighters; some are early birds and specialize in morning meals, often the bargain meal of the day. Some even serve breakfast at any hour. Your server can answer any questions about the food or the area.

If you have kids in tow, you'll find most restaurants are very child friendly, and if they don't have a kids' menu, they are usually more than willing to bring out something that will please a picky youngster. Let price be your guide. The less expensive the restaurant, the more likely it will cater to kids. Wheelchair accessibility varies greatly, but since many of the restaurants were built during the "boom period," they are readily wheelchair accessible. Older establishments may have narrow doors, steps, or other obstacles, or bathrooms too tiny to accommodate wheelchairs. If wheelchair facilities are of concern to you, be certain to call the restaurants to see what arrangements might be made to fit your needs.

Most restaurants are open seven days a week during the busy season (April through Christmas), and the season has gotten longer over the years. When things slow down during January and February, many restaurants cut back on their serving hours or close completely. If you're in town the first three months of the year, it would be a good idea to call ahead, just to make certain where you want to eat is open. That also goes for reservations. Hardly any place requires them, but it's smart to call the nicer restaurants during the busy season or if you're trying to catch a show right after dinner.

Most establishments will accept major credit cards (MasterCard, Visa, Discover), cash, or traveler's checks. Some even accept personal checks, though others won't accept personal checks at all, not even from locals. Unless otherwise noted, your plastic is accepted at the restaurants we list. Note the price code assigned to each restaurant listing. The little dollar signs are a hint at the bottom line for your evening dining—an indicator of the usual amount you can expect to pay for dinner for two, not including appetizers, dessert, drinks, or gratuity. You can expect lunch prices to be a third to half as much.

We've grouped restaurants according to major fare offered (American, Asian American, Fine Dining, Italian and Pizza, Seafood, Steak Houses and Barbecue, Tex-Mex, and More than a Meal), though some establishments offer fare from more than one category. We've also included a category called Out of the Way, but Worth the Drive for places that you'd have to work to fit into your schedule. And for your sweet tooth, we've created a category called Sweets.

Price Code

$	Less than $20
$$	$21 to $40
$$$	$41 to $60
$$$$	More than $60

AMERICAN

BALDKNOBBERS COUNTRY RESTAURANT $
2846 Country Blvd.
(417) 334-7202
www.baldknobbers.com
Right next to the Baldknobbers Theatre and the Baldknobbers Motel! You can get a good package deal, right in the center of the Strip! They advertise "Food so good, you'll want to say grace twice!" The buffet is fantastic, for price and quality: $5.99

breakfast, $7.99 lunch, or $11.99 dinner, or order off the menu. The hillbilly burger is great, but Stub's liver and onions is the best in Branson if you are a liver and onions lover! (I know there are some of us out there!)

BLEU OLIVE MEDITERRANEAN BISTRO $$
204 N. Commercial St.
(417) 332-2538
www.bleuolive.com
Chef-owner Sam Papanikas serves a variety of Mediterranean dishes in this out of the way place in downtown Branson. It's underneath the Chappy Mall and not visible from the street. Because it's good, you'll find it. The Grilled Chicken Panino with caramelized onions on homemade focaccia bread is especially noteworthy. So is the Shrimp Tourkolimano: shrimp sautéed with plum tomatoes, capers, spinach, served with feta cheese over parmesan rice pilaf.

CHESTER'S RESTAURANT $
1166 Country Blvd.
(417) 334-7838
Perry Chester knows how to build a burger. His "stuffed burger" vies with Billy Bob's as "best of Branson." He offers plenty of burger options: Cajun, classic, mariachi, Mediterranean, Western; and a variety of sandwiches (we suggest the reuben), great fried chicken, fish and chips, and "greens and things." For those who are not into greens, try the flash-fried spinach. Chester's is a great place to start the day with a country breakfast. It's right next to the Hillbilly Inn.

CLOCKERS CAFÉ $
103 South Commercial St.
(417) 335-2328
Clockers advertises itself as "the locals' choice for atmosphere, service and quality food." You'll also find a lot of tourists who have discovered this homey cafe, decorated with nostalgic, "backroadsy" Scott Coleman and O. Winston Link photographs, as well as their signature item: vintage wall clocks. Clockers serves juicy burgers, timely sandwiches, and tasty dinners at a modest price.

FARMHOUSE RESTAURANT $
119 West Main St.
(417) 334-9701
Come at 7 a.m. and you can get a great breakfast. The Farmhouse is one place you can get breakfast anytime, and the lunch and dinner menu lists catfish, shrimp, chicken-fried steak (their specialty), and ham steak. They also have daily specials. Save room for the blackberry cobbler, the dessert they're famous for. A close second is the apple dumpling—great with cinnamon ice cream and tea, our favorite.

MCFARLAIN'S RESTAURANT $
3562 Shepherd of the Hills Expressway
(417) 336-4680
www.bransonimax.com/bigfood
At the IMAX Entertainment Complex, this restaurant has established a strong reputation for good food. McFarlain's says there is no secret to their great food, they just make it the old-fashioned way, like it was made at home—breakfast, lunch, and dinner. That means gathering fresh-as-you-can-get ingredients and serving them in great menu selections, delivered as soon as the food is done. That also means no buffet lines. It may take a bit longer, but McFarlain's believes life's too short to eat bad food. But for all their being down-home, they are really uptown—you can download the menu from their Web site. The restaurant is known for fried green tomatoes, sweet potato fries, pot roast, and chicken potpie. They make great desserts, and pies are their specialties: apple, cherry, strawberry-rhubarb, coconut, chocolate, and even some sugar-free varieties. When it comes to pie, McFarlain's motto, on a prominently placed sign, is, "Life's too short. Eat pie first." Not bad advice. Try the Branson Traffic Jam pie!

i You'll find the cream-of-the-crop recipes, the best of area cooks, and even "pioneer recipes" in cookbooks published by our local churches, societies, and service organizations. Watch for them in gift shops and bookstores.

PENNY GILLEY'S LOUISIANA FIXIN'S $
2005 W Hwy 76
(417) 334-8626
www.pennygilley.com

Right on The Strip, across from Wal-Mart, locals are getting a taste of red beans and rice and Abita root beer by the gal who has a show in Branson. There're the usual po'boys, gumbo, jambalaya, and other Cajun foods. We especially like the raisinless bread pudding there.

THE PLANTATION $$
3460 76 Country Blvd.
(417) 334-7800

Right across from Whitewater, the Plantation offers southern cookin' at its best. Perhaps that's why theater folks drop in to enjoy the fried chicken, all-you-can-eat catfish, hush puppies, and fried okra at its lunch and dinner buffets. You may like it so much you'll want to come back for breakfast. The southern breakfast buffet offers pancakes, eggs in a variety of ways, bacon and sausage, hash browns, biscuits and gravy, and various fruits. If you're not in the mood for the delights of the buffets, you can always order from the menu: breakfasts, steaks, and seafood.

RAFTERS STEAK & SEAFOOD GRILLE $$
3431 Country Blvd.
(417) 334-7535

Expect Ozarks casual elegance and quality with the good fare at the Rafters in Lodge of the Ozarks—right across from the Jim Stafford Theatre. Specializing in steaks and seafood, the Rafters has a local reputation for tender, juicy steaks, cooked to perfection, and the best fish and shellfish dishes from streams and oceans, all served in an elegant atmosphere. We've heard from more than one that they have the best Kansas City strip in the state. Top that off with one of their luscious desserts—we recommend the bread pudding or the crème brûlée—and you'll experience Ozarks elegance!

RUBY LENA'S TEA ROOM & ANTIQUES $
224 West Main St.
(417) 239-2919

This old house downtown is a great place for lunch. The atmosphere is homey (handpainted murals, fieldstone fireplace, kitchen chairs and tables), and the food is good: sandwiches, soups, salads, quiche. Our favorite is the strawberry soup—sweet and cool but calorie-laden. Enjoy the collection of for-sale antiques. Parking is limited, but so is the seating. Any wait is worth it, however.

SADIE'S SIDEBOARD & SMOKEHOUSE $$
2830 76 Country Blvd.
(417) 334-3619

The old yellow farmhouse they advertise as Sadie's isn't like the farmhouse that used to be there before the Branson Boom, or else it had an extreme makeover! But prepare to roll up your sleeves and show your farmer's tan and dig in. Here you'll find a steaming hot buffet piled high with goodies such as macaroni and cheese, chicken livers, roast turkey, ham, fried catfish, and more. You can also order from the menu, which offers a variety of additional options. The dessert menu holds its own with any in Branson. Impressive is the number of cobbler selections—try the peach, blackberry, apple, or cherry. It's easy to find—right across from the Baldknobbers Jamboree Theatre.

THE SHACK CAFE $
108 South Commercial St.
(417) 334-3490

The Shack is the oldest cafe in town. Though it moved years ago from a shack across the street (now part of a bank's parking lot) to bigger and better quarters, the food is still the same good homemade comfort cookin'. Your friendly waitress takes your order and puts it on the cook's spin wheel. The cook takes the requests in order. Dishes come out, usually with an accompanying bellow from the cook in "restauranteeze," and the waitress delivers your meat loaf or fried chicken with a smile and a "Here you are, honey." You can have a ringside seat for this Branson show at the counter in the back, where locals gather for coffee and conversation or to read the newspaper. More deals have been struck in the Shack than on all the golf courses and in all the real-estate offices in town. The Shack offers breakfast, lunch (with daily specials), and dinner (the pan-fried chicken is our favorite). For dessert try the gooseberry cobbler or the raisin cream pie. No credit cards.

STAGE DOOR CANTEEN $
1984 MO 165 South
(417) 336-3575

Located in the Welk Resort Center, the Stage Door Canteen serves typical "American fare." Popular menu items are pan-fried trout or prawns and pasta. They also make some fine salads topped with blackened chicken. It's a convenient place to eat before any of the shows there.

STARVIN MARVIN'S $$
3400 West 76 Country Blvd.
(417) 334-7402
www.starvinmarvinsbranson.com

With more than two decades of experience, locally owned and operated Starvin Marvin's knows what it takes to keep customers coming back, and that's delicious meals at affordable prices. It's a country restaurant that serves ample servings of country-fried steak, tender roast beef, and smothered chicken breast, brown beans, fried okra, biscuits and gravy—the works! Marvin's seafood buffet "with a Cajun attitude" may leave you a bit overwhelmed. They change the menu every day, but one thing that remains constant is the great quality of the dishes and seafood buffet, a favorite of Cedric Benoit, who helps advertise it. The fried oysters are our favorite.

UPTOWN CAFE $$
285 MO 165
(417) 336-3535

Art deco and chrome, lots of it, is the motif for this theme cafe that serves favorites from the 1940s and 1950s. People go to the Uptown as much for the unique atmosphere as the delicious food, and everyone has to check out the little yellow taxi (a 1953 Henry J. Kaiser). It's a classy and classic diner from that time, but with a contemporary touch. The Uptown is known for its Kansas City steak

i "If It Ain't Fried, It Ain't Food" is a song by country star Ray Jones. Ever hear of him? He's the fictional creation of the late detective novelist Donald E. Westlake, whose *Baby, Would I Lie?* takes place in Branson. It's fun to check out the landmarks and places he mentions and to take in his elbow-in-the-ribs humor about Branson and our tourists.

burgers, patties fixed on a greaseless griddle. A broiler favorite is the Hawaiian chicken. The breakfast buffet has all you want or need for breakfast, plus fruits and right-from-the-oven breads, biscuits, and rolls.

ASIAN AMERICAN

GREAT WALL CHINESE SUPER BUFFET $
1343 76 Country Blvd.
(417) 334-8838

This Chinese super buffet advertises "great food at a great price." Certainly they have variety, and the "extensive" all-you-can-eat dinner buffet is impressive and just might convince you. First, there is Mongolian barbecue. (For those who don't know, the Mongolian barbecue is a buffet of the raw materials; you pick what you want; they fix it for you.) Then there's an Italian, American, and Chinese buffet, with sushi, salad, and a fruit bar—and a dessert bar. Great Wall always has lunch specials (combination plates) and a lower-priced lunch buffet. You can also order from an extensive menu (seventy-eight options!)—everything from orange beef to Szechuan-style shrimp and chicken. Anyone who goes away hungry from the Wall and its Chinese cornucopia must have dead taste buds!

HONG KONG BUFFET $
1206 76 Country Blvd.
(417) 334-2727

Only in Branson! Chinese cuisine right next door to the down-home Ozark cooking of Chester's Restaurant. This small but efficient restaurant packs a lot of variety in its newly remodeled and expanded space: moo goo gai pan, shrimp and pea pods, Hong Kong Delight (shrimp in a sweet and sour sauce), and beef with oyster sauce. There are more than 100 Chinese dishes, from the well-known to the exotic.

LOTUS VALLEY $
3129 76 Country Blvd.
(417) 334-3427

This restaurant attracts a number of workers from The Strip in that area and pulls in crowds from nearby theaters—they're open until 11 p.m. The buffet has lots of fried entrees, but there are lighter, low-fat dishes as well. Lunch and dinner are served daily.

SHOGUN JAPANESE STEAK AND
SUSHI RESTAURANT $$
3265 Falls Parkway, MO 165
(417) 332-0260

With all the theaters in town, it's only natural that dining in Branson would become a show of its own. Shogun Japanese Steak and Sushi Restaurant is the "show," serving both lunch and dinner under the direction of master chefs-performers. Most diners don't get to see the quality of the raw materials of their meal, but at Shogun's, you see it all. And the preparation at your table is a show unto itself, with juggling and comedy by your individual chef/actor.

The menu at Shogun includes a variety of beef, chicken, and seafood: shrimp, scallops, or lobster. All meals are served with soup, salad, appetizer, vegetable, and steamed or fried rice. For the hearty eaters there are other appetizers on the menu: shrimp or beef or pork dumplings, various tempuras, and, of course, egg rolls and sushi.

For beverages there's a variety of soft drinks, a full line of bar and mixed drinks, and domestic and imported beers, including, of course, Japanese beers, notably Sapporo, Kirin, and Asahi.

Dessert is ice cream: vanilla, chocolate, and green tea. (That's right! Green tea ice cream! Try it! You'll like it!)

Get there early and you can relax with an appetizer and drink on the trumpet-vine-covered patio and watch an Ozark sunset before your dinner.

To get to the Shogun Japanese Steak and Sushi Restaurant, take MO 165 south from its junction on The Strip. You'll find Shogun in the Falls Center on the left, less than a mile from the MO 76/165 junction.

FINE DINING

BUCKINGHAM'S $$$
2820 76 Country Blvd.
(417) 337-7777

Buckingham's, in the Clarion Hotel next to the Grand Village, is our nod to Africa with its safari decor, forest plants, animal-skin prints, and carved wood totems. The cuisine might be labeled as modern continental. Appetizers are good and big enough to serve as light fare for those with a modest appetite. The menu is clever, and food ranges from what you would expect (steak, fish, and prime rib) to the exotic. The wine list is good, with more than thirty selections. Desserts are rich and flamboyant, so expect to see flaming dishes even if you don't order them. Buckingham's serves only dinner. (Also see the Oasis Lounge in the Nightlife chapter.)

CANDLESTICK INN $$$
127 Taney St.
(417) 334-3633
www.candlestickinn.com

One of the oldest restaurants in the area, the Candlestick has an established reputation, winning "best restaurant," "best view," and "best romantic dinner" awards over the years. Because of the food and the view, it's the place we locals go to celebrate a special occasion. Perched atop Mount Branson, it offers a panoramic view of Lake Taneycomo and the city of Branson and Branson Landing. When the weather is nice, you can eat out on the large deck. Check the menu and the wine list (best in Branson) online. Lunch and dinner are the only meals served at the Candlestick, and we suggest you make reservations well in advance. To dine at the Candlestick, cross the Lake Taneycomo Bridge and turn left onto MO 76 east toward Forsyth. When you start up the steep hill, look for the sign on the left about halfway up and turn left onto Candlestick Road to Taney Street.

CHATEAU ON THE LAKE RESORT
AND CONVENTION CENTER $$$
415 MO 265 North
(417) 334-1161, (888) 333-LAKE
www.chateauonthelakebranson.com

The Chateau Grill in Branson's newest luxury hotel overlooking Table Rock Lake features fine dining for breakfast, lunch, and dinner. The plush carpet, fine stonework, and cherry paneling absolutely reek of richness and elegance. The hotel has been awarded AAA's four-diamond rating, the only hotel in Branson and one of only four in Missouri to achieve the rating. (See the Accommodations chapter.) The Atrium Lounge Bar provides full service for any drinks with your dinner. The ten-story Chateau, on a high ridge just north of Table Rock Dam, offers a dining room with a view—and what a view! The restaurant, on the entry level, provides a panoramic and serene view of the lake, but you may want to see the landscape from higher up after you finish dining. Chef Anthony Burke has an equally spectacular menu that melds the best of various cultures and nationalities. One of the grill's many outstanding appetizers is fruit de mer: smoked scallops, shrimp, and Alaskan crabmeat, with three different types of caviar in lemon vinegar. A local favorite that has gained a national reputation is the sorghum-glazed salmon with caper-whipped potatoes and candied beets (glazed in butter and honey with lemon butter sauce). Another popular selection is the pecan-seared Colorado rack of lamb with pancetta potato tower and porcino mushroom pan juices. For those who want to "eat rich," the mushroom-dusted veal tenderloin with pan-seared fois gras in oxtail cabernet reduction is a creation that doesn't count calories. There are also lots of vegetarian items—including roasted vegetable frittata with wilted greens in a balsamic reduction. Desserts are made in-house, and our

i Want to prevent your child from spilling a water glass at your table, and keep yourself from a mess and embarrassment? Restaurants are generous with king-size water glasses, but many haven't caught on to the fact that toddlers can't easily handle those monster glasses. Unless your youngster has hands like a professional basketball player, request a smaller glass.

favorite is the chocolate-raspberry truffle with a vanilla bean sauce and anglais glaze. The grill's signature dessert is a rich southern pecan torte with chocolate-caramel sauce. Reservations are suggested for this one!

DEVIL'S POOL RESTAURANT $$$
Big Cedar Lodge
Devil's Pool Road, Ridgedale
(417) 335-5141
www.big-cedar.com

You don't have to be a member of the occult to dine at the Devil's Pool. The restaurant gets its name from the nearby Devil's Pool Spring, reputed by locals to be bottomless and, according to some, the place where several "revenooers" met their end after meddling in area moonshine making. The restaurant is on the grounds at Big Cedar Lodge, and it is well worth the drive out to it, if only to have a drink at the Buzzard Bar. We like it for the fresh shiitake mushrooms and goat cheese from nearby farms and the smoked trout appetizer (great with horseradish). The chef curries good food contacts and makes them into memorable dishes. If you're a trout lover, you'll like the Devil's Pool's specialty—trout fixed in a variety of ways that they order in the morning and serve that night. You can also get steaks, pastas, and soups (a different one every day). The Devil's Pool is famous for its smoked prime rib. They serve all three meals, and some people go there just for the old hunting-lodge decor. You can admire the antiques and the spectacular stonework while enjoying a drink from the full-service Buzzard Bar. When you see it and taste the food, you'll know why St. Louis and Kansas City folks come down here just to dine. You can check out the impressive batch of chefs at the Web site.

To get to the Devil's Pool, take US 65 10 miles south to MO 86. The turnoff to the restaurant, about a half mile down MO 86, is well marked.

THE WORMAN HOUSE RESTAURANT $$$
Big Cedar Lodge
Devil's Pool Road, Ridgedale
(417) 339-5214
www.big-cedar.com
Once the home of railroad magnate Harry Worman and his wife, Dorothy, the restaurant is one of the newest and swankiest in the area. The menu features American Harvest cuisine, perhaps because it presents the best of our bountiful land: hot waffles with a variety of syrups (pecan is one of our favorites), omelettes to order (and they can put just about anything in them, from ham and cheese to mushroom and jalapeños). There's a great view of Table Rock Lake, and the mood and decor are right out of the Roaring '20s. See the menu and meet the chefs at the Web site.

The Worman House is located on the grounds of the Big Cedar Lodge. Take US 65 10 miles south to MO 86. The turnoff to the restaurant, about a half mile down MO 86, is well marked.

ITALIAN AND PIZZA

LUIGI'S PIZZA KITCHEN NORTH $$
1447 MO 248 #F
(417) 339-4544

LUIGI'S PIZZA KITCHEN SOUTH
1972 MO 165 #P
(417) 334-3344
www.luigispizzakitchen.com
Branson's proud of Luigi's Pizza Kitchen because it is a locally owned and operated business and a great success story. Owners Chris and Michelle Jordan bring the best in pizza and other Italian foods to Branson. Specializing in St. Louis–style thin-crust pizza, Luigi's has positioned itself as the best in Branson, as shown by its recent award of Best Dining in Branson by *417 Magazine*. Luigi's

serves up great pizza, sandwiches, and other Italian dishes in a casual atmosphere. Locals like it because of the daily lunch specials. Our favorite is the ATM (All The Meats): Italian sausage, hamburger, pepperoni, Canadian bacon, and bacon. Cutting back on the meats? Try the veggie deluxe: onions, mushrooms, green peppers, black olives, artichoke hearts, and marinated roma tomatoes.

Luigi's North is in the Cedar Ridge Shopping Center; South is located in the Marketplace Center next to the Welk Resort. You can see the menu and specials, order online, and print out coupons by visiting Luigi's Web site.

MR. G'S CHICAGO STYLE PIZZA $
202 North Commercial St.
(417) 335-8156
If you're a Chicago fan, you'll enjoy the ambience of the sports memorabilia, pictures, and newspaper clippings, as well as the food at Mr. G's. Pizza styles include both thin crust and pan style, with homemade sauce and Italian sausage. Large and mini pizzas are available for big or small appetites, with toppings as exotic as pineapple and jalapeños. Try the tomato bread, Italian bread with tomatoes, oregano, basil, and Parmesan cheese. Mr. G's also serves pasta dishes, sandwiches, soups, and salads, and beer from the bar.

ROCKY'S ITALIAN RESTAURANT $$
120 North Sycamore St.
(417) 335-4765
Rocky's is a great place for the locals for lunch and dinner. Many locals can remember when it was a feed store. You can still see evidence of the plank loading dock at the entrance. Its limestone creek rock exterior has a rustic, continental interior that is interesting and homey without being pretentious. Before you order, notice the local artwork on the walls and the sculptures, including the blue heron fountain by artist Tim Cherry. Rocky's has a full range of good pasta dishes, and you can sip a variety of wines (no Missouri or Arkansas wines, though) and mixed drinks from the bar. We recommend the chicken noodle soup, simply

Close-up

Branson Battlin' Buffets

In addition to being the "live music capital of the world," Branson very well may be the buffet capital of the United States, perhaps rivaled only by Las Vegas. There are plenty of buffets in Branson—in fact, most restaurants have buffets—probably because it is an inexpensive and fast way to feed lots of people. It has to be fast because it seems that everyone in Branson has a show or attraction to catch. You can get good food cheap because the competition is fierce. It seems that restaurants have buffet spies to check out their competition, not only for quality and quantity but for price. It is good food served fast, but you still should be prepared for some time waiting in line during the busiest times of the tourist season.

If you have a show date, you might want to consider the buffet approach to dining because you have control over not only how much you are served but also when you are served. You won't have to sit and look at your watch, worrying about the speed of the cook who is frying your chicken or mashing your spuds. Bus tours make frequent use of the Branson buffet venues, so you do have to be careful not to get behind a large group of "bus people." If you are on a limited budget, buffets are an inexpensive route. Some have children's prices or senior prices. We've known some people who tank up at a bountiful breakfast buffet and have only a light snack or picnic for lunch.

We might point out some "buffet fare play" for those not used to this type of eating. It is true that most of the buffets are all you can eat, but that doesn't mean that when you belly up to the bar you need to overload your plate or try to build sideboards with the celery sticks. You can go back for seconds—and thirds—or for various courses. Use a clean plate each time. It's polite to leave your plate on your table and pick up a clean one for your seconds, or for the next course, in spite of what your mother may have preached to you about "dirtyin' up dishes."

Just because it's all you can eat is no reason to be wasteful. (We Ozarkers are a thrifty, even a tight lot. At butcherin' time, everything from the hog but the squeal was used in some way.) A good rule might be, "Eat all you want, but eat all you take."

When getting your food, don't lean on the sneeze guard to examine the food or reach for food on the other side. It's important to keep the line moving because, like you, the other people have a show to catch. Use only the spoon or ladle that is in an entree, so that you don't "contaminate" a dish with some undesired and flavor-changing addition. And, finally, keep in mind that though you are serving yourself, a server brings your beverage and keeps your water glass filled and clears your used plates, so don't forget to tip. You can even feel good about the tip because you'll probably be helping a local college or high-school student.

There is buffet fare for about every taste, but don't expect to find dainty and delicate dishes on the buffet table. A high soufflé or a delicate meringue won't stand up over time and under the buffet heat lamps. Most buffet food, such as ham and beans and soups and fried chicken, are on the buffet because they have endurance qualities and can stand up for a period of time without serious changes in quality or taste. There are buffets that are somewhat specialized: southern buffets, Asian American buffets, seafood buffets, barbecue buffets, and breakfast and lunch and dinner buffets. If you are a picky eater, there is always enough variety within a buffet to tickle your taste buds.

So when you are in Branson, taking in the shows and seeing all the attractions, and you are trying to fill your time with as much activity as possible, the buffet may be the food service of choice.

because it has an Italian zest in what is often thought of as a rather bland dish. Also good are the salads, especially Rocky's special salad and the tortellini salad. If it's Italian, you can order it at Rocky's: spaghetti, lasagna, fettuccine, and ravioli. Service is so quick, you probably won't have time to have a game of darts at the bar, but it's great fun to watch. Rocky's also has live music entertainment. With the new Branson Landing across the tracks, Rocky's is part of the "old town" next door to the new.

TONY Z'S ITALIAN RISTORANTE
& LOUNGE $$
300 Terrace Rd.
(417) 332-0610
www.tonyzbranson.com
Located across from Pointe Royale next to the Welk Resort, Tony Z's is known locally for its authentic Italian cuisine. The food is good because Tony's uses the finest ingredients in their cherished family recipes. Choose from homemade Italian pasta and pizza, aged steak and seafood, chicken and lamb, and Caesar salad prepared tableside. Tony Z's is also a fixture of Branson's nightlife with the nightly jazz, blues, and rock entertainment in the lounge. (See the Nightlife chapter.)

SEAFOOD

LANDRY'S SEAFOOD HOUSE $$$
2900 76 Country Blvd.
(417) 339-1010
Landry's has the atmosphere of an old-time 1940s coastal seafood house, a bit of the seashore here in the Ozark hills. The Landrys came here from Katy, Texas, down near Houston, and they bring their reputation for great seafood inland. You'll enjoy their special recipes for tasty appetizers, and they have such entrees as red snapper, stuffed flounder, lemon pepper catfish, crawfish étouffée, gumbo, and spicy crawfish, all served in a laid-back atmosphere. Their specialty is shrimp, and you can have it your way: fried, boiled, chilled, served in gumbo, combined with pastry stuffed in a po'boy. In fact, depending on

the season, shrimp lovers here will go through 80 to 275 pounds of shrimp a day! For those who aren't the seafarin' type, Landry's offers certified Angus steaks and tempting chicken delicacies. They're open for lunch and dinner, and you can call ahead for takeout.

THE RAILS $$
433 Animal Safari Rd.
(417) 336-3401
Nearly every place to eat in Branson, it seems, has a buffet, but the Rails is one of the best all-you-can-eat fish and seafood buffets we know of. The comfortable booths and tables may seem a bit close together, but that contributes to the homey atmosphere and attests to the popularity the Rails holds among the locals. You can fill up on both boiled and fried shrimp, delectable catfish, Cajun fries, clam strips, seafood gumbo, stuffed crab, clam chowder, grilled chicken breasts, and barbecue pork roast. Then top it off with a dessert of fruit cobbler and ice cream. It's all southern comfort food, but what do you expect: Owners Buddy and Jane Hurst came to the Ozarks from southern Arkansas, and they were close enough to Louisiana to have a major Cajun influence. The Rails is on the left, just after you turn off on Animal Safari Road from MO 165, just down from the intersection with Green Mountain Road.

WHITE RIVER FISH HOUSE
1 Bass Pro Dr.
(417) 243-5100
www.whiteriverfishhouse.com
Johnny Morris gave another reason for visiting Branson when he built this restaurant on Lake Taneycomo by the Bass Pro Outpost on the south side of the Branson Landing development. It's one of a number of good eateries in the new shopping venue, but it's the only one built on the water. Well-appointed with turn-of-the-twentieth-century White River float-fishing memorabilia, the Fish House features catfish and trout, as well as their saltwater relatives. You can even get "dry land" ribs and and steaks. Our favorite is the Ozarks pan-fried trout almondine with a beer

of choice. The corn bread itself is worth the visit. Check the menu online and learn some float-fishing history and about the man that "started it all," Jim Owen, at the same time.

STEAK HOUSES AND BARBECUE

B. T. BONES $$
2346 Shepherd of the Hills Expressway
(417) 335-2002
www.btbones.com
"A Little Taste of Texas in Branson" and "Great Steaks! No Bull!" are accurate B. T. Bones slogans. The ranch decor fits the steaks, prime ribs, and fajitas that are the favorites since 1992. You can also get shrimp, trout, catfish, salmon, and mahimahi, which doesn't sound very western, but neither does the meatless, cholesterol-free garden burger. It's that influence by outsiders! Although B. T. Bones doesn't advertise it, the meals come with a show, as there is always dancing to live music by some good off-The-Strip talent. The bar is raised so you can get a better view, and it has typical finger food: nachos, buffalo wings, "Texas bullets" (stuffed and fried jalapeños). Locals come by after the show, and B. T. Bones attracts the college crowd, not only locally but also from Springfield.

CHARLIE'S STEAK, RIBS & ALE $$
3009 West 76 Country Blvd.
(417) 334-6090
A bit hard to find but worth the hunt! The name says it all, but without mentioning the great appetizers, Texas-size salads, giant sandwiches, or the tangy barbecue and tasty chicken and seafood dishes—plus full-service bar and its own microbrewery, all in a western decor. There's also a kids' menu, and for those in the fast lane, there's the convenient takeout. They serve up a bucket of peanuts, but don't fill up on them! We think it has some of the best ribs in Branson, and definitely the most catchy TV ad jingle! You'll find Charlie's by looking where the giant John Wayne on the Hollywood Wax Museum is gazing across The Strip: right at Charlie's!

FALL CREEK STEAK AND
CATFISH HOUSE $$
997 MO 165 at Fall Creek Road
(417) 336-5060
www.bransonsbestrestaurant.com
Bring your catcher's mitt here, as you have to catch your high-rise, softball-size rolls. It's all part of the fun of eating steaks grilled with real hickory chips. Newly rebuilt after burning in 2006, the restaurant features the old steak and fish favorites with baked sweet potatoes as well as traditional spuds served every way imaginable. You can also try fried dill pickles and fried green tomatoes. Lunch and dinner are served daily, and a kids' menu is offered. The back porch overlooking Fall Creek is a great place to eat and watch the raccoons that come up for a free handout.

OUTBACK STEAK AND OYSTER BAR $$$
1914 76 Country Blvd.
(417) 334-6306
www.outbacksteakhouse.com
You'll almost pick up an Aussie accent with the meal and atmosphere of the Outback. There are Down Under favorites such as lamb chops, snaggers (large spicy sausages), steaks, oysters, and even alligator tail. The food is served in an atmosphere of flags, tools, musical instruments, signs, and Australian antiques with primitives on the weathered barn-board interior. Bread is served in the metal buckets it's baked in, and you'll swear the khaki-clad servers look like they're ready for a safari into the Outback. (They even have the accent right!) The menu has interesting alligator and oyster "teasers" (appetizers) and drinks from the full-service bar, including a number of Australian brews. Locals have found it's a great place for after-the-shows gatherings, especially when you can eat, sit, drink, and talk on the deck during summer nights or hang out in the Outback Pub next door. It seems to be a favorite of local college students, perhaps because they have noticed there actually are 99 bottles of beer on the wall (count 'em if you don't believe us)—and all of them different. (See the Nightlife chapter.)

SHORTY SMALL'S $$
3270 Yellow Ribbon Rd.
(417) 334-8797
www.shortysmalls.com

"Short on name, but big on barbecue," Shorty's has juicy burgers (a favorite is the mushroom cheeseburger), steaks, macho nachos, "jumpin' off the bone barbecue ribs," tender barbecue brisket, and tasty salads, including a heroic-size taco salad. Proportions are generous at Shorty's, perhaps to make up for the diminutive name and perhaps to make you want to buy an "I Pigged Out at Shorty Smalls" T-shirt. Shorty's serves lunch and dinner daily in a plain southern smokehouse atmosphere just down from the Falls shopping center before Fall Creek Road.

TEX-MEX

CANTINA LAREDO $$
1001 Branson Landing Blvd.
(417) 334-6062
www.cantinalaredo.com

Cantina Laredo, in Branson Landing, and looks out over Lake Taneycomo and the fountains/fire show at the Landing. A great place for a drink, it offers authentic Mexican dishes in a sophisticated atmosphere with daily fish specials, grilled chicken, and steaks complemented by signature sauces such as chipotle-wine with portobello mushrooms or sautéed artichoke hearts and roasted red bell peppers. We recommend the Enchilada Veracruz: chicken and spinach with rice and a mixed vegetable medley that has an amazing flavor. The Cantina has happy hour 4–7 p.m. weekdays. Check the menu at their Web site.

CASA FUENTES $
1107 76 Country Blvd.
(417) 339-3888
www.casafuentes.com

This casual cantina offers authentic Mexican cuisine, and locals like it for lunch. Quite a few have even been convinced to try spicy dishes for breakfast, and, of course, the good food attracts the evening crowd. The Casa Fuentes

was actually established in Mexico City in 1920 by Manuel Fuentes Martinez, who had worked as head chef in hotels and restaurants in New York, Chicago, and Dallas for more than 20 years. His son, Manuel Fuentes Alvarez, continues his tradition in Mexico City and Puebla, and now his son, Manuel Fuentes Rodriquez, continues the tradition in Branson, somewhat adapted to American tastes. We're learning to desert our traditional biscuits and gravy for *huevos con chorizo* (eggs with Mexican sausage, rice, and beans) or the *enfrijoladas* (soft tortillas rolled in bean sauce and topped with onion, cheese, and sour cream), and other delectable day-starters. For lunch there is a variety of traditional specials, or you can order a la *carta*: chiles rellenos (poblano peppers stuffed with beef and cheese and served with rice and beans) or the Taco Loco (three tacos with shredded beef, rice, and beans). Dinner can be one of a dozen Casa Fuentes specialties. A favorite is Bisteck a la Mexicana—thinly cut steak, stir-fried with tomatoes, onions, and jalapeño peppers and served with refried beans, Mexican rice, guacamole, and hot tortillas. If any of this fare proves to be too hot, the fire department is only two doors down The Strip. Good to know.

GILLEY'S TEXAS CAFE $$
3457 76 Country Blvd.
(417) 335-2755
www.gilleys.com

Mickey Gilley eats here. He says the food's good, and that's good for business. It's his restaurant, next door to his theater. His usual is Hot Tex buffalo wings with iced tea or a light draft beer. Locals like Mickey's chili and buy Gilley's chili seasoning mix to replicate their restaurant favorite in their own kitchens. Beef or chicken fajitas, the famous El Toro burrito, homemade enchiladas, and Texas nachos are popular menu items, but other options include steaks, burgers, ribs, and salads. Gilley's frozen margaritas are popular during the heat of the day and after the show.

MORE THAN A MEAL

For you Type A people who like to cram in as much as you can and do something while eating, here in Branson you can take a cruise, watch a horse show, or see the antics of some redneck good ol' boys (and their gals). You have to be able to rubberneck, laugh, clap, chew, and swallow at the same time at these places. Note that our price guide includes your meal and the show or attraction.

BRANSON SCENIC RAILWAY $$$
206 East Main St., Branson Depot
(417) 334-6110
www.bransontrain.com
Take a train ride up Turkey Creek Valley or the Roark Creek Valley on this candlelight excursion into our Ozarks past. The dinner train is Saturday evening only, leaving at 5 p.m. and returning at 7:15 p.m., just in time for you to make a show. This sit-down dinner offers traditional train fare, which includes a salad; a beef, fish, or chicken entree; vegetables; and a drink. The train will take you back in time to when the railroads set the standard for luxury. You'll see the seasonal splendor of the Ozark Mountains. The conductor will point out some of the interesting highlights along the 40-mile round-trip and let you know when you'll plunge into the darkness of a tunnel. With the fine china and linen in candlelight, this is what we call romance. It's an Ozarks version of the *Orient Express* without the murder. During the day, you can make the same journey without the dinner. Dinner trip: $53.75 per person; excursion trip, $24 for adults (13 years and older) and $13.75 for children (3 years to 12).

DIXIE STAMPEDE $$$
1525 76 Country Blvd.
(417) 336-3000, (800) 520-5101
www.dixiestampede.com
"The most fun place to eat in Branson," says Dolly Parton of her 1,000-seat restaurant. You get a four-course meal of hickory-smoked barbecued ribs and rotisserie chicken, plus veggies, dessert, and drinks, served while you watch a horse show.

i Before tourism and during Prohibition, the making of moonshine was a profitable underground Ozarks enterprise. "Taney County scotch" and "Booger County bourbon" were slang names for the product. (No one knows why or how, but nearby Douglas County, named after Lincoln's opponent in the Lincoln-Douglas debates, acquired the nickname Booger.)

The service for that many people is fast, and if you get so caught up in the show that you forget to chew and swallow, you can take the rest home in a doggy (make that a horse) bag. The architecture of the Dixie Stampede theater gives an idea of the theme. It's antebellum Old South, with horse races, roping, trick riding, chicken races (and races with birds bigger than chickens—would you believe ostriches?), and a fireworks finale. Dolly does it big for you. Of course, she's had some experience, with similar venues in Pigeon Forge, Tennessee, and Myrtle Beach, South Carolina. We suggest reservations for this one, and get there in time for the preshow entertainment in the alcohol-free saloon. There are two Stampedes each night, at 5:30 and 8 p.m., with the preshow starting at 4:30 and 7 p.m. This southern spectacle with food is served up nightly March through December with some exceptions. Call for show nights and times for a gallopin' good evening!

MEL'S HARD LUCK DINER $
2800 Country Blvd.
(417) 332-0150
If you're shopping in the Grand Village and happen to need breakfast, lunch, or dinner (or just a snack), stop in at Mel's Hard Luck Diner. They serve up fabulous food with a song. That's not for a song, but with a song. Expect your waitperson to burst into song. A classic 1950s-style diner—great food, good times, fun music, and Branson's original singing servers provide a unique dining experience for the whole family. They're so good you'll wonder why they aren't in the entertainment business! (Perhaps they are!) The basic food

in this diner is homemade plate specials (Jimmy Crack Corn and Chicken Chowder and the All Shook Up Salad) and the inevitable burger and fries, with variations. You can get dessert from their authentic soda fountain. Our favorite singer-server?—Sharon Robinson!

PLAYTIME PIZZA $$
3101 Gretna Rd.
(417) 332-1112

Visitors to Branson know all about the wonderful shows and amazing entertainers, but what about when it's time for dinner and the kids are bored? Well, meet Pete Za! Walk into this race car garage for your dining experience. As the "legend" goes, Pete was a former race car driver who was banned from the sport due to his use of olive oil in his fuel. He took his olive oil elsewhere and created fabulous Italian food recipes with it. Pete Za's "former garage" can seat 520 and has a go-kart race track, two levels of arcades, shops, and tons of food: several buffets, including pizza, pasta, dessert, and more. You might have to drag the kids away from the games to eat, but once they get there, they will enjoy the food just as much.

SHOWBOAT BRANSON BELLE $$$
4800 MO 165, near Table Rock Dam
(417) 336-7171, (800) 831-4FUN
www.silverdollarcity.com

Ride the biggest boat in the world launched on bananas. (Get the captain to tell you how they got that big stern-wheeler off the bank and onto the lake!) You can have a cruise, meal, and show all in one to pack lots into a short time on your vacation. You can do breakfast, lunch, dinner (two evening cruises), or Sunday brunch. Meals aboard the Branson Belle come right from the ship's galley, and the various courses are served by the singing and dancing servers while you watch the current stage show. The menu is set, with breakfast of ham, egg, and cheese casserole; muffins; fruit; juice; and coffee. Lunch and dinner both feature a green salad, hot bread, vegetables, chicken, and brisket, plus dessert and coffee. The ship has no bar, so go expecting tea and soft drinks. Plan a block of two hours for the cruise, dinner, and show. There is time before and after the meal to go out on deck and take in some of our magnificent scenery. Cruise times vary according to the season, so call ahead for departure times. (See the Attractions chapter.)

OUT OF THE WAY, BUT WORTH THE DRIVE

DEVITO'S RESTAURANT
350 Devito's Loop, Harrison
(870) 741-8832

It's not far to Harrison, and Deivito's is worth the trip. Sights around Harrison make a great day trip, and dinner at Deivito's on the way back would top it off. There is a large spring there that forms Bear Creek, which eventually makes its way to Bull Shoals Lake. But there is more to Bear Creek Springs than that. Two of the more famous things are Devito's Restaurant and trout fishing. Devito's is renowned for their wonderful Italian food and, naturally, their trout. In fact, you can fish there, catch a trout, and they will prepare that very one for you to have for dinner. No fishing license is required and the entire family can do it. Fishing is by appointment. Call 870-741-8832. Some of their greatest dishes include the chicken almondine, trout, Fettuccine Devito, and the chicken parmesan. Boone County is dry, so they don't serve alcoholic beverages, but you can bring your own wine and they will provide you with corkscrew and glasses. Deivito's is open Tuesday through Saturday.

HEMINGWAY'S BLUE WATER CAFE $$
1935 South Campbell St., Springfield
(Third floor of Bass Pro Shops)
(417) 891-5100
www.hemingwaysbluewatercafe.com

"I have discovered that there is romance in food when romance has disappeared from everywhere else."
—Ernest Hemingway.

Papa would have found it in this namesake restaurant: alligator tail appetizer (one among many), steaks, and seafood (including Ozark Mountain trout), a variety of pasta dishes from "Pastabilities," and salads (the Hemingway Caesar salad is locally famous). There is a great selection of laureate sandwiches from "Between the Breads," and Hemingway's is famous for its buffet: breakfast, lunch, dinner, and Sunday brunch. Your favorite drink can come from Hemingway's bar. And check out that huge aquarium as part of the back-bar decor. You can spend hours relaxing and lowering your blood pressure!

LAMBERT'S CAFE $$
US 65 and County Road J/CC, Ozark
(417) 581-7655
www.throwedrolls.com

Here's another road show, but you have to go up the road almost to Springfield for this one! The Ozarks now has its own version of the famous Bootheel Cafe in Sikeston. The first one opened in 1942 and made famous the "throwed roll," originated by a customer who yelled to a server, "Just throw it to me!" You'd think a lot of great yeast rolls would be dropped by butterfinger catchers, but not many are. Now number two has the same good food, in a barnlike structure decorated with Missouri roadside advertising art from the 1930s, 1940s, and 1950s, and with items from barns and toolsheds. Lambert's features down-home comfort food—steaks, ribs, pork chops, ham, and meat loaf—for lunch and dinner. Not everyone would agree, but high on our list is liver and onions. Keep filling your plate with "pass-alongs"—helpings of fried okra, black-eyed peas, and fried apples—until you're filled and just have to pass them along. This place is so popular and so famous that the wait can be long (30 to 45 minutes) during the busy season, but people don't seem to mind.

PAPOULI'S $$$
725 MO 248, Reeds Spring
(417) 272-8243

Tom and Betsy Haldoupis came here from Greece so many years ago that they almost have a hillbilly accent, and they've been cooking most of those years using old family recipes. They had other restaurants, but Papouli's has been attracting those who take eating seriously since 1986. It's said that St. Louis and Kansas City have "Papouli Clubs," groups of devoted diners who meet and talk about the food they've eaten at this Reeds Spring restaurant. The Greek salad is legendary, loaded with feta cheese and covered in a family-recipe dressing that is out of this world. The lamb kabobs are also famous. The menu includes more traditional American fare as well. The plain blue exterior of the restaurant (a remodeled bait shop, Tom told us) doesn't prepare you for the fine-dining experience inside, but you know something is up because the parking lot is always packed.

THE RIVERSIDE INN $$$
2629 North Riverside Dr., Ozark
(417) 581-7051
www.riversideinnrestaurant.com

Those interested in fine dining have been coming to the Riverside since 1923, when rumors circulated that people drove down from St. Louis and Kansas City just for famous fried chicken, corn fritters, and "Taney County scotch," the local moonshine from the hills south of Ozark. The Riverside and its food have stood the test of time. In its 80-year history, the Riverside has been flooded several times by the Finley River, most recently in 2008, but it has always reopened. Owner Eric Engel doesn't like to think about floods, but he keeps his flood insurance paid! With the Finley River flowing just outside your window, friendly for the moment, you can enjoy steaks, frog's legs, seafood, that famous fried chicken, and sinful desserts. A great favorite is chateaubriand for two with Rutherford Hill merlot; the steak is a 24-ounce choice cut, and they carve it for you at the table. Enjoy the ambience of the Riverside's antiques, stained glass windows, mirrors, and greenhouse, home to the mint plants that add zing to your tea, salads, and sauces. Ask your server about the restaurant's famous floods, and you'll be shown the high-water marks on the wall and told stories of bygone days. The wall murals by original owner, artist-businessman Howard Garrison, make for some interesting yarns, too. You can get fine food and an easy local history lesson in a single evening at this dinner-only classic.

SWEETS

This is the dessert section of our list of local eateries, and it is only a small gathering of the best. We have plenty of ice-cream chains: Ben & Jerry's, Maggiemoo's, Cold Stone Creamery, TCBY, Baskin-Robbins. New ones pop up each season like spring Ozark wildflowers. Being a tourist must be hard work, because we have so many restaurants and even more stands and kiosks for snacks and sweets. Indulge your sweet tooth at a couple of them.

How much is your sweet tooth going to cost you in Branson? That depends on you and the number of kids you have in tow. You can get a foot of chocolate at the Fudge Shop for 99 cents (a great gag gift for chocoholic friends), but if you're paying by the pound for fudge and nut candies, expect to pay $2.50 to $4.00 at most places.

Hard ice cream runs about $1.50 a scoop, and you get a big one. A double is about $2.90, and a triple may cost $4.25. A malt, shake, or sundae can cost $2.75 to $2.90. So all things considered, you can get by as cheap as a buck and a half a head (or should that be mouth?), but count on spending more like $2.75 per mouth. Now you look at the kids in tow, judge their appetites, and you do the multiplication!

ANDY'S FROZEN CUSTARD
3415 W 76 Country Blvd.
(417)377-5501
www.eatandys.com
Branson was delighted to get the delectable Andy's—saving a drive to Springfield for our favorite summer treat! You won't know what you're missing until you try it. Our favorite is the Ozark Concrete.

CAKES 'N' CREAM DESSERT PARLOR
2805 76 Country Blvd.
(417) 334-4929
Half the fun of this place is the atmosphere, which is decidedly 1950s, with vintage records on the wall, a Wurlitzer jukebox with tunes of the time, and intimate round tables with sweetheart chairs. You can get homemade cobblers, pies, cakes (try the Black Forest cake), funnel cakes (topped with vanilla ice cream, fresh strawberries, and whipped cream), banana splits, and sundaes. They serve 'em up from midmorning to midnight seven days a week during the busy tourist season. They also have sugar-free ice cream and fruit pies for those with special dietary needs. When you see the costumed servers work at getting that rock-hard ice cream out of the containers, you'll know why we wouldn't wager anything on a blacksmith who might get into an arm-wrestling contest with one of them.

DELICIOUS DELIGHTS
2925 76 Country Blvd.
(417) 337-9328
Hot dogs, funnel cakes, ice cream, and delicious strawberry shortcake are the hot items for people with a sweet tooth. It's a busy place, because they also established a reputation for great deli sandwiches, but while you're indulging your sweet tooth, you may want to check out some of the gift items for friends back home.

DUTTON DELI AND DESSERTS
3454 76 Country Blvd.
(417) 332-2772
www.theduttons.com
Next door to the Dutton Family Theater, the Dutton Deli features hearty soups (broccoli and cheese, chicken noodle, and others) and chili, along with a variety of sandwiches. They also stock homemade specialty desserts: cream and fruit pies, great cobblers, cheesecakes, right-from-the-oven cookies, and a variety of ice creams. A local favorite is the blackberry cobbler. Before or after their show, or any other time, it's a great place for lunch, dinner, or a late-night snack. Open 11 a.m. to midnight.

THE FUDGERY
3562 Shepherd of the Hills Expressway
IMAX Entertainment Complex
(417) 336-3887

300 Tanger Blvd., Tanger
Outlet Center
(417) 337-9899

100 Branson Landing
(417) 239-0136

The Fudgery promises (and provides) fudge and fun, the only free show in town. Watch the singing, wise-cracking candy makers make up a batch and roll it out on the big marble slab. They might even offer you a free sample. The Fudgery gives you three chances to indulge that sweet tooth while you're here in Branson. They have the richest, creamiest fudge around, including New Orleans praline fudge, vanilla, chocolate, peanut butter, and other types you could only dream of.

THE FUDGE SHOP
106 South Second St.
(417) 334-5270

For more than 30 years, Barry and Pat Dautrich at the Fudge Shop have satisfied Branson's sweet tooth. You can get a variety of homemade hard candies and fudge, including peanut clusters, pecan logs, caramels, and taffy. Order a foot of chocolate—a great gag gift to take back, if you don't eat it first. Take a look at their famous Dolly Parton suckers. Sample their creamy, rich fudge, and you'll know why everyone who goes in comes out carrying a box.

MR. B'S ICE CREAM PARLOR
102 Second St.
(417) 336-5735

A cheerful red-and-white-checked decor is splashed around this small, old-fashioned ice-cream shop at the corner of Main Street and US Business 65. It's not just desserts though. You can get hot dogs, chili dogs, and deli sandwiches. But it's the ice cream that Randy and Judy Dees are famous for. They serve up old-fashioned ice-cream sodas, malts, and shakes. They have hand-dipped ice creams (more than 23 flavors) and yogurts. Favorites are apple pie, cherry-almond, and death-by-chocolate. They even have no-sugar/no-fat ice creams for the diet-conscious. Let them know it is your birthday, and you'll get a free ice-cream cone. They also have fruit cobblers and real stirred-in-copper-kettles fruit butters—apple, plum, peach. If it takes more than ice cream to satisfy that sweet tooth, the Fudge Shop is right next door!

NIGHTLIFE

If you ask locals what kind of nightlife there is in Branson, they'll probably tell you to see an 8 p.m. show. That's because most folks go to bed fairly early around here. Those of you who are looking for action even after the shows have let out will find a fair mix of local taverns and glitzy nightclubs. Up until the last couple of years, the choices for late-night entertainment in Branson were slim. However, as the number of annual visitors steadily increases, so does the demand for more late-night establishments.

Most of the nighttime activity in Branson actually takes place in about a dozen or so restaurants with full-service bars. We have grouped them together in this chapter, but you'll also find most of them listed in the Restaurants chapter. Some have live entertainment from time to time, but most of them do not. Unless otherwise noted, there's never a cover charge at these places. If you're really looking to kick up your heels and are younger than 30, you should probably head on up to Springfield, where there's a plentiful supply of dance clubs and taverns that are frequented by mostly 20- and 30-somethings. Check out the *Springfield News-Leader*'s weekend section that comes out on Friday for a list of the places hosting live bands or other special events. Branson does have a few places where you can go to cut a rug. Most notable is B. T. Bones.

The legal drinking age is 21 in Missouri, and many of these places will ask for identification. Nondrinkers will find a few places that serve a selection of nonalcoholic concoctions.

If you've had one too many of the altering kind, ask the bartender or waitperson to call a cab for you. Why spoil an otherwise perfect vacation?

During the winter months, most of our bars and nightclubs close up well before midnight, and even during the busy summer and fall, not too many stay open past then. After 1 a.m., you may have to settle for cable TV.

Local entertainers like to frequent the nightspots after the shows. They catch up on gossip while enjoying a beer with their evening meal. At Tony Z's or B. T. Bones, you never know whom you might see at the bar or at the microphone.

If you belong to the under-21 dating crowd and want to cuddle up to your sweetheart in the dark, see a movie. Skateworld stays open until 10 p.m., and some of the go-kart tracks stay open until midnight in the summertime, which can be great fun for a date (see the Kidstuff chapter). If all else fails, take your other half down to Sunset Park, on the Taneycomo lakefront just west of the US 65 bridge. A stroll on the park path, listening to the night critters, may do more for your love life than some loud, smoky evening spent in a bar.

EATS AND DRINKS

APPLEBEE'S NEIGHBORHOOD BAR & GRILL
1836 Country Blvd.
(417) 336-5053
www.applebees.com
This one's got everything you would expect to find at any other Applebee's franchise, but what sets it apart is its huge parking lot at the Apple Tree Mall location—close to another nightlife hot spot, Club 57, and Dick Clark's American Bandstand Theater and the Dixie Stampede. You can watch cable TV at the bar and have dinner, take in a show at Club 57, and walk back to your parked

car. This is a popular hangout for local college students and other barely 21 guests.

BUZZARD BAR (BIG CEDAR LODGE)
612 Devil's Pool Rd., Ridgedale
(417) 335-2777
ww.bigcedar.com

This is the kind of place where you might have found Teddy Roosevelt after one of his hunting trips, if it had been around back then. In keeping with true Big Cedar Lodge style, the Buzzard Bar is a dark and cozy place where you can enjoy Irish coffee and other imported alcoholic beverages. Head on upstairs to the Devil's Pool Restaurant (see the Restaurants chapter) for a dinner feast, or skip dinner altogether and get to know the bartender on a first-name basis. Be sure to check out the view of Table Rock Lake out the west side of the building.

CANDLESTICK INN
127 Taney St.
(417) 334-3633
www.candlestickinn.com

Thinking of popping the question? You won't find a more romantic spot than the Candlestick Inn. And that's no bluff, because it's perched 250 feet above Lake Taneycomo just east of downtown Branson overlooking the Branson Landing. This casual but gourmet restaurant boasts the best sunset scenery in town. You and your special someone can choose from a long list of fine wines, liquors, and imported beers to celebrate the occasion (assuming the answer is yes). You won't find any loud bands or karaoke at Candlestick, just great atmosphere, food, and service.

LONE STAR STEAKHOUSE
201 Wildwood Dr.
(417) 336-5030

Popular with tourists and locals alike, Lone Star Steakhouse serves up food and liquor in the Texas tradition: big. If you've come just to drink, try one of their giant margaritas. You may need only one. Their grilled chicken is out of this world, and unless you have a Texas-size appetite, you'll have plenty to take home. You never know whom you might run into at Lone Star. Many of our local entertainers stop by after the shows for a well-earned steak dinner. If you're looking for a place to celebrate a birthday, the staff at Lone Star will make enough noise to let everyone in the place know you're there.

OASIS LOUNGE
2820 76 Country Blvd.
(417) 337-7777

It's okay to bring your camera to the safari-themed Oasis Lounge. More than one local has been known to do it. You'll see why when you step into this upscale bar, adjacent to the Clarion Hotel. From the wicker ceiling fans to the wall murals to the palm trees and zebra-print upholstery, this place carries the term "themed decor" to new heights. They keep a well-stocked bar of imported wines and liqueurs on hand for the most discriminating palates. The food comes picture-perfect and tastes just as good. Food is served until 9 p.m., and the lounge stays open until 11 p.m. Monday through Saturday.

OUTBACK PUB
1922 76 Country Blvd.
(417) 334-7003

Name your favorite brew, and the Outback Pub probably has it. With more than 100 beers, wines, and beverages, the hard part will be making the decision. Aside from the beer, this is a great place to go for big-time Australian atmosphere. They've got live entertainment, darts, billiards, and unique appetizers and sandwiches for lunch and dinner. We like the alligator tail. It's a little like chicken, but more like fish. When the weather's nice, you can sit outside on the veranda or, on cool evenings, cozy up to the fireplace. The Outback is a great spot

i If you get lost easily and suffer from insomnia, by all means hop in the car and check out the town after 1 a.m. There's hardly any traffic, so it's a great time to get to know your way around.

to come and hear some energetic live music in a casual, easygoing atmosphere. Played most nights, the live music is a mix of different styles. Guests can choose between two different bands—one on the outside upper-level deck and one in the lounge area. Happy hour is 4–7 p.m. Monday through Friday. If you're looking for a more substantial meal, try the Outback Steak and Oyster Bar next door (see the Restaurants chapter).

ROCKY'S ITALIAN RESTAURANT
120 North Sycamore St.
(417) 335-4765

This is where the downtown business crowd gathers for lunch and where they unwind after 5 p.m. You can order from their full-service bar any time of day. In the evening, test your hand-eye coordination with a game of darts, and then decide if it's time to call a cab. From time to time Rocky's brings in a local combo band for weekend evening entertainment. The atmosphere is great, and the food is even better. By the time you finish with the homemade bread they bring to your table, you'll be lucky to have room for anything else.

i If you know you'll be out partying late and will need a ride home, check with the front desk of your hotel to find out if they offer shuttle service. Many of the area's hotels will be happy to bring you back in for the night.

LIVE ENTERTAINMENT

ANDY WILLIAMS MOON RIVER GRILL
2600 W Country Blvd.
(417) 337-9459

You can enjoy dinner at the grill, then go next door to Andy's Moon River Theatre for a show, and come back to the grill for a nightcap and lounge entertainment. Andy himself or performers in the show often make appearances or have lunch and dinner there. Gail Lennon and the Buzz Boyz, a group of locals (Bruce Hoffman, Tom Dos-

tal, Mike Cathcart) in various shows, have been playing the mellow and avant-garde as well as old favorites late night once a week.

CHARLIE'S STEAK, RIBS & ALE
3009 West 76 Country Blvd.
(417) 334-6090

Drop by this local favorite across from the Hollywood Wax Museum for a little late-night Big Band and swing dancin'. There's a $3 cover charge, but you'll get to hear music performed by members of the bands of local shows. The great thing about our local bands is that they're made up of top musicians and singers from the theaters. If you arrive early for dinner, you'd better come hungry, because the food at Charlie's is piled high. We like the ribs best.

CLUB 57
1600 W. Country Blvd.
(417) 332-1960

Club 57 is a show lounge at Dick Clark's American Bandstand Theater playing live music from the '50s, '60s, and everything up to today. There are many guest appearances from the stars playing the Dick Clark American Bandstand Theater as well as popular local talent.

ERNIE BIGGS CHICAGO STYLE DUELING PIANO BAR & GRILL
505 Branson Landing Blvd.
(417) 239-3670

Ernie Biggs Chicago Style Dueling Piano Bar is your classic sing-along piano bar. At Ernie Biggs the show revolves around your requests, and audience participation is a must. If you don't think they can play your type of music—just try 'em. These "walking jukeboxes" hate being stumped and hit the stage every night with an "if you can say it, we can play it" attitude. From oldies and classic rock to the '80s and songs still on the charts today, these guys are here to play what you want to hear and some old favorites that we bet you've forgotten. There is no better place for birthdays, bachelor and bachelorette parties, reunions, or just a great night out. They can handle and appetite, too, with a full menu including appetizers, soups, salads, sandwiches, and "Chicago-style" pizza.

TONY Z'S ITALIAN RISTORANTE & LOUNGE
300 Terrace Rd.
(417) 332-0610
www.tonyzbranson.com

Located across from Pointe Royale next to the Lawrence Welk Resort, Tony Z's has quickly become a fixture of Branson's nightlife with the nightly jazz, blues, and rock entertainment in the lounge. Groups and entertainers vary each week and change since many also perform in shows on The Strip. Recent acts have included "the voice" Nedra Culp and the Stilettos, pianist Johnny Johnson, and Chance and the Chasers. Sometimes things start as early as 6:30 p.m. and sometimes as late as 10:30 p.m. Tuesday at 9 p.m. is karaoke night, so you provide the entertainment!

The food is good, too: homemade Italian pastas, pizza, aged steaks, seafood, lamb, and fresh homemade bread.

DANCE FLOORS

B. T. BONES
2346 Shepherd of the Hills Expressway
(417) 335-2002

If you can find a spot on this dance floor, cowboy hats off to you. You'd better get there early, because floor space is rare after about 8 p.m. when the band strikes up and the two-steppers and line dancers take over. Joni Carter, Carl Bird, and the Route 66 Band cover all your favorite country songs plenty loud enough for you to hear 'em. Sundays are karaoke nights, and folks from all over come to make their Branson debut. It's not unusual for this 300-seat place to be packed right up until closin' time (1 a.m. Monday through Saturday, midnight on Sunday). There's never a cover charge here, but they make it up on steaks and cocktails.

i Although Branson police officers may be friendlier than most, they do enforce the law. Don't drink and drive.

MOVIE THEATERS

BRANSON MEADOWS CINEMAS
4740 Gretna Rd.
(417) 332-2884
www.bransonmovies.com

Branson's largest first-run movie theater opened in March 2000 at the Factory Shoppes at Branson Meadows. This Shopro Theatre features 11 screens, and each theater has plush continental stadium seating and digital sound. They're calling it "stealth cinema design" and saying it's the first one of its type in Missouri. All we know is that the new design provides for a great moviegoing experience. The seats are comfortable, and you will have no trouble seeing over the person in front of you. The theaters are so small that every seat is close to the screen. They even have cup holders, and we know how important those are when you're trying to juggle popcorn and soft drinks and hold hands at the same time. There's an arcade room and a private party room as well. Tickets for movies beginning before 6 p.m. are $5 per person. Movies starting after 6 p.m. are $7 for adults, $6 for adults 55 and older, and $5 for children 3 through 11. Children two and younger always get in free. Each Tuesday is "bring your own bag" night. They'll fill it with popcorn for free.

i Ozark writer Daniel Westrell's novel *Winter's Bone* was being filmed in the Forsyth area in early 2009. Look for it in theaters.

ELITE CINEMA III
IMAX Entertainment Complex
3562 Shepherd of the Hills Expressway
(417) 335-4832
www.bransonimax.com

The Elite Cinema III is the newest addition to the Branson moviegoing experience. Each of the three 35 mm theaters features stadium-style seating, oversized seats with adjustable armrests, ample leg room, and an impressive digital sur-round-sound system. Tickets are $6.70 for adults and $4.75 for children 3 through 11. Students and seniors pay $5.55. Children two and younger get in free. Shows before 5 p.m. cost $4.75.

IMAX ENTERTAINMENT COMPLEX
3562 Shepherd of the Hills Expressway
(417) 335-4832, (800) 419-4832
www.bransonimax.com

For the ultimate moviegoing experience, try IMAX. Its six-story screen and surround-sound system and 75 mm films will knock your socks off. Beginning at 9 a.m. each day, the theater runs a different IMAX film every hour. Recent films we saw include *Grand Canyon: The Hidden Secrets, Ozarks Legacy & Legend, Alaska: Spirit of the Wild, and Everest.* At 8 p.m. they run a major 35 mm motion picture. There's a new full-length movie every week, so be sure to call ahead to find out what's playing. Adult tickets for the regular IMAX films are $8.50 plus tax and $4.95 for children 4 through 12. Feature film prices are $7.37 plus tax for adults and $4.95 plus tax for children. (See the Attractions chapter for more information.)

THE SHOWS

When the popular *60 Minutes* television show proclaimed that Branson was the "live music capital of the entire universe" on December 8, 1991, there were only 22 theaters in operation. Today we have more than 40. Morley Safer reported that Branson hosted an estimated four million people per year. Today the number is eight million; a startling fact when you consider the town's population is just over 7,000. We have more theater seats than Broadway and Las Vegas combined, around 59,000 in all. Branson has been consistently rated by groups such as the American Bus Association and the National Tour Association as one of the top three vacation destinations in the United States. Family-wise, Branson is the most economical of all these vacation spots. Needless to say, Branson is a popular place!

When the Baldknobbers started the first show five decades ago, little did they know that their show would be joined by more than 120 other shows in the years to follow. Today the entertainment offerings in Branson range all the way from community theater productions and amateur talent shows to extravagant Las Vegas style productions complete with 3-D special effects, dazzling costumes, laser lighting systems, and surround sound—and who can forget the big-name stars! Over the years Branson has played host to some of the biggest names in country and pop music both past and present—mostly past, but nevertheless still some of the most famous. Try getting a ticket to Andy Williams's Christmas show after about November 1 and then decide if the term "has been" isn't a little premature.

If you ask people why they come to Branson, the majority of them will say to see the shows, but what they really enjoy is getting to meet the stars face-to-face. You see, in Branson there are no walls between the entertainers and their audiences. They sign autographs, pose for pictures, board motor coaches, and listen intently as people tell them stories about hearing their songs for the first time. If it's your birthday or your anniversary, the stars will announce your name from the stage, or they might even invite you to come up and join them. Veterans are recognized from the stage of almost every theater in town, and no

matter what state you're from, you'll be made to feel as if it were the only one in the Union.

Since most of the entertainers have homes in Branson and live here at least nine months out of the year, you're as likely as not to run into Yakov Smirnoff at Wal-Mart or see one of the Grand Ladies of Country at the supermarket. When Mel Tillis is in town, he and Shoji Tabuchi are regular Table Rock Lakers. Moe Bandy and Mickey Gilley spend most of their free time on one of the area's golf courses. If you see a really good-looking group of 20-something guys and gals at one of the area restaurants, you can probably bet they make up the chorus or dance troupe at one of the shows. Go over and say hello. They'll be glad to shake your hand and tell you about their show. Branson is a small town, and the entertainers don't have many places to hide—not that too many of them even try.

One of the best things about the shows in Branson is that because the entertainers are not constantly packing up to get to their next gig, they have time to really work on their presentations and develop new and creative ways to show off their talents. Comedian, musician, and all-around creative genius Jim Stafford is the perfect example of someone who takes full advantage of the time he has to develop his product. His show is constantly changing through the addition of new numbers, special effects, cast members, jokes, and other neat tricks. You could go to his show five times a year and see something new every time.

Most performers do two shows a day. The most common showtimes are 9:30 a.m., 10 a.m., 2 p.m., 3 p.m., 7 p.m., and 8 p.m. The shows usually last around two hours with a 15-minute intermission. Some of them have pre-shows that begin as much as 30 minutes ahead of the main show. Pre-shows generally feature some type of specialty act, emcee, or comedian.

The theater season in Branson runs from March through December; however, many of the shows are staying open during January and February for Hot Winter Fun (see the Annual Events chapter). For a list of these shows, call the Branson/Lakes Area Chamber of Commerce at (417) 334-4136. Most of the theaters offer Christmas shows that begin around the second week of November and run through the end of the week before Christmas. Ticket prices may be slightly higher for some shows during this time. The custom in Branson is for the shows to devote the second half entirely to Christmas-themed entertainment, while the first half remains the same as the regular season show. There are some exceptions. We have not included specific information for Christmas shows in this book, so your best bet is to call the theater directly to find out what's in the works.

Holidays are a big deal in Branson, especially Veterans Day. Veterans receive discounts to most shows during the week of Veterans Homecoming each year and are treated to some type of special recognition at each venue. New Year's Eve is fast becoming another biggie. Many of the theaters present special late shows to ring in the new year and offer additional shows on New Year's Day.

The showtimes and dates listed in this section are intended to give you a general idea of the days and times a particular show plays at a particular theater. Most shows run six days a week, one or two times a day. Specific dates and times vary frequently throughout the year, so be sure to call the box office if you have a particular date in mind. Also remember that if you call in

April about a show in October, you'd best call back to confirm the information two to three weeks before the show.

Not only do the entertainers change their show schedules during the year, they also change theaters as well. One observer said that Branson shows are as "jumpy as frog legs fryin' in a skillet." Most performers lease a theater or a time slot, and they're always looking for a bargain or a better location. Yakov Smirnoff's theater became too small for his sold-out shows, so he bought the old Will Rogers Theatre, originally built by Mel Tillis. Mel Tillis sold the new theater he built for himself and "retired" (but still plays dates at specified times throughout the year); his old theater is now a church. Sounds confusing, doesn't it? Don't panic if you dial the number of a theater only to find out that the name has changed or the show you were looking for is no longer playing there. Some theaters are "dark" for a season as they change owners or remodel. Again, your best bet is to call the Branson/Lakes Area Chamber of Commerce to find out who is where. (See the Close-up in this chapter on Branson's game of "musical theaters.") But shows open and they fold. Acts come and go. Theaters are sold, and new shows and talent are showcased, leaving the earlier shows looking for new venues. The theater scene is in a state of constant flux in Branson, so much so that even the weekly papers find it difficult to keep abreast of the changes.

The ticket prices we have listed here include tax unless otherwise noted and are subject to change. Fortunately, more shows are now allowing children 12 and younger in for free, but for others the children's ticket prices listed here generally apply to those 12 and younger. There are some exceptions, so be sure to call the box

i **The very first musical show to make its debut in Branson was the Baldknobbers Hillbilly Jamboree. Celebrating its 50th anniversary in 2009, it's as popular as ever and features country and gospel music as well as sidesplitting comedy routines.**

office for specific information. Some of the theaters admit children for free during the summer months but charge at other times of the year. Babes in arms are usually admitted free.

The easiest way to purchase tickets is to call the box office directly or go online to the theater's Web site. Some theaters ask for a credit card number before they will reserve your seats, while others simply require you to pick up and pay for your tickets 30 minutes to one hour before showtime. If you don't show up in time, you risk losing your reservation unless it has been guaranteed with a credit card. The earlier you call, the better your chances of getting good seats. Good seats vary widely from theater to theater. Front row center may be great in one venue but too close to the stage in another. If you have time, you might want to stop by the box office the day before the show and ask to see a seating chart. If you have special needs, you can ask to take a peek inside the auditorium. Let the box-office staff know if you have seriously impaired vision, need a wheelchair space, or require hearing assistance equipment. Staff members will do their best to accommodate you.

A number of ticket brokers and tourist information centers in town will be happy to make all of your show reservations for you. Some of them charge a small fee, and others purchase tickets from the theaters at a wholesale price and then mark the tickets up. These companies are a good source of information about the shows and will even deliver your tickets to your hotel room. Hotels, campgrounds, RV parks, resorts, and other overnight lodging facilities also make reservations for guests. If you know what shows you want to see at the time you make your lodging reservation, the place will often have the tickets waiting for you when you check in and simply add the cost of the tickets to your final bill. If you have tickets in your hand before you arrive at the theater, you can avoid the line at the box office right before showtime.

Most all of the theaters have some type of concessions area where you can purchase soft drinks, popcorn, candy bars, coffee, and water. A few serve hot dogs, muffins, and cookies, but

that's about it. You can take food and drinks into all the theaters, but listen closely for their audio and video recording policies, usually mentioned at the beginning of each show. Some shows ban the use of flash cameras inside the auditorium during the performance.

ALL NEW AMERICANA THEATRE
2905 West Country Music Blvd.
(417) 339-4663
www.thehaygoods.com
www.redhotblue.com
www.tonyroiexperience.com

The Haygoods, one of the most energetic families on the face of this planet, made a move a few years ago from Silver Dollar City to Music City Centre on the Branson strip. This year marks a new chapter in the life and times of the Haygoods. They have purchased and remodeled the Americana Theatre just a little further up the strip. They have redone the lighting, sound, and have made a super roomy lobby for your enjoyment and comfort.

The Haygoods are seven boys and one girl who, with a high-energy show, perform their hearts out for you. You will simply marvel at the abilities and talent of these young people.

They came by their talent honestly because their mom and dad both had their roots in show business long before the first little Haygood was a glint in anyone's eye.

The Haygoods also share their stage with other performers such as Cassandre.

The Voice of an Angel is a brand new production that features the profoundly beautiful voice of Cassandre Faimon-Haygood. Cassandre has been the featured vocalist in Silver Dollar City's productions of *For The Glory*, *Dickens Christmas Carol*, and *Headin' West* for the last 11 years, and has been become a must-see favorite! Now, she boldly steps into the heart of Branson concertgoers with a full production show for all ages featuring pop, Broadway, and classical songs.

Red, Hot and Blue!, one of Branson's most-popular shows that won awards for "Best Morning Show" and "Best Vocal and Dance Group," is back for the full 2009 season, bigger, better and more exciting than ever.

These incredible entertainers provide a high-energy, beautifully costumed production featuring the timeless melodies everyone loves. This "Hardest Working Cast in Branson" takes you on nostalgic journey back to the classic jazz era of the 1940s, the hilarious 1950s, the rockin' 1960s, the disco flash of the 1970s, and into the new century,

Tony Roi's Elvis Experience is an unforgettable tribute to the King of Rock 'N' Roll.

When you watch Tony Roi, you have to keep reminding yourself that you're not actually witnessing a real live performance by the King of Rock 'N' Roll. Tony Roi becomes Elvis Aaron Presley the moment he makes his dramatic entrance at the beginning of every performance!

Backed by one of Branson's hottest bands, Tony Roi puts on an incredible two-hour tribute of the world's greatest music legend. He has the look, the voice, and the swagger that make you believe you are watching Elvis live on stage. Tony Roi has won more awards than anyone in Branson. His show was voted Branson's show of the year for 2006 and 2007, and he was voted Branson's performer of the year for 2004, 2005, 2006, and 2007.

Call the theatre box office or visit the web sites for information, schedules, reservations or tickets.

ANDY WILLIAMS MOON RIVER THEATRE
2500 West Country Blvd.
(417) 334-4500, (800) 666-6094
www.andywilliams.com

You've heard the saying "Everything old is new again"? Well, maybe Andy Williams, who turns 82 in 2009, isn't old (and never will be, in our opinion), but he's certainly enjoying a career renewal in Branson. It's not like he ever disappeared from the entertainment scene. He had a string of gold records and silver screen appearances in the early 1960s, followed by a very popular TV variety show that ran from 1963 to 1971 on NBC. In the decades that followed, his annual Christmas special on television became an institution. In between he played to audiences all over the world, because, as the song says, "there's such a lot of world to see."

Having his own theater in Branson, though, has put Williams back in the spotlight in a big way, and what's good for Andy is good for Branson. By now you've probably figured out that Branson isn't just about country music anymore, and frankly Andy Williams is a large part of the reason why. Most folks consider him to be the first pop music star to call Branson home, and his arrival in 1992 helped pave the way for other non-country performers such as Wayne Newton, Tony Orlando, and the Welk show.

It's been nearly 44 years since "Moon River" became a hit song, and the fact that it now has its own namesake theater is a testament to the influence that a mere piece of music can have on our popular culture. It also has its own little stream of the same name, flowing over the limestone in front of the theater.

Inside, the lobby boasts some impressive pieces from Andy's private art collection, including an original Henry Moore and three from Willem De Kooning.

The year 2009 marks a different schedule in the Moon River Theatre. Andy will be taking some time off to work on his autobiography while other shows will be playing. For the first time since it's opening, Moon River Theatre will have shows on-stage without Andy being a part of it.

Also at the Moon River, Bill Haley's Original Comets will be appearing, as well as Paul Revere and the Raiders. These guys are the real deal. Bill Medley, of the Righteous Brothers, and his daughter will be appearing on their shows as well. Bell Medley's son appears with Paul Revere as the "Baby Raider." It is a line-up you will not want to miss. These are the guys and gals that started the whole rock 'n' roll era.

Andy will be back in the fall, as he usually teams up with another "golden oldie" star, such as Glen Campbell, Ann Margaret, or Petula Clark.

Andy is still bringing Branson a Christmas show that's a virtual sellout year after year. The show changes each season, and it includes contemporary songs as well as oldies. Andy's Christmas shows usually run from the beginning of November through the second week in December. During September and October for the last several years, Andy has shared half of his show with country music superstar Glen Campbell and with a variety of other acts, and folks have come to expect the double billing. Please call the box office or visit their Web site for information and ticket prices.

BALDKNOBBERS HILLBILLY JAMBOREE
2845 76 Country Blvd.
(417) 334-4528
www.baldknobbers.com
The Baldknobbers are celebrating their 50th year in Branson in 2009 and don't show any signs of slowing down. If you know anything at all about Branson, you've probably heard their story, but just in case you haven't, we'll recap it for you. In 1959 four brothers—Bill, Jim, Lyle, and Bob Mabe—started a little show in downtown Branson on the second floor of City Hall. The room had 50 folding chairs and a small stage where the brothers entertained locals and visiting anglers and others who had come to enjoy Lake Taneycomo and the Ozarks outdoors. The group's instruments—a washtub bass, a banjo, a Dobro, and a washboard with a jawbone for rhythm— were mostly homemade. Tickets were 50 cents for kids and $1 for adults. After they outgrew City Hall, they moved to the 200-seat Sammy Lane Pavilion on the lakefront and then on to an old skating rink that accommodated 600 people. In 1968 they built their current theater on The Strip and put in 864 seats. After five remodelings, a lobby renovation, and the addition of 836 seats to total 1,700, the Baldknobbers' nest was made.

Bill and his wife, Joyce, and Jim and his wife, Katie, still run the business operation of the theater, while the younger Mabes now dominate the stage. Guitar player Dennis Mabe, son of Bill and Joyce, is the lead male vocalist. Brent Mabe, Lyle's son, plays bass guitar, and Tim Mabe, who is Jim and Katie's son, carries on his father's legacy as Droopy Drawers Jr. Veteran performers such as Mike Ito, who grew up in Tokyo, Japan, and joined the group in 1979; Gene Dove, emcee, singer, and guitar player; and Milt Quackenbush,

piano player, along with several other seasoned musicians and singers, round out the cast.

The show's formula has deviated little from its humble beginnings. The instruments are fancier, the costumes are flashier, and the sound and lighting systems are high-tech, but the musical styles and comedy routines are much the same. Each year the show gets completely overhauled, and new songs are added and old ones are taken out. Don't be surprised to hear the "Orange Blossom Special" though. It seems to be a mainstay. They do old country songs by the greats and hot new country songs by current chart toppers. The comedy skits evoke riotous laughter show after show. Droopy Drawers Jr. and Stub Meadows fire off one hillbilly joke after another.

Life magazine wrote, "Branson is the Baldknobbers." To find out where the name Baldknobbers came from, check out the History chapter. You can see the Baldknobbers Monday through Saturday at 8 p.m. March through December. Call the box office or visit their Web site for information and ticket prices.

BRANSON MALL MUSIC THEATER
2206 76 Country Blvd.
(417) 335-4400

BRANSON HALL OF FAME THEATER
(417)-464-8497
This theater, adjoining Wal-Mart on The Strip, is changing faces for 2009. This year new shows will grace the stage of the Branson Mall Music Theater. The Branson Mall complex has also integrated a mini theater, the Branson Hall of Fame Theater.

Marvin Short, previously with *50's At The Hop*, gathered up an able and willing group to put together a new show for 2009 called the *Top Ten Rock and Roll Revue*. It's a hot show bringing you the greatest songs of rock and roll. This is a show with something for all ages, from the beginning of rock and roll, to doo wop and on through the '70s and '80s. It has Darrell Croy, who looks a tad bit like the young Jerry Lee Lewis, and he plays the piano and sings remarkably like him. "Marvelous Marvin Short," voted saxophone player of the year several years running, is the one with the outlandish hairdo. You will have no trouble picking him out of the cast. High energy and feel good: these are the hallmarks of the *Top Ten Rock and Roll Revue.*

Another perennial Branson favorite is Denny and Shelia Renee Yeary, known as the "Sweethearts of Branson." Denny, a former bass singer with the Blackwood Brothers, has a voice that literally will shake you in your shoes. Denny and Shelia have won numerous awards for their great production and incredible vocals. This trip down memory lane will not only entertain you but will forever be in your heart as one of the best shows you have ever seen.

The Branson Mall Music Theater will also host the *Mike Walker Show.* Mike is billed as the World's Greatest Singing Impressionist. Mike, who just came from the Mickey Gilley Theatre, pays tribute to many of your favorite singers: Ray Charles, Stevie Wonder, Elvis, and many more. You will be glued to your seat wondering what or who he will do a tribute to next. Sometimes Mike reminds one of a young John Travolta, just an added bonus. Paying attention gals?

The "Flying Warnocks," having finished a successful season with Andy Williams, will bring their family talents to the Branson Mall Music Theater for 2009. The Warnocks are Jamie and Sandi Warnock, along with their five daughters, Katherine, Ashlee, Anna, Rhonda, and Emilee, and they will sing their hearts out for you. Just about every genre of music from the fifties, sixties, and beyond is represented. The Warnocks are high energy, very easy on the eyes, and an extremely talented family who will win your heart after the first couple of songs. They are irresistible.

The Branson Mall is also opening a new "mini" theater called the Branson Hall of Fame Theater. It will house the *Wings of Magic,* starring David Silverman.

It will also be a showcase for the talents of Keith Allynn and his wife, Diana Lynn, as they present the *Diamond Experience.* Theirs is a tribute to Neil Diamond. Keith not only resembles Neil Diamond, but he has Neil's voice down cold. Keith and Diana Lynn do the famous Neil Diamond and Barbara Streisand duets. They are unbelievable.

Please call the theaters' respective phone numbers for information, schedules, and tickets.

BRANSON VARIETY THEATER
2701 West Country 76 Blvd.
(417) 334-2500, (888) GO-BRANSON
www.bransonvarietytheatre.com

Branson "old-timers" will remember the Branson Variety Theater as Bobby Vinton's Blue Velvet Theater, until he "retired." It's the same 1,600-seat theater, located right across from the Grand Palace. It has the same two-story lobby in blue with the Italian floor tile and cherubic ceiling and wall murals. The carpeting inside still bears the initials BV, but rather than standing for Bobby Vinton or Blue Velvet, they stand for its new name: Branson Variety. It has the same problems it did before, being built on the side of a very steep hill. The parking lot in back can be difficult to maneuver, especially if you're in a wheelchair or have trouble walking up an incline. There's a nice flat spot right in front of the front door where you can be dropped off, though.

The Branson Variety Theater lives up to its name with its shows. *Broadway: The Star Spangled Spectacular* is a show that is snippets of famous Broadway musical and literally "breathes" *New York, New York!* A massive skyline; the melting pot of the world; streets awash with a sea of yellow cabs; Times Square, lit up with a million neon and other lights; and, of course, Broadway. The Great White Way is a 12-block stretch of chophouses, restaurants, markets, and, of course, theaters. The Great White Way has been going constantly since 1810 and has produced more culture for our enjoyment than any other single source in the world.

Spirit of the Dance is another show at this theater. Winner of nine Global Awards, including Best Choreography and Best International Production, this spellbinding show has smashed box office records in 15 different countries. It is a breathtaking production that masterfully weaves together dramatic Irish dance with the exhilarating forces of classical ballet, flamenco, red-hot salsa, and jazz. The electrifying troupe of dancers performs with military precision. You won't see one shoe step out of line as the thunderous feet perform as one in this foot-stomping show.

Also in 2009, Twelve Irish Tenors will be performing. This hugely talented group of Ireland's finest singers are taking the concert world by storm as they perform their award-winning show in concert halls everywhere. Sold out tours in Europe and America have made this show one of the "hottest" production in years. Fans go wild over the Twelve Irish Tenors, and theaters everywhere just love them! From opera to pop, from jazz to classical, this show is a spine-tingling fabulous smash hit! Songs include "Danny Boy," "That's Life," "You Raise Me Up," "Hey Jude," "Twist and Shout," "Yesterday," "Cockles and Mussels," "Nessun Dorma," "Music of the Night," and lots more.

CARAVELLE THEATRE
3446 West Country 76 Blvd.
(417) 334-5100
www.carvellc.com
#1 HITS OF THE 60'S is bringing an all new show to the Caravelle stage for 2009! All of Branson has come to know this fun-filled, fast-paced, high-energy production show and its award-winning cast and live band. You can join the cast and crew for a nonstop party as they continue to celebrate the good vibrations of the '60s with music and dance, comedy, timely trivia, and unique video segments, including their very special tribute to Vietnam Veterans.

4 Ever Motown will take you back to the days of Motown and many of their celebrated recording artists. If you like the Motown sound, this show's for you. Call the box office or visit their Web site for information, showtimes, or tickets.

CIRCLE B CHUCKWAGON THEATRE
200 Jess Jo Pkwy
(417) 336-3540
www.circlebshow.com
www.redheadexpress.com
Old cowboy movies and free freshly popped corn at 4:15 p.m. begin your Circle B Cowboy Supper and Show with the Horn family. Then a wild west shootout leads to a fabulous meal served by their hombres. The Horns are proud to prepare the meal from scratch, serve everyone at their tables at 5, and bring out seconds before begining the show. They serve the food right to your table on old-fashioned tin plates. Then the Riders bring around buckets of seconds to refill your plate until you say "Whoa!" The meal is slow-roasted beef, barbecue beef sausage, cowboy baked beans, foil-wrapped spuds, chunky applesauce, fresh-baked biscuits, and hot peach cobbler for dessert! Your admission price also includes complimentary iced tea, cool water, and hot coffee. For a small fee, you may also enjoy an old-time sarsaparilla or other soft drinks from our Sarsaparilla Saloon. The Riders of the Circle B then take the stage for sweet cowboy harmonies, rollicking humor, and put a smile on everyone's face. The Riders have been joined by two-time Louisiana State Fiddle Champion Louis Darby. At 7, you're free to depart the centrally located venue, making it easy to get to your other evening program or to your hotel. Great food, grand music, gosh darn good comedy! Will ya have a good time? You're darn tootin'!

Also at the Circle B Theatre this year is a family straight from Alaska. The Redhead Express is a husband, plus wife, plus their seven kids who take you on a musical ride with harmonies, instrumental skills, and good old-fashioned, close-knit family values. Their type of music is called, "Alaska Grass" and is a show you will not soon forget.

The Circle B Theatre is just about halfway down the hill on the street, on your left, by the Branson Variety Theater.

CLAY COOPER THEATER
2215 West Country 76 Blvd.
(417) 332-2529
www.claycooper.biz
www.paulharriscomedy.com
www.johntweedshow.com
www.jimowenmusic.com
www.bobnelson.com
This is an old theater with a new name. For several years it was the home of Moe Bandy. Then it

was the home of Paul Harris, the comedian who used to be with Pierce Arrow. This represented a different twist to the evolving Branson entertainment scene, as it was the home to a stand-up comic. In the past, comics had been relegated to segments in music shows. Clay Cooper, takes center stage, along with several other shows.

Clay Cooper and his Country Music Express now headline at the Clay Cooper Theater, and Clay dresses in black from his boots to his western hat and wears a 10-gallon smile. He never played second fiddle to anyone, he is it.

Clay was a featured male vocalist at *Country Tonite!* for nine years and lent his smooth voice to the Texas Goldminers. He has also performed with the Ozark Country Jubilee. His high-energy show features a six-piece band, a female vocalist, and dancers, along with trick roper Johnny Lonestar and 16-year-old singing sensation Jenna Crispin.

The lineup of shows at Clay Cooper's Theater would not be complete without Clay's forever sidekick, Paul Harris.

Paul, in one way, is a very simple guy. He farms, sings songs, tells jokes, plays a guitar, and generally enjoys what he does in life. You can picture him, can't you? You can see this guy, with a bunch of friends, sitting around a blazing campfire, strumming a guitar, singing ballads of times past and telling stories of life and times experienced. For Paul, life is good. He is likely, while brush-hogging his land, to stop the tractor, get off, jump in his pickup and head for town. Not to get a cup of coffee or grab a beer with the locals at the saloon, but rather he goes to town to entertain a lot of folks, who appreciate his down-home brand of humor.

Paul has a smile that starts bluegrass growing. A smile that dogs like, women would die for, and men envy. It is also a sincere smile that is set below a couple of moon pie eyes on a solid, square, granite-like face. Paul likes to look at the fun side of life, or as they would say around Mountain Home, Ark., where his roots run deep, "the green side of grass." He actually looks at every side of life, and his way of looking at life is hilarious. He is basically a good ole boy who tells of life back

home in the Ozarks of northern Arkansas. You might say that Paul is the modern day Will Rogers, who just happens to be from Arkansas. Paul Harris is not average in any way you look at it. He thinks outside the box and says pretty much what he thinks. That is good for all of us, because we enjoy listening to him. You will, too.

Another show in the lineup at Clay Cooper's Theater is the *John Tweed Show*. John is a fabulous singer with a vocal range that few in the world can match. John does everything from rock, to down and dusty country to Broadway. You will come away from his show amazed and asking yourself, how can one man sing like he does. Well, you are just gonna have to see and hear it for yourself.

Jim Owen does another show. Jim has garnered a Grammy for his portrayal of Hank Williams. Jim wears many hats in his life. He is a recording star, singer, musician, comedian, and comes from the admittedly, funniest family who ever was. Jim's show starts off with laughter and ends with even more hilarity. Jim is also blessed with songwriting talent, having written many songs featured by other artists. One song he wrote for Conway Twitty, "Louisiana Woman, Mississippi Man," was recorded by Conway and Loretta Lynn and became a country hit.

Jim is a person of many, many talents, and this is one show you want to be sure to see while in Branson.

Bob Nelson has been all over the place in television and movies before landing in Branson at the Clay Cooper Theater. Johnny Carson once said of Bob, "You won't laugh any harder in five or six minutes than you will with that guy." Rodney Dangerfield started Bob's career by including him in a couple of his HBO specials. From that time forward, Bob has taken the proverbial bull by the horns and wrestled the critter to the ground. His

> **i** Check out www.BransonWorld.com before coming to Branson. It gives you the latest scoop, headlines, rumors and facts, and show synopses and schedules. There's even a message board for Branson fans.

career is one to be literally laughed at. He doesn't mind it at all. Bob can also be caught on the family show, *Bananas,* that airs throughout the United States and Canada.

Call the theater or visit their individual Web sites for information, showtimes, ticket prices, or reservations.

DICK CLARK'S AMERICAN BANDSTAND THEATER
1600 West 76 Country Music Blvd.
(417) 332-1960
www.dickclarksbranson.com
www.legendsbranson.com
The newest of the new is this venue, an 85,000-square-foot theater complex with a 900-seat theater, a 12,000-square-foot Dick Clark American Bandstand Grill, and the 30,000-square-foot exhibition hall of flawlessly restored automobiles and memorabilia from the year 1957 from the Patch Collection.

For several years, *Legends in Concert* has been at different Branson venues. The latest in "theater hopping" has landed the show in Dick Clark's American Bandstand Theater, just across the street from Dixie Stampede. Night after night *Legends* is providing the best of the great pretenders.

"Dolly Parton," "Marilyn Monroe," "Roy Orbison," "Michael Jackson," "Garth Brooks," "Reba McEntire," "Shania Twain," "Elvis Presley," "Little Richard," "Frank Sinatra," "Bette Midler," and "Judy Garland" are among the superstars of the past and present who might make an appearance at any given performance. Remember, they're not the real things, but as you watch the show you may find yourself forgetting that little point. "Elvis," of course, almost always gyrates on stage to close out the show. What makes this presentation so eerily realistic is the fact that not only do the impersonators look like the stars, they also can sing like them or play their instruments. Many are called but few are chosen, and those few are usually quite talented in their own right, apart from the coincidence of being a look-alike.

The "star" lineup changes four times a year to coincide with audience preferences. The summertime show is geared more for younger crowds with "Madonna" and "Shania," and in the spring and fall older audiences are treated to the likes of "Marilyn Monroe" and "Frank Sinatra." Showtimes are March through December. Check the Web site for dates and prices.

The morning show at the Dick Clark Theater is the Brett Family Singers. The Brett family members are all talented in song and dance and even poetry. Brianna dances and sings like a dainty pixie. Sports? Brydon and Garon, when not in college, put on an exhibition with a basketball that would make you wish they were on your team. The family sings together and in solo, and the backup musicians are just as talented. They present a squeaky-clean family image that makes the Cleaver family look like dysfunctional degenerates!

If you see a show, don't miss the non-singers. Open for the first time to the public, the Patch Collection is the world's finest collection of flawless 1957 automobiles and memorabilia. Visitors will step back in time as they tour this collection of 55 automobiles, all from 1957, complete with an entire re-created "Small Town America"—authentic settings where these cars would have been seen in their glory days. The automobiles represent every major American manufacturer from 1957, including Buick, Chevrolet, Ford, Cadillac, DeSoto, Hudson, Nash, Studebaker, and Packard. You can see it more than once, as models and brands will rotate in and out of this big and beautiful collection.

DIXIE STAMPEDE
1527 West Country Blvd.
(417) 336-3000, (800) 520-5101
www.dixiestampede.com
Whether you go there for the food or the show (you can't get one without the other), you'll leave plenty happy with both. The Dixie Stampede is a 35,000-square-foot arena with seating for 1,000. Audience members dine at tiered tables that surround the 12,000-square-foot dirt floor on three sides. The show and the meal kick off at the same time. Thirty-six costumed servers bring out huge tubs of chicken, ribs, potatoes, corn, soup, and

dessert. The catch is that they don't bring out any flatware. That's right, no knives or forks. They do offer a moist towel for cleaning up after the meal. (See the Restaurants chapter for more information about the meal.)

The cast of more than thirty performers presents a show reminiscent of the days when folks hosted parties on the grounds of grand southern plantations. Singers dressed in 1850s-style costumes enter via horse-drawn carriages. There's plenty of flirting and singing between the belles and their beaus. Trick riders race their horses around the arena, all the while flipping, turning, and standing in the saddles. The cavalry charge features six riders with swords who attempt to spear hanging 3-inch rings. There's even an ostrich-riding competition and a "buffalo stampede." Audience members can get in on the fun when they are invited to toss horseshoes, chase chickens, and ride the horses. The patriotic musical finale last season featured a 35-foot Statue of Liberty, a 30-by-50-foot American flag, and 30 white doves.

There's a music and comedy pre-show in the Carriage Room adjacent to the arena that starts one hour before showtime. You can purchase a soft drink while you wait for the arena doors to open. The 32 horses at the Dixie Stampede are held in stalls along the west side of the building from 10 a.m. right up until showtime. You are welcome to stop by and visit them anytime, and you don't need a ticket.

Come for Christmas and see a dramatic live Nativity with three kings atop live camels, holiday music, and a visit from Santa. Elves from the North and South Poles serve up your holiday feast.

THE DUTTON FAMILY THEATER
3454 76 Country Blvd.
(417) 332-2772, (888) 388-8661
www.theduttons.com

Boxcar Willie entertained audiences from his theater at 3454 76 Country Blvd. for more than 10 years before losing his battle with leukemia in April 1999. The Dutton Family, who first performed in Branson at the Barbara Fairchild Theatre, took over the Boxcar Willie Theatre in 1998 when Boxcar became too ill to perform. Now they call it their permanent home.

Boxcar Willie would be proud to know that country music is still being performed in his theater, and Dean and Sheila Dutton, parents of Benjamin, Abigail, Timothy, Judith, Amy, and Jonathan, go the extra mile to present the same kind of heart-warming, hand-clappin', feel-good show that Boxcar was known for.

The Duttons are a mighty talented bunch of musicians, singers, and dancers. The kids (who are hardly kids anymore) play a variety of instruments, such as the violin, guitar, bass, viola, cello, banjo, mandolin, keyboard, harmonica, and drums. Sheila and Dean are right there on stage with them, plucking out traditional country, gospel, pop, and patriotic songs. Pretty soon the grandkids will be joining them. Before settling in Branson, the family traveled throughout the world, performing hundreds of dates each year. In the off-season, they still manage to squeeze in a few concert dates as well. They've performed on PBS, were in *America's Got Talent* competition, and don't show any signs of slowing down. Their shows are at 2 and 8 p.m. Monday through Saturday from April until December. The exact days and times vary throughout the year.

Go online for a schedule or to check ticket prices. They also offer special combo vacation packages for the show and lodging at the nearby Dutton Motel.

ℹ Many of the area's music shows have coupons in local guidebooks. A few good ones to check out are *Best Read Guide, Travel Host,* and *Sunny Day Guide Book,* all usually available in stands or at your hotel front desk.

'50S AT THE HOP SHOW & THEATRE
The Shoppes at Branson Meadows
4230 N. Gretna Rd.
417-335-5300
www.50satthehop.com
www.taylorreed.com
www.bartrockett.com

Two hours of sock-hop. That is essentially what *'50s at the Hop* is all about. Young, eager, bright, freshly scrubbed faces adorn the stage with non-stop music throughout the show. The music is doo-wop, gospel, Motown, Elvis, and, of course, good, old-fashioned rock 'n' roll.

'50s at the Hop is a must-see, feel-good show. In this time of wars, terrorism, stock market plunges, and financial bailouts, let a couple of hours of *'50s at the Hop* bail you out of the world lurking outside the theater doors. You'll leave with a little more spring in your step and a couple of oldies kicking around in your head.

It is not often that two performers, who are used to having their own show, team up to produce a blockbuster. That is exactly what happened when Bart Rockett and Taylor Reed got together. Each of these guys has entertained millions around the globe and are waiting to show you their stuff. Each has his own brand of magic and combined, they are dynamite. The show is touted to have the "World's Largest Touring Illusion." As it says on their rack card, you will definitely get more magic for your money.

GOD AND COUNTRY THEATER
1800 West 76 Country Blvd.
(417) 334-6806
www.gacbranson.com
The God and Country Theater is a movie theater that has been renovated so live shows could be performed there. It is next door to Applebee's and across the street from Music City Centre. Several shows now play in the theater.

The Branson Brothers, an award-winning quartet; *Goldwing Express;* Wade Landry, the wild Cajun fiddler; *A Tribute to Jim Reeves* by his nephew, John Rex Reeves; *Eagles Tribute; Timeless Treasures* with Ralph Kuster; and *Cowboy Church* with one of the Grand Ladies of Country, Norma Jean, along with her husband, Al Martin.

ℹ The Live Music Capital of the World, Branson boasts more than 40 theaters and features more than 100 shows. With 56,797 seats, Branson has more theater seats than New York's Broadway.

GRAND COUNTRY MUSIC HALL AND RESORT
1945 West 76 Country Blvd.
(417) 335-2484
www.grandcountry.com
www.bucktrent.com
Wouldn't it be neat if there were a place where you could see a show any season of the year, any day of the week, and any time of the day? And if you could do a little shopping and enjoy a meal while you were there—and see the world's largest banjo?

There is such a place, and it's called the Grand Country Music Hall and Resort. Previous visitors might know it as the 76 Mall Complex, but that was before a series of renovations. And, yes, it's still got the indoor miniature golf, video arcade games, and plenty of motel rooms. (See the Kidstuff and Accommodations chapters.)

The morning starts with Buck Trent and his cast of musicians and singers. You probably remember Buck from his days on the *Porter Waggoner Show* or for his picking and grinning on *Hee Haw*. You remember, he's the fuzzy-headed guy who could play the daylights out of a banjo. Buck brought his talents to the Grand Country Music Hall.

Buck's multitalented cast delivers nonstop action with bluegrass, gospel, country, and plenty of laughs. From the fiddlin' duo of Bruce Hoffman and Melody Hart to the Yakety Sax of Jonathan Black to the sensational country sounds of featured vocalists Kenny Parrott and Melody Hart, it's hand-clappin', toe-tappin' fun! As the beat goes on with Rob Blackwood and Dave Clark, the powerful pickin' just gets better with mandolins, steel guitars, and Buck's legendary banjo tunes, guitar strummin', and knee-slapin' comedy! Buck's show starts at 9:30 with a great breakfast buffet at 8. Come on, get out of bed, it's worth it.

Grand Country Music Hall's evening show is a group that many consider Branson's best quartet, New South. New South has recently released a country album, *It's a Good Thing*, and a gospel album, *Somebody Must Be Praying for Me*. This hot and harmonious group, comprised of tenor Scott Leven, bass Mark McCauley, lead singer Trey Wilson, and baritone Jason Pritchett, sing timeless quartet classics and today's country hits. Bring your flags and get ready to sing "Dixie"; you'll have memories of the Old South and Lee, Jackson, and Beauregard with this New South that has risen.

What is a Comedy Jamboree? Well sir and madam, let's go to *Websters* and see what the people in-the-know say about it. *Comedy* is defined as being something that causes laughter. *Jamboree* is a large festive gathering or celebration. Both of these descriptions pretty well fit Comedy Jamboree.

Comedy Jamboree is a mixture of great music, singing, dancing, comedy, and cornball with *Hee Haw*. Yup, you heard right, *Hee Haw*. Straight from the heart of Cornfield County comes the sounds of a Minnie Pearl as she shouts, "Hoooowdy! I am just so proud to be here," and "BR-549," as Junior Samples tries to get someone—anyone— to buy a used car from him. Others in the cast are Nurse Goodbody, Jim and John Hagar (the Hagar Twins), Stringbean, and Don Herron, who relates the latest news from the studios of CORN Radio. Corn is good—and not just in Iowa.

Branson has gone to the dogs (and cats) with Gregory Popovich's Comedy Pet Theatre. Popovich was there in 2005 for the morning show with 15 house cats and 8 amazing dogs that do about everything except play country music. Adults like the show. Kids love it—and they get to meet the stars when the curtain goes down.

Grand Country Square prides itself as being a total family vacation experience, with lots of stuff for the kids. With four live shows daily, 36-hole indoor minigolf, pizza, custard, homemade fudge, Grand Country Buffet, the world's largest banjo and violin, 35,000 square feet of shopping, and Splash Country Indoor Waterpark, you could spend the entire vacation there.

The shows sometimes switch times during the season, so it's always best to check a theater schedule or call the box office.

i You can read "quick summaries" and reviews of Branson's 100 plus shows (and add your own comments) at www.bransoncritic.org.

HAMNER BARBER THEATER
3044 Shepherd of the Hills Expressway
(417) 334-4363, (888) 335-2080
www.bransonvariety.com

This theater is small and sits off the Shepherd of the Hills Expressway behind the Victorian Village. Under several different names, it has been the home of several groups in the past, including the Braschlers and the Sons of the Pioneers. Perhaps it has found the right match for its intimate qualities with two shows.

The Hamner Barber Variety Show is one for the birds. Dave and Denise Hamner have headlined many major production shows around the world but are best known for their one-of-a-kind act in which they produce ten enormous exotic birds. Their beautiful macaws and cockatoos appear amid flying cards, flaming swords, and falling coins and jewels, and then perform an incredible flight over and around the audience before gracefully returning to the stage. Other original illusions to be featured in the new variety show include the Stargate, the Lightning Levitation, and Vertigo: The Fall of Death.

The Hamners have performed these effects on many national television shows, including NBC's *World's Greatest Magic*. Dave Hamner is also an ordained minister with extensive educational training. He and his wife, Denise, have held special theater worship services in Branson whenever they appear here locally, and they are first in line to volunteer talent for benefit shows.

The other portion of the show has a dummy for its act. Recognized as one of the world's great ventriloquists, Jim Barber has been honored as the International Ventriloquist of the Year and Comedy Entertainer of the Year by the National Association of Campus Activities. Jim was first introduced to Branson as the featured comedian in Glen Campbell's *Goodtime Show*, and he has since been featured in other successful Branson productions with the Osmonds, Tony Orlando, Kirby Van Burch, and the late Eddie Rabbitt. He served as a national cohost for the Jerry Lewis "Stars Across America" Labor Day Telethon and has appeared on many national television shows on the Nashville Network, A&E, Fox, ABC, and NBC.

It's best to be up front and center, as close as possible, to get the full effect of this fellow, who reverses the usual roles, with Jim playing the dummy and his "dummy" playing the ventriloquist. And when he gets a third dummy involved, the lip and voice work really become complicated!

Jim also combines his creativity with computers as co-owner of Image Works, Inc., a video production, graphic design, and publishing company and has personally developed projects for Silver Dollar City, Big Cedar Lodge, Glen Campbell, Jimmy Osmond, Yakov Smirnoff, Pierce Arrow, Paul Harris, and many other businesses in the Branson area and around the country.

HOT HITS THEATER (OWEN THEATER)
203 South Commercial St.,
Downtown Branson
(417)337-RICO, (417) 336-2112,
(800) ELVIS-95
www.bransonhothits.com
www.elvisinbranson.com
www.lalliebridges.com
This venue was the first theater in town, a movie theater operated by float trip operator Jim Owen. (You can see the Bass Pro tribute to him and his float service on Branson Landing.) No movies are shown, but there's a lot of live shows now!

Here's the low down on *Motown!* Rico J and his hearty cast and crew will delight you with a romp through the historical Motown label. You will hear hits from the Motown era that are endless and will bring back many memories. Be sure to check it out.

If the King were alive, he'd probably have his own theater in Branson by now, but fortunately for us we have Dave "Elvis" Ehlert to stand in for him. Ehlert's show, called *Elvis and the Superstars* is now in its 15th smash season. Dave "Elvis" Ehlert has been featured on *Oprah, CNN Showbiz, CBS Nightwatch,* and on Legend's stage in Las Vegas. Fox Television calls this "Great Entertainment!" Alan Solomon of the *Chicago Tribune* says Dave "is one of the very cool things about Branson." Audiences are treated to a full hour of "Elvis," fol-

lowed by impersonations of 12 other "Superstars" . . . Dean Martin, Sonny & Cher, Roy Orbison, Tom Jones, Johnny Cash, Willie Nelson, The Blues Brothers, Neal Diamond, and many more.

Hank & Patsy, Together Again: A live musical tribute to Country Music's First Superstar, Hank Williams Sr. and America's Sweetheart, Patsy Cline, starring Randy Steffen (aka Dave Ehlert) whose uncanny talent captures the very essence of Hank as he takes you from the live radio shows to appearances on the Grand Ole Opry and Branson's very own "Patsy" performs Patsy's hits with the same feeling and emotion that propelled the star into the Country Music Hall of Fame. Enjoy all your favorite Hank & Patsy songs: You'll have "Sweet Dreams" about "Honky Tonkin." You'll go "Crazy" for "Your Cheatin' Heart."

Lallie Bridges joins Dave and wants to thank all of her fans who come to see her perform in Branson. Right now Lallie is working on her originals CD and plans to release it this fall. After the release of the CD you'll be able to see her perform somewhere near you on her thirty-city tour. Between studio times and until December, you can find Lallie at the historic Owen's Theater in downtown Branson performing in the following shows: *Hank & Patsy Together Again, Elvis and The Superstars, Loretta Lynn Tribute,* and *Elvis in the Morning.*

THE HUGHES BROTHERS THEATRE
The Hughes Brothers and Six
3425 West 76 Country Blvd.
(417) 336-3688, (888) 518-9925,
(877) 749-2767
www.hughes-brothers.com
www.sixrealbrothers.com
Up until the Hughes Brothers purchased the theater from its original owner, Jim Thomas, in early 2000, it was the one theater in town that had managed to stay out of the name game for the most part. That is—its name had changed just twice since 1983. First it was the Roy Clark Celebrity Theatre, and then just the Celebrity Theatre. In the early years the theater hosted some of the biggest names in entertainment, such as Tanya Tucker, Glen Campbell, T. G. Sheppard, Ray

Price, the Smothers Brothers, Lucy Arnaz, and Roy Clark, of course. A few of the stars who now have their own theaters first played in Branson at the Roy Clark Celebrity Theatre. Jim Stafford, Bobby Vinton, and the late Boxcar Willie all met with such success during their limited runs here that they decided to put down roots in the little town none of them had heard of before.

The Hughes Brothers show is packed with hot country songs, gospel favorites, Broadway show tunes, and even some patriotic music to boot. The group, which started as an act out at Silver Dollar City in 1994, has garnered an impressive following, winning Best Morning Show and Best Vocal Group in the Branson Entertainment Awards. Their vocal harmonies and smooth dance moves, not to mention their instrumental talents, are quite impressive, and the theater and its lobby, Grandma's Parlor, exude "family values." And the show is a family affair. The five brothers even work four wives and 12 children into the show. The Hughes Brothers perform from March through December, Monday through Saturday.

Another show on the theater line-up is Six. Six real brothers who do the seemingly impossible by not only singing songs popular with different decades, but they also provide the instrumentation with their mouths. Your eyes won't believe your ears. Six-itement, fun, and frenzy are the three words that come to mind. They sing a capella while at the same time furnishing the percussion section with their vocal cords, lips, and tongues. The bottom line is this: if you have never seen or heard an orchestra of human voices, please go to the Hughes American Family Theater and take in the Knudsen brothers, who are also known simply as Six.

JIM STAFFORD THEATRE
3444 76 Country Blvd.
(417) 335-8080
www.jimstafford.com
www.douggabriel.com
www.moebandy.com

When vaudeville went out of fashion decades ago, it seemed that the days of an entertainer who could do it all were past. And so it remained until Jim Stafford hit town.

Reasonable people could disagree on whether Jim is a singer-songwriter who does comedy or a new American humorist who is also a musician. Reciting a list of his credits would do nothing to settle the argument, because he's done so much in both fields. Even so, it's worth noting that he's had hit records such as "Spiders and Snakes" and "Cow Patti," starred in his own TV show (*The Jim Stafford Show* in 1975), and served as head writer for the *Smothers Brothers Comedy Hour*.

Nothing can prepare you for seeing the Jim Stafford show at his theater in Branson. Most people are surprised to see whirling blimps and flying saucers and 3-D movies in a town full of music shows. They do, however, get a good dose of music, and Jim delivers that on guitar, fiddle, and harmonica, just to name a few instruments.

The show has something new every year, and that's what keeps folks coming back. Our favorite part is the black-light segment, but in 1998 it was the real-live tornado effect that really blew us away. Now Jim's added a 3-D movie he created, shot, and edited all at his theater. It's shown on a stereoscopic 3-D rear projection screen. Sounds high-tech, huh?

Jim talks a lot about family during the show, and his own is incorporated in a major way. His wife, Ann, who is the theater manager, joins him on stage, and his son Sheaffer demonstrates budding prowess on the drums, fiddle, guitar, and bagpipe! Even little G. G. gets into the act. It's all calculated to tug at the audience's heartstrings, and it works. It's shameless, really, but Jim knows it's shameless, and we know he knows—and that's part of the fun of it. Corn is okay if it's well tempered with cleverness. By the time you add up the jokes, stories, songs, and a 3-D show, you've got what we consider the rebirth of the vaudeville-type variety show, with a definite technological twist.

Check out Pie-Annie's upstairs at the theater. It's a sandwich and dessert shop with an old-fashioned soda shop feel. It's also a gift shop, which is very convenient since that's where Jim signs autographs after the show.

The morning show at the Jim Stafford Theatre is the *Doug Gabriel Show*. Doug shares not only his talent, but also his tremendously talented family. Whatever your taste in music, you will hear it all, and long before you leave the theater, you will know why Doug's show was voted Best Morning Show three years in a row. And why Doug is the five-time winner of Male Vocalist of the Year, and why he was awarded Entertainer of the Year and Instrumentalist of the Year in 2000. Not only will you be awed by his voice, but you will also be amazed at his ability on guitar and piano. You'll also see Doug play his world-famous "muftar," a guitar made out of a 1969 Thunderbird muffler! Branson's Ripley's Believe It or Not! Museum has even added a replica of the muftar to its collection (see the Attractions chapter). Doug's wife, Cheryl, joins him on stage for touching vocal duos, as do their children, Joshua, Jordan, and Jasmine. Doug is backed by what is possibly one of the best bands in Branson. His horn section adds a special flair to many of the musical numbers. When Roy Clark is in town, he frequently shares the stage with Doug, so sometimes you get a "bonus."

Moe was raised in San Antonio, Texas, and labored as a sheet metal worker while playing the local nightclubs. After a stint in the rodeo, he began to hit it big with such chart-toppers as "Bandy the Rodeo Clown" and "Americana." Like many of his Branson colleagues, he's won numerous awards from such prestigious outfits as the Academy of Country Music and the Country Music Association.

After more than a decade in Branson, Moe's blend of country and patriotic music is as well received as ever. His show includes all his country hits as well as the comedy of his sidekick, "Hargus Marcel." Moe likes to sign autographs after the show, and that might be a good time to ask him about his fishing exploits. He enjoys relating the story of how he once took Mel Tillis and Shoji Tabuchi out fishing but had to bring them back after only 15 minutes because, "I couldn't understand either one of them."

Sharing the spotlight with Moe is his beautiful and talented wife, Teresa. Her powerful voice and their chemistry in song and life is evident on stage. Teresa is from Laredo, a small town in Missouri. She grew up in the theater business and started performing in her parents' music show when she was six. In 1996, Teresa came to Branson and performed at the 76 Music Hall (now called The Grand Country Music Hall). Moe says that he heard her sing and just fell in love with her. In fact, they were married in 1998, and so she not only became a part of Moe's life, she joined Moe on stage!

KIRBY VANBURCH MAGICAL THEATRE
2353 MO 248
(417) 337-7140
www.kirbyvanburch.com
You won't believe your eyes! A thrill-a-second production packed full of astonishing disappearing acts, huge illusions, and exotic animals. Expect royal white tigers, leopards, lions, a unicorn, a helicopter appearing in three seconds flat, assistants cut in half, mind-reading, and more!

LITTLE OPRY THEATRE
IMAX Entertainment Complex
3562 Shepherd of the Hills Expressway
(417) 335-4832, (800) 419-4832
www.bransonimax.com
Branson's smallest and most intimate live theater (it only seats 210) is nestled inside the IMAX Entertainment Complex. It is so intimate that the first row of people is invited to rest their feet on the stage during the shows. How's that for up close and personal to the entertainers?

James Garrett has one of the finest tribute shows we have had the pleasure of seeing in Branson. He pays tribute to John Henry Deutschendorf—who you say? John Denver, that's who. The same man who wrote 146 songs with one of them, "Rocky Mountain High," being chosen as the Colorado State Song.

James spent a lot of time in past years with John Denver and is the ultimate knowledge base for anything to do with him. He also is very careful not to detract from Denver's songs and does them as the master himself would have done. I have to say, he does a marvelous job. We're sure John Denver is looking down on the Little Opry Theater with that wide grin of his, nodding his head and saying, "Well done, my friend!"

James also does a separate show called *Strait Country*, a tribute to George Strait, featuring the music of George Strait. Strait is a living legend with 57 #1 country hits, along with the timeless hit songs of Patsy Cline. Sing along with classics like "Ocean Front Property," "Amarillo by Morning" and Patsy Cline's hits like "Crazy," "Sweet Dreams," and many more! You'll hear music from other great artists, with a little bluegrass, comedy, and gospel sprinkled along the way!

Leroy New, a local boy made good from Kirbyville, and his band perform in a show called *New's Country*. Leroy will take you back to earlier times with a lot of songs you will not normally hear in Branson shows. Leroy is also known as the guitar wizard, and when you hear him play, you will understand why.

Enjoy *Crossties Bluegrass and Gospel* with Jim Glaspy and his talented family. It's acoustic bluegrass music at its best! This family band, with their award-winning musicians, will charm you with three part harmonies and traditional and original bluegrass material! A refreshingly old-fashioned bluegrass show the whole family can enjoy!

The *Branson Divas* are three long-time friends and "Branson Stage Veterans." Combined, their resumes would stretch as long as the famous "76 Strip" itself. Singing solo, they are magnificent, whether it is Big Band, Broadway, blues or pop. But when they join together for their patriotic and gospel numbers, their harmonies will blow you away! Add in some yodeling and a hilarious country segment, guaranteed to keep you in stitches

Good New's Gospel Hour with Leroy New and Friends is a one hour service that features the various gospel stylings of Leroy New, Ken Christen, and Jim Glaspy. From time-to-time other Branson stars may even come and drop in to share a song and testimony in this must-experience gospel service. This entertaining and inspirational Sunday service is complimentary, and seating is on a first-come basis. Every Sunday morning at 9 a.m.

Crossties Country Cathedral is the perfect late morning Sunday service if you are in the mood for some good "old-time" bluegrass and gospel! Come as you are and join Jim Glaspy for this non-denominational Christian gathering every Sunday morning worship service. This lively and passionate Sunday service is complimentary and seating is on a first come basis—every Sunday morning at 11.

MANSION AMERICA THEATER
187 Expressway Lane
(417) 239-1333, (866) 707-4100
www.themansiontheatre.com
www.gatlinbrothers.musiccitynetworks.com
www.skeltontribute.com

Mansion America has plans for 2009. Those plans consist of several special events along with a couple of regular shows.

Starting in May, Cathy Rigby will be performing her Broadway role as Peter Pan on the Mansion stage. The original sets from Broadway are being used as well as several of the original crew of the play. This is something very different for Branson and may possibly light the path for others to follow. We certainly hope so.

Tom Mullica, who worked with Red Skelton for many years, will open each day with a *Tribute to Red Skelton*. When Tom first enters from stage right, you will swear it is Red Skelton. It is a fascinating show, and Tom is the perfect person to present Red to you. It is, as was the original show, a good, clean, family show. Red proved throughout many years of performing, one did not have to use foul language or off-color stories to get rollicking laughter from an audience.

In the fall, Larry Gatlin and the Gatlin Brothers will bring you *All the Gold in California,* a big hit for them and their signature song. They will also perform many of their other hits as well. Larry is like a loose cannon, and one never knows what he might pull during the show. Larry, Steve, and Rudy Gatlin will bring you the very best they have to offer in entertainment.

Special guests at the Mansion, from time to time, scheduled for 2009, are Engelbert Humperdinck, Kenny G, Johnny Mathis, and Asleep at the Wheel. Call or visit their respective Web sites for current showtimes, information, or tickets.

MICKEY GILLEY THEATRE

3455 West 76 Country Blvd.
(417) 334-3210, (800) 334-1936
www.gilleys.com
www.joeyriley.net

When people talk about Mickey Gilley's music show, one of the first things they mention is the comedy. And it's no wonder. Throughout the show, Mickey and his steel guitar player, Joey Riley, swap barbs and jokes and stories until you think you're gonna bust. Rubber-faced Joey playfully bashes straight man Mickey (who can sling back his own barbs), and their hilarious ad-libbing is a chemistry that works wonderfully.

Joey also proves himself to be quite an adept fiddle player on "Orange Blossom Special," and he finally ends the show with the song he continually refers to throughout, the incredibly funny "Ever Since You Left, Baby, I Don't Have to Put the Seat Down Anymore," topped with a hilarious ending.

Mickey may have been an *Urban Cowboy* in the 1980 movie that made him famous, but today he is as urbane as he is witty. He strolls on stage decked out in a tuxedo and some serious jewelry, including a necklace bearing a diamond pendant that spells out "MG." But then he mentions that his cousins are Jerry Lee Lewis and Jimmy Swaggart, and we realize the joke's on him after all.

Still, Mickey has come a long way from the rough-and-tumble days of growing up in Texas. His mama, he says, bought the piano that he and his famous cousins all learned to play on because she hoped Mickey would take a shine to gospel music and become a minister. We don't know why or when he went astray, but we're glad he did. For more than two decades, Mickey has been preaching about the heartaches and hard breaks of the honky-tonk life. No one knows more about honky-tonks than Mickey. His nightclub in Pasadena, Texas, Gilley's, was an institution long before the movie cameras dropped in to capture John Travolta ridin' the mechanical bull. And speaking of hard breaks, both the Gilley's

nightclub in Texas and Mickey's first theater in Branson were destroyed by fire, the latter in 1993. (Maybe that's what cousin Jerry Lee was forecasting when he sang about "Great Balls of Fire.") Undaunted, Mickey rebuilt in 1994, and his 996-seat theater is frequently sold out.

Joey Riley is the other show. We all know every cowboy worth his white hat had a sidekick: Roy Rogers and Gabby Hayes; the Lone Ranger and Tonto. For years it was Mickey Gilley and Joey Riley, who served as the comedy sidekick to Branson's Mickey Gilley Show. For two years now he's been standing on his own. It only takes an audience of one to prop him up. The crowd loves him, and he loves a crowd. But it all goes back to individuals. Joey has intimate contact with all members of his audience. If he sees you have a camera pointed his way, you will get what he calls "a Kodak moment," and he'll mug one of the million of his funny faces. He sings silly songs and impersonates those from the Grand Ole Opry, but he's a serious fiddle performer in his own right. Call the theater for schedules and prices.

ℹ If you're going to be in Branson over the weekend, pick up Friday's *Springfield News-Leader*. Their "Weekend" insert gives a listing of all Branson shows with contact information and suggestions and ideas of all sorts about other area activities and attractions.

MUSIC CITY CENTRE

1835 West 76 Country Blvd.
(417) 336-1600
www.musiccitycentre.com

This prime location on The Strip has been remodeled into a theater-motel complex consisting of Branson's La Quinta Inn and Suites, plus shops and a Starbucks.

A new era for Music City Centre begins in 2009, as they will be having various guest stars throughout the year. Please call the box office or visit their Web site for schedules, showtimes, and/or reservations.

NEW SHANGHAI THEATRE

645 MO 165

(417) 336-8888, (877) 212-4462

www.newshanghaicircus.com

This new Branson venue, home of the New Shanghai Circus, was helped to fruition by Bill Dailey (wife of author Janet Dailey) before his death in 2005. Bill Lennon, of Branson's Lennon Brothers, designed it. Bill Dailey said, "This theater is being built specifically for the New Shanghai Circus as their show requires extra rigging and large space for their backdrops. The back of the theater is 50 feet tall." The new theater, which seats about 900, is "classic Chinese architecture with a modern twist," and it certainly has added a broad new look to the Branson Strip, which is lined with some 49 theaters performing more than 100 live shows.

The theater features a giant sculpture of an early example of Chinese bronze ware, along with modern Chinese artwork, cascading water-falls, and Chinese gardens.

The New Shanghai Circus features aerial bal-let, modern Chinese performance art, tumblers, magicians, spinning plates, bicycle aerobics, pole climbing, and more. New Shanghai Circus per-formers begin training at the age of six and come from the same school as Chinese Olympic gym-nasts. In addition to their shows in Branson, the New Shanghai Circus presents shows year-round in Shanghai, China, and also tours internationally and across the United States.

More than 40 acrobats of China showcase dramatic interpretation of classic Chinese dance and physical performance art in this new Branson theater. These contortionists will keep you tied in knots with their amazing physical feats. Fabulous backdrops, state-of-the-art lighting, and a fast-paced, exciting production celebrate the exotic wonders of China: playful lion dances, awesome jar juggling, incredible hoop diving, daring tra-peze, and an amazing, gigantic dancing dragon. This is a huge production show that is a spec-tacular extravaganza of elegant Eastern dance, dazzling acrobatics, mysterious magic, and more.

The troupe has amazed the locals, and because the local supermarkets have had to cater to a new clientele, area folks have been introduced to some interesting new vegetables and foods!

Call the theater for showtimes, dates, and prices, or visit the New Shanghai Circus Web site.

OAK RIDGE BOYS THEATRE

464 MO 248

(417) 335-2000

www.orbtheatre.com

www.oakridgeboys.com

www.dalenaditto.com

www.gatlinbrothers.musiccitynetworks.com

For 2009 the Oak Ridge Boys Theatre morning starts off with the *Dalena Show*. Her show is a real trip through country, bluegrass, Texas swing, pop, with just a touch of Iowa culture. Dalena has several people on the show that add just the right amount of spice and garnish to an already highly flavored revue. Those other people, or maybe we should say people and critters on the show, are in the form of one person, Patty Davidson. Patty has a troupe of dummies at her beck and call. She's one of the most remarkable ventriloquists we have ever seen.

Country Tonight has been voted the best live country show in America: this high-energy produc-tion is guaranteed to keep you tapping your feet to the music and laughing at the comedy! *Country Tonight* is unparalleled in the entertainment com-munity. A cast of twenty talented performers will keep your full attention for two hours.

Then, of course, there is the namesake of the theatre, the Oak Ridge Boys. The Mighty Oaks play selected dates at the theater so you would be wise to check their Web site for information and schedules. The Oak Ridge Boys Theatre will have special guests throughout the year includ-ing T. G. Shepherd, Little Texas, Restless Heart, Debby Boone, and Collin Raye. Again, be sure to call or visit the theatre Web site for scheduling, showtimes, and information.

OSMOND FAMILY THEATER
3216 West 76 Country Blvd.
(417) 336-6100
(800) 477-6102
www.magnificentvariety.com
www.osmond.com

The Magnificent Variety Show, having moved to the Osmond Family Theater for the 2009 season, takes you on a delightful stroll through the musical part of each decade with color, animation, and lively music, ending with the new turn of the century and its first decade—now. All this is accomplished with nearly 300 costume changes. Amazing, truly amazing. In the fall the Osmonds will return to their home stage with a musical treat for everyone. The Osmond Family Theater is located at the junction of MO 76 and 165, next door to Walgreen's. Check individual Web sites or call the theater for reservations, information, scheduling, or tickets.

PIERCE ARROW THEATER
3069 Shepherd of the Hills Expressway
(417) 336-8742
www.piercearrowtheater.com

This venue is easy to find; it's right across from the landmark Shoji Tabuchi Theatre. The group, named after the classy car, is a class act. Pierce Arrow has gained a cult following in Branson and the nation, with its overtones of the Statler Brothers and the Oak Ridge Boys. The new Pierce Arrow show opened in Branson on May 22, 2000, and was sold out, despite the fact that the fresh paint had barely dried and the theater signage hung mostly incomplete. This high-energy show features a talented male quartet, including Dan Britton, the world's lowest bass singer, according to *The Guinness Book of World Records*. Jerod Daugherty provides comedy. The Pierce Arrow

i In 2009, Branson's state-of-the-art stages offered more than 100 live shows, including country, pop, gospel, blues, rock, western, classical, swing, Big Band, Cajun, Motown, Broadway, comedy, magic, and more.

Band provides backup vocals and solid musical accompaniment to keep this fast-moving show right on track. Call the theater or visit the Web site for a schedule, dates, and ticket prices.

PRESLEYS' COUNTRY JUBILEE
2920 West 76 Country Blvd.
(417) 334-4874
www.presleys.com

The Presley family is truly an icon for Branson. They built the first theater on The Strip in 1967 and have entertained millions of visitors every year since. Their show stars three generations of incredibly talented musicians, singers, and comedians.

It all started when the patriarch of the family, Lloyd Presley, made somewhat of a name for himself in the 1940s with his live performances on KWTO radio in Springfield. In the 1950s he and his family performed in the Underground Theater, a cave just north of Kimberling City. In 1967 Lloyd and his wife, Bessie May, their son, Gary, and his wife, Pat, paid $15,000 for ten acres on The Strip. The building they designed had a level concrete floor and no permanent seats. In the event that their music-show idea didn't float, they planned to turn the space into a boat storage facility. Slowly but surely folks did come to see their show. They sat in folding chairs and purchased their tickets out of Gary's home just behind the theater. The family continued to keep their day jobs while the audiences grew. Lloyd worked as a professional fishing guide on Table Rock Lake. Gary commuted to Springfield, where he worked at a typewriter factory.

Bessie May kept her job as a secretary, and Pat worked for Security Bank. By 1975 the theater had been expanded to hold 1,300 people, and the shows were selling out. After a total of six expansions, including the addition of a balcony and wings, the total capacity reached 2,000. The shows still sell out.

With 20-plus cast members, the Presleys' show is one of the hottest tickets in Branson. The 30-minute comedy pre-show alone is worth the price of admission. Gary, also known as the sequined, overall-clad "Herkimer," gets out and works the crowds. (He even makes his wife work! She's Branson's mayor!) The show that follows features a variety of hot new country music and old favorites along with southern gospel and swing, all performed on such instruments as the banjo, fiddle, guitar, bass guitar, drums, and harmonica. Greg Presley, Lloyd's grandson, gets our vote as one of the best harmonica players in town. The entire cast wears superb-looking costumes complete with fringe, sequins, and beads. What started out as a homemade show in a metal warehouse is now not only one of Branson's best but also as good of a show of its kind as you'll see anywhere.

The Presleys play March through December at 8 p.m. Monday through Saturday. Call or check the Web site for tickets, reservations, or information.

RFD-TV THE THEATRE
4080 West 76 Country Blvd.
(417) 332-2282
www.rfdtv.com/Theatre
The RFD-TV theater and TV studios will be entertaining you with special events and special guests to be announced throughout the year. Please check with their box office or visit their Web site for scheduling, information, reservations, or tickets.

ROY ROGERS AND DALE EVANS MUSEUM AND HAPPY TRAILS THEATER
3950 Green Mountain Dr.
(417) 339-1900
www.royrogers.com
The Happy Trails Theater opened in the summer of 2003 when the Roy Rogers and Dale Evans Museum relocated in Branson from Victorville, California (see the Attractions chapter). This intimate 308-seat theater creates a personal connection with Roy and Dale. Roy "Dusty" Rogers Jr. and the High Riders perform the music made famous by these icons of Western culture and traditional family values. You'll hear "Cool Water," "Tumbling Tumbleweeds," "Blue Prairie," "Sky Ball Paint," and many more classics.

Roy, Dale, and the rest of the original gang are gone now, lost to the ages and to us, but fortunately we have Dusty Rogers, Roy and Dale's son, right here in Branson, telling us what life was like in the Rogers' household and what it was like to grow up in one of the most famous homes of their time.

When you go to the Roy Rogers and Dale Evans Museum, you will want to visit the gift shop and attend one of two daily performances of the Happy Trails Theater.

The museum will teach you all about Roy, Dale, Trigger, Bullet, Buttermilk, Nellybelle, and the life and times of Roy, Dale, and their family as shown in displays, photos, and memorabilia. For an afternoon of nostalgia and a ride down life's trail with Roy, Dale, and other voices of the past, you need to go to the Roy Rogers and Dale Evans Museum and Happy Trails Theater. For showtimes, information or reservations, please call their box office or visit their Web site.

SHEPHERD OF THE HILLS OUTDOOR THEATER
5586 West Highway 76
(417) 334-4191
www.oldmatt.com
The Shepherd of the Hills Outdoor Theater is located adjacent to the Inspiration Point Tower, which can be seen for many miles in every direction. Take Highway 76 straight past the RFD-TV Theater for about 3 miles. The entrance will be on your right.

At Tthe Shepherd of the Hills Outdoor Theater, Harold Bell Wright's epic story of love, loss, power, hardship, and the true meaning of life is brought to life every night on their star-lit stage. It takes a crowd of actors and actresses, a gaggle, flock, herd, and bunch of livestock, an armory of guns and rifles, a log cabin that will be set on fire during the play, plus a classic 1908 DeWitt automobile to make the live action performance what it is—a legend.

So, come enjoy a legend in its own time. *The Shepherd of the Hills,* by Harold Bell Wright, is the fourth most published book in the world. It has been translated into seven languages and made into four movies, one starring John Wayne in his first Technicolor film. Come see the book brought to three-dimensional and living color life on the largest stage in Branson.

SHOJI TABUCHI THEATRE
3260 Shepherd of the Hills Expressway
(417) 334-7469
www.shoji.com

Guess who's the most talked-about entertainer in the live country music capital of the world? Nope, it's not some Nashville recording artist; it's a violinist from Japan.

If you don't know who Shoji is, don't feel bad. He's the biggest star nobody ever heard of. He's never written or recorded a hit song, and outside of Branson he's virtually unknown. But here he's the Godzilla of the Ozarks, attacking all our preconceived notions of what a music star looks and sounds like.

We might as well tell you about the theater bathrooms first, because that's probably one of the first things a visitor hears about anyway. The women's room features live cut orchids at every granite and onyx pedestal sink. There's stained and jewel-adorned glass and exquisite chandeliers. The men's restroom contains a hand-carved mahogany billiard table, black leather chairs, a marble fireplace, a walnut mirror built in 1868, and black lion-head sinks. Those who forget to take their camera into the bathroom needn't worry, because the restrooms are featured on picture postcards in the gift shop.

On the other hand, perhaps the lavish lounges aren't so unusual when you consider that the exterior of the building is decked out in purple neon. It's our guess that this particular shade did not exist on the planet before Tabuchi, or perhaps it's just that so much of it has never been assembled all in one place. Those who might complain that the decor of the theater exceeds the bounds of acceptable gaudiness should be reminded that this is not a museum; it's an entertainment hall.

What we like most about Shoji is that his success epitomizes the American dream. He immigrated to the United States after being inspired by a Roy Acuff concert in Osaka, then waited tables in San Francisco while waiting for his big break. Eventually he landed in Branson in 1981 and steadily worked his way up from theater to theater. In 1990 he built his showplace at a convenient location on Shepherd of the Hills Expressway, where he has enjoyed unfathomable success.

Shoji fiddles in every style of music you can think of. Besides the obligatory "Orange Blossom Special," Shoji does classical, Cajun, Broadway, and bluegrass. Each season brings something new to the production, due in large part to his wife, Dorothy, who is credited as producer and choreographer. She often sings and emcees as well.

In recent years Shoji's daughter Christina, also a singer, has been featured in an increasingly prominent role. Shoji sings some, too. His Japanese accent is still cute as ever, even when sung, but we think this would be a good time to point out again that Shoji is a first-rate fiddler. By the way, it's pronounced SHOW-gee Ta-BOO-chee.

You can see him March through December at 3 and 8 p.m., Monday through Saturday. During the fall and Christmas season he also performs on select Sundays and adds 10:30 a.m. shows as well. Check the Web site or call the theater for showtimes and ticket prices. It's the most expensive ticket in town, but on the other hand, the show itself is one of the longest. It clocks in at two hours, thirty minutes, give or take a little, so you'll get your money's worth.

I urge you to call ahead for showtimes, schedules, tickets, information, or reservations.

SIGHT & SOUND THEATRE
Noah the Musical
1001 Shepherd of the Hills Expressway
(800) 377-1277
www.sight-sound.com

The scale of this particular production is very large, literally big; it is hard to imagine the amount of effort it took to pull it off. The theater housing this production is more than three times the size of the average Wal-Mart. The average Wal-Mart is 102,000 square feet. The Sight and Sound Theatre is 339,000 square feet. Does that begin to sink it as to how large it is? The stage this production is presented on is over one quarter the size of that same average Wal-Mart or 26,550 square feet and the distance from the stage floor to the roof is 110 feet—imagine, an 11 story building can sit on the stage. It is quite possibly the largest stage in the world. The show is illuminated with two million watts of light. That is enough light to provide for 300 average homes. That is enough lighting to provide for a small town of around 1,200 people. It takes 16 lighting engineers to control the production. The interior of the Ark alone contains 500 lights. The sound part of Sight and Sound is provided by 70 surround sound speakers. It is superb and awe inspiring. Sometimes the sound seems to go right through one's body. During the second half of the show, you will be surrounded on three sides by the interior of the Ark in an amazing set. Call the box office or visit their Web site for information, schedules, tickets, or reservations.

STAR THEATRE
3750 West 76 Country Blvd.
(417) 334-7131
www.bransonstartheatre.com
This venue, located near the Olive Garden, has two stages, "large and small," and shows on both of them. It's back off The Strip a tad, so you could miss it—but don't. It has some great shows.

"Trailer for sale or rent—dum, dum—rooms to let, fifty cents." Remember those famous lyrics by Roger Miller? When was the last time you heard that song played on the radio? A long time ago, we bet. Keith Allen, as Redneckers, brings back to life the songs of our past and in doing so re-kindles emotions and images that were buried in the back recesses of our minds oh, so many years ago. Jeff Foxworthy claims a redneck is "a person with a glorious lack of sophistication"— and goes further to say we are all guilty of it at one time or another. In other words, just as there is a little bit of "Bubba" in all of us.

Keith Allen, in his show, is certainly not sophisticated, to the delight of Foxworthy. He tells his tales with the simplicity of a child and that makes it all the more understandable and enjoyable. His stories are real, taken from his own life experiences, and those stories take us back

to our salad days as we were learning about our neighborhood, the town down the road—not yet understanding there was a world on the other side of that town.

You might remember Keith from seeing him at Silver Dollar City. He's a local boy with a comic storytelling ability, a big red guitar (that he can play the dickens out of), and a big baritone voice. When you see Keith Allen's Redneckers show, you will never think of a redneck in the same way again. Trust us on that one.

David Lomascola was winner of Branson's Best Instrumentalist of the Year Award for 2008. However, Lomascola's *Million Dollar Piano Variety Show* 2009 spring season has been cancelled. David Lomascola, star of the show at the Branson Star Theatre was involved in an automobile accident and sustained injuries that will require months of therapy. The show will resume its regular fall 2009 schedule starting in September. We wish David a speedy recovery, suggest you check the Web site or call the theater for a progress report and schedule.

Another show at the Star is *Breaking Up Is Hard To Do,* a fun-filled musical featuring a sweet comic story woven together with the classic hits of Neil Sedaka including "Laughter In the Rain," "Calendar Girl," "Sweet Sixteen," and (of course) "Breaking Up Is Hard To Do"—and other Sedaka hits. This show will bring back memories of your past life like few can. It is a fun, fun romp through the decades that meant so much to all of us.

Branson Blast! is a show in the Crystal Show Room. This crazy little variety show includes illusion, acrobatics, juggling, music, and loads of fun! The show is a little over an hour in length and starts at 5 p.m., giving you a chance to take in a second show later in the evening. Be sure to visit their Web site or call the box office for tickets, reservations, scheduling, or information.

STARLITE THEATRE
3115 West 76 Country Blvd.
(417) 337-9333, (877) 336-7827
www.starlitetheatre.com
Out with the old Barbara Fairchild Theatre and in with the new Starlite Theatre. This venue on

Close-up

Branson Performers Play "Musical Theaters"

Imagine this. You've finally saved the money for the ultimate Branson vacation. You've plotted your route, made hotel reservations, received the information you've requested from the Branson/Lakes Area Chamber of Commerce, gassed up the car, and set off on your merry way. Along the way, you see billboard after billboard adorned with the faces of one of the entertainers that you had planned to see.

You arrive at your hotel at 7:15 p.m., in plenty of time to make it to that 8 p.m. show over at such-and-such theater. You break out the Branson map, locate your destination, and rush out the door. When you arrive at the theater, you notice that the marquee lists the name of a different performer. "That okay," you think, "they share theaters in Branson. Maybe they've got two stars playing here." You approach the friendly box-office clerk and ask for four tickets to your favorite singer's show. Instead of handing you the tickets, she flashes you a puzzled look.

"I'm sorry, he's moved down The Strip to the so-and-so theater," she says.

A lump rises in your throat as you realize you don't have time to make it down The Strip before the curtain rises.

Welcome to Branson. The entertainers here have come up with the game called "musical theaters." It's a slightly modified version of musical chairs. Every so often, some of them pack up their bags and bands and move two or three doors down the street. At the beginning of every new game—or season, as we call it—some of them end up without a place to sit down. They're usually replaced with new, faster-moving players.

Since the Baldknobbers opened the first show in Branson in 1968, lots and lots of players have come and gone. Big-name stars such as John Davidson, Glen Campbell, Cristy Lane, Ray Stevens, Barbara Fairchild, and Anita Bryant all had theaters bearing their names. Headliners such as Kenny Rogers, Willie Nelson, Louise Mandrell, Larry Gatlin, and Ray Price even had their own shows here, but they are no more. They've been replaced by other big-name stars and ensemble productions shows such as *Country Tonight, The Promise, Spirit of the Dance,* and *Dino Kartsonakis.*

As with life, just about the time you get used to something, it changes. The theater business in Branson is no exception, and the billboards often don't change as fast as the theater hopping. But that's what makes it dynamic and interesting. While entertainers such as Jim Stafford, Andy Williams, and Yakov Smirnoff own their own theaters, many do not. When they get a better offer from another theater owner, they do the smart business thing and move. That was the case with Tony Orlando and Wayne Newton, who moved from the Tony Orlando Yellow Ribbon Theater to play at the former Glen Campbell Theatre from 1998 to 1999, when the owner filed bankruptcy. Now Wayne is in Las Vegas and Tony is touring. Much the same thing happened with the Charley Pride Theatre in 1997. It changed hands and became the home of *The Promise* for several years. In 2002 it sold to Bob Wehr, who sent the cast of *The Promise* packing and opened it as the White House Theatre. Sad to say, the White House Theatre is being sold again. Stay tuned.

Critics often try to use the announcement of a Branson theater bankruptcy to conclude that the town is drying up and that big-name stars are on their way out. This couldn't be further from the truth. As with any industry, there are businesses that come and go. Restaurants around the country go out of business, motels go out of business or change hands, and T-shirt shop owners file bankruptcy. The only difference is that they don't make the front page of the newspaper, and theater closings do. The Branson boom of the early 1990s is now an echo, but the economy it generated is alive and well—just different.

The overall face of Branson entertainment is changing, however. When Roy Clark first moved to town in 1983, he was the first nationally known entertainer to call the place home. Up until that time, the Baldknobbers and Presleys and other family shows ruled the roost. Some said Clark would never last, that Branson was not the place for stars. Well, Clark and others who joined him, such as the late Boxcar Willie, Mel Tillis, and Jim Stafford, proved them wrong. Then, when Andy Williams opened in 1992, some said his style of pop music would never appeal to the country fans that were coming to see Roy Clark and Boxcar Willie. Williams and others such as Bobby Vinton and Tony Orlando proved them wrong. Today, such variety production shows as *Country Tonite, Lost in the Fifties, Legends in Concert, Dixie Stampede,* and *Pierce Arrow* have tested the waters and show no sign of sinking. Their success may be the reason Dick Clark built his American Bandstand Theater, new in 2006.

Jim Thomas, former owner of the Roy Clark Celebrity Theatre and the Remington Theatre, said he believes the days of stars in concert are over in Branson. A bare stage and spotlight used to do the trick, but not today. What he means is that the audiences want to see the stars surrounded by glitz, flash, fancy costumes, dancers, props, ice skating, variety acts, comedy, pyrotechnical stunts, animals, and other bells and whistles.

Entertainers such as Andy Williams, Jim Stafford, Mickey Gilley, Mel Tillis, and other Branson veterans know that in order to appeal to audiences year after year, they have to give them what they want—fancy productions. And they do. That's not to say that traditional shows such as the Baldknobbers and Presleys don't offer big production value. They do. But they have had to change, too. Drive by the Presleys' theater and take a look at their marquee with its enormous video screen, or stop in and check out the Baldknobbers' sound and lighting systems. You'll quickly see that these shows have found a successful recipe that tempers hillbilly charm with showbiz glitz.

The stars who have been here the longest are the least likely to participate in the game—of musical theaters, that is. It's the new players or the locally known shows like *Pierce Arrow; Red, Hot . . . & Blue!;* the Hughes Brothers; and the Duttons that have had a hard time locating from season to season. Even some of them have begun to settle into more permanent homes. The Duttons bought the old Boxcar Willie Theatre, for example, and have remodeled and comfortably settled in.

The old switcharoo usually takes place between December and March, when many of the theaters are closed for the winter. Sometimes entertainers move in the middle of the season, but not too often. Your best bet for finding out who is where is to call the Branson/Lakes Area Chamber of Commerce at (417) 334-4136 before you leave home. Since the information in this guide is compiled well before it makes it into your hands, some of the listings may even be out of date, thanks to Branson's game of "musical theaters." You can't even believe the billboards you see on your way here or on The Strip. Frequently, they don't get painted in time to reflect the current reality.

So when coming to Branson for the shows, be aware of the Branson switcharoo. Check things out so you don't find yourself writing down directions at the show box office for the show that didn't show where you thought it would show!

The Strip was erected in 1999 on the very spot the Barbara Fairchild Theatre used to sit. It was decided the old venue had seen all of its better days, so down it came and up went the 900-seat Starlite Theatre, with an 11,000-square-foot glass-enclosed five-story lobby that sits so close to the street you can see your reflection in the glass as you drive by. The architects attempted to re-create the look and feel of a 1950s Main Street America inside the atrium. There's an authentic 1950s soda fountain, complete with shakes, sundaes, floats, and even a soda jerk. For you younger folks in the crowd, a soda jerk is the guy who actually concocts and serves the soda. He is NOT really a jerk.

Here Louise Harrison presents *Liverpool Legends, the Ultimate Beatles Tribute.*

These four lads are talented musicians and actors hand picked by Louise to re-create the band that changed the face of music forever. Everything is performed live with precise attention to every detail, *Liverpool Legends* will make you believe you are seeing and hearing the real thing. Experience Beatlemania in Branson with songs like "She Loves You," "I Wanna Hold Your Hand," "Yesterday," "Hey Jude," and many more.

Celebrate *Motown's 50th Anniversary* with the World Famous Platters at the Starlite Theatre. With amazing new production and the addition of a live four-piece band you will experience fifty years of Motown music and Platters favorites as they take you back to hot cars and drive-in movies, sock hops and slow dancing with songs like "Only You," "The Great Pretender," and many more soulful classics.

The Rankin Brothers *Classic Music Revue* voted Best New Show in 2008. This multimedia experience showcases the Rankin Brothers musical talent on everything from pop to country, rock 'n' roll to folk, blues, soul, and everything in between. Time will stand still as the Rankin Brothers take you on a memorable journey with hits from Elvis, Buddy Holly, Neil Diamond, Conway Twitty, George Strait, and many more of your favorites.

With their talented cast of three female vocalists, five musicians, and an outstanding comedian, The Rankin Brothers authentically replicate the classic songs the way you remember hearing them. They will take you on a trip down memory lane, with their favorite classic songs of the last five decades. Hear classics from Elvis, Buddy Holly, The Everly Brothers, Neil Diamond, The Righteous Brothers, Simon and Garfunkel, all the way to Billy Joel, Eric Clapton, and Faith Hill. Also enjoy gospel music and even relive a classic high school prom.

Ticket prices vary for the shows at the Starlite, so call the theater or visit their Web site for tickets, reservations, information, or schedules.

TRI-LAKES CENTER
2527 MO 248
(417) 335-5715
www.trilakescenter.com

This theater was the house that Mel built. It is a 2,500 seat mega-theater built just on the north edge of Branson. The former Mel Tillis Theater was sold by the country music great and is now a church.

The Tri-Lakes Center will be having special guest stars along with special performances throughout the year. For 2009 the lineup includes: Mary Duff, Ray Price, Roy Clark, Merle Haggard with Gene Watson, Daniel O'Donnell, and of course, M-M-M-M-Mel Tillis. Call the box office or visit their Web site for further information, tickets, reservations, or schedules.

WELK RESORT THEATRE
1984 MO 165
(417) 337-SHOW, (800) 505-WELK
www.welkresortbranson.com
www.sullivanshows.com

The fizzle went out of the champagne at the Champagne Theatre at the Welk Resort. Many of the stars of the *Lawrence Welk Show* are gone;

i If you're a "Branson Fan," you can sign up for weekly e-mail "Branson News"—reviews, tidbits, and entertainment updates—by going to www.Branson.net.

the Lennon Sisters have retired, and audience tastes have perhaps changed. The Welk Resort continues, however, and the venue there continues to pack them in, but with special-event concerts, such as the Beach Boys, Pam Tillis, Larry Gatlin and the Gatlin Brothers, B. B. King, and Three Dog Night. Check the theater Web site for a schedule of shows, dates, and tickets, or call the box office.

YAKOV'S AMERICAN PAVILION
470 MO 248
(417) 33-NO-KGB, (800) 33-NO-KGB
www.yakov.com

After eight seasons in Branson with shows at the Cristy Lane Theatre, the Osmond Family Theater, and the Grand Palace, Russian comedian Yakov Smirnoff finally got a theater bearing his own name in 1997. The 1,300-seat former Ozark Theater, at the west end of The Strip, became Yakov's American Pavilion. His sold-out shows necessitated another move in 2004—to the former Will Rogers Theater. Yakov's show is full of comical yet touching stories about growing up in Russia and adjusting to life in America. In 1977, shortly after Yakov graduated from college in Russia, where he studied art, he and his parents traveled to New York in search of their freedom. One of Yakov's first jobs was as a bartender in a hotel with a 2,000-seat theater. With a little encouragement from one of his coworkers, Yakov soon mustered up the nerve to take the stage. While in Russia, Yakov had spent a few years as the emcee of a band that worked cruise ships in the Black Sea. He wasn't exactly a stranger to the stage, but most of his jokes were in Russian. Nevertheless, Yakov was a hit at the hotel.

This experience led to a move to Los Angeles, where he found work in comedy houses before being cast in the 1984 movie *Moscow on the Hudson*, starring Robin Williams. Two more feature films followed in 1986—*Heartburn*, with

Jack Nicholson and Meryl Streep, and *The Money Pit*, with Tom Hanks and Shelley Long. A few years later, while he was performing at a Farm Aid concert in Iowa, Yakov ran into Willie Nelson, who told him about Branson. In 1993 Yakov opened at the Cristy Lane Theatre and has been in town ever since. Branson has embraced him and voted him comedian of the year three times.

Yakov's particular brand of comedy pokes fun at communist Russia and at the idiosyncrasies of his everyday life as a husband, father, and now an American. His show includes comedy, music, and Russian dances. Comedian David Hirschi, aka Slim Chance, who is also a fantastic juggler, defected from the *Country Tonight* show and joined Yakov in 1998. Yakov's so sure you'll like his show that he offers a money-back guarantee if you're not satisfied.

The gift shop inside the lobby of the theater contains items imported from around the world. You'll see handpainted glass collectibles from Holland, breakfast teas from Ireland, pottery from South America, hand-carved wooden boxes from Poland, and beer steins from Germany. You can also get a copy of Yakov's book, *America on Six Rubles A Day*, which is now in its fifth printing and has sold more than a quarter of a million copies. You may also purchase prints of Yakov's impressionistic paintings. Both he and Mel Tillis are accomplished painters. And if you're an AARP member, read Yakov's column in *AARP Magazine*.

Call the theater or check the Web site for tickets, information, or show schedules.

Well folks, that's it. We hope we have been helpful in guiding you through the many theaters of Branson and more importantly, what to expect. Have a great time while you are in Branson and please come back and see us when you can stay longer. You'll always get a heapin' helping of hospitality.

ATTRACTIONS

From the bottoms of our caves to the tops of our hills, the Ozarks is packed with a huge selection of attractions both natural and man-made. Long before there were automobiles and airplanes, folks came on horseback and in wagons to see the rivers, caves, and wildlife. Thanks to a little modern technology, now you can see our oldest attractions from our newest attractions. Railway cars will take you through tunnels and over natural bridges deep into the Ozarks outdoors. Paddle-wheel boats will take you down Lake Taneycomo and across Table Rock Lake. Hot-air balloons will take you 2,000 feet above the hills. Ducks (World War II amphibious vehicles) will take you across both land and lake. And from the 230-foot-tall Inspiration Tower, you will see a far wider view of the Ozarks than Harold Bell Wright ever did.

Not only do our attractions let you see the Ozarks from all possible angles, but at the same time you can see a live music show, enjoy a meal, or sit in a high-tech IMAX movie theater. Our two largest theme parks will show you a view of the Ozarks' past. Silver Dollar City and the Shepherd of the Hills Homestead have preserved turn-of-the-20th-century pioneer life in their shops, live shows, crafts, music, and hospitality. These two world-class attractions offer much more than a history lesson. Silver Dollar City has sensational thrill rides, full production shows, fine gift items, and great water attractions for kids. At Shepherd of the Hills you can watch the outdoor drama with its pyrotechnical special effects, and modern sound and lighting systems.

Although many of the area's attractions are deeply rooted in the Ozarks' past, places such as the Hollywood Wax Museum and Ripley's Believe It or Not! Museum rely on the appeal of their bizarre contents and wax movie star figures to attract visitors. These places, along with the IMAX Entertainment Complex, are real hot spots with the younger generation. You might want to flip to the Kidstuff chapter for other great attractions for kids. You'll find a listing for White Water, Cool Off Water Chute, and the Track in that chapter. Nearby Springfield also has a number of great attractions, such as Bass Pro Shops, the Discovery Center, the Wonders of Wildlife Museum, and Dickerson Park Zoo. You'll find them listed in the Day Trips chapter.

The attractions listed in this chapter range from a free stop at the Shepherd of the Hills Historical Evergreen Cemetery to a $180 hot-air balloon ride and everything in between. Many of the places offer season passes, combo tickets, and group discounts. The hours of operation can change during the year, as can available space. Be sure to call in advance before your trip to town so you won't wind up like Clark Griswold at Wally World in *National Lampoon's Vacation*.

Most of the attractions publish their ticket prices excluding tax. We have noted those that include tax in the published price. While Branson is still a seasonal town, many of the attractions are extending their winter hours, and some of them even stay open year-round. They often close earlier in the winter, however, so again, call ahead.

THEME PARKS

Silver Dollar City

Indian Point Road
(417) 338-2611, (800) 831-4FUN
www.silverdollarcity.com

From the moment you step off the tram at the entrance gate, you'll be transported back to a day and time when folks lived simpler lives, free from modern-day stress. There's plenty of hustle and bustle at Silver Dollar City, only it's of the 1880s type. You'll see "citizens" dressed in authentic-looking pioneer outfits rushing to and from their craft stations; musicians roaming the streets playing fiddles, guitars, and other homemade instruments; and wide-eyed children taking in the sights, sounds, and smells in a kind of place many of them have never seen before.

Over the past 40-plus years, Silver Dollar City has grown from a small family operation into a booming commercial enterprise. It has been voted one of the top theme parks in the world (1998–99) by the International Association of Amusement Parks & Attractions, and it plays host to more than two million visitors each year. Even with the addition of five annual festivals; a 1,800-seat exhibition and performance center; newer attractions, including the explosive launch coaster, Powderkeg; and the multilooping thriller roller coaster, Wildfire; and more than 50 live shows each day; Silver Dollar City has consistently maintained its commitment to old-fashioned authenticity and style. No trip to Branson would be complete without at least a peek into Ozarks pioneer life, and there's no better place to experience it than at Silver Dollar City.

A Short History

What started out simply as a geological wonder is now a booming tourist attraction. Marvel

i Want a "straight shot" to Silver Dollar City? Take exit 1b, the Ozark Mountain Highroad (MO 465), 6 miles north of Branson on US 65. It connects to MO 76 just east of Silver Dollar City.

i Traffic really stacks up on MO 76 coming back into Branson at the close of Silver Dollar City each day. To avoid the snarl, you might want to leave a little early or take the scenic route east from Indian Point Road on MO 76 to MO 265 and then to MO 165 where it intersects US 65 south of Branson. From there it's a straight shot north back into town.

Cave, as it is now known, was discovered by the Osage Indians around 1500. After hearing unusual noises coming from within the cave, the Indians opted not to enter it, but they did give it the name Devil's Den. A group of miners, led by Henry T. Blow, ventured inside the cave in 1869, hoping to find lead. While they discovered no lead ore, they were convinced the cave must be full of marble. When word spread, the locals began referring to it as Marble Cave. The cave was later renamed Marvel Cave since no marble was ever mined from its walls.

In 1894 archaeologist William Henry Lynch bought the cave and opened it to tourists. After Lynch's death in 1932, his two daughters took over the business and by the late 1940s were entertaining 5,000 guests a year. In 1946 two vacationing tourists from Chicago, Hugo and Mary Herschend, fell in love with the cave and in 1949 signed a 99-year lease on the property. They planned to turn the cave into an entertainment center with live music and square dancing since the constant 58-degree temperature in the cave made it a perfect summertime retreat. But, just four years later, Hugo died at the age of 55 and left the task of operating the business to his wife and two sons, Jack and Peter.

Their entrepreneurial skills served them well. Acting on a tip from a traveling salesman who claimed to have been born in the general store of the town that had once stood near the cave, the Herschends decided to re-create an 1880s Ozark Mountain village in order to encourage more tourists to visit the cave.

In 1960 Silver Dollar City opened with a blacksmith shop, general store, ice-cream parlor, doll shop, and stagecoach ride. As a marketing ploy, each park visitor received his change in silver dollars. When they left the area and spent the silver dollars, people would ask where they got them. The idea worked. In its first year, Silver Dollar City attracted more than 125,000 people.

Getting Around

After you pass the entrance gate and pick up a map of the park, the first thing you'll come to is the Hospitality House. Here you'll find an abundant assortment of souvenirs and snacks as well as the line that forms for Marvel Cave. The Mine Restaurant is not far inside the park on the right as you exit the Hospitality House. This is a good place to stop for breakfast or lunch before you begin the hike through the park. The "streets" at Silver Dollar City twist and turn amid the trees and hills, but just remember as a general rule, if you're walking downhill, you're going deeper into the park, and if you're walking uphill, you're heading back to the entrance. Strollers, wheelchairs, and electric carts are available for a nominal fee, and the latter two can be reserved by calling (800) 225-0222. Ask for the stroller booth. Strollers are available on a first-come, first-served basis. Fortunately there are many places to sit and catch your breath at SDC, and the trees that Mary Herschend insisted be spared more than 30 years ago shade many of them. Only service animals are allowed in the park. The average visit to Silver Dollar City takes at least one day, two if you come during a festival or are one of those types who likes to see and do it all.

Shows

With 50 live shows a day at Silver Dollar City, you're never more than a few feet away from some of the liveliest entertainers in the Midwest. Most of the shows feature performers who can sing, dance, play a musical instrument, and tell a quick joke to boot. Some of the shows move from venue to venue during the course of the season. The days and times for a particular show also change frequently, so be sure to call in advance or check the Web site if you are interested in seeing a specific show. The shows change from

year to year, and here we've listed a few of the SDC venues with examples of the types of shows they feature. The Silver Dollar Saloon show is usually one of the best at the park, a favorite for nearly four decades, featuring high-kickin' gals and boot-scootin' cowboys. Hilarity reigns supreme at the tongue-in-cheek, fast-paced, and always comical half-hour show.

After park closing, the stars come out overhead and on the stage of the 4,000-seat Echo Hollow Amphitheater. The nightly show is included in the admission price to the park. The Horsecreek Band combines bluegrass, Western swing, and Ozarks hospitality at the Gazebo. During the summer months, championship cloggers from throughout the United States perform at the Gazebo stage. Pure Heart is the park's resident sister duet that harmonizes like only family can, and the Cajun Connection presents the rollicking upbeat music of the bayou. Another favorite is the Homestead Pickers, presenting front-porch picking. The 1,800-seat Red Gold Heritage Hall, a performance and exhibition center themed to reflect the Ozarks tomato canning and shipping history, often features festival shows, special exhibits, and crafts.

Rides and Attractions

Adrenaline junkies rejoice at the many opportunities to catch a buzz at Silver Dollar City's rides and attractions. From the Grand Exposition of 1882 with 10 new family rides open in 2006 to the eight-story, high-speed Wilderness Waterboggan flume, there are plenty of ways to raise your blood pressure at Silver Dollar City. In 2005 the park debuted its newest wild ride, the explosive launch coaster Powderkeg, which takes riders from 0 to 53 mph in 2.8 seconds. Another thrill coaster is Wildfire, a 0.75-mile roller coaster that reaches top speeds of 66 mph with five inversions, two full loops, and one leave-your-stomach-behind drop of 15 stories (155 feet). BuzzSaw Falls, a wet-dry coaster, combines sharp twists and turns at speeds of approximately 50 mph with a nine-story plunge right into a reservoir. Other thrill rides include Lost River of the Ozarks, where passengers are taken on a white-water adventure through the Ozark hills; Fire in the Hole, a ride through a burning town; and the Great Shoot-Out at the Flooded Mine, a float through a flooded mine full of bandits and outlaws. Another favorite is the American Plunge, where passengers board a hollowed-out log and ride it to the bottom of a water chute. (It's just a fancy way to get wet, really.) The good news for some of us is that not all of Silver Dollar's City's rides and attractions will scare the living daylights out of you. The Frisco Silver Dollar Line Steam Train is about as tame as they come. You'll be treated to a 20-minute trip through the woods as a narrator provides commentary on the scenery. Watch out, though—it seems bandits such as Alf Bolin are still a hidin' out in them thar Ozark hills (see the History chapter for more about Mr. Bolin). They usually don't take any prisoners, and their robbery attempts are comical at best.

i **Be sure to waterproof your camera at Silver Dollar City. On some rides, you *will* get wet!**

The Cave

Early Spanish explorers came to the cave looking for the Fountain of Youth. Miners hoping to find marble called it Marble Cave but were surprised to find nothing but a plentiful supply of bat guano. The guano was mined, however, for fertilizer. Open for more than a century as Missouri's oldest continuously operating cave tour site, Marvel Cave was once home to the Ozark Jubilee, the Presley family music show, and hundreds of square dances. Jack Herschend was married in it. The gigantic Cathedral Room has even seen hot-air balloon competitions. That's right, it's that big. A complete tour of the cave is included in the admission price to the park. There are a few tight squeezes, but for the most part it's not a bad hike, around 60 minutes. If you have a special medical condition, we suggest you talk to a cave guide before attempting the tour. There are 600 stairs you'll have to maneuver. The good news is that you go in on foot and come out on a train.

The cave is fully lit and a great place to cool off on a hot summer's day. Tours depart a number of times a day from the Hospitality House just near the entrance of the park.

Kidstuff

Tom Sawyer's Landing is a play area designed especially for kids too young for the thrill of Thunderation. Inside Tom Sawyer's Landing are a number of mechanical rides, such as the Sky-chase Balloon Ride and the classic Becky's Carousel, with hand-carved wooden horses and bears to ride. A Petting Zoo provides real live animals, but not to ride. There is a four-story Rope Tower for the aspiring climber. Children with boundless energy appreciate Geyser Gulch, the world's largest tree house, with three towers of mazes, rope crawls, foam blasters, and water cannons, as well as Splash Harbor, a three-story boat and four-level dockside tower outfitted with enough water toys to douse the entire state.

McHaffie's Pioneer Homestead

Experience life in the 1880s firsthand at McHaffie's Pioneer Homestead, where you'll see authentic-looking pioneers tending the animals, carving wood, sewing, square dancing, cooking over an open fire, and more. The homestead is an authentic Ozark log cabin built in 1843 at Swan Creek near Forsyth. Opal Parnell donated it to the Herschends and insisted that it be used only as a working homestead. The inhabitants will be happy to answer questions, and they'll even throw in a tall tale or two. At 4 p.m. daily you can stop by for the musical jam session. The nice thing about a visit to Silver Dollar City is that the entire staff is ready, willing, and able to interact one-on-one with visitors. No one leaves a stranger.

Wilderness Church

Authenticity is the name of the game at Silver Dollar City, and the Wilderness Church is no exception. The walls of this 1800s-style structure are made out of old logs. The pews are carved out of logs, and the podium is even made out of a huge old tree. Guests are always welcome to stop in for a little spiritual reflection or to peer out the large window overlooking a garden. Church services are held on Sunday at 9:30 and 11 a.m. Drop in to join the singing of hymns a number of times each day. If you've finally found that special someone, Wilderness Church has served as the setting for hundreds of weddings and vow renewals over the years, and if you make your reservation early, it can host yours, too. Call the central reservation number listed for SDC for information. You can renew your vows Monday through Saturday at 4 p.m. You must sign up at the Angel Shop to participate.

Shops and Crafts

There are a few places where you will find a selection of run-of-the-mill souvenir items at Silver Dollar City, but for the most part each shop carries entirely unique handcrafted items. The Hospitality House and Ozark Marketplace carry an assortment of T-shirts, trinkets, and seasonal merchandise. The other 60 shops carry the products of Silver Dollar City's 100 craftspeople. You'll find blown-glass items from perfume bottles to vases to Christmas ornaments in a variety of colors at Hazel's. Handmade white oak baskets from pie baskets to full-size picnic baskets can be found at D. Ellicon's shop. Handmade oak furniture, stoneware pottery, candles, carved wood, leather, knives, ironwork, and even lye soap are some of the products and crafts you can see made daily at the park. If you're worried about carrying all those treasures around with you all day, you can arrange to have them delivered to the entrance of the park. Just remember to pick them up on your way out.

The demonstrating craftsmen at Silver Dollar City help ensure that there is a plentiful supply of young craftspeople being trained in the variety of arts displayed at the city. Many of the craftspeople employed at Silver Dollar City are master craftspeople with decades of experience who teach their skills and techniques to the apprentices of the next generation.

Food

After a big meal at the Mine or Mill Restaurant, you probably won't have room for much else for a few hours, but when you are ready there are a number of places to grab a snack or sample old-fashioned pioneer cooking. When we say snack, we don't mean a bag of chips. If you are looking for a snack, you can get a bag full of fresh corn popped in a cast-iron kettle over an open fire at the Sawmill Kettle Corn shop. The pastries at Eva and Delilah's Bakery are to die for, and the Black Angus char-grilled burgers at the Garden Cafe are a real treat. The Tater Patch serves up calico fried potatoes, curly fries, chicken strips, and pork tenderloin sandwiches. During the festivals you will find additional food offerings according to the season. Our favorite is the hot wassail served during the Christmas festival. For a more substantial meal, try Mary's Springhouse Restaurant, where you'll find salads and pastas with freshly made cheese, five-layer lasagna, and rosemary pork loin sandwiches. The Riverside Ribhouse has barbecued ribs, barbecued chicken, and hand-pulled pork sandwiches.

Festivals

With the exception of a few weeks between the six festivals, there is always something special happening at Silver Dollar City. (See the Annual Events chapter for more information.) The fun starts in mid-April each year with World-Fest, a four-week festival featuring hundreds of performers from around the globe who bring their music, dance, costumes, and culture to the park. Bluegrass and Barbecue follow mid-May to early June, with the upbeat sounds of bluegrass music and the aromas of an all-American barbecue.

The National Children's Festival, held each year from mid-June through the end of August, is fast becoming one of the park's top draws. Silver Dollar City routinely brings in special displays and interactive exhibits for kids as well as new shows and hands-on crafts and games. Bluegrass and Barbecue brings in some of the best bluegrass performers in the nation in May.

Added in 2006 is the Southern Gospel Picnic, with gospel music and classic picnic cuisine for the summer months.

The Festival of American Music and Craftsmanship, which begins each year in early September and lasts through October, features the creations of visiting craftspeople and the unique sounds of musicians from around the country. You'll find artists who specialize in such forms as raku pottery, copper smithing, carousel horse carving, and stained glass. And you can hear regional music from all areas of the nation, from New York Irish pub singers to New Orleans jazz and Mississippi blues.

One of the most popular seasons in the Ozarks and one of the most popular festivals at Silver Dollar City takes place as Christmas approaches. The Old Time Christmas Festival begins in early November and runs through the end of December. Each evening at 5:30 p.m. guests can watch the lighting of the five-story Christmas tree on the square. The tree has more than 160,000 lights. Guests may sing carols at Wilderness Church or catch a special Christmas show at the Silver Dollar Saloon. Perhaps the best part of the celebration is the fact that the entire park is filled with tiny lights, Nativity scenes, traditional Christmas ornaments, and the smell of hot mulled cider and wassail, as well as other tasty holiday treats.

Vital Statistics

- **How to get there:** Silver Dollar City is 4.5 miles west of Branson, just off MO 76 on Indian Point Road. Turn left at the entrance sign at the intersection on MO 76 and Indian Point Road.
- **Parking:** The first parking lot you'll come to is for handicapped licensed vehicles. Just show the parking attendant your tag. The other lots sit on both sides of Indian Point Road just past the main entrance to Silver Dollar City. Regular parking is free, with valet and close-up parking available for fees from $5 to $20, but it isn't necessary. Trams run every few minutes to and from the lettered lots. Be sure to remember which lot you parked in to save time at the end of the day searching for your car.
- **Admission prices** (including tax) in 2009 are $53 for those 12 and older, $43 for children 4

to 11, and free for children three and younger. Seniors 62 and older get in for $51. Season passes for 2009 are $85 for adults, $74 for children, and $78 for seniors. If you also plan to visit White Water, the *Showboat Branson Belle,* the Dixie Stampede, or the Radio City Christmas Spectacular, you can save money by purchasing combo tickets in various combinations. Tickets and passes can be ordered online at SDC's Web site.

- **Hours of operation:** Silver Dollar City is open from early April through the end of December. The week after Christmas is a great time to pick up sale items at the more than sixty shops. From opening day in April to mid-May, the park is open Wednesday through Sunday from 9:30 a.m. to 6 p.m. On Saturday the park is open from 9 a.m. to 7 p.m. From mid-May to the end of August the park is open daily from 9:30 a.m. until 7 p.m. From late August to late October the park closes at 6 p.m. every day except Saturday, when it stays open until 7 p.m. Beginning on Labor Day the park is closed on Monday for the rest of the year. From early November until the end of December, the park is open from 1 to 10 p.m. Wednesday through Sunday. There are a few exceptions to this schedule, so be sure to call in advance to check exact dates and times.

Shepherd of the Hills Homestead and Outdoor Theatre

5586 MO 76 West
(417) 334-4191, (800) OLD-MATT
www.oldmatt.com

No visit to Branson would be complete without a visit to Shepherd of the Hills Homestead and Outdoor Theatre. The traditional sights, sounds, and smells of the Ozarks are alive and well at this turn-of-the-20th-century theme park. You won't find the commercialism you might expect at one of the country's most popular attractions. (More than seven million people have seen the outdoor drama to date.) You will find gentle rolling hills, mature trees, flowers in the summer and fall, and the same kind of hospitality Harold Bell Wright encountered more than a century ago. What you get from a visit to Shepherd of the Hills is more than a history lesson. It's a trip back to a state of mind when families thought nothing of opening their homes to strangers and even less of defending their farms with their very lives. The best part of Shepherd of the Hills Homestead and Outdoor Theatre is the people who steadfastly perpetuate its wholesome environment and take pride in their Ozarks heritage.

A Short History

What tourists know today as Shepherd of the Hills Homestead and Outdoor Theatre all began with a minister, a farmer, and a flood. The minister was a man by the name of Harold Bell Wright, who traveled from his home state of New York to the Ozarks in 1896 to contemplate his diminishing career and improve his ailing health. During his journey into the Ozarks on horseback, Wright was stopped short by the flooded White River. Farmers John and Anna Ross offered to let Wright stay a night on their farm (which would today be located just east of the Country Tonite Theatre on MO 76 near Mutton Hollow) until the river subsided, but his visit extended for an entire summer. During the next eight years Wright returned to the Ross home each summer, where he began compiling the events and characters for his novel, *The Shepherd of the Hills*. The book was published in 1907, and its success was immediate.

When the Missouri-Pacific Railroad completed the track of the White River Line through the Roark Valley in 1906, the area became more accessible to tourists. By 1909 travelers stopping in Branson or Reeds Spring began asking to see Old Matt's Cabin, as the Ross homestead was called in the book. After the deaths of John and Anna Ross around 1923, the daughter of a Springfield banker, Lizzie McDaniel, bought the homestead and set about the task of restoring the cabin. The first dramatizations of Harold Bell Wright's story were told on the cabin's lawn. She also named the cornfield where Wright had once camped Inspiration Point. Dr. Bruce Trimble and his wife, Mary, acquired the property in 1946 after McDaniel's death and added a number of attrac-

tions, including a gift shop called Aunt Mollie's Cupboard and the outdoor amphitheater called the Old Mill Theatre. In 1941 a film was made of the story, which starred John Wayne in his first Technicolor film.

Performances of *The Shepherd of the Hills* began in 1960. The drama became the leading outdoor performance in the country under the direction of the Trimble family. In 1985 the son of Mary and Bruce Trimble, Mark, and his wife, Lea, sold the property to its current owner, Gary Snadon. During the late 1960s Snadon played the villainous Wash Gibbs in the outdoor drama while maintaining his day job as a teacher and football coach at Branson High School. In 1989 Snadon added Inspiration Tower, and in 1990 he had the Morgan County Church relocated to the homestead to signify the churches where Wright used to preach. Each year since, Snadon and his family have added new attractions to the park to reflect the growing and ever-changing demands of the public. In 1997 the 100-member cast of *The Shepherd of the Hills* celebrated the play's 5,000th performance.

Touring the Park

The Jeep-drawn guided tours of the homestead take visitors on a journey back to the days of Bald Knobbers, traveling preachers, and subsistence farming. Among the stops is the Morgan Community Church, built in 1901, where visitors spend a few moments with a recorded impersonation of Harold Bell Wright in an inspirational presentation.

The National Historic Landmark Old Matt's Cabin is a highlight of the tour. A photographer will take your photo on the front porch steps. Along the tour you'll also see Inspiration Point, Harold Bell Wright's Circle of Legends, Lizzie McDaniel's home, a moonshine still, the backstage area of the amphitheater, and the Waves of Glory Flag Museum.

No visit to the homestead would be complete without a trip to the top of Inspiration Tower. Built in 1989, the structure is 230 feet tall and weighs more than three million pounds. Its flagpole is 1,608 feet above sea level. As you look through a telescope on the open-air observation deck, you can see people in boats on Table Rock Lake. The enclosed observation deck contains 4,400 square feet of glass—enough to cover a third of a football field. The ground level houses a gift shop, snack bar, and restrooms. The tower has 225 stairs and two elevators. During the Christmas season the tower is adorned with 25,000 lights, transforming it into one of the Ozark's largest Christmas tree–shaped displays.

Other attractions at the homestead include the Shepherd of the Hills Clydesdales. In 1997 they made an appearance in the Macy's 71st Annual Thanksgiving Day Parade. There are pony rides for the kids and a City Kids and Country Cousins playground, where little ones can burn off energy. A fire at the Shepherd of the Hills in spring 2002 destroyed the Pickin' Parlor, Aunt Molly's Restaurant, and the Precious Moments Animated Gallery and Gift Shoppe—all of which have now been rebuilt. Expect the usual Ozarks' favorites such as fried chicken, mashed potatoes, gravy, beans, roast beef, corn, salad, and hot bread. There are demonstrating craftspeople scattered throughout the park and live musical entertainment all day long, including the Sons of the Pioneers in a dinner show ($39 for adults, $19 for children, and $36 for seniors).

The Outdoor Drama

The original goal of *The Shepherd of the Hills* outdoor drama was to bring to life the characters, events, and setting of *The Shepherd of the Hills* novel. When the play was first presented in the 1960s, it was considered one of the most ambitious theater projects in the Midwest. Through the use of "living" props such as horses, a functioning steam engine, a mill, and a dirt stage, the theater concept called ultrarealism came to the Ozarks. Set against a natural backdrop of stars, trees, moonlight, and the echo of frogs and crickets in the nearby woods, the play would have made Harold Bell Wright proud. Many generations of cast members have grown up playing the characters Wright described in his novel. Some of the current cast members have been in the show for thirty years and now share the stage

with their children and grandchildren. The story has all the elements of a good old-fashioned romance. Conflict, young love, music, dancing, tragedy, fighting—you name it, it's there. The current production has a cast of eighty actors and actresses, thirty-two horses, twenty-eight revolvers, twenty-two double-barreled shotguns, and a nightly pyrotechnical display of Dad Howitt's cabin. The play is presented nightly at 8:30 p.m. from April through August and at 7:30 p.m. from late August until October. When it's raining, there's no show.

Special Events

Each year Shepherd of the Hills Homestead offers a number of special events. August features gorgeous antique cars and hot rods in the Shepherd's Super Summer Cruise. Car collectors travel from miles around to take part in the daily show 'n' shine, mall crawl, and rallies. Visitors come to gawk at and drool over the cars. September through October is the Cowboy Roundup. November through early January is the Trail of Lights. Old Matt's 160-acre homestead is transformed into a spectacular holiday wonderland of lights, sound, and motion. Life-size animated displays are set to festive holiday music, and the entire park is outlined in multicolored lights.

Vital Statistics

- **How to get there:** Go 1 mile past the Country Tonite Theatre on MO 76. The parking lot is on the south side of MO 76. There is a walkway underneath the highway that leads to the entrance to the park. Parking is free.
- **Admission:** Admission to the site is free, but the various attractions have individual prices. A Jeep-drawn day tour plus a visit to Inspiration Tower and a ticket to the play is $39 for adults and $19 for children 4 to 16. Children younger than four get in free. Tickets just to Inspiration Tower are $6 for adults and $3 for kids 4 to 16. Tickets to the play are $37 for adults and $18 for children younger than 16. Children younger than four get in free. Trail rides on horses are $20 for adults and children seven and older. Kids six and younger can ride

Harold Bell Wright: Shepherd to the Opening of the Ozarks

"This, my story, is a very old story.

"In the hills of life there are two trails. One lies along the higher sunlit fields where those who journey see afar, and the light lingers even when the sun is down; and one leads to the lower ground, where those who travel, as they go, look always over their shoulders with eyes of dread, and gloomy shadows gather long before the day is done.

"This, my story, is the story of a man who took the trail that leads to the lower ground, and of a woman, and how she found her way to the higher sunlit fields.

"In the story, it all happened in the Ozark Mountains, many miles from what we of the city call civilization."

So begins the novel that opened up the Ozarks to the tourist industry. What *Midnight in the Garden of Good and Evil* did for tourism in Savannah, Georgia, in the 1990s, *The Shepherd of the Hills* did for the Ozarks in the first two decades of the 20th century. The book, by minister Harold Bell Wright, was part of the social gospel of the time, spread as much by fiction as by sermons from the pulpit during the Third Great Awakening, a middle-class response to a nation worried about the rising tide of immigration and the theories of Sigmund Freud, Karl Marx, and Charles Darwin.

The inspiring story of the muscular Young Matt, the lovely Sammy Lane, and the wise Old Shepherd, set in the purity of the isolated Ozarks, was not greeted with praise by the critics, but it struck a responsive chord with the book-buying middle class. It still does.

After its publication in 1907, it quickly became a best seller, selling a phenomenal 1.2 million copies. Railroad cars loaded with copies of the book departed daily from Chicago to satisfy the public's reading appetite. Action-packed with vividly drawn characters and a moral that many can still believe in, the novel is quite readable 100 years later. Fueled in part by the popularity of the Ozarks tourism industry, an interest in history and the early Ozarks, and the outdoor drama based on the play, the book still sells enough copies to keep it in print, and it has sold enough copies over the years to make it one of the best sellers of all time.

Wright, who became the John Grisham of his day, studied for the ministry two years at Ohio's Hiram College, but left in 1884 because eye trouble and pneumonia prevented him from working to pay for his tuition. During the next three years, Wright made his way westward, earning his keep by doing farm work and painting landscapes on the sides of delivery wagons. He ended up in the Ozarks, having come by horseback from Marionville, where the railroad ended. Turned back from a flood-swollen White River, he took shelter at the homestead of John and Anna Ross on a ridge above Mutton Hollow. He intended to spend only the night but stayed the summer. He returned to the Ross homestead each summer for the next eight years.

It was in the Ozarks where he first began preaching, initially because the local minister missed a community Thanksgiving dinner. According to Wright in a 1917 account, "A long, lean hillbilly approached me. 'You got an education, mister, why can't you preach to we-uns?'" Wright took the pulpit, delivered a successful message, and began preaching regularly. He was soon offered a pastorate at a Disciples of Christ church in Pierce City, Missouri. Wright preached there from 1897 to 1898, and he had other pastorates in Lebanon and Kansas City, but he was always drawn to the Ozarks and to writing.

It was at the Ross homestead that he met some of the hill folk that would be transformed into the characters of his novel. John and Anna became Old Matt and Aunt Mollie, and their son, Charles, is the acknowledged Young Matt. Several local women later claimed to be the model for Sammy Lane, but it seems that Grace Shear may have been Wright's model. Truman Powell was the prototype for the Old Shepherd. Levi Morrill, a general store operator at Notch, provided the pattern for Uncle Ike. It's easy to see that Wright's characters were deeply rooted in the Ozarks hills and its people. If you stop at the Evergreen Cemetery beside MO 76 near Silver Dollar City today, you can find the final resting spot for many of Wright's models. You can also find the names of the characters from the novel embedded in the names of dozens of businesses and place-names in the area.

Whether they shaped or reflected American values, Wright's best sellers certainly embody the values of his readers, a group who represented a mainstream in the American culture. They still do. Wright pitted the corruption of cities and civilization against the purity of person and environment found on the vanishing American frontier. The Ozarks was isolated enough to be uncorrupted.

The Old Shepherd, who finds strength in the hills and regeneration after leaving Chicago, says at the end of the book that the coming railroad will taint the mountains with city ways. "Many will come and the beautiful hills that have been my strength and peace will become the haunt of restless idlers and a place of revelry." Many people, looking at the phenomenal growth of the Branson area and the live entertainment industry, with its Vegas-style lights on The Strip, would say that the Old Shepherd's prediction came true. But as he preached the purity of the isolated Ozarks, Wright himself was the initial impetus of a string of events that opened up the Ozarks, the others being better roads and the building of the White River dams. The book's popularity caused visitors to come and see firsthand what they had experienced vicariously in the book. Ironically, they came on the newly opened White River railway.

By 1920 the novel's influence in bringing travelers into the region had slowed. Pearl "Sparky" Spurlock helped keep the legend alive with her taxi service from Branson, taking visitors to the former Ross homestead over the rugged Dewey Bald Road, later to become MO 76 and The Strip. Lizzie McDaniel, the daughter of a Springfield banker, bought the homestead in the 1920s and hunted for memorabilia connected to the Ross family and Wright. Dr. Bruce Trimble, a professor at the University of Kansas, and his wife, Mary, and their son Mark acquired the homestead after McDaniel's death. Their outdoor theater on the site that told the story of Wright's novel soon became a major area attraction and one of the largest outdoor theaters in the nation.

A Branson football coach, Gary Snadon, who played the evil Wash Gibbs in the play, bought the Shepherd of the Hills Homestead and Outdoor Theatre from Mark Trimble and his wife, Lea, in 1985. By that time the outdoor drama and the combined attractions in the area were putting such a burden on the section of MO 76 between Branson and Silver Dollar City that Snadon built his own road (see the History chapter).

Wright had resolved that if *The Shepherd of the Hills* was successful, he would give up the ministry. It was his most successful book, and Wright became a full-time novelist. His book was so popular that he even directed a film based on his novel in 1919. The book has been filmed as a movie several other times, once with John Wayne in the early 1940s, his first Technicolor movie. Copies of it are readily available, and it is interesting viewing, but anyone who knows the Ozarks can recognize that it wasn't filmed there!

Wright's novel allowed him to leave the ministry and become a major popular writer in the early decades of the 20th century. Its success brought the first wave of tourists to the isolated Ozarks, and many people still refer to the area as Shepherd of the Hills Country.

Wright died in 1944. Though he could see at that time the effect his novel had on opening the Ozarks to the outside and its influences of the big city, one can only wonder what he would think today were he to travel the old trail as he did a hundred years ago as it leaves the White River Valley and begins its climb into the hills and skirts around Dewey Bald. It was the trail that became MO 76 and The Strip. Would he recognize it?

What hath Wright wrought?

the ponies for $3. Prices for the Trail of Lights are $10 for adults and $5 for children younger than 16. Season passes are $75 for adults and $30 for children 4 to 16, and $70 for seniors. Children younger than four get in free.

- **Hours of operation:** The park is open from the last Saturday in May through October, Monday through Saturday. Jeep-drawn tours run from 10 a.m. to 5 p.m. The ticket office opens at 8 a.m., and the gift shop opens at 9 a.m. The park closes for about 10 days at the end of October and opens back up for the Christmas season through December. During the Christmas season, the park is open seven days a week. The Trail of Lights is open from early November until the first week in January from 6 p.m. until midnight. The Inspiration Tower is open seven days a week year-round and stays open until midnight during the Trail of Lights. During January and February the tower closes at 4 p.m.

MUSEUMS

HOLLYWOOD WAX MUSEUM BRANSON
3030 West 76 Country Blvd.
(417) 337-8277
www.hollywoodwax.com

The facade of the Hollywood Wax Museum is fashioned after Mount Rushmore, except that the larger-than-life faces are of famous movie stars, not presidents. The 115-foot-long, 50-foot-high stone front is adorned with the likes of Marilyn Monroe, Charlie Chaplin, John Wayne, and Elvis Presley. If you happen not to see that, you surely won't miss the marquee of a man and an old-time movie camera perched high on a beam facing the building. The collection of 170 wax figures inside the building is equally impressive. From the 60-foot-tall King Kong in the entry to the Hall of Presidents to the moving display of the Last Supper, the museum is packed with uncanny likenesses of dozens of notable TV, movie, sports, political, and historical figures. There's a Land of Oz display complete with Dorothy, a set from the *Tonight Show* with Johnny Carson, and even a display of Grand Ole Opry

stars. The crypt room houses the Alien, Dracula, Elvira, and a dead ringer for Jason of the *Friday the 13th* movie series. (No pun intended.) You'll find Kate Winslet and Leonardo DiCaprio figures from *Titanic,* and there's even a Mark McGwire figure poised for a home run. You can get your picture taken with Jack Black, Ben Stiller, and other "wax celebrities." The Hollywood Studio Store, located inside the museum, is the area's largest celebrity-merchandise shop. Self-guided tours usually take one hour. The museum is open seven days a week, year-round, from 8 a.m. until midnight. Tickets are $11.95 for adults and $5.95 for children 4 to 11. Kids younger than four get in free.

RALPH FOSTER MUSEUM
College of the Ozarks, Point Lookout
(417) 334-6411, ext. 3407

Known as the Smithsonian of the Ozarks, this museum contains the lifetime collections of radio pioneer and philanthropist Ralph D. Foster, who donated much of the museum's contents to the college. Housed in a former boys dormitory on the campus of College of the Ozarks, the museum takes up three floors and includes objects representing archaeology, history, antiques, numismatics, natural history, fine arts, geology, and mineralogy. A collection of Foster's 1,500 guns fills the second floor and includes a Thompson submachine gun, Pancho Villa's pistols, and a handgun once owned by Hollywood cowpoke Slim Pickens. Natural-history exhibits, mostly taxidermy animals from Africa and North America, line the walls. On the third floor you can see rocks, minerals, and preserved birds and butterflies.

Other exhibits in the museum trace the history of the Ozarks and the more-recent Branson boom. The famous jalopy owned by the Clampett family in the 1960s TV series *The Beverly Hillbillies* can be found on the first floor. The collection of fine art at the museum ranges from Kewpie dolls created by Rose O'Neill to paintings by Thomas Hart Benton, M. E. Oliver, and others. There's also a collection of Native American art (see also the Arts and Culture chapter). Admission to the museum, including tax, is $4.50 for adults and $3.50 for adults 62 and older. Children younger than 18 get in free. The museum is open year-round Monday through Saturday from 9 a.m. to 4:30 p.m., with a few exceptions.

RIPLEY'S BELIEVE IT OR NOT! MUSEUM
3326 76 Country Blvd.
(417) 337-5300, (800) 998-4418, ext. 2
www.ripleysbranson.com

If the first thing you saw when you arrived in Branson was Ripley's Believe It or Not! Museum, you might think the New Madrid fault had finally given way. The building is as much of an attraction as the weird collection inside. There's a crack right down the middle of it, and the marquee lies half-cocked on one side. Huge chunks of missing mortar reveal the wood framing, and the water fountain out front is even split in half. Inside the second floor, the faux-earthquake theme continues with exposed ceiling beams and cracked Sheetrock. Once you finally dare to enter the building, you'll encounter an immense collection of odd artifacts and unusual art based on the findings of Robert Ripley.

Ripley spent 40 years traveling the world, from New Zealand to Tibet, in search of the unbelievable and inexplicable. A self-taught artist, Ripley started his "Believe It or Not" cartoon feature in 1918, and at the height of his popularity the cartoons could be found in more than 300 newspapers with a combined readership of 80 million—a feat Ripley himself would have been amazed to report. In 1933 he opened his first Odditorium at the Chicago World's Fair, and nearly two million people came to view such objects as a shrunken head from Ecuador, a two-headed calf, and photos of the world's tallest man.

Today, people's fascination with incredible facts, strange artifacts, and "impossible feats" continues to thrive. There are 26 Ripley's museums around the world, each with a different list of contents. In Branson you'll find cool collectibles from many local celebrities. Doug Gabriel's first muftar, a musical instrument crafted by his father out of a muffler and guitar parts, is on display, as well as one of Shoji Tabuchi's fiddles. There's even an intact candy bar that survived scorching temperatures in the Mickey Gilley Theatre fire in 1993.

In April 1998 the museum added a gallery with 45 new exhibits, including a replica of an ancient Chinese emperor's dragon ship. It is one of only eight existing hand-carved jade ships in the world. It stands 9 feet tall and 12 feet long and weighs more than 1,800 pounds. The gallery also contains a carving called Universal Celebration that is almost as large as the jade ship. Made out of camel bones, the carving contains intricately detailed pagodas, flying cranes, and bonsai trees. There's also a rice-grain painting of the four Beatles, a Last Supper painting on a coin, a toothpick carving made to look like Dracula, handpainted potato chips, and a purse made out of cigarette wrappers.

Robert Ripley makes an appearance on each self-guided tour in a short holographic presentation from his study. There are plenty of other high-tech interactive displays at the museum, such as the tongue-rolling test. Kids will get a kick out of the giant jelly-bean portrait of Mary Poppins, the figure of Liu Ch'ung (the man who had two pupils in each eye), and the stretch limousine with its heart-shaped hot tub. From time to time Ripley's rotates some of its more popular exhibits among the various locations around the world. One of the most popular exhibits ever to go on tour was the African fertility statue. When it was on display in the Branson museum a few years ago, women who touched it were asked to fill out a card to send back to the company if they found themselves pregnant in the months following the encounter. While the statue was on tour, Ripley's headquarters reported attendance was up 30 percent, and during a 14-month period, 14 women became pregnant after touching the statue. Was it coincidental, or did the statue really have magical powers? Believe it or not!

Plan to spend at least two hours at the museum in order to get the full flavor of the place. There's a unique gift shop to visit at the end of the tour. Tickets are $16.95 plus tax for adults, and children 4 to 12 get in for $8.95. Children younger than four get in free. The museum is open daily from 9 a.m. until 11 p.m. March through December and from 9 a.m. until 7 p.m. January and February.

ROY ROGERS AND DALE EVANS MUSEUM
3950 Green Mountain Dr.
(417) 339-1900
www.royrogers.com
Branson is proud to be the home of the Roy Rogers and Dale Evans Museum, formerly of Victorville, California. Lovers of the old Western show and Sons of the Pioneers music will delight in the memorabilia and interactive exhibits on display at the museum.

Right out front is the larger-than-life Trigger, a reminder of the famous couple who devoted their lives to making young and old happy by keeping the spirit of the American West alive. Housed inside the exhibit walls are memories and treasures of two lifetimes and all the couple loved—a permanent reminder of a simple and innocent time when many Americans dreamed of living the King of Cowboy's exciting adventures. You'll find family photos dating from Roy and Dale's childhood, colorful costumes, parade saddles, memorabilia from the silver screen and the "golden age" of television, artifacts from Roy's real-life safari adventures, fan mail, comic strips, Roy and Dale's Remington gun collection, tributes to his friends and sidekicks, and much, much more.

The museum is open from 9 a.m. to 5:30 p.m. year-round, but it's usually closed on Sunday and in winter months on Monday, so call ahead. Admission is $13 plus tax for adults, $6.50 for children, ages 13-17. The Happy Trails Theater is $27 plus tax for adults. Children 13-17, $13.50, and those younger than 13 get in free. Save $3.50 per person on a combo ticket for both the museum and show.

TITANIC MUSEUM ATTRACTION
3235 MO 76 West
(417) 334-9500, (800) 381-7670
www.titanicbranson.com
Take an emotional journey back in time to the world's most famous sunken ship. New in 2006, the museum houses more than 400 artifacts and historic treasures from the *Titanic*. Walk the grand staircase, see a first-class stateroom, and touch an iceberg. Find out in the museum's memorial room whether or not the passenger named on your boarding ticket survived. Check the Web site for special events and guests during the year.

The museum is open year-round seven days a week from 9 a.m. to 6 p.m. January to March 15; 9 a.m. to 11 p.m. March 16 to December 17; and 10 a.m. to 6 p.m. December 18 to 31. Admission, plus tax, is $18.82 for adults and $9.99 for children 5 to 12. Children younger than five get in free.

VETERANS MEMORIAL MUSEUM
1250 76 Country Blvd.
(417) 336-2300
www.veteransmemorialbranson.com
This museum isn't easily missed. A full-size World War II P-51 Mustang fighter plane that looks like it is about to strafe your car marks the museum's location on The Strip. This attraction offers 18,000 square feet of authentic, thought-provoking exhibits and dramatic art in 10 great halls covering conflicts fought during the 20th century, including World War I, World War II, Korea, Vietnam, Desert Storm, and more. Sculpture, murals, historical artifacts, objets d'art, and thousands of authentic memorabilia honor all branches of the service, major battlefronts, campaigns, industrial defense, and others. More than 500,000 names of the men and women killed in action to defend our freedoms in World War II, Korea, Vietnam, the Persian Gulf, and other recent conflicts of the 20th century are displayed on the walls of the halls. In fact, the WWII Hall is the only place in the world where you will see these names displayed.

Fred Hoppe, internationally renowned bronze sculptor, researched and traveled the world collecting these special exhibits. The world's largest bronze sculpture (70-plus feet long, weighing 15 tons) is a hallmark of the museum and features 50 life-size statues storming a beach. Each life-size statue is modeled after a combat veteran from each state.

The Veterans Memorial Museum is open 8 a.m. to 9 p.m. daily year-round. Hours may vary in January, February, and March. Admission prices are $13.50 plus tax for adults and $4.50 plus tax for children 6 to 12. Veterans get a $1 price reduction.

WORLD'S LARGEST TOY MUSEUM
3609 76 Country Blvd.
(417) 332-1499
www.worldslargesttoymuseum.com
Remembering your childhood has never been so much fun! For kids and adults, this museum is like Christmas morning every day! Rediscover the joy of your favorite toys and reminisce about childhood heroes such as Shirley Temple, Tom Mix, and Groucho Marx. You'll find toys as old as the 1800s and as new as *Star Wars,* as tiny as a thimble and as big as a genuine, full-size Rolls Royce. There are thousands of toys including dolls and doll house furniture, toy cars and trucks, action figures, die cast toys, antique bicycles, die cast cars, a doll museum, an Elvis display, Ertl farm toys, General Lee, John Deere, Johnny Lightning, kaleidoscopes, miniature museum toys, miniatures, tin toys, toy trains, wind-up toys, toy tractors, and cap guns. The toy museum has toys on display dating from the Civil War period to present day. There's a toy gift shop to browse when you finish your tour. Admission: adults, $11.10, children, $8.87.

HISTORIC SITES

BONNIEBROOK HISTORICAL SOCIETY AND KEWPIE MUSEUM
485 Rose O'Neill Rd., Walnut Shade
(417) 561-1509, (800) 539-7437
www.kewpie-museum.com
One of Missouri's most famous residents, Rose O'Neill, was also one of the early 20th century's most remarkable women. By 1914 her illustrations and cartoons in such magazines as *Harper's Monthly, Harper's Bazaar, Good Housekeeping,* and *Twentieth Century Home,* along with her novels and poems, had earned her $1.4 million. She is perhaps best known for her Kewpie drawings and sculptures, which have been collectors' items since the early 1900s. The annual Kewpiesta festival sponsored by the International Rose O'Neill Club is held in Branson each April to commemorate O'Neill's works (see the Annual Events chapter), and the 2009 Kewpiesta was bigger than usual, being the 100th anniversary of the Kewpie doll. O'Neill's reconstructed home, Bonniebrook, just north of Branson, is one of the area's most visited places. The impeccably maintained grounds, gift shop, and nature trails provide a glimpse into the life of this enormously talented and unique individual.

The original home burned to the ground three years after O'Neill died in Springfield in 1944, but thanks to the Bonniebrook Historical Society, Inc., and other collectors around the world, the home has been restored and filled with O'Neill memorabilia, including illustrations, sculptures, and numerous Kewpie pieces. It is listed on the National Register of Historic Places. The top floor of the home was O'Neill's studio, where she spent hours contemplating new creations and even designing her own clothing. She was often seen wearing her own designs when she visited the local movie theater, as she did often. A short distance from O'Neill's home and just across the "bonnie brook" for which the house is named lies the family cemetery where Rose, her siblings Callista and James, and their mother, Meemie, are buried.

Admission to the home tour and museum is $7 per person. Children younger than 12 get in free. The 20-minute home tours are given seven days a week between 9 a.m. and 4 p.m. except from noon to 1 p.m. The museum and grounds are open from 9 a.m. to 4 p.m. Monday through Saturday and closed Sunday and holidays. A 30-minute home tour is also given. The gift shop has copies of O'Neill's illustrations, art, books, poems, and dolls.

Bonniebrook is approximately 9 miles north of Branson just off US 65. Rose O'Neill Road is on the right, just past the bridge at Bear Creek. Once you turn onto Rose O'Neill Road, look for a sign leading you left to the park entrance.

SHEPHERD OF THE HILLS HISTORICAL EVERGREEN CEMETERY
MO 76 West, between Indian Point Road and MO 265

After you've seen *The Shepherd of the Hills* outdoor drama and gotten to know the characters who formed the basis for Harold Bell Wright's wildly famous novel *The Shepherd of the Hills,* you can visit their final resting places at the Shepherd of the Hills Historical Evergreen Cemetery. A small sign just west of Indian Point Road on MO 76 marks the entrance to the cemetery. If you get to the intersection of MO 265, you've gone too far.

You'll see the graves of J. K. and Anna Ross (Uncle Matt and Aunt Mollie), Levi Morrill (Uncle Ike), and his wife, Jennie, and Truman Powell (the Old Shepherd). Morrill donated the land for the cemetery in 1894, and a memorial stone was erected in 1925 in memory of these legendary Ozarkians, whose mark on the area remains alive and well today. In an appropriately tree-shaded portion of the cemetery at the easternmost corner lies a granite stone bearing the names of Mary R. (1899–1983) and Hugo Herschend (1899–1955), founders of Silver Dollar City.

SEE THE SIGHTS

BRANSON SCENIC RAILWAY
206 East Main St.
(417) 334-6110, (800) 2-TRAIN-2
www.bransontrain.com

Take a trip back in time to the days when rail travel was one of the best modes of transportation, in Branson Scenic Railway's restored 1940s dome cars. The 105-minute excursions take you 20 miles from the depot in downtown Branson south to Arkansas or 20 miles north to Galena, depending on the schedule. The glass-bubble-topped cars offer a great view of the rugged countryside, especially during October, the railway's busiest month, when the leaves have turned their fall shades of orange, gold, and red. Along both routes you pass through tunnels, over bridges, and next to meandering streams. You may even see a bobcat, a bald eagle, or a deer along the way.

Up to four trips are offered Monday through Saturday from early April to mid-December. Trips are added on Sunday in October and on select holidays during the year. From April through December, departures are at 9 a.m., 11:30 a.m., and 2 p.m. During the summer a 4:30 p.m. run is added on select dates. During the Saturday-evening excursions, passengers are treated to a full-course dinner with an entree of prime rib, chicken, or fish for $53.75 per person, plus tax. This trip lasts 145 minutes. A concession car offers sandwiches, coffee, and sodas on all other trips for an additional charge. Tickets for the regular trips are $24 for adults and $13.75 for kids 3 through 12, plus tax. Children younger than three ride for free.

OZARK BALLOON PORT
2235 Smyrna Rd., Ozark
(417) 581-7373, (417) 725-3449

Ozark Balloon Port owner Jim Herschend says a ride in a hot-air balloon is a popular gift idea, according to his customers who often come to celebrate anniversaries, birthdays, and other notable occasions high above the Ozark hills. Since the experience is a bit pricier than, say, a trip to Waltzing Waters—it costs $195 per person for a typical flight—you'd better make sure your gift recipient would approve of the idea before plunking down that 50 percent deposit, which is due at the time the reservation is made. For the past two decades Herschend has been taking folks up, up, and over the treetops 2,000 feet in the air in his five hot-air balloons. The visibility factor and wind speed make each ride unique. Herschend says he has a perfect safety record and won't go up if there's any precipitation or too much wind. If it's windy enough to fly a kite, it's too windy to go up in a balloon, he says.

An award-winning pilot himself, Herschend knows all about balloon safety. In 1992 he and a copilot won the oldest hot-air balloon race in Europe to take home the Gordon Bennett Cup. This marked the first time Americans had won the contest in 33 years. In 1994 he was entered in the *National Aeronautic Book* for inflating and flying five hot-air balloons underground in Marvel Cave at Silver Dollar City.

There are about a dozen sites in and around Ozark from which Herschend launches his balloons. Many of the flights take passengers near the banks of the Finley River, where white-tailed deer and beaver are often spotted. Each balloon holds two to four passengers, and children are welcome as long as they are old enough to follow directions, Herschend says. Balloons may be launched seven days a week, 12 months a year, conditions permitting. The typical flight takes about three hours total, with half of the time spent setting up and the other half in the air. The Ozark Balloon Port business office is open Monday through Friday from 9 a.m. to 5 p.m., except for January through April, when the office is closed on Monday, Wednesday, and Friday.

RIDE THE DUCKS
2320 76 Country Blvd.
(417) 334-3825
www.ridetheducks.com

One of the best ways to orient yourself to Branson and Table Rock Lake all in one shot is aboard a Duck. These World War II–era amphibious vehicles, originally called DUKWs by the military, have been modified to accommodate sightseers on an 80-minute land-and-lake adventure. From the time you leave the home base, next to Wal-Mart on The Strip, to the time you splash down in Table Rock, your U.S. Coast Guard–approved captain booms across the loudspeaker, pointing out interesting places and scenery along the way. He'll even throw in a joke or two and some fun facts about the history of Branson you may not hear anywhere else. The Duck route takes passengers along The Strip, down MO 165 past Table Rock Dam and the Shepherd of the Hills Fish Hatchery, and atop Baird Mountain, the area's highest peak, where you can get a magnificent view of Table Rock Lake. The captain will even treat you to a look at the Ducks' own outdoor museum of vintage military vehicles.

From there it's splashdown time. The captain may let you try your hand at the wheel as you cruise by the *Showboat Branson Belle*. If you

make it to the driver's seat, you'll get a nifty-looking honorary captain's license. Each passenger receives a free wacky quacker with each ticket purchase. These yellow plastic duck-lip spit collectors make a rather obnoxious noise when you blow into them, sort of a whiney quack. If you have kids and want any peace at all during the trip home, you may want to pack the quackers in the trunk. There's a Lake Taneycomo and downtown Branson trip available, too. Tickets for both versions are $20 plus tax for adults and $12 for children 3 to 12. Ages two and younger ride for free. Ride the Ducks is open March through December from 9 a.m. to 5 p.m. seven days a week. During the busy summer months, the hours are extended. Tours depart every 15 minutes or so, and reservations are not required.

SHOWBOAT BRANSON BELLE
4800 MO 165 at
White River Landing
(417) 336-7400, (800) 831-4FUN
www.silverdollarcity.com

One of the Silver Dollar City–owned properties, the *Showboat Branson Belle* is a 1990s version of a turn-of-the-20th-century paddle wheeler, sans the rats. At 278 feet long, 78 feet wide, and three stories tall, this 700-passenger vessel is an impressive sight on Table Rock Lake. When it was launched from White River Landing in 1994, bananas were used to grease down the path to the water in keeping with Silver Dollar City's environmentally correct modus operandi. You won't find any alcohol or gambling on this luxury ship, but you will find a live show, meals prepared onboard in the galley, and a breathtaking view of the lake during the day and a star-filled sky at night. Radio personality Paul Harvey was presented the official maritime captain's bell on board the Showboat, making him an honorary captain on one voyage.

The ship moves so slowly (an average of 6 mph) and quietly that once you're inside you hardly notice the movement at all. On deck, however, the cool breeze rising off the lake is the perfect prescription for unwinding at the end of a long day of sightseeing. The ship's interior spans three open stories with balconies on the second and third floors looking down on the stage. Fine draperies partially conceal the view from the dozens of windows overlooking the water. The tables are tastefully adorned with white table-cloths and attended to from the moment you arrive by a most courteous wait staff. Cruises are at noon, 4 p.m., and 8 p.m. They run mid-March to December.

The live entertainment lineup in 2006 includes *Showstoppers!,* celebrating the most memorable musical performances in entertainment history. The 4 and 8 p.m. cruises feature nationally acclaimed comedian Todd Oliver and his talking dogs.

The food aboard the showboat rivals any restaurant in town. The full-course lunch or dinner features a beef or chicken entree, salad, sourdough bread, and a specialty dessert.

After the show and meal have ended, passengers have plenty of time to take a stroll on the upper decks and visit the pilothouse, where the captain welcomes questions about the ship. Lunch is $46–$58 for adults and $23–$29 for children; the Early Escape dinner cruise and the sunset dinner cruises are $54–$66 for adults and $27–$33 for children. All prices are plus tax.

Private dining and menu service are available in the Paddlewheel Room. Boarding begins 30 minutes before departure, and cruises always leave on time, so don't be late. Before or after the cruise you might want to visit the gift shop at White River Landing. You'll find nautical-themed trinkets and other neat collectibles. To get to the *Showboat Branson Belle,* take MO 165 south of Branson. As soon as you cross the Table Rock Dam, look for the entrance sign to the parking lot on your right.

TABLE ROCK HELICOPTERS
3309 76 Country Blvd.
(417) 334-6102
www.tablerockhelicopters.com
Right in the heart of The Strip, across from Ripley's Believe It or Not! Museum, Table Rock Helicopters offers a variety of tours, starting with the basic

5-mile flight to the edge of Table Rock Lake and up to the 50-mile round trip to Eureka Springs, Arkansas. The 5-mile flight gives you about three minutes in the air. Along the way you'll see MO 165, the Welk Resort, Point Royale golf course, and, during the peak season, motorists patiently crawling along in traffic. The 10-mile flight lasts twice as long as the 5-mile flight and takes you on both sides of Table Rock Dam, past the Shepherd of the Hills Fish Hatchery, over Lake Taneycomo, and near Chateau on the Lake. The 15-mile flight takes you to Baird Mountain and out to Indian Point, where you can get a better idea of exactly how many resorts and marinas line the shoreline. This flight lasts approximately eight minutes. The 20-mile tour includes views of Table Rock Dam, downtown Branson, and the 76 strip. The 25-mile tour passes Shepherd of the Hills Homestead, Silver Dollar City, Table Rock Lake, and Lake Taneycomo. The 30-mile flight goes east to Powersite Dam, south of town to Table Rock Dam, and past the Chateau on the Lake. The 50-mile tour takes passengers over the historic town of Eureka Springs and near the Passion Play.

Both of Table Rock Helicopters' birds can seat up to six passengers and are operated by experienced pilots who offer a narration of the scenery on each trip that guests can listen to through headphones. Reservations are not necessary, and prices are the same for adults and children. Children two and younger ride for free on all flights. Table Rock Helicopters opens at 10 a.m. in the spring and fall and closes each day when the crowds begin to thin out. During the summer they are open from 9 a.m. until 9 p.m. No flights December through February.

TALKING ROCKS CAVERN PARK
Talking Rocks Road
(417) 272-3366, (800) 600-CAVE
www.talkingrockscavern.com
Talking Rocks Cavern, considered one of Missouri's most beautiful caves, is just a few miles west of one of the state's most famous caves, Marvel Cave at Silver Dollar City. To get to Talking Rocks, drive west on MO 76 out of Branson. Turn

left onto MO 13 at Branson West. Go 1 mile and turn left onto Talking Rocks Road. Look for the signs leading you to the entrance.

The cave, on a 400-acre natural preserve, is said to have been discovered in 1883 by hunters when they chased a rabbit under a rock. In 1892 Truman Powell, the pioneer immortalized as the Old Shepherd in Harold Bell Wright's novel *The Shepherd of the Hills,* named the cavern Fairy Cave. Waldo Powell, Truman's son, opened the cave and the land surrounding it to the public in 1921. Today we know it as Talking Rocks Cavern and as one of the unique geological sites in the area. The main chamber is 100 feet tall and extends over 600 feet. The wall formations are thick with stalactites and helectites that curl down from the ceiling like a candlemaker's creation. Colorful stalagmites dot the floor of the cave. Be sure to bring along your camera, as you'll want to capture these magnificent crystal creations on film. Although bats do not inhabit Talking Rocks Cavern (be sure to ask your guide why bats do not reside there), it is a sanctuary for the Ozark blind cave salamander. This unique creature is on the rare and endangered species list, so be careful not to touch or otherwise disturb it should it make its presence known.

A well-trained guide leads each 50-minute walking tour. The cavern is open to the public year-round from 9:30 a.m. to 6 p.m. seven days a week from March through November. It is closed Wednesday and Thursday all other times of the year. Before or after a tour of the cave, you can enjoy a picnic or a hike along the nature trails at the Talking Rocks nature park. There's a gift shop and a Wings of the World bird park. Admission to the cave is $16.95 for adults and $8.95 for children 4 through 12. Children three and younger get in free.

If the trek through Talking Rocks Cavern has left you wanting more, and you've got the guts for it, you can explore one of the other caves on the Talking Rocks property. Ask for the Wild Cave Tour into Indian Creek Caverns. There's no electricity in this cave, which means no lights, no concrete paths, and no handrails. This is real spe-

lunking, by George! A pair of experienced cave guides will accompany you on the tour. You'll get a flashlight, a hard hat (you pay to rent), and a real sense of what Truman and the rabbit hunters felt like on their first peeks into Talking Rocks Cavern. Call for prices. The guides are ultra-cautious when it comes to safety. Caves are not nice places to be during or following rain.

SHOWS AND PRESENTATIONS

THE BUTTERFLY PALACE AND RAINFOREST ADVENTURE
MO 76 and Shepherd of the Hills Expressway
(417) 272-8899
www.thebutterflypalace.com
This attraction is designed to place you in an Eden-like setting that could be found in one of the planet's rain forests. An accessible curving ramp leads to one of two theaters where you can view a 3-D film about the life of a butterfly. Your next stop is a 7,000-square-foot greenhouse–butterfly refuge filled with tropical plants, shimmering water, and thousands of colorful, free-flying butterflies. Next, the Emerald Forest provides a rain forest experience. At the final stop you can view rain forest insects, all contained in habitat enclosures. Call for prices and hours.

> **i** In Branson, comfortable walking shoes are a must. Most places are casual—even at the big shows people are seen in shorts and T-shirts.

IMAX ENTERTAINMENT COMPLEX
3562 Shepherd of the Hills Expressway
(417) 335-4832, (800) 419-4832
www.bransonimax.com
For the ultimate moviegoing experience, you should definitely check out the IMAX theater. With a six-story screen that projects an image ten times larger than standard 35 mm theaters, forty-four speakers with a combined total of 22,000 watts of digital surround sound, and a seating arrangement that puts you right in the middle of the action, IMAX is a movie buff's dream. In

1997 the theater added a projector fitted with a special lens that made it possible to show 35 mm feature-length motion pictures. What an idea that was! Since then, IMAX has shown such first-run movies from *Titanic* and *The Fellowship of the Ring* to *The Dark Knight* and *Slumdog Millionaire*. The image area of the 35 mm films fills more than half of the IMAX screen and takes full advantage of the surround-sound system. New feature films arrive every few weeks. Showtimes range from 7 to 9 p.m. depending on the season. Tickets are $9 for adults, $6 for children 2 through 12, and free for children younger than two.

The signature film shown throughout the year exclusively at the Branson IMAX Theater is called *Ozarks Legacy & Legend*. Directed by Academy Award–winning director Keith Merrill and produced for a mere $3 million (cheap by today's titanic movie-making standards), the film tells the story of the fictional McFarlain family (after whom the complex's full-service restaurant is named), who inhabited the Ozarks between 1824 and 1950. They experience the triumphs and tragedies of pioneer life in the Ozarks with a touch of humor and a great deal of faith. The beauty of the untamed Ozarks is captured extremely well in a number of memorable scenes. The camera takes viewers on a ride with the vigilante Bald Knobbers into the depths of an unexplored cave, aboard a flight on the first biplane in the Ozarks, and along for a chase involving a revenuer and a moonshiner. The Civil War battle scenes are meticulously re-created, right down to the last detail. (See the History chapter for more on the Civil War in the Ozarks.) All of this is underscored with original music and numerous realistic sound effects. *Ozarks Legacy & Legend* is presented a number of times each day.

Films are shown on the hour, every hour, beginning at 9 a.m., seven days a week year-round. Ticket prices for the large-format IMAX films are $8.50 for adults and $4.95 for children four through twelve. Children younger than four get in free.

Before or after the show you can pop into McFarlain's Restaurant. They serve up good old-fashioned home-style meals and some of the best pie in town. (See the Restaurants chapter for more information.) The specialty shops at the IMAX complex offer everything from costume jewelry to grandfather clocks. There's even a fudge shop that hands out free samples. (For more on the shops at IMAX, see the Shopping chapter.)

LITTLE OPRY THEATRE

Inside the IMAX complex you'll find live performances in the 210-seat Little Opry Theatre. It's a great venue for those who like to be "up front and personal" with those on stage. You don't need the Hubble telescope to see a performer's eyebrows arch. Shows change, so always check the current schedule at www.bransonimax.com or a local newspaper.

Bluegrass and country music are on the menu with *New's Country*, starring singer-songwriter Leroy New, known as "Branson's Guitar Wizard." Leroy performs bluegrass, country, and gospel in this spectacular show.

Catch "diva fever" with Janice Copeland and two friends who make up the "Branson Divas" to present comedy and songs that run the range from country, Big Band, rock, and gospel.

Crossties Bluegrass and Gospel with Jim Glaspy and his talented family provide traditional and original acoustic bluegrass and three-part harmonies in a show the whole family can enjoy.

Strait Country is a show that's not straight country but has elements of gospel and comedy by George Strait. Past meets present in this combination of great country hits with some of the latest on the country scene.

A Tribute to John Denver and Country Music Legends is a show with songs we all know and love by John Denver, including "Rocky Mountain High" and "Leavin' on a Jet Plane." Join James Garrett as he pays tribute to his long time buddy John Denver and other country music legends.

Showtimes may vary throughout the year, so call for specifics. Tickets are around $23 for adults. Children under 12 get in free.

Sunday mornings at 9 and 11 are free "country church services." *Good New's Gospel Hour* with

Leroy New and Friends is the 9 a.m. service that features the various gospel stylings of Leroy New, Ken Christen, and Jim Glaspy. From time-to-time other Branson stars may even come and drop in to share a song and testimony. *Crossties Country Cathedral* is the perfect late morning (11) Sunday service if you are in the mood for some good "old-timey" bluegrass and gospel. Come as you are and join Jim Glaspy for this non-denominational Christian gathering every Sunday morning worship service.

MOUNT PLEASANT WINERY
3125 Green Mountain Dr.
(417) 336-9463
www.mountpleasant.com
Mount Pleasant Winery was established in 1859 and is in the heart of the Augusta Appellation wine district of Missouri. As the winery celebrates its 150th anniversary, it is pulling out all stops (or stoppers!) for the big event. Mount Pleasant's Branson location is a wineshop, art gallery, and hands-on bottling experience, all rolled into one. In addition to touring the facility and tasting award-winning wines, visitors have the unique opportunity to bottle their own dessert wine from a specially designed 600-gallon French oak barrel. The bottles of wine are the perfect souvenir or gift with a personal touch, and at only $9.99 are a great buy.

Mount Pleasant prides itself as a viticulturally sustainable business and practices and encourages efforts to reuse and recycle. Bring in an empty bottle from any winery and get 10 percent off your take-home purchase. Bring in as many bottles as you'd like, but the discount limit is 10 percent per customer. Mount Pleasant's Branson facility is open Monday through Saturday 8:30 a.m. to dusk and Sundays 10 a.m. to 6 p.m.

STONE HILL WINERY
601 MO 165 at Green Mountain Drive
(417) 334-1897, (888) 926-WINE
www.stonehillwinery.com
Like many of the businesses in Branson, Stone Hill Winery is family owned and operated. Thomas Held, the son of Jim and Betty Held, who bought the original Stone Hill Winery in Hermann in 1965, runs it. At one time the Hermann winery, built in 1847 by settlers from the German Rhineland, was the third-largest winery in the world, until Prohibition shut it down. From 1933 until the Helds bought it, the winery's cellars were used to grow mushrooms. Today the Held family operates three wineries in Hermann, Branson, and New Florence. Cream sherry and two types of spumante are made here in Branson. The 40-minute free tour of the winery includes a tasting session, where adults can sample dry and sweet wines while the kids sip grape juice. There is a short video presentation at the beginning of the tour that tells about the parent winery in Hermann. Along the tour you'll be treated to a winemaking course and a short history of winemaking in Missouri. The tours begin every 15 minutes from 8:30 a.m. until dusk Monday through Saturday year-round. On Sunday tours are given from 11 a.m. to 6 p.m. The gift shop stocks great gift packages that include meats, cheeses, and biscuit mix. You can pick out a bottle of wine, and the staff will package it for you. They'll even throw in a glass or two. The winery is closed on Thanksgiving, Christmas, and New Year's Day.

i Did you know the French wine you drink owes its existence to Missouri? During the 19th century, Missourian Hermann Jaeger discovered that Ozark grape root stocks were immune to the root louse that was devastating French vineyards. An estimated 10 million root stocks were shipped to France for grafting. In 1889 a grateful French government bestowed the Cross of the Legion of Honor on him for "saving the French wine industry." Visit Branson's two winery outlets, *Mount Pleasant* and *Stone Hill,* and raise a glass in appreciation!

WALTZING WATERS THEATRE

3617 76 Country Blvd.
(417) 334-4144, (800) 276-7284
www.waltzingwaterstheatre.com

The folks at Waltzing Waters are so convinced that their attraction is one of the best you'll ever see that they will give you your money back if you disagree. This colorful 40,000-gallon water fountain display synchronized to music is certainly unique, you have to admit. With a ticket price of $6 for adults and children 12 and older, $3 for children 3 to 11, and free for kids 2 and younger, the 42-minute Fountains of Fire show is as good an entertainment value as you'll find. Continuously changing colored lights are aimed at the water fountains, which are manipulated to rise and fall with the rhythm of popular taped music. The term "liquid fireworks" appropriately describes the splashy scene. Fountains of Fire is presented every hour on the hour each day.

SPEND THE DAY OUTDOORS

COLLEGE OF THE OZARKS

Point Lookout
(417) 334-6411, (800) 222-0525
www.cofo.edu

Built on a bluff overlooking Lake Taneycomo, Point Lookout, just 2 miles south of Branson on US 65, is College of the Ozarks, one of the area's more unusual attractions. The campus grounds, with their rose gardens and gently rolling hills, are immaculately maintained by students who work on campus in return for their tuition (see the Education and Child Care chapter for more information about the work program). The buildings include everything from an old-fashioned working gristmill to a neo-Gothic chapel to a modern greenhouse.

Pick up a free map at the Keeter Center at the college entrance and take a self-guided tour of the campus. The Keeter Center is your starting place, and it's a great place for lunch or dinner (www.keetercenter.edu). It is designed to resemble the first building on the campus,

Dobyn's Hall. It also has a gift shop that contains items made by the students, crafts, and other Branson souvenirs. Edwards Mill is an authentic working gristmill powered by a 12-foot waterwheel, which is turned by runoff water from Lake Honor. You can watch as student workers grind whole grains into meal and flour. On the second floor of the mill, students use old-fashioned weaving machines to produce rugs, place mats, and shawls. All of the items produced at the mill are available for sale. The greenhouses at the college contain more than 7,000 plants, including orchids. Clint McDade, one of the school's first students, donated the bulk of the orchid collection. You can purchase orchids and other houseplants at the greenhouse.

The icon for the college is Williams Memorial Chapel, an impressive piece of architecture designed in the neo-Gothic style with an 80-foot vaulted ceiling and magnificent stained-glass windows. The structure was dedicated in 1956 and is one of the area's most popular wedding sites. Ask locals and they'll tell you they've either been to a wedding there or were married there themselves. Attached to the chapel is Hyer Bell Tower, where carillon concerts are played at noon and 6 p.m. Sunday services at the chapel are open to the public every week at 11 a.m.

Students who work in the fruitcake and jelly kitchen produce more than 40,000 cakes a year, which are shipped throughout the country for sale. Visitors can watch as students prepare apple butter and other jellies in the kitchen. And, yes, you can buy any of their products on the spot. Other notable sites on the campus include the Taney County Airport (see the Getting Here, Getting Around chapter), the Lake Honor Fountain, the Star Schoolhouse, Memorial Fieldhouse, and Ralph Foster Museum. The campus even has a working dairy farm where students arrive before their morning classes to tend to the livestock. If you're interested in getting some great photos of the campus, you can pick up one of the college's brochures that lists the best places to shoot.

(Q) Close-up

Getting High in Branson

Missouri leads the nation in the number of meth-lab busts. It's not a statistic we're proud of. Police in Branson take a dim view of locals and tourists who believe in chemical highs, but we have some interesting alternatives. Most folks coming into Branson from the north don't realize they are coming "down" into the Ozark Mountains. Branson, at 779 feet above sea level, is a bit lower than Springfield, at 1,150 feet. The "mountains" are the result of long-term erosion by our meandering rivers (see the History chapter).

There are ways to get high legally while here, and unless you suffer from acrophobia, you can try them: parasailing on Table Rock Lake; taking a ride in a hot-air balloon; getting a bird's-eye view of the area on a helicopter ride; or taking the elevator to the top of Inspiration Tower.

Inspiration Tower at the Shepherd of the Hills Homestead reaches 230 feet into the sky above the Ozark mountains, giving visitors a bird's-eye view of the area. The tower was built in 1989 to celebrate the 100th anniversary of author Harold Bell Wright's first visit to the Ozarks and reputedly sits where Wright first placed his tent and where he first penned the parts of his famous novel, *The Shepherd of the Hills*.

Forty-three cement trucks were required to lay the massive foundation, and the tower is solid enough to withstand constant winds of 172 mph and gusts up to 224 mph. More than 4,000 squares of glass frame the fantastic views.

The circular glassed-in observation deck is reached by a glass elevator that provides a dazzling view of the country as it ascends. In air-conditioned comfort, viewers can look 360 degrees from the top. Telescopes are available for a closer look, but many sites are visible without any aid. Nearby Springfield can be seen, as can the Forsyth water tower and neighboring Arkansas. On a clear day, it's possible to see 90 miles.

Visitors are literally higher than the birds—eagles and buzzards can be seen sailing through the air and riding air currents below. Now that's high! Call (417) 334-4191.

OZARK SHOOTERS SPORTS COMPLEX
759 US 65 North, Walnut Shade
(417) 443-3093
www.ozarkshooters.com

This 45-acre gun-sport attraction 11 miles north of Branson offers everything from basic target ranges to competitive tournaments for the advanced shooter. The complex has sporting clay ranges with everything from bouncing bunnies to snipe to gobbling turkeys to charging crows—10 forms in all. You can bring your own gun or rent a shotgun for around $10 a day. The south ridge sporting-clay course has 10 fields and 21 stations. For around $50 an hour you can enlist the services of an instructor who will teach you how to fire a shotgun. If you're looking to buy a weapon, you can pick one out at the clubhouse, where owner and gun dealer Peggy Siler will set you up.

The complex hosts a number of special events each month year-round, including the Valentine Sweetheart Shoot in February, the Women's Recreational Shooting Association in May, the Quail Unlimited Bass Pro Shoot in October, and many other cash-prize tournaments. The entry fee for most of the competitions ranges from $4 to $50 per person. The cost for trap skeet, ball trap, and wobble trap is $5.50 for 25. Sporting clays are $18.50 for 50 or $30 for 100. Ozark Shooters Sports Complex opens at 9 a.m. seven days a week year-round. In the summertime the complex stays open until 6 p.m., but during the winter it closes at 5.

KIDSTUFF

Plant a seedling of an idea in a child's mind, give him or her the tools to cultivate it, the time to nurture it, and the confidence to weather it, and a child can create a vast garden of dreams and convictions strong enough to withstand the world's most turbulent storm. What starts out as a simple family vacation can grow into a life-changing experience for a child. A trip to a zoo, a stroll through a theme park, or an early-morning horseback ride through the Ozark hills may be all it takes to sow new life in a child's mind. The tri-lakes area is as good a place as there is to set a child's imagination loose in the world. With our balanced mix of high-tech attractions, performance arts, history museums, wildlife centers, and natural playgrounds, children have fertile ground in which to cultivate their ideas.

The listings in this section by no means make a complete list of the interesting or appealing things available for children in the Branson area. We hope that you will consider flipping through the Lakes and Rivers as well as the Recreation and the Outdoors chapters as you begin your quest to find activities for children.

The attractions you'll find at Silver Dollar City combine the best of nature, history, technology, science, and art. The National Children's Festival, held each year during the summer months (see the Annual Events chapter), showcases exhibits by Crayola, Hallmark, the Smithsonian Institute Traveling Exhibition Service, and the National Geographic Society. Even before the Children's Festival began in 1995, Silver Dollar City was a perennial favorite among children. Many other outstanding activities for children are listed in the Attractions chapter. Ride the Ducks, IMAX Entertainment Complex, Ripley's Believe It or Not! Museum, the Hollywood Wax Museum, and the area's caves (including Fantastic Caverns) are hot spots for kids. There are also plenty of free and inexpensive things to do in Branson. With three lakes and a fish hatchery as well as a public playground on nearly every corner, kids have plenty of room to get out and explore the Ozarks. Many of the area music shows now admit children at no charge. Lodging facilities are also stepping up their efforts to attract families by letting children stay for free in a parent's room.

Nearby Springfield offers a number of interesting as well as educational kiddy attractions, including Discovery Center, portions of the Bass Pro Shops, Dickerson Park Zoo, and the Wonders of Wildlife Museum. The Day Trips chapter contains other attractions, such as Wilson's Creek National Battlefield and the Springfield Art Museum, that are popular destinations for school groups.

The list of activities in this chapter runs the gamut from arcades to zoos. You will undoubtedly find some treasures we left out. This listing is meant to serve only as fertile ground for your children's growing imaginations. Who knows what may come of their ideas? Maybe they'll decide to grow up to be country music stars or fishing guides. Or they'll do what a few native Ozarkers did and become both.

SPLASH IT

BUMPER BOATS AMUSEMENT CENTER
1715 76 Country Blvd.
(417) 335-2628

At Bumper Boats Amusement Center, pint-size sea captains can board floating bumper vessels and set sail for nautical adventures on the mighty Atlantic. Okay, it's only a swimming pool, and the surf is none too mighty. Nevertheless, kids get a kick out of banging into each other in maneuverable inner tubes. Drying off after the big sea battle is great fun in the gyro-force orbiter as it whirls you head over heels. If that hasn't brought back memories of lunch, you can bounce around on the trampoline for a while. Bumper Boats Amusement Center is open seven days a week from mid-morning until midnight, April through October.

COOL OFF WATER CHUTE
2115 76 Country Blvd.
(417) 334-1919

This 560-foot water slide is built into the side of one of our famous Ozark mountains. It's got more twists and turns than a snake on hot asphalt. Kids with plenty of energy won't mind the long trek up the staircase to the top of the chute. They can slide 30 minutes for $6 or one hour for $8. The attraction is open daily from 10 a.m. to 10 p.m., Memorial Day through Labor Day. It is the oldest water slide in Branson.

WHITE WATER
3505 76 Country Blvd.
(417) 334-7487, (800) 475-9370
ww.bransonwhitewater.com

One of Branson's premier attractions for summertime kiddy fun is this 12-plus-acre tropical paradise. White Water boasts 14 water attractions, including Kalani Towers, a 6-lane freefall and racing slide. Surfquake Pool is a 500,000-gallon wave pool, great for a little surf action or tubing. Fast-paced rides include Raging River Rapids, an enclosed slide that sends guests racing down a 400-foot plunge, and Tropical Twister, a float trip with rafts large enough for the entire family. Lazy River offers rafters a slower ride down a gently moving river.

A recent attraction is RainTree Island, a 20,000-square-foot island with more than 60 different types of water elements, including aqua shooters, water blasters, splash geysers, a 150-foot-long slide, and a tipping bucket that showers guests with 700 gallons of water. This expansion provides space for an additional 800 guests per day. A park favorite is the Little Squirts' Waterworks area, which is full of colorful mazes of tunnels, slides, waterfalls, nozzles, and pools. The park also has a sand volleyball area, beach-gear shop, and snack bar. Life jackets are free, and certified lifeguards are always on duty.

The park is open May through early September from 10 a.m. to 6 p.m. daily.

Operating hours are extended during June, July, and August. Admission is around $36 for those 12 and older. Children 11 and younger get in for around $30. Kids younger than four are admitted for free. Season passes are available, as well as combination tickets to other Silver Dollar City properties including Silver Dollar City, *Showboat Branson Belle,* Dixie Stampede, and the Radio City Christmas Spectacular. (See the Attractions and The Shows chapters.)

DRIVE IT, PUTT IT, RIDE IT—JUST DON'T BREAK IT

GRAND COUNTRY SQUARE
1917 76 Country Blvd.
(417) 334-3919
www.grandcountry.com

Formerly known as 76 Mall Complex, this recently renovated, 319-room resort features 18-hole public indoor minigolf courses (adults pay $6.00, children younger than 13 are charged $4.50, and children 5 and younger are $1.50), a deluxe video arcade, and music shows. An interactive water-play area called Splash Country is free to motel guests, or $18 per person for those three and older. It contains waterfalls, water slides, water guns, a floating river, and a special area for toddlers. Children younger than 17 stay free with a parent at Grand Country Inn (see the Accommodations chapter).

KIDS KOUNTRY
2435 76 Country Blvd.
(417) 334-1618

Little tykes can step into their favorite fairy tale along the Mother Goose–themed miniature golf course or enter a house-size shoe to look for the Old Lady. Kids can also enjoy jungle gym equipment and electrical rides such as the train, carousel, bumper boats, and kiddy go-karts (the go-karts are only for kids weighing less than 40 pounds). Rides range from $1.50 to $4.50 plus tax a pop. You can also purchase a wristband for $15 that allows unlimited riding all day. Kids Kountry is open all year, except for January, from 10 a.m. to dark daily, weather permitting. The attraction extends its hours to midnight during the busy summer months of June, July, and August. Mom and Dad may want to stay next door at the Cobblestone Inn so they can keep an eye on the little ones. (See the Accommodations chapter for more information.)

PIRATE'S COVE
2901 Green Mountain Dr.
(417) 336-6606

If Tarzan played miniature golf, this is where you would expect to find him. He'd feel right at home amid the tropical plants, palm trees, rock waterfalls, and mountain caves. Golfers have two 18-hole courses to choose from: Blackbeard's Challenge Course, for the experienced golfer, and Captain's Course, with its gradual slopes and numerous props. You can play daily from 9 a.m. until 11:30 p.m., weather permitting. The indoor Fun Center is packed with video machines and games. If you're really into the jungle theme, you can spend the night across the street in the Safari suite at the Settle Inn Resort and Conference Center (see the Accommodations chapter).

i Looking to save a buck? Area publications such as *TravelHost's Happy Camper, Best Read Guide,* and *Sunny Day Guide* offer coupons for area restaurants and shows. Look for them in the entryways of restaurants, retail shops, and hotels.

THE TRACK RECREATION CENTER
www.bransontracks.com
No. 1, 2505 76 Country Blvd.
(417) 334-1611

No. 2, 3345 76 Country Blvd.
(417) 334-1617

No. 3, 3525 76 Country Blvd.
(417) 334-1619

No. 4, 1116 76 Country Blvd.
(417) 334-1613

No. 5, 1655 76 Country Blvd.
(417) 334-1610

One of the great debates among insiders is which one of the Track's go-kart tracks is the best. If you've got little speed demons in your family, let them be the judge. Each of the Track's five locations has a different list of amenities. Number one has miniature golf, bumper boats, and an arcade room. Number two also has a miniature golf course, complete with statues of lurking alligators. Racers must be at least 54 inches tall, otherwise they'll have to stick to the bumper boats and golf. A few of the Track locations stay open year-round, but most of them close in January and February. During the summer, they are open seven days a week from 9 a.m. until 10 p.m. Days and hours vary other times of the year. Prices vary for each activity, but a great value is the Go Card. Guests purchase a set number of points that apply to any activity at any location, and cards can be refilled for half the price of the walk-up rate. The Go Card also comes with discounts at other area attractions, so it could add up to big savings for families!

PICK IT, SING IT, SADDLE IT, STAY OVERNIGHT

BOYS AND GIRLS CLUB OF THE OZARKS
1460 Bee Creek Rd.
(417) 336-2420
www.bgcozarks.org

Kids visiting the Branson area for a day, a week, or a month can find great fun at the Shirley M. Schaefer Boys and Girls Clubs in Branson, Forsyth, and Reeds Spring. This nonprofit organization offers a supervised gathering place for kids to enjoy computers, basketball, racquetball, swimming, fitness equipment, games, crafts, and a library. The Branson facility can accommodate 250 children a day, but it is often packed in the summer. Call ahead for availability before dropping off your child. During the school year, the facility is open from 3 to 7 p.m., and during the summer it is open from 7 a.m. to 7 p.m. The annual membership fee is $10 for children 6 through 18. (For more information on this organization, see the Education and Child Care chapter.)

KAMP KANAKUK AND KANAKOMO
1353 Lakeshore Dr.
(417) 266-3000
www.kanakuk.com

One of the most popular attractions for kids in the Branson area is Kamp Kanakuk and Kanakomo. Kids have been spending their summers at these camps since the 1920s. Known for their Christian ideals and emphasis on physical activity, these camps offer 7-, 14-, and 26-day terms May through August. Kids enjoy camping, boating, archery, climbing, basketball, and other sports. Parents of kids 7 to 18 must make reservations months in advance. The cost varies according to length of stay and the type of camp the child plans to attend.

PERSIMMON HILL FARM
367 Persimmon Hill Lane, Lampe
(417) 779-5443, (800) 333-4159
www.persimmonhill.com

Too many hours at the video arcade can turn your children into techno-zombies. Treat them to some fresh Ozark Mountain fruit at Persimmon Hill Farm. They'll experience the taste of blueberries, blackberries, raspberries, and gooseberries right off the vine. You pay for what you pick. The farm also grows shiitake mushrooms, and employees make jams, jellies, and barbecue sauces while you watch. Their Blueberry Barbecue Sauce took first place in the American Royal International Barbecue Contest in Kansas City in 1994,

and their other products have received numerous awards each year since. You can have a gift pack sent to grandma filled with a variety of their top-selling products, including Thunder Muffins made with ripe blueberries that were picked just hours before. Call ahead to find out what's ripe for the pickin', and be sure to wear a hat on a hot summer's day and plenty of sunblock if you plan to stay awhile. The farm is open from May through December. The hours vary according to the season. To get there from Branson, take US 65 south to MO 86. Turn right on MO 86 and follow it to Lake Road 86-63. Go 1.5 miles, and the farm is on the left.

i The Dixie Stampede houses its show horses in outdoor pens from 10 a.m. until showtime. There's no charge to come by and look.

SALOON PHOTOS
2817 West 76 Country Blvd.
(417) 334-4928

If you're into the outlaw look, this is the place to go. Be sure to hold back on that smile if you want your photo to look authentic. Prices start at $14.95 for one person and $2.00 for each additional person you want in the shot. They are open March through November seven days a week at 10 a.m. Closing hours vary.

SKATEWORLD
100 Truman Dr.
(417) 334-1630
www.skatebranson.com

Want to become an Olympic ice skater someday? You can get started on four wheels at Skateworld. Little hopefuls can get in plenty of practice for around $5. The center has both in-line and speed skates. If you've got a special event coming up such as a birthday or graduation, call for rates on private parties. Skateworld is just west of Dixie Stampede. It's open daily year-round from 7 to 10 p.m. Ask about private skating lessons.

UNCLE IKE'S TRAIL RIDE
MO 76 West, Notch
(417) 338-8449
www.uncleikestrailride.com
The days of Tonto and Silver may have long passed, but kids of all ages can still enjoy a good game of Cowboys and Indians at Uncle Ike's Trail Ride, just a half mile west of Silver Dollar City in the community of Notch. Ike has 40 horses available for the 2.5-mile rides, which last about 45 minutes each. Rides depart from 9 a.m. to 4 p.m. daily Memorial Day weekend through Labor Day. Children younger than 6 must ride with a small adult (less than 150 pounds). Each ride costs $25 per horse. Breakfast rides are available for groups at $45 per horse. You get a hearty breakfast of eggs, hash browns, biscuits, and gravy. Dinner rides are $47.50 per horse. The menu includes a pulled pork plate with two side dishes, lemonade, and coffee. All meal rides require reservations. An experienced guide accompanies each tour.

LEARN IT

BRANSON GHOST AND HAUNT TOUR
By Reservation: (417) 423-7812
www.bransonghosttours.com
Learn about the history of Branson in a hair-raising 90-minute walk with a guide who takes you on a search along the shadowy streets of the historic downtown area of Branson to hear stories of the strange and unexplained. Hear about the Jake Fleagle, a bank robber, who was captured and shot in a sting operation at the Branson train depot and how he still haunts it to this day. You'll visit Branson Cemetery hear tales of Branson's founding fathers. It's not hokey, and it's not scary—no lanterns or costumes or folks jumping out of bushes to scare you. It's great exercise for parents and a way to work off children's excess!

COLLEGE OF THE OZARKS POINT LOOKOUT
(417) 334-6411, (800) 222-0525

EDWARDS MILL
(417) 334-6411, ext. 3355

RALPH FOSTER MUSEUM
(417) 334-6411, ext. 3407
Two attractions on the campus of College of the Ozarks might be of interest to school-aged children: the Ralph Foster Museum and Edwards Mill. The mill is an old-fashioned, water-powered gristmill, where college students grind flour and cornmeal while you watch. You can buy a bag to take home with you. On the second floor of the mill, students use weaving looms to make table-cloths and place mats. The Ralph Foster Museum houses three floors of antique trinkets and gadgets, including exhibits on nature and Ozarks history. (For more information on the museum, see the Attractions chapter.) Both attractions are open Monday through Saturday. Admission is free for children younger than 18.

DEWEY SHORT VISITORS CENTER
MO 165
(417) 334-4101
A trip to the Ozarks wouldn't be complete without a good dose of education about the area and its wildlife. The U.S. Army Corps of Engineers operates the Dewey Short Visitors Center just for that reason. Kids can look at the wildlife exhibits, learn about native flora along the nature trail, take in a film or lecture, pick up a book in the bookstore, and visit nearby Table Rock Dam and Powerhouse. There is no charge to the visitor center. The center is open seven days a week April through October from 9 a.m. to 5 p.m. Both the dam and visitor center are open on Saturday and Sunday November through March. (For more information on the visitor center, see the Recreation and the Outdoors chapter.)

SHEPHERD OF THE HILLS FISH HATCHERY
483 Hatchery Rd.
(417) 334-4865
http://mdc.mo.gov/areas/hatchery/shepherd/
If your kids spent all their money on video games at the Track (see earlier listing), they'll surely hit you up for more change to buy fish food at the Shepherd of the Hills Fish Hatchery. It's a real thrill to throw a handful of pellets into a tank filled with growing trout. They devour it so fast and

furiously, it's almost comical. Try not to be disappointed if you show up about the time a school-bus load of kids pulls out—the fish may not be hungry anymore. In addition to the huge open-air holding tanks, the hatchery has educational exhibits, multimedia presentations, literature, and nature trails. If you're here in February, take in the hatchery's "Vulture Venture," a program about the black vultures and turkey vultures that winter over in the hatchery area. You can always find a helpful conservation agent on hand to answer questions about fish and the vultures. (For more information on the hatchery, see the Recreation and the Outdoors chapter.) Admission is free to the hatchery, which is just off MO 165, 6 miles south of Branson.

TITANIC MUSEUM ATTRACTION
3235 West MO 76
(417) 334-9500, (800) 381-7670
www.titanicbranson.com

Kids of any age will enjoy touching an iceberg and unlocking the secrets of the world's most famous sunken ship. This new museum includes interactive experiences and opportunities to follow the personal stories of the *Titanic*'s passengers. The museum is open year-round, seven days a week. Admission is $18.82 plus tax for adults, $9.99 for children 5 to 12. Children four and younger get in free. Check the Web site for all of the special events and shows at this museum. (Also see the Attractions chapter.)

DAY TRIP IT

The listings in this section, although not in Branson, are well worth the trip if you can afford the time. We have focused primarily on the aspects of these attractions that appeal to children. You can find a more complete write-up of each one in the Day Trips chapter.

Springfield Area
BASS PRO SHOPS
1915 South Campbell Ave., Springfield
(417) 887-7334
www.basspro.com

You probably never saw as much wildlife in your entire life as you can see in one hour at Bass Pro Shops. To say the place is as much a museum as it is a retail store is an understatement. You'll get a concentrated dose of taxidermy at Bass Pro. They've got grizzly bears, moose, bobcats, caribou, birds, fish, and many large predatory animals on display among the wares for those addicted to about any sport you can name. And there are live animals, too. You can see plenty for free at Bass Pro, including the 64,000-gallon freshwater aquarium. Kids can watch as divers feed the inhabitants by hand. There is also a 30,000-gallon saltwater aquarium filled with lobster, moray eels, and sharks. Experts offer free seminars from time to time in the 250-seat auditorium. Topics include everything from bass to water safety, so there's more than just sports shopping here. Throughout the facility plaques encourage patrons to respect the environment and preserve wildlife. You can learn more about Ozark wildlife and the Ozarks right next door at the Wonders of Wildlife Museum.

DICKERSON PARK ZOO
3043 North Fort Ave., Springfield
(417) 864-1800
www.dickersonparkzoo.org

This 40-acre zoo includes a wide range of exhibits, including gazelles, European white storks, East African crowned cranes, ostriches, giraffes, lions, cheetahs, and Asian elephants, to name just a few. Throughout the year the zoo offers a number of special events. April's Teddy Bear Rally offers free admission to anyone carrying a teddy bear. In May there's Reptile Mania, with educational activities throughout the zoo addressing the fear and fascination people have with reptiles. On Grandparents Day in September children get a 75-cent discount when accompanied by their grandparents. On October 31 of each year, the zoo throws a Halloween party for children.

If you plan your vacation well in advance, you might want to call ahead to find out what special events may be coming up at the zoo. Admission is free for children 2 and younger and $5 for ages 3 to 12. Adults are admitted for

$7. Adults 65 and older get in for $5. The zoo is open from 9 a.m. to 5 p.m. daily, April through September, and from 10 a.m. to 4 p.m. daily, October through March, except during inclement weather and on major holidays.

DISCOVERY CENTER OF SPRINGFIELD
438 East St. Louis St., Springfield
(417) 862-9910
www.discoverycenter.org
Inquiring minds will get plenty of neuron stimuli at Springfield's Discovery Center, a museum with dozens of interactive displays and exhibits on topics from archaeology to TV technology. Plan to make a day out of this one. School-aged children as well as preschoolers find plenty to do at this state-of-the-art facility. You can even rent the entire facility for birthday parties and special events. Admission is $7 for adults, $6 for adults older than 60, and $5 for children 3 through 12. Children two and younger get in free. The museum is open from 9 a.m. to 5 p.m. Tuesday through Thursday; from 10 a.m. to 5 p.m. Saturday; and from 1 p.m. to 5 p.m. Sunday. Closed on Monday.

EXOTIC ANIMAL PARADISE
124 Jungle Dr., Strafford
(417) 859-5300
www.goanimalparadise.com
You won't spot any singing purple dinosaurs at Exotic Animal Paradise, but you will see plenty of exotic animals as you drive through this 40-acre park. They've got ostriches, longhorns, big cats, birds, monkeys, and more varieties of deer than you can count. These animals really love automobiles and think nothing of planting big slobbery kisses on your windshield. Kids can stretch their legs in the petting zoo, where they'll find goats, geese, ducks, and llamas among other creatures. Admission prices are $11.95 for children 4 through 12 and for seniors and $15.95 for adults. To get there from Springfield, go east on I-44. Look for the signs 3 miles east of Strafford.

WONDERS OF WILDLIFE MUSEUM
500 West Sunshine St., Springfield
(417) 890-9453, (877) 245-9453
www.wondersofwildlife.org
Next door to Bass Pro, and officially named the American National Fish and Wildlife Museum, Wonders of Wildlife is an exciting, educational experience on the past, present, and future benefits of wildlife conservation. The 92,000-square-foot museum has 160 species of live animals in realistic habitats. Children can test their strength against that of a bald eagle; come face-to-face with river otters, bobcats, and beavers; walk through the digestive system of a 32-foot largemouth bass (now that's a lunker!); and hook their own blue marlin on an interactive video simulator. They can enter a replica of an Ozarks cave (complete with bats), see real wild turkeys that roam the lower level of the museum, walk a swinging rope bridge, and marvel at the 19-foot waterfall flowing in the 140,000-gallon community pond. You can see lots of the same things in the real outdoors of the Ozarks, but it might take lots longer. The WOW Museum is currently closed for renovations and expansion, so be certain to call to see if it has opened before making the trip to Springfield.

Eureka Springs, Arkansas
TURPENTINE CREEK
239 Turpentine Creek Lane
Eureka Springs, AR
(479) 253-5841
www.turpentinecreek.org
Turpentine Creek exotic wildlife refuge is a little out of the way but well worth the drive. With 450 acres inhabited by lions, tigers, cougars, leopards, bears, monkeys, exotic birds, and other wildlife, Turpentine Creek is a haven for previously neglected or unwanted animals. The facility is USDA licensed, and donations and guest admission fees ($15 for adults and $10 for kids 2 through 12 and senior citizens 65 and older) support it. Guides offer up-close and personal information on each resident creature. The facili-

ties allow you to get about as close as you dare to these animals. On one recent trip we even got to pet a litter of tiger cubs in the petting zoo. Turpentine Creek is 7 miles south of Eureka Springs on AR 23. Follow the signs out of town. The refuge is open to guests March through December from 9 a.m. until dusk.

EAT IT

PLAYTIME PIZZA
3101 Gretna Rd.
(417) 332-1112
When it's time for dinner and the kids are bored, head for Playtime Pizza and step into the race car garage of driver Pete Za. The "garage" is a go-kart race track with two levels of arcades where kids can play Skee-Ball, air hockey, driving games—you name it. The tons of pizza, pasta, desserts, and other foods will delight the kids, too. (See also the Restaurants chapter.)

BUY IT

Since Branson is fast becoming known as one of the top shopping destinations in the country, kids can find a number of places to plunk down their savings on everything from comic books to school clothes. The three outlet malls offer a variety of clothing stores for kids and carry name brands such as OshKosh B'Gosh, Eagle's Eye, Healthtex, and P.S. Originals. See the Shopping chapter for information on the Tanger Outlet Center, (417) 337-9328, the Red Roof Mall, (417) 335-6686, and Branson Meadows, (417) 339-2580.

Specialty stores abound in Branson, and we think your little shopper will have a blast at the Disney Store (417-335-5307) in the Tanger Outlet Center, where they carry loads and loads of movie, music, and mouse memorabilia. Show your kids what a real old-fashioned dime store is like at Dick's 5 & 10, (417) 334-2410, 103 West Main St. in downtown Branson, where plastic knickknacks, candy, and other treasures line the shelves. Kids on a budget looking for souvenir T-shirts are in luck in Branson. We've seen prices as low as three shirts for $5 at some stores.

Just down the hill from the five-and-dime, The Branson Landing sprawls along the banks of Lake Taneycomo. Shoppers can start at Branson's branch of Bass Pro on the south end and work their way along the brick-lined avenue of exclusive and up-scale stores to Belk on the north end. Fancy the fashions at nationally-known venues like Lane Bryant, White House Black Market, and Coldwater Creek. Pick your favorite flavors at Marble Slab Creamery, enjoy a pint at O'Shay's Irish Pub, or sink your teeth into a steak at Texas Cattle Company. Parents love the break from shopping for kids at the central playground, and kids will love the opportunity to add to their collection of stuffed animals with one they create at Build A Bear. Tired toes can hop aboard the free trolley that cruises the Landing, or you can park your pockets on a bench and enjoy the complimentary fountain and fireworks show each hour. Evening is a terrific time to stroll the boardwalk and enjoy the play of lights on water before having a bite on one of the many patios that restaraunts offer overlooking the lake.

OUTDOOR FUN

With three lakes, dozens of marinas, public swimming beaches, and plenty of on-call fishing guides, the Branson area gives kids lots of opportunities to enjoy the great outdoors. Moonshine Beach, just off MO 165 near Table Rock Dam, with its picnic area and playground equipment, is a favorite among local kids. For a list of swimming beaches on Table Rock Lake, see the Campgrounds and RV Parks chapter. If you want to learn how to Jet Ski, scuba dive, or parasail, try State Park Marina, (417) 334-2628, on MO 165 just south of Moonshine Beach, or Indian Point Marina on Indian Point Road, (417) 338-2891, for rental equipment. These places can even hook you up with fishing guides who enjoy working with kids. See the Lakes and Rivers chapter for more information on guides and marinas.

Is an Ozark shower raining on your parade? Never fear, the Butterfly Palace is here! Enjoy outdoor nature in the great indoors of the Butterfly Palace and Rainforest Museum. Children and adults alike will marvel at the winged wonders in flight within the domed tropical habitat. Newly-emerged beauties are released daily—and cocoon-keepers often let kids assist! Indoor adventurers can also see a 3-D movie all about bugs, get lost in the mirror maze, and investigate the insect zoo. Explore the extraordinary! 4106 West MO 76, (417) 332-2231.

TOTALLY FREE

Kids can enjoy a variety of free things to do right in the city limits of Branson. We have a number of public parks with playground equipment, basketball courts, tennis courts, picnic tables, fishing docks, and softball fields. Two of our favorite public playgrounds are located at Stockstill Park on James F. Epps Road, just north of Roark Valley Road, and at Alexander Park, east of the US 65 bridge on the Taneycomo lakefront. (For more information on these parks and others, see the Recreation and the Outdoors chapter.) If you're heading down to the lakefront, take along some dried bread or crackers to feed the geese that meander up and down the shoreline. Be sure to bring along a camera so you can capture any Kodak moments that may arise.

MUSIC SHOWS

Never before have kids had a better selection of live entertainment in Branson. Many of the theaters now routinely feature children in their shows and offer lower ticket prices or free tickets to children. Jim Stafford features his young son, Schaefer, who is already wowing crowds on the drums, piano, and fiddle, and daughter G. G., who will wow the grade-school set. The *Country Tonite* cast has a number of child performers who do everything from sing to dance to perform rope tricks. A number of pint-size performers steal the show in the Hughes Brothers show at the Hughes Brothers Theatre. The brothers put their wives and children to work in the show, and the cast is increasing in size all the time. One show made up entirely of kids is the *Starlite Kids Review* show at the Starlite Theatre. These talented singers and dancers, between the ages of 5 and 17, come from throughout the United States. The cast is constantly rotated, so new performers get a chance to be on stage in Branson.

Some of the most popular shows for kids are the *Kirby VanBurch Show, the Acrobats of China,* and *Waltzing Waters.* Illusionist Kirby VanBurch is known for using exotic animals in his show, and the Chinese acrobats perform absolutely amazing physical feats. The *Waltzing Waters* show is a spectacular presentation of 40,000 gallons of choreographed vertical water streams that are colorfully lighted and synchronized to live piano music.

KID-FRIENDLY ACCOMMODATIONS & RESTAURANTS

Many of the lodging facilities in the Branson area allow children younger than 18 to stay in a room with a parent for no additional charge. These include Cascades Inn, 3226 Shepherd of the Hills Expressway, (417) 335-8424, (800) 588-8424; Barrington Hotel, 263 Shepherd of the Hills Expressway, (417) 334-8866, (800) 760-8866; and the Savannah Hotel, 165 Expressway Lane, (417) 336-3132, (800) 383-3132. A number of restaurants also offer kids' menus with meals starting as low as $1.99. See the Accommodations and Restaurants chapters for more information.

ANNUAL EVENTS

It seems like every little community in the Ozarks has an annual event designed to celebrate something or another, more an excuse to have a get-together and renew acquaintances, make new ones, and blow off a bit of steam than anything else. These celebrations are as Ozarkian as pie suppers, Saturday-night fish fries, and gospel sings. Whether it's Gainesville's Hootin' N Hollerin', Houston's Emmett Kelly Clown Festival, or Nixa's Sucker Day (not the kind that's born every minute, but an ugly but good-eatin' fish found in local streams), the affairs have contests, races, food, drawings, exhibits, and other events that are interesting and fun for locals and visitors alike. Perhaps it's even more fun for the outsider, who can see the events with a fresh perspective.

Whatever we celebrated, major holidays like Christmas and Veterans Day or just the simple things like apple harvests or dogwood blossoms, we usually did it just for ourselves and our communities. With the advent of tourism as a major industry, we've opened ourselves up and accepted those who want to join us. And recognizing that there might be a buck to be made at the same time while having our fun, we've actually begun to market some of the events. Some are even designed to attract outsiders of a certain type, like Eureka Springs's Corvette Weekend or the UFO Convention there. It's a great way to meet folks (perhaps even some aliens!) who have similar interests.

We've put together a collection of the big and the small (and the bizarre) of our area's annual traditions. Use our list as a guide, keeping in mind that often the best experience of being a tourist and sightseer is taking the road less traveled. Doing so can result in a serendipitous experience of making a new friend or finding that just-right antique or perfect crafts product that would never have happened if you had stuck to the main roads.

If you're planning a trip to Branson, check out our list in this chapter for sources that can help you in your travel plans. Or check the Web address we give for an annual event; you may find some events we didn't mention that will tickle your own special interest. Our own Branson/Lakes Area Chamber of Commerce, (417) 334-4136, is a great source for information about the area's annual events.

Some of the towns that host annual events are listed in the Day Trips chapter, but not all. So pack a good Missouri road map, because some of these small burgs won't be on your interstate highway map, but they'll all be within easy driving distance of Branson.

If the event is always a specific weekend or date, we've mentioned that fact, and we've arranged them in approximate chronological order. It's best to call ahead for costs, if any, and the exact dates.

JANUARY

HOT WINTER FUN
Branson
(417) 334-4136, (800) 214-3661
www.explorebranson.com

January through March is the off-season in Branson, and many theater, restaurant, and shop owners take a rest to remodel, do some deep cleaning, or just relax and go on vacation themselves. However, we've found that some people like to visit Branson at that time, and there are entertainers who have decided that Branson needs a bit of hot winter fun to liven up the scene. Bargain-hunting travelers will appreciate the reduced rates at hotels and restaurants during this off-season. If you call the Branson/Lakes Area Chamber of Commerce, you can get a list of year-round entertainers and businesses, but don't expect to find the full-scale activity that you'd find the rest of the year.

FEBRUARY

THE CHOCOLATEFEST
Eureka Springs, AR
(479) 253-2001
www.eurekasprings.org
Spend a weekend in Chocolate Heaven! Chocolate tasting, chocolate treat demonstrations, even a chocolate buffet! (To get in the mood, you may want to rent the movie *Chocolat* before attending!)

SPRING FISHING CLASSIC
1935 South Campbell Ave., Springfield
(417) 887-1915 or www.basspro.com
Near the end of February or early March, when thoughts lightly turn to fishing, Bass Pro Shops Outdoor World hosts this free show to provide everything you always wanted to know (or see) about fishing. You'll find all the latest gear and boats. There are professionals to offer tips and sign autographs, as well as plug their latest lures and books. There are even special programs for the kids to lure them into becoming addicted anglers.

MARCH

ANNUAL "GONE WITH THE WIND" KITE FESTIVAL
Eureka Springs, AR
(479) 253-6596
www.eurekasprings.org
Go fly a kite in Eureka Springs! Enjoy the first breezes of spring with a colorful and relaxing day of kite flying. Be a kid again or teach your own kids how to fly a kite. See the unique, the tiny, the

great, the colorful, and the unexpected take to the air during this day of fun and frolic.

EUREKA SPRINGS ANNUAL ANTIQUE SHOW AND SALE
Inn of the Ozarks Convention Center
US 62 West and Historic Loop
Eureka Springs, AR
(479) 253-7551, (866) 566-9387
www.eurekasprings.org
During the third weekend in March (and again the third weekend in November), vendors from more than 10 states converge at the convention center at the Inn of the Ozarks with a full range of quality antiques, from small items (buttonhooks, coin purses, postcards, and snuffboxes) to furniture. It's a great place to perhaps find the bargain of a lifetime.

BEER CAN COLLECTORS FESTIVAL
Eureka Springs, AR
(479) 756-6756
www.eurekasprings.org
Would you believe that some of them are empty? The Progress Chapter of Oklahoma and the Ar-Can-Sas Brewery Collectibles Club have a collector festival in the Arkansas town, and they always seem to meet close to St. Patrick's Day. Both organizations are chapters of Beer Can Collectors of America (www.bcca.com). All collectors of beer cans and breweriana are welcome, as are the simply curious. Call for admission prices.

ST. PATRICK'S DAY PARADE
Eureka Springs, AR
(479) 253-8737
www.eurekasprings.org

The Branson/Lakes Area Chamber of Commerce publishes Slip Away, a colorful magazine about Branson and events in the area. Stop by the chamber office to pick up a copy plus other area information. Call (417) 334-4136 or (800) 214-3661 and have a copy sent to you before your trip, or check www.explorebranson.com.

Bring a float! March in the parade! Win a prize! Or just enjoy the fun, and frolic on the streets of Eureka. It's a nice time to enjoy the wearin' o' the green and do some early season shopping and dining in America's Victorian Village.

WHITE BASS ROUND-UP
Upper end of Bull Shoals, Forsyth
(417) 546-2741
www.forsythmissouri.net
When the white bass are running (March through early May, depending on the weather, water temperature, phase of the moon, and your luck), there is a fishing frenzy on Bull Shoals Lake and its tributaries, such as Swan Creek and Beaver Creek. If you don't catch a mess, you can always come back in May for the Forsyth White Bass Fish Fry and have them already fixed.

APRIL

EASTER EGG HUNT
Shell Knob
(417) 858-3300
www.shellknob.com
If you're in the Ozarks at Easter, you may want to drive around Table Rock Lake to Shell Knob and let the kids hunt for eggs at the old CCC Camp in the Mark Twain National Forest. It's good free fun!

FORSYTH ART GUILD SPRING CHINA SHOW
Forsyth Art Guild building, Forsyth
(417) 546-5439
www.forsythmissouri.net
For about as many years as we can remember, local porcelain and china painters have show-cased their work at the Forsyth Art Guild building on US 160 from mid-April to mid-May. It's the perfect place to get a Mother's Day present.

THE GREAT PASSION PLAY
Eureka Springs, AR
(479) 253-9200, (800) 882-7529
This outdoor drama is, for many, the highlight of their trip to the Ozarks. See the Day Trips chapter for specifics.

Resources

We put together a list of names and phone numbers to help you plan your Branson visit.

Branson/Lakes Area Chamber of Commerce
269 MO 248 West at US 65 North
(417) 334-4136, (800) 214-3661
P.O. Box 1897
Branson, MO 65615
www.explorebranson.com

Table Rock Lake/Kimberling City Area Chamber of Commerce
MO 13 North at MO 00
(417) 739-2564, (800) 595-0393
P.O. Box 495
Kimberling City, MO 85686
www.tablerocklake.com/chamber

Springfield Convention & Visitors Bureau Tourist Information Center
(417) 881-5300, (800) 678-8767
3315 East Battlefield Rd.
Springfield, MO 65804
www.springfieldmo.org

Missouri Division of Tourism
(573) 751-4133
P.O. Box 1055
Jefferson City, MO 65102
www.missouritourism.org
For a free travel-planning kit,
call (800) 877-1234.

Arkansas Department of Tourism
(800) NATURAL
1 Capitol Mall
Little Rock, AR 72201
www.arkansas.com

KEWPIESTA
Branson
(417) 334-1548, (888) 322-2786
www.explorebranson.com
The International Rose O'Neill Club preserves the

memory and work of one of Branson's best known and most influential artists, and for 2009, the 100th birthday of the Kewpie doll, the town pulled out all the stops for the celebration. The rebuilt home of Rose O'Neill at Bonniebrook, north of Branson, becomes a mecca for Kewpie collectors and Rose scholars from around the world, and the entire town commemorates our own Wild Irish Rose.

OZARK MOUNTAIN COUNTRY DOGWOOD TRAIL
Forsyth
(417) 546-2741
www.forsythmissouri.net
This is a bloomin' good experience! Take a self-guided tour on back roads and through small towns into the Mark Twain National Forest to find the dogwoods. Blossom time can vary a week or so from year to year, but mid-April is the usual time to take a peek at the peak-season whites of the woods. You can pick up a map at the Forsyth Chamber of Commerce at 16075 US 160 or call the number above.

OZARK UFO CONVENTION
Inn of the Ozarks Convention Center
US 62 West and Historic Loop
Eureka Springs, AR
(479) 354-2558
www.eurekasprings.org
Calling all aliens and saucers seekers: The truth is out there! Uncover some of it during the second weekend in April at the convention center at the Inn of the Ozarks, as lectures, audiovisual presentations, and panel discussions on all aspects of the UFO phenomenon (abductions, crop circles, etc.) seek to answer some of life's most unusual questions. Authors, researchers, vendors, and those who have experienced phenomena will be on hand. This event gets bigger each year. The registration fee of $40 covers the weekend.

WORLD-FEST
Silver Dollar City
(417) 338-2611, (800) 952-6626
www.explorebranson.com
www.silverdollarcity.com

World-Fest is the season kickoff event at Silver Dollar City, and it begins the second weekend in April, just as dogwoods are ready to bloom, and lasts a month, into May. The Ozarks area celebrates world diversity as more than 350 performers from 18 countries come to the theme park. You can hear dozens of languages and many varieties of English as you take in the art of national dancers, singers, and performers, from an Israeli folk dance troupe to an a cappella boys choir from Zambia. You can find flag throwers, sword dancers, and bagpipe and tin-whistle maestros, as well as old-world glass blowing, armor construction, and egg decorating. The international flavor also involves food, and you can sample the culinary delights of the world in the confines of the park. Regular admission prices to the park apply.

MAY

ANNUAL WHITE BASS FISH FRY
Shadow Rock Park, Forsyth
(417) 546-2741
www.forsythmissouri.net
Share all those white bass you caught earlier, or if you didn't catch any, come anyway for a taste at the Forsyth Chamber of Commerce fish fry. Meet at Shadow Rock Park, but call the chamber for the exact date.

ARTSFEST ON WALNUT STREET
Walnut Street, Springfield
(417) 831-6200, (877) 900-ARTS
www.springfieldarts.org
During the first weekend in May (10 a.m. to 6 p.m. both days), Springfield's historic Walnut Street district puts on a celebration at which more than 150 local and regional artists display their work or perform. The Artsfest features food, dancing, art (paintings, sculpture, pottery, jewelry), crafts, and hands-on activities for children. Performers of all ages present ballet, theater, ethnic and folk music and dance, and choral and instrumental music from several venues—the Show Wagon Stage, the bandstand, porches. Even the street itself becomes an arena for roving street performers.

Admission is $2 for adults. Children twelve and younger get in free.

EUREKA SPRINGS BLUES FESTIVAL
Various locations, Eureka Springs, AR
(479) 253-8737
www.eurekasprings.org
Nationally known blues artists perform in clubs, hotels, and the city auditorium the last weekend in May and the two days before. This all-indoor event of world-class blues makes for a long weekend of great music in a unique setting. There are artists' parties and special events galore. Prices vary, but there are also free concerts at Basin Park, and you can wander around on Spring Street and just soak up the blues and the atmosphere.

EUREKA SPRINGS DOLL & TOY SHOW AND SALE
Inn of the Ozarks Convention Center
Eureka Springs, AR
(479) 253-8737
www.eurekasprings.org
Come as you are or get all dolled up. Antique, collectible, and artist dolls, along with old toys, doll clothes, wigs, furniture, and anything doll related, will fill the main level of the Inn of the Ozarks Convention Center the third Saturday in May. New, old, and artist-made bears of all sizes also have a special place in the show. Appraisals are available for dolls that you may have, and door prizes, dealers from several states, and fellow hobbyists make this a fun weekend for children and collectors. Call for admission prices.

ℹ️ Branson has an annual rainfall of 43 inches. January is driest (1.79 inches) and coldest (31 degrees). June is the wettest (5.09 inches). June, July, and August are the hottest months with an average of 78 degrees, but you can expect some days to be 90 to 100 degrees.

FORSYTH CITYWIDE GARAGE SALE
Various locations, Forsyth
(417) 546-2741, (417) 546-4763 www.forsyth missouri.net

Hang around the area for another week after you visit the Nixa citywide garage sale, and you can also take in Forsyth's. It's always the third Saturday in May, and it attracts people from near and far, as local folks, artists, and crafters reduce inventory and clean out the attic and garage. It's a citywide party, arts and crafts event, and flea market!

GREAT AMERICAN MUSIC FESTIVAL
Silver Dollar City
(417) 338-2611, (800) 952-6626
www.explorebranson.com
www.silverdollarcity.com
Beginning the third weekend in May and lasting for three weeks, you can celebrate American music with award-winning musicians as more than 200 musicians and groups from across the nation and around the world (ever hear an Austrian bluegrass group?) perform bluegrass, country, gospel, and Dixieland throughout the park at Silver Dollar City. Regular admission prices apply to this special event.

MAY FINE ARTS FESTIVAL
Downtown Eureka Springs, AR
(479) 253-8737
www.eurekasprings.org
The arts are everywhere here. Eureka turns on the creativity all month, celebrating the arts with special events, including an outrageous parade, kids' activities, performing arts, workshops, demonstrations, displays, weekend nighttime gallery walks, receptions, a changing roster of featured artists, and much more. Most events are free.

NIXA CITYWIDE GARAGE SALE
Various locations, Nixa
(417) 725-5486
www.nixa.com
On the second Saturday in May, the Nixa Parks Department sponsors a citywide garage sale. Every house in town seems to participate. People from Springfield and towns around Nixa flock to this small burg for the bargains, and Nixans get a lot of spring cleaning and clutter clearing done that day.

PLUMB NELLIE DAYS
Downtown Branson
(417) 334-1548, (888) 322-2786
www.branson.com

This is when locals play stereotypical hillbillies for themselves and the tourists. This downtown Branson celebration gets us out in our bib overalls and calico and gingham dresses for the parade, the children's pet contest, and the contest for king and queen of Plumb Nellie Days. We even have a beard-growing contest and an outhouse race. In fact, we have "plumb nellie everything" at this event, including more than 120 booths in large tents in the crafts festival and the merchants' sidewalk sale. Look for this event the third weekend in May!

SUCKER DAY
Downtown Nixa
(417) 725-1545
www.nixa.com

That good-eatin' but ugly fish that spawns in the spring here in the Ozarks is the excuse for this celebration. During mid-April, if you see people in trees along Ozark rivers and on bridges looking down into the water, they are probably trying to grab suckers. The third Saturday in May is Nixa's celebration of all things sucker, and thousands descend on the town to get their fill of fried suckers and a chowder they call sucker soup. There is a parade to kick off the day's events, and you can find craft booths, entertainment, and amusement rides that last into the night.

WAR EAGLE MILL SPRING ANTIQUE AND CRAFTS SHOW
11045 War Eagle Rd.
Rogers, AR
(479) 789-5343
www.wareaglemill.com

Two times a year folks flock to War Eagle Mill, a working gristmill, which plays host to the biggest crafts and arts fair in Arkansas. The spring show has a focus on antiques and crafts, while the fall show features more arts and crafts. Serious collectors, dealers, and buyers, as well as lots of lookers and gawkers, come out in full force for this three-day show. Some people just go for the food and the flavor of the Ozarks found there. The old mill opens early for War Eagle Biscuits, made from flour ground at the mill, and gravy. You'll also find great barbecue, Indian tacos, cornbread and beans, and a host of other delectables and snacks. War Eagle Mill is 25 miles southwest of Eureka Springs, Arkansas, in a secluded valley south of AR 12 and north of US 412. You can get to War Eagle on Benton County Road 98 from the north, but traffic is slow and is often backed up because of the one-lane bridge over the War Eagle River. We suggest you take AR 303 from the south for easy access to free parking and the fairgrounds.

JUNE

ALL CONVERTIBLE CAR SHOW AND PARADE
Downtown Eureka Springs, AR
(479) 253-8737
www.eurekasprings.org

Go topless in Eureka Springs the third Saturday in June. This is the ultimate one-day convertible car show, with 14 classes in competition for trophies and prizes. Convertibles from 1915 to the present will be on display and will parade through the historic district at 2 p.m. Special classes include 4x4s, VWs, street machines, and more. There's a preregistration fee for cars, but if you're just going to gawk, admission is free.

ANNUAL '50S–'60S STREET DANCE
Taneycomo lakefront
(417) 334-1548, (888) 322-2786
www.branson.com

The third Saturday in June is the date for this big event held along the Taneycomo lakefront. This is a late-night affair; it does not start until 9 p.m., and it goes until midnight. Many local entertainers provide live music for this nostalgic event for people of all ages. Bring lawn chairs, a blanket or cushion for sittin', and shoes for dancin'!

ANTIQUE TRACTOR AND ENGINE SHOW
Tapjac Home Center, MO 39, Shell Knob
(417) 858-3300, (800) 658-0328
www.shellknob.com

Whether you go for the tractors and steam engines or the country music and barbecue doesn't matter. You can get it all at this free show, usually held at Tapjac Home Center in Shell Knob. You'll see old Case steam engines, Molines, Fords, and Deere "Johnnie Poppers," plus other antique farm machinery.

DR. MARY LONG SCHOLARSHIP
Ice Cream Social
Taney Center, Forsyth
(417) 546-2741
www.forsythmissouri.net

Who can resist homemade ice cream? Don't feel guilty about what you eat here because it's for a good cause: proceeds from the event, which honors one of the area's pioneer doctors, provide medical scholarships for students. Bring your appetite to the Taney Center, 2 miles south of Forsyth. Call for the exact date.

INSPIRATION POINT OPERA
US 62 West
Eureka Springs, AR
(479) 253-8595
www.eurekasprings.org

Opera in the Ozarks has a long tradition and a devoted following. Call for the summer schedule and ticket information, and see the Arts and Culture chapter for more information.

MSU SUMMER TENT THEATRE
Springfield
(417) 836-7678
www.missouristatetix.com

This summer theater under a tent is where Kathleen Turner, John Goodman, and Tess Harper got started in their careers, and it's on the Missouri State University campus outside Craig Hall. Productions are top quality, and during June and August it's a great way to spend an evening. In 2005 ticket prices were $9 for adults, $6 for students and seniors. See the Arts and Culture chapter for more information.

NATIONAL CHILDREN'S FESTIVAL AT SILVER DOLLAR CITY
Silver Dollar City
(417) 338-2611, (800) 952-6626
www.explorebranson.com
www.silverdollarcity.com

This relative newcomer of events has grown up to become a favorite of ours because it keeps its kids' outlook. It always starts the third weekend in June and runs through August. It is now recognized as one of the nation's largest children's festivals. There are games and activities galore, more than 100 of them, with interactive games from Nickelodeon—the only television network just for kids. Earth 2U: Exploring Geography is an interactive geography adventure from the Smithsonian Institution, and the traveling exhibit gives kids a new way to explore geography facts and history through models, computer programs, and videos. Adults will have fun, too, and the events and activities are guaranteed to bring out the kid in you. Regular park admission prices apply. (See the Kidstuff chapter.)

OINKLAWN DOWNS PIG RACES AND BARBECUE
Cape Fair
(417) 538-2222

Porker pride, we have it here. After all, the Ozarks is home to the Razorbacks down in Fayetteville, but in Cape Fair during the second weekend in June, local businesses are thinking pigs, not pigskins, in competitive races run by porkers. You'd think that by mid-June the sap would have finished flowing, but Cape Fair is a slow, laid-back sort of place. It's all great fun—eating, wandering about, watching the races, and squealing for your favorite hog. We won't comment about all the informal wagers placed on this competition; officially no betting is allowed. You can expect more than pig races. There are craft booths, entertainment of various types, and a barbecue. (Losers in the races aren't eaten; they are merely trained harder for next year's event!)

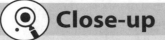 **Close-up**

Veterans Are Welcome in Branson

In an attempt to establish Branson as the year-round, national home for all veterans, active-duty military personnel, and their families, the nonprofit Branson Veterans Task Force, Inc., has mobilized more than 150 businesses and countless volunteers to offer special events, conferences, music shows, parades, and traveling exhibitions during the year.

More than 20 events take place during the year, but the big ones are centered around Memorial Day, the Fourth of July, and Veterans Day, and they are the most popular.

Veterans may seek out old comrades through the reunion registry, held each year at Grand Country Square, the shopping complex at Grand Country Music Hall and Resort (see The Shows chapter). Not only does the free computerized service allow veterans to obtain the home addresses of others who served in their units, but it also allows them to find out where old friends are staying while visiting Branson during Veterans Homecoming weekend. Many military units and organizations hold reunions in Branson during the weekend. Some of them, such as the Tuskegee Airmen, have presented programs and served as resources in the local school systems.

In the past, the Veterans Patch Wall has proved popular, with its branch, division, and unit patches collected from veterans. The collection spans the Civil War to the latest conflicts, including the war against terrorism. By encouraging veterans and their families to donate to the Patch Wall, the sponsors hope to produce the largest veterans patch collection in the world.

Veterans and their families have also liked visiting the Welk Resort Center to see the traveling Vietnam Veterans Memorial, better known as the Wall. This half-scale replica of the Vietnam Veterans Memorial in Washington, D.C., stretches nearly 240 feet. And like its big brother, it lists the names of more than 58,000 servicemen and servicewomen who made the ultimate sacrifice in that war.

Veterans and Bransonites were instrumental in a community-wide effort to raise money for the National World War II Memorial in Washington, D.C., and many attractions and shows in Branson offered premiums to those who made contributions to the memorial.

OZARK VILLAGE DAYS
Ozark Square, downtown Ozark
(417) 581-6139
The third weekend in June, Ozark has a festival that features arts and crafts and a Hillbilly Olympics, including an outhouse relay race, rolling pig toss, log chuck, and wheelbarrow race. There's also a petting zoo, games, and food. It all takes place on the Ozark Square, and it's free. If this isn't exciting enough for you, stroll down to the Finley River Park for the annual Missouri State High School Rodeo Finals, always held on the same date.

ROCKAWAY BEACH HYDROPLANE RACES
Rockaway Beach
(417) 561-4280, (800) 798-0178
www.runaway.to/rockawaybeach
Waves, wakes, and the roar of powerful engines! Always in early June, the races are exciting to watch from the safety of the beachfront, and there's always food and dance at the city park. You might even enjoy the swimsuit contest.

RODS & RELICS AT ROCKAWAY BEACH
MO 176, downtown Rockaway Beach
(417) 561-4280, (800) 798-0178
www.runaway.to/rockawaybeach
Rods & Relics is a car club that has had its com-

The Paralyzed Veterans of America association holds an annual 10K race and 5K Run, Walk, Roll and Remember to raise funds for the Spinal Cord Research Foundation. Other similar fund-raisers are scheduled during the year.

Festivities during the three big veterans events include segments to honor visiting vets. In the fall, during the weeklong festivities of A Veterans Homecoming, Branson is home to the nation's largest Veterans Day parade, always beginning at the 11th hour of the 11th day of the 11th month. It's been a Branson tradition for 70 years, but only recently has it become so large and attracted so much attention. In 2001 entertainer Jennifer Wilson (known for her USO work) and the Branson Scenic Railway had a special "troop train" welcome for visiting vets. The IMAX theater usually offers a special movie on its six-story screen.

Veterans are especially interested in the Veterans Memorial Museum. (See the Attractions chapter.) It is composed of 10 great halls covering the five main wars and other conflicts fought during the 20th century, including World War I, World War II, Korea, Vietnam, Desert Storm, and more. Sculpture, murals, historical artifacts, objets d'art, and thousands of authentic memorabilia honor all branches of the service, major battlefronts, campaigns, industrial defense, and others.

The Radisson Hotel and others cater to veterans with special rates during the events, and many vets like to gather at the R & R Bar there and at Mike Radford's "Remember When" Veterans Cafe. Of special interest there is a hallway of pictures, clippings, patches, and memorabilia left by many visiting vets—a veritable museum.

Of course, Branson has been honoring veterans before it recently became the patriotic, "in thing" to do, and the nation's vets have returned the gesture by making Branson, with its center-of-the-nation locale and its varied and family entertainment, a sort of veterans meeting place and playground. The entertainment industry and all the locals cater to vets and love it. They feel it's the least they can do for those who have given the most for the nation.

Veterans and visitors interested in the upcoming veterans activities can call the Veterans Task Force at (417) 337-8387 or visit www.bransonveterans.com.

petition and meetings for 30 years at Rockaway, and they have been joined by several other car clubs on Father's Day to bring to this small town the best of antique cars and rebuilt, custom, and street rods. Come for the show, or come to flex that muscle car! Call for information.

JULY

FIREBURST
Kimberling City
(417) 739-2564, (800) 595-0393
www.tablerocklake.com/chamber
Fireburst is a spectacular fireworks show that you can view from car, boat, or on foot. The fireworks burst into the sky, reflecting beautifully over Table Rock Lake. A show in itself is the flotilla of 1,000 boats gathered to party and experience this popular event.

FIREFALL
5000 West Kearney St., Springfield
(417) 864-1049, (800) 678-8767
www.springfieldmosymphony.org
Attend Firefall, and you'll know why the Springfield Symphony Orchestra has such strong community support. This is some Fourth of July party—though it's not always held on the Fourth of July. Call to find out the exact date. It's an all-day-into-the-night affair, so pack a blanket and a

picnic lunch, or buy lunch at the site. Entertainment is held throughout the day in the open fields near Springfield/Branson Regional Airport, and entertainers from shows on The Strip almost always participate. The climax of the evening is music by the Springfield Symphony with synchronized fireworks. There is always a large crowd (part of the fun), and parking is at a premium (not fun), but shuttle buses run from sites in Springfield to Firefall. The admission price is usually $5 per family or carload.

Other fireworks displays to celebrate Independence Day are held in Hollister, (417) 334-3050; Kimberling City, (417) 739-2564; Point Lookout, (417) 334-6411; Rockaway Beach, (417) 561-4280; and Shell Knob, (417) 858-3300.

OZARK EMPIRE FAIR
Ozark Empire Fairgrounds, Springfield
(417) 833-2660
www.ozarkempirefair.com
This is the mother of all fairs in the Ozarks, second only to the Missouri State Fair at Sedalia. It always begins on the last Friday in July and extends through two weekends at the Ozark Empire Fairgrounds near Dickerson Park Zoo.

And what a fair! There's always a great midway and the usual fair fare of food, livestock, family-living exhibits, booths, and entertainment at the grandstand—usually a big-name star from rock or country music and sometimes both. Our fair favorites are the produce exhibits; the livestock; shows (where you can see a calf born if you want to hang around long enough); the fish, snakes, and mammals at the Department of Conservation exhibit; and the Pineapple-Whip stand—not just for the cool, tasty delight, but also for the amazing hula girl who dances atop the stand. Admission is usually $5 plus parking. Kids 12 and younger get in free.

TANEY COUNTY FAIR
Fairgrounds, Forsyth
(417) 546-2741
www.forsythmissouri.net
You'll like the livestock and agricultural exhibits, sheepdog trails, festival rides, games, and delicious smells that permeate the air on the banks of Bull Shoals Lake. Have some cotton candy, order a tasty Lion Burger (grilled by the local Lions Club), and visit the petting zoo. The summer may be hot, but the nights are always cool by the lakeside fairgrounds.

AUGUST
ANNUAL OLD TIME FIDDLE CONTEST
(417) 334-1548, (888) 322-2786
www.branson.com
Held on the third Saturday in August, this is always a great way to spend an evening. Amateur fiddlers from throughout the United States compete for more than $3,500 in cash and prizes.

CRANE BROILER FESTIVAL
Downtown Crane
(417) 723-5104
www.bransonshows.com
This small town is home to one of the biggest, oldest festivals in the Ozarks. For almost half a century, chicken has been cock of the walk the last Friday and Saturday of August, and you can smell it sizzling on the open charcoal pits for miles around. Perhaps that's what brings the 26,000 people who descend on this small Stone County town north of Galena on MO 13. Or it could be the beauty pageant (in which local lovelies vie for the title of Little Miss Chick and Miss Chick), craft booths, fireworks, country music entertainment (past performers have been Minnie Pearl, Red Foley, Merle Travis, Gene Shephard, Hank Thompson, and Jerry Clower), horseshoe pitching tournament, and carnival. Whatever the reason, it's a just an excuse to have some August fun in Crane.

FALL HUNTING CLASSIC
Springfield
(417) 867-1915
www.basspro.com
Prepare for hunting season and that trophy buck by getting information and tips from the nation's

top hunters. Each year Bass Pro Shops Outdoor World sponsors this free event, not only for area hunters but also for all those willing to make the trek to that mecca of sport in Springfield. You can see the latest and greatest in hunting and camping gear as well as learn how to keep hunting safe and enjoyable. Call for specific dates.

NIKE GREATER OZARKS OPEN
Highland Springs Country Club
Springfield
(417) 887-3400
The Highland Springs Country Club is the field for up-and-coming PGA tour players. There are four levels of competition in the tournament, which has a guaranteed purse of $125,000 and is traditionally held in mid-August, the hottest time of the year in the Ozarks. Lots of area golfers go just to watch the big dogs play and perhaps pick up a few pointers to improve their own games.

OLD FIDDLERS CONTEST
Golden
(417) 271-3769, (417) 271-3532
August 2000 marked the 50th year of this contest for amateur fiddlers, always the last Saturday in August. Folks come from miles around to eat the home-cooked food prepared by the Golden Circle Shores Association and listen as the best fiddlers from all over strut their stuff on strings. There are divisions for senior and junior fiddlers. Admission in 2005 was $3 for adults, $2 for children 5 to 16, children younger than 5 admitted free.

WHITE RIVER VALLEY ARTS AND CRAFTS FAIR
Shadow Rock Park, Forsyth
(417) 546-2741
www.forsythmissouri.net
Exhibitors from across the country let you look for free at their art and wares, but be certain to bring your wallet, because you're sure to find that perfect one-of-a-kind gift or that just-what-you-needed item. You'll find basket makers, knife smiths, cornhusk-doll artists, and other craftspeople.

SOUTHERN GOSPEL PICNIC
Silver Dollar City
(417) 338-2611, (800) 952-6626
www.explorebranson.com
www.silverdollarcity.com
Southern gospel music has always resounded through our Ozark hills, from country churches and county fairs to porch-side pickin' sessions and Sunday services. Now, we offer a whole festival of such music with a bonus of our popular theme park.

SEPTEMBER

ANNUAL ANTIQUE AUTOMOBILE FESTIVAL
Pine Mountain Village, US 62 East
Eureka Springs, AR
(479) 253-8737
www.eurekasprings.org
Vintage vroooom takes over the city as hundreds of antique cars gather at Pine Mountain Village in Eureka Springs for this event the second weekend in September. There are judging classes for cars 25 years and older in both original and modified categories, with trophies and prizes. The weekend also includes a reenactment of a 1922 bank robbery and much more, including the city's annual toy, doll, and train show. Admission for the Antique Automobile Festival is free, but if you have a car you want to enter, registration is $18.

ANNUAL EUREKA SPRINGS JAZZ FESTIVAL
Various locations, Eureka Springs, AR
(479) 253-8737
www.eurekasprings.org
Enjoy one cool, long weekend of jazz and the beginnings of the fall color on historic Spring Street. The Jazz Festival is always the third weekend in September. There's jazz around town indoors and out in clubs, bed-and-breakfast inns, restaurants, parks, and other venues. Renowned jazz headliners will appear in concert at the city auditorium on Saturday night. Prices vary at venues, and there are always free concerts in the Basin Street Park.

APPLE FESTIVAL
Seymour Square, Seymour
(417) 935-2257
www.seymourmissouri.org
All things apple fill the menu for this festival on the Seymour Square. Expect all kinds of apples, apple cider, apple pie, apple cobbler, apple butter, apple bobbing, and an apple-peeling contest, as well as Johnny Appleseed himself. Seymour is 20 minutes east of Springfield on US 60.

AUTUMN DAZE CRAFT FESTIVAL DOWNTOWN
Downtown Branson
(417) 334-1548, (888) 322-2786
www.branson.com
During the third weekend in September, Branson's downtown area is turned into a craft-lover's paradise. More than 150 crafters from throughout the United States have displays and demonstrations, and the parking lots and sidewalks are filled with them and their work. This 30-plus-year tradition is one of the best crafts shows in the nation.

BANJO RALLY INTERNATIONAL
Downtown Eureka Springs, AR
(479) 253-8737
Finger-pickin' good could describe this event the first weekend in September and the two days before it. It's a gathering of top-rate banjo players, replete with concerts, jam sessions, educational sessions on old-style techniques, workshops, and specialty vendors for banjo players or those who just love to hear a banjo. A concert on Saturday night is open to the public for a minimal fee (about $5). Call for information about workshop fees.

COUNTRY FAIR DAYS
Shell Knob
(417) 858-3300
www.shellknob.com
You may be surprised what we do in small towns to have fun. This event is worth it just for the Ugly Dog Contest, but you can also find a car show, arts and crafts, and food and fun. Call the Shell Knob Chamber of Commerce at the number above for the exact date.

NATIONAL HARVEST FESTIVAL
Silver Dollar City
(417) 338-2611, (800) 952-6626
www.explorebranson.com
www.silverdollarcity.com
The cream of the crop of American craftspeople is invited to display talents and arts at Silver Dollar City's big annual harvest festival. Held in September and October when the Ozarks area is changing to its colorful fall wardrobe, this show has been ranked as one of the top tourism events in the nation. There are doll makers, wheat weavers, basket weavers, woodcarvers, potters, raku pottery makers, and glassblowers who do what they do best and answer questions from the curious. There is always a cornucopia of not only crafts and arts but also interesting and exciting foods. One nice thing about this big event is that regular park admission prices apply.

GRAPE AND FALL FESTIVAL
Downtown Hollister
(417) 334-3050
www.hollisterchamber.net
Hollister is not a grape-growing region anymore, but that's no excuse not to have a fall festival on Downing Street in the "English Village of the Ozarks." Look for entertainment, eats, and arts and crafts, usually the second weekend in September.

GREATER OZARKS BLUES FESTIVAL
Downtown Springfield
www.greaterozarksbluesfest.com
Downtown Springfield sponsors the Greater Ozarks Blues Festival the second weekend in September. Legendary blues artists and fans gather at various venues in downtown for the bluesy event. In the past, it has featured artists such as Tommy Castro, the Cate Brothers, Delta Groove Blues Revue, Rich Berry, ABS Band, and Teeny Tucker.

HOMETOWN HARVEST DAYS
Webster County Fairgrounds, Marshfield
(417) 468-3943
The County Fairgrounds is the site of this arts, crafts, and entertainment show that attracts people from near and far in Webster County. Marshfield is only minutes east of Springfield on I-44.

HOOTIN' N HOLLERIN'
Town square, Gainesville
(417) 679-4913
www.ozarkcounty.net
Gainesville is the county seat of Ozark County, just east of Taney County. The drive on US 160 is slow and crooked, but going over there the third Thursday, Friday, and Saturday in September will give you some of the prettiest fall colors and scenery the area has to offer. The fall festival there celebrates everything hillbilly as the residents let down their hair and have fun in their local celebration with bed races, a quilt show, crafts and demonstrations (spinning, basket weaving, lye soap making, etc.), a turkey shoot, a pet contest, a costume parade, square dancing, and country music jam sessions on the courthouse lawn. Outsiders and flatlanders are welcome! Admission is free.

OZARK MOUNTAIN MULE & DONKEY DAYS
Ozark Empire Fairgrounds, Springfield
(417) 833-2660
www.ozarkmountainmuledays.com
Over 500 mules and 100 miniature donkeys will converge at the Fairgrounds to compete in over 60 events in this celebration of the Show-Me state's official animal. There is no way to actually describe this event. It's part mule and donkey show, part test of skills, part Wild West show, and pure fun.

LAURA INGALLS WILDER FESTIVAL
Mansfield
(417) 468-3943
www.lauraingallswilder.com
All of Mansfield turns out to celebrate its most famous citizen. The arts and crafts fair is at the homesite of author Laura Ingalls Wilder, famous for her Little House books. There are all sorts of Laura-inspired activities: fiddle contests, pioneer children's games, costume contests, and an outdoor drama based on Wilder's books.

MISSOURI FOX TROTTING HORSE BREED
Association Show and Celebration
Show grounds, Ava
(417) 683-2468
www.mfthba.com
This annual meeting of the Missouri Fox Trotting Horse Breed Association, the group that promotes the Ozarkian's horse of choice, always starts on Labor Day and is a six-day event. Thousands of fox-trotting breeders and horse lovers congregate at the Douglas County seat for one of the biggest shows in the nation. You don't have to own one to enjoy the show, and it's possible you might get caught by the fox-trotting bug.

i The "Cadillac of Horses," the Missouri Fox Trotting Horse, was developed in the rugged Ozark hills during the 19th century by settlers who needed easy riding, durable mounts that could travel long distances at a sure-footed, ground consuming gait. The breed's national headquarters is located in Ava, Mo.

OZARKS STEAMORAMA
Republic
(417) 732-3356
www.steamorama.com
For almost 50 years, the Ozarks Steam Engine Association in Republic has hosted Ozarks Steamorama. It's held on US 60 on the south side of the road, with entrance to the grounds from FR 170. It is usually held the second weekend in September. They have a 35-acre site that features more than 400 old tractors, 20 steam-driven traction engines, 300 gasoline engines, 40 crawler tracts, 55 garden tractors, and 40 antique and classic trucks, plus threshers and shingle and sawmills.

STATE OF THE OZARKS FIDDLERS CONVENTION
Compton Ridge Campground, MO 265
800-233-8648
www.branson-missouri.com
Three days of fiddling fun can be found at the Compton Ridge Campground. Fiddlers from around the country meet and perform day and night at various locations around the campground and at the Gathering Place, the campgrounds meeting center. Awards are presented for oldest, youngest, most-improved, and farthest-traveled fiddlers. Come to play or just listen. Call for the exact dates and details. (See the Campgrounds and RV Parks chapter for information on Compton Ridge Campground.)

OCTOBER

ANNUAL FALL ART SHOW
Forsyth Art Guild building, 1600 US 160
Forsyth
(417) 546-5439
www.forsythmissouri.net
During the entire month of October, you're invited to stop by the Forsyth Art Guild building and see work of local artists and crafters. You'll find woodcarvings, watercolors, oils, sculpture, and china paintings. Much of the work is for sale, so bring your wallet.

APPLE BUTTER MAKING DAYS
Town square, Mount Vernon
(417) 466-7654
www.mtvernonchamber.com
Just the aroma is worth the trip to the Lawrence County seat, named after George Washington's home and host to one of the sweetest festivals in the Ozarks the second Friday, Saturday, and Sunday of October. It's free, but you'll want to pack some apple butter (made before your eyes in 60-gallon copper kettles) back with you so you can enjoy it at home. While there on the Mount Vernon square, admire the old courthouse, enjoy the parade, watch the terrapin race (or maybe bring your own entry), enter the tall-tale-telling contest, take in the crafts and demonstrations—more than 370 booths—and listen to the live entertainment. Mount Vernon is west of Springfield but is only a bit more than an hour's drive from Branson via the back roads of MO 13 and 265.

CORVETTE WEEKEND
Pine Mountain Village
Eureka Springs, AR
(479) 253-8737
www.eurekaspringscorvette.org
More than 350 Corvettes will purr their way into Eureka Springs for this annual show and parade. See Vettes of all ages on display at Pine Mountain Village or out on a timed road rally. The sheer number of these classic cars all in one place is a sight to behold. Attendance is free, but if you want to enter your Vette, registration is $35 and $45.

FALL FESTIVAL OF THE ARTS
Kimberling City-Area Library
Kimberling City
(417) 739-2564, (417) 739-5829
www.visittablerocklake.com
Sponsored by the Tablerock Art Guild for 30 years, this arts and crafts show is a great way to get some Christmas shopping done. You'll find oil and watercolor paintings, sculptures, and a host of crafts and homemade items. Call the guild at the number above for exact dates and details.

GLADE TOP TRAIL FLAMING FALL REVUE
Various locations, Ava
(417) 683-4594
www.avachamber.org
Mother Nature gives a show of color in the Ozarks that rivals that of an Ozark Mountain Christmas. You can catch the dogwoods, sumac, hickory, and various oaks at their finest in the Glade Top Trail Flaming Fall Revue when you drive the ridge roads in sections of the Mark Twain National Forest near Ava. The town has special events, and you can still catch the great farmers' market on the town square Saturday morning. Stop at the Ava Drugstore where you can get an ice-cream cone for a nickel.

OZARK MOUNTAIN COUNTRY FALL FOLIAGE DRIVE
Forsyth
(417) 546-2741
www.forsythmissouri.net

See the Ozarks' "golden oldies": great hickory nut trees plus the reds and rusts of oaks and sweet gums as well as the scarlet of dogwood, sumac, and cinquefoil in this 75-mile drive. It's a great way to see the area, a world so different from that of The Strip, so pack up a picnic lunch and the camera and plan on taking the whole day. There are always fruit stands and antiques stores as well as country stores to provide a change of pace. You can pick up a map at the Forsyth Chamber of Commerce at 16075 US 160.

i For up-to-the-moment foliage reports for the Ozarks, suggested drives, photos, and fun folliage facts, visit: www .ozarkmtns.com/foliage/reports.asp

OZARK NATIVE ARTS & CRAFTS FESTIVAL
Ozark City Park, Ozark
(417) 581-6139
www.ozarkchamber.com

Always the first full weekend in October, this event has grown to become one of the larger craft fairs in the Ozarks. Almost 400 vendors, crafters, and artists pack in 10,000 people in the Ozark City Park. While there, you may want to take in some of the many flea markets and antiques shops in Ozark.

PUMPKIN DAZE
Republic
(417) 732-3356
www.republicmo.com

Republic gears up for its Pumpkin Daze celebration every year on the first Saturday in October. This small town grows some of the biggest pumpkins in the nation. A recent winner, named the "Big Ugly" by its owner, was 838.5 pounds. It took four men and a forklift to move it to the weigh-in. Competition is fierce, and water bills

i In 2007, the Missouri Ozarks suffered severe tree damage from an ice storm. In 2009, the Arkansas Ozarks had a similar disaster. That accounts for many of the broken trees and limbs and the large amount of forest floor debris you'll see.

must be high. The "Big Ugly" was estimated to gain 35 pounds each night and "drank" about 200 gallons of water a day.

WAR EAGLE MILL ARTS AND CRAFTS FAIR
Rogers, AR
(479) 789-5398
www.wareaglemill.com

For more than half a century, crowds have flocked to the biggest crafts fair in the Ozarks. Each year an estimated 135,000 people come to the free four-day fair. You'll find more than 300 exhibitors from Arkansas, Missouri, Oklahoma, and Kansas. You'll see woodworkers, weavers, sculptors, and stained-glass artisans, as well as basket makers, painters, and jewelry artisans. It's a great way to catch the fall colors on the drive down, see the old mill there (and perhaps buy lunch or sample some exotic items from food vendors), and pick up one-of-a-kind items at the fair for Christmas presents.

The mill is 25 miles southwest of Eureka Springs, Arkansas. (See May listing for specific directions.)

NOVEMBER

ANNUAL FOOD & WINE WEEKEND
Various restaurants, Eureka Springs, AR
(479) 253-8737
www.eurekasprings.org

Eureka's finest restaurants offer special multi-course menus for three days of epicurean delight in America's Victorian Village during the second weekend in November. From exotic wines by the glass to a seven-course Renaissance feast, you can find a taste to suit your palate almost anywhere in town. Prices vary according to the restaurant, but you can find a feast to fit any size pocketbook.

CANDLELIGHT CHRISTMAS OPEN HOUSE
Downtown Branson
(417) 334-1548, (888) 322-2786
www.branson.com
Although downtown Branson stores are open all year, the second weekend in December is a special time, when merchants help everyone get in the Christmas spirit by dressing in Dickens-style costumes. You'll hear carolers on the streets, get a chance to visit with Father Christmas, enjoy the fruits of the window decorating contest, and sample cookies and hot cider.

EUREKA SPRINGS ANNUAL ANTIQUE SHOW AND SALE
Inn of the Ozarks Convention Center
US 62 West and Historic Loop
Eureka Springs, AR
(479) 253-7551, (866) 566-9387
www.eurekasprings.org
A repeat of the spring show; see the entry under March.

FESTIVAL OF LIGHTS
Branson/tri-lakes area
(417) 334-4136, (800) 214-3661
www.explorebranson.com
Branson decks the streets and businesses with millions of lights, and folks come from all around to take in the multicolored lights and the animated light scenes. Kimberling City has its Port of Lights, a spectacular 1.5-mile drive through an animated light display with the lake on three sides. Silver Dollar City is like a fairyland at night, with rides, buildings, fences, and trees covered in lights. Indian Point, just past Silver Dollar City, has its Enchanted Forest Light Display. The Shepherd of the Hills Homestead features millions of lights. And Branson has various lighting displays scattered around town, by Lake Taneycomo, and on the Branson Landing. Pack up the kids and a thermos and plan to make a night of oohing and aahing at what has become a major tourist attraction in itself.

OZARK MOUNTAIN CHRISTMAS
Branson-Lakes area
(417) 334-4136, (800) 214-3661
www.explorebranson.com
A decade ago this was part of the off-season in Branson. Not anymore. More than 450,000 people come to see the lights, shop, and take in the special Christmas shows in November and December. It's no wonder that the American Bus Association has included Ozark Mountain Christmas in its list of Top 100 Events in North America for several years running. Most of the theaters have special and spectacular Christmas shows, and Santa is certain to make an appearance at all of them. Silver Dollar City presents its Old Time Christmas, celebrating the Christmas traditions of different nations and cultures from November 4 to December 30. The festival features a five-story special-effects Christmas tree, a 17-foot talking Christmas tree that interacts with children, holiday shows, and more than two million lights. And everybody loves singing carols at the Wilderness Church and drinking mulled cider! You can take in the lights all around the area (see the next entry), do your Christmas shopping, and see some Christmas specials. The events vary from year to year, but you can get a complete list of holiday programs and events by calling the Branson/Lakes Area Chamber of Commerce at the numbers above.

PORT OF LIGHTS
Kimberling City
(417) 739-2564, (800) 595-0393
www.tablerocklake.com/chamber
The Port of Lights is one of the most spectacular light displays in the state. The 2-mile lighted loop of fantasy at the U.S. Army Corps of Engineers Highway 13 Park in Kimberling City is a must-see for all ages, with dozens of colorful animated and artistic displays and a gorgeous, sparkling, 120-foot-long tunnel of snowflakes.

VETERANS HOMECOMING
Citywide locations, Branson
(417) 334-4136, (417) 334-1548,
(800) 999-8839
www.bransonveterans.com

The week of Veterans Day has become a special event to many of us and our nation's veterans, as Branson welcomes with open arms all those who have served their country. It's an opportunity to reflect on our nation's history, have an old-fashioned parade down the renamed Veterans Boulevard (US Business 65), and give thanks to those who served. The parade is always held on November 11 and begins at 11 a.m. Many of the theaters have a veterans salute, with special tributes and music, that gives meaning to being an American.

DECEMBER

ANNUAL ADORATION PARADE AND LIGHTING
Downtown Branson
(417) 334-4136, (800) 214-3661
www.explorebranson.com

Mark the first Sunday in December for this event. Started in 1948, this noncommercial community parade has grown to include dozens of bands and bugle corps, floats, and antique cars. The event attracts thousands of people from the surrounding areas. The parade starts at 5:30 p.m., and the event climaxes with the lighting of an adoration scene with 40-foot figures atop Mount Branson. If you miss it, you can often catch it the next day on one of the local television stations.

FIRST NIGHT
Downtown and MSU areas, Springfield
(417) 831-6200
www.springfieldarts.org

For over a decade Springfield has thrown a big nonalcoholic New Year's Eve party that starts early in the afternoon and lasts until the new year. Events are scattered all about town but are centered in the downtown and MSU area. Activities include storytelling, rock, jazz, mimes and clowns, magic, ballet, drama, and stand-up comics. You can walk about, sampling various events and activities, and shuttle buses run between distant activities. A great way to usher in the New Year, this family affair has a single admission fee that gets you an admission button for all events.

ARTS AND CULTURE

Missouri has produced its fair share of our nation's artists and writers. Scott Joplin, George Caleb Bingham, T. S. Eliot, Langston Hughes, Kate Chopin, Robert Heinlein, Howard Nemerov, Maya Angelou, and—oh, yes—Mark Twain. And many of them—Thomas Hart Benton, Vance Randolph, Laura Ingalls Wilder, Rose O'Neill, Harold Bell Wright, Zoe Akins, Janet Dailey—have had connections to that little area of our state known as the Ozarks. There is something about the Ozarks that has nourished the individual artist. Maybe it is the beauty of the hills, the many greens of trees in the spring, the riot of color of those same trees in the fall. Perhaps it is the strength and endurance of the hills themselves, or perhaps it is our great oral storytelling tradition. Others would say simply that it's because of "something in our pure spring water."

In any event, the Ozarks area has produced art and artists from an environment that did not offer the best support system for the artist. There has always been an anti-art element in the Ozarks. Many schools did not allow school plays to be produced, even until fairly recently, and prohibited dancing (some still do). The fiddle was sometimes looked upon as "the devil's instrument." That was part of our early settlers' puritan heritage, and it still is strong, as evidenced by controversy over Missouri State University's production of *The Normal Heart* and the banning of a large photographic reproduction of the Venus de Milo in Springfield's Battlefield Mall some years ago. That heritage of an innate suspicion of the arts may explain why so often local public schools practice a benign neglect of the arts and humanities. They without question will buy uniforms for sports programs but insist that the music program conduct fund-raisers to buy new uniforms for the band. But that's changing—if only gradually and grudgingly. The artists and performers on The Strip have been a positive influence. The new Branson High School has an acoustically perfect stage and 750-seat intimate auditorium that would rival many Branson theaters, one that can even mount traveling off-Broadway productions.

But equally strong has been the faction that has pushed for arts education and encouraged development of the individual in the arts. As soon as crops were planted and cabins built, some settlers organized amateur theatricals, Friday-night literaries (declamations, debates, and readings), and "kitchen sweats" (in-home dances). A remnant of these gatherings can be found in "mountain jam sessions," gatherings in homes, old rural schoolhouses, and community centers where Ozarkers gather to play "just for the fun of it." Music and storytelling are part of our folk culture. The traditional hardscrabble Ozarks existence, a general independence, and isolation from outside influences have developed a crafts tradition. The individual desire for perfection and decoration have produced utilitarian objects that border on fine art. Writers from Harold Bell Wright in the past and Janet Dailey and Jory Sherman today have found solace and seclusion in the hills around Branson.

As contact with outside influences has increased with better roads and travel, there has been change in the arts as well as attitudes toward the arts. The music of old-time barn dances has evolved into a new country style "that built The Strip." Branson may not have fine examples of old architecture like Eureka Springs, Springfield, and

Carthage, but we have some fine new buildings as a result of becoming a tourist town.

The development of the tourist industry has created a greater appreciation of art and design because theater owners, banks, and businesses recognize that architecture and decor are important for satisfying the aesthetic eye of visitors. For example, the bronze *Freedom Horses* monument created by world-famous artist Veryl Goodnight of Santa Fe, New Mexico, greets visitors in the circle drive at Mansion America Theater. The Moon River Theatre and the Moon River Grille feature some of modern art collection of Andy Williams. Sculptures by Frederic Remington can be viewed in the lobby of the Remington Theatre, and ceiling murals by Arthur Congero and wall murals by Antonio Arechega can be viewed at the Branson Variety Theater. Even plantings and landscaping are being used more artistically to catch the eye of the tourist. Many theaters and businesses have landscaping displays that are artistic delights. Blossoms of Branson is a program that encourages planting flowers to brighten up the scene and give Branson more "eye appeal."

The old has not been abruptly replaced or obliterated by the new. Instead, there has been a melding, a flowing together that's incongruous but not infelicitous, rather like the unique blend of nectars that makes Ozarks wildflower honey so tasty.

Today, Branson is home to well-known country and pop artists, who lure hundreds of thousands to a small town that has more theater seats than New York City. What other town in the nation the size of Branson can claim so many artists and so much entertainment? In a sense, the area's performance art, as well as its history and natural beauty, is what brings people here. Increasingly, the local theaters are offering music that can hardly be called strictly country, and there are now more variety and theatrical entertainment than ever. More people has meant changed entertainment; it has also meant more galleries and more artists—not just musicians, but also writers, dancers, and directors moving

to the area. These artists find they feel welcome, comfortable, and inspired by the area. Consumers of the artists' products are finding quality, an exciting blend and evolution, as well as an increasing variety in the artistic culture of the area. Branson is a great place for the artist and the art lover—and it's getting better all the time.

ART GALLERIES AND STUDIOS

Art galleries here in Branson tend to reflect the tastes of the buying public and probably the majority of the artists. The art tends toward pastoral, bucolic, wildlife, and western themes, sometimes of a super-realist nature. Functionalism is in, and galleries frequently offer a mix of art and crafts. However, one can find "newfangled art" including cubism, impressionism, expressionism, and minimalism that sometimes reflects a regional quality. We've included some of the better-known galleries and studios in Branson and the immediate vicinity. You may want to see the Day Trips chapter for information about Eureka Springs, as this small town has a number of shops, studios, and galleries that would entice the art lover.

ART SHOWCASE: A GALLERY OF FINE ART
144 East Main St.
(417) 334-8490
Mary Ravitz has a delightful new gallery, located conveniently in downtown Branson just up the street from the railroad depot and the new Branson Landing. The gallery features works by many artists, including some who are internationally known. You can find Murano glass hand-signed by Novarro and Veni, whimsical works by Pierre Matisse, and portraits by Royo. Also featured are Missourians who work in oils, photography, and wood carving, including Native American artist Doug Hall and award-winning artist Margaret Myers.

Art Showcase is open from 10 a.m. to 5:30 p.m. Tuesday through Saturday from March through December and Thursday through Saturday in January and February.

BOGER GALLERY
Jones Learning Center,
College of the Ozarks, Point Lookout
(417) 334-6411

This gallery frequently has visiting and traveling shows as well as student art shows. Exhibits are free. Call the college's art department at the number above or the Branson Arts Council, (417) 336-4255, for its current featured exhibit.

BURLINGTON STORE ANNEX
201 South Commercial St.
(417) 335-4789

In this downtown Branson store, you'll find a full array of stained-glass work, as small as sun catchers and as large as windows, doors, and ceilings. It also carries an interesting variety of other quality gift items. What started as a basement stained-glass project for artist Suzy Aikman has now grown into a production studio with several retail locations and commissions from churches and businesses across the nation. The Yellow Ribbon stained-glass window in the old Tony Orlando Yellow Ribbon Theater is an example of the work they do.

HESS POTTERY AND BASKETS
MO 413, Reeds Spring
(417) 272-3283
www.hesspottery.com

Potter Tom Hess has a wide local following for his beautiful, earthy clayware. His unique open-air, twelve-sided yurt serves as the workshop and sales gallery for Tom and basket maker Lory Brown. Tom specializes in making a smooth red clay pie plate that produces an evenly-browned bottom crust. His pie plate has been featured in the New York Times and Fine Cooking magazine and enjoys a reputation of excellence that is worldwide. Lory makes baskets and ornaments from coils of longleaf pine needles she stitches together with strips of raffia palm leaf. The two artists also work together to create combination clay and pine needle wall pieces and baskets.

MITCH YUNG CERAMIC DESIGN, INC. & HOT FRESCO POTTERY
141 Sunset Dr., Hollister
(417) 337-9227, (877) 337-9227
www.mitchyung.com,
www.hotfrescopottery.com

Mitch creates custom stoneware wall sculpture, decorative objects, and custom tile. Also available: custom sinks and fountains for interior and exterior use. His work has been installed in various locations, including banks, hotels, and hospitals. He sells through interior designers, art consultants, retail art shows and directly from his studio by appointment. His Hot Fresco Pottery is a collection of stoneware serving pieces made by the potters at Mitch Yung Ceramic Design, Inc. Its best-selling item is a wheel-thrown dip cooler that keeps dips and cheeseballs cold for four to six hours. Much of the pottery has a colorful Mediterranean theme. A retail shop within the existing studio is open by appointment.

OMEGA POTTERY SHOP
MO 248, Reeds Spring
(417) 272-3369
www.omega-pottery-shop.com

Playing in the mud since 1972, Potter Mark Oehler has almost become a landscape feature. He produces everything from bathroom sinks to lamp bases and from dinnerware to canister sets in his dishwasher-safe, ovenproof, and microwave-safe high-fired stoneware. In addition to the utilitarian, there are beautiful, unique, and exotic sculptural items. Oehler's palette of glazes leans toward earth tones, but he also likes cobalt blue. Omega is open year-round from 10 a.m. to 5 p.m. but is closed Wednesday.

PETE ENGLER'S DESIGN SHOP
2800 76 Country Blvd.
(417) 335-6862
www.peterenglerdesigns.com

Peter Engler has been carving since 1962 and specializes in carving Santas. In fact, he is known as Branson's Santa Carver and has been featured on HGTV and in *National Geographic* magazine.

i If you want some real Ozarks products made by genuine Ozarkers, not some China knockoffs, and don't have time while visiting Branson to do some shopping, order online when you get home at www.ozarks emporium.com.

His small shop in the Grand Village features regional and folk art—mostly wood carvings reflecting the major interest of this owner and master woodcarver. The work of more than 200 Ozark wood-carvers is represented, including that of wood sculptor Bob Robertson from Hollister. The shop is open year-round, but call for winter hours.

TABLEROCK ART GUILD GALLERY
Kimberling City Shopping Center
(417) 739-5829
www.tablerockartguild.com
The Tablerock Art Guild is a local support group of area artists who operate a membership gallery. The eight members of a 1980 oil-painting class who decided to form an art guild didn't know that their efforts would turn into an organization with 100 members and its own art gallery. Formed "to promote the advancement of art in the local area and encourage members to further their talents," the guild has monthly meetings and offers educational programs, workshops, and art shows. The gallery displays and sells members' artwork. It is open Monday through Saturday from 10 a.m. to 4 p.m.

If you are moving to the area or already live in the area and are interested in joining the guild, call the number above for membership information.

TIM CHERRY SCULPTURE DESIGNS
609 Parnell Dr.
(417) 335-3870
www.timcherry.com
Sculptor Tim Cherry always has a few bronze pieces lying around the workshop of his home in the subdivision across from the Skaggs Com-

munity Health Center, but most of his work is cast in Colorado and sold in galleries across the nation and Canada. The blue heron fountain in Rocky's Italian Restaurant is a good example of Cherry's work (see the Restaurants chapter). His years of experience as a professional guide in British Columbia show in his love of simple and graceful lines, a hallmark of his sculpture. Cherry says, "My sculptural approach involves the use of simplified shapes and lines to produce curvilinear forms. I enjoy orchestrating these elements into sculpture that is rhythmical, flowing, and inviting to the touch." Cherry and his wife Linda in 2008 were sponsors of the Springfield Symphony Orchestra's Branson Landing concert, at which the sculpture *Bruin Ball* was presented to Andy Williams for his contribution to the city.

i Rose O'Neill, best known for creating the Kewpie doll in 1909, was also a sculptor. You can see two of her sculptures, *Embrace of the Tree* and *The Fauness*, on the grounds of the artist's rebuilt home, now operated as Bonniebrook Home, 9 miles north of Branson on Bear Creek.

MUSEUMS

BRANSON CITY HALL
110 West Maddux St.
(417) 334-3345
Obviously, the seat of our city government isn't a museum, but if you're in the vicinity, stop in and see some of the buildings and scenes of early Branson reflected in the fine watercolors of Eloise DeLaval. City Hall also has a permanent collection of photographer-journalist Townsend Godsey's photographs of people, events, and activities of the early days of Branson. Godsey chronicled Ozarks culture through photography in his book, *These Were the Last*.

RALPH FOSTER MUSEUM
College of the Ozarks
(417) 334-6411
www.rfostermuseum.com

This museum is a veritable attic of interesting items and collections (see the Attractions chapter for more information). For the art lover it houses an interesting collection of Rose O'Neill's Kewpies and a small collection of paintings and drawings by O'Neill, Louis Freund, Thomas Hart Benton, M. E. Oliver (whose drawings for years graced the pages of *The Ozarks Mountaineer*), and others. For those interested in Native American art, the museum has a large collection of work by the artist Shipshee.

The museum also hosts the annual White River Painting Exhibit to showcase and encourage area artists. Many area businesses offer purchase awards, and you can see a fine collection of art in some area businesses.

While on the college campus, go over to the library and see the mural on the second floor by Steve Miller (friend of Benton), a local artist who was longtime curator of the Ralph Foster Museum.

i | **The Springfield Area Arts Council publishes a calendar of arts events for the Springfield area. Call (417) 869-8380 to get on the mailing list.**

SPRINGFIELD ART MUSEUM
1111 East Brookside Dr., Springfield
(417) 837-5700
www.ci.springfield.mo.us/egov/art/index.html
Sculptures in this park setting immediately attract the eye. The lawn sculptures are by Jim Sterrit, Ernest Trova, and John Henry. Located on the edge of Phelps Grove Park, the original structure of the Springfield Art Museum opened in 1958, but the newer Jeannette L. Musgrave Wing dates from 1994. It was built to house works from the museum's permanent collection of drawings, etchings, prints, and paintings, some 8,895 art objects representing thousands of years of culture. Special collections include 19th-, 20th-, and 21st-century American paintings, watercolor, sculpture, and prints. Thomas Hart Benton,

George Burchfield, and Red Grooms are just a few of the artists represented, but there are also works by Dürer, Rembrandt, and other masters. The museum is home of the Gertrude Vanderveer Spratlen Collection, an eclectic assortment of more than 450 paintings. It has more than 20,000 square feet of exhibit space, a museum shop, a 400-seat auditorium, classrooms, and studio space. In 2008, a new wing with an entry hall, galleries, gift shop, and a new library was completed. Educational activities include preschool to adult groups studio classes.

Each summer the museum is home to *Watercolor U.S.A.*, a nationally known juried show of watercolors. The show was started in 1961 and has grown to become one of the major watercolor shows in the nation. Recently the show drew more than 1,545 entries by 815 artists.

Artists from nearly every state in the Union were represented. The show usually consists of 100 to 115 pieces and is a summer highlight. Every two years the museum features the *Moak* (for Missouri, Oklahoma, Arkansas, and Kansas) *Exhibition*, an open, competitive, and juried all-media show.

THEATER AND FILM

The evolution of The Strip has presented us with materials to make some interesting observations and predictions. Branson from its earliest days as a tourist destination has had theatrical attractions, whether stage and street shows at Silver Dollar City, The Shepherd of the Hills outdoor drama, or, for many years, the summer repertory productions at the Beacon Hill Theatre (1960–89) of the School of the Ozarks (now College of the Ozarks). In the last several years, other shows and dinner theaters have come and gone. Area residents and visitors can find student productions at College of the Ozarks and in Springfield at Missouri State University and Drury. More and more, The Strip is diversifying its entertainment offerings to include something other than country music.

For decades, the only movie theater was the old Owen in downtown Branson. That changed when Branson became a tourist destination. The Factory Shoppes at Branson Meadows, 4562 Gretna Rd., has a 30,000-square-foot, eleven-screen movie-theater complex showing first-run movies. The cinema complex features stadium seating in a specially designed pie-shaped "stealth cinema" auditorium, digital surround sound, the latest projection technology, and a party room so you can plan special events, such as kids' birthday parties, at the cinema and mall. The cinema also features a large video arcade and game area. Call (417) 332-2884 for their latest cinema offering.

Elite Cinema Three, (417) 335-4832, is the most recent movie-theater venue. It is housed in the IMAX Entertainment Complex on the Shepherd of the Hills Expressway. The $1.7 million expansion added three standard-size movie theater screens, all with state-of-the-art sound and seats, which show first-run movies. One theater has a stage and can be used for conventions and other special events.

Branson has the big-screen IMAX Theater, (417) 335-4832, on the Shepherd of the Hills Expressway that shows spectacular 70 mm movies on its six-story-tall screen (see the Attractions chapter), and it recently installed a 35 mm projector and shows Hollywood productions using the theater's 22,000-watt surround-sound system. (For a really awesome experience, you ought to see some of the latest action spectaculars on this screen!)

INSPIRATION POINT FINE ARTS COLONY
US 62 West
Eureka Springs, AR
(479) 253-8595
www.opera.org
In the beauty of the Arkansas Ozarks, 7 miles west of Eureka Springs, is a summer opera treat. Top-notch college/graduate-level musicians and vocalists enroll for classes in this summer workshop, conducted by well-known names in opera, and residents and tourists reap the benefit of nightly outdoor full-length orchestra-accompanied opera performances. There are also orchestra concerts, opera scenes, and children's

opera performances. In 1999, IPFAC offered some painting classes, and some years they run a high-school vocal jazz camp. You can enjoy a great sunset on the hills overlooking the White River 600 feet below and opera by some surprising and developing talent. For fifty-plus years now, we've enjoyed our "opera in the Ozarks." Call or visit their Web site for their summer schedule or if you are interested in participating.

MSU TENT THEATRE
801 South National Ave., Springfield
(417) 836-7678
www.missouristatetix.com
For almost 50 years Tent Theatre on the MSU campus has provided summer repertory entertainment that presents the best of Broadway in an intimate, outdoor setting. Tent Theatre alumni have gone on to become well known in professional theater and film or active in area theater and education.

Recent productions have included *Damn Yankees, Altar Boyz, The Miss Firecracker Contest,* and *Joseph and the Amazing Technicolor Dreamcoat.* The season is late June, July, and early August. Give a call for shows, dates, and curtain times.

SPRINGFIELD LITTLE THEATRE
311 East Walnut St., Springfield
(417) 869-1334
www.landerstheatre.org
The historic Landers Theatre is home to Springfield Little Theatre, one of the Midwest's finest community-theater organizations. Built in 1909, the Landers is a prime example of Baroque Renaissance/Napoleon-style decoration. Audiences have seen touring artists and vaudeville stars ranging from Lillian Russell to John Philip Sousa and Fanny Brice on the Landers stage, and more recently, Tess Harper, Kathleen Turner, and John Goodman have performed there. Springfield Little Theatre, founded in 1934, was bought by the Landers in 1970, who began to nurture it back to its original elegance. In the newly restored showcase theater, SLT brings a mainstage season of seven plays and musicals. Recent

productions were *Misery, Narnia, The Music Man, The Boys Next Door,* and *The Buddy Holly Story.*

There's a variety of entertainment activities in the adjacent 200-seat Vandivort Center Theatre, including YES (for Young Entertainment Series), a performance series geared for young audiences, and the Studio Series, offering nontraditional theater works in an intimate setting. Call for current shows, ticket prices, and curtain times.

> **i** The Branson area is home to a number of novelists of some note: Daniel Woodrell, Janet Dailey, Lois Kleinsasser (aka Cait London and Cait Logan), Lori Copeland, and Suzann Ledbetter. Look for their books next time you're in your local bookstore.

SPRINGFIELD REGIONAL OPERA
411 North Sherman, Springfield
(417) 863-1960
www.sropera.com

The stage of the Hammons Center is home to most of the productions of the Springfield Regional Opera. The opera began in 1979 and was the impetus of its first director, Dawin Emanuel. It has done much to further opera in the Ozarks and has performed much of the traditional operatic literature in some not-so-traditional performing spaces, including Fantastic Caverns (see the Day Trips chapter). Past productions have included *Madame Butterfly, The Elixir of Love, Carmen,* and *The Girl of the Golden West* and operettas *H.M.S. Pinafore,* and *The Merry Widow.* The latest production of *Rigoletto* featured internationally known tenor, Michael Spyres, a local boy from nearby Mansfield who has become a shining star in the opera world.

Currently the SRO mounts two productions a year, with a fall and spring operatic offering. Casts are drawn from the extended area. The operatic chorus is volunteer but auditioned. Members come from communities as far flung as Gainesville, Marshfield, Branson, and Ozark,

and local church and college choirs actively participate. Principal roles are auditioned from the general community, with some roles performed by imported stars.

STAINED GLASS THEATRE
1996 West Evangel, Ozark
(417) 581-9192
www.sgtheatre.com

For over twenty years, Ron Boutwell, cofounder and executive director of the Stained Glass Theatre, has been bringing Christian drama to the Ozarks area. Productions are not "bathrobe drama" but high-quality performances of quality plays at reasonable prices. (Tickets are $5 to $8.) The promise of entertainment with a moral message has drawn people who otherwise might not step into a theater. Stained Glass Theatre offers instruction in acting, directing, and playwriting through its Christian Drama Institute and operates the Stained Glass Theatre-West in Joplin. Like the traveling theater companies of yore, Stained Glass Theatre takes shows into churches, stores, and communities in the Ozarks to audiences who might not ever get to see a live theater production otherwise. Recent productions were *The Lord of Two Requests* and *The Last Oasis.* Call the above number for shows and information.

TRI-LAKES COMMUNITY THEATRE
P.O. Box 1301, Branson, MO 65615
(417) 335-4241

Founded in 1983, the TLC Theatre draws from a wealth of area talent and from shows on The Strip during the winter season, when some venues are closed. The organization is run by a board of nine directors, and all the work, from directing, acting, and building sets to box office and ushering, is performed by TLC Theatre volunteers. It does two shows a year, and past productions have included *Steel Magnolias, Oliver, Fiddler on the Roof, Lil Abner, Follies, Big River, Bus Stop,* and *Plaza Suite.* Productions usually take place in one of the local music theaters. Call the above number for current shows and ticket prices or if you want to become involved as a volunteer.

DANCE AND MUSIC

SPRINGFIELD BALLET
400 South Ave., Springfield
(417) 862-1343
www.springfieldballet.org
Incorporated in 1976, Springfield Ballet has been upgrading the quality of area ballet and bringing fine examples of dance art to area audiences. A community favorite for years has been its annual production of *The Nutcracker*. Also important is the School Concert each May. Call the number above for a current schedule and ticket prices.

SPRINGFIELD MID-AMERICA SINGERS
P.O. Box 3239, Springfield, MO 65808-3239
(417) 863-7464
This group of talented amateurs with a healthy mix of professional singers directed by Sharon Wilkinson makes community appearances during the year with concerts and recitals.

SPRINGFIELD SYMPHONY ORCHESTRA
1536 East Division St., Springfield
(417) 864-6683
www.springfieldmosymphony.org
Directed by Ron Spigelman, the SSO features an eight-concert season that is a mix of pop and classical music. Recent guest artists and conductors have included violinist Michael Ludwig, cellist Mark Kosower, jazz vocalist Nancy Kelly, soprano Arianna Zukerman, and pianist Andrew Russo. A number of special-events concerts, including performances at the Branson Landing, are featured each year. Call for current concerts and ticket information.

SUPPORT ORGANIZATIONS

No matter where you live, funding for the arts is meager to scarce. Although dance, music, and theater add much to what we call a civilized life, our orchestras, music schools, and dance companies frequently have a hand-to-mouth existence, especially at a time of a sagging economy and declining federal support.

i The Branson area is not just country-music country. Jazz guitarist Charlie Haden is from Forsyth. Check out his CDs, including *Under the Missouri Sky*, at music stores.

Most support organizations in the Ozarks have found creative ways to promote that which makes civilizations noble. If you visit the Ozarks, support the arts by attending a show or buying artwork. If you are new to the area as a resident, ask around: you can be sure there is some way you can get involved in the arts and culture of our area.

BRANSON ARTS COUNCIL, INC.
201 Compton Dr.
(417) 336-4255
www.bransonartscouncil.com
The BAC's mission is "to make available artistic, cultural, and education opportunities and support, strengthen and enhance these opportunities for all community citizens." It does that through membership and grants. The BAC has been active in purchasing arts educational materials for the local library as well as sponsoring plays, workshops, exhibits, and concerts, including popular Milk and Cookies concerts for kids at the Taneyhills Library. It has established historical markers for Branson sites, sponsored art-safety workshops for area artists and craft workers, developed a summer drama camp for children, and sponsored public murals and sculptures. The recently restored Old Stone Presbyterian Church at the corner of Fourth and Pacific Streets has become an intimate venue for BAC-sponsored recitals, concerts, and lectures. It publishes *BAC Tracks* for members. A call to the BAC can get you information about current shows and arts activities and information about becoming a member.

OZARKS WRITERS LEAGUE
P.O. Box 1433, Branson, MO 65615
(417) 334-5615
www.ozarkswritersleague.org
The Ozarks Writers League is open to writers of all

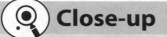

Close-up

Storyteller Judy Dockery Young

"TELLRZ" tells it all. That's the license plate of storyteller Judy Dockery Young and her storytelling husband, Richard Young. For more than 25 years, Judy has been "Branson's Storyteller," relating tall tales and stories she had heard and collected throughout the years, following a tradition that is as old as the folks who settled the Ozark hills.

Her homespun appearance and versatile voice, which can range from a deep bass for a bear or a scary "haint" to the soprano squawk of a scared chicken, masks a solid scholarly background in speech and theater. After a B.A. at Southwest Missouri State University in Springfield and an M.A. from Trinity University in San Antonio, with a concentration in Children's Theater, Judy taught for two years in a local high school. She was convinced by one of her students, who worked summers at Silver Dollar City, to audition for the post of "entertainer." She has been entertaining ever since, as a street character, train robber, and finally, as a master storyteller, at the park and for libraries, clubs, and conventions.

"A good teacher is a good actor and entertainer, and a good entertainer is part teacher," she says of her career as resident storyteller at the famous theme park. "Most folktales are not told for mere entertainment only but have a moral or a lesson buried in them. It was through stories that hill people demonstrated a creative, dramatic capacity and also passed on to the younger generation their basic beliefs and morals, as well as techniques for getting on in life. These techniques would serve them whether they became teachers or store owners, or if they ran for local political office."

She became interested in storytelling as an art when asked to do an impromptu, audience-participation sketch called *The School Marm and the Bear* at the theme park. Recalling the experience, she said, "It was great fun, getting children to play parts as crows, bears, skunks, elephants, even trees, and I was director and ad-libber." Gradually she began telling some of the stories she had heard growing up in Oklahoma and Missouri before or during the sketch, with great success—and she found the career that was the love of her life. She also learned she had to search for materials. She told favorites from *The Grandfather Tales*, collected by Richard Chase, stories such as "Old One-Eye" and "Mean John and the Devil."

It was stories like these that entertained urban visitors to the theme park, but locals and hill folks who came eyed her like she was a rattlesnake sunning itself—harmless but not trustworthy. When they realized that she was having fun telling the story and wasn't poking fun

stages of development, from aspiring beginners to published professionals. It meets quarterly and features programs and workshops by members and outside experts for its 350 members, drawn from a 150-mile radius. It publishes a quarterly newsletter, *The OWLs Hoot,* and features writing contests for members. Call or write for membership information.

Writers within the Ozarks region network on an e-loop, the Ozarks Regional Writers Loop (ORWL), to share information about markets and writing. Membership in the e-loop is open to all writers in the Ozarks region, and registration information can be found at http://groups.yahoo .com/group/ORWL.

SPRINGFIELD AREA ARTS COUNCIL
Creamery Arts Center
411 North Sherman Parkway
Springfield
(417) 862-2787
www.springfieldarts.org
This nonprofit organization "fosters, promotes, and encourages the existing cultural and edu-

at the hillbilly stereotype but passing on orally the values and traditions and stories they felt comfortable with, they began telling her stories they had heard or that they themselves loved to tell. One, "The Dog's Tale" (with a pun on tail), became a favorite of hers to tell, and she has collected more than 19 variations of it. Gradually she began to gather a large collection of tales that had never been written down but that had been passed down in families or a community for generations.

"I would sometimes get pages and pages from a Big Chief tablet written in a shaky scrawl from some old person who had finally found someone who could appreciate the art of a tale and could be trusted to tell it in the spirit it had been told. I felt like I was being given a legacy," she says. "They knew I would take care of their stories."

"Such treasures should be shared. I can do that through storytelling, but I can't tell the story to everybody. I can record it for future generations, though." And she has. She and her husband, Richard, have ten audio cassettes of the storyteller's art. She has also further safeguarded these gems from the hills, for oral art can be ephemeral, in published collections, such as *Ozark Ghost Stories and Outlaw Tales from America's Middle Border* published by August House. She and Richard have nine collections of folktales and stories to their credit.

Both she and Richard have brought their art to conventions and workshops, and to the general public on radio and TV. They are often invited to do workshops for teachers and drama departments, and of course they are in demand as after-dinner speakers.

Like Oscar Wilde, who would polish his bon mots before they would appear in his work, a good storyteller is always working and polishing. "I would say 98 percent of my material is 'set' and learned. But you have to learn to tell it not like it is memorized but like it's 'just off the cuff.' The other 2 percent is improvising, playing on the audience and the moment, seizing the day—carpe diem. That's why I never get bored with telling a story I've told before. 'The Old Woman and Her Pig' is a story I must have told 10,000 times, and it's my signature piece. But it's different every time—and I enjoy it every time."

Judy's gusto for her work and for life is contagious. She can hold an audience of children who would normally squirm like snakes on a stove in rapt attention as they hang on her every word. That's power. That's art.

And for Judy there is satisfaction in that aspect as well as knowing that you are preserving while you practice an art that is as old as the Ozark hills.

cational endeavors of Springfield and its environs." It sponsors the annual Artsfest on Walnut Street the first weekend in May and First Night, a citywide New Year's Eve gala (see the Annual Events chapter). It helps coordinate arts events in Springfield and publishes a calendar of events and arts directory.

SPRINGFIELD VISUAL ARTS ALLIANCE
P.O. Box 11113 GS, Springfield, MO 65808
(417) 862-2787
www.springfieldvisualartsalliance.org

One of the enjoyable activities in Springfield is finding an art display in an unexpected area, often sponsored by the SVAA. Founded in 1988, the nonprofit alliance seeks to create "a richer environment for the visual arts in the Springfield region." It offers professional exchange and exhibition for local and regional artists by displaying artwork in public locations. Membership is open to artists within 180 miles of Springfield, working in any medium and at any stage of artistic development. The group publishes a quarterly newsletter, *The Visual Voice*.

SPRINGFIELD WRITERS' GUILD
(417) 883-4647
www.swgsite.org
This writers' support group for Springfield and area writers is a chapter of the Missouri Writers' Guild and sponsors an annual poetry/prose contest in October and often hosts an annual conference at the same time. The Guild meets the fourth Saturday monthly at the Heritage Cafeteria, 1364 E. Battlefield, at 1 p.m. (except December) with a speaker and business meeting, and publishes a monthly newsletter, The Freelancer. Annual dues are $15. Writers of all genres are welcome.

VENUES

JUANITA K. HAMMONS HALL FOR THE PERFORMING ARTS
Cherry Street and John Q. Hammons Parkway
(417) 836-7678
www.missouristatetix.com
www.hammonshall.com
Performing arts in the area got a big boost with the opening of this fine facility in 1993. (You'll find the Hammons name on a lot of Springfield real estate.) It is the home of the Springfield Symphony, and the hall presents a concert and stage series that provides fare for every taste. Recent shows in the Give Your Regards to Broadway series included *The Rat Pack, To Kill a Mockingbird,* and *Cherish the Ladies.* Recent performers have included Hal Holbrook in *Mark Twain Tonight,* Bela Fleck, Bebe Neuwirth, Russian cellist Alexandre Bouzlov, the Trinity Irish Dance Company, and Jerry Seinfeld. If you don't find it on The Strip in Branson, you can find it "at the Hall"!

Call the box office or visit the Web site for shows, curtain times, and prices. The site also includes events at Coger Theater, Hammons Field, Guilloz Theatre, and JQH Arena.

RECREATION AND THE OUTDOORS

No matter how many shows you take in or how much shopping you do while here in Branson, take the time to try athletics and outdoor sports. Mix a little exercise into even your busiest trips, or at least take a look around. Even if you don't venture off The Strip, try walking it. It isn't all that long, and you may be surprised at how much you can see on foot while walking that you miss when in your car surrounded by traffic.

The great outdoors here in the Ozarks is so great that we actually have two chapters devoted to it. If you miss fishing, floating, boating, and waterskiing in this chapter, that's because the Lakes and Rivers chapter covers those outdoor activities. In this chapter we cover "the land activities" in the great outdoors and other types of recreation you'll find in the Branson area.

Most of the folks who live in the Ozarks are into the outdoors, and it's easy to see why the Ozarks would be home to Bass Pro Shops (see the Day Trips chapter). Lots of folks like to hunt, fish, boat, golf, or hike in what has been described as a sport lover's paradise. Our highways and roadsides are lined with wildflowers. People inside the Branson city limits put out salt for deer that nibble the shrubbery; sometimes you can see the deer even from motels on The Strip. We may have the neon glitz and glitter of The Strip and traffic so thick during the season you can't stir it with a stick, but we are also only a half hour's drive from some of the best free-flowing floating streams in the nation and wilderness areas so untouched that you can hike for days and not see a soul.

Development in Branson has changed the nature of the hills, and we do have some raw-looking road cuts that have not yet had the softening weathering experience of rain, frost, and lichens. But the nature that drew visitors here at the turn of the 19th century is still abundantly evident. As soon as high-pressure boilers allowed small steamboats to come up the White River in the 1850s, anglers and hunters came to the Ozarks. Often they'd have to spend a year because the river was only navigable in spring during high water. Sometimes they'd choose to leave via wagon or horseback later in the year rather than wait until the next spring to take a steamboat back down the White. With the coming of the railroad, the Ozarks became more accessible to sports enthusiasts. Game was plentiful. The scenery was breathtaking. The plow's touch was confined to the fertile bottomlands. That which attracted Harold Bell Wright into the Ozarks at the turn of the 20th century can still be found. *The Shepherd of the Hills* has a cast of characters that are as big as the Ozarks' out-of-doors, and Young Matt, the hero, and Sammy Lane, the heroine, still cast a romantic shadow on our landscape.

Dams on the White River have changed forever the terrain and nature of the Ozarks (see the Lakes and Rivers and the History chapters), but the area continues to invite exploration. Our rivers and streams, lakes, woods, and balds are becoming more accessible than ever to today's hikers, bikers, campers, and nature lovers. Thanks to better roads, a better appreciation by locals of their own outdoor environment, and the development of private, city, state, and federal parks and wilderness areas, more people than ever can appreciate the beauty that we who live here have so often taken for granted.

CITY PARKS AND RECREATION

"Parks will always improve the quality of life in a community," says Cindy Shook, Branson's parks and recreation director. And in Branson, the community is blessed with a large number of parks for a town of just more than 7,000 residents. Branson has 1,817 acres of parkland encompassing 17 parks and natural wilderness areas. These parks provide green, open space and allow for the city's parks and recreation programs.

"Parks and natural open spaces generate many fond memories for people," said Shook. "Picnics, playgrounds, Little-League baseball, and family fun are synonymous with parks." More than 150,000 participants enjoyed programs offered by the Branson Parks and Recreation Department in 2008. Adult sports such as softball, basketball, and volleyball; youth sports such as baseball, softball, soccer, and basketball; along with various community and specialty events are just the basics of the Parks Department program.

With the realization that tourists list "trees, scenery, and environment" as the fourth most important reason for visiting the Branson area, according to a Branson/Lakes Area Chamber of Commerce survey, residents recognize the need to provide adequate green space and plantings that make the area attractive. A city ordinance that encourages builders and developers to save as many trees as possible on a building site has met with great success. Developers increasingly use interior and exterior green space. Older busi-

nesses, which were exempt from the new requirement, are choosing to meet the code because it makes their locations more attractive. Recreation and environment are both important concerns.

Likewise, the recreational features of Branson's parks are balanced with environmental concerns. Many Branson parks take into consideration continuing community changes and wheelchair accessibility. Landscaping puts the emphasis on native materials to harmonize with the surroundings, and park trails are designed to minimize erosion.

In Branson, many park users come from outside the city, which underscores how important parks are to not only the city but also the region. Any child, no matter what economic background, can participate in Branson Parks and Recreation programs. Psychologists have found that pleasant events such as a walk in the woods or a park give a boost to the immune system that lasts two to three days. When visiting Branson, we invite you to not only enjoy the neon side of our city, but also the nature side. You'll be healthier for it.

ℹ The Canada geese and the mallard ducks on the Taneycomo lakefront are welfare birds and don't migrate. They are tourists who stayed—and they enjoy handouts.

ℹ The Missouri Department of Conservation publishes a number of good, inexpensive books that deal with the state's recreational activities: hiking, floating, bird-watching, and nature study. (See the Lakes and Rivers chapter.) They are available at bookstores and the state's four nature centers. If you are coming to Branson from the north, stop at the Springfield Nature Center at 4600 South Chrismon Rd. on the south side of Springfield, just a mile off US 65.

ALEXANDER PARK
Sunset Street
Situated on the banks of Taneycomo Lake, this park can be seen on the east from the bridge as you cross the lake on US 65. The facilities at the five-plus-acre park include a playground with a variety of equipment, two baseball fields, and tennis courts. The park is a whirl of activity on summer evenings, for the light lasts longer on the east-west valley of Lake Taneycomo, and when it does get dark, electric lights allow for league games until late. Neighbors and area residents use the perimeter streets for walking and biking.

BRANSON LAKESIDE RV PARK
300 South Boxcar Willie Dr.
(417) 334-2915
On the shores of Lake Taneycomo, this campground has rental sites, restrooms, shower facilities, and a public fishing area. RV fees help fund activities sponsored by the Branson Parks Department. The campground can be seen from US Business 65 as you cross the old Taneycomo Bridge. (See the Campgrounds and RV Parks and the Retirement chapters.)

BRANSON NORTH PARK
Lake Street
This is a one-acre neighborhood pocket park with playground equipment in one of Branson's established residential areas, Branson North. It's largely a gathering place for neighborhood kids.

BRANSON RECPLEX PARK
1500 Branson Hills Parkway
(417) 335-2368
The "new kid on the block" of the Branson park system, the $12 million Branson RecPlex opened its doors in June 2005 and instantly became a gathering place for the entire community. The facility is truly a campus of recreation, featuring a one-stop location for health, fitness, recreation, and organized sports.

Located on 42 acres in Branson Hills, north of the city, it features a 44,000-square-foot recreation center consisting of two gymnasiums, locker rooms, community rooms, a game room, offices, and a concession area. The second floor consists of a 7,500-square-foot fitness center with aerobics room and a 0.5-mile track above the gymnasiums.

Adjacent to the RecPlex is a 12,000-square-foot aquatic center. The state-of-the-art swimming pool features a zero-depth entry leisure pool, play features, a lap pool, water slides, and a diving well. The 30-foot-high water slides can be seen from US 65 when traveling to and from Branson.

The additional outside portion of the campus features soccer fields, a large children's playground, and four picnic pavilions. A 1.5-mile walking trail circles the entire complex. A four-field softball complex and concession building complete the complex.

The facilities allow Branson to host regional, state, and national sporting events throughout the year that and draw additional visitors to Branson.

Like the parks, the RecPlex is open to those visiting Branson, but for a fee, depending on what facilities are used.

CANTWELL PARK
Oklahoma and Walnut Streets
This neighborhood park in the Cantwell Addition neighborhood features nearly one and a half acres of grassy slopes, with huge old walnut trees, playground equipment, picnic tables, and a basketball court. You'll often see area youngsters rolling down the green slopes in summer and sliding down them whenever we get snow. It's a great place to take a picnic lunch.

CAUDILL PARK
Caudill Way
This new five-acre neighborhood park features a picnic area and gazebo and is currently under development. Parking is available.

EISERMAN PARK
Compton Drive
Eiserman Park, near the Branson Community Center, is one acre that includes a basketball court, playground, and covered pavilion. Adjacent to the park is the nine-hole Don Gardner Pitch and Putt Public Golf Course, named after an early golfer who brought the sport to Branson with the development of the Holiday Hills Golf Course in 1939. Each hole is a par 3, and the course is great for sharpening short-iron skills.

JOHN NYGARD MEMORIAL PARK
Adams Street
This two-acre park in central Branson was acquired in 2001 from the old Branson primary school. The old school ground has a large playground area and seating for local neighborhood use.

i The Branson RecPlex swimming pool is a great place to cool off during the hot summer and allow the kids to work off some energy—and lots cheaper than a water park. And at $4 a head for kids, $5 for adults, it's a great bargain. Call (417) 335-2368.

LAKESIDE FOREST WILDERNESS AREA
Fall Creek Road

This 130-acre park opened in 1999, a gift of Dr. Lyle Owen, a retired college professor who bought the land in the early 1930s and built the 340 stone steps from the top of the bluff above Lake Taneycomo down to about 60 feet above the water's edge. It was no easy task carrying the stone and mixing the mortar at that time. Owen inscribed one step: "Let those who tread here not forget that these steps were not made of stone and mortar alone, but of sweat and blood and agony."

The area contains two trails. Trail number one (0.5 mile one way) is a trail to the steps, but if you go down the steps, you have to come back up them, and though it's only 340 steps down, it seems like 3,400 on the climb up! Plans are to extend the trail along the bluff and have it loop back to its start. The trail and steps offer a scenic view of the Lake Taneycomo valley and feature a natural waterfall and several caves, including one called Old Soldiers Cave, which served as a hideout for a gunsmith during the Civil War. It takes about an hour to take the trail walk and the steps.

Trail two winds its way through forest and glades. The 1.3-mile trail is fairly level, accommodating families with children and folks who desire an easier stroll. A picnic area can be found halfway down the trail.

The Lakeside Forest Wilderness Area is open during daylight hours only in the fall and winter and from 7 a.m. to 7 p.m. during the spring and summer. Access to the area is from Fall Creek Road, about 0.2 mile south of MO 76. Turn left off MO 76 at the stoplight just before Dick Clark's American Bandstand Theater. Then look for the park sign on your left.

MURPHY PARK
John G. Neihardt Drive

This five-acre park in the Murphy Addition features a basketball court, children's playground, and two picnic pavilions. It's a centerpiece of neighborhood activity.

i If you plan a float trip in Arkansas, you can get a free Floater's Kit from the Arkansas Department of Parks and Tourism. The kit identifies 17 rivers and 9,700 miles of floatable water, providing maps of all locations and giving access points. Get the Floater's Kit by calling (501) 682-7777 or writing the Arkansas Department of Parks and Tourism, 1 Capitol Mall, Little Rock, AR 72201.

OLD BRANSON SCHOOL PARK
Country Boulevard

Located on The Strip near the Dixie Stampede, this one-acre park is a popular site for visitor picnics. There are picnic tables, a covered pavilion, and playground equipment. A public restroom resembles the old one-room schoolhouse that was once at this site.

PARNELL PARK
Parnell Circle

Located in the Parnell Neighborhood across from Skaggs Community Health Center, the one-acre park features two tennis courts, picnic tables, and playground equipment. Close by is the Branson Community Center.

STOCKSTILL PARK
Melody Penner Lane

The largest of Branson's public parks at 62 acres, Stockstill is on the north bank of Roark Creek, west of the US 65 bridge that crosses the creek. It is accessed from James F. Epps Road. Amenities include restrooms, two adult softball fields, a large children's playground, two covered picnic pavilions, a 0.3-mile walking path, six tennis courts, a soccer field, and a skate park.

For locals and visitors who like to live "on the edge," Stockstill is the home of Branson's first skateboard facility, featuring ramps, curbs, rails, and other challenges for both the experienced and novice skater. The skate park is free and open during daylight hours. Skaters are urged to wear helmets and pads that they must provide.

For those less adventuresome, this "center of Branson's Parks and Recreation activity" has shallow Roark Creek flowing on its south side, which gets lots of little visitors, who chase minnows and crawdads while parents and older siblings are on the playing fields.

SUNSET PARK
Sunset Street

This park is the large area of green space seen to the west as you cross Lake Taneycomo on US 65. It is reached via Alexander Park by going under the US 65 bridge. The 10 acres of open space and trees contain a 0.6-mile walking path along Taneycomo, where former president George H. Bush jogged during a 1992 campaign stop in Branson. Sunset also holds a 9-hole Disc Golf Course. Score cards are available on the Web site: www.bransonparksandrecreation.com. The park, along with Alexander Park and nearby Branson Lakeside RV Park to the east, is a favorite cycling place since it is one of the few large, flat areas with little traffic.

OTHER PARKS AND RECREATION AREAS

Glades and Balds

Although hardwood forests cover much of the Branson area, one of the most notable and interesting features is the glades. Glades are frequently called balds by locals, and we noted their historic function as meeting spots for the vigilante justice gang the Bald Knobbers in the 1880s in the History chapter.

Glades are islands of semi-desert and prairie plants within the sea of oak and history that covers the Ozarks. Glades often occur on the south- and west-facing slopes of hills. The sunlight is intense and prolonged there, and the thin soil barely covers the dolomite bedrock, which breaks down slowly. Parts of the stone weather more quickly than others, resulting in fantastic, gargoylelike shapes that resemble tiny gnarled totems.

Decomposition of organic materials takes a long time, and there is little buildup of organic materials like you might find on northern and eastern slopes, which are largely forested. In early days, fires started by lightning or set by Indians or early settlers enlarged these sites and kept them almost free of trees. With burning curtailed, many of the areas have become overgrown with the only trees that can survive in the semiarid environment—cedars. It was difficult to make a living from the hardscrabble land, so many of the glade areas were virtually wilderness regions. Many have come under the protection of the Missouri Department of Conservation. The fragile environment of the glades is easily damaged. In order to maintain the integrity of the land, the department regularly sets prescribed, controlled burns of sections of the glades.

Though they seem barren, glades harbor a vast array of plants and wildlife. Spring rains produce a profusion of wildflowers, including the Missouri state flower, the yellow Missouri primrose, which thrives in the rocky, thin, dolomite soil. When you hike glades in the spring, look for some of the unusual wildflowers and specially adapted plants, such as prickly pear cactus and the endangered glade bladderwort with its tiny yellow flowers. More common are mayapples, pussy toes, serviceberry, Solomon's seal, and Indian paintbrush. Other seasons produce fewer and less showy but equally interesting flowers. Even the hot summer can provide an interesting and pleasurable hike.

Keep your eyes open for our largest spider, the tarantula, especially in the fall when it searches for a winter home. The tarantula, black or brown and very hairy, can be 5 inches across. Though they look scary and they can bite, they are generally harmless. Good advice is not to turn over rocks, which can uncover spiders, scorpions, and the black-and-orange giant centipede, which can be

10 inches long. Some of these creatures have potentially fatal bites or stings, so you are better off leaving them alone—and so are the critters.

You may see our fastest snake, the slim coachwhip snake, which can reach lengths of 6 feet and slither faster than you can run. You'll also find other reptiles: skinks, fence lizards, garter snakes, three-toed box turtles, and eastern collared lizards. Locals call the 10-inch-long critters that look like a miniature T. Rex, especially when they rear up and run only on their hind legs, "mountain boomers." However, the lizard is voiceless, not at all like some of the spring tree frogs you may hear that "baa" like sheep. You may even see a roadrunner, which preys on the glade's reptiles and insects.

The glades are an interesting, wonderful, and fragile ecosystem. We love to have visitors, and we want you to learn about our unusual areas. However, do respect them. Follow the old adage: "Take only pictures. Kill only time. Leave only footprints."

BUFFALO NATIONAL RIVER
402 North Walnut St., Suite 136
Harrison, AR
(870) 741-5443
www.nps.gov/buff
The Buffalo River in the Boston Mountains is the last major undammed river in Arkansas, and it's going to stay that way. The 97,750 acres that make up the Buffalo National River and its tributaries became a national park in 1972. There had been plans all that century to build a dam on the river, and the Corps of Engineers had plans to build several dams on the Buffalo during the 1930s. World War II put those plans on hold. After the war, when the dam projects were reconsidered, a coalition of locals and canoeists, who had discovered the white-water experience of the Buffalo, made an outcry that called national attention to Arkansas's scenic gem. The Buffalo National River Park was the result. When you are in Branson, you can glimpse the peaks of the Boston Mountains from Inspiration Tower on the Shepherd of the Hills Homestead (see the Attractions chapter). It is worth a day trip to hike the park or float a portion of the 148-mile Buffalo

River. The bluffs, rising from the water's edge to a sheer rock-face height of 400 to 500 feet and an additional 300 feet of outcroppings and trees, are best experienced from the river while dipping your paddle in its clear waters (see the Lakes and Rivers chapter), but a bird's-eye view of the river from Big Bluff or Jim Bluff while hiking can be an equally thrilling experience. You can walk through thick forests, shallow-soiled glades, and spring-filled hollows.

The Buffalo National River in Arkansas is a recent addition to the nation's park system, and development of walking and hiking trails is progressing as people recognize that the park offers interesting and challenging hiking and walking as well as floating. There are more than 135 miles of trails, some maintained by the park, and others unmaintained (old logging roads, footpaths, etc.), with more planned. Some trails are for horse riders only. Eventually, the Buffalo River Trail will traverse the entire length of the park. Some trails are short walks that provide access to a particular bluff or interesting geological feature, but others offer miles of hiking along the 148-mile course of the river for those who want to experience the Ozarks before development. A hike along the river trails takes you up on the bluffs and provides spectacular views of the river, such as the one from Big Bluff, which at 500 feet is the highest bluff in the Ozarks. From some of the river's bluffs, you might catch a glimpse of the park's elk herd. The aptly named Goat's Trail, 350 feet above the river along Big Bluff, provides a heart-in-your-mouth hike. All parkland is open to walkers and hikers, and you may want to walk up the bed of a stream that enters the Buffalo.

The hike up Hemmed-In Hollow, a large box canyon, provides a glimpse of one of the highest waterfalls (200 feet) east of the Rockies, and it is always spectacular after a heavy rain. A hike into Lost Valley (just above Ponca) and back can take half a day. A walk into Hawksbill Crag (near Boxley) is shorter, and the view of the upper Buffalo River valley is spectacular. Standing on the crag, you can watch eagles and buzzards drifting in flight below you. Hiking is most popular in fall after the first frost (when ticks and chiggers have been eliminated), and with our mild winters and the greater visibility after the leaves have fallen, hikers can experience a facet of the Ozarks that is unavailable to summer hikers. Before venturing on the hiking paths of the Buffalo National River, know your limits and stamina, and make certain you have an up-to-date map of the areas you plan to hike.

You can download maps of the river and hiking trail maps at www.harrisonarkansas.org. The park publishes maps and *Buffalo National River Currents*. This annual magazine is chock-full of pictures and advice, and it has the latest information about the river and hiking trails. It is free at any park office. You can call the park headquarters at the number above for information about the river and the park and maps of the hiking trails. They'll be glad to send you an information packet about the Buffalo River.

The Buffalo River is just an hour and a half drive south of Branson. Park headquarters are in Harrison, Arkansas. Take US 65 to Harrison. A number of Arkansas highways enter the 148-mile-long park, including AR 43, 7, 123, 374, and 14.

BUSIEK STATE FOREST AND WILDLIFE AREA
US 65, 15 miles north of Branson
(417) 895-6880

This rectangular, 2,505-acre site has topography typical of the Ozark plateau, with steep rocky hills and gravel-bottomed creeks. Woods Fork of Bull Creek flows across 2.5 miles of the area, and Camp Creek flows 2.5 miles to its confluence with Woods Fork. More than 90 percent of the area is forested. It is open to camping, hiking, birdwatching, hunting, outdoor photography, and picnicking (no tables are provided). There are 15 miles of self-guided nature trails. An unattended public shooting range is 0.25 mile west of MO 65 near the access road.

You can obtain information and a map of the Busiek Wildlife Area by writing the Mark Twain Forest district forester at 2630 North Mayfair St., Springfield, MO 65803 or calling the number above.

To get to the Busiek Wildlife area, go 14 miles north of Branson on US 65 and make the first right (east) immediately after crossing Camp Creek. You'll see the sign on your right.

i Don't try to transplant wildflowers and native shrubs back home. Most don't transplant well when in full bloom (when you'll notice them), or they thrive in a very limited microenvironment with specific soil conditions. Besides, it's illegal to dig up native plants along Missouri highways. You can get many varieties of wildflower seeds and plants and learn if your planned home for them is suitable by calling Missouri Wildflowers Nursery at (573) 496-3492 or visiting www.mowildflowers.net.

CURRENT AND JACKS FORK RIVERS
Ozark National Scenic Riverways
P.O. Box 490, Van Buren, MO 63965
(573) 323-4236
www.nps.gov/ozar

It's a long drive over to the Big Springs country, in a whole different watershed where the river flows east, but it's a pretty area—and pretty spectacular. It offers hiking and floating (see the Lakes and Rivers chapter). The area is 125 miles east of Springfield, but since US 60 through Van Buren is a main conduit for folks coming to the Branson area from southern Illinois and Kentucky, you may want to make it a stop when you're coming (or going) that direction. A two-day float trip on the Jacks Fork or Current River could be your most memorable experience. The Current is fed by some of the largest springs in the world, and so it is floatable even in our dry summer months. The Jacks Fork, its major tributary, has less water but offers some excellent spring and early summer floating as it flows through a canyon in its upper reaches. The middle Jacks Fork valley is home to herds of wild horses, now protected by the National Park Service.

Like the Buffalo National River in Arkansas, the Current and Jacks Fork Rivers Ozark National Scenic Riverways is a recent addition to the national park system, and since most people come to float the river, development of walking and hiking trails has been slow and not widely publicized. However, more and more, people are

i All dirt roads and marked trails are available for horseback riders in the Current and Jacks Fork Rivers Ozark National Scenic Riverways. You can bring your own horse, or rent one. You can download a horse trail map at www.nps.gov/ozar or contact park headquarters at 573-323-4236, ext 0.

recognizing that the parkland along the river has interesting features not easily accessible to floaters, and so hiking is becoming more popular.

Currently there are 43 trails covering 48 miles, with more being developed, and existing trails are being upgraded. There are 23 miles of horse trails. Some hiking trails are merely short walks that provide access to a particular or interesting feature, but others offer miles of hiking for those who want to backpack in and camp and experience the Ozarks up-close and personal. Walking the Jacks Fork trails provides contact with the quiet environment of the Ozarks that author Sue Hubbell wrote about with such awe and admiration in *A Country Year*.

A hike along the river trails takes you up on the bluffs and provides spectacular views of the river and the valley below. You can look down on twisted junipers—scrawny, gnarled evergreens that rival California's redwood tree as the nation's oldest living plants. Frequently, they are draped with fisherman's beard (a plant much like Spanish moss), which provides an Old South–like atmosphere. In the spring, bright flowers, including the intense yellow of wild coreopsis, dot the shallow soil of bluff tops. You might catch a view of wild horses in the valley below. Along the trail, you may see white-tailed deer, a reclusive bobcat or red fox, or hear the calls of crows or pileated woodpeckers. Since all land is open to walkers and hikers, you may want to leave the trail where a small stream enters the river and hike up the stream course to catch glimpses of ferns, wild orchids, and other shade-loving plants. Such excursions often provide intimate glimpses of wildlife and serene sights of quiet pools or little waterfalls in a setting reminiscent of a Japanese

garden. Hiking along the bluffs of the rivers often provides you glimpses of some of the state's many caves. Jam-Up Cave (see the History chapter) has an awe-inspiring entrance. Trails closer to the river are cooler and provide intimate contact with the many springs that feed the river. Before venturing on the hiking paths, make certain you provide yourself with an up-to-date map of the area you plan to hike.

Write or call the National Park Service at the address/phone number above, and they can send you an official map of the river, with the hiking trails and recreation areas, as well as a current list of canoe rental concessionaires.

DEWEY SHORT VISITORS CENTER
MO 165
(417) 334-4101
Situated at the south end of Table Rock Dam, the center is a great place to learn about Ozark flora by hitting the 0.8-mile wheelchair-accessible nature trail that winds by the lakeshore. The center itself has wildlife exhibits (they usually have raccoons, snakes, insects, and other local wildlife), films, wildlife art shows and photography exhibits, special lectures, and other educational programs offered by the U.S. Army Corps of Engineers. There's a 20-minute free film about the construction of the dam shown on request. Named after Missouri congressman Dewey Short, who lobbied his colleagues for years to build flood-control dams in the White River valley, the center is one of the 10 most-visited centers operated by the corps. It's a great place—and a free one—to take the kids for the obligatory educational experience (see the Kidstuff chapter).

DOGWOOD CANYON NATURE PARK
2038 MO 86 West, Lampe
(417) 335-2777, (417) 779-5983
www.dogwoodcanyon.com
Dogwood Canyon is a 10,000-acre private wilderness refuge developed by John L. Morris, founder of the Bass Pro Shops. This incredible area is readily accessible to nature lovers. Crystal-clear Dogwood Creek flows through a high-bluffed, narrow canyon. The ridges on either side are

forested with large trees. You can see herds of buffalo and elk—and Texas longhorns. You can learn about Fire Pit Cave and Great Spirit Rock Shelter, where the oldest human remains in Missouri have been found.

Guest attractions include a Civil War museum, a long-abandoned lead mine worked by early settlers, the Dogwood Canyon General Store, and a handcrafted covered bridge built by the Amish. You don't have to be a fit mountaineer climber to experience the beauties of this Ozark area. You can take a guided tour of the canyon via a Jeep-pulled tram. You can hike, bike and fish for trout in the stream or take an Orvis fly-fishing course and learn on the job, all for the single "Adventure Pass" of $35.95 per day for adults, $20.95 per day for children, ages 3 through 12. Horseback rides are an additional $17.95. To get to Dogwood Canyon from Branson, take US 65 south to MO 86 and follow it west, going over the Long Creek Arm of Table Rock Lake toward Blue Eye. You'll see the turnoff to Dogwood Canyon a mile after you pass the MO 86/MO 13 junction.

DRURY-MINCY CONSERVATION AREA
MO 76, 6 miles east of Branson
3347 Gunnison Rd.
Kirbyville, MO 65679
(417) 334-4830
This 5,559-acre conservation area in southern Taney County is only minutes from downtown Branson. It is named for early landowner Frank Drury and the settlement of Mincy. It was the Missouri Conservation Department's first deer refuge. By the 1920s Missouri's deer numbers had dwindled to only 14 herds. One of these lived in the Mincy area on the private Skaggs Game Preserve, and Frank Drury worked with the department to increase deer numbers. From 1939 to 1959 deer from the preserve were successfully used to restore populations statewide. Turkeys from the preserve also provided the stock for statewide restoration projects during the 1960s. The department leased the land in 1939 and purchased it in 1987. Fox, Bee, and Mincy Creeks meander through stands of wild cane on their way to Bull Shoals Lake in this wilderness area,

which is in the heart of the White River glade region. It is open for hunting, frogging, stream fishing, hiking, bird-watching, nature study, picnicking, and outdoor photography. Camping is allowed in the Mincy portion only. The area has miles of foot trails for hiking. You can obtain information and a map of the Drury-Mincy Conservation Area by writing the Drury-Mincy Area Manager, HCR 2, Box 1040, Kirbyville, MO 65679 or by calling (417) 334-4830.

To get to the preserve, go 3 miles east of Branson on MO 76. As soon as you pass the Kirbyville School, turn south (right) onto MO J, which will take you right into the preserve. At Mincy you see the signs for the preserve.

GLADE TOP TRAIL
MO 125, Bradleyville
(417) 683-4428
www.ozarkmtns.com/gladetop/
The Glade Top Trail in the Mark Twain National Forest is Missouri's only National Scenic Byway. The 23-mile trail weaves along the narrow ridgetops and glades above the surrounding rolling countryside. The Glade Top Trail's historical significance is very important to many of the Douglas, Taney, and Ozark County residents who worked for the Civilian Conservation Corps in the late 1930s, and the trail has changed little since the CCC workers constructed the two-lane, all-weather gravel road. Now paved, the trail is a scenic nature getaway from Branson, and it provides an excuse to pack a picnic lunch and see the country. The drive is especially pretty in the spring, when numerous dogwood, smoke, and redbud trees are in bloom. Fall has its own spectacular show and provides a Flaming Fall Revue (see the Annual Events chapter) and an excuse for another drive.

You can obtain more information about the Glade Top Trail and a map by writing the Mark Twain Forest Ava Ranger District, P.O. Box 186, Ava, MO 65608, calling the number above, or visiting the web site. The easiest way to access the Glade Top Trail from Branson is by taking MO 75 east past Bradleyville, turning south (right) onto MO 125 and then crossing Beaver Creek. About

4 miles south of the junction of MO 125 and US 160, you'll turn left onto the Glade Top Trail (Forest Service Road 149).

HERCULES GLADES WILDERNESS AREA
Eastern Taney County
(417) 683-4428
www.fs.fed.us/r9/forests/marktwain/
recreation/sites/hercules_glades_trail/
Just 20 miles east of the glitter of The Strip in Branson is the Hercules Glades Wilderness. It's a varied and complex area of woods, glades, balds, springs, and creeks. This beautiful but hard-to-make-a-living-in area is so undisturbed that the glades were declared a federal wilderness in 1964 and are protected by federal law.

The Hercules area of 12,315 acres, more than 20 square miles, falls within the Ava District of the Mark Twain National Forest. If the neon lights of The Strip don't attract you—or if you want a diversion from them—the Hercules Glades is worth a trip for a day or longer. Hiking and horseback trails are the only way into the glades. From the trailheads there is a network of over 31 miles of maintained trails, so hikes ranging from two hours to two to three days can be planned. Cross-country hiking in other parts of the area is allowed. Camping is available in areas of the surrounding Mark Twain National Forest and also just south of the glades at the U.S. Army Corps of Engineers campground at Beaver Creek. Primitive camping is available everywhere in the glades, as long as you are at least 100 feet off a trail. Don't bring electrical equipment such as radios or cell phones, as such items are forbidden and lessen the wilderness experience for you and spoil it for others. Campfires are permitted, but be certain to obliterate all traces of your campfire and site.

In the spring the glades have wet-weather springs and branches, and the hillsides are covered with a profusion of rare and beautiful flowers. Spring rains show off the cascading waterfalls, shoals, and splash pools that eons of time have cut into the limestone bedrock. The glades contain sculptured totems and gargoyles of limestone, weathered into fantastic shapes by time. Spring is the most comfortable time to hike in the area.

During the summer the shallow-soiled south-facing hillsides become almost semidesert, with a whole array of plants and animals. You'll see yucca, prickly pears, lizards, and roadrunners. Summer hikes can be hot, so pack plenty of water.

In the fall you can experience the vast array of colors contrasted with the greens of cedars and junipers, as well as a totally different crop of late wildflowers. The fall season offers a more comfortable hike than in summer. Winter provides special attractions, and after a wet snow or an ice storm, the area is transformed into glittering beauty. Many people who like landscape photography find winter their favorite time to explore the glades.

The Hercules Glades lie between MO 125 and US 160, with MO 76 forming the eastern border. Tower Trailhead is on MO 125, 8 miles south of MO 76. Coy Bald Trailhead is on Fairview Church Road, a gravel road 3 miles north of US 160 and MO 125. For more information you can call the Ava Ranger District at the number above. You can also obtain information from the Mark Twain National Forest supervisor in Rolla, Missouri, by calling (573) 364-4621, and you can purchase U.S. Geological Survey maps for $4 each. Ask for the Hilda and Protem NE Quadrangle Maps.

PINEY CREEK WILDERNESS
Northeastern Stone County
(417) 847-2144
www.fs.fed.us/r9/forests/marktwain/
recreation/wilderness
Cut over for lumber and railroad ties in the late 1800s, this 8,142-acre preserve has reverted to its original primitive state. The area is the entire watershed for Piney Creek and a favorite haunt for local hikers, naturalists, and bird-watchers who prize seclusion and solitude. The wilderness has 13 miles of primitive trails. Piney Creek is crystal clear and runs over gravel beds and solid rock. The holes at beds and beneath root wads harbor fish, turtles, frogs, and mink. Songbirds nest along the creek, while the ridges are favorite places for hawks, eagles, and buzzards.

You can obtain additional information on Piney Creek Wilderness Area by writing the Cassville Ranger District, P.O. Box 310, Cassville, MO 65625, or by calling them at the number above. A map of the wilderness with trails is available from the office for $3. U.S. Geological Survey maps of the area can be purchased for $4 each by calling the Mark Twain National Forest supervisor's office in Rolla, Missouri, at (573) 364-4621. Ask for the Shell Knob and Cape Fair Quadrangle maps.

ROARING RIVER STATE PARK
MO 112
(417) 873-2539
www.mostateparks.com/roaringriver.htm

A river roars through this state park, just an hour's drive from Branson. A $5 million lodge overlooks it, and trout fishing in the cold, spring-fed waters is always good at this 4,093-acre park deep in the forested hollows of Barry County. Stonework laid by the hands of CCC workers more than 70 years ago still channels the fury of Roaring River spring and hatchery. You can catch a nature program, enjoy the cool air at the spring (20.4 million gallons per day), fish, swim, dine, or bike or hike the park's seven trails, including the Devil's Kitchen Trail, a challenging 1.5-mile trail that climbs 325 feet to the ridgetop. The name is derived from an odd rock outcrop that forms a roomlike enclosure. You may want to take a flashlight to explore some of the shallow trailside caves.

Nearby Cassville has some flea markets and antiques shops you can check out, and the Pea Ridge National Military Park at Pea Ridge, Arkansas, on AR 72, isn't far away. The park and some area attractions make a good day trip (see the Day Trips chapter).

RUTH AND PAUL HENNING STATE CONSERVATION AREA
MO 76 West
(417) 334-3324
www.exploresouthernhistory.com/henning1.html

One of the nicest aspects of Branson is that you are so close to two totally different worlds. Only half a mile from where 76 Country Boulevard ends with the Butterfly Palace is the near-wilderness experience of the Ruth and

Paul Henning Conservation Area, a 1,434-acre preserve of glades, hills, and valleys between the west end of The Strip and the Shepherd of the Hills Homestead—and it's within the Branson city limits! From the top of Dewey Bald, there is a lovely view of Mutton Hollow, Roark Creek Valley, and the lights of The Strip back east. Because the area is so close to activities on The Strip, it's easy to work in a half-day trip to get your exercise or to let the kids burn off extra energy.

Development farther west of The Strip was effectively stopped when the land, owned by Paul and Ruth Henning, was donated to the Missouri Conservation Department. Paul Henning was the producer of *The Beverly Hillbillies* and *Petticoat Junction* TV series. Ruth is a native of Eldon, Missouri, near the Lake of the Ozarks.

Features of this conservation spot were immortalized in *The Shepherd of the Hills*: Dewey Bald, Boulder Bald, Sammy Lane's Lookout, Mutton Hollow, and Little Pete's Cave.

In the parking lot is a display that illustrates plants and animals you might see in the preserve and explains the ecology of glade areas. The Henning Conservation Area has several short hiking trails. Be sure to take your camera, not only for the great vistas but also for the unusual plants and animals you might encounter.

The 1.75-mile Streamside Trail may take you about an hour. The Glade Exploration Trail is a 1-mile loop of this trail that takes you around the top of an Ozarks glade where you can see firsthand the grasses, cacti, and shrubs found on a glade. A 0.5-mile section leads to the top of Dewey Bald, where you can climb a fire tower for a panoramic view. There is a 1-mile section of the trail that takes you to an overlook deck and back to the parking lot where you started.

A longer loop, the Henning Homesteads Trail, constructed primarily by Boy Scout Troop 2001, is 3.7 miles long. It is a moderately difficult trail and should take you about three hours to complete. You can pick up a brochure before you start that describes some of the features of the walk, which takes you by hand-dug wells, fieldstone home foundations, log barns, springs, and other relics of some of the early homesteaders in the area.

i There are only four members of the pit viper family found in the Ozarks: the copperhead, timber rattlesnake, and pygmy rattlesnake, all found usually in wooded or glade areas, and the cottonmouth, found along creeks and rivers. You're not likely to encounter any snakes at all, for they are shy and unobtrusive. If you do happen on a snake, don't bother it. Give it a wide berth and go on your way. You will probably scare the snake more than it will scare you.

During the season a naturalist is on duty to answer questions about flora and fauna and lead descriptive walks. This is a natural area, so smoking, fires, fireworks, and camping are not permitted. If you visit http://mdc.mo.gov/documents/area_brochures/8208map.pdf you can print out a trails map.

SHEPHERD OF THE HILLS FISH HATCHERY
483 Hatchery Rd.
(417) 334-4865
http://mdc.mo.gov/areas/hatchery/shepherd/
The Shepherd of the Hills Fish Hatchery is the largest trout-rearing facility in Missouri and produces 1,125,000 catchable trout annually, weighing 301,000 pounds. Nearby Lake Taneycomo receives 700,000 catchable trout per year. The hatchery complex includes a free visitor center, where you can learn more about trout culture, aquatic life, fishing, and wildlife resource management. Fishing access areas and a public boat launch on Lake Taneycomo are available. Trails near the hatchery are appropriate for hiking and wildlife viewing, and many locals make the short drive just for a walk along the lake and amid the wildlife. The area has become a winter roost for hundreds of turkey and black vultures, seagulls, redwing blackbirds, and robins. Missouri's state bird, the bluebird, is often seen around the hatchery, as are such fish predators as the great blue heron, green heron, and belted kingfisher. The hatchery area is also home to a variety of other wildlife, including deer, turkeys, squirrels, raccoons, foxes, minks, muskrats, and beavers.

The hatchery is a good place for the kids to get a close-up look at native Ozark fish in large aquariums and to feed the trout in hatchery pools (see the Kidstuff chapter). Picnicking is allowed, and tables are located near Lake Taneycomo. The hatchery is 6 miles southwest of Branson on MO 165, just below Table Rock Dam.

TABLE ROCK STATE PARK
Off MO 165 near Table Rock Dam
(417) 334-4104
www.mostateparks.com
Table Rock State Park consists of 356 acres and is operated by the Missouri Department of Natural Resources. It's just south of the Showboat Branson Belle's White River Landing on MO 165. For more information about the full-service marina, including scuba diving and sailboat rentals, see the Lakes and Rivers chapter; for more on the camping facilities, check the Campgrounds and RV Parks chapter.

The park has several miles of walking trails along the lakefront and in the forest, a boat launch area (at which people frequently swim), picnic tables, a covered pavilion with barbecue grills and tables, and playground equipment, including a volleyball court and softball field.

You can obtain information about Table Rock State Park and other parks operated by the Missouri Department of Natural Resources by calling (800) 334-6946 or writing P.O. Box 178, Jefferson City, MO 65102.

BIKING

Because of the topography and the traffic, Branson is not a very friendly place for bikers to enjoy their sport. Pleasure biking isn't very popular here, in spite of the fact that we have had a good turnout for the racers in a Branson leg of the Tour de Missouri. Rides along Branson's Taneycomo lakefront from North Back Park to Sunset Park are level and pose few traffic problems. Although it's not a good idea to venture out on The Strip with a road bike, a number of the less-traveled roads and highways can be a good deal of fun to ride, so we don't discourage you from bringing your road bike. Definitely bring your mountain bike. Mountain biking is beginning to catch on in this area, as rugged individuals with their rugged bikes find that rides in our mountainous terrain are equal to those found in many other areas of the nation. If you are willing to drive a few miles, you'll find some pretty trails.

In the works is a proposal for a lakeside bike trail along portions of Table Rock Lake. It will connect with the bike trail that was constructed with the Ozark Highroad, which loops around Branson. In the future when you come to Branson, you'll find that we cater to bikers better than we do now.

While in the area, you can always stop at the DBA bike shop (see listing) and talk to Craig Erickson, who is more than willing to provide maps, suggest rides for road bikers, and share information about area trails for mountain bikers.

DBA: DOWNHILL BIKES AND ACCESSORIES
116 Flynn Rd., #C
(417) 335-4455
www.downhillbikes.biz

Up close and personal! Downhill Bikes offers guided cycling tours, half- and full-day trips for all skill levels. Beginners are welcome!

Owner-manager Craig Erickson is one of the area's biggest fans of mountain biking, and he is spreading the word that the sport is fun and a great way to see the landscape. His store carries a variety of bikes—Trek, Giant, and Gary Fisher—and biking accessories. If you find yourself in need of bike repair or bike rental ($20 for half day, $30 for full day), Craig can take care of you.

BOWLING

DOGWOOD LANES
2126 MO 76 East
(417) 336-2695

Dogwood Lanes is a nice, clean 16-lane bowling alley and video arcade near the Holiday Hills Golf Course. The lanes host both day and night leagues and open bowling with glow-in-the-dark pins. The place is a favorite hangout for area teenagers on Saturday nights for Rock 'n' Bowl, when you bowl with black lights to rock 'n' roll music.

They have a snack shop and a small pro shop. Dogwood Lanes is located 1 mile east of the Lake Taneycomo bridge on MO 76.

GOLF

We never thought that people would actually be coming to Branson just for the golf, but now that Branson has nine courses, we've begun to attract golf fanatics. If you are interested in golf, it's easy to work in a tee time during the day and the shows at night. Many of the new courses are part of resort complexes, so you could have a condo on the fairway for your stay. It was Missouri's Mark Twain who said "Golf is a good walk spoiled," but some of the newer courses are beautiful themselves. Coupled with the natural Ozark scenery, they make for a great walk even if you aren't a gung ho golfer. If you're the competitive type, local courses give a wide range of challenges: tricky doglegs, narrow fairways, and shots over water that will test the best. We've listed clubs that are open to the public as well as to their guests (who often get reduced rates and priority on tee times). All courses accept credit cards. Information and fees are for 2009, but it's best to call before you go.

> ℹ️ You can find information for a "test drive in Branson" at the Golf Council's Web site, www.golfbranson.com; it provides information about area golf courses, including current greens fees. Most of the condo developments have "stay and play" specials that are good for that test drive in Branson.

BRANSON CREEK GOLF CLUB
144 Branson Creek Dr.
(417) 339-4653, (888) 772-9990
www.bransoncreekgolf.com

Branson Creek, was designed by noted course designer Tom Fazio, his first venture in the Ozarks. He has designed such prestigious courses as Las Vegas's Shadow Creek; the Quarry in La Quinta, California; Champion Hills in North Carolina; and Hammock Dunes in Florida. Given virtually free rein as to cost and "as much land as needed," Fazio designed a 7,000-yard, par 71, championship-level golf course that incorporates the natural terrain of the Ozark Mountains, creating exciting challenges for both low- and high-handicap players. Greens are bent grass with zoysia grass fairways. The 18th hole has been described by Fazio as "the Midwest version of the 18th hole at Pebble Beach—a tricky par 5 that doglegs left—but in place of water, there's a sea of trees."

The course is part of the network of more than 40 courses managed by Troon Golf worldwide. The course is a spikeless course, and course rules require "appropriate golf attire." There is a driving range and practice facilities. Greens fees, which include golf cart, vary from $45 to $95, depending on the season. The course has a pro shop and snack shop. The clubhouse, with elevated patios and decks, sits high atop a hill, commanding a panoramic view that overlooks the golf course and offers a fabulous vista of Branson to the north. Branson Creek is located 4 miles south of Branson on the east side of US 65.

DON GARDNER PITCH AND PUTT PUBLIC GOLF COURSE
201 Compton Dr.
(417) 337-8510

Eiserman Park, near the Branson Community Center, is one acre that includes a basketball court, playground, and covered pavilion. Adjacent to Eiserman Park is the nine-hole Don Gardner Pitch and Putt Public Golf Course. It's named after an early golfer who brought the sport to Branson when he built the Holiday Hills Golf Course in 1939. Each hole is a par 3, and lots of folks sharpen their short-iron skills there. The course is open to the public and costs $10 for residents and $15 for nonresidents to play the nine holes. Pull carts and clubs can be rented.

FISHER CREEK GOLF COURSE
42 Golfcrest Drive Dr., Kimberling City
(417) 739-4370

This is a great nine-hole golf course if you don't have much time or want to work on your short game. The 2,100-yard, par 34 course is in the midst of some grand mountainous terrain. The course has no par 5s, but hole 6 with a hard left dogleg is a very difficult par 4.

The course is open seven days a week and charges $15 per person, plus a $11 per person cart fee. Carts are not required, so you can get the full exercise benefit of the game. Pull carts are available. The course has a pro shop.

To find the Kimberling Golf Course, turn south onto MO 13 at the intersection of MO 76 and MO 13 in Branson West. As you're coming down the long hill into Kimberling City, you'll turn right at the fifth light.

HOLIDAY HILLS RESORT & GOLF CLUB
630 East Rockford Dr.
(417) 334-4838, (800) 225-2422
www.holidayhills.com

Holiday Hills is one place in Branson you can drive all day and never be stuck in traffic! On MO 76, 3 miles east of downtown Branson, the city's first golf course is now one of its newest. Chicago golf pro Don Gardner and his wife, Jill, moved to Branson and established the course in 1938, but a 1997 multimillion-dollar renovation has brought it up to PGA standards. In the old days, Forrest Tucker and Charlton Heston flew in to the grass strip that was nearby and joined Don Gardner in a threesome, and now many of Branson's music stars who live here play the course. It has bentgrass greens and hybrid Bermuda grass fairways and tees. This 5,771-yard public course is now par 68, with more than 50 large bunkers and water obstacles on 6 holes. The course meets the challenges of all levels of golfers, but hole 1, a par 4, might intimidate you with its long 432-yard drive with water on the left and sand on the right. However, if you do well on this difficult hole, you may have your confidence boosted to meet lesser challenges!

The course has a restaurant and bar, the Grille on the Green, and a fully stocked golf shop that offers club repair and club rentals. Greens fees including a cart are $59 for 18 holes in the morning ($45 after noon) and $39 after 3 p.m. Holiday Hills is a spikeless course, and a collared shirt is required for play. Holiday Hills also offers condo rentals and golf vacation packages. (See the Accommodations chapter.)

JOHN DALY'S MURDER ROCK GOLF & COUNTRY CLUB
Golf Club Drive
Hollister, MO 65672
(417) 332-3259
www.murderrock.com

If you read our History chapter, you know about Murder Rock. Bushwhacker Alf Bolin's favorite place for road robbery has been incorporated into Branson's newest golf course and semi-private club in the Branson Creek Residential Community. Located near the new Branson airport, the golf club is designed to serve Branson Creek's multiple neighborhoods and has a community clubhouse with dining with the longest view in Branson, a members lounge and bar, pro shop, fitness room, tennis, and swimming. Designed by Landmark Land Company Inc., the 18-hole Championship Golf Course enhances the magnificent landscape of the Ozarks, incorporating the natural beauty of the land with lush fairways and pristine greens.

The course plays to a par 71, and ranges in length from 6,600 yards from the tournament tees to 5,000 yards from the forward tees. Patrons are treated to a wonderful variety of golf holes by design: exciting par 5s, challenging par 4s, and dramatic par 3s. Rates are $50 to $80, including cart rental, depending on the time of the year and the day of the week. To find the Murder Rock Course, go 4.2 miles south of Branson on US 65 to the Branson Creek Development Entry, then east on Branson Creek Boulevard. Continue on Branson Creek Boulevard to Golf Club Drive and turn right following to the property's highest elevation. As we say in the Ozarks, "You can't miss it."

LEDGESTONE GOLF COURSE AND COUNTRY CLUB
Intersection of MO 76 West and MO 365
1600 Ledgestone Way
StoneBridge Village
Reeds Spring
(417) 335-8187, (800) 817-8663
www.ledgestonegolf.com

This course is the heart of the gated community of StoneBridge, which is near Silver Dollar City. The 18-hole, 6,800-yard, par 71 championship-style course was designed by the renowned golf course architectural firm of Ault, Clark and Associates. It was nominated as Best New Course in 1995 by *Golf Digest*, calling it "a masterpiece of mountain golf architecture." When you play this course, you never have to see other groups because there are no adjoining holes anywhere on the course. Much of the course meanders along the upper reaches of Roark Creek and incorporates its still pools, bluffs, and rock outcroppings into the overall design. Ledgestone, however, is more than just a pretty face; it is one of the Midwest's more demanding courses, with such features as narrow, tree-lined fairways, sand bunkers, and numerous water hazards. Hole 15 is a real challenge. It's a 177-yard, par 3 hole that has you teeing off from a 100-foot-high-cliff.

Along with golf, you can enjoy the large 20,000-square-foot clubhouse with pro shop, restaurant, activity rooms, and exercise and fitness areas.

Greens fees are $90 at peak time, including cart fee, but are $79 for guests staying on the property. The course's driving range is reserved for people playing the course that day. There is also an 8,000-square-foot putting green. Ledgestone takes tee-time reservations up to one week in advance.

OAKMONT HILLS RESORT AND GOLF COURSE
769 MO 86, Ridgedale
(417) 334-8424
www.bransonloghomes.com

This course is located on MO 86 right across from the turnoff to Big Cedar Lodge. Established in 1987, this course of 2,939 yards is par 36 for nine holes and can provide a memorable short round. The fairways are Bermuda grass and mixed grass, with bent-grass greens. Local golfers rate holes 2 and 4 as the most difficult.

Hole 4 is a 395-yard, par 5 challenge that has a dogleg left requiring a 190-yard drive from the tee down a narrow fairway.

Greens fees are $20 for nine holes, plus $15 for cart rental.

PAYNE STEWART GOLF CLUB
100 Payne Stewart Dr.
(417) 337-2963
www.paynestewartgolfclub.com

The Payne Stewart Golf Club is a tribute course in progress honoring local golf legend Payne Stewart. Payne Stewart Golf Club is located in one of the area's newest development, Branson Hills, and is just minutes from the Branson Landing which offers restaurants, shopping and entertainment on lake Taneycomo. The course currently has 9 holes open for play (1–8 and 18). The remainder of the course will open in 2009. The clubhouse is currently open and is being managed along with the golf course by Hilton Golf. Call the number above or go to the Web site for pictures and the latest details about construction and the grand opening.

POINTE ROYALE GOLF COURSE
142 Pointe Royale Dr.
(417) 334-4477, (800) 962-4710
www.pointeroyale.com

Pointe Royale advertises the course as "where the stars live and play." It's true that Branson's first gated community is home to a number of Branson's stars, and it's true that Andy Williams, Moe Bandy, and Mickey Gilley play regularly at the course, which was established on Lake Taneycomo just below Table Rock Dam in 1986. The course is right across from the Welk Resort Complex on MO 165.

The 18-hole, 6,250-yard course is a par 70. It has bent-grass greens and Bermuda grass fairways, with out-of-bounds stakes lining most holes. It offers one of the wettest courses in the Midwest—12 holes with water obstacles—plus a number with sand traps. Veteran golfers contend that you'll use every club in your bag if you play the course properly. One of the most challenging holes is the last one, a par 4, 411-yard uphill hole that requires a 200-yard drive to get to the top. Costs for condo guests playing at Pointe Royale

are $54 for 18 holes and $32 for 9 holes. A "twilight fee" (after 2 p.m.) is $42. Cost is $79 for 18 holes for "walk on players not staying at Pointe Royale." Prices include the required cart.

The course has a complete pro shop and offers lessons and club rentals. Pro shop owner and golf pro Jeff Wallster says the course is challenging because it is hilly and has so many water hazards. He is always available for advice. The Pointe Royale course has a restaurant and clubhouse with meeting rooms.

Pointe Royale offers weekly and nightly condo rentals or golf with condo packages. Call (800) 962-4710 for reservations and information.

THOUSAND HILLS GOLF CLUB
245 South Wildwood Dr.
(417) 334-4553, (800) 864-4145
www.thousandhills.com

This public course was inaugurated by Andy Williams in 1995, and it's just over the next ridge from his Moon River Theatre on one of Branson's Wildwood Drive. It's one of two courses within the city limits.

The 18-hole course has a championship tee of 5,111 yards and is par 64 with bent-grass greens and zoysia fairways and tees. Wildwood Branch meanders through the course to nearby Cooper Creek and provides some special kinds of water hazards. Golf Pro Cliff Easum says hole 3 has been described as "the hole from hell"—a 460-yard par 4 that has a long 260-yard drive to the green. The green, carved out of a bluff, has a bluff in front of it and a bluff behind it. Miss it and you're up the creek by being in the creek or on the cliff. Hole 16 is the second hardest hole of the course, with a sharp dogleg to the right.

Greens fees in 2009 were $59 to a low of $39 for 18 holes, depending on time of the year, and that includes cart expenses. Look into the early bird and twilight specials, about half the going rates. Resident pro and pro shop manager Easum will answer any of your questions (and rent you clubs if you forgot yours). The course has a clubhouse with meeting and group facilities and a snack bar, full-service lounge, and grill. Thousand

Hills offers nightly and weekly "stay and play" condo rentals. Call (417) 334-4553 or (800) 864-4145 for information.

TOP OF THE ROCK GOLF COURSE
150 Top of the Rock Rd.
(417) 339-5312
www.bigcedar.com
This course is currently closed for renovation. All those scars and the scraped earth you see to the south will be changed into an additional nine holes with new pars on the first half and with a brand new pro shop. Check the Web site for renovation updates and grand opening information. In the meantime, we can tell you this: Jack Nicklaus designed this nine-hole, par 27 course on one of Taney County's highest hills overlooking Table Rock Lake. Established in 1996 by John Morris of Bass Pro fame, the course is 47 acres, with more than 38 percent of the area kept in a natural state or planted with native grasses, wildflowers, or native trees. The water features of the course were created not only to add a challenge but also to enhance wildlife habitat. Giving new meaning to the word *birdie*, the course planners worked with the Audubon Society and incorporated interpretive tools into the landscaping, pro shop, and clubhouse, so you can learn about our Ozark birds and wildlife as you play. The course is the only Audubon Society signature course in the state and the fourth in the nation.

Golf Equipment

If you forgot your clubs, most of the courses will rent clubs or they have pro shops where you can buy gear. Of course, you can always visit Branson's sport section in Wal-Mart or Target.

GIBSON'S GOLFWORKS
2078 MO 76 East
(417) 334-8989
Wayne "Hoot" Gibson of Gibson's Golfworks likes to talk golf, and although he can fix or improve your golf gear, he leaves it up to you to improve your game. He can regrip, reshaft, refinish, or reweight your clubs. Hoot was nominated for Golf Club Maker of the Year of the Professional Club Makers Society in 1993. If your clubs are in need of professional repair, you can find Gibson's Golfworks two sharp curves before the Holiday Hills Golf Course, one mile east of the Lake Taneycomo bridge on MO 76.

HORSEBACK RIDING

One of the best ways to take a break from the glitz and activity of The Strip and see the "real" Ozarks is to take a trail ride. Horses are able to get you back into hollows and recesses of the beautiful Ozarks that can't be reached even by four-wheel-drive vehicles. Trail riding is an easy, interesting, and fun outdoor activity. You can see the blush of red buds and the bloom of dogwood blossoms up close in the spring, and in the fall you can be right in the midst of the flaming fall review of oaks, sweetgums, sumac, and dogwoods. There are trail rides available at the Shepherd of the Hills Homestead. (See the Attractions chapter.) In addition, there are other local horseback riding opportunities.

BEAR CREEK TRAIL RIDES AND STABLE
3400 US 65, Walnut Shade
(417) 337-7708
Bryan and Sherri Caperton have this family-owned and family-operated business in connection with their ranch on Bear Creek, 7 miles north of Branson on US 65. In fact, as you cross Bear Creek going south, just before going up to the deepest road cut in Missouri on Bear Mountain, you'll see the horses and stables to your right. They offer family fun at reasonable prices and have a wide variety of horses that are gentle and easy to handle. The trails are shaded, beautiful, and exciting. Rides are on their 500-acre private ranch along Bear Creek. A one-hour trail ride is $19, a two-hour trail ride, $37.

SHEPHERD OF THE HILLS TRAIL RIDES
Shepherd of the Hills Outdoor Theatre
5586 MO 76
(417) 334-4191, (800) 653-6288
www.oldmatt.com

Take a trail ride through history! This 30-minute ride on horses used in the action-packed drama *The Shepherd of the Hills* runs through the historic homestead and will take you on some of the same trails the Bald Knobbers rode. See the majestic Ozark hills, "the Trail Nobody Knows How Old," and ride down in the holler in the beautiful shade of the Ozark woods and see the places of Harold Bell Wright's novel. This is your chance to ride a real "show horse!"

Rides run Monday through Saturday, some Sundays. Call for availability and rates. Must be seven years old or older, at least 4 feet tall, and weigh no more than 250 pounds.

UNCLE IKE'S TRAIL RIDE, INC.
8393 MO 76, Notch
(417) 338-8449
www.uncleikestrailride.com

Uncle Ike's Trail Ride, the oldest in the area with more than 25 years in operation, is named after a character in *The Shepherd of the Hills* and is actually located at Notch, where the prototype for Uncle Ike carried mail over some of the same trails you'll be riding.

The 2.5-mile daily ride takes about 45 minutes. It's available on a first-come, first-served basis; no reservations needed. The cost in 2009 was $25 per person. There's also a 7 a.m. breakfast ride, which is 4.5 miles and takes just a little more than two hours. Breakfast, cooked at about the halfway point, consists of sausage, biscuits and gravy, scrambled eggs, hash browns, coffee, and juice—all you can eat, or at least all that the pack horses can pack in! Cost for the breakfast ride is $45, with children younger than six charged $8. Dinner rides, with scrumptious dinner fare, are $47.50. Uncle Ike's Trail Ride is 0.5 mile past the entrance to Silver Dollar City on MO 76.

HUNTING

At the turn of the 20th century, hunters from St. Louis, Kansas City, and Chicago came by train into the Ozarks to hunt. In fact, one of the early buildings on the College of the Ozarks campus at its Point Lookout location was a log hunting lodge, the Maine Exhibition Hall at the St. Louis World's Fair, moved down here by a group of St. Louis sportsmen and reassembled for a clubhouse. Hunting and float fishing were big business for locals, who served as guides and knew how and where to find game because it provided fare for their own dinner tables. They hunted deer, turkey, and small game: rabbits, squirrels, and raccoons.

Today our forests provide better hunting for white-tailed deer than they did back then, but these pursuits are no longer the main reason tourists come to the Ozarks. Hunting is licensed and regulated by the Missouri Department of Conservation. We Ozarkers do share our forests with "comehere" hunters, and we know there are more than enough deer to go around. In fact, if you hunt in other counties in Missouri, you are probably hunting whitetails descended from Taney County stock. When the Conservation Department began its restocking of both whitetails and wild turkeys in the 1930s after much of the state had been depleted by overhunting, they came to the Branson area to the old Skaggs Game Preserve near Mincy to obtain the restocking animals.

Licenses and Seasons

In order to hunt in Missouri, you must have a permit. All hunters born on or after January 1, 1967, must have a certificate from an approved hunter education program. You must give evidence of this certificate before you can purchase a firearms hunting permit. Permit fees and season lengths vary from year to year for firearms, muzzle-loading firearms, and archery, so it's best to contact the Missouri Department of Conservation at (573) 751-4115 for the latest information. You may also access the department's Web site: www.conservation.state.mo.us.

Most permits for residents are fairly inexpensive ($19 in 2009) but more expensive for nonresidents. In 2009 fees for nonresidents were: firearms (includes muzzle-loading firearms) deer-hunting permit, $175; archery deer-hunting permit, $150; and fall firearms turkey-hunting permit, $105.

More than 2,000 stores, bait and tackle shops, resorts, and other locations sell permits, but you can also contact a Missouri Conservation Department office or one of the four Missouri Department of Conservation nature centers in the state. You can also purchase a permit by phone by calling (800) 392-4115. The Conservation Department accepts major credit cards.

Dates vary each year for the season. Contact the Missouri Department of Conservation for the latest season information: (573) 751-4115.

During the firearms white-tailed-deer season and both parts of the muzzle-loading firearms white-tailed-deer season, hunters must wear a cap or hat and a shirt, coat, or vest of hunter orange that is plainly visible from all sides. The only exception to the hunter orange attire is for archers. The bright color will keep you from being mistaken for game, like Capt. Meriwether Lewis was by one of his hunters on the return leg of his famous expedition with William Clark. Fortunately, Lewis was only shot through the buttocks! Missouri wants its hunters to get game, not be game!

Migratory Waterfowl Hunting

The Ozarks is a flyover zone for most migratory waterfowl, so hunting of ducks and geese is not as prevalent or popular here as it is in the southeast and central portions of Missouri. A migratory-bird hunting permit and a federal waterfowl stamp are necessary if you want to hunt birds in Missouri. Costs were $6 in 2009 for the Missouri permit and $15 for the federal waterfowl stamp. These permits can be obtained at the U.S. Post Office or any Missouri Department of Conservation office. Penalties are stiff for violating state migratory bird regulations, so have the necessary permits before you pack your bird vest and shotgun.

Contact the Missouri Department of Conservation, P.O. Box 180, Jefferson City, MO 65102 for complete information on waterfowl seasons and hunting regulations.

TRAP, SKEET, AND SPORTING-CLAY SHOOTING

There was a decline in quail and dove hunting in the Ozarks in the last half of the 20th century, largely because local farmers didn't plant as much grain, which served as cover and food for the birds. However, another reason was the recognition that increasing human population and habitat destruction has put a strain on bird species. The result has been the evolution of several fast-growing sports derived from bird hunting. One type of shooting, calling sporting-clays shooting, is based on flying targets (sporting clays), designed to simulate an actual hunting situation. The targets fly in from all directions and heights. Sporting-clays shooting differs from skeet shooting (in which the clay targets come from only two locations) since shots are fired from eight different stations in a 180-degree field.

Trap shooting has the target come from one spot, and shooters rotate through five positions. With both skeet and trap shooting, the slight angles and speeds of targets are constant. That isn't so with sporting clays, which mimics the actual field conditions of bird hunting and is thus more of a challenge. It provides the thrill of bird hunting without the kill.

OZARK SHOOTERS SPORTS COMPLEX
759 US 65
(417) 443-3093
www.ozarkshooters.com
This complex at Chestnut Ridge, about 11 miles north of Branson, is the only shooting range in the area. Dale and Peggy Siler have an indoor handgun and rifle range and sponsor celebrity shoots at which you can join some of the stars from The Strip for a round or two to test your marksmanship.

Many country musicians are outdoors types (they either come by it naturally or think it's good for the image) and hunt or fish. Ozarks Shooters sponsors shooting competitions, often for some charitable cause, and Branson's stars are often involved. In 1995 Ozark Shooters Sports Complex was the site of the U.S. Open Sporting Clay Championship, the first time the event had been held in the Midwest. As the second-largest event of the National Sporting Clay Association, the five-day competition attracted shooters from across the nation and brought a good deal of local publicity to this rapidly growing sport. Ozark Shooters is open seven days a week, 9 a.m. to 5 p.m., year-round, and you can participate in trap, skeet, and sporting-clays shooting. The complex has a clubhouse, a gunsmith service, a small shooters' shop, and a gun rental service. It offers classes in handguns and shotguns for men, women, and kids and often sponsors hunter safety classes.

ICE SKATING

MEDIACOM ICE PARK
635 East Trafficway
(417) 866-7444
www.parkboard.org

Ice skating doesn't come easy to Ozarkers; open waters here seldom freeze solid enough to support the sport. But in September 2001, an estimated 8,000 people attended free skating sessions to "test the waters" (to mix a metaphor) when the Jordan Valley Ice Park opened its doors in the latest development phase of Jordan Valley Park in Springfield. An exhibition hockey game between the St. Louis Sting and St. Louis Blues Alumni was a success.

The result was that a local hockey team was formed. The Jordan Valley Ice Park is now home to a junior amateur hockey team, the Springfield Spirit. The Spirit is affiliated with the North American Hockey League, with players ages 16 to 20. The ice park is also home to the Missouri State University Division II hockey team, the Ice Bears. The ice park was the 2005 site of the Junior National Hockey Tournament.

The ice park has skating times and programs available for residents and visitors. It has a pro shop, two regulation ice sheets, snack areas, and meeting rooms. Family and group skating packages are available, as are public skating sessions, Learn to Skate programs, freestyle sessions, Learn to Play programs, and adult hockey sessions.

You don't have to be a skater to appreciate the ice park. There are, of course, the hockey games for spectators. In addition, the ice park sponsors the "Snow Fest" in June and a December Christmas figure-skating program. Check the Web site for details and dates.

SPECTATOR SPORTS

Bransonites were as proud as anyone in the state when the St. Louis Rams won their first Super Bowl honors in 2000, and quarterback Kurt Warner and lineman Grant Wistrom (from nearby Webb City) are local heroes. However, it's a four-hour drive from Branson to St. Louis or Kansas City, the nearest cities with professional teams, and you'd have to be a real die-hard fan to make it to all the games, so most folks are content to follow football and baseball via radio and TV.

Bransonites, of course, root for the Cardinals and the Royals, but interest in the minor league Springfield Cardinals has been high. Developer John Q. Hammons was willing to step to the plate and built a baseball stadium in downtown Springfield, to be used by the Missouri State University Bears and the Cardinals. Construction on the $9 million project, with seating for about 8,000, was completed in 2004. The project, in conjunction with Springfield's Jordan Valley Park project and the Springfield Spirit hockey team, has changed not only the Springfield downtown area but also spectator sports in the southwest Missouri area.

Folks focus on local teams, and high-school basketball is the big spectator sport. Though some of the area schools are quite small, they have won state championships throughout the years. Branson High School has had notable football teams. Folks in Branson are more likely to be in the stands at Alexander Park rooting for a Little League team or in the school gym backing the local basketball team than cheering on the Chiefs in Kansas City. They follow the Arkansas Razorbacks and the Missouri Tigers, but they tend to take more interest in the College of the Ozarks Bobcats or the Missouri State University Bears—especially the Lady Bears.

Branson is deluged by basketball fans when the College of the Ozarks hosts the NAIA Division II men's basketball national championship each March. The NAIA tournament draws more than 30,000 fans, who also see Branson and attend shows and shop.

Spectator sports are important to us in the Ozarks, but for most of us it is purely a local thing. However, recent events in the Ozarks have broadened the opportunities for sports spectators.

i **Want to know the best natural, public-access swimmin' holes, far from the madding crowd? This book by Glenn Wheeler provides pictures, descriptions, directions, and maps: *Swimming Holes of the Ozarks: A Guide to the Best Places to Cool Off in Arkansas and Missouri*. It's available in local bookstores or from www.glenn wheeler.com.**

SWIMMING

Swimming here in the Ozarks is more of an excuse to get the family out to the river or lake during the heat of summer and have a picnic and cool off than it is a serious sport. It's more splash and play than swimming, and you'll see families on gravel bars at various holes on local creeks or at beaches or recreation areas on Table Rock or Bull Shoals Lake. Lake Taneycomo is too cold, even in 100-degree August weather, for swimming. Check out the Lakes and Rivers chapter for other water activities available in the area.

You can swim about any place in Table Rock and Bull Shoals Lakes, but use your common sense. Lots of folks swim at the boat launch area and the lakeshore at Table Rock State Park and at the lakefront by Table Rock Dam at the Dewey Short Visitors Center. The water is refreshing and the beach rocky at both sites, and there are sudden and dramatic dropoffs at the underwater

bluffs in Table Rock Lake. Since there are no lifeguards for such swimming areas, the play is always at your own risk.

Moonshine Beach, just north of Table Rock Dam, is a favorite public swimming area. This quiet cove faces west, so the afternoon sun is intense, and it is light until even after the sun has set. The swimming area is roped off, so no boats can enter, and sand and pea gravel have been hauled in to make the beach easy on the feet. It's a great place to take a picnic lunch and spend the afternoon, and it's shallow enough for even toddlers, but there are no lifeguards, so you should be on your guard. Amenities include a picnic shelter, playground, sand beach, volleyball, swimming area boat launch, restrooms, and outdoor showers. A special area fee of $4 per car is charged. To reach Moonshine Beach from Branson, take MO 165 south from MO 76. You'll see the turnoff to Moonshine Beach to the west, just after you pass the entrance to Chateau on the Lake and before you start to cross Table Rock Dam.

Most hotels and motels have pools for their guests (see the Accommodations chapter) to cool off and play in. There are several water slides and water chutes in the area, and White Water is a large water theme park on 76 Country Boulevard (see the Attractions and Kidstuff chapters).

The newest swimmin' hole is a big "concrete pond" that's part of Branson's new RecPlex on the Branson Hills Parkway between US 65 and MO 248 north of Branson. Everyone is right proud of the new facility, which opened in the summer of 2005. (See the City Parks and Recreation section earlier in this chapter.) Outside and adjacent to the 44,000-square-foot recreation center is the "aquatics park," with pool, water slides, diving boards, lap pool, and kiddy area. Visitors to the area can use the pool and other facilities on a per-day, per-person basis. Call (417) 335-2368 for more information.

LAKES AND RIVERS

Long before the belch of the tour bus echoed off the highways, the purr of the motorboat reverberated across lakes and the whir of the fly reel competed with the gurgle of streams. For those who know Branson only as the home of music shows, a production of an entirely different kind awaits in nature's own amphitheater, with a cast of thousands, a score that is truly surround sound, and lighting of the most spectacular subtlety and beauty. The prologue to the modern-day drama that is Branson tourism can be found in the lakes and rivers that wind in, around, and among the Ozark hills, valleys, and plateaus. Because of the dams and lakes created in the 20th century, the White River in Missouri is no more, but its legacy is the advent of tourism in the Ozarks.

When the first railroads lumbered into the area around the turn of the 20th century, they brought more than just the timber industry and commercial agriculture. They brought the angler, hunter, and outdoor lover, who saw a bottomless pool of recreational natural resources in the crystal-clear waters of the lakes and streams. Waterfront resorts sprouted from the hillsides, and vacationers from all over came in ever-increasing droves to enjoy swimming, boating, fishing, hiking, and camping. Each new dam-made lake brought a new burst of pleasure boaters, who left economic growth and even more commercial development in their wake.

To provide the tourists with a little after-hours diversion, the first music show made its entrance some three decades ago. Today, Branson is a glittering, internationally renowned entertainment city, with scores of performers who strut their stuff upon the stage nightly. From season to season they come and they go, followed into town today and out of town tomorrow by the fan clubs, the tour buses, and the whole neon hype of show business. Through it all, the lakes and the rivers remain, as popular today as yesterday, with no more advertisement needed than their very existence.

In the following sections we merely skip stones across the vast surface of the river of knowledge about Ozark lakes and rivers. Words alone cannot impart the thrill of hooking your first big trout on Lake Taneycomo; they cannot describe the serenity of a shady afternoon float down Swan Creek. The magnificence of the Ozark lakes and rivers can only be truly experienced in person. Once experienced, perhaps you will find yourself returning to the Ozarks again and again for an encore performance of what might turn out to be your favorite show of all, with yourself cast in the leading role and played out upon the scenic splendor of our beloved Ozarks waterways.

THE LAKES

Lake Taneycomo

Only in the Ozarks could you call a lake a stream—or call a stream a lake. Actually, Taneycomo is neither—and both. It was born in 1913 when the White River was impounded just south of Forsyth by Powersite Dam, creating the first major dam-made lake in Missouri. The name Taneycomo is derived from the abbreviation for Taney County, Missouri. At 2,080 acres of surface area, it's small by modern reservoir standards, but its impact on the area is big indeed. This early flooding of the White River valley was the precursor to the flood

ℹ️ In 2001, Missouri Department of Conservation biologists, in a sampling of Lake Taneycomo, netted a record trout: 36.5 inches long, with a girth of 28.5 inches. They had no scales, but calculated the weight at 37 pounds, well above the current state record of 26 pounds, 13 ounces. After his physical examination, the fish was released back into the lake for an angler to catch him so he can go into the record books. He hasn't been caught yet.

of tourists to come. Hotels and summer resorts sprang up in Branson and Rockaway Beach, powered by electricity from the Empire District Electric Company's new dam. The accommodations offered fishing, boating, and, of course, swimming. For nearly a half century, the summertime flopping and splashing in the warm waters of Taneycomo was a familiar sight.

There's still plenty of flopping and splashing in Taneycomo these days, but now it's of the ichthyoid, not humanoid, variety. In 1958 the erection of Table Rock Dam, 22 miles upstream from Powersite, had a chilling effect that would make Lake Taneycomo world famous for trout fishing. The water for Taneycomo is now drawn from the bottom of Table Rock Dam, some 140 feet below the surface of Table Rock Lake. The temperature never exceeds 58 degrees, which is cold enough to make insulated waders a really good idea. The resorts along Lake Taneycomo are still there, but now they cater more to anglers than swimmers.

Fishing Lake Taneycomo

Though the warm-water crappie and bass are gone, even first-timers should have no trouble reeling in the trout, thanks to the Missouri Department of Conservation. Each year the department stocks Lake Taneycomo with more than 750,000 rainbow trout and a smaller number of brown trout. They are raised at Shepherd of the Hills Fish Hatchery on MO 165 (for more on the hatchery, see the Recreation and the Outdoors chapter) and lowered into the lake every month just below Table Rock Dam. The best spot to reel in

these fish is usually not too far downstream from Table Rock Dam, where the water tends to be shallowest. But only fish until the siren blows! When you hear it go off, that means they're sending water through the hydroelectric generators just upstream from where you're standing, and it's time to move quickly back toward the bank. Those who do not heed the warning will find that peaceful Lake Taneycomo can be "dam dangerous."

When the water is running, of course, the fly fishing is excellent on this well-stocked little lake. That's good, because state regulations require that only flies and artificial lures may be used on the upper portion of Taneycomo, defined as the area from the closed zone 760 feet below Table Rock Dam to the mouth of Fall Creek. Soft-plastic baits and natural and scented baits are prohibited in this area.

Drift fishing remains one of the most popular methods when the water is running. You simply motor up the lake to a particular starting point, then drift back down with the current. Drag your bait or lure behind the boat. Watch your sinker placement so that the bait will float just above the bottom, perhaps bumping it occasionally. A miniature marshmallow threaded on the hook can help provide the right amount of buoyancy to keep it off the bottom.

In still water, baits of all types can be effective, and we've heard of success stories with everything from canned corn (whole-kernel only!) to salmon eggs. When fishing from shore, the traditional carton of live nightcrawlers is still effective, and you can take it to the bank (so to speak). Despite the scores of fishing magazine articles and late-night infomercials touting miracle lures, bait selection remains a highly personal decision. Go to any trout dock on Taneycomo, and we can almost guarantee that an old-timer hanging around will be happy to offer an opinion, even if you haven't asked for it.

The same goes for finding a favorite fishin' hole—everybody has an opinion and is willing to share it. Ask around, but keep in mind that Taneycomo is a dynamic living river, and last year's lucky lunker site may be too shallow, too deep, or too overgrown this year. Frankly, much of the fun of fishing a place like Taneycomo is the challenge of exploration and the thrill of discovery. So you might want to do what locals do: put in with a small johnboat someplace, and seek out the many nooks and eddies that finger off the lake all up and down the shoreline. Sooner or later you're bound to reel in something.

Table Rock Lake

What Lake Taneycomo is to trout, Table Rock Lake is to bass—and crappie, walleye, bluegill, and catfish. But if you think Table Rock is only about fishing, you'll miss the boat entirely.

Let's start with its size. At more than 43,100 acres (67.34 square miles) of surface area and with a shoreline of 800 miles, Table Rock seems as big and as blue as the Ozarks sky on a summer afternoon. Lined by cedar-covered bluffs and framed by rolling hills, it is an august sight indeed, which helps explain why skiers, boaters, swimmers, scuba divers, and Duck-riders are themselves such a common August sight. Table Rock seems tailor-made for summer fun, and in fact it was. In 1958 the U.S. Army Corps of Engineers completed Table Rock Dam and Powerhouse, which is 6,523 feet long and a spectacular 252 feet high. It signaled the end of the White River in Missouri, but it also brought the beginning of a new era in water sports and outdoor sightseeing in the Ozarks.

Even if you're coming to Branson only for the music shows, set aside a few minutes to drive south on MO 165 from The Strip. Almost without warning, you'll find yourself driving over the dam itself, with Table Rock Lake stretching away to your right. Now look to the left. It's amazing how very far below Lake Taneycomo seems to be. Keep going south on MO 165 as it loops to the east, and you'll come to a scenic overlook where

i To check on current water conditions, call these recorded messages: Table Rock/Beaver Lakes, (417) 336-5083; Bull Shoals/Norfolk Lakes, (870) 431-5311.

you can pull off and get an unparalleled view of the dam to the west and Taneycomo below.

Along the way you'll pass the Dewey Short Visitors Center (see the listing in the Recreation and the Outdoors chapter). Practically next door to the visitor center is Table Rock State Park, one of the nearly 25 public-use areas on Table Rock Lake. It has a marina, boat-launch ramp, and camping and picnicking areas, as do many of the other public-use areas (see its listing in the Campgrounds and RV Parks chapter for more information). Other areas feature swimming beaches and playgrounds, and some have a marine gas facility, bait shop, or boat and motor rentals. There are also a number of private marinas where you can rent Wave Runners, ski boats, and bass boats and purchase fishing tackle.

You can also hire a fishing guide, but here are a few suggestions for the do-it-yourselfer: Start with a medium-weight casting rod, outfitted with jig and eel or jig and pork and 12- to 15-pound test line. Although with crappie and catfish you'll have the best luck at night, largemouth and smallmouth bass can be caught during the day about 30 feet deep. They tend to cluster around the cedar flats or timber submerged when the lake was first flooded. When the water cools in the fall, try shallower areas in the many coves and feeder creeks that line the lake. For up-to-date fishing reports, visit www.branson.com or www.ozarkanglers.com.

Table Rock Lake is about the only place where the indoor world of live entertainment and the outdoor world of fishing and recreation can share common ground or, in this case, common water. Many of the big music stars have homes overlooking the lake, so don't be surprised if you see a famous face trolling by on a bass boat. Around here performers Shoji Tabuchi and Mel Tillis are almost as well-known for their fishing exploits as their music shows. Where else can you be a bass angler by day and a bass singer by night?

Although most people think of the theaters when they think of Branson nightlife, insiders know that the lakeside is just as much the place to be as dusk falls. The roar of the powerboats has subsided to be replaced by the plaintive call of the solitary loon. The deep orange and violet of sunset is projected in 3-D beyond the far horizon of the lake, accompanied only by nature's own cricket-and-wave-ripple soundtrack. No wonder romance can spring into bloom at the lakeside, even as the water flowers are folding their own blossoms for the night. Indeed, more than one transplanted city boy has been known to stroll down to the water's edge in the fading light and slip a ring on the finger of his best girl, with only the rustling cedars to bear witness.

So whether you're young or just young at heart, don't think of Table Rock Lake only as a place for sports lovers and sunbathers. Have a quiet honeymoon dinner overlooking the cozy cove at Big Cedar Lodge, or celebrate your anniversary with an evening cruise on the *Showboat Branson Belle* (see the Attractions chapter). Once you've spent an evening at Table Rock, we think you'll view the lake in a whole new light. Even if it's dark.

Bull Shoals Lake

Most of Bull Shoals Lake is in Arkansas, a little farther from Branson than either Table Rock or Taneycomo. But for the serious angler, it's worth checking out. The northern end of the lake touches popular Shadow Rock Park near the mouth of Swan Creek in Forsyth, Missouri.

Bull Shoals is well known for white, largemouth, and spotted bass, as well as channel catfish, bream, walleye, bluegill, and crappie. Even so, it has been overshadowed by the later arrival of its sister lake, Table Rock, and some say that has made Bull Shoals an underfished lake by comparison. But over the years Bull Shoals has yielded more than its share of trophy fish and state records.

The floodgates closed on Bull Shoals Dam in 1951, creating a 45,440-acre sports lover's paradise with 740 miles of shoreline. At flood-control stage, the size nearly doubles to 71,240 acres of surface area. With the surrounding steep bluffs and rock ledges, it almost seems like a highland mountain lake. Most of what little brush was on the original lake bottom has rotted away, leaving the chunk-rock banks and drop-offs to suffice as cover. The lake is deep, and it's not unusual to be in 50 feet of water when you're no more than 20 feet from the bank.

As with Table Rock, scuba divers and swimmers are attracted by the clear waters of Bull Shoals. The clarity also makes light tackle and light line the best choice for anglers. Both the depth and clarity of the water make night fishing the preference of many anglers. In the summer, night fishing is also a great way to beat the heat as well as prove that slower fishing in summer doesn't always have to be the case. Channel cat fishing is best in the spring, with September through December and March through May considered the preferred times for black bass.

Boat ramps, beaches, and campgrounds abound, with more than 20 local, state, and federal public-use areas. Still, Bull Shoals Lake somehow lacks the feeling of being overcrowded or overcommercialized, though there are plenty of motels and resorts scattered around it in Missouri and in the surrounding Arkansas towns such as Mountain Home and Bull Shoals.

All the White River Flood Control Dams proved their purpose and worth in 2008 during a spring flood over the general watershed. Rainfall for the entire year was almost 58 inches, more than our usual average of 38, the wettest year since record keeping started in 1870. Some areas exceeded the general average. Nearby Miller, Missouri, recorded 72 inches. Most of the lakes filled to capacity, resulting in Table Rock and Beaver Dams' floodgates all being opened, at least to partially. There were lots of lakeshore boat docks that had to re-tether, but relative little property damage as the result of water.

THE RIVERS

Bull Creek

Bull Creek empties into Lake Taneycomo near the town of Rockaway Beach. It is one of the clearest streams in the Ozarks, which makes it a favorite of snorkelers and underwater photographers. The occasional deep pools are home to smallmouth and largemouth bass. For a leisurely float, put in at a low-water bridge off MO 176, 3.5 miles north of Walnut Shade, and take out at the MO F bridge, some 10 miles downstream.

Swan Creek

On the day following a heavy rain, this creek can be a great ride for the true white-water canoeist. Normally in the summer, though, it is either not floatable or a low-water float at best, with some walk-through required. The total distance is only 21 miles, from the MO 125 bridge at Garrison, Missouri, to the Shadow Rock Park campground at the town of Forsyth. For a shorter float, around 8 miles, you can put in at the bridge at MO AA and take out at Shadow Rock Park.

Beaver Creek

Traditionally the realm of fly fishermen, Beaver Creek is now a canoeist's favorite as well. Due to fluctuating water levels, both the fishing and floating are best after mid-June below Bradleyville, Missouri, where you can put in at the MO 76 bridge and take out at the MO 160 Kissee Mills Public Access, about 19 miles downstream. You can find black bass and white bass in a series of pools just before take-out. For canoe rentals call Beaver Canoe Rental & Sales at (417) 796-2336. For an all-day trip, put in instead at the MO 76 bridge 8 miles southwest of Ava, Missouri. For a shorter all-day trip, put in at the MO 76 bridge at Brownbranch and float to the MO 160 bridge or take out even earlier at the MO 76 bridge at Bradleyville.

The James River

A major tributary of the former White River, the James is best known for float fishing. Float fishing is popular in the Ozarks, and some say it was invented on the James River at the town of Galena. Using a johnboat, a long flat-bottomed boat squared off at both ends, the angler drifts down the river in ease and comfort. Before the advent of Table Rock Dam, johnboats could make a 25-mile float trip from Galena to Branson, but now most float fishing is done on a 22-mile stretch from Hootentown to Galena. Swimming on the James is not recommended on any portion below the city of Springfield due to wastewater runoff. The smallmouth bass fishing is good, but we recommend that you catch and release. The Department of Natural Resources has deemed 28 miles of the James River impaired by both urban point and nonpoint sources. The experienced canoeist will enjoy the tremendous scenic variety of a winter float. The craggy bluffs, broad valleys, and trunks of dark trees are quite majestic after snowfall. Canoeists can contact Hootentown Canoe Rental, MO O, Crane, (417) 369-2266, or James River Outfitters, 110 Y Bridge Rd., Galena, (417) 357-6443, for floating gear and shuttle service as well as RV hookups and campsites.

Buffalo National River

If there can be such a thing as a river that is too magnificent, this is it. Magnificence translates into popularity, and frankly the upper Buffalo is simply overrun by recreators on weekends in the summer. Why? Because the scenery simply takes your breath away for nearly 150 miles. From its source in the Boston Mountains to Lost Valley and Buffalo Point downstream, the Buffalo riverscape is unparalleled and virtually untouched. In the years following World War II, a coalition of outdoorsmen and environmentalists successfully opposed damming the Buffalo, and ultimately most of it was designated a National Scenic River under the supervision of the National Park Service. It remains the last major unimpounded river in Arkansas.

i **If you're interested in the beauty of the Buffalo River Country, check out the hiking and photography publications by Tim Ernst at www.cloudland.net. You can order online or toll-free at (800) 838-HIKE (4453).**

Floaters come from all over to revel in the Buffalo River's 500- to 1,000-foot wooded bluffs, clear green pools, and blue and white riffles. Fishing, swimming, canoeing, and camping all have their share of enthusiasts. You'll need a guidebook, and there are two in particular we recommend. For floating see *The Buffalo National River, Canoeing Guide* published by the Ozark Society, P.O. Box 2914, Little Rock, AR 72203. Order from its Web site: www.ozarksociety.net. The landlubber will enjoy *Buffalo River Hiking Trails* by Tim Ernst, available from his Web site: www.cloudland.net. (For hiking information see the Buffalo National River listing in the Recreation and the Outdoors chapter.) Both books are also available at the listed park headquarters address, where you can also get maps and information on boating, canoeing, camping, commercial outfitters, and park facilities. The Buffalo is about a one-and-a-half-hour drive from Branson but well worth the trip. For more information contact Park Headquarters, 402 North Walnut St., Suite 136, Harrison, AR 72601; (870) 741-5443; www.nps.gov/buff.

Current and Jacks Fork Rivers

The Current River and its major tributary, the Jacks Fork, are located several hours east of Branson in a sparsely populated area of east-central Missouri. Major portions of both rivers have been incorporated into Ozark National Scenic Riverways and thus receive federal protection and management under the National Park Service. Park headquarters is in Van Buren, Missouri. Commercial development is minimal, yet you can still find sufficient lodging and commercial outfitting services.

Fed by big springs (hence the regional name Big Springs Country), the Current remains floatable even during the dry days of summer. The water is deeper than other Ozark streams, but it is a relatively safer float because there are fewer hazards. The scenery is remarkably diverse over the course of the two rivers' combined floatable length of 180 miles, with natural beauty that has remained virtually unchanged since it was first discovered. The Jacks Fork is unusual in that it flows between canyonlike bluffs. Later it develops meandering qualities, with high bluffs on one side and broad valleys on the other. The float allows one to see huge caves, large springs, and perhaps a glimpse of the valley's herd of wild horses. Below Van Buren on the Current River be certain to check out Big Spring, one of the world's largest springs. (See the History chapter for more information.) The spring supplies the Current with 276 million gallons of water a day. Hiking and camping are favorite riverside activities. (For hiking information see the Recreation and the Outdoors chapter.)

The Jacks Fork joins the Current at a point known as Two Rivers. Jacks Fork is a much smaller stream than the Current, but it's well noted for the steep limestone bluffs that crowd the edge of the river canyon. For more information on the Current and Jacks Fork Rivers, contact Ozark National Scenic Riverways, 404 Watercress Dr., Van Buren, MO 63965, or P.O. Box 490, Van Buren, MO 63965; (573) 323-4236; www.nps.gov/ozar.

ACTIVITIES AND GEAR

Canoeing and Kayaking

Ozark rivers offer something for both the whitewater canoeing or kayaking enthusiast and the pleasure floater. Some of the waterways offer a true thrill ride, especially in winter and spring or after a few days of heavy rain. But in the summer, water levels can be low enough on many area waterways as to make for a perfect day trip or camping trip. It's an ideal outdoor activity for the family, with a leisurely pace and spectacular landscapes full of varied and sometimes noteworthy flora and fauna.

Guides are available but probably unnecessary for an afternoon float trip, and for the shallower summer runs, no expertise or even equipment of your own is needed. Canoes, kayaks, and other gear can be rented by the day at any number of commercial outfitters throughout the Ozarks, even in the smallest of towns, as long as there is a popular put-in spot nearby. Typically, you park your car at rental headquarters (often a take-out point), and the outfitter shuttles both you and the canoes upstream, 7 to 15 miles for a day trip, to put in. Many offer inner tubes or rafts as well as camping gear and supplies. It's a good idea to call the rental company in advance, especially if you are planning a float during a holiday.

The novice canoeist or kayaker should observe a few safety tips. Wear a life jacket in preparation for the unexpected because a flowing river can be as deep and treacherous in some spots as it is calm and shallow in others. Seal your wallet, fishing license, camera, and other valuables in waterproof bags or containers, and stow your gear low in the center of the craft. When selecting a scenic gravel bar as a campsite, keep in mind that river conditions can change without warning, and flash flooding from rains upstream is always a possibility.

Finally, know your river. The best way is to acquire a copy of *Paddler's Guide to Missouri* ($6) , available from the Missouri Department of Conservation, P.O. Box 180, Jefferson City, MO 65102; (573) 751-4115, or online at www.mdc natureshop.com. This guidebook contains detailed maps of some 52 major float streams in the Ozarks, together with distance information, difficulty ratings, and suggested put-in and take-out points. You should also talk to the rental company staff, who can alert you to any recent changes in the river and forecasted weather conditions.

i Some of the most beautiful and genetically pure McCloud River rainbow trout can be caught in Crane Creek in Stone County. The trout were stocked from railroad cars in the 1890s from the McCloud River in California and have been successfully reproducing for more than a hundred years.

Fishing Guides

Fishing is always more fun when you catch something, and hiring a guide goes a long way toward ensuring that you do. Of course, there's no guarantee, but an experienced guide will be familiar with the current hot spots and the best baits and lures to use.

Most marinas can refer you to a guide or make the arrangements for you. Some guides, like the ones listed here, can be telephoned directly. Usually they will meet you at a marina or other lakeside location, or they may pick you up at your waterfront lodging. Typically, the guide provides the boat, gas, bait, and fishing gear (if you don't have your own). Some will also provide lunch on request. Most guide boats can carry two, or at most three, passengers. Half-day excursions start at around $200 and full-day trips at $250, but the price can depend on what is included, so make sure you always ask first. Advance reservations can help you avoid disappointment. The prices we have listed here are starting prices for guides. More than two anglers in a party, snacks, meals, live bait, and transportation to and from your hotel may be extra. You must provide your own fishing license or trout tag prior to embarking on a trip.

As with any service of this nature, there may be those who hold themselves out as guides but may not have much experience; that's why a specific referral from a knowledgeable marina or resort is recommended. All of the guides listed here carry a current Coast Guard certification. In 1999 Coast Guard officials began stepping up their efforts to make sure fishing guides possessed current licensing and instated random drug tests to weed out unscrupulous guides.

BOB'S FISHING GUIDE SERVICE
8722 MO 76, Notch
(417) 338-2316
www.shadyacremotel.com
294-7248

Full day or half, Bob Juneman provides the boat and all equipment for one or two persons to troll for bass on Table Rock or trout on Taneycomo. Rates start at $160 for five hours or $250 for eight hours. Bob says 40 percent of his business is from repeat customers. On a good day of fishing you can expect to reel in between 15 and 30 bass. You need to call two weeks in advance for summertime fishing excursions with Bob.

HOOK'S TABLE ROCK FISHING GUIDE SERVICE
129 McIntosh Lane, Reeds Spring
(417) 338-2277, (800) 603-4665
www.hooksbass.com
Your captain is Jim Van Hook, and he specializes in assisting the beginning angler. He's also a favorite among tournament participants. His rates start at $225 for a half day, all equipment included. Live bait is an extra charge, as is picking you up at your hotel or resort. Jim goes out only on Table Rock Lake.

PETE'S PROFESSIONAL GUIDE SERVICE
681 Hardin Hills, Galena
(888) 214-1767
www.hookedonbass.com
Pete Wenners is a 1999 qualifying participant in the Kmart Bassmaster 150 tournament. He's been a professional fishing guide for more than a decade and specializes in helping to educate anglers on the ins and outs of fishing. He said he and his other guides try to help clients understand why fish bite when they do and what factors contribute to success. Rates begin at $220 for four to five hours and $325 for eight hours for up to two people. Pete or one of his other guides will pick you up at your hotel for no extra charge and take you out on Table Rock Lake or Lake Taneycomo.

RIVER RUN OUTFITTERS
2626 MO 165
(417) 332-0460, (877) 699-3474
www.riverrunoutfitters.com
River Run Outfitters is a full line fly fishing shop (full line? Does that include the fish?) about a half mile north of Table Rock Dam. It is owned and operated by Stan and Carolyn Parker, each of whom have fished the area lakes and rivers for more than three decades—and they probably can almost guarantee it will include a fish. They offer wade guide trips starting at $165 for four hours for one person. Their instructional fly-fishing trips are great for beginners and include nomenclature, basic casting, line tending, fly selection, and water reading. Rates start at $165

for one person for a half day. These rates include all equipment. Their shop offers a good variety of fly-fishing equipment, such as wading wear, rain gear, fly-tying materials, gifts, and many accessories for the fly fisherman.

Fishing Licenses

The Wildlife Code of Missouri, which governs fishing, is what is known as a permissive code. The regulations tell you what you are permitted to do, in terms of what species you can take, when, and how; everything else is off-limits.

Everyone who fishes must have a permit, except those age 15 or younger and Missouri residents older than 65. In 2009 an annual fishing permit was $12 for residents and $42 for non-residents. A daily permit is $7.50, but if you think you'll fish for more than a week, you're better off purchasing the annual permit. In addition, a trout permit of $3.50 is required of all persons to possess and transport trout on Lake Taneycomo between US 65 and Table Rock Dam. In some state parks a $2 daily trout tag is required. You can buy the various permits at marinas, bait and tackle shops, and convenience stores, or get one directly from the Missouri Department of Conservation by calling (573) 751-4115. Visit their Web site for more information at www.missouri conservation.org. Always carry your permit while fishing or transporting your catch.

The daily aggregate limit for bass on Table Rock and Bull Shoals Lakes is six, with a minimum length of 15 inches (12 inches for spotted bass on Bull Shoals). In streams, the black bass daily limit is six, with a length minimum of 12 inches. The daily limit for crappie is 15 with a minimum length limit of 10 inches on Table Rock and Bull Shoals. On Lake Taneycomo there is a daily limit of four trout, only one of which may be a brown (minimum length: 20 inches). Any rainbow trout between 12 and 20 inches must be released between Table Rock Dam and the mouth of Fall Creek.

These limits are intended only as basic guidelines, of course, since it is always good practice to confirm the season and any limits in whatever particular lake or stream you intend to fish. Also, when fishing Table Rock or Bull Shoals Lakes, which are each partly in Missouri and partly in Arkansas, ask locally about which, or if both, state permits might be required.

In Arkansas the fees and limits are similar. A nonresident annual fishing license is $40, and the nonresident trout permit is $12. Again, the licenses and a copy of the state regulations are available over the counter at sporting goods, fishing supply, and other stores. Or call the Arkansas Game and Fish Commission at (800) 364-GAME or visit their Web site at www.agfc.com.

Both states are emphasizing catch-and-release (pleasure) fishing as a conservation measure that helps fish populations. And since you will probably be hooking some undersized fish anyway, it's a good idea to know the guidelines for survivable release. The fastest and best method is simply to cut the line without ever lifting the fish out of the water; the hook will usually fall off or be expelled by the fish. Or use barbless hooks, and always avoid excessive handling of the fish.

Fishing Tournaments

What would a spring or fall weekend be without a fishing tournament on an Ozarks lake? The tradition is long-standing, and some tournaments often seem to grow in popularity year after year. Many tournaments are sponsored by area marinas, boat manufacturers, or tackle suppliers, with lucrative prizes of their brand-name goods as well as cash. Others are held to benefit charities, with thousands of dollars raised each year.

Earlier in this chapter we mentioned how catch-and-release fishing is catching on, and nowhere does it receive more prominence than in the tournaments. Boats are outfitted with live wells, which are small aerated water tanks to keep the fish alive and well until final weigh-in.

Tournaments can be either single-competitor events or buddy tournaments, in which the catches of two anglers in a boat are weighed together. Most tournaments are open events, with the only prerequisite being payment of the entry fee ($70 to $500 a person for single events, $90 to $150 a boat for buddy tournaments).

Same-day registration is usually available.

On Table Rock Lake many of the major tournaments originate at Port of Kimberling Marina (see the subsequent Marina and Houseboat Rentals section) in Kimberling City. The Table Rock Lake/Kimberling City Area Chamber of Commerce helps keep track of these events; you can contact them at P.O. Box 495-98, Kimberling City, MO 66686; (417) 739-2564 or (800) 595-0393. Visit their Web site at www.tablerocklake.net or find tournament listings at www.sportfishermen .com. Also check bulletin boards at marinas, bait and tackle shops, and convenience stores for postings.

Marinas and Houseboat Rentals

All three area lakes have a number of full-service marinas. Unless otherwise noted, the marinas listed sell bait and tackle, marine fuel, fishing licenses, and sodas and snacks. They also rent fishing boats or bass boats and pontoons. Rates range from $35 per hour to $290 a day. Fishing advice and tall tales are free. When you call, you might want to ask if the marina is affiliated with or adjacent to a campground or other services.

Many marinas also have houseboat rentals, and these are noted. Today's houseboats usually have the same modern conveniences you find in motor homes, such as TVs, microwaves, air-conditioning, and electric generators. Most come fully outfitted with bed linens and table service for the kitchenette. Some even have VCRs, cellular phones, and gas grills. They sleep anywhere from 4 to 12 people or more. Make your reservations well in advance, and be prepared to pay a substantial deposit—around $300 or more. Don't expect to get any one-night or even two-night rentals during the summer; most rentals are by the week or for a minimum of three or four nights. Houseboats are usually available March through late October.

Most marinas can arrange a fishing guide for you or at least make recommendations and give you names and phone numbers. See the previous Fishing Guides section for a partial list of guides in the area.

BAXTER BOAT DOCK
MO H, Lampe
(417) 779-4301
www.tablerocklake.net

Baxter is on the south side of Table Rock Lake, where it's a little quieter and less congested. The marina sells groceries and offers wet and dry boat storage. You can rent a fishing boat for $95 for four hours or get a pontoon for $140 for four hours or $270 for eight hours. Ski boats go for $135 for four hours or $260 for eight hours. Rent a personal watercraft for $65 an hour. Owner since 1986, Sue Pollard will be glad to recommend a fishing guide if you need one. The marina is closed December through March, but they do answer the phone and pump gas if you stop by.

CREEKSIDE MARINA AT LONG CREEK
1368 Long Creek Rd., Ridgedale
(417) 334-4860
www.creeksidemarina.com

Gage's offers groceries, fishing guides, ski boats, Wave Runners, and boat slips by the day or year. Call in advance for reservations, especially in the summer. Rental prices are on their Web site.

HITCH-N-POST TACKLE
5439 MO 165
(417) 334-3395

Landlocked and not a marina, the Hitch-N-Post is still without peer as a place to load up on bait, marine fuel, camping supplies, life jackets, groceries, and anything else you might need. The shop also offers fishing-guide referral and an up-to-the-minute daily fishing report. Hitch-N-Post is across from Table Rock State Park.

INDIAN POINT MARINA
3443 Indian Point Rd.
(417) 338-2891, (866) 218-0417
www.indianpointmarina.com

Located on the north side of Table Rock Lake near Silver Dollar City, Indian Point Marina is open year-round. This is the area's "dive center" for those interested in going underwater. Those who want to just skim on top, Jet Skis rent by the hour for $65 for a three-seater. Indian Point has twenty wet storage stalls, a snack shop, and tackle and live bait.

K DOCK MARINA
295 Marina Dr., Kirbyville
(417) 334-2880

On Bull Shoals Lake, the marina rents boat slips and fishing and pontoon boats. Fishing boats are $60 per half day, $100 full day. Pontoons are $90 per half day, $150 full day. Fuel is additional.

LILLEYS' LANDING RESORT & MARINA
367 River Lane
(417) 334-6380, (417) 334-2263
www.lilleyslanding.com

Lilleys' is a one-stop trout angler's dream. You can spend the night at the resort and then hook up with a fishing guide for a variety of different types of fishing adventures. Trips are on Lake Taneycomo or Table Rock with an experienced guide. Check the Web site for guest rates. If you'd like to go out on your own, they have johnboats starting at $75 for four hours, pontoons for $129 for four hours, and bass boats for four hours at $119. The marina's specialty is selling artificial lures and flies. Their Web site is chockful with advice, tips, information, and other links.

PORT OF KIMBERLING MARINA
49 Lake Rd., Kimberling City
(417) 739-2315
www.mypok.com

Touted as Table Rock Lake's largest marina, it also offers boat slips, dry storage, and a complete ski shop with sales, service, rental, and instruction. You may call the Ski Shack directly at (417) 739-2628. What's Up Dock rents speedboats and personal watercraft as well; call (417) 739-4511. Or you can rent a houseboat at Tri-Lakes Houseboat Rentals, (800) 982-2628. Table Rock Lake Pontoon Rentals is also here at (417) 739-2732 or (800) 652-9884. For the Water's Edge Campground, call (417) 739-5377. See the listing under Scuba Diving for the dive shop.

RIVERLAKE RESORT
146 Riverlake Circle, Hollister
(417) 334-2800, (888) 891-2720
www.riverlakeresort.com
Bring the entire family to Riverlake on Lake Taney-como for a summertime reunion and fishing trip. A stay at the 35-unit resort ranges from $65 to $180 per night. All units feature a kitchenette. There is a 360-foot dock with fishing, a fully equipped bait shop, and a heated fish-cleaning room. The marina features 16-foot aluminum fishing boats for $50 for a full day or $35 for a half day, plus gas. You can get a family-size pontoon for $75 for four hours or $105 for eight hours. The bass boats go for $37 for a half day and $65 for a full day. Fuel is extra.

SCOTTY'S TROUT DOCK AND MARINA
395 North Lakefront Rd.
(417) 334-4288
www.scottystroutmarina.com
Sometimes it's just as much fun to fish from the dock as from a boat, and Scotty's is located right on the Taneycomo lakefront next to a large public-access fishing dock. If you're not having much luck, you can get a fishing boat from Scotty's for around $49 for four hours or $74 a day, a pontoon boat for $129, $199. Scotty will set you up with a fishing guide for a half or full day starting at around $135 for two people.

STATE PARK MARINA
State Park Marina Road, MO 165
(417) 334-3069
www.stateparkmarina.com
When the marina boasts everything on the water, it's not kidding. Besides the usual fishing water-craft, it also rents canoes, Wave Runners, and ski boats. Or sign up for a little parasailing. It also has a general store and a dive shop, which is listed in the subsequent Scuba Diving section. This marina is at Table Rock State Park. The marina is closed November 1 through March 1.

TRI-LAKES HOUSEBOAT RENTALS
50 Marina Way, Kimberling City
(417) 739-2370, (800) 982-2628
www.tri-lakeshouseboat.com
One of the many marine services at Port of Kimberling, Tri-Lakes Houseboat Rentals features a full range of houseboats that sleep anywhere from 6 to 12 people. There is a two- or three-night minimum depending on size. You can get boats by the week. Rates vary depending on boat size and season. Reservations are recommended, and a deposit is required.

Where to Buy a Boat
BASS PRO SHOPS
1935 South Campbell Ave., Springfield
(417) 887-7334, (888) 442-6337
www.basspro.com
People come from around the world to visit Bass Pro Shops in Springfield, and no doubt many of them come for the boats. Beginning when you drive by their huge outdoor showroom, you are sure to be impressed by their overwhelming list of models, features, options, and prices. You can basically spend as much money on a boat as you so desire. You name the option, and they'll customize the boat any way you like it. Want lime green stripes to match the ones on the RV? No problem. At Bass Pro you can find a full selection of Tracker boats, including the popular Tracker, Sun Tracker, Tahoe, and Nitro models, as well as other brands The sales reps at Bass Pro will help you wade through the vast sea of options so that you've got enough left over for bait.

Scuba Diving
Snorkeling, scuba diving, spearfishing, and underwater photography are popular in the crystal-clear streams and lakes of the Ozarks. At Table Rock, Bull Shoals, Beaver, and Norfork (in Arkansas) Lakes, visibility is often as much as 15 to 25 feet. The Ozarks has a surprising diversity of underwater wildlife, and its waters attract dive groups from as far away as Kansas City. Remember, safety first when div-

ing. The following shops can help provide proper training and equipment maintenance.

AQUASPORTS SCUBA CENTER
5601 South Campbell Ave., Springfield
(417) 883-5151
www.aquasports.ws
Aquasports provides instruction from snorkeling and basic open-water scuba to instructor-level classes, as well as many specialty classes such as underwater photography, spearfishing, dry-suit diving, and ice diving. Before you buy or rent scuba gear, you can try it out in the center's heated indoor pool. Group excursions are available to Table Rock, Bull Shoals, and Beaver Lakes.

PORT OF KIMBERLING SCUBA
49-A Lake Rd., Kimberling City
(417) 739-5400
This is a well-known, full-service dive shop, providing instruction at all levels, chartered dive trips, scuba supplies, and rental equipment.

SCUBA SPORTS
4550 Gretna Rd., Branson Meadows Mall
(417) 334-9073
www.scuba-sports.com
Scuba Sports sells and rents scuba equipment, refills tanks, and repairs gear. They are the largest dive store in Missouri and offer classes for beginners and advanced divers, as well as dive vacation packages. They offer a weeklong PADI Seal Team summer camp for youngsters 8 to 10, popular with residents as well as tourists. They do guided dive tours for certified divers in Table Rock Lake. If you might be interested in diving, Scuba Sport offers a summer program called Discover Scuba Diving. For $65, they provide a short classroom session in a pool, then take you to the lake for an actual dive with an instructor.

STATE PARK DIVE SHOP
State Park Marina Road at intersection of MO 165
(417) 334-3069
Full-certification instruction is offered here, but before you jump in with both feet for extended

lessons, you might try out what the shop calls a "scuba experience," a two-hour trial run. The shop also offers dive tours and group tours. It rents dive boats and scuba gear and provides sales and repair services.

Sailing and Parasailing
It's not uncommon to find a sailboat or three on Table Rock Lake during a windy summer day. Your best bet for rental equipment is the State Park Marina at Table Rock State Park or the Port of Kimberling Marina in Kimberling City (see previous listings). If sailing is what floats you, make the trip to Stockton, Missouri, home of the state's top sailing lake, Stockton Lake. For information call the Lake Stockton Association at (417) 276-5161. If the air on Table Rock Lake is a little too calm for sailing, you might want to try parasailing instead. Many of the area marinas have rental gear and are willing to offer helpful tips for both the driver of the boat and the parasailer.

Swimming
Many of the public-use areas at Table Rock and Bull Shoals Lakes have imported sandy beaches. The best known is probably Moonshine Beach on Table Rock, just north of the dam off MO 165. The U.S. Army Corps of Engineers campgrounds also have public swimming beaches. Nominal day-use fees are charged at the rate of $1 per person 13 and older, with a maximum of $3 a car. These rates are subject to change throughout the year. For a complete list of public-access areas operated by the corps, see the Campgrounds and RV Parks chapter or visit the corps Web site at www.swl.usace.army.mil/parks/tablerock/camp groundpages.htm.

Resources
ARKANSAS GAME AND FISH COMMISSION
2 Natural Resources Dr.
Little Rock, AR
(501) 223-6300, (800) 364-GAME
www.agfc.com
Call the toll-free number to order a fishing license

or to get free brochures on fishing in Arkansas, boating regulations, and area wildlife.

MISSOURI DEPARTMENT OF CONSERVATION
(573) 751-4115
www.missouriconservation.org
The Fisheries Division publishes an annual fishing report called Fishing Prospects, which lists some of the more popular lakes and streams for fishing in Missouri as well as information on fish populations. It is available free by writing the department at P.O. Box 180, Jefferson City, MO 65102 or from any fisheries office throughout the state.

U.S. ARMY CORPS OF ENGINEERS
(417) 334-4101, (870) 425-2700
(for Bull Shoals and Norfork Lakes)
Dock permit information, a list of campgrounds and public-use areas, corps regulations, maps, and other information are available from the Table Rock Lake Office, 4600 MO 165, Suite A, Branson, MO 65615 or Mountain Home Project Office, 324 West Seventh St., Mountain Home, AR 72653. Visit the Web site at www.swl.usace.army.mil/parks/tablerock/campround pages.htm.

Trout-Fishing Organizations

Whether you're a novice or a fishing pro, join a trout-fishing organization and you will enjoy the many club activities and the chance to exchange fishing stories and techniques. There is always something new a person can learn about trout fishing, and the best way to learn is from a friend. If you are new to the sport of trout fishing, there is no better way to learn more about it than by joining a club. If you are an experienced trout fisherman, share your knowledge with other club members. You can find a complete list and links at www.missouritrout.com/clubs/index.htm.

Publications

Many of the libraries in the tri-lakes area have copies of the following guidebooks. Some are out of print but are readily available from www.amazon.com. *The Greatest Ozarks Guidebook,* by Harry and Phyl Dark, published by Greatest Graphics, Inc., features plenty of information on rivers, streams, and lakes as well as camping, state parks, and national recreation areas; *The Ozarks Outdoors,* by Milton D. Rafferty, University of Oklahoma Press, is a well-researched and comprehensive resource about the Ozarks, with chapters on floating and fishing the lakes and rivers, hiking, and camping. There are also maps and addresses to write for more information on a region-by-region basis. *Ozark Trout Tales, A Fishing Guide for the White River System* by Steve Wright can be ordered from the White River Chronicle, P.O. Box 4653, Fayetteville, AR 72702-4653 and is an excellent history and how-to about trout fishing in tailwaters below each of the following dams: Table Rock, Bull Shoals, Beaver, Norfolk, and Greer's Ferry. It is available in area bookstores or at the above address. *Pro's Guide to Fishing Missouri Lakes,* by Monte Burch, Outdoor World Press Inc., provides lake-by-lake descriptive information, maps, and fishing tips, including plenty of quotes from the pros who fish them. *Two Ozark Rivers,* by Oliver Schuchard and Steve Kohler, University of Missouri Press, Columbia, has great photographs and a detailed historical and ecological perspective on the Current and Jacks Fork Rivers. A good Web source for Missouri and Arkansas trout fishing information is www.whiteriverandnorforktrout.com.

CAMPGROUNDS AND RV PARKS

Long before the word tourism entered the vocabulary of native Ozarkians, people were coming to these parts to escape city life, fish in the rivers, hunt in the woods, and take in the clean, natural air of the Ozark Mountains. Some of them stayed with their country relatives, but most camped out along the White River, the James River, and, after 1913, Lake Taneycomo. After Table Rock Lake Dam was completed in 1958, small commercial campgrounds began popping up around the newly impounded lake to meet the demand of outdoors lovers, who by now were making regular trips to the area. When the Mabe brothers began offering these campers a little weekend musical entertainment out of an old roller-skating rink, the word tourism became common around here.

In a sense, not much has changed. The Mabe brothers are still entertaining, only now they have a fancy place on The Strip called the Baldknobbers Jamboree Theatre, and campers are still coming to enjoy the scenery and to hunt and fish. The major difference today is that their reason for coming has changed. They come for the entertainment, and while they're here they camp out.

Campgrounds and RV parks are big business in Branson. People aren't just coming to camp lakeside anymore. Many of the more than 5,000 campsites in the area are smack-dab in the middle of town. The list of amenities at these places would make one of the earliest campers either jealous or offended. We've got campgrounds with swimming pools, laundry facilities, grocery stores, car rentals, video arcades, full-service marinas, and more electricity than you can shake a stick at. Some of them are so popular they even host entire conventions.

Fortunately for those who prefer primitive camping, we still have plenty of places without cable television and phones. They are more the exception than the rule, however. If you're looking to really rough it, we suggest the nearby Mark Twain National Forest or the Hercules Glades Wilderness Area within the forest. (See the Recreation and the Outdoors chapter for more on these areas.) You can call the National Park Service at (417) 732-2662 for information.

WHEN TO COME AND HOW MUCH TO PAY

If you're bringing your own recreational vehicle to town, be sure to make a reservation before you leave home. Many places require a minimum stay and a deposit. If you're coming in peak season—June through August for camping—you could have trouble finding an available spot. The rates are also higher in the summer than in the spring and fall. The best times to come are early spring and late fall. You'll get the best rates and won't have any trouble finding space. Since Branson is quickly becoming a year-round destination, many of the parks are staying open all year, especially those in town. Rates are the absolute lowest in January and February, but you may get what you pay for as far as the weather is concerned. Our heaviest snowfalls don't last for more than a couple of days, but it's not uncommon to have several days in a row with temperatures in the low to mid-30s.

If your vacation is scheduled for August, never fear, most of the campgrounds and RV parks offer a number of discounts. They routinely offer Good Sam, AAA, and AARP discounts. They also offer fishing packages and extended-stay packages, which can include show tickets and meals. Be sure to pick up brochures when you arrive because some of them have coupons attached. The average cost for a full RV hookup is around $25 a day (some places charge more if your party is larger than two people). Tent sites cost less, and cottages and cabins go for slightly more.

> **i** Interested in seeing Branson and other vacation spots for almost free? Ozarker Arline Chandler's book, *Road Work II: The RVer's Ultimate Income Resource Guide,* explains the hows, whats, and whys of jobs and volunteerism for workampers.

POLICIES

Many RV parks also have mobile homes, cabins, pop-up campers, and hotel units. Although they usually don't mind if you bring your pet along in your own rig, pets are generally not welcome in the rentals. The same goes for smoking. Be sure to ask about policies when you make your reservations. Some places prohibit alcoholic beverages, so again ask if you're planning on bringing any.

If you're going to need phone service, you are generally out of luck. America's Best Campgrounds will hook up a private phone for a fee, but most of the others either have one or two pay phones or none at all. Again, don't wait until you check in before you ask. Check-in time runs around 3 p.m., and checkout is generally 10 a.m. or earlier. A few places have offices that stay open 24 hours a day, but most do not. However, owners tend to stick nearby and often live on the properties year-round.

Many of the listings in this section are located within a few blocks of The Strip. The ones a little farther out generally offer shuttle service into town, either for free or for a small charge. Or you can arrange to have a rental car delivered to your campsite before you arrive. (See the Getting Here, Getting Around chapter for a list of rental-car companies.)

LOCATION

The commercial campgrounds and RV parks in this section are listed according to location. The Branson Lakeside campgrounds, listed in the Public Campgrounds section, are on Lake Taneycomo. All the Indian Point Road commercial campgrounds are on or near Table Rock Lake. Since many of the places do not have numbered addresses, be sure to call for specific driving directions. We have given our directions based on the assumption that you will be leaving from The Strip; however, if you are coming from out of town, there may be a better route than the one we have described.

PUBLIC CAMPGROUNDS

BRANSON LAKESIDE RV PARK
300 South Boxcar Willie Dr.
(417) 334-2915
www.bransonparksandrecreation.com
A campground close to downtown Branson can still be found in spite of the new Branson Landing development project on the Taneycomo lakefront. Retirees have long enjoyed the superb location with the "air-conditioned breeze" from Taneycomo and the camaraderie with the other residents. There is a table for each of the 180 campsites. The folks in the campground enjoy feeding the geese that gather along the riverbanks and fishing for trout from one of several fishing docks. A marina and two shelters are provided. The showers and restrooms include central heating and air-conditioning. A 30- or 50-amp site with cable TV is available for $26 per day, with the seventh day free.

> **i** Many of the theaters and restaurants have special parking places for RVs. But if you're taking your rig into downtown Branson, better think twice. You can't park along the streets, and some of the parking lots do not accommodate long vehicles. Call the Downtown Branson Main Street Association at (417) 334-1548 for information on RV parking.

TABLE ROCK STATE PARK
MO 165
(417) 334-4704
www.mostateparks.com
This 356-acre park, located just south of the Table Rock Dam near the *Showboat Branson Belle,* is run by the Missouri Department of Natural Resources. Its 165 campsites come with basic and full hookups, available only on a first-come, first-served basis. You can use the concrete boat launch for free. The park has a full-service marina with rental boats and scuba-diving equipment. The marina can be reached by calling (417) 334-2628, or you can write to the Missouri Department of Natural Resources at P.O. Box 176, Jefferson City, MO 65102. Call them at (800) 334-6946 for more information about Table Rock State Park and other state-run parks.

U.S. ARMY CORPS OF ENGINEERS CAMPGROUNDS
Main Office, MO 165 adjacent
to Table Rock Dam
(417) 334-4101,
(877) 444-6777 (for reservations)
www.reserveusa.com

AUNT'S CREEK, REEDS SPRING
(417) 739-2792

BAXTER, LAMPE
(417) 779-5370

BIG M, CASSVILLE
(417) 271-3190

CAMPBELL POINT, SHELL KNOB
(417) 858-3903

CAPE FAIR, GALENA
(417) 538-2220

CRICKET CREEK, OMAHA, AR
(870) 426-3331

EAGLE ROCK, EAGLE ROCK
(417) 271-3215

INDIAN POINT, BRANSON
(417) 338-2121

LONG CREEK, RIDGEDALE
(417) 334-8427

MILL CREEK, LAMPE
(417) 779-5378

OLD HIGHWAY 86, BLUE EYE
(417) 779-5376

VINEY CREEK, GOLDEN
(417) 271-3860

VIOLA, SHELL KNOB
(417) 858-3904
The U.S. Army Corps of Engineers operates 13 public recreation areas on Table Rock Lake. All come outfitted with toilets, showers, drinking water, fire rings, picnic tables, swimming beaches, boat-launching ramps, and parking spaces. The campgrounds have electric hookups and dump stations for your travel trailer. The Corps of Engineers campgrounds open between April 1 and May 15. A few close after Labor Day, but some of them stay open until the end of October.

The corps allows up to 90 percent of the campsites in any given park to be reserved in advance. The remainder are available on a first-come, first-served basis. The fees vary according to what type of site you request but generally run between $14 and $20 per night, plus an additional $3 administrative fee. You can make reservations by mail with a check or money order, or reserve by phone with a credit card. The corps offers a central reservation service for all corps campgrounds. You can make advance reservations by calling toll-free at (877) 444-6777 or visiting the Web site at www.reserveusa.com. Area-use fees for the swimming beaches and picnic areas are $1 per person with a maximum of $4 per car.

Visitors older than 62 can request a America The Beautiful Passport, which entitles the holder to a 50 percent discount off camping and day-use fees at any corps-operated facility on any of the area's lakes. The lifetime pass costs $10 and is available at any park attendant booth or at the Corps of Engineers Visitors Center on MO 165 adjacent to Table Rock Dam. A Golden Access Passport, for anyone permanently disabled, is free and can be picked up at the visitor center.

Campers can get a guidebook, which lists each campground's location and amenities, at the visitor center. For driving directions you may call the campgrounds individually.

COMMERCIAL CAMPGROUNDS

In and around Branson

ACORN ACRES RV PARK & CAMPGROUND
159 Acorn Acres Lane (MO 76 West)
(417) 338-2500, (800) 338-2504
www.campbestbransonrvpark.com
To get to Acorn Acres from Branson, follow The Strip west out of town. After you pass the Indian Point/Silver Dollar City turnoff, go 1 mile and look for the signs on your left. The park has 55 full-hookup RV sites, with 15 pull-through sites and 2 tent sites. You can get 30- or 50-amp electrical service and cable TV with your hookup. The park features a swimming pool, private showers, laundry facility, covered pavilion, concrete patios, game room, playground, horseshoe pit, and plenty of shaded picnic tables. Rates range from around $24.00 a day for a tent site to $34.50 a day for a 50-amp luxury full hookup. The manager will be happy to make your show ticket reservations. Acorn Acres is open year-round.

AMERICA'S BEST CAMPGROUND
499 Buena Vista Rd.
(417) 336-4399, (800) 671-4399
www.abc-branson.com
This large campground is well off the beaten path, but only 0.5 mile north of the Tri-Lakes Center Theater on MO 248. You can't see it from the highway, so look for the red, white, and blue sign on MO 248 directing you west to Buena Vista Road.

There are 158 pull-throughs with full hookups, concrete patios, picnic tables, and grills. Sites have 30, 50, and 100 amps of electricity. Satellite TV and Wi-Fi are available at every site. Six well-kept cabins come with air-conditioning, heat, and TV, but no restrooms or linens.

The amenities at ABC include a swimming pool with a hot tub, phone hookups, picnic tables, barbecue grills, laundry facilities, a gift shop, a convenience store, basketball courts, horseshoe pits, a playground, an air-conditioned recreation room, and a closed-circuit camera for security. They also have a 1,200-square-foot pavilion, which can be reserved for large group events. Sites run between $29 and $35 a day, depending on what type of services you choose. The cabins run close to $36 and can sleep up to four. The campground is open all year. Be sure to take advantage of their valet parking.

BRANSON MUSICLAND KAMPGROUND
116 North Gretna Rd. (MO 165)
(417) 334-0848, (888) 248-9080
www.musiclandkampground.com
Just 1 block off The Strip, Musicland Kampground caters to RVs only, but does have five four-person cabins with no plumbing. Huge trees provide great shade in the summertime, and guests can cool off in the swimming pool or step inside the recreation room. With 120 sites in a prime location, the park fills up fast. Guests are usually advised to make reservations well in advance.

Rates range from $22.95 for a basic hookup to $32.95 for a 50-amp site. The cabins go for $37.95 a night. Amenities include a laundry facility, cable television, restrooms, and a small gift shop. The campground is closed December through February.

BRANSON SHENANIGANS RV PARK
3675 Keeter St.
(417) 334-1920, (800) 338-7275
www.bransonrvparks.com
Branson Shenanigans boasts the most private bathrooms of any RV park in the area. Each bathroom has a private entrance, sink, toilet, and shower. You'll also find a luxurious clubhouse with plenty of comfortable furniture, a fireplace,

and a deck overlooking a shaded creek. The park has 40 sites with 25 pull-throughs and sits just off The Strip near the Dutton Family Theater. The hookups have 30- and 50-amp electrical service, free cable TV and Wi-Fi, and barbecue grills. Shenanigans also has a laundry room and picnic areas. They offer valet parking and shuttle service in town.

The park is open year round, and rates run between $29 and $33 a night, with discounts for veterans and AAA members.

i January through March provides the least-expensive camping rates. Remember, however, that many of the shows and attractions will be closed then.

BRANSON STAGECOACH RV PARK
5751 MO 165
(417) 335-8185, (800) 446-7110
www.bransonstagecoachrv.com
Located just 1 mile south of Table Rock Dam, Branson Stagecoach RV Park is far enough out of town to be well secluded but less than 15 minutes from The Strip. The park has 50 full-hookup sites that come with 30- or 50-amp electrical service and wi-fi Internet access and average $36 per day. The park has large, level sites and can accommodate the largest of RVs. On the grounds you will find a swimming pool, spa, picnic tables, recreation room with video games, library, 24-hour laundry facility, playground, dump station, public telephone, private showers, and a meeting room for up to 36 people. There is also a restaurant adjacent to the park. They will cater your next group gathering or set you up with a rental car if you need your own wheels. The office has dial-up and broadband Internet access, and the park is open year-round.

BRANSON KOA AND CHASTAIN CONVENTION CENTER
397 Animal Safari Rd.
(417) 334-4414, (800) 467-7611
www.bransonkoa.com

To get to Ralph and Kim Newel's Branson KOA RV Park and Campground from The Strip, take MO 165 south past the New Shanghai Theater. Turn right onto Animal Safari Road. Look for the signs on the left leading you to the entrance road. At Branson KOA, you'll find a variety of accommodations including cabins, mobile homes, tent sites, and RV hookups. There is a shaded swimming pool (children younger than 12 are not allowed to swim without an adult present), grocery store, laundry facility, pavilion, restrooms, playground, and picnic tables. The RV sites are paved or have concrete runners and come with 30- and 50-amp electric service, cable TV, and propane. They will arrange to have your show tickets delivered before you arrive. The air-conditioned conference building accommodates 600 people. They'll be happy to help you find catering services for your next event.

The rates at Branson KOA start at $12.50 for a basic tent site with water and electricity. RV sites are from $22.50 to $27.50, and the cabins start at $30.00 per night. The fully equipped mobile homes are $55 a night and can sleep six.

COMPTON RIDGE CAMPGROUND
5040 MO 265
(417) 338-2911, (800) 233-8648
Lodge, (417) 338-2949
North Park, (417) 338-2747
www.comptonridge.com
Fiddlers from across the country gather each May and September at the 85-acre Compton Ridge Campground for the State of the Ozarks Fiddlers Convention (see the Annual Events chapter). Spectators are welcome to drop by the 350-seat convention building and listen to these musicians play their fiddles, which are among the area's most popular instruments.

The campground is divided into three sections. The main campground is reserved for tents and coaches up to 45 feet. The Lodge has large guest rooms with kitchenettes. The North Park has full-hookup sites, barbecue grills, and picnic tables. All guests can take advantage of their three swimming pools (one of them is heated), the kiddy wading pool, tennis court, playground, laundry facility, and hiking trail. They also have an 80-square-foot covered kitchen shelter with most sites. Rates vary according to the type of site you request but average around $32 to $42 a night. If you need to make show ticket reservations, courtesy phones are available. Rental cars are available nearby.

Compton Ridge is 1 mile south of Silver Dollar City and 5 miles north of Table Rock Dam. To get there from The Strip, go west to MO 265, then turn south and look for the signs.

THE WILDERNESS AT SILVER DOLLAR CITY
MO 265
(417) 338-8189, (800) 477-5164
www.thewildernesslogcabins.com
The Silver Dollar City Campground is now called the Wilderness. To reach it, go west on MO 76, turn left on MO 265, and go south 0.5 mile. Buy a season pass to Silver Dollar City, and you become a member of the Camper Club, which entitles you to a 15 percent discount on a campsite or cabin reservation.

The Wilderness cabins vary in price, depending upon amenities. If you like "roughing it," rent a Pioneer cabin, with no indoor bathroom, at $65 per day for two adults. Go the "luxury" route and rent a cabin at $175 for four adults and get a queen bed, two full beds, and one twin, with a loft, fireplace, shower, and Jacuzzi bathtub.

Or bring your own RV. If you don't have one, you can rent a Coachman camper. Full hookup 30-amp sites rent for about $33 a night for two campers; it's an extra $2 for each camper 12 and older. You can get pull-through access and free shuttle service to Silver Dollar City. And if you want to simply pitch a tent, rent a site for $18 and up.

The Wilderness has a general store, swimming pool, three playgrounds, a game room, and free high-speed wireless Internet at most campsites.

Just be aware to call ahead, because rates change with the season and a five-day cancellation notice is required.

Indian Point Road
To get to Indian Point Road from Branson, go west on The Strip past the Shepherd of the Hills Homestead. Go 5 miles and look for the signs leading to Silver Dollar City. When you come to the second stoplight, turn left onto Indian Point Road, just as if you were going to Silver Dollar City. You will come to the SDC parking lots on your right and left, but go right past them, and within 200 yards or so you will begin to see signs directing you to the resorts and marinas on Indian Point. Indian Point Road is quite narrow in places and can be treacherous in bad weather. There are very few places to turn around or pull off.

ANTLERS RESORT AND CAMPGROUND
162 Antlers Lane
(417) 338-2331
www.antlersresort.com
Antlers Resort and Campground has one-, two-, and three-bedroom cabins and RV hookups. Some of their cabins can hold up to 12 people. They come fully furnished with kitchens and decks. A full hookup runs about $22 a day. These rates are for two people. Each additional person costs $2. The campground is located right on Table Rock Lake just 1 mile south of Silver Dollar City. From Indian Point Road turn left onto Jakes Creek Trail, then go 0.75 mile, and Antlers will be on your left.

Antlers has free-of-charge paddleboats, but rental boats available, including pontoon boats. The campground has a launch ramp and a covered dock.

The campground also has a swimming pool, picnic tables, barbecue grills, and a recreation room with pinball, a pool table, and video games. Antlers is open April to mid-December.

INDIAN POINT RESORTS
Indian Point Road
(417) 338-2633, (800) 888-1891
www.indianpoint.com
The lodging possibilities here range from RV hookups to cottages and cabins to two-bedroom mobile homes. The park has RV sites with 20-, 30-,

or 50-amp electrical service; water and sewer; a picnic table; and a barbecue grill. You can also rent RVs from the park. Each RV comes fully furnished with a queen-size bed, full bath, kitchen, cable TV, air-conditioning, picnic table, and barbecue grill. The mobile homes also come fully furnished. The resort's grounds feature a swimming pool, volleyball net, horseshoes, tetherball, shuffleboard, playground, hiking trail, and boat dock with rental boats. The full-hookup sites run around $18 to $22 a day, and the mobile homes go for up to $98 to $195 in peak season. There is no charge for children younger than four.

Lake Taneycomo

COOPER CREEK RESORT & CAMPGROUND
471 Cooper Creek Rd.
(417) 334-4871, (800) 261-8398
www.coopercreekresort.com
To get to Cooper Creek from The Strip, take Fall Creek Road south approximately 1 mile. Look for the signs on your left. Cooper Creek offers 75 RV sites and 22 one-, two-, and three-bedroom cabins that come with decks, fully equipped kitchens, ceiling fans, air-conditioning, and cable TVs. Most of the sites have a view of Lake Taneycomo, depending on how thick the leaves are. The roads are paved at Cooper Creek, so you don't have to worry about getting your rig stuck in the mud on a wet day. The hookups come with 30- or 50-amp electrical service and run about $28 a day. The one-bedroom cabins start and $69; two-bedroom cabins start at $99; and three-bedroom cabins start at $159.

The campground caters to anglers at Cooper Creek and offers bait and licenses, two lighted fishing docks, boat and motor rental, and a concrete launch ramp. Other amenities at the park include two swimming pools, laundry facilities, a grocery store, picnic tables, video arcade, and playground. Trout-fishing enthusiasts are catered to at this resort. The campground is open March through November, and the cabins are open year-round.

SHOPPING

We can remember when Branson had little more than stores for the locals that provided the basics, plus a couple of cafes and a few bait shops that catered to anglers. Gradually, visiting country-music shows developed to provide evening entertainment for the visiting anglers and their nonfishing spouses, and then began to attract others who were more interested in the music than in the fishing and lake activities. Then came more shops and outlet malls, so many that now shopping has become a major reason why tourists come to our town. (See the History chapter.)

The outlet malls have changed Branson, and they may change your idea of shopping. Savings of 40 to 60 percent might change any shopper! Many manufacturers have shops in the outlet malls, and you'll have to check each mall for your particular quarry or just browse and see what interests you. We've divided the Branson area into several different types of shopping, and we hope the list serves as a general guide.

Branson and its environs are home to scores of talented artists and craftspeople. Some of your best buys in crafts can be had at the many area crafts shows (see the Annual Events chapter). If you're in the market for handcrafted treasures, check the shops at Silver Dollar City, Branson Mill Craft Village, and the Grand Village, which we've listed in this chapter. We don't want to imply that our list is a comprehensive directory of all the shopping places in Branson. Far from it! It seems like every time we go out we discover another neat store tucked away somewhere. However, our list should get you started. We've included phone numbers for the stores. If a store doesn't have a number, that's because it's in a mall with a central phone number or because it is written up more fully in another section of Shopping or another chapter (see the Index).

Unless we mention it, all stores willingly accept your plastic as well as cash, and many accept checks, but ask before writing one. Lots of the little retail shops, especially those in the theaters, may be closed during the slower months of January and February, but the bigger shopping centers and major stores are open year-round.

MALLS AND SHOPPING DISTRICTS

Downtown Branson

Since the turn of the 20th century, locals have made the trek from the outlying areas for their store-bought staples, hardware, and tools, as well as Levi's and Big Smiths. The whole area is only about 4 square blocks, and it caters a bit more to the outsiders and tourists than it used to. That has changed. Everything east of the railroad tracks in the Branson Landing is "new." The $300-million

Branson Landing lakefront development is attracting shoppers and gawkers. (See the Close-up in this chapter.) Locals continue to shop and eat downtown and look forward to changes "across the tracks" by Lake Taneycomo. Still, Main and Commercial Streets could easily be a movie set for Middle Town, America.

Exploring the couple dozen shops by foot in old downtown is an adventure in itself, and you'll find yourself wanting to poke in just about every store. About half are open six days a week (closed Sunday), and many are open seven days a week, with reduced hours during the off-season of January and February.

Check out some of our favorites in the old downtown area. Dick's 5 & 10 is worth poking in just for the vintage music on the jukebox. Its creative clutter of 50,000-plus items gives rise to the local saying, "If Dick's doesn't have it, you don't need it." (See the Specialty Shops section in this chapter for more on Dick's.) Reish Shoe Store, (417) 334-3635, has been fitting Bransonites' feet for more than 60 years; it has a great bargain basement. Branson Landing's 100 shops, restaurants, hotel accommodations, and marina give a new aspect to downtown. Taking a stroll down the 1.5-mile boardwalk, visitors and locals alike can enjoy the six intimate themed districts, a fountain, and entertainment.

Anchored on one end of the square is a Belk Department Store, with Bass Pro Shops anchoring the other end. In between, browse at shops such as Ann Taylor Loft, Christopher & Banks, Rack Room Shoes, Hat World, Sunglass Hut, Brighton Collectibles, Pacific Sunwear, Victoria's Secret, Hollister, and Finish Line.

From fine dining to casual eateries, you can choose from restaurants such as Sullivan's Steakhouse, Joe's Crab Shack Restaurant, Bass Pro's White River Fish House, Hilton's Liberty Tavern, Famous Dave's BBQ, and Charley's Grilled Subs. Or enjoy a sweet treat at the Fudgery, Häagen-Dazs, Rocky Mountain Chocolate Factory, the Big Popper, Gloria Jean's Gourmet Coffee, and the Marble Slab Creamery.

Shopping for a Branson gift or other specialty item is easy on the boardwalk. With shops such as Best of Branson, featuring Branson souvenirs; Build-A-Bear Workshop; Cardinals Clubhouse for the sports fans; and Oh My Goddard! Gallery; you'll have to hire someone to carry all your bags!

Outlet Shopping

Since the first settlers made their way into the remote Ozarks, we hill folk always had to look beyond the hills for our store-bought necessities. Going to Springfield to do some shopping was a big deal for some of us, and for a real adventure, St. Louis and Kansas City beckoned. After becoming accustomed to leaving the hills for our "serious shopping," never in our wildest dreams could we have imagined that folks would be coming to Branson for the shopping. But that is exactly what has happened. Now fishing and country music aren't the only things that'll make you feel good when you come to Branson.

Outlet shopping is now a major reason for folks to make Branson their destination. Our first outlet store was the Carolina Mills Factory Outlet way back in 1975, and its dry goods products were of great practical value to residents and visitors alike. Then in 1988 the Factory Merchants of Branson, or Red Roof Mall as we locals call it, opened. The first year there were so few customers it was like shopping in a ghost mall. But like a field of dreams (build it and they will come!), the mall was soon crowded, and it even expanded to include more shops. When the Factory Shoppes of America (referred to as the Branson Meadows Mall by locals) opened in 1995 in Branson Meadows, Branson became one of the nation's major outlet-shopping destinations.

Outlet shopping has changed Branson, and it may change you because few things make you feel better than saving money. The savings are nothing to sneer at, so you may want to spend a few hours in each, checking out what is tempting and finding that special something that you just can't live without.

CAROLINA MILLS FACTORY OUTLET
3615 76 Country Blvd.
(417) 334-2291
If you think only of sheets and towels when you think of this outlet, think again. Yes, you can get lace, upholstery fabric, pillowcases, and sheets and towels, but this 5,000-square-foot, barnlike store also has a host of other items: gift closeouts from major stores and men's and women's ready-to-wear clothing, with an emphasis on Western wear. (It's a great favorite for square dance clubs to buy costumes!) Lots of entertainers from The Strip check in every so often to see what's new,

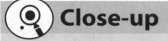

Close-up

Branson Landing

The Branson waterfront has changed quite a bit in the last century and a half. It was once the summer camp of Indians on the White River. After the railroad came to Branson (1906) and Powersite Dam (1912) stilled the white-water rapids, it became the industrial part of town, where railroad ties and cedar logs and box cars of mussel shells and fruit were shipped out. It also became the scene of camping tourists and early tourist resorts, like the Sammy Lane Resort, which catered to water-skiers, boaters, and fishermen. And when Lake Taneycomo became a cold-water lake after the construction of Table Rock Dam above it (1958), it became a prime trout-fishing destination. And with some seven million visitors a year coming to Branson, the naturally air-conditioned Branson lakefront is reinventing itself once again.

The Branson Landing has changed forever the lakefront and created a mystique all its own. Waterfront condo residences, retail shops, dining, recreation, entertainment, and relaxation come together in this new development that springs from the roots of nostalgia now gone. Stretching from where Roark Creek flows into Lake Taneycomo and 1.5 miles upstream to the MO 76 bridge that connects Hollister and Branson, the 95-acre project has been open since the spring of 2006.

A 243-room boutique hotel and convention center (operated by Hilton), is enveloped by more than 100 shops. Anchor stores include a Belk department store and Bass Pro Shops, which offers fishing-guide services on Lake Taneycomo. A "town square" light and water display is in the center of the development and a 2,600-foot-long boardwalk meanders by the shops and Lake Taneycomo. The town square area can accommodate some 6,000 people who can enjoy outdoor musical events and the free water display. Other entertainment opportunities await, like the dueling pianos at Ernie Biggs, and live music at Shorty Small's or Waxy O'Shea's Irish Pub. Check the Web site for current schedules (www.bransonlanding.com).

and area Elvis impersonators buy scarves by the gross to throw to audiences after a sweaty encore of "Love Me Tender." There is also a large selection of ladies' denims. A great favorite is the $5 room, where every item is $5 or less or two for $5.

FACTORY MERCHANTS OF BRANSON
1000 Pat Nash Dr.
(417) 335-6686
www.premiumoutlets.com

Located just off The Strip by White Water, this two-story red-roofed complex has nearly 100 factory outlets, making it one of the largest outlet malls in the state. Locals refer to it as the Red Roof Mall. It's large, and since it's on two levels, we suggest that you stop by the mall office to pick up a guide and map. Besides, outlets come and go, and that way you'll have the latests offerings. Shoppers will find children's and maternity fashions, home furnishings, jewelry and cosmetics, luggage and leather goods, shoes, women's and men's clothing (including full-size fashions), and accessories in a host of stores with internationally recognized brands: Samsonite, Corning, Reebok, Carter's Childrenswear, Hush Puppies, and others.

The do-it-yourselfer can find the latest tools and gadgets at Tools & More. The Chicago Cutlery and Case Pocket Knives outlets have blades for both hunting camps and the finest home kitchens. If you need sustenance for a renewed bout of shopping, there are four restaurants and snack places, including Auntie Anne's Pretzels and the Rocky Mountain Chocolate Factory.

Stores are open most of the year from 9 a.m. to 9 p.m. except Thanksgiving and Christmas, but with reduced hours of 10 a.m. to 6 p.m. during January and February.

THE SHOPPES AT BRANSON MEADOWS
4562 Gretna Rd.
(417) 339-2580, (800) SHOP-USA
www.factorystores.com

This Victorian-themed outlet mall of Chelsea Outlet Centers is Branson's newest, opening in 1995. It has handsome buildings in a nicely landscaped arena. An added attraction is the Cinemas of Branson Meadows, an 11-screen movie theater complex showing first-run movies. There is a 30,000-square-foot VF Factory Outlet. For those not in the know, VF is the world's largest publicly held apparel manufacturer, encompassing such brands as JanSport, Vanity Fair, Lee, Wrangler, Jantzen, and Healthtex. Around these two large anchor stores are more than 40 other outlets that include men's, women's, and children's apparel; footwear; jewelry; cosmetics; and home accessories. Here's our favorite: the spacious atmosphere and inexpensive books at Metz Bookstore. The mall at Branson Meadows is open all year, usually from 9 a.m. to 9 p.m., with reduced hours in January and February. It's closed Easter, Thanksgiving, and Christmas.

TANGER FACTORY OUTLET CENTER OF BRANSON
300 Tanger Blvd.
(417) 337-9328, (800) 407-2762
www.tangeroutlet.com/branson

Carved right out of a hillside and not visible from the highway, this outlet mall with 90-plus shops has its entrance just before you reach Andy Williams' Moon River Theatre on The Strip. Watch for the sign that tells you when to turn off on Tanger Boulevard. Brand-name merchandise is featured at cut-rate prices, including Ralph Lauren, Coach, Tommy Hilfiger, Van Heusen, Levi's, Haggar, SAS, NIKE, Harry and David, and others. Appealing to the younger set are Tommy Girl, Gap, Polo Jeans, and Disney outlets. You can find hosiery and intimates, housewares, home furnishings, accessories, books, CDs, and men's, women's, and children's apparel and footwear. One of our favorites is the Kitchen Collection, which has everything from the practical to the interesting to the slightly bizarre to furnish your kitchen just the way you want. If you feel faint from shopping, the Fudgery can provide sustenance. Lots of folks do their Christmas shopping in July, outfit the kids for school, or load up with the year's birthday and wedding presents at Tanger. Whether you call it smart shopping or guilt-free shopping, Tanger advertises that if you find any item you buy advertised for less than you paid for it within 30 days of your purchase, bring in a copy of the ad and the Tanger merchant receipt to any of the 26 Tanger Outlets in the nation, and they'll refund the difference in cash.

Tanger is open from 9 a.m. to 9 p.m. every day of the week most of the year, with reduced hours in January, February, and March. It's closed Easter, Thanksgiving, and Christmas.

Strips on The Strip

When you drive down The Strip, you'd think that it is one gigantic strip mall interspersed between live music theaters. Closer inspection proves that it is an adventure for the exploring shopper, jammed as it is with quaint shops and stores, shopping centers, and mini-malls. Lots of the shops offer the same souvenirs and T-shirts, but some are unique, and we've mentioned some of the best in the Specialty Shops section of this chapter.

We've mentioned some of the malls on The Strip for your convenience, but it's up to you to explore and plunder all the stores in each one. Happy shopping!

BRANSON HEIGHTS SHOPPING CENTER
1557 76 Country Blvd.
No central phone

This was Branson's first shopping center, built way out in the country when there was nothing but barren roadside to the west and woods between it and downtown Branson. It has the usual mix of professional offices and shops. It has the Koin-O-Matic Laundromat in case you need some clean duds during your Branson visit. Gary's Coiffure's, (417) 334-2184, takes walk-ins, and you may see some of the stars from The Strip getting a trim there. Worth checking out is Quilts & Quilts Country Store, (417) 334-3243, one of the largest quilt shops in the tri-state area. The center is also home to the Branson Heights Flea Market (see the Antiques, Crafts, and Flea Markets section later in this chapter).

BRANSON MALL
2206 76 Country Blvd.
(417) 334-5412

The 25-something shops and kiosks are packed in like books between the bookends of Wal-Mart and Jubilee Market, the two big stores in this shopping center. Everyone knows about Wal-Mart, and Jubilee's is one of the largest grocery stores in the area. If you stay here from three days to a week, you'll find yourself taking advantage of the necessities of the two bookend stores, but don't neglect the shops between them. There's an arcade where the kids can park while you investigate the place. There are kiosks that cater to odd and interesting items as well as lots of comfortable chairs and benches so you can take a load off your feet and watch the tourists and locals pass by, or relax and dine at the same time at Ruby Tuesday's. Locals say, "You can do it all at the Branson Mall!"

GRAND COUNTRY SQUARE
1945 76 Country Blvd.
(417) 334-3919
www.grandcountry.com

Shop here just to gawk at a local landmark. Branson's "Eiffel Tower" is located in the Grand Country Market, part of the Grand Country Square

i **One of the best ways to see the sights of The Strip and shops, meet people, and get a bit of exercise is to become a Branson Strip walker. Park at a designated point, walk down one side, poking into what interests you, then when you're half played out, walk the other side back. You'll see more this way, discover things you might have passed up in your car—and you'll help reduce traffic on The Strip!**

complex. The world's largest banjo has gained worldwide attention for Branson. The neck, holding five fiber-optic strings, is 47 feet long. A true replica of a collectible Gibson banjo, the huge fiberglass shell has a sturdy frame of more than 3,000 pounds of steel. Be sure to check out the autographs on the back of the banjo—and bring your camera for this photo opportunity!

There's shopping at the Grand Country Market, (417) 335-2454, a sort of supermarket of interesting items for the Branson visitor. Before you catch a show in the Grand Country Music Hall in the complex (or after the show), you can eat or snack at several places. The big feed is at Grand Country Buffet. Pizza fans delight in the selection at Papa Grand's Pizza, (417) 336-6709, where a vast selection of pizza and salad is featured in an all-you-can-eat buffet. Glenn's Frozen Custard, (417) 336-6709, is made fresh daily in the open kitchen setting. All the combinations of flavors and treats are on the menu.

Popular during rainy days and ultra-hot afternoons is the area's only indoor minigolf course.

THE GRAND VILLAGE
2800 West Highway 76
(417) 336-7280
www.grandvillageshops.com

You could easily miss the Grand Village, but you shouldn't. It's tucked away next to the Grand Palace. It's not exactly a strip mall, but a small shopping center, tastefully decorated and landscaped, conducive to wandering about in specialty shops and sitting on park benches in the miniparks on the streets. You'll like the comfortable and casual style, fitting like an old pair of jeans and just as down-home. The Grand Village gives you shopping in style—no barns or warehouses. There's a central clock tower, a fountain, and cobblestone streets, all slightly reminiscent of old Charleston.

If you're shopping for the home, the Grand Village has a wide assortment of perfectly quaint shops. Peter Engler's Design Shop, which features unique work by Branson's most renowned woodcarver, has carvings and one-of-a-kind gifts and items (see the Arts and Culture chapter). Pretty

Victorian accents can be found at Mulberry Mill, (417) 332-3400. If you're into Coca-Cola collectibles, stop in at Coke 4 U & More, (417) 336-7253, where you can find anything connected with old Coca-Cola advertising—and even get a Coke! Browse the spacious bookshelves of T. Charleston & Son Books, (417) 334-7931, Branson's largest family bookstore. The Grand Glitz, (417) 336-7251, carries flashy fashions and is not for the conscious conservative. Even if you don't buy, it's fun to check it out! Kringle's, (417) 337-5426, is Missouri's largest Christmas store—three spacious rooms of Christmas decorations, including Department 56 collectibles. Check the Specialty Shops and the Unusual section in this chapter for more details on some of our favorites. If you tire of shopping, and it's snack time, the Village Cafe has pastries and cappuccino, and the Hard Luck Diner, (417) 336-7217, features treats and meals.

No motor traffic is permitted on the village streets, and you can wander, shop, or just relax. The Grand Village is open seven days a week from May through December, with shorter hours January through March. Call the number above for hours of operation.

Strips off The Strip

You'll have to venture off The Strip to find these places, but with more of our visitors learning about and using the alternative routes now (see the Getting Here, Getting Around chapter), you may just find yourself right in front of some of these shopping centers. Stop and check them out.

BRANSON HILLS PLAZA
Branson Hills Parkway
No central phone

Coming into Branson from the north, you'll notice an impressive amount of retaining wall rockwork at the Bee Creek Road/Branson Hills Parkway exit. The top of that hill is the home of Branson's newest shopping venue and hosts Home Depot, Target, and T.J. Maxx. New in 2009 is the nationally known craft mecca, Michaels, as well as a Wal-Mart Supercenter, Best Buy, Books-A-Million, Kohls, Bed, Bath, & Beyond, and

a host of smaller shopping opportunities. Eating options currently include Chili's Restaurant and a Wendy's, but many more offerings are scheduled for the near future.

BRANSON MILL CRAFT VILLAGE
3300 Gretna Rd.
No central phone
www.bransonmill.com

New in 2005, Branson Mill Craft Village presents some of the nation's finest crafts and heirloom-quality work. More than just a craft mall, this unique, 60,000-square-foot village features fine-quality artwork, live artisans, upscale home decor, boutiques, and dining.

As you stroll through the mall, see live demonstrations with master craftspeople. You can watch while they create beautiful blown glass, carved leather, personalized wood signs, woven baskets, oil paintings, custom frames, silver jewelry, pottery, candles, leather goods, etched and sandblasted stone carving, and scrimshaw.

Many one-of-a-kind items can be found among the 150 showrooms throughout this specialty retail center. One of our favorites is the Mountain Man Nut & Fruit Co., where you can sample (free) gourmet chocolates, coffee, and soups; hear live entertainment; and enjoy gifts, coupons, and giveaways.

If shopping makes you hungry and the freebies at Mountain Man aren't enough, there's Bandana's Bar-B-Q Restaurant.

CEDAR RIDGE PLAZA
1447 MO 248 at Epps Road
No central phone

The local Kmart is found here, plus Country Mart, a very large grocery store. Country Mart has the usual groceries and features a large fresh fruit and vegetable section, an in-store bakery, and a spectacular deli. It's a great place to hit if you plan a picnic or an in-room dinner. They have smoked fish and meats, pickled herring, barbecue, and an array of cheeses and deli meats. The bakery is a wonderful source of a variety of rolls, breads, and desserts to go with your meal. The Wine Company next door has a big selection of vintages (see the Specialty Shops section in this chapter) to round out any alfresco dining.

The center is also home to the usual array of stores and Luigi's Pizza Kitchen, (417) 339-4544, which offers both dine-in and takeout and is a favorite for some quick pizza or pasta.

THE FALLS SHOPPING CENTER
3265 Falls Parkway
(417) 343-3400
Less than a mile south of the MO 165 junction at The Strip, this shopping center has more than a dozen shops, restaurants, and businesses. One of the eateries is Shogun's Japanese Steak House (see the Restaurants chapter). Dressin' Gaudy, (417) 336-3465, is a favorite place of college students who want to make a splash in fashion without the cost. They have the sequined, flashy fashions, but they also have stylish imports, hip fashions, and swanky costume jewelry at rock-bottom prices. Have an extra hour? Schedule a massage, tanning session, or manicure at Saigon Nails & Tanning, (417) 336-6595. The Falls Shopping Center is a great place to spend some time just looking before you catch the next show.

IMAX ENTERTAINMENT COMPLEX
3562 Shepherd of the Hills Expressway
(417) 335-4832
www.bransonimax.com
When you think IMAX, you think big movies, and that's the big draw here (see the Attractions chapter). It's also home to the Little Opry Theatre (see The Shows chapter). However, the 21 shops and kiosks in the center provide some interesting diversion before the shows as well as some excellent buys. Shadow Box Gifts, (417) 335-4832, provides home appointments and decorations. It's Unique, (417) 334-5008, offers odd and interesting gifts and items "for kids 1 to 90." Fabulous Finds, (417) 336-2983, allows you to buy that ostentatious diamond without being a millionaire—and some great fragrances that smell like the real thing but at a lower cost. The Clock Shop, (417) 336-8777, offers clocks from grandfather to

mantle and miniatures as well as a variety of time-theme collectibles. If you get hungry, you'll find help at the Fudgery (always a show there!) and at McFarlain's Restaurant.

ANTIQUES, CRAFTS, AND FLEA MARKETS

Branson has just a small number of shops that deal only with antiques, but you're not likely to find the fine-quality antiques that are sold in shops in the eastern half of the nation. You will find, however, a wide selection of primitives, including furniture and tools—frequently handmade—and other objects that were part of the early settlers' lives, at reasonable prices. You'll find lots of crafts stores and outlets. The major theme parks of Silver Dollar City and Shepherd of the Hills (see the Attractions chapter) have practicing artisans who make and sell their works in the parks. There are several small malls and shops devoted to crafts, and virtually every area festival celebration in the Ozarks will have its share of crafts booths (see the Annual Events chapter). Though the dividing line between crafts and arts is often not finely drawn, especially in the Ozarks, we've put those shops and galleries specializing more in the fine arts in the Arts and Culture chapter, but they also tend to have crafts items.

As for flea markets, the area has more of them than a dog in August has fleas, and you can find some amazing treasures if you are willing to spend the time exploring. Ozark, between Springfield and Branson, has recently developed as a major stopping point for those interested in antiques, flea-market items, and collectibles. There are no fewer than five large stores within yards of each other at Finley River Park at the junction of MO 14 and US 65 in Ozark. If you come into Branson from the north, you'll notice them on your right (west side) just before you cross the Finley River. If you go east on MO 14, you'll find another half dozen antiques stores and flea markets. If such treasure hunting is on your agenda, you can see why it is worth stopping in Ozark or making it a whole day trip.

We've not begun to list all of the stores, but we've featured the cream of the crop. We've put antiques, crafts, and flea markets together because many of the stores in the Ozarks are a strange but interesting conglomeration of all three. Most places will accept your plastic; some will not accept out-of-state checks or any checks; all will accept the green stuff. A caveat: We found that most places keep pretty standard 8 a.m. to 5 p.m. business hours, but some tend to keep what's known locally as banker's hours, 9 a.m. to 3 p.m., and when the white bass are running or deer or turkey season opens, don't count on some shops being open at all.

ANTIQUE EMPORIUM
1702 West Boat St., Ozark
(417) 581-5555

Just north of the Tracker Boat Factory in Ozark on US 65, take the CC exit, and right behind Lambert's Cafe (home of the "throwed rolls"; see the Restaurants chapter) you'll find the Antique Emporium. The two together would make an afternoon and evening, with dinner down-home style at the cafe after you've tuckered yourself out shopping. With more than 100 booths, the Antique Emporium has more than the usual assortment of old tools and small farm machinery, fishing tackle and gear, boat motors, old advertising items (we wondered if Lambert's had done some shopping for their decor there!), and sporting antiques such as old golf and billiard gear. They also offer a variety of antique housewares, china, glass, and clothing.

THE APPLE TREE MALL
1830 76 Country Blvd.
(417) 335-2133

An old supermarket building has been converted into one of the largest crafts malls in the area, though some booths feature antiques and flea-market type items. The mall has more than 400 different booths, and you can find everything from local honey and homemade jams and jellies to handpainted crosscut saws and mailboxes, dried flowers and woodland wonders, fossils,

and rock paintings, as well as handmade quilts, afghans, and doilies. It's a great place to wander about and explore and big enough to almost get lost.

BRANSON HEIGHTS FLEA MARKET
1139 76 Country Blvd.
Branson Heights Shopping Center
(417) 335-3165

Jack Wallace has converted the old grocery store of the shopping center into one of the biggest flea markets in the Branson area. You can find it all: books, records, tools, dolls, collectibles, crafts, antiques—just a bit of about everything. One of our prize purchases was a first edition of Ernest Hemingway's *In Our Time* for a dollar.

CADWELL'S FLEA MARKET
116 East Main St.
(417) 334-5051

This large flea market is just up Main Street from the Branson Landing's Hilton Hotel. For more than two decades it has attracted Branson visitors and locals with its large selection of the old and new. We know of a local girl who financed a semester of college with a 1930s Mickey Mouse toothbrush holder and cup that she bought for $25 and resold.

GREEN LANTERN ANTIQUES
15 Downing St., Hollister
(417) 334-7541

This small shop is crammed with a lifetime of antiques and collectibles buying, and the crowded, cluttered atmosphere invites long and loving looking. It's a rare person who doesn't find something to add to a personal collection.

MAINE STREET ANTIQUE MALL
1994 Evangel St., Ozark
(417) 581-2575

The first of the antiques and flea markets in Ozark, this store opened in 1988, and locals thought Carl Miller, an out-of-the-area developer, was an out-of-his-mind entrepreneur. Now the 27,000-square-foot mall has 100 dealers from five states, and business is better than ever because of nearby competing malls. Carl sold out to Interstate Antique Malls of America, who knew a good thing when they saw it, and retired. You can find all sorts of collectibles and upscale antique items. Recently we saw a booth that had the biggest collection of cookie jars we have ever seen, including a rare Casper the Ghost jar. The Maine Street Mall also has the General Store, which features decorator items, coffees, teas, sweets, and eats.

OZARK ANTIQUE MALL
200 North 20th St., Ozark
(417) 581-5233
In the complex of antiques shops in Ozark, this 17,000-square-foot store has a mix of old and new. The atmosphere is friendly, and the store encourages browsers and talkers. We liked the fact that you can pick up cards to keep notes about potential buys as you do your browsing. You can actually learn about items here. If you don't know what it is, Dan and Kathy Walter do, and they say they spend as much time "talkin' and educatin' as sellin'." But they admit they wouldn't have it any other way. The store seems to carry lots of collectibles from World War II and from the 1930s and 1940s. They also have furniture, lots of vintage signs and advertising, carnival and Depression glass, and watches and clocks.

MUSIC AND INSTRUMENTS

Branson has become known as the "live music capital of the universe," and with so much music and so many musicians, you'd expect to find more than just a few shops that cater to music lovers. For professional songwriters and musicians, there are music publishers and professional recording studios. A number of shops (including area pawnshops) carry musical instruments, records, and music-related items, from T-shirts to guitar picks. We've highlighted the notables for you.

CEDAR CREEK DULCIMERS
3010 West Highway 76
(417) 334-1395
www.cedarcreekdulcimers.com
Sandwiched between the Presley Theater and the Hollywood Wax Museum, Cedar Creek Dulcimers is in tune with what musicians want. Whether you are a professional picker or a rock star wannabe, this shop offers quality instruments from around the world. Their wide selection of instruction books, accompaniment CDs, and beginners' kits are sure to inspire songsters of all ages and abilities. Even if you are more into music appreciation than performance, don't miss the chance to see the Irish penny whistles, Australian didgeridoos, Native American flutes, or Indian sitars on display!

MUSIC FOR A SONG
300 Tanger Blvd.
(417) 336-4420
www.musicforasong.com
Located in the Tanger Mall, Music for a Song has music videos, CDs, cassettes, and DVDs. No matter your taste, they have it. Jazz and classical, rock and rap, and, of course, country! What they don't have they'll order for you. And they carry the cases and boxes to store and carry your music collection. There's a special section devoted just to Branson-area musicians.

i The Branson Police Department reports that the most common crime is shoplifting. Don't get your name in the local paper in the "Court Report" section by forgetting to pay for an item you've picked up.

SPECIALTY SHOPS AND THE UNUSUAL
ALASKA DOWN SOUTH
1150 76 Country Blvd.
(417) 339-2800
Just south (opposite) of Branson Heights Shop-

ping Center is Alaska Down South, tucked "down under the hill." It's a store that you could easily miss while gawking on The Strip. But it is one of the gems you can discover shopping in Branson and then go back home and rave about. It has nature-themed art, crafts, home decor, and furnishings—including unique wildlife decor from Alaska to Zimbabwe.

BEEHIVE TATTOO & BODY PIERCING STUDIO
210 West College St.
(417) 339-9155
www.beehivetattoos.com
If you're looking for a souvenir to take home that will never get lost or broken, we suggest a trip to Susan Keller's Beehive tattoo studio. It is just one of three in Branson. The studio has thousands of designs to choose from, or the tattoo artist will customize something new just for you. (How about a permanent Branson bracelet?) A basic tattoo starts at around $40, but the average cost ranges from $50 to $200. Some of the more popular designs include dragons, flowers, butterflies, unicorns, hearts, and military-style tattoos. The studio is open every day.

DICKENS GIFT SHOPPE
3630 76 Country Blvd.
(417) 334-2992
This shop is a bit like Charles Dickens's Old Curiosity Shop—it has a bit of everything. You'll find everything from upper-end collectibles such as Department 56, Boyd's Bears, Cherished Teddies, Precious Moments, Emmett Kelly clowns, and Norman Rockwell items to Branson souvenir key rings and T-shirts, birdbaths, lawn ornaments, and concrete deer, frogs, and gorillas. (Now you know where McGuffey's Restaurants got their gorillas!) Dickens is a great place to spend some time between shows.

DICK'S 5 & 10
103 West Main St.
(417) 334-2410
Here's a store where you can easily spend several hours strolling the narrow aisles, gawking at the

more than 50,000 different items in stock, and listening to the old-time tunes on the authentic jukebox. Not only the items for sale but also the museum-type displays will bring back memories of the old five and dime. It's been a landmark store since 1929. You can find what you need and lots that you don't, but we bet you won't leave the store without buying something! Blue Waltz perfume, fragrant rose pod sachets, paper dolls, soap-on-a-rope, Necco candy, pant creasers, marbles, mothballs, Clark's Teaberry gum: you'll see why Dick's says, "We've got what you forgot!"

THE FLAGSTORE
212 S. Commercial St.
(417) 334-1776
www.frontierflags.com
With the International Festival at Silver Dollar City and the Veterans Day and Independence Day celebrations (see the Annual Events chapter), Branson is frequently awash in flags and color, and the place to get it is from Betsy Ross (honest!) at the Flagstore. For flags from every nation and every occasion and for historical flags, people seek out one of Branson's most unusual stores. The store also has flagpoles from 12 feet to 120 feet, wind socks, religious flags, seasonal flags, patriotic bunting and decorations, decals, bumper stickers, and pens. If you don't find the flag that you want, they'll make it to order.

KRINGLES
2800 76 County Blvd.
The Grand Village
(417) 336-7246
Christmas in July and August? Yes! Believe it or not, next to December, that's the busiest time at Missouri's largest Christmas store. There are three large rooms devoted to Christmas decorations, ornaments, and wrapping paper. One caters to a Victorian theme, one to the comical and whimsical, and the third to Christmas collectibles, including Department 56. During the hot summer, stepping into Kringles may just be the way to cool off!

MOUNTAIN MAN NUT & FRUIT CO.
3300 Gretna Rd., Branson Mill Mall
(417) 336-6200, (800) 336-6203
www.mtmanbranson.com
The Mountain Man says "Nuts to you!" and this store provides all kinds of nuts for you, imported as well as the king of nut meats, the Ozark black walnut. The stores also have a wide array of dried fruits, jams, and jellies (our favorite is the muscadine jelly), more than a dozen different types of trail mixes, honey, regular and sugar-free candies, gourmet coffees (ever try Fuzzy Navel coffee?), and exotic and unusual foods. It's fun to taste the free samples and wander around the gift-filled nooks and crannies of the store, and it's a great place to shop for a special snack to take back with you.

STONE HILL WINERY
601 MO 165 at Green Mountain Drive
(417) 334-1897, (888) 926-WINE
www.stonehillwinery.com
Early in the 20th century, Missouri was one of the major wine-producing states, and the Stone Hill Winery at Hermann, Missouri, which dates from 1847, was the third-largest winery in the world and the second largest in the nation. This thriving industry became illegal with Prohibition in 1920, and it is now just beginning to recover its former glory. At this outlet you can taste various vintages and take a tour of the wine room to learn how grapes are processed into vino and bottled. There are tours every 15 minutes, and large groups are welcome. It's a great place to taste the grape, discover some new varieties, and pick up some vintages to take back home for yourself or for gifts. Stone Hill is open all year, from 8:30 a.m. to dusk, except Sunday, when hours are 11 a.m. to 6 p.m. (Also see the Attractions chapter.)

THE WINE COMPANY
1447 MO 248, Cedar Ridge Plaza
(417) 334-4551
The Wine Company has a large selection of domestic wines, including Arkansas and Missouri vintages (Stone Hill, St. James, Les Bourgeois, and Wiederkehr), as well as imported wines and micro-brewery and specialty beers—more than 133 and still growing. They have some great wines and great labels. A bottle of Toad Hollow or Fat Bastard is worth the price just for the label. The store advertises itself as having "Taney County's largest wine selection," and it seems an undisputed fact. They also feature premium cigars and imported cigarettes. They have wine gift packages, and gift wrapping is available for other purchases.

BOOKSTORES

BOOKS-A-MILLION
985 Branson Hills Pkwy
(417) 239-3702
booksamillioninc.com
This is Branson's newest bookstore. It's small enough to be comfortable but not large enough to get lost in. It has a small cafe. Go in and have latte and read when you need to rest. They don't mind.

HALF PRICE USED BOOKS
1819-C 76 Country Blvd.
(417) 334-7970
Heidi Sampson has a large selection of all sorts of used books, paperbacks, and hardcovers, which run the range from romance to science fiction to local history to biography in this crowded but comfortable book outlet. In the almost two decades it's been here, the store has become a local fixture, and it also features antique books, maps, and collectibles. It's a great place to browse on a rainy day. When you stop in, be certain to give Calvin the cat a pat.

METZ BOOK OUTLET
4540 N. Gretna Rd.
Factory Shoppes at Branson Meadows
(417) 339-2424
Metz is large, well-lit, and made for wandering. They have the area's greatest selection of

children's books and travel guides, but they also have a good selection of books, guides, and self-help for the computer user. Though discounted books are their specialty (up to 80 percent off), they also carry the latest best sellers and a large selection of local and regional books. It's a favorite gathering place for quick readers, and readers are encouraged, but it is a rare person who can resist the book bargains found there and walk out without one in hand.

T. CHARLESTON & SON
2800 76 Country Blvd.
The Grand Village
(417) 334-7931
T. Charleston is one of the several shops in the Grand Village where you can while away an entire afternoon. It's Branson's largest family bookstore, and it certainly looks booky—with browsing sections, tall shelves, ladders, and ready and knowledgeable service. Tourists like the wide variety of selections, especially those on local history and subjects, and locals like the "if we don't have it, we can get it for you" order service.

DAY TRIPS

Branson may be the reason and the focus of your visit to the Ozarks, and we'd be the first to admit that there are more than two weeks' worth of exciting things to do just in town. We've lived here for years and haven't seen it all, and with the way the area is growing, we probably never will. However, there are only so many shows you can take in before becoming satiated. (Still, we know of folks who have seen two or three shows a day for a week and not gotten tired!)

Branson is an ideal center for exploring Ozark Mountain country, that area roughly within a 100-mile radius of Branson. We stress that that's not all of the Ozarks, and we encourage you to trek beyond and discover what the rest of the Ozarks have to offer—country lanes, meandering creeks, small-town general stores—the best of bucolic rural America. We had to limit ourselvesto keep this book from becominga travelogue encyclopedia! Our day trips are just that: trips that will fill your day, often from daylight to past dark. In some areas you might want to spend the night or even longer, as you'll find that towns that do not have Branson's fame offer their own uniqueness for the adventuresome traveler.

Better roads in the area have made travel faster and exploring easier in the local environs, but remember that once you get off the main arteries, the roads are much more meandering and thus slower. That's often their beauty and charm, a virtue high on the list of some visitors but low on a highway engineer's. We've organized such trips according to the name of the surrounding communities, and we provide you with a bit of history and background on some of our near neighbors. For some areas we've listed area attractions, and you can pick and choose as your time allows. For others we've provided a suggested itinerary.

SPRINGFIELD AND IMMEDIATE ENVIRONS

The "Queen City of the Ozarks" has had her royal nose tweaked by upstart Branson in the last decade, as millions have passed by Springfield or seen the city only as a stopping point on their way to the tourist playground of the Midwest. Now that Branson has become a shopping mecca as well as "the live music capital of the universe," there has been mild concern in Springfield at the competition and the loss of sales tax revenue. That concern has increased now that the Branson Airport opened in May 2009.

In spite of beneath-the-surface rivalry and competition, there is a sense of shared community and cooperation. We Bransonites respect and appreciate Missouri's third-largest city (population 154,777) and fastest growing of our state's "Big Three" for the services, cultural activities, and amenities that a larger city offers—and for its citizens who come down to shop and take in our music shows. The "big city" nearby merely makes Branson a better place to live. That close relationship will undoubtedly get closer as Springfield expands south and Branson expands north along the US 65 corridor, especially since all of US 65 is four-lane, making travel time between the two cities quicker. We'll share more of what each has to offer if regional planners are correct in their speculation that the Springfield-Branson megalopolis will continue to grow.

There will be much more to share in the future. Springfield's downtown area is undergoing a huge, multimillion-dollar "green space addition," with the 260-acre Jordan Valley Park. The first phase of 35 acres opened in the fall of 2001 and included a recreational ice-skating facility with twin ice rinks.

Springfield has had a $100 million-plus burst of construction activity the last several years: the 83,000-square-foot, state-of-the-art Library Center; the 92,000-square-foot Wonders of Wildlife Museum; the $32 million Jordan Park Hammons Field, the home of the Springfield Cardinals; and the new $67 million Missouri State University JQH Arena. More is projected.

Springfield is where we go for "serious doctorin'." Its "medical mile" (National Avenue) on the south side makes it convenient for Bransonites. It's also where we go for our "high culture," including Broadway plays and concerts and the Springfield Symphony at the Juanita K. Hammons Center and the Springfield Little Theater at the downtown historic Landers Theater. The new JQH Arena, which opened in November 2008 with a concert by the Eagles, provides a large venue home for programs not possible in Branson. Springfield is still the major mercantile center, and if we can't find it here at Wal-Mart or Dick's Oldtime 5 & 10 and still think we need it, we drive up to see the Queen. Its Battlefield Mall, with 150 stores and a six-plex theater, is the only large climate-controlled mall short of the four-hour drive to Kansas City or St. Louis.

With its major university (Missouri State University, enrollment just more than 19,000) and two private liberal-arts colleges (Drury and Evangel), it is a major education center. We send our grown youngsters there for a liberal-arts education—far enough for them to be independent and close enough for us not to worry too much. The city has 13 parks, with activities frequently scheduled in them (Springfield's parks are used!). It has a nationally recognized zoo and an art museum that hosts one of the best watercolor shows in the nation every summer.

There's enough in Springfield alone to make a week's worth of day trips, so pick and choose from the smorgasbord! Springfield also, we've been told, has more restaurants and fast-food places per capita than any city in the nation (cashew chicken was invented there). You won't starve in Springfield!

Attractions

BASS PRO SHOPS
1915 South Campbell Ave., Springfield
(417) 887-7334

BASS PRO SHOPS WHITE RIVER OUTPOST
1 Bass Pro Dr., Branson
(417) 243-5200
www.basspro.com
Don't think "shop." Think a gigantic department store devoted to sports. We feel obligated to put a store in Attractions because "the world's largest sporting goods store" has become Missouri's premier tourist attraction, pulling in more than four million visitors a year. You'll see license plates in the parking lot from every state and Canada, and tour buses have a special "bus lot." You'll find acres of fishing tackle and guns and camping gear and boats, but you'll also find aisle upon aisle of sports and casual wear for women and children as well as men.

If you tire out, there is always space to sit and listen to the roar of the four-story waterfall and watch native fish and the lifelike stuffed animals that serve as the theme decor. Half the fun is wandering about the store, gawking at the mini-exhibits of wildlife in near-real settings. Especially good picture points are marked, so be sure to bring your camera.

Hemingway's Blue Water Cafe on the third floor is a great place for lunch, as you could make this an all-day experience. Or you can rest at the smoke-free marble and mahogany bar and sip a drink and watch the bartender work in front of a floor-to-ceiling, 30,000-gallon saltwater aquarium that serves as the back bar.

If it has to do with sports—golf, canoeing, basketball, cricket, soccer, you-name-it—Bass Pro will have it. There's an indoor shooting range—both archery and gun. Wildlife experts hold seminars in a 250-seat auditorium on the lowest level. There's an art gallery, devoted to wildlife art, of course. You can even get a haircut at the Tall Tales Barber Shop on the balcony overlooking the main showroom—a great place to people-watch. And if you are so inclined, you can take a lock of your hair to the fly department and have it incorporated into a custom-made fishing fly!

Right next door is the Wonders of Wildlife Museum. Closed for renovations, the museum promises to be even more spectacular by Fall of 2009. Between Bass Pro and the museum, you could spend an entire day.

i If you crave the Bass Pro experience, but need to stay closer to Branson, check out the new store location at the Branson Landing. The 40,000 square foot Ozark Lodge theme presents many of the favorite features of its northern sister. Young and old alike enjoy the "old" mill and waterwheel, aquarium stocked with rainbow and brown trout, and abundance of wildlife depicted in various scenes throughout the shopping area. Serious boaters can peruse the array of Tracker, Nitro, Tahoe, Mako, Kenner, and other brand-name water vehicles, while backyard enthusiasts can revel in the bird feeders and home decor items. Not to be missed is the unique White River Fish Company Restaurant, a 4,000 square foot floating dining option, complete with outdoor seating overlooking Lake Taneycomo, a children's fishing pier, and marina. There is truly something for everyone at this newest addition to outdoor recreation giant, Bass Pro.

CRYSTAL CAVE
7225 North Crystal Cave Lane, Springfield
(417) 833-9599
www.crystalcavemissouri.com
Crystal Cave was one of the area's first tourist attractions, opened for tours by Alfred Mann back in 1893. The cave remained in the family until the 1960s. Now operated by Loyd and Edith Rich-

ardson, the cave offers a guided 80-minute tour. Wear your Nikes for the trip that takes you down into limestone that was the seabed of the Ozarks millions of years ago. You can actually see the fossils! You'll also see evidence of Native American inhabitants, marvel at the Upside Down Well, and see the Rainbow Falls and the Cathedral. Crystal Cave is a "living cave" (one that is growing), so note the spelotherms in many unusual shapes and forms.

To get to the cave, take exit 80B off I-44 on Springfield's north side. It continues out of the city and becomes MO H. Weather permitting, the cave is open year-round. Admission is $9 for adults and $5 for children 4 through 12.

DICKERSON PARK ZOO
3043 North Fort Ave., Springfield
(417) 864-1800
www.dickersonparkzoo.org
The zoo owns 175 acres, much of it undeveloped, but it's home to a variety of species. The land for the zoo was purchased in 1922 and grew during the late 1920s and 1930s. Dickerson Park has continued to grow over the years and has become an attraction worthy of a half-day's trip.

The zoo has developed an international reputation for its work in breeding elephants and in the past has involved area schoolchildren in contests to name newly arrived pachyderms. A 1995 addition, now a thriving pachyderm toddler, was christened Asha, Hindu for hope. An important arrival appeared on November 28, 1999: a bouncing 378-pound baby named Haji, after a pregnancy of 674 days and a 34-hour labor. Haji was the first Asian elephant in the world born as the result of artificial insemination. Baby elephant births have almost become commonplace today.

During its annual Teddy Bear Rally in April, free admission to anyone carrying a teddy bear packs the zoo. Of course, the spring weather and the trees and shrubs in bloom are big draws, too. Other events during the year include Mother's Day and Father's Day activities; a Reptile Mania Day in May, with educational activities throughout the zoo addressing the fear and fascination people have with reptiles; and an Ice Cream Safari in July. On Grandparents Day in September, children get a 75-cent discount when accompanied by their grandparents. And on October 31 of each year the zoo throws a Halloween party for children! The zoo hosts Zoofari, an early fall outdoor fund-raiser dinner to which many come in costume. It's the one time people are more exotic than the animals! There is a gift shop at which you can purchase animal-related items and books. You can even take home a bag of "zoo-doo" for your flower bed!

To get to the zoo, take the MO 13 exit off I-44 and immediately turn right at the light on Norton Street. You'll see the zoo on your left in a few blocks. The zoo is open from 9 a.m. to 5 p.m. daily April through September, and from 10 a.m. to 4 p.m. daily October through March, except during inclement weather and on major holidays. Admission: $6 adults, $4 for children 3 to 12. Children two and younger get in free. Although the Playground Park is free, there is an additional charge for the train ride, as well as wagon, stroller, or wheelchair rentals.

EXOTIC ANIMAL PARADISE
124 Jungle Dr. at MO OO, Strafford
(417)859-5300
www.exoticanimalparadise.com
Don't let the Strafford address worry you! It's only 8 miles east of Springfield on I-44. Open to the public since 1971, this 400-acre park is home to more than 3,000 wild animals and birds. It's a great hot-day activity, as you can drive in air-conditioned comfort in your car or catch the complimentary bus tour, through a landscape dotted with lakes and ponds. The animals roam free in the wilderness park, except for the dangerous big cats and bears, which are kept in a large fenced area. The animals are curious and expect treats. More than 400 animals can be seen in their "wild" surroundings, including rhinoceros, tigers, hyenas, zebras, lemurs, bison, and even ligers! Animal feed is available for purchase, as well as tokens for the arcade, and go-cart rides (open seasonally).

Halfway through your trek, you can stop at the Safari Outpost, an outback compound with two gift shops: one with basic curios and souvenirs, and the other, the Kenya Connection, with authentic items from not only Kenya but also countries all over the world. There is also the inevitable (but appreciated) snack bar, and what is even more attractive to the kids, a baby-animal nursery and petting zoo. You can wander among (and feed) potbellied pigs, goats, deer, geese, ducks, and llamas.

You get to the Exotic Animal Paradise by taking I-44 east 8 miles to exit 88. Signs along the south outer road will direct you. The park is open every day except Christmas, from 10 a.m. to 5 p.m. Admission is $16 for adults and $12 for children 3 through 11.

FANTASTIC CAVERNS
4872 North FR 125, Springfield
(417) 833-2010
www.fantastic-caverns.com
If you want to see the Ozarks underground without having to walk, this is the place! Propane-powered Jeep trains take you right through the cave, billed as "America's Only Ride Thru Cave." (We have BIG caves in Missouri! Beat that, Texas!) This also is probably the only cave in the nation that is wheelchair accessible.

On hot summer days, there can be a line, and if you have to wait, a good side trip to hike off the kids' excess energy is Canyon Trail, a mile walk through the woods to the Sac River.

The facility operates a research program that tracks, by the use of dyes, the flow of underground water. The program has discovered, through tracing rainwater and sinkhole drainage, that the cavern has a watershed of about 15 square miles. The program helps educate groups and schoolchildren about our Ozarks underground by demonstrating this drainage and by taking them into parts of the cave not normally toured.

To get to Fantastic Caverns, take MO 13; exit off I-44 on Springfield's north side. Go 1.5 miles north on MO 13, turn west onto Fantastic Caverns Road, and follow the signs. As we say in the Ozarks, you can't miss it! Admission in 2009 was $21.50 for adults and $13.50 for children 6 through 12.

MISSOURI SPORTS HALL OF FAME
3861 E. Stan Musial Dr., Springfield
(417) 889-3100, (800) 498-5678
www.mosportshalloffame.com

Whether it's the late golf great Payne Stewart or former pitcher "Preacher" Roe who draws you, you can find the entire gallery of Missouri's sports legends memorialized here. The Hall of Fame and the nearby Highland Springs Development, one of Springfield's most exclusive, was developed by John Q. Hammons. (You'll see his name plastered on a number of MSU campus buildings and community developments.) The Hall of Fame is right next to the Highland Springs Country Club on Springfield's south side. The spectacular homes are also worth the short drive through the park setting.

To get to the Hall of Fame, as soon as you cross Lake Springfield on US 65, turn east on US 60. After a 0.25 mile drive to the top of the hill, you'll turn right. Admission is $5 for adults, $3 for students, and $4 for senior citizens.

SPRINGFIELD CONSERVATION NATURE CENTER
4600 South Chrismon Rd., Springfield
(417) 888-4237
www.mo.gov

The 80 acres of woods and park are Springfield's urban homage to the natural world that exists beyond the city's sprawl. There are 3 miles of wood-chip hiking trails. (No pets are allowed; they'll disturb the natural critters!) During your hike you can observe birds from the trail and from blinds, and you can hear more than you can see—your walk is accompanied by a symphony of birdsong. There are boardwalks over the marshy parts of Lake Springfield (James River). If you're lucky, and quiet, you might catch a glimpse of the many deer that make the center their home.

The center's complex, near the entrance, is a wood and rock building that seems to be part of the ground it emerges from. Inside are exhibits, both permanent and traveling, and a small auditorium that often features programs and speakers.

It's a challenge getting to the nature center, but don't despair if you first miss it. As you come up US 65, take the second exit on the right (US 60 west) after you cross Lake Springfield. After a mile, take the Glenstone Avenue exit. Turn left (south), cross the James River Expressway, and go through the traffic light, keeping a lookout for the next left, the outer road, which takes you back east to the nature center. It's a bit tricky, even if you know the way, but the center is well worth it.

Museums and Historic Attractions

AIR & MILITARY MUSEUM OF THE OZARKS
2305 East Kearney St., Springfield
(417) 864-7997
www.ammomuseum.org

World War II buffs and vets will find this 3,600-square-foot museum a treasure trove of over 5,000 artifacts, mostly from World War II to the present. There are airplane models and uniforms from the various military branches. There's even a PX where you can get military memorabilia and that inevitable vacation T-shirt! Admission is $3 for adults, $1 for children. Call first to check hours of operation. The best way to get to the museum is to take the Kearney Street exit from US 65 and head west.

i Events at the Springfield Conservation Nature Center are free. You can pick up a copy of *The Harbinger*, which lists the upcoming schedule of events.

DISCOVERY CENTER OF SPRINGFIELD
438 East St. Louis St., Springfield
(417) 862-9910
www.discoverycenter.org

This hands-on, interactive museum is fun for children and adults. It features science, architecture, archaeology, energy, and health exhibits. Don't expect your typical museum with behind-the-glass displays. You'll get down and "get dirty" and learn and have fun as you explore a variety of interest areas, including the Exploratory Lab.

A special display is Discovery Town, which features a miniature supermarket, bank, newspaper, TV station, doctor's office, and various other town features. Kids can write their own news story about themselves, take their picture, and print the paper right there, appearing on page one! In the TV studio, they can operate the camera, see themselves on the monitor, and do a newscast as a TV news anchor. You can marvel at the giant 8-foot eyeball model or learn about different cultures in a rotating multicultural exhibit. There's a special area called Wonderland for preschoolers. EnergyWorks has a life-size statue of Benjamin Franklin flying a kite, and the museum store features educational toys, games, puzzles, and puppets. The Discovery Center has group tours for area schoolchildren and special classes during the school year for area youngsters to explore and discover in an interactive way. It has become an important educational asset to schools.

The center was helped on its way by donations from Springfield citizens. Former Springfieldian Brad Pitt pitched in with a $120,000 donation to help fund what has become one of the state's most kid-friendly museums.

To discover the Discovery Center, take the Chestnut Expressway exit from US 65. Turn left (west) onto Chestnut and travel until you come to Glenstone Avenue. Turn left (south) onto Glenstone, and just after passing over the railroad tracks, turn right onto St. Louis Street. The Discovery Center is on your left, about a mile and a half down, just after you pass the Shrine Mosque and before you reach Park Central in downtown Springfield.

Admission is $7 for adults, $6 for adults older than 60, and $5 for children 3 through 12. Children two and younger get in free. There is an additional charge for the Highwire Bike Ride and

i If you know you're going to be exploring some areas of Missouri before you come to Branson or after you leave our town, you can get a *Missouri Travel Guide,* which provides a state highway map and information about our state and its areas of interest. To request a copy (do so several months before you travel), write the Missouri Division of Tourism, P.O. Box 1055, Jefferson City, MO 65102, or call (888) 925-3875, ext. 124.

Immersion Cinema. The museum is open 9 a.m. to 5 p.m. Tuesday through Friday and 10 a.m. to 5 p.m. weekends.

HISTORY MUSEUM OF SPRINGFIELD–GREENE COUNTY
830 Boonville Ave., Springfield
(417) 864-1976
www.springfieldhistorymuseum.org

If you want an overview of the area's history—from Ozark cave dwellers to today's condo dwellers—this is the place. A favorite feature of the museum is the Native American Room. A ten-minute video provides a history of Native American life in the Ozarks. The kids can grind Indian corn using a mano, a handheld stone for grinding grains on a metate. In the main gallery they can dress up in uniforms from the Civil War period and clamber on a real, honest-to-goodness Springfield wagon.

In addition to its many public displays and hands-on activities, the museum is home to the Fulbright Family Archives, which contains more than 30,000 books and documents and 20,000 historical photographs that relate to Springfield's past, making it a major research source for local historians. The three-story building itself is something of a museum piece. The handsome dressed limestone structure dates from 1894, when it was the U.S. Customs and Post Office building. From 1938 to 1992 it served as Springfield's city hall, and many people even today refer to it as the old city hall building. The building dons festive Christmas apparel for the holidays, when the museum hosts its annual gingerbread house contest. Organizations, businesses, and individual bakers offer their best in the tasty culinary-architecture contest.

The museum is on the third floor but is wheelchair accessible by elevator. It's open Tuesday through Saturday from 10:30 a.m. to 4:30 p.m. and by appointment. Group tours can be arranged. You can reach the museum by taking the Chestnut Expressway exit from US 65 and turning west (left). The museum is on the corner of Chestnut Expressway and Boonville Avenue. Admission is free, but a donation of $3 for adults and $2.50 for students and seniors is suggested.

SPRINGFIELD ART MUSEUM
1111 East Brookside Dr., Springfield
(417) 866-2716
www.springfieldmo.gov/egov/art/index.html
Springfield Art Museum has a small but fine collection and hosts *Watercolor U.S.A.,* a nationally known watercolor exhibition each summer. (See the Arts and Culture chapter.)

SPRINGFIELD NATIONAL CEMETERY
1702 East Seminole St., Springfield
(417) 881-9499
The large, parklike area is ablaze in fall color with red maples and sweet gums, and in spring with redbud, dogwood, and crab apple and pear blossoms. This old cemetery is the final rest for both Confederate and Union soldiers and a lone Revolutionary War veteran who made it this far west. It is also the cemetery for veterans from conflicts after the Civil War, including five Medal of Honor recipients, whose headstones are engraved in gold.

The cemetery is decorated with small flags on Memorial Day, and many area families make the annual trek there to honor their nation's soldiers.

WILSON'S CREEK NATIONAL BATTLEFIELD
FR 182 and MO ZZ, Republic
(417) 732-2662
www.nps.gov/wicr
You can enjoy the park anytime, but August 10 is a great day to do so because it's then that the annual commemoration of the Battle of Wilson's Creek takes place with an army of Civil War reenactors.

That date, in 1861, marked the serious beginnings of the Civil War in Missouri.

The battlefield, just south of Springfield, is a park operated by the National Park Service. The visitor center features a film about Missouri's biggest Civil War battle, a battle map, and a museum. In 1999, on the 138th anniversary of the battle, it was announced that funding had been secured to double the size of the visitor center. The center is visited by 250,000 tourists each year. The enlarged center houses the nation's largest Civil War library collection, a multipurpose educational room, and offices. It also houses an impressive collection of Civil War artifacts and memorabilia and recently acquired the extensive collection of Dr. Tom Sweeney.

During the summer, there are weekend events, living-history events, demonstrations of 19th-century medical treatments, and Civil War firearms demonstrations. There are hiking and biking paths that wander through the park, or you can drive along a road tour of battle sites such as Bloody Hill and the Ray farmhouse, used during the battle as a field hospital by the Confederates.

To get to the park, if you are already in Springfield, just follow Sunshine Street (US 60) west out of town to MO M. Turn left onto MO M and then right onto MO ZZ. The park is 2 miles south on this road. If you're coming up from Branson and want to avoid the Springfield traffic, take the MO 14 exit at Ozark. Turn left (west) onto MO 14. You'll go through Nixa and cross US 160. The rest of the way is a pretty drive on MO 14 to MO ZZ, where you'll turn right (north).

WONDERS OF WILDLIFE MUSEUM
500 West Sunshine St., Springfield
(417) 890-9453
www.wondersofwildlife.org
The museum is currently closed for some renovations and refurbishing. Call to check if it has opened. Officially named the American National

Fish and Wildlife Museum, Wonders of Wildlife is an exciting educational experience focusing on the past, present, and future benefits of wildlife conservation. The $52 million, 92,000-square-foot museum has 160 species of live animals in realistic habitats. Visitors can test their strength against that of a bald eagle; come face-to-face with river otters, bobcats, and beavers; walk through the digestive system of a 32-foot largemouth bass; and hook their own blue marlin on an interactive video simulator. They can enter a replica of an Ozarks cave, see real wild turkeys that roam the lower level of the museum, walk a swinging rope bridge, and marvel at the 19-foot waterfall flowing in the 140,000-gallon community pond. There's also a 220,000-gallon Out to Sea Gallery, which features three varieties of sharks and assorted rays and 300 other saltwater species. The Conservation Heroes Library spotlights famous historical conservationists Aldo Leopold, Theodore Roosevelt, John James Audubon, and others through video books. By opening a book's cover, visitors can view a video profile of each conservationist.

CARTHAGE

Carthage is a right smart piece from Branson, but it's a right smart town that can easily fill your day. This county seat of Jasper County, with a population of 11,000, is about 100 miles northwest of Branson, and the quickest way to get there is to take US 65 north to I-44 and drive west toward Joplin. Carthage is 6 miles north of I-44 on US 71A.

Carthage was a handsome town when Branson was just a group of log homes on the White River. It gained its prosperity from lead and zinc mining after the Civil War. At the end of the 19th century, Carthage had more millionaires per capita than anywhere in the United States. It was "their town," a good place to raise a family while the rough and ready mining camps just a little bit south made the money. Area granite and the famous Carthage marble made beautiful and durable building materials. You can see some of the old homes, restored to their original splendor, and even stay in some that operate as bed-and-breakfasts.

It wasn't always so splendid. Founded in 1842, the village had a rough childhood. You can compare the Old Cabin Shop, which was used as the first county courthouse, with the present beautiful white marble courthouse built in 1894. Early growth came to a halt when the Civil War started. Carthage was the site of the first major battle of the Civil War, July 5, 1861, preceding the first Battle of Bull Run by 16 days and Missouri's biggest battle at Wilson's Creek by more than a month. The town was occupied several times by both Union and Confederate forces, and most of the buildings in the town were torched. Bands of guerrillas and bushwhackers terrorized the surrounding countryside.

The 1860 census counted 6,883 residents in Jasper County, but by the end of the war only 30 were left. After the war, farmers and settlers returned and began rebuilding. Then the miners came. Mineral wealth had been discovered and was exploited, and when the railroad came in 1872, Carthage was on its way to becoming a major cultural and architectural center. Today, it's a quiet, thriving town, proud of its Victorian beauty and past.

The chamber of commerce will be glad to send you information if you call (417) 358-2373, or you can pick up brochures and information in the office at 107 East Third St. Here are some things you'll want to see in Carthage.

BATTLE OF CARTHAGE CIVIL WAR MUSEUM
205 East Grant Ave.
(417) 358-6643
www.carthage-mo.gov/index
Start here on your study of Carthage and the Civil War. The museum provides artifacts and information about the Battle of Carthage. Its focal point is an elaborate 7-by-5-foot mural by local artist Andy Thomas. Admission is free, and the museum is open all year, seven days a week.

BATTLE OF CARTHAGE STATE HISTORIC SITE
East Carter Street
(417) 682-2279
www.mostateparks.com/carthage.htm
Events of this first major battle of the Civil War are highlighted in a kiosk of text and graphic illustration at the park, located next to Carter Park on East Chestnut Street.

i Missouri has more than 5,000 reasons to be known as "the cave state," and a dozen new ones are discovered every year. Caves are a great way to beat the summer heat. Remember that although it may be 90 degrees outside, a cave will be a constant 60 degrees. When it's hot outside, the cave will seem cool; in winter when it's cold outside, the cave will seem warm. Wear a sweater and your comfy walking shoes.

JASPER COUNTY COURTHOUSE AND DOWNTOWN CARTHAGE SQUARE
Grand Avenue
(417) 358-0421
www.jaspercounty.org
The turrets, towers, and arches of this Romanesque Revival masterpiece evoke the feel of a medieval castle. Designed by M. A. Orlopp Jr. of New Orleans, the courthouse, which has been called "one of the handsomest in the country," dominates the town square. The building is on the National Register of Historic Places. Inside is a wrought-iron cage elevator, an array of military artifacts, and local mining and mineral specimens. A prominent feature is artist Lowell Davis's *Forged in Fire* mural, which vividly portrays the county's history.

The downtown Carthage square is lined with specialty shops: a 1950s-style deli, tearoom, espresso bar, antiques and collectible shops, and craft and gift shops.

KENDRICK PLACE
MO 571 and MO V
(417) 358-0636
www.kendrickplace.com
A mile north of Carthage is Kendrick Place, one of the few structures in the county to escape the Civil War unscathed. Built in 1849 and used as a command post by both Union and Confederate forces during the conflict, it has now been restored to its pre–Civil War appearance. Call for tour or group meal information.

OLD CABIN SHOP
155 North Black Powder Lane
(417) 358-6720
This cabin from the 1830s served as the county's first courthouse. You can browse through the retail shop and check out the large collection of Native American artifacts. There's also a large collection of guns of the types used by Jasper Countians on both sides of the law.

PHELPS HOUSE
1146 Grand Ave.
(417) 358-1776
www.phelpshouse.org
The late-Victorian Phelps family mansion recalls the opulence and elegance of old Carthage. Constructed in the 1890s of huge blocks of gray Carthage limestone, it conveys the image of solid strength so important to the wealthy of that era. The interior displays elaborate and unique features: handpainted wallpaper, beautiful tile mosaics, gold-trimmed woodwork, a Shakespeare stained-glass library window, and a hand-operated rope pulley elevator that serves the four floors. The home has ten fireplaces, all with different color tile.

Phelps House is open for tours on Wednesdays, April through November, and can be rented for special occasions. A step-on tour guide for touring buses is available with advance request. Admission is $5 for adults, $2 for children 6 to 12.

POWERS MUSEUM
1617 West Oak St.
(417) 358-2667
www.powersmuseum.com
The free museum displays a variety of textiles (quilts and fashions), furnishings, decorative arts, archival resources, and Powers family memorabilia that highlight Carthage's history from the late 19th and early 20th centuries. If you have an interest in the Victorian era as reflected in Midwestern culture, this is the place for you. The museum was a gift to the community by Marian Powers Winchester in honor of her parents, Dr. Everett Powers and Marian Wright Powers. The museum and gift shop are open February through December, Tuesday through Sunday.

PRECIOUS MOMENTS CHAPEL COMPLEX
480 Chapel Rd.
(417) 358-7599, (800) 543-7975
www.preciousmoments.com
More than a mere chapel, Precious Moments chapel is a theme park based on characters and ideas of Sam Butcher. Artist Sam Butcher's waif-like ceramic figurines and drawings have a following around the world. Butcher fell in love with the rolling hills near Carthage when he pulled off the interstate in 1984. So he bought land along Center Creek, a parcel big enough to take in its broad meanderings and large enough for his grand plan, and he created a chapel that has become one of Missouri's most popular attractions, drawing more than a million visitors a year. You're likely to encounter tourists from around the world at the Spanish Mission–style chapel, which features more than 50 spectacular murals and 24 stained-glass windows. It's a quiet place of beauty and inspiration in a parklike setting. Sam Butcher's vision is a growing one. There's the recently added inspirational Fountain of Angels, featuring 120 one-of-a-kind Precious Moments sculptures cast in bronze, and a sound and light show. Near the chapel is the Precious Moments Gallery, which houses Butcher's original art, out-of-production figurines, and mementos and gifts he has received throughout the years.

A three-story Victorian home has been moved from Carthage to Dusty's Honeymoon Island (like all of the islands and green spaces, Dusty is named for one of Butcher's grandchildren), which is smack-dab in the middle of a 40-acre lake. It's available for honeymooners, and if you're planning on getting married, there's even a wedding chapel nearby to accommodate you. Tiffany's is a restaurant on the grounds that provides tasty fare for the many visitors, and Royal Delights provides deli items and desserts for those who need only a snack. You can even tour Butcher's home (there's an admission charge for that) and see how an artist decorates a house! The complex is even competing with Branson's music shows with its own gospel music shows by Al Brumley Jr. (son of the famous gospel songwriter) and a group called the Chapelaires.

This amazing complex is cared for by a friendly staff of more than 300, who answer questions from curious visitors and keep the flowers fresh and watered and the grounds groomed. If you need a place to stay, there's a 90-unit RV park and the Best Western Precious Moments Hotel, (417) 359-5900 or (800) 511-7676.

Precious Moments is easy to find. After you exit off I-44 onto US 71 going to Carthage, you'll turn at MO HH. Just follow the signs. Admission is free, but a donation is requested. There are admission charges for the house tour and the Fountain of Angels show.

VICTORIAN HOMES DRIVING TOUR
Various sites
(417) 359-8181
The Victorian Homes Driving Tour is a leisurely drive-by tour of Carthage's most beautiful and architecturally significant mansions, built between 1870 and 1910. Stop by the Carthage Chamber of Commerce at 107 East Third St., or call them at the number above for a map and descriptive brochure. It's an especially nice drive during the height of the fall leaf color. Several of the mansions have been converted into bed-and-breakfast inns, including the Grand Avenue Inn, (417) 358-7265,

at 1615 Grand Ave., and the Leggett House, (417) 358-0683, at 1106 Grand Ave.

JOPLIN

Though larger, Joplin isn't as well known to tourists as Carthage, but as the state's fourth-largest metro area and with its colorful lead-mining past, it's worth the short 8-mile drive from Carthage for a bit of exploration.

Worth the excursion alone is the Thomas Hart Benton mural Joplin *at the Turn of the Century, 1886–1906* in the Joplin Municipal Building at 303 East Third St. The building is open Monday through Friday, 8 a.m. to 5 p.m., and admission is free. Benton began his artistic career in Joplin and visually celebrates his memories of the rough-and-tumble town of his youth in his only autobiographical mural. This is the last mural completed by the artist, the only one on panels, and the only one he ever signed. Support exhibits show the models Benton created for the piece.

Of course, with the town's rich mining past, there are many antiques stores located in and around the Joplin area, rumored to slowly sell off antiques of the town's old families who are down on their luck. Our personal faves: the Antique Mansion and the Gingerbread House—the latter still particularly good for astounding finds. The Antique Mansion, (417) 781-0300, is at 4830 East 32nd St. at the I-44 crossover. The Gingerbread House, (417) 623-6690, is located at 4060 Coyote Dr.

The Joplin Convention and Visitors Bureau, at 222 West Third St., offers shopping and tourist information. Call (417) 625-4789 or (800) 657-2534, or log on to www.joplincvb.com for updates of events in and around Joplin.

GEORGE WASHINGTON CARVER NATIONAL MONUMENT
Diamond
(417) 325-4151
www.nps.gov/gwca
Administered by the National Park Service, this park includes the birthplace and boyhood home of the famous agronomist, botanist, and "stove-

top chemist" George Washington Carver (1864–1943). Carver, born a slave, is best known for his development of many uses for the peanut and soybean. The park includes the Carver family cemetery, a museum, and a self-guided nature trail. Picnic facilities are available, and the park often sponsors special afternoon and weekend programs. Hours are 9 a.m. to 5 p.m. daily. The park is closed Thanksgiving and Christmas. Admission is free.

To reach the Carver National Monument, take US 71 to Diamond, Missouri. Go west 2 miles on MO V and then south about 1 mile. Watch for the signs.

i Did you know that Eureka Springs, Arkansas, ranks number three—right behind Las Vegas and Gatlinburg, Tennessee—in "marriage destinations" in the United States? Being number three doesn't mean you don't get first-class treatment, however. There are a number of "wedding chapels" and romantic honeymoon spots in Eureka Springs. You can go to www.eureka springsbride.com for wedding tips, plans, places—even photographers.

JOPLIN MUSEUM COMPLEX
P.O. Box 555, Joplin, MO 64802
(417) 623-1180
www.joplinmuseum.org
The Joplin Museum Complex, located in historic Schifferdecker Park, consists of the Dorothea B. Hoover Historical Museum and the Everett J. Ritchie Tri-State Mineral Museum. The Mineral Museum focuses on the what is historically known as the Joplin District—the lead and zinc mining camps that peppered southwestern Missouri, southeastern Kansas, and northeastern Oklahoma and that poured wealth into the town near the end of the 19th century. Mineral specimens on display show the amazing purity of the lead and zinc deposits of the area, as well as other minerals found locally. The Historical Museum

focuses on the history of Joplin, especially the effect of "instant wealth" on the homes and businesses in the area. Other highlights are the Merle Evans Circus Tent #24, Circus Room, and a fine collection of porcelain and bisque dolls.

The museums and their gift shops are open Tuesday through Saturday 9 a.m. to 4 p.m. and Sunday 1 to 4 p.m. Admission is free.

The easiest way to reach the museum complex is to take the Schifferdecker Street exit (exit 4) north from I-44 to Old Route 66 (Seventh Street). You'll see the museum buildings on your left.

EUREKA SPRINGS, ARKANSAS

It would be nice to spend several days in Eureka Springs, but it is close enough that you can get a good taste in a single day. It's a pretty drive through the winding wilderness of Arkansas to this "Little Switzerland of the Ozarks," and you'll love the meandering streets, quaint shops, and Victorian-era homes.

There is no single attraction that makes this town remarkable; the attraction is the entire town. People were coming as tourists to Eureka Springs when Branson was only a couple of log cabins in the White River wilderness. Eureka Springs developed as a spa town when people traveled from all over the country to bathe in the town's many mineral springs, hoping to find cures to everything from blindness and rheumatism to "the vapors," the then-popular term for female depression.

American Indians had known about the many springs in the area and shared the secret of their cures with settlers. Soon people began coming to the "Indian Healing Spring," also known as Basin Spring because the water flowed into a natural stone basin. During the Civil War, Dr. Alvah Jackson established a hospital in the Rock House, a cave near the spring, treating the wounded of both sides. He must have done some good. After the war news of the springs' cures spread, and people came from miles away to camp nearby and "take the waters."

By July 4, 1879, more than 400 people were camped nearby, and they decided to form and name a community. Trees on the hillsides furnished lumber for permanent homes, and the sawmills quickly stripped the area of trees. The hills were so steep and the houses so close together that they were stacked in layers upon layers up the sides of the steep slopes. In fact, according to local history, the first lawsuit in Eureka Springs resulted when a woman carelessly threw dishwater out the back door and down the chimney of her neighbor, damaging the furniture.

Basin Spring water was bottled and sold nationwide, and the face of the "Ozarka Girl" became a familiar trademark and spread the town's growing fame.

The railroad came to the town in 1883, and connections with the Frisco line at Seligman, Missouri, assured the success of Eureka Springs as a health spa. Six trains a day came into the town, and its population of 5,000 full-time residents made it the fourth-largest city in Arkansas.

By 1885 the gas-lighted streets were graded and paved or sprinkled daily during the summer to keep down the dust. In 1910 streetlights were electric, and the town had a new Carnegie library. Hotels were built, and by the 1890s Eureka Springs had become one of the most fashionable spa towns in the United States, rivaled only by Hot Springs in central Arkansas. Bathhouses and hotels that featured hydrotherapy attracted the rich and famous, along with those who preyed on them and provided services for them.

The town whose fame was founded on water attracted people who wanted something stronger than water, and area moonshine found a ready market. Interestingly, temperance crusader Carrie Nation spent her last years in Eureka. She died there in 1911 after a stroke, following one of her famous fire-and-brimstone temperance speeches at Basin Park.

The town, which grew like wildfire, paid the price, suffering four major fires in the years 1883–93. The fires destroyed large sections of the town but resulted in building codes and general rebuilding in stone rather than wood. But the rebuilding, plus expensive civic luxuries that saddled the city with debt and a general decline in the public's belief in the curative powers of spring waters, put the city in a depression that began in 1907. By the time the Great Depression came upon the nation in 1929, Eureka Springs was still struggling. The town dwindled from its former glory. Of the 30 hotels during its heyday, only three were still in business in the 1930s, and by the 1950s, the town's population had shrunk to fewer than 200.

The impounding of the waters of the White River behind Beaver Dam in the 1960s, and the attraction of the Ozarks in general as well as the development of Branson in particular, have brought new life and prosperity to this quaint town. It has grown to almost 2,000 residents now. Today you can enjoy its colorful and ornate Victorian architecture in newly restored stores and homes. You can shop the variety of specialty shops and galleries, more than 150 of them, along meandering Spring Street, mentioned by Ripley's Believe It or Not! museums as the street that contains more S curves than any street in the nation. We suggest you obtain a map of the town when you get there, as the winding streets make it easy to become disoriented. You can get information ahead of time by calling the Arkansas Chamber of Commerce at (800) 638-7352 or stop by the visitor center on AR 62 West.

Start your adventure at the base of the valley along Main Street, then walk up Spring Street, stopping at sites and stores that interest you. Walk until you get to the top (or get tired), and come back down the other side. On the way enjoy the 12 spring sites, of more than 63 in the town, that have become miniature parks.

The Eureka Springs Preservation Society publishes a series of six self-guided walking tours. At $1.25 they are worth their weight in gold, not only for the historical information, but also to keep you from getting lost. If you do get lost, don't worry. The town is small enough that you can't wander far before you'll be back in familiar

i Don't take RVs on the streets of Eureka Springs. Plan on parking and walking, or use the trolleys to get around town. Bring your most comfortable shoes because there are lots of steps and the streets are steep. Besides, walking is by far the best way to take in this town's charming ambience.

territory. Besides, getting lost can be the most interesting way to discover the town!

Another way to become oriented is to buy an all-day trolley pass and ride the loop once just to scope out the situation. The pass is only $3, and by the end of the day your feet will think it was money well spent. The trolleys stop in front of virtually every hotel and motel and have regular stops downtown. Tickets can be purchased at many shops and at the downtown trolley depot on Spring Street.

There are lots of restaurants, delis, and dessert shops in the town, so there is no danger of not finding a good place to eat. No matter how eclectic or discriminating your taste, Eureka Springs has a restaurant that will tease your palette. The town is a mecca for chefs, many of whom have established their own restaurants. You can eat out every meal for weeks in Eureka Springs and never tire of the variety—continental to Asian, barbecue to baklava. An Annual Food and Wine Weekend has become one of the most popular events in Eureka Springs and one of our favorites. (We love our food!) Chefs around town showcase their talent, matching food and wine at different meals throughout the day. Brunch, lunch, and dinner, along with simple "splash in the glass" tastings, are available. You'll find a listing of Eureka Springs' culinary offerings at the Web site.

As you walk the town, you'll pick up a New Orleans atmosphere without the flat ground. It's a quality that is emanated by the wrought-iron work on some of the buildings and perhaps by the large number of musicians, artists, and general character types that have come to live in the town. In fact, the town owes much of its revival to the fact that large numbers of the "hippie element" of the 1960s were attracted to the town, liked it, and stayed to become more staid town elders.

If you happen to be in town in September, you can catch the Eureka Springs Jazz Festival, and in May there is an annual blues festival (see the Annual Events chapter).

It's about a 45-minute drive to Eureka Springs. The simplest way to get there is to take US 65 south to Harrison and pick up US 62 west just after Bear Creek Springs. The other option, a more scenic route, is to take US 65 south to MO 86 West, then AR 23 South. We suggest, just for variety and to see more of our beautiful Ozark country, you take the scenic route down and the other route back.

EUREKA SPRINGS & NORTH ARKANSAS RAILWAY
North Main Street
(479) 523-9623
www.esnarailway.com
The depot is on North Main Street (you may want to check out some of the flea markets on that street) as you come into town via AR 23 North. You'll enjoy the historic station, gift shop with train memorabilia, and vintage railroad car and steam engine display—all free. The ride itself lasts about an hour. You'll be pulled in vintage steam locomotive comfort and enjoy lunch in a restored dining car while a panorama of scenery passes by your window. Check the depot for the schedule and prices.

GAZEBO BOOKS
86 Spring St.
(479) 253-9556
This bookstore carries everything from best sellers to odd, interesting, and off-the-wall selections. The store advertises itself as "the bookstore with the world view," and you can increase your view of the world with art books, exotic geography, travel, and cookbooks and books on religion and history. Gazebo Books also stocks local-interest books, children's books, and a fine selection of how-to books.

THE GREAT PASSION PLAY
Passion Play Road
(479) 253-9200, (800) 882-PLAY
www.greatpassionplay.com
The play usually runs from April through October. It's a spiritual and theatrical extravaganza done in pantomime (with professionally recorded voices). More than 200 actors, sheep, donkeys, and camels re-create the life, death, and resurrection of Jesus Christ in a two-hour show. There are also two pre-play performances: gospel concerts and Parables of the Potter presentations. These are free to the public on the nights the play is performed.

In 2009 Passion Play tickets cost $25 for ages 12 and older and $12 for ages 6 to 11. All seats must be reserved, so call ahead for tickets at the number above. The drama is performed nightly, except Sunday and Wednesday, with curtain time at 8:30 p.m. After Labor Day, the show begins an hour earlier. There is also a *Top of the Mountain* dinner theatre show. Check the Web site for a value package that includes both shows.

On the grounds are other attractions, including a 10-foot section of the Berlin Wall on which an East Berliner inscribed a line from the 23rd Psalm. There is a Bible Museum with more than 6,000 Bibles in 625 languages and a life-size reproduction of Da Vinci's *Last Supper*. The museum features an interesting video about the history of the Bible. At the end of Passion Play Road, you can't help but see the 67-foot *Christ of the Ozarks*, used as a landmark by aviators. It weighs more than a million pounds and is the product of Emmit Sullivan, one of the sculptors of Mount Rushmore. Some say that the statue looks like Willie Nelson. Others say it looks like a milk carton with outstretched arms. Others say that its eyes follow you. Many of the attractions on the grounds are free.

QUIGLEY'S CASTLE
Quigley Castle Road
(479) 253-8311
www.quigleyscastle.com
Albert Quigley had not been delivering on his promise to build his wife a new house. One day when he went to work, the missus and her five

kids demolished the old house and moved all their stuff into a chicken coop. Construction on the new house began immediately, based on a model built by Mrs. Quigley out of cardboard and matchsticks. Rightly known as the Ozarks' strangest dwelling, this curiously designed home (built in 1943) includes suspended rooms, secret passageways, floor-to-ceiling windows, and inside planting areas. The eccentric Mrs. Quigley loved collecting and incorporated into the walls of her home, and even on the furniture, her rock, arrowhead, and butterfly collections. The castle has been open to the public for more than 40 years. Hours are 8:30 a.m. to 5 p.m. April through October, but the castle is closed Sunday and Thursday. Admission is free for children 14 and younger, $6.50 for adults.

ROSALIE HOUSE
282 Spring St.
(479) 253-7377
In the middle section of Spring Street where it levels out (yes, it runs sideways along the hillside at times!), you may want to tour the colorful Rosalie House. The burgundy brick house has ivory, gray, and green ornate gingerbread. It's open daily for tours and weddings. Admission is free for children 12 and younger and $5 for adults.

SPRING STREET
Greater Eureka Springs
Chamber of Commerce
(479) 253-8737, (800) 638-7352
www.eurekaspringschamber.com
Eureka Springs is an artsy town. Spring Street alone boasts almost two dozen studios, galleries, and shops. You'll like No. 83, the Spring Creek Pottery Shop, where you can buy the practical as well as artistic and even fantastic sculptures in clay. It's the flagship gallery of sculptor Mark Hopkins. Quicksilver Nature Gallery at 73 Spring St. sells art with a natural theme. You will marvel at how everyday items and natural objects are transformed into art. Wildlife artist Susan Morrison has a gallery that features her own work as well as a number of great local artists at 60 Spring

St. There are others: Fusion Squared Gallery, Zark's Fine Design, Iris at the Basin Park, Eclectic Edge—and that's just on Spring Street. Check the Web site for a complete listing.

THORNCROWN CHAPEL
US 62
(479) 253-7401
www.thorncrown.com
The chapel is just west of Eureka Springs on US 62. Designed by world-renowned Arkansas architect E. Fay Jones, the chapel seems like a jewel of light in its Ozark mountainside setting and has been called one of the finest examples of religious space in modern times. It rises to the sky like the forest that surrounds it. The chapel, majestic in its simplicity, has 425 panes of glass divided by a lattice of native pine. The chapel was honored as Building of the Decade in 1991 by the American Association of Architects and has been featured in numerous magazines. Since the chapel opened in 1980, more than four million people have visited this woodland sanctuary. Thorncrown Chapel is open daily from 9 a.m. to 5 p.m. There is no admission fee, but donations are accepted.

TURPENTINE CREEK
239 Turpentine Creek Lane
(479) 253-5841
www.turpentinecreek.org
With 450 acres inhabited by lions, tigers, cougars, leopards, bears, monkeys, exotic birds, and other wildlife, Turpentine Creek is a haven for neglected or unwanted exotic animals. The facility is USDA licensed, and it's supported by donations and guest admission fees. The facilities allow you to get about as close as you dare to these animals, and in the petting zoo you can even pet tiger and lion cubs. An Education Station lets you get hands on with the Touch and Feel Center, while Feeding Time is an event not to be missed (usually between 4 p.m. and 5 p.m.). Guided tours of the habitats begin at 11 a.m. each day, and Keeper Talks conducted by biologists and zoologists answer all your questions about this

awesome attraction. Turpentine Creek is 7 miles south of Eureka Springs on AR 23. Follow the signs out of town. The refuge is open to guests March through December from 9 a.m. until dusk. Admission is $15 for adults and $10 for kids 12 and younger and senior citizens 65 and older.

MOUNTAIN VIEW, ARKANSAS

Everywhere you go in Mountain View, you'll hear the sound of authentic mountain music. Banjos, dulcimers, guitars, harmonicas, and other unplugged instruments play century-old folk songs. Thousands of visitors come to the area each year to hear music on the square. The town is the proclaimed "Folk Music Capital of the World," and so the tradition of impromptu music by pickers and singers on the town square was born. The Mountain View square has been the site of a spring music festival for decades, and purists insist that the amateurs who jam on the courthouse lawn are as good or better than the folk artists at the nearby Ozark Folk Center. One of the first and most obvious factors that attracts people to Mountain View to live or just to visit is its location. The town is nestled into the hills and valleys of the beautiful Ozark Mountains. Touched by the White River and several year-round creeks, streams, and springs, the area around Mountain View is truly majestic. You'll enjoy the drive down to Mountain View, though it is 150 miles over roads that would not qualify as even moderately straight for more than a mile stretch.

Because it's a rather long (and slow) drive, you may want to make this out-of-Branson excursion an overnighter. Mountain View has a number of motels and bed-and-breakfast inns, and overnight accommodations at the Ozark Folk Center are available at the Dry Creek Lodge, (870) 269-8871. Baxter and Stone Counties of Arkansas have been two of the state's fastest-growing counties, and there is a world of natural beauty and several attractions to tempt the tourist. For more on attractions in this area, contact the Arkansas Chamber of Commerce, P.O. Box 133, Mountain View, AR 72560; (870) 269-8068.

The quickest way to get to Mountain View and the Ozark Folk Center from Branson is to take the scenic drive down US 65 south to Harrison, Arkansas, and then to the town of Leslie, Arkansas. There you'll turn east on AR 66, which will take you into Mountain View. Just so you can have an equally scenic and different drive back, take AR 5 to Mountain Home, and come back to the Branson area via Gainesville. As we mentioned, this is our longest day trip, and we suggest you make this an overnighter. There's just too much to cram into a single day when you have to travel our slow roads.

BLANCHARD SPRINGS AND BLANCHARD SPRINGS CAVERN
Blanchard Springs Cavern Road
Blanchard Springs, AR
(870) 757-2211
www.fs.fed.us/oonf/ozark/recreation/
bsc.html

Only 14 miles from the Ozark Folk Center is a natural wonder. More than a dozen new caves are discovered each year in the Ozarks, but nothing has been as spectacular as this 1963 discovery. Blanchard Springs Cavern's lower level had been known for years. In fact, the explorers who found the "new cave" were on their 27th trip into the cave when they noticed the tell-tale red clay at the top of a large room. Red clay is normally found only on cave floors, and some caves are entirely filled with the clay, waiting to be washed out and reveal a new cave. Recognizing that an upper cave might exist, they poked around and found the cave discovery of the century. The cave has many awe-inspiring rooms and passages, including a beautiful Dripstone Tour, and is impressive because it is totally uncorrupted and not vandalized. In order to keep it that way and not disturb humidity and cave life, visitors enter through specially constructed "air locks." Nearby Blanchard Springs is impressive, as is the river that emerges from the cavern. The walk up the trail to the source is especially pretty in the spring when the dogwood and redbud are in bloom.

The cavern is in the Ozark National Forest and is operated by the U.S. Forest Service. There is an excellent movie presentation about the cave—its past and formation and discovery—in the cavern visitor center. The center also carries books about caves and the flora and fauna of the area. The cavern is on MO 14 west of Mountain View. Call for information or directions.

CALICO ROCK, ARKANSAS
AR 9
(870) 297-4129

Calico Rock is a tiny town whose main street is on the National Register of Historic Places. Calico Rock is named for the colorfully splotched 200-foot bluffs of the White River, the same White River that flows through Branson. Calico Rock was at one time an important river town when steamboats were the only method of transportation into the White River country. Later it became an equally important rail town after the railroad snaked its way up the White River valley. It is worth the drive to check out the several craft stores and the best old-time hardware store we've ever found.

If you need an overnight stop because you've worn yourself out, our favorite place is the old 1923 Riverview Hotel, (870) 297-8208, right in the town near the bridge, now a quaint bed-and-breakfast operation overlooking the valley below.

OZARK FOLK CENTER
P.O. Box 500, Mountain View, AR 72560
AR Spur 382 off AR 9
(870) 269-3851, (800) 264-3655
www.ozarkfolkcenter.com

The center is an expansive park with restaurants and shops, demonstrations of folk arts and crafts, a conference center with classrooms, landscaped grounds, and even overnight accommodations. The center's intent is to give the visitor an insight into Ozark history, crafts, and arts in a frozen-in-time re-creation. It contrasts with Branson, which represents the eclectic and evolving Ozarks with electric guitars and music influenced by rock ele-

ments, plus neon, bright lights, and glitz. They're two different versions of the Ozarks: one past, the other present.

The Ozark Folk Center, an Arkansas state park that opened in 1973, is dedicated to preserving the music, crafts, art, and history of our mountain way of life from about 1850 to 1930. You can see Ozark craftspeople at work, weaving baskets, throwing pots, shoeing horses, and forging tools and knives. You can listen to unplugged country music and sample Ozark cuisine or get some quick lessons in jam and jelly making and home canning. If you want to spend more time, you can learn some of these old skills, including sorghum making to herb gardening. The conference center is the setting for the classes, Elderhostel programs, workshops, and seminars, and if you're planning your trip well in advance, you may want to write the center for information. It has three large meeting rooms, a small (160-seat) auditorium, and an impressive Ozark Folklore Research Library.

Admission prices vary a good deal because you can purchase tickets just for the music performances, and there are one- and three-day combination tickets or season passes. It is best to call for prices, but a family pass costs $27.50 for a day's visit to everything the center has to offer. The regular season is mid-April through October, and the center is closed December through March. Call for more information.

HOLLISTER

We've come to think of Branson's "sister city" across the lake as if we were Siamese twins. The two towns, with separate but cooperating city governments, are looked upon by natives as extensions of each other. To get to Hollister, take US Business 65 (or Veterans Boulevard) in downtown Branson east. As soon as you cross the Taneycomo Bridge, turn right.

Before Branson, there was Hollister, which developed as the area's first tourist attraction after the coming of the St. Louis Iron Mountain & Southern Railroad. It had the area's first iron bridge, the first paved street, electric lights, a movie house, and a steam-heated hotel. Named after a Hollister in California, the town developed as the result of nearby vineyards, orchards, and truck farms. J. W. Blankenship started the development of an English-style village to attract tourists, and the Tudor Revival architecture along Hollister's Downing Street was placed on the National Register of Historic Places in 1978.

In pre-dam days, Turkey Creek and the White River frequently flooded the town. Vintage photographs show trains plowing through water and johnboats floating in the dining room of Ye English Inn. You can inspect the old Ye English Inn, built in 1912, without danger of being flooded. Ask to see the fossilized fish built into its cobblestone walls, which are made from rock from nearby Turkey Creek. It was a popular stopover for the area's early travelers, and though it can't claim George Washington slept there, it can claim that Clark Gable slept there. While strolling down Downing Street, stop at No. 10 and have your picture taken. One of the most picturesque train stations in the nation is now Hollister's chamber of commerce.

Green Lantern Antiques is a shopping stop. (See the Shopping chapter.) If you want to inspect a real old-time country feed mill, stop at the Mule Barn under the US Business 65 bridge over the railroad tracks. Reading the local bulletin board and talking with the proprietor about his jumping mules is worth the short walk to it.

Information and a map of the town are available from the Hollister chamber of commerce. Call (417) 334-3050. You can visit the Web site at www.cityofhollister.com for a variety of information about the town.

OZARK/MANSFIELD/SEYMOUR

Here's a way you can work in a number of sights and activities in a single day if you've had an overload of shows in Branson—and have a pleasant drive in the process. You can take in some antiques shops, visit a shade garden and the Laura Ingalls Wilder house museum, and inspect Amish country at Seymour.

Start early—by 8 a.m.—and drive north on US 65 to Ozark. After you cross the Finley River, you'll take MO 14 east through Ozark. You might want to stop and take in some of the antiques shops and flea markets in Ozark, but don't dawdle too long. Continue east on MO 14 toward the towns of Sparta and Ava. Your first stop will be the Garden of Dreams. The Garden of Dreams, (417) 683-3733, is a gardener's delight and is only 1 mile south of MO 14 between Sparta and Ava. Look for the signs. You'll enjoy the shade garden on a hot day. Though there are lots of sun-loving plants and gardens, Dr. Bill Roston, the owner, is known for his "hosta hobby." There are more than 10,000 hosta plants encompassing some 600 varieties in the garden, plus dozens of different types of ferns, impatiens, and other shade-loving plants. You may want to buy some plants for your own shady area.

After you leave the Garden of Dreams, continue east on MO 14 and enjoy the scenery on the way to the small community of Dogwood. When you get to MO 5 in Ava, turn left (north) and drive toward Mansfield. Watch for the signs directing you to the Laura Ingalls Wilder Historic Home and Museum, located a mile east of Mansfield.

LAURA INGALLS WILDER HISTORIC HOME AND MUSEUM
3068 MO A, Mansfield
(417) 924-3626
www.lauraingallswilder.com

Wilder's *Little House* books are classics of children's literature, and because of the TV series (still aired in Europe and Japan) you're likely to see a bus of Japanese tourists at this site. Laura lived most of her life on the farm she named Rocky Top. She moved to the Ozarks in 1894 but never wrote a Little House in the Ozarks. When she settled down, she stayed. The home was listed on the National Register of Historic Places in 1957, the year that Laura died at age ninety. She and her husband, Almanzo, and daughter, Rose, are all buried in the Mansfield Cemetery. You can see the writing desk where she penned her *Little House* books and some of her handwritten manuscripts. You

ℹ Missouri has a connection to the stars, and we don't mean those in Branson. Marshfield was the birthplace of Edwin Hubble (1889–1953), known as the Columbus of the Cosmos. You can see a one-quarter-size replica of the telescope that bears his name and is now in space sending back pictures. And astronaut Tom Akers is from the small town of Eminence, east of here.

may feel a bit like Gulliver in the land of the Lilliputians because Almanzo custom-built counters and much of the furniture to accommodate the diminutive 4-foot, 11-inch Laura. Next door is the Laura Ingalls Wilder–Rose Wilder Lane Museum, which has Laura's earliest needlepoint sampler, Pa's famous fiddle, collections of household and farm implements, and memorabilia from Rose, a celebrated author in her own right. You'll also like the Little House Bookstore, where you can purchase books in the *Little House* series, as well as books by Rose, dolls, posters, T-shirts, puzzles, and games.

If you come in late August, you might want to take in the community production of *Little House Memories* at the Mansfield City Park in the evening. Call for information about times. The house and museum are usually open daily during the season, March 1 to October 31. During November the museum and house are closed, but during December there is a special Christmas open house. Call for dates. Tickets to the house and museum are $3 for those ages 6 to 18, $5 for seniors, and $6 for everybody else except kids younger than 6, who get in free. Signs will direct you to the home and museum, which is only a mile east of the Mansfield town square on MO A.

After leaving the Laura Ingalls Wilder Historic Home and Museum, continue north on MO 5. At the junction of US 60, you'll turn left (west) toward Springfield. Your next stop is Seymour.

Seymour, in Webster County, is a typical small Missouri town built around a square. Just north of the town, in Wright County, are the headwaters of Bryant Creek, which flows south to the White River. Though you would never know it from your view from the highway, the incline at Cedar Gap, north of town, is one of the longest and steepest in the state.

Marshfield, the county seat, can boast being the highest county seat in the state at an elevation of 1,490 feet. In fact, of all the towns along I-44, Marshfield is the highest town east of the Rocky Mountains. The county was named after Massachusetts senator and orator Daniel Webster, and the county seat was named after Webster's hometown, Marshfield, where he died on October 24, 1852, three years before the county was formed from Greene County.

Because Webster County has such a high elevation in comparison to surrounding counties, it is also the "mother of rivers." Five noteworthy streams originate in Webster County, flowing to various points of the compass. The James and Finley Rivers flow west and southwest. The Pomme de Terre River takes off to the northwest. The Niangua River flows to the north toward the Lake of the Ozarks. The Osage Fork of the Gasconade River meanders to the northeast.

In Seymour, you may want to investigate the town square and poke in at some of the antiques shops. Murphy Orchards, (417) 935-2270, right on US 160, is worth a stop, especially during apple season, and Seymour hosts an annual apple festival (see the Annual Events chapter).

There is a sizable Amish community in the vicinity, and you may want to check out the J & A Country Amish Store. The market features arts, crafts, and items made by the local Amish community. The Amish themselves run a store—no phone number, of course! Just turn right off US 160 on MO C and drive 5 miles.

You may find that you don't want to make it back to Branson that night! If that's the case, try the bed-and-breakfast experience at Amish Country Inn, (417) 935-9345, www.amishinn.com. This barn, built in 1915, serves as the comfortable inn and has a gift shop with lots of Amish-made items. Turn left off US 160 onto MO K. After the first sharp bend to the right, you'll see the bed-and-breakfast on your left.

With this day trip, you'll have had a full day and will have seen a lot of country. On your way back to Branson, you'll continue on US 60 west to Springfield, then take US 65 south to Branson. If you haven't dawdled around too long, you may even be able to take in a show that night!

REEDS SPRING

To get to Reeds Spring, go west on MO 76 to Branson West. Turn right onto MO 13. It's just a short mosey down the road. There is a new bypass around the town, but you won't want to miss the quaint burg. According to newspaper editor Truman Powell, Reeds Spring in 1883 consisted of only a log cabin, which was used for a school. Named for two brothers who settled there in the 1870s and gave their name to the spring (still flowing), the town came to life with the building of the railroad. Just east of the town is a 2,000-foot-long tunnel, 18 feet high and 24 feet wide, that was drilled through the solid rock of an Ozark mountain. Italians, Austrians, and African Americans, some 250 of them, working on each end with steam drills and dynamite, removed 10 feet of rock a day. When they met in the middle four years later, they were only a fraction of an inch from each other. The payroll of $700 a day brought prosperity to the developing town.

In the early 1900s, Reeds Spring was the tie capital of the United States. Before the railroad reached the area, ties were hacked and rafted down the James River. Later they were loaded on the new railhead in the town and shipped all over the country. By 1915 most of the big timber had been logged off, and the tomato industry developed to replace it. Hundreds of acres of tomatoes were grown on farms in the area for the two canneries in the vicinity of Reeds Spring, but that industry too declined with depleted land and changing markets.

When Table Rock Dam was completed in 1959, tourism became an important part of the economy. The town changed little until recently. The 1930 and 1950 censuses both listed the town with a population of 313. The Branson boom changed all that. Reeds Spring now has a population of more than 500, and Stone County has been one of the fastest-growing counties in the state the last decade.

Now Reeds Spring calls itself "the City of Art." You'll see why when you stroll the rustic Main Street, MO 13, of this artsy, laid-back burg. There aren't many side streets, as the town is built in two very steep, narrow valleys, and you won't get lost in Reeds Spring. There are fine-art galleries, silversmiths and coppersmiths, jewelers, and stained-glass artisans. As you come into town on MO 13, you can't help but notice the Castle. It turns heads. The black, wrought-iron fence at the valley floor contains a 10-acre private estate that climbs the ledges and bluffs of the steep hillside on your right. From MO 13 you can see a large waterfall, a giant bronze eagle with a 12-foot wingspread, and endless native rock retaining walls in a landscape of pools surrounded by natural and sculptured shrubs.

If you like antiques and flea markets, there's the Old Barn, a veritable museum of interesting and odd items. If it is fine art you're interested in, drop in at the New Coast Gallery. You'll like the little sculpture garden beside the shop at 10 Main St. Check out the spring that gave the town its name, newly refurbished with a gazebo made by the shop students at the local high school. The Sawdust Doll is also certainly worth a stop. Turning right onto MO 248 and going under the road trestle on the leg home, you'll find the Omega Pottery Shop. They sell finely crafted products the world over.

We suggest you go back to Branson via MO 248, perhaps stopping for a Greek lunch at Papouli's, on the left just past the Omega Pottery Shop. (See the Restaurants chapter.) When you drive up the other narrow valley, notice the ruins of several old canneries. Turn right when you get to the stop sign at the top of the hill, and you'll have a meandering, picturesque drive back to Branson, experiencing what it was like to drive "Old Highway 65." On the way back you may want to make a short detour and stop at the Sycamore Log Church. Turn right onto Sycamore Log Church Road and make the short drive downhill to sample what early churches were like in the Ozarks: small, sincere, and serene. Several miles before you come back into Branson you'll cross over the Ozark Highroad, constructed as a giant loop around Branson with exits for its major attractions.

ROCKAWAY BEACH

Only 9 miles from Branson, Rockaway Beach, like Hollister, is a town with a past. Just a mile or so upstream from Powersite Dam, the first dam on the White River, Rockaway Beach was the first resort on Lake Taneycomo. To get to Rockaway Beach, go 4 miles north on US 65 and take the MO F exit. After crossing Bull Creek and going up the hill, MO F meets MO 176. Turn right onto MO 176, and in a few hundred yards you'll see signs to Rockaway Beach. Bear right, and after you pass Merriam Woods, the road turns and drops sharply downhill, makes several hairpin curves, and becomes Beach Boulevard. You're in Rockaway! (Don't be confused. Natives almost always drop the "Beach" from the name.)

Willard and Anna Merriam (Merriam Woods was named after her) had the little town, originally called Taneycomo, renamed after the famous New York resort. They had big visions. They adapted the Adirondacks architectural style—knotty pine interiors, native stonework, and bent-limb furniture—to the Ozarks and attracted the developing tourist trade, including famous defense lawyer Clarence Darrow and writer Sherwood Anderson, who came down to enjoy the serenity and the then-warm waters of Lake Taneycomo. Several large hotels sprang up, and some of them were run by former vaudeville stars who settled in Rockaway after the developing movie industry killed old-time vaudeville.

Business boomed during the 1920s through the 1950s. Vacationers took the train to Hollister and boarded a boat to cruise down to Rockaway for several weeks of serenity and swimming. They hiked, fished, water-skied, participated in archery, badminton, and golf, and listened to hot jazz in the cool evenings. All this came to an end when the lake turned cold because of the release of water from the base of Table Rock Dam. Gone are the grand hotels and the activity, but Rockaway is in a revival because of some gung-ho newcomers and tourists who discover the town's past and seek some solitude, knowing they are only minutes away from the bright lights of Branson's shows.

The town's cabins and kitchenettes are reasonably priced, and the quiet family atmosphere with the lakefront park make it a good place to hold family reunions. You can fish off the town pier and keep an eye on the kids as they feed the geese and ducks. If you need gear and tackle, they can be had at the Taneycomo Market.

Check out one of the area's most interesting flea markets, the Wild Goose, for bric-a-brac and treasures. (See the Shopping chapter.) The Dockside Cafe and the Pizza Cellar are good local eateries.

An interesting day's excursion to Rockaway Beach would be to skip the drive and rent a boat in Branson. That's the way folks used to get there before roads, disembarking at the Hollister or Branson depot, and completing the journey by boat. You can fish for trout on the 6-mile cruise down the lake and watch great blue herons, ducks, geese, and the landscape. You can tie up in Rockaway, spend the day browsing the shops, and take your boat back that evening. Not a bad way to spend the day, even if you don't catch any fish!

During the year, the town has a number of special events. For information on Rockaway Beach and a special-event schedule, call the Rockaway Chamber of Commerce at (417) 561-4289 or (800) 798-0178.

FORSYTH

If you drive to Rockaway Beach, you may want to come back to Branson through Forsyth, the county seat of Taney County. When in Rockaway, just take Beach Boulevard (MO 176) east to US 160. Turn right at the junction with US 160, and the highway will take you right through Forsyth.

Forsyth sits safe, comfortable, and sleepy atop a bluff overlooking Swan Creek's confluence with the White River (now the upper part of Lake Bull Shoals). When the town was founded in 1837 as the county seat, with high hopes that steamboat traffic would eventually make it that far up the White River, it was down at the present-day Shadow Rock Park, where Swan Creek flows into the lake. When the lake is low, you can see the old steamboat tie-ups, though it wasn't until 1852 that a steamboat was able to make it as far as Forsyth. (See the History chapter.)

The Civil War saw Forsyth changing hands several times between the North and the South. By 1863, nothing was left of the town except the burned-out brick walls of the courthouse. After the war, the area was plagued by bushwhackers and the later Bald Knobber problems, but gradually it rebuilt itself—only to be forced to higher ground as a result of the 1947 decision by the U.S. Army Corps of Engineers to build Bull Shoals Dam. By 1950, the entire town had been relocated atop the bluff. Today, Forsyth tenaciously keeps its old-fashioned small-town charm.

The town doesn't have any major tourist attractions, but there are several antiques shops. The Forsyth Art Guild Gallery, (417) 546-5439, is an interesting "poke-in," a place where you can find some interesting and inexpensive art. If you would like to see Forsyth's quaint old business district, turn left (east) at the junction of US 160 and MO Y. If you decide to eat in Forsyth, we recommend the Forsyth Flower Cottage and Tea Room, 16052 US 160, (417) 546-5848, for good food as well as local atmosphere.

To check out Powersite Dam, go west on MO Y. After following the ridgetop, the road will head downhill and lead you to Empire Electric Park—a great area for a picnic lunch, fishing, and camping. Bull Shoals Lake begins at the low side of the dam, and Lake Taneycomo ends on the high side. When the Table Rock Dam generators are producing electricity and releasing water from Table Rock Lake, or during high water, Lake Taneycomo spills over the dam.

By today's standards, the dam isn't very impressive (546 feet long and 70 feet high), but when it was finished in 1912, it was one of the nation's largest privately owned dams, and it was important in bringing electricity to the area, as well as helping start the Branson-area tourist industry.

When you leave the dam, continue following MO Y along the lowlands. (Just don't take any road that forks off to the left.) You'll come to the old bridge that crosses Swan Creek; turn left after crossing the bridge and follow the road that heads under the higher steel bridge across the creek.

You are now in Shadow Rock Park. The park gets its name from the high bluff on the north side of Swan Creek. The area that is now the park was an important Indian trading post in the early 19th century and later was Old Forsyth. It now has playground equipment and a reconstructed old log home. Two commemorative plaques to the right of the cabin will give you some of Forsyth's historic highlights.

When you leave the park, follow the main road uphill and turn right. Turn right again at the stop sign at US 160/MO 76, and immediately turn left at the light and go over the MO 76 bridge over Bull Shoals Lake. The next 12 miles is up and down and around, but you wind up on the Hollister side of the Taneycomo bridge in Branson. After you go over the bridge, you're in downtown Branson.

ROARING RIVER STATE PARK AND CASSVILLE

Roaring River State Park features the rugged and scenic terrain of the southwestern Ozarks, and a day trip over that direction gives a respite from the glitz of The Strip and allows you to see what folks came to the Ozarks for in the early part of the 20th century.

The best way is to make a loop. Take MO 76 west early in the morning to Branson West, Reeds Spring, Cape Fair, and then Cassville. You'll be passing through part of Piney Creek Wilderness Area. (See the Recreation and the Outdoors chapter.) Cassville has some flea markets and antiques shops you can check out (Cassville Chamber of Commerce, 417-847-2814, or e-mail Cassville@mo-net.com).

If you are so inclined, Crystal Springs Trout Farm, (417) 847-2174, just north of Cassville, is open year-round for family trout fishing. There's no license or fee required, no limit, and you pay only for what you catch: $3.95 a pound. Trout are cleaned and iced free. Your bait is free, and even your tackle is free if you don't bring your own. Take MO 37 north out of Cassville, turn right onto Barry County Road Y, right onto Partridge Drive, and go 0.25 mile. Watch for the signs.

If you have your tackle and don't mind the cost of a fishing license and trout stamp (see the Lakes and Rivers chapter for details), you might want to try your luck at Roaring River State Park. Take the scenic MO 112 south out of Cassville to the park. A river roars through this 3,354-acre state park, and a $5 million lodge overlooks it. Stonework by CCC workers more than 70 years ago channels the fury of Roaring River Spring, gushing out more than 20 million gallons a day to form the headwaters of Roaring River. In the spring, a waterfall pours from the mountainside into the river. The stream is stocked daily during the March through October trout season and provides excellent fishing for rainbow trout.

If you're not the fishing type, you can catch a nature program, enjoy the cool air at the spring, horseback ride (a one-hour trail ride costs $12 per person), swim, dine, bike, or hike the park's seven trails, including the Devil's Kitchen Trail, a challenging 1.5-mile trail that climbs 325 feet to the ridgetop. The name comes from the odd rock outcropping that forms a roomlike enclosure, once used as a hideout by bushwhackers. Take along a flashlight to explore some of the shallow trail-side caves. There are 20 caves within the park and 15 alongside the hiking trails. Lunch can be a picnic, packed before you start for the day, or eat at the Tree Top Grille (from $3.50 to $7.00) in the park. Don't forget to take in the park's nature center, which has changing exhibits and programs.

If you're not too tired, you can take in the show about the Mountain Maid of Roaring River (call 417-847-4639 for admission prices and information) in the evening before driving back.

If you're not the hiking type but still want to see some scenery, take MO 76 farther south toward Seligman. There's a free observation tower about 3.5 miles from the park. Turn on FR 197 and follow along 8 miles to MO 86. This is the Sugar Camp National Scenic Byway of the Mark Twain National Forest, noted for its scenic quality. Leave in time to take dinner at the Devil's Pool Restaurant on the way back to Branson (see the Restaurants chapter) via MO 86. You may wish to make reservations before you take this day trip.

Coming back to Branson from the south will complete your loop. You'll take MO 86 east through Blue Eye. The turnoff to Big Cedar Lodge, a mile before MO 86 joins US 65, will take you down to Devil's Pool Restaurant. After dinner, continue on MO 86, turn north on US 65, and drive the 10 miles back to Branson. You'll have had a full day!

RELOCATION

Folks have been relocating to the Ozarks since the frontier days, and for much the same reasons as they do today: peace, quiet, solitude, the "we mind our own business" attitude of the natives, and of course the clear rivers, springs, and "cheap land" to settle on and build one's own castle—or cabin.

Cherokees on the Trail of Tears to Oklahoma, attracted by the game and remoteness, frequently disappeared to settle in out-of-the-way hollows. Outlaws from Jesse James to Ma Barker and Pretty Boy Floyd found the Ozarks attractive for some of the same reasons "hippies" found (and revitalized) Eureka Springs during the 1960s.

The more recent retirees and the comeheres of the past three decades have made the Ozarks a growing place while some counties in southern Arkansas and northern Missouri have actually lost population. People in other areas will continue to vote with their feet as long as they think there is something attractive about the Ozarks. Some folks come for the "old" reasons that attracted the outlaw types and early settlers. But more and more, the area is attractive because of increasing job opportunities, low taxes, good medical care, and the entertainment and recreation possibilities. These have made the Ozarks attractive to retirees and the young "still-working" group.

One interesting recent phenomenon has been the influx of a Hispanic minority. The most significant increases from 1990 to 2000 occurred in McDonald County (from 121 to 2,030—an increase of 1,577 percent), Barry County (from 152 to 1,713—an increase of 1,027 percent), Jasper County (from 797 to 3,615—an increase of 353 percent), and Lawrence County (from 211 to 1,195—an increase of 466 percent).

"Those counties have all attracted Hispanic workers as a result of major meat-processing plants located in the county. Hispanic workers have migrated to those counties to take employment in the processing plants," says Daryl Hobbs, professor emeritus of rural sociology, Office of Social and Economic Data Analysis, University of Missouri Outreach and Extension.

An exception was Taney County, in which the Hispanic population increased from 194 in 1990 to 962 in 2000, a 396 percent change. The increase has accelerated. The attraction in Taney County has been the tremendous employment growth

associated with the Branson entertainment industry. The growth in general has caused the local school system to have to scramble to find kindergarten and early-grade teachers, and the Hispanic migration has increased the number of non-English-speaking students in the early grades.

The retired set has always found the Ozarks attractive, but increasingly so as retirees are "more active" during their retirement years and are living longer. And they have different reasons for relocation: we know of some retirees who have decided to settle within "60 miles of Springfield" (to be close to medical care) or "40 miles of Branson" (for the entertainment) and then began casing out the acreages and small burgs until they found their dream location.

If you're a retiree planning to relocate, you may want to check out the Health Care and Retirement chapters in addition to this one. If you're a "young" relocator, take a closer look at the Education and Child Care chapter. And both types will be interested in the Real Estate section of this chapter.

REAL ESTATE

Aint' nothin' to a flat country nohow. A man jest naturally wears hisself out a walkin' on a level 'thout ary hill t'spell him. An' then look how much more there is of hit! Take forty acres o' flat now an' hit's lest a forty, but you take forty acres o' this here Ozark country an' God 'lmighty only know how much 'twould be if hit war rolled out flat. Tain't no wonder 'tall, God rested when he made these here hills; he jest naturally had t'quit, for he'd done his beatenest an' war plumb gin out.

—Harold Bell Wright,
The Shepherd of the Hills,
chapter 1

There's something about the Ozarks that has always attracted people. Whether it's something in the water or the air, or the sight from a hilltop of fog in a valley, or the sound of a stream falling over itself on its wandering way to something larger, the ineffable result is love that can only be felt and never explained. We admit that it never was easy to eke out a living on this hardscrabble land, but it's a lot easier now with tourism and related industries. It sure beats tie hacking, stavebolt cutting, and growing tomatoes for the canneries! Early settlers in the area used wood from the abundant forests for cabins, but these rude dwellings have largely rotted away after being abandoned for better sawmill-lumber homes. However, some older homes have remnants of old log cabins. Many older homes were built of native fieldstone, creek rocks, or quarried stone, and those with a keen eye and a knowledge of the area can tell you precisely where the stone came from. Such stone construction is less prevalent now, except in more expensive projects, because it's labor intensive and therefore costly.

Movin' to Missouri has a nice ring to it, and moving to the Ozarks is more attractive than ever. The Branson area has become a desired place to live for lots of reasons: clean air and water, low property taxes, quiet towns, and good neighbors. It's secluded but not desolate, with a rural atmo-sphere yet close to big-city services and plenty of entertainment and activities. Many come for lakeside living. Table Rock Lake covers 52,000 acres to create nearly 750 miles of shoreline. The lake has been proclaimed one of the three cleanest in the United States. Fishing for bass, crappy, catfish, and a host of other game fish is a year-round sport. Water sports are abundant also (see the Lakes and Rivers chapter). With a usually mild climate, Table Rock Lake is used 12 months every year. The lake never freezes, and you can leave your boat at the dock. Close by, just below Table Rock Dam, you will find Lake Taneycomo, which is famous for trout fishing. Below Taneycomo's Powersite Dam begins Bull Shoals Lake, known for years as one of the best striped bass lakes in the nation, with much of its waters in Arkansas. Above Table Rock Lake, the newest dam (and the one highest up on the White River) backs up the waters of Beaver Lake in Arkansas. Check the Lakes and Rivers chapter for detailed information on these areas. You'll understand why lots of people find the laid-back lake living here in the Ozarks appealing.

Rental Housing

If you're moving to Branson, you might want to try it on for size first by renting and living in the area for a short time to see if you really like it. Use the rental time to do some homework and find your dream home or acreage. If you plan on renting, we suggest two things: contact a property management agency to see what is available and get a local paper for the housing rental section. Branson has several property management firms, some of which are: Apple Real Estate, (417) 334-7888; Bart & Brown Realty, (417) 336-0300; Branson Tri-Lakes Property Management, (417) 739-1902; MO-Zark Realty, Inc., (417) 334-5253; and Shepherd of the Hills Realtors, (417) 739-4333.

Other real estate companies may also manage rentals; check with them if you call around. We can tell you that good, clean, fair-priced rentals are not abundant in Branson, especially during the season of March to December, in spite of the building boom several years ago. If you plan on renting, January and February are your best months to sign a lease. You can expect to pay $500 to $750 a month for a two-bedroom apartment. Some rentals may include water and trash service in their price, but others may expect you to pay all utilities. A two-bedroom house may rent from $500 to $900 a month, and a three-bedroom house, $800 to $1,300 a month. Recently, there has been a lot of new apartment construction targeted to affordable housing. With income restrictions, some apartments rent as low as $350 per month for two bedroom units.

Another rental alternative is a condo. The Branson area is as well stocked with condos as Lake Taneycomo is with trout. Many offer nightly and weekly rentals (see the Accommodations chapter). Here's a selection of condos that offer nightly, weekly, and long-term rentals: Treehouse on the Lake on Table Rock Lake's Indian Point, (417) 338-5199; the Village, also on Indian Point, (417) 338-5800; Foxpointe, just north of Branson, (417) 334-1990 or (800) 334-6590; Thousand Hills, just south of The Strip in Branson, (417) 336-5873 or (800) 864-4145; Plantation at Fall Creek, (417) 334-6404 or (800) 562-6636, on MO 165; and Pointe Royale, on MO 165 just north of Table Rock Dam, (417) 334-6181 or (800) 962-4710. A condo rental is a good way to "try out" Branson as you investigate longer-term commitments. The price of a condo varies a good deal depending on location, quality, amenities, and whether it is furnished or unfurnished. Rates for a one-bedroom are between $500 and $600, and a two-bedroom can cost $700 to $800 a month. A three-bedroom condo in a desirable location with fireplace, Jacuzzi, and other amenities can run $1,300 and up. With any rental you can expect to pay first and last months' rent or a security deposit, but again, that varies a good deal. Renting is a good way to become acclimated to the area, and it is also a good way to get your foot in the door to home ownership.

Buying a Home

Branson has changed more in the last decade than in the previous century, and that includes size and area, as well as economics and culture. At the 1990 census, Branson's population was less than 4,000; now it is 7,435 per the 2005 census. In 1999 the city limits of Branson grew by more than four square miles to 16 square miles, due to voluntary annexations of Pointe Royale and other areas on the southwest side of the city. The city limits now touch Table Rock Lake.

Branson's real estate market has been compared to a roller coaster ride with tremendous highs associated with its first boom in 1992–94. Between 1992 and 1993, 4,500 new motel rooms were built (a 40 percent increase), 3,100 new restaurant seats were added (a 14 percent increase), and 12,228 theater seats were constructed (a 37 percent increase). Construction went from $10.6 million in 1990 to a high of $119.5 million in 1993.

Between 2003 and 2005 there was another large construction and development boom in the tri-lakes area. Many new residential and commercial developments came on line or finally started to boom such as Branson Hills, Branson Creek, and the Branson Landing.

Growth has continued, but more steadily. In the city limits of Branson as of December 31, 2007, there were 53 theaters with a total of 59,757 seats; 207 lodging facilities with 18,808 rooms; 13 golf courses (8 championship); and 458 restaurants with 38,813 seats.

This peak in construction in 1993 actually marked an overbuilding of several segments of the market. A flood of nightly rental condominiums were sold to vacation owners during the 1993 period. With an oversupply of nightly rental condos all over town, the individual revenues dropped very quickly. New owners then flooded the market again, attempting to sell their almost new investment condo. The years 1995 to 1999 witnessed many of these owners selling their investment condos for close to half of what the original purchase price had been. In recent years, these same properties have finally appreciated back to and above the original 1993 prices. Prices soared between 2003 and 2006 as interest rates were low and the economy surged across the country. The economic downturn which has been felt nationwide in 2008 has slowly trickled into Branson as well. Currently there is a large supply of residential real estate for sale including a limited number of bank foreclosures. We have not seen the significant drops in prices that many other parts of the country have experienced, however. Branson's home prices, in general, have stayed very stable with some areas continuing to appreciate annually unlike most other parts of the country.

Branson's trademark live-entertainment theaters also experienced an oversupply situation with little demand from buyers. With a very limited number of potential buyers, several theaters built during the 1993 boom have sold for far less than what their original construction costs were. Many former music theaters have been converted to church facilities in fact. However, a smaller venue, the New Shanghai Theatre, opened in 2005, and the Dick Clark American Bandstand Theater had its grand opening in March 2006.

Much of the new construction between 1992 and 2008 has been in the timeshare industry. Time-share condominiums maintained a steady amount of new construction, with more than 80 percent of Missouri's 3,100 time-share units located in Branson. In 2004, time-share construction of $13.5 million accounted for a large portion of the $76.5 million in construction dollars. Most notable of the new construction in the Branson area is the Branson Landing project, located downtown, which opened for business in 2006.

The city purchased several properties along the downtown lakefront in order to construct this commercial and residential development. Branson Landing includes retail shops, restaurants, lodging, condominiums, and a convention center. Springfield-based Bass Pro Shops anchors the southern end, and Belk, a large nationwide fashion store, anchors the northern end. The convention center is a small portion of the development, but it is a vital step in an ongoing effort to expand the marketability of Branson while appealing to a younger demographic and remaining a family-oriented destination. A Tax Incremental Financing (TIF) bond, approved by Missouri's legislature, was used to help finance the convention center.

A second "boom" appears to be associated with the renewed growth spearheaded by the Branson Landing project. The first boom in 1993–94 experienced a heavy amount of home construction and sales. For example, there were 730 homes sold in 1993 and 814 in 1994 in the Tri-Lakes Multiple Listing Service. In 2004 there were 1,982 homes sold in this same geographic area. Low interest rates and Branson's affordable nature attracted a multitude of new residents moving into the community from all over the country. Other real estate markets across the nation have experienced "hyper-appreciation" of home prices brought on by the 40-year-low interest rates. During this time, the local Branson residential real estate market has appreciated at a smaller but steady pace. Consequently, the prices in Branson have not dropped through the floor as being witnessed in California, Florida, and Nevada. The Tri-Lakes' "affordable" nature with respect to other markets appears to be what differentiates the local and national markets. An influx of prospective buyers from outside Missouri seems to be a large portion of the continued growth. With an average home price of $152,000, the Branson area is has been and still is attractive to retirees and other home buyers leaving the congestion of urban areas.

Those interested in moving or retiring to Branson and the surrounding area will find they can pick and choose, and there are bargains to be found. Statistics and averages are misleading for this area because prices can vary widely, depending on zoning and location. There is high-priced commercially zoned property on The Strip that has sold for more than $25 a square foot, which is over a million dollars per acre, but then there are acreages in the eastern part of Taney County that can be had for less than $1,500 an acre.

Price depends not only on what others are willing to pay, but also on what you're looking for and how badly you want it. Housing in the Kimberling City, Branson, and Table Rock Lake areas includes small lake cabins for vacations and weekend getaways, condos, and full-time residences. Permanent residences range from the moderate price of modulars to more elabo-

ℹ️ Looking for a view of the water? The tri-lakes area provides Lake Taney-como, Table Rock Lake, and Bull Shoals Lake, as well as a number of year-round streams and creeks, for those who want to see water from their windows.

rate two- and three-bedroom abodes for the retiree to upper bracket four- and five-bedroom homes for larger families. You can live way back in the woods with complete privacy, or you may wish for a lakefront or lake-view location. For some the hustle and bustle of Branson is more important. If that's the case, you can find a home right in the middle of town. Building-lot prices generally start from a low of about $7,000. Homes, lots, and acreages with a lake view or lake access are, of course, more expensive. Lake-view lots range from $25,000 to $60,000. Very special lakefront lots are priced in the $80,000 to $200,000 range.

Although Branson's population in the city proper is just more than 7,000, an additional 18,000 people live within a 4-mile radius. There are homes on acreages, in tiny subdivisions with three or four homes, and in large developments with hundreds of homes. Weekend cabins can be purchased for less than $100,000 in the extended market area while a small three-bedroom (starter) home can be purchased for as low as $100,000. In general, a modest home can be purchased at or under $200,000 with homes in the $300,000 to $500,000 range being located on the lake or on a golf course.

There appears to be a large supply of higher-end homes (over $350,000) at the current time. At the end of 2008, there were 378 homes listed for sale in Stone and Taney Counties that were over $350,000. In the last six months of 2008, only 52 homes sold in the MLS for this same price category. This segment of the economy appears to have taken a decline, but affluent visitors will discover that the beauty of the Branson lakes and golf courses and the relatively inexpensive cost of living could prove to be a good combination for them to find their dream home. A $350,000 home

in Branson is often in excess of 3,500 square feet and is on a lake or the golf course. That price wouldn't get you near the greens in many other areas of the nation.

In general, the four-county area of Taney, Stone, Christian, and Greene has seen the average price of a home rise over the last decade. The booming economy has prompted people to build bigger and more expensive houses. For the four-county area, the average cost of a home rose from about $100,000 in 2001 to $152,000 in 2008. Figures we offer are ballpark averages, and anything we present has two caveats: do your homework and ask questions. If you're coming from either of the coastal areas, you may consider the real estate here cheap. On Commercial Street and Main Street you may see tourists and potential retirees gawking at the pictures and prices of homes posted on the windows of real estate offices. We still hear, "Wow, that's really cheap!" and "What I'd give to have that house on my lot back home!" In fact, the complaint by locals is that people retiring from Chicago, New York, or California can buy twice the house they had there for half as much—and in so doing drive up the price of real estate for local home buyers. However, others from small towns in the Midwest wonder why the prices are so high. It all depends on where you come from and what you're willing to do and pay to move to the Ozarks.

If you're city folk and not used to buying rural property, get advice from your Realtor. Learn to ask questions, the more the better. How deep is the well? How many gallons per minute does it produce? Where's the septic field? When was it built? Does it meet the current standards and code? We recommend that you hire a property inspector. When you move to a rural area, don't assume that you'll have full-time paid police and fire departments. Sometimes there are only a sheriff and a few deputies to cover an entire county. As for fire protection, often you are the fire department, if you want to serve with your neighbors as one of several volunteer firefighters. Your local real estate agent can give you the lowdown on such issues, but you have to know the questions to ask.

The drop in the market after the boom in the early 1990s was a long one, and the professional mortality rate among real estate agents was high. Only the best survived, and they did so by cutting back and tightening their belts. We are expecting the same during this current recession/depression time frame, however short-lived it may be. The number of companies declined, with quite a few going out of business, and there were lots of mergers and buyouts in the 1990s. Unfortunately, the current tourism economy is based upon how much tourists spend on vacation. With everyone tightening their belts, Branson's employers have had to as well. In any event, the local real estate market has, over the years, gone through a number of cycles, as the market has slacked off, only to rise again on the next wave.

The local tourist economy drives the real estate market. Several long-term development projects indicate that some people with big bucks are bullish about the area's development. One development project, the 8,500-acre Branson Creek, south of Hollister, saw its opening in 1999 and now offers a variety of residences with its two championship golf courses. This is also the location of the new Branson Regional Airport which opened in May of 2009. This new airport will enable both charter service scheduled air service from other hubs like Atlanta, Chicago, and Denver.

Since any future development depends on getting more people into the area, the city has taken on a massive effort of building "feeder roads" and street widening. US 65 from Springfield to Branson is completely four-lane now, making the commute between the two towns just 25 minutes. The first segment of the new Highroad, MO 465, is complete from north US 65 over to MO 76, just east of the entrance to Silver Dollar City. This cuts the drive time to Silver Dollar City significantly. The MO 13 bypass around Reeds Spring opened in 2003. A second bridge has been built across Lake Taneycomo, and US 65 is four-laned to the Arkansas border. Plans are in place to build a second MO 76 bridge to relieve the congestion that accumulates on the old "arch bridge" built downtown in 1930. Tourists will find that the "road to Branson" is paved and increasingly straight. These better ways to drive into Branson combined with the new Branson airport are the foundation for keeping tourism and retirement growing in the tri-lakes area as a whole.

The Branson/Lakes Area Chamber of Commerce marketing budget is at an all-time high and is aimed at increasing Branson tourist counts to record levels. The future of tourism in Branson looks good, and that means the long-term real estate market will likely be bright. Look in the yellow pages of the local phone directory, and you'll see several pages of real estate companies, all of them eager to sell you a piece of the Branson action, that retirement home or an Ozarks summer home. Most of the companies we have listed belong to the multiple-listing service (MLS) of the Tri-Lakes Board of Realtors, but you might want to ask an individual company if it has all local listings available. Even though the Ozark Mountain country encompasses many towns, we've listed only, in alphabetical order, the major companies in Branson and the immediate surrounding communities.

Neighborhood Areas and Developments

Though Branson is known as a neighborly town and prides itself on that reputation, only about 17 percent of the area within the city limits was actually zoned residential. With the annexing of the Branson North subdivision and the Pointe Royale development, that figure has gone up to about 28 percent.

Most of the people here live outside the city proper. Like the Ozarks—which has a myriad of micro-environments, depending on the elevation, slope, and geology—neighborhoods cover a wide range. There are subdivisions of up to a dozen homes, large subdivisions of more than a hundred homes, neighborhood areas of several blocks in town, and gated golf communities that are out in the country but have all the amenities of a big city. A home in Omaha, Arkansas, Forsyth, or Branson West still puts you close to Branson's activities and entertainment as well as its shopping. You can find a wide variety of options, so if you're looking for a particular kind of lifestyle, community, or environment, it's best to let your Realtor know.

A local wag remarked that "Branson has been growing so quickly, we could have a subdivision of the month club." There is truth to his remark. In fact, a computer survey of subdivisions and developments in Taney and Stone Counties turns up more than 700 developments. We have River Bluff Estates, Country Bluff Estates, Friendly Hills, Savannah Hills, Cougar Trails, Skyline Drive, Blue Meadows, Woodridge Estates, Notch Estates, the Woodlands, the Patterson Duck Club, and other names designed to attract the ear and give one "the right address." We've listed only some of the larger, better-known developments, both old and recent, and areas that we locals consider a neighborhood or area by name, even though it may consist technically of a number of old adjacent developments.

Such neighborhoods may not be for you; you may find the home of your dreams on a small acreage or tucked away in some hollow or atop a hill with virtually no neighbors. Or you may like the quiet of some of the tiny subdivisions with no more than a half dozen homes. Look around; the variety will surprise you!

Inside the City Limits of Branson and Hollister

BRANSON NORTH

Developed in the 1960s before US 65 bypassed downtown Branson, the town has grown to enclose this large, wooded area. It has James F. Epps Road as a border on the west and MO 248 on the north, with entrance to the development from MO 248. Pioneer developer Dwayne Henss promoted the area as "Branson's best address," and in spite of many newer developments, it still is one of the best. Moving to Branson North almost symbolizes to the community that you've made it. Most streets are curbed and guttered. The modern and upscale construction, with many of the original forest's trees remaining and established plantings that have matured, presents a cultivated but woodsy environment. Skaggs Community Health Center and down-

town shopping are close, and it's easy to get to The Strip, too. Homes start at about $150,000 and top out at $600,000.

CANTWELL ADDITION AREA

The Cantwell Addition Area takes in several subdivisions that grew over the years around Cantwell Park. It is bounded by MO 76 on the south, US 65 on the east, Roark Valley Road on the west, and Roark Creek and the railroad tracks on the north. Because the area has developed over many years, some homes date from the late 1950s, while other homes were built within the past year. The neighborhood is quiet, with large trees and established home landscaping. It has easy access to downtown, Cedar Ridge Shopping Center, and The Strip. Stockstill Park is close by, on the north side of Roark Creek. Homes are neat and well kept and range from $60,000 to $230,000.

COUNTRY BLUFF ESTATES

Located off Fall Creek Road on approximately 50 acres, this is an upscale subdivision with paved and guttered streets and central sewer and water. It is only minutes from the east side of The Strip and MO 165 to the west. Homes are new and modern, mostly of brick construction, and are built on large lots. It is obvious that great effort has been made to preserve large, existing native oaks and walnuts. There are approximately 106 restricted lots. Homes range from $150,000 to more than $300,000.

COZY COVE CONDOMINIUM COMMUNITY
341 Loganberry Rd.
(417) 335-2644

On the banks of Bee Creek at its confluence with Lake Taneycomo is the gated condominium community of Cozy Cove. Cozily situated on 35 acres in the Bee Creek valley beneath Oak Bluff, the development consists of 58 two- and three-bedroom units. It's north of Branson's city limits just off US 65 and is only minutes from Branson Junior High School, downtown Branson, and MO 248. The development has county water and its own community sewage system. Streets are paved and curbed. Amenities include a boat dock with access to Lake Taneycomo, a swimming pool, and a 12-acre private park at the mouth of the creek. Units range from $75,000 to $100,000. Access to Cozy Cove is the first right (Loganberry Road) off Bee Creek Road before you cross the creek.

HIAWATHA HEIGHTS NEIGHBORHOOD

Once considered way out in the country, this area is now in the heart of the town. This area has US 65 as a border to the east, 76 Country Music Boulevard to the north and west, and Cliff Drive to the south. The homes on Cliff Drive have a spectacular view of Lake Taneycomo, and the Cliff Drive address was considered the place to live when Branson was very tiny. Most of the streets are curbed as part of Branson's efforts to curb and gutter all city streets. The area still has some forest, and giant established trees in many of the yards of older homes make for a feeling of being in the woods.

The neighborhood offers insulation from the commercial development on The Strip, yet residents are only minutes from downtown Branson, the hustle and bustle on The Strip, and any point north or south of Branson via US 65. The neighborhood is close to Alexander Park on the Taneycomo lakefront and the jogging track at adjacent Sunset Park (see the Recreation and the Outdoors chapter). Homes range from $70,000 to $300,000.

LAKEWOOD ESTATES
700 Parnell Dr.
(417) 334-4170

One of Branson's earlier high-quality developments, this neighborhood of 53 duplex condos (106 units) has a private entrance and maintains its own streets. Right on the banks of Lake Taneycomo, only 2 blocks from Skaggs Community Health Center and a block from the Branson Community Center, this neighborhood has been the choice of retirees and professionals who don't want to bother with home maintenance. The neighborhood is totally managed by the home owners. The assessment fee includes

i We all know that trees clean the air and add beauty to any community. Most developers take pains to preserve existing trees, and Branson has a tree ordinance that encourages builders and developers to do so and to plant replacements for those destroyed during construction. According to a poll of tourists, the fifth-ranked reason for visiting the Branson area was "nature and the beauty of the environment."

trash pickup, home maintenance, insurance, and ground maintenance. The development is on the city sewer system. Amenities include a pool clubhouse, small fishing dock, and workshop for hobbies and crafts. Parnell Park, with its tennis courts, is only a block away. The development is unusual in Branson: it is one of few totally flat areas in the city. Units in Lakewood Estates sell from $75,000 to $133,000.

McGEE ADDITION, HOLLISTER

This old, established neighborhood is nestled between Lake Taneycomo on the north and a steep hill and bluff on the south. Its eastern boundary is the railroad and trestle over Lake Taneycomo, and its western line is US 65. Entrance to the area is via Railroad Avenue from US Business 65 in Hollister. The neighborhood evolved and developed during a period of 40 years or more. It has homes that range from trailers and modest summer cabins to older expensive homes with enviable boat docks and slips on Lake Taneycomo. It is right across the lake from the homes that border Alexander Park and Sunset Park in Branson. The new neighborhood's location makes for easy access to downtown Branson or Hollister, yet it's only minutes from The Strip and its activities. More recent development west of US 65 is accessed through the subdivision's Wilshire Drive, which goes under the highway. The newer area includes Taneycomo Terraces, condominiums for those 55 and older. Homes in the McGee Addition can range from a low of $35,000 to a high of $170,000.

MURPHY ADDITION

Developed largely during the 1970s, this area is near the heart of Branson's entertainment activity on 76 Country Boulevard, which forms its southern boundary. Roark Valley Road provides its northern boundary. Dr. Good Drive, named for a respected president of College of the Ozarks, forms its western edge. Murphy Park, with its five acres of playgrounds, picnic area, and sand volleyball courts, serves as the neighborhood's center. It has easy access to The Strip and downtown Branson. The Branson Heights Shopping Center is nearby. Homes range from $80,000 to $150,000.

OAK BLUFF

Located on the bluff point formed by the cut Bee Creek makes to enter Lake Taneycomo, the development boasts a spectacular east view of Lake Taneycomo 350 feet below and the valley across the lake. It is one of Branson's most exclusive home sites. Streets are paved but not curbed and the area is on city water and sewer. Homes in Oak Bluff start at $240,000. Access to Oak Bluff is via Fagan Drive off Bee Creek Road near Branson High School and then turning onto Oak Bluff Road.

ROCKWOOD HILLS

Rockwood Hills, located north of Branson just off MO 248, offers quick access to the west end of The Strip via the Shepherd of the Hills Expressway and is only 2 miles from downtown Branson. The subdivision is on the north side of Branson, just outside the city limits. Rockwood Hills is accessed from MO 248 via Eagle Rock Road. The neighborhood surrounds a five-acre lake, which is a favorite playground and fishing hole for neighborhood kids. Roads are paved, community water is available, and sewage service is via individual septic tank. Homes in Rockwood Hills are priced between $70,000 and $190,000.

POINTE ROYALE VILLAGE AND COUNTRY CLUB
MO 165
(417) 334-0634

People stopping at the scenic view on MO 165 south of Hollister see a bucolic community spread out beneath them in the White River valley. That's Pointe Royale Village and Country Club on MO 165 opposite the Welk Resort. Pointe Royale sets the Branson standard for country club–style living and gated-community security. It is the home or second home for 961 families. Developed on 290 acres along upper Lake Taneycomo, Pointe Royale is only 3 miles from Table Rock Lake and 2 miles from Branson's 76 Country Boulevard. Clearing of land began in the spring of 1985, and construction started on condominium units and the 18-hole championship golf course that fall. The course opened in October 1986. Nearly 200,000 square yards of sod were used in building the challenging 6,175-yard, par 70 course. There are 12 holes with water hazards.

Created by a master plan to achieve harmony with the environment, Pointe Royale condominiums, patio homes, custom-built homes, golf-front, and lakeside-site homes make for an idyllic living area. Golfers like the pro shop. A clubhouse, swimming pool, and tennis courts complement the heart of Point Royale. The golf course weaves ingeniously through the entire development. Pointe Royale currently has 249 single-family residences and patio homes as well as almost 600 condominiums. It is home for both year-round residents and seasonal visitors, and building construction and real estate sales continue at a high growth rate. Pointe Royale offers nightly condo rentals, too. Pointe Royale Realty handles the listings. Call (417) 334-0079.

NEIGHBORHOODS OUTSIDE THE CITY LIMITS OF BRANSON AND HOLLISTER

BRANSON CREEK
100 Branson Creek Blvd.
(417) 336-0940, (866) 334-7817
www.privatecommunities.com/missouri/bransoncreek
Go figure. Branson Creek is an impressive new development of 7,500 acres south of Hollister in the Turkey Creek valley and watershed, a premier

residential community sculpted into the natural beauty of the Ozarks. Perhaps they wanted to capitalize on the Branson fame when choosing the name, but then they kept the local name of Murder Rock for one of the two golf courses. But you can't poke fun of the fact that Branson Creek was voted in the Top 100 Master Planned Communities by *Where to Retire* magazine. Perhaps the name is symbolic of the mini-metropolis that the several small local communities of Branson, Hollister, Kirbyville, and Point Lookout are becoming, as access to the new Branson Airport is through this development. Branson Creek blends breathtaking surroundings, community amenities, and outdoor recreation into an upscale development, consisting of distinct neighborhoods each designed to appeal to a specific lifestyle. The community offers a unique combination of nature and recreation, from a stroll up to the greens of their championship golf courses, to hiking, tennis, swimming, and boating. Homes start at about $250,000. Drive south on US 65. Look for the Branson Creek and Airport exit to the left.

EMERALD POINTE
MO 265
(417) 336-8700, (800) 872-7889

Emerald Pointe, developed by Branson businessman and theme-park owner Gary Snadon, is the area's newest planned community of more than 600 acres. It is just 4 miles south of Hollister on County Road 265-20, just off MO 265. All lots have views of Table Rock Lake, and the development includes single-family homes as well as town houses and condominiums. The architectural restrictions ensure strong property values. It has underground utilities, sewer and water service, and curbed and guttered streets. The development includes a spacious marina, gated entry, and clubhouse with complete amenities, including tennis courts and a swimming pool. Big Cedar Lodge and the Jack Nicklaus signature golf course are close by. The location gives views, privacy, and seclusion, yet easy access to all that Branson offers.

> **i** If you're looking at property around the area, a good map that has all the roads less traveled is the Taney County 911 map. You can obtain a copy at the Branson/ Lakes Area Chamber of Commerce office on MO 248 for $2.80.

OAKMONT COMMUNITY
2308 MO 86, Ridgedale
(417) 334-2106

One of the first really big developments around Table Rock Lake, Oakmont is south of Hollister near the Arkansas line. It is between US 65 and the Long Creek Arm of Table Rock Lake. It consists of a variety of pocket developments and communities, from mobile home clusters to large exclusive lake-view and lakefront lots with homes as expensive as you'll find anywhere in the area. Amenities include the Executive Timbers Resort and Golf Club (see the Recreation and the Outdoors chapter) and a community recreation center.

The development is near the Big Cedar Lodge and Top of the Rock restaurant and golf course (see the Restaurants and Accommodations chapters). Most of the streets and roads are paved. Water is by individual or community wells. Sewage is by individual septic systems. Prices of homes depend on restrictions, lot sizes, and lake access and views.

RIVERSIDE ESTATES, HOLLISTER

Nestled on the low-water side of a bend in Lake Taneycomo, Riverside Estates provides a great view of a bluff across the lake and easy access to the lake with a community launch ramp. Pointe Royale development is just around the bend on the opposite side of the lake. Short Creek forms the eastern boundary of the neighborhood, and Lake Taneycomo completes the western and northern boundaries. Streets are paved, and some are guttered; it has community water and a community sewer system. Both homes and condominiums are in the development, with homes ranging from $90,000 to $400,000-plus, depending on view and lake access.

The neighborhood is neat and clean, with lots of large trees along the lakefront and in the yards of homes. The area offers seclusion but is only five minutes from Branson and Hollister. Riverside Estates can be reached via Acacia Club Road from MO V south of Hollister and Point Lookout or by Iowa Colony Road from MO 165.

SADDLEBROOKE
15111 US 65 South
(417) 443-6500

Saddlebrooke is a master-planned community located on US 65 14 miles north of Branson, just on the Christian County line. Not only does it have its own zip code, it has paved roads, underground utilities, swimming pool, tennis courts, four parks, full equine stable, hiking and biking trails, and 15 miles of streams and creeks. Large building sites ranging from one to three acres are available, with lot prices starting at $39,900. New homes in the development start at $289,900. Coming into Branson from the north, you can't miss the rustic log-cabin rest stop, information center, and Saddlebrooke sales center.

SPRING MEADOWS, HOLLISTER

Spring Meadows is another popular subdivision that is conveniently located 1 mile east of Branson just off MO 76. It overlooks a small wet-weather creek valley and is accessed from MO 76 via Meadow Parkway. Holiday Hills Golf Course is only a quarter mile away, and Forsyth is only 12 miles farther east. Downtown Branson is only a three-minute drive to the west. Streets are paved and curbed, and community water is available. Sewer service is handled by a community sewage plant. Homes are priced between $60,000 and $180,000.

STONEBRIDGE VILLAGE
1600 Ledgestone Way, Reeds Spring
(417) 336-1700

A 3,200-acre development just east of Silver Dollar City at the intersection of MO 76 and MO 265, StoneBridge Village is Branson's newest gated community. Developed by Cooper Communities, this still-growing neighborhood has the 18-hole Ledgestone Championship Golf Course at its heart (see the Recreation and the Outdoors chapter). Cooper Communities has been building master-planned communities since 1954, and property owners enjoy access to four other private recreational communities in Arkansas, Tennessee, and South Carolina. StoneBridge offers homesites, townhomes, and condominiums. StoneBridge has vacation exchanges with RCI in more than 2,900 locations around the world. For those owners and StoneBridge's permanent residents, it offers amenities of a 20,000-square-foot clubhouse, lighted tennis courts, a swimming pool, an exercise room, and a nature trail. The carefully planned community is only minutes from Silver Dollar City and Branson's famed entertainment on The Strip, and it's 20 minutes from the three major lakes (Bull Shoals, Table Rock, and Taneycomo), with more than 90,000 acres of combined water surface area.

SUMMERBROOKE AND MILL CREEK

Location is the key for these two subdivisions, just north of Branson at the intersection of US 65 and MO F, and the Highroad 465. Summerbrooke continues with the trend of affordable housing in the Branson area, with homes ranging from $130,000 to $190,000. Adjoining Mill Creek has larger half-acre lots with homes ranging from $200,000 to $300,000. Steve Matlock of Matlock, Inc., states that the location, near the new Branson High School with easy access to US 65 and the Branson Highroad, and affordable, quality-built homes are the keys to these subdivisions' success.

TABLE ROCK HEIGHTS, HOLLISTER

Table Rock Heights is aptly named. This hillside community has a panoramic view of Table Rock Lake and Dam and the Taneycomo Valley. The development is about 300 feet higher than the scenic view overlook on MO 165 south of Hollister. Entrance to the neighborhood is via Table Rook Heights Road from MO 165 and MO 265. The neighborhood is only an eight-minute drive from

Branson and Hollister. Lots are large, and the steep hillsides are thickly wooded. Community water is available; sewage is by individual septic systems. Homes range from $100,000 to $220,000.

i Some rural properties have community water but most do not. If your dream lot doesn't, you should know that drilling a well to the necessary 400 to 600 feet, casing it, and buying a pump will add $4,000 to $6,000 to the cost of constructing your home.

TANEYCOMO ACRES, BRANSON

Just down the lake and across from Point Lookout, Taneycomo Acres is on the ridge between Cooper Creek and Lake Taneycomo and is about as near to the city of Branson as can be without being in it. The neighborhood offers seclusion but is only four minutes from downtown Branson and the east end of The Strip. Nearby is the Thousand Hills Golf Course, and there is easy access to MO 165 and Table Rock Lake via Fall Creek Road. Access to the area is by several streets off Fall Creek Road. The development has paved streets and community water and sewer. Lots are large, and there are large areas with forest. Since this is a fairly recent development, homes are modern and range from $100,000 to $300,000.

Real Estate Companies

APPLE REAL ESTATE
180 Mall Rd., Hollister
(417) 334-7888
www.applerealestate.com
Suzy Samsel's business card says she "specializes in honesty," and this area native has a long track record of selling commercial and residential properties in Arkansas and Missouri. Apple Real Estate is especially active with property listings south of Hollister and in the Missouri-Arkansas border area. She and her husband also handle rentals management and nightly condo rentals.

AUX ARCS REAL ESTATE
14678 MO 13 North, Kimberling City
(417) 739-5487, (800) 296-LAKE
www.aux-arcs.com
Pronounced simply "Ozarks," this firm was founded more than ten years ago by seasoned area Realtors to provide comprehensive, professional real estate services to Ozark Mountain country. Aux Arcs specializes in sales of residential and commercial properties on Table Rock Lake and in Branson and Kimberling City. The Aux Arcs office is equipped with an up-to-date computer system. Every agent has a personal computer linked to the local multiple-listing service. Agents can find property in the area that fits your needs, instantly. All office computers are networked so that each agent is able to access the others' files and offer service to another agent's customers and clients when necessary.

BRANSON BEST REALTY, INC.
1033 West Main St.
(417) 339-1770
www.bransonbestrealty.com
This is one of the newest offices in the area, but not new in the business. Shawn and Don Boushehri bring their combined ten-plus years of experience working with two of the largest corporations to this family-run business, where they emphasize personal customer service. Lisa Boushehri is broker and, along with three sales associates, personally answers phones from 8 a.m. to 9 p.m. seven days a week. They specialize in condo sales, as well as residential and commercial properties.

i Branson usually has several snowfalls each winter, with the deepest ones in February or early March, but they usually don't last more than several days. Average annual snowfall is 15.9 inches. Usually school districts build five snow days into the schedules for adverse weather conditions.

BRANSON HOMETOWN REALTY
499 Coffee Rd.
(417) 230-0567

Rex Asselin got off the water and into land. This third-generation Branson resident and his parents created the Sammy Lane Pirate Cruise, and Asselin was Captain Rex for a number of years. His grandparents and Don Gardner helped bring golf to the Ozarks in the development of the Holiday Hills Golf Course in 1938. Vintage photographs of his ancestors and interesting things they did or witnessed decorate the office walls. Co-owner of Branson Hometown Realty with Rex is Pamela Ledbetter, a fifth-generation native. Thus the agency's motto is "Our hometown heritage is your advantage." The company, founded in 1989, handles both commercial and residential listings. Branson Hometown Realty is active in developing Meadow Brooke Ranches, just northeast of Branson near Walnut Shade.

BRANSON REALTY
205 W Atlantic St., #E
(417) 337-3141
www.bransonrealty.com

Richard T. Hall is the owner of Branson Realty, the oldest real estate company in Branson, in business since 1948. Hall and his staff deal in both residential and commercial property, with the bulk of their listings being commercial.

CAROL JONES REALTORS
45 Notch Shopping Lane,
Branson West & Reeds Spring
(417) 338-2022

1484 State Highway 248
(417) 335-5180, (417) 335-5950
www.caroljones.com

Carol Jones, which has its headquarters in Springfield, also has offices in Branson and Branson West. It is one of the older established companies in the area, specializing in both residential and commercial properties. More than 30 sales associates work out of the Branson area offices. Carol Jones has had great success because of a multimedia approach to advertising, including newspapers, direct mail, distinctive signs, magazines, the Internet, and a TV program, *Homebuyer's Guide*. The company even makes copies of the program to mail to potential customers moving into the area.

COLDWELL BANKER FIRST CHOICE
16205 US 160, Forsyth
(417) 546-4766

Owner Rick Brown and his team of five brokers cover the area, but they specialize in properties in the Forsyth, Rockaway Beach, eastern Taney County, and Lake Bull Shoals areas. The company prides itself on its personal service and in a decade has established a reputation for reliability.

ERA TABLE ROCK REALTY
2101 MO 248
(417) 334-3138
www.era.com

The original Table Rock Realty was formed in 1950 when the U.S. Army Corps of Engineers needed to purchase land for the new Table Rock Lake. The office was in downtown Branson until 1996, when the firm moved to its present location on MO 248. Jim Asbury is the broker-owner, with an additional twelve sales associates. The firm mostly services Stone and Taney Counties, but it is also licensed to serve outside of its home area.

FOGGY RIVER REALTY
122 Symington Place, Hollister
(417) 334-5433, (888) 934-5433
www.foggyriver.com

Broker-owner Anne Symington has established, in just a decade, a reputation for finding the just-right property or house for her clients. She and Booker Cox III take the time to ask the right questions so they know what you're looking for and won't waste time showing you something that doesn't fit your needs. Symington was a top seller for other area firms and finally set out on her own with great success. From her office on Turkey Creek on the east side of the bridge in Hollister, she has built a reputation that ranks high among locals.

i **There have been cases of mosquito-borne West Nile virus in the Ozarks. If you are bringing horses into the area, make certain they are vaccinated. To protect yourself, wear long-sleeved clothing in mosquito-infested areas and apply repellent that contains DEET.**

GERKEN & ASSOCIATES REALTORS
1157 MO 76 West
(417) 334-1892
Owner-broker Duane Gerken served as president of the Tri-Lakes Board of Realtors in 1985, and in 1998 he was installed as president of the Missouri Association of Realtors. He's been active in the real estate scene for three decades, and he helped start the Tri-Lakes Board's multiple-listing service. Kay Gerken is following in her husband's footsteps and was inducted as the Missouri Association of Realtors President for 2004. Both manage the firm, whose staff of six has a solid community reputation. Gerken & Associates deals with all facets of local property—residential and commercial.

KIMBERLING HILLS REAL ESTATE
12907 MO 13 South, Kimberling City
(417) 739-4367, (800) 659-4687
www.kimberlinghillsrealestate.com
Just south of the Kimberling Golf Course, Kimberling Hills Real Estate can boast of being one of the oldest companies in the Table Rock Lake area. It was founded in 1976. John and Michelle Nordin, Dennis Wood (Stone County-area state representative), Connie Emmons, and nine other representatives specialize in that area of Table Rock Lake real estate. They have a high degree of customer loyalty because Kimberling Hills Real Estate knows its people are what sells real estate.

RE/MAX ASSOCIATED BROKERS
109 North Sixth St.
(417) 334-1374, (800) 220-2302
www.realtor.com/branson/remax

Since the company's inception in 1988, owner Kelly Grisham, with a staff of 12 sales associates, has consistently ranked in the top three in Branson in number of transactions and dollar volume sold. RE/MAX lists and sells not only residential property but also lots, acreages, condominiums, commercial development, motel/resorts, and business properties.

RE/MAX TOWN AND LAKE REALTY
14788 MO 13 Branson West
(417) 739-3636
www.notchrealty.com
Owner-broker Tammy Cooper specializes in lake properties as well and has quickly become one of the top-selling agents in the Branson area. Property management for rentals is another service Notch Realty offers investors and potential tenants.

ROUND THE CLOCK REALTY, INC.
138 Wintergreen Rd.
(417) 334-1980
Round the Clock has lived up to its name by working around the clock for its clients. Its unusual name and sign have been associated with the Branson area for more than 20 years. Owner Don Horner and the staff of 10 salespeople have earned a reputation for success, honesty, integrity, and hard work. Round the Clock deals in both residential and commercial property.

SHEPHERD OF THE HILLS REALTORS
Kimberling City Shopping Center
Kimberling City
(417) 739-4333, (800) 748-8163
MO 76 West
(417) 338-8400
www.shepherdhillsrealtors.com
Shepherd of the Hills Realtors first hung out a shingle in Kimberling City in 1963, anticipating great development as the result of the recently impounded Table Rock Lake. Owned by fourth-generation Ozarks native Layne Morrill, Shepherd of the Hills Realtors is one of the oldest companies in the area, specializing in both residential and commercial properties. The Branson office,

just west of Silver Dollar City, was opened in 1992. Broker-owner Morrill is past president of the National Association of Realtors.

TRI-LAKES REALTORS, INC.
18062 MO 13, Suite B, Branson West
(417) 335-5253

MO 39, Shell Knob
(417) 858-3344
www.trilakes.com/
Tri-Lakes Realtors, with offices in Ridgedale, Cape Fair, Branson West, Shell Knob, and Branson, specializes in selling residential, land, and commercial properties. The company is bullish on the area's growth and expects increased volume of sales due to the increased interest in Branson as a major retirement region.

WEISZ COMMERCIAL REALTY, INC.
180 Mall Rd., Suite K, Hollister
(417) 334-3310
Mark Weisz is president of Weisz Commercial Realty and is Branson's first full-time commercial broker. Those seeking commercial or investment properties in Branson call Mark first. He is a member of the Commercial Investment Real Estate institute and has earned the Real Estate Cyberspace Specialist designation from the Real Estate Cyberspace Society. Weisz is the past president and the 1998 commercial chair for the Tri-Lakes Board of Realtors and is currently the Realtors' Political Action Committee chair for the Missouri Association of Realtors. He also serves on the Branson/Lakes Area Chamber of Commerce's Community and Economic Development Council and is the past president of the Tri-Lakes Community Theatre.

Real Estate Publications
A handsome, glossy publication about the area that contains relocation and demographic information is *Slip Away*, published by the Branson/Lakes Area Chamber of Commerce. If you are moving to the area, call them for a copy at (417) 334-4136 or fax (417) 334-4139. You should also request a relocation packet and visitor packet. The materials will give you a broad perspective on the area. Requesting the publication will also get you on the list of the Tri-Lakes Board of Realtors, with more than 500 members, and you'll start receiving brochures and information from area real estate companies.

Discover Real Estate Magazine, (417) 334-3161, is a monthly publication with information about the area and lists of properties and real estate companies. It is published by the *Branson Tri-Lakes Daily News*, which includes the magazine with subscriptions.

Parade of Homes, (417) 334-6671, is a monthly publication that's available free in local real estate offices and on racks in restaurants, malls, and local grocery stores. It contains area demographic information and other facts and figures of interest to people who might be moving to the area or buying property. It also contains a number of local companies' real estate ads and listings. *Parade of Homes* is distributed nationally by subscription, $25 per year, by calling the number above.

i **If you're interested in Ozarks history and culture as well as the shows and crafts fairs scene, *The Ozarks Mountaineer* is a bimonthly magazine that covers the entire Ozarks, in both Missouri and Arkansas. Check the Web site www.ozarksmountaineer.com for information.**

RETIREMENT

The National Tour Association and the American Bus Association have rated Branson among their top tour destinations for the last 15 years. Since most motor-coach travelers are older than 55, it is clear that people in this age bracket consider Branson one of their favorite places to visit.

It is also fast becoming one of their favorite places to live. In the last few years, Branson has been rated by publications such as *Money* and *Where to Retire* as one of the best retirement cities in the United States. Recent population figures reflect the growing interest in the tri-lakes area. In the decade 1990–2000, towns in Stone and Taney Counties registered population increases from 15 percent to 129 percent. And growth since the last census has continued. Robin Amoker, professor of sociology at Missouri State University, projects a half million new Ozarkers by 2020, with most of the growth being in Stone, Taney, Christian, and Webster Counties. "Increasingly, the growth will be fueled by retirees looking for the 'good life,'" says Amoker.

The percentage of people older than 60 in Stone County is estimated at more than 65 percent, and the average age in Taney County is 45. Big-name stars, entertainment, golf courses, and outlet malls may lure visitors here, but it's the scenery, climate, fishing, availability of health care, and good old-fashioned Ozark Mountain hospitality that lure retirees.

Local county governments have done their share to attract older residents. The Stone County Senior Services Fund is a five-cent-per-$100 assessed valuation tax on real estate, which was passed in 1992 for the sole purpose of providing services to citizens older than sixty. The goal is to help people stay at home and out of nursing homes. Most of the revenue goes to the Stone County Council on Aging, the agency responsible for delivering meals to home-bound seniors and providing them with housekeeping services. In addition to providing money to the Stone County Council on Aging, the service fund helps support the Ozarks Lake Country Senior Center in Kimberling City and the Crane Senior Citizens Center.

The list of natural amenities in Ozark Mountain Country rivals that of other major retirement areas across the United States. We have four

distinct seasons here, unlike Florida and Texas, and the winters are much milder than in the New England states. From your retirement condo overlooking one of the area's three lakes, you can watch the leaves turn in mid-October, the snow fall in January, the flowers bloom in late April, and the grandkids water-ski in July. Trout fishing on Lake Taneycomo outdoes any in the Midwest. With a golf course practically on every corner, retired golfers can spend their days tearing up the greens and their nights taking in free music shows. That's right, free shows. Each year, when the theaters open in March and April, some offer what are called area-appreciation shows. Residents of Stone and Taney Counties get in for free. A donation is sometimes requested, often a contribution of a local charity, and seats are usually based on availability. The entertainers like local residents to see their shows so they can make recommendations to tourists during the year. Some of the theaters even offer area-appreciation shows at the beginning of the Christmas season as well.

The undeniable hubs of activity for seniors are the community centers in Branson, Forsyth, and Kimberling City. These centers are partially funded by the Southwest Missouri Office on Aging and serve lunch each weekday for a donation of $3. Home-bound seniors can have lunch delivered. The centers offer a variety of activities ranging from bridge games to tennis matches. Many of the area fraternal organizations and clubs meet at the centers.

One thing the tri-lakes area is not short on is clubs. Each week the *Branson Tri-Lakes Daily News* publishes a listing of club meetings and reports. We have a club for just about every interest imaginable, from amateur ham radio operators to Rose O'Neill fans.

Condominium developments, time-shares, apartments, and housing developments all seem to attract retirees. Many retirees choose to live near Kimberling City, Forsyth, or Reeds Spring instead of inside the Branson city limits, due to the shortage of housing in Branson as well as the shortage of available residentially zoned property. Besides, only a few neighborhoods in Branson can boast a view of the lake.

Many part-time residents enjoy campground living during the summer and fall. Branson has a number of campgrounds, RV parks, and mobile home parks that attract retirees. (For more information see the Campgrounds and RV Parks chapter.)

After you've seen all the shows and visited all the antiques shops, you may be looking for something a little more meaningful to do with your time. Consider volunteering at one of the many area libraries, senior centers, home health agencies, charities, or adult basic education centers. If you need help finding your niche, call RSVP in Springfield at (417) 862-3595. (For more information see the listing later in this chapter.) They should be able to put you to work right away.

Whether you choose to spend your time enjoying the quiet beauty of the Ozark hills from your assisted-living facility or volunteering to work on the Christmas parade, the tri-lakes area is a retiree-friendly place. After all, almost eight million people a year come here, and many of them choose to stay.

SENIOR SERVICES

SOUTHWEST MISSOURI OFFICE ON AGING
1735 South Fort St., Springfield
(417) 862-0762, (800) 497-0822
www.swmoa.com
The Southwest Missouri Office on Aging (SMOA) provides funding, training, and support for senior centers in 17 counties in southwestern Missouri. SMOA sponsors the Daily Bread program at the senior centers in Stone and Taney Counties. SMOA also provides help with housekeeping, shopping, and meals for a nominal donation. If you would like to volunteer or need assistance, call SMOA or one of the senior centers listed in this section. You can find links and addresses for all community centers in the counties they serve at their Web site.

i If you're retiring to the southwest Missouri Ozarks, you can get a free *Directory of Resources for Seniors and Caregivers* by calling toll free (800) 497-0822 or requesting online at www.swmoa.com.

TANEY COUNTY HEALTH DEPARTMENT
1440 MO 248, Suite J
(417) 334-4544

15479 US 160, Forsyth
(417) 546-4725
www.taneycohealth.org
The Taney County Health Department provides free blood pressure clinics a number of times each month at various locations in Branson. Check the local *Branson Tri-Lakes Daily News* for dates and times. If you are planning a trip to Forsyth, you can drop by for a blood pressure check without an appointment. The Taney County Health Department's breast and cervical cancer control program provides examinations for seniors 55 and older who meet income guidelines. For more information on the health department's immunization and family-planning services, see its listing in the Health Care chapter.

i Learn and vacation at the same time! Branson is host to at least 18 Elderhostel programs for seniors during the year, from Branson Show Biz to Ozark Culture and History. If you're older than 55, you may want to look into various programs by writing Ozark Adventures, P.O. Box 366, Branson West, MO 65737; checking the Elderhostel Web site, www.elderhostel.org; or calling toll-free (877) 426-8056.

SENIOR CENTERS

Residents in Branson, Forsyth, Kimberling City, Branson West, Hollister, Rockaway Beach, Kirbyville, Taneyville, and Reeds Spring are served by three senior centers, each of which offers a variety of social and health programs. All of the centers serve lunch each weekday to people older than sixty for $3, or they will deliver the meal to your home hot or frozen. If you need transportation to or from the senior center in your area, you may call OATS Transportation Service at (800) 770-6287 or the senior center. For more information on OATS, see our listing later in this chapter.

i Be sure to give your age when you make your ticket reservations for shows. Many theaters offer senior discounts, and restaurants and motels also give as much as 15 percent off.

BRANSON COMMUNITY CENTER AND BRANSON SENIOR CENTER
201 Compton Dr.
(417) 337-8510, (417) 335-4801 senior center
www.cityofbranson.org
The Branson Community Center is the place to go if you want to rub elbows with the natives. Located just off US 65, and near the banks of Lake Taneycomo, the community center is where seniors gather for lunch, duplicate bridge, china-painting classes, ceramics classes, exercise classes, and square and ballroom dance classes. If you're

into something a little more adventurous, you can join the mixed doubles tennis club, which meets at Stockstill Park. The Don Gardner Pitch-n-Putt Golf Course is a nine-hole course located next to the community building. The Branson Parks and Recreation Department oversees the course, as well as all the city sports programs. You can reach them at (417) 335-4801. Administrator Christine Thompson would be happy to send you a brochure.

FORSYTH SENIOR FRIENDSHIP CENTER
13879 US 160, Forsyth
(417) 546-6100
www.swmoa.com
Located 2.5 miles north of Forsyth, the Forsyth Senior Friendship Center offers just what the name implies. Friends gather here for activities ranging from billiards to cards to exercise classes. Not only does the center provide a hot lunch each weekday for a suggested donation of $3, but you can also have it delivered to your home hot or frozen. Call the center to find out more about their health-screening workshops and tax-counseling sessions. If you'd like to volunteer, the center always needs people to help community members with transportation or housekeeping chores.

OZARKS LAKE COUNTRY SENIOR CENTER
63 Kimberling Hills Blvd.
Kimberling City
(417) 739-5242
The seniors at the Ozarks Lake Country Senior Center rarely sit still. While you will find some playing cards, carving wood, and making handicrafts, more often than not they're line dancing, exercising, or off seeing the shows in Branson. The 16-passenger OATS bus (see the listing in this chapter for more details) comes by each Thursday to take passengers around town for errands and doctor's appointments. Lunch is served at the center each weekday for $3, or you can call and have it delivered to your home hot or frozen. In the spring the center offers income tax consulting. The Ozarks Lake Country Senior

Center building is located just off MO 13 next to the Shepherd of the Hills Lutheran Church. With 10,000 square feet of space, the center includes an exercise room, billiards room, and plenty of elbow room.

HOME HEALTH SERVICES

A number of home health-care services have sprung up in the tri-lakes area in the last few years. Licensed health-care workers staff each of the companies listed here. A few of the companies use the services of trained volunteers. The average daily rate for a visit from a home health-care worker is $100. Most companies accept Medicare and Medicaid. It may be a good idea to call the Better Business Bureau, 2101 MO 248, (417) 335-4222, for a reference when deciding which home health-care company to use.

ACCESS HOME HEALTH AGENCY
1315 E. Montclair St., Springfield
(417) 863- 7100
Access serves Barry, Christian, Dade, Dallas, Douglas, Greene, Lawrence, Ozark, Polk, Stone, Taney, Webster, and Wright Counties.

AMEDISYS HOME HEALTH CARE
500 West Main St., Suite 303
(417) 336-6661
www.amedysis.com
This local home health-care serves only Taney and Stone Counties.

HOME INSTEAD SENIOR CARE
1936 East Sunshine St., Suite B, Springfield
417-227-9977

INTEGRITY HOME CARE
2331 Business Hwy 65 South, Hollister
1-888-793-1795
www.integrityhc.com
Integrity Home Care serves many counties in southwest Missouri. They also have a Springfield office.

OXFORD HEALTH CARE
3660 South National, Springfield
417-883-7500
523 State Highway 248
417-336-6996
www.OxfordHealthCare.net
Oxford's experienced, specially trained hospice staff understands the unique emotional, spiritual, social, and physical needs of patients, and families, coping with a terminal illness.

SKAGGS PROFESSIONAL HOME CARE
611 South Sixth St.
(417) 335-7203
www.skaggs.net
A service of Skaggs Community Health Center, this organization serves the Branson, Forsyth, and Kimberling City areas with sixty employees. It provides services in physical therapy, speech therapy, occupational therapy, and skilled nursing. A nurse is on call 24 hours a day.

VISITING NURSE ASSOCIATION
531 South Union St., Springfield
(417) 866-3211, (800) 595-7167
Affiliated with St. John's Regional Health Center, the Visiting Nurse Association provides medical assistance to approximately 180 residents in the tri-lakes area. Their staff includes registered nurses, occupational therapists, and medical social workers. They make nursing-home referrals and can assist patients in securing financial aid. You may call them directly or have your doctor arrange for a visit.

HOUSING

The availability of low-income senior citizen housing in Branson is rather limited due to the lack of facilities, and both Oak Manor and Branson Manor have long waiting lists. However, other low-income apartment housing in Branson, not specifically for seniors, is available. (See the Real Estate section in the Relocation chapter for more information.) Many seniors enjoy campground life and find the city-owned campgrounds as good as any in town.

BRANSON APARTMENTS
406 Judy St.
417-332-2788

BRANSON MANOR
218 Old County Rd.
(417) 334-3800

Don't let the address fool you. This low-income senior housing development is located in the heart of Branson just south of The Strip. The five-floor high-rise often has a waiting list of more than 20. Residents here enjoy potluck meals, church services, and regular bingo. The OATS bus makes two stops here each week.

BRANSON HOUSING AUTHORITY
320 W. Main
(417) 334-4236

i Retired residents should be leery of potential scam artists. If someone calls you on the phone and asks for a credit card number or bank account number, don't give it out. Call the local police department if you suspect you may have been the target of a crime.

BRANSON LAKESIDE RV PARK
300 South Boxcar Willie Dr.
(417) 334-2915
www.cityofbranson.org

Lots of folks "test the waters" before relocating by living a month or more in an area campground. Relocators and retirees have long enjoyed the "air-conditioned breeze" from Taneycomo and the camaraderie with the other residents as they check out the area or simply vacation here. Each of the 160 campsites has a table, and you can feed the geese that gather along the lakeside and fish for trout from one of several fishing docks. A marina and two shelters are provided. The showers and restrooms include central heating and air-conditioning. A 30- or 50-amp site with cable TV is available for $26 per day, with every seventh day free.

GOLDEN OAK APARTMENTS
1600 Bird Rd.
in the Branson Hills area
(417) 337-5803

The Branson Hills area is just north of old town Branson. These apartments are close to the hospital and old downtown, as well as some new development: The Branson Hills Shopping Center with its Wal-Mart Super Center, Target, Home Depot, Books-a-Million, Kohl's, and Bed, Bath, and Beyond. It's even a short drive to the Branson Rec-Plex. Rentals start at $575 and go up to $625 for these 2-bedroom, appliance-furnished units. Water, sewer, and trash collection are included in the price. The 92 units at Golden Oak have a community swimming pool and clubhouse.

LAKEWOOD ESTATES
700 Parnell Dr.
(417) 334-4170

One of the oldest developments in Branson, Lakewood Estates is located just off US 65 across from Skaggs Community Health Center. The homes range in price from $90,000 to $140,000. The Lakewood Estates Condominium Association oversees the operation of a clubhouse, swimming pool, and fishing dock on Lake Taneycomo. Although the association does not have any age requirements for home ownership, most of the residents are at least fifty-five years old.

LOST TREE CONDOS
150 Lost Tree Dr.
(417) 335-3936
5 miles north of downtown at intersection
US 65 and MO F

These 1-, 2-, or 3-bedroom condos are located near the Ozark Highroad, giving you a clear, non-stop drive to the west end of the Strip, yet only 5 miles to downtown Branson, and just 4 miles to the Branson Hill Shopping Center. There are 264 units, unfurnished, but with a washer and dryer hookup. Prices range from $375 to $550, including trash service. Renter pays water and electric. Amenities include a swimming pool and on-site day care center.

OAK MANOR
320 West Main St.
(417) 334-4236
This 40-unit apartment complex consistently has a waiting list of more than 20, with an average move-in time of approximately six months. Applicants must meet income guidelines. All units are unfurnished. The complex is near the library, and downtown Branson is within easy walking distance. Each year the complex hosts Thanksgiving and Christmas dinners as well as monthly birthday parties for residents. The OATS bus stops at Oak Manor once a week. A Social Security representative from Springfield stops at Oak Manor twice each month to accept Social Security applications from area residents. Call for specific days and times.

RESIDENTIAL HOUSING

Residential care centers are great alternatives to nursing homes, provided you're fairly self-mobile. The residential care centers in the tri-lakes area cater to affluent seniors who can afford to pay anywhere from $400 to $12,000 per month in rent. All the facilities in this section welcome drop-in visits by prospective tenants and family members.

TABLEROCK HEALTHCARE
HCR 3, Box 116, Joe Bald Road
Kimberling City
(417) 739-2481
Country living at its best is at Tablerock Healthcare. Seniors at this 120-bed skilled-nursing facility live in one- and two-bedroom apartments, with decks overlooking the beautiful Ozark Mountains. Each unit has a kitchenette, but when you're not in the mood to cook, you can enjoy a meal planned by the full-time dietician. The facility features a variety of medical services, including physical therapy, occupational therapy, speech therapy, psychotherapy, dental care, and ophthalmology. In addition to the 150 staff members, the facility welcomes volunteers. The Pink Ladies are volunteers who are always on hand to assist residents with their various needs. One of the most interesting features of the facility is

its employee housing complex. Twenty duplexes located in what the staff calls the Upper Village are reserved for employees and their families.

WEDGEWOOD GARDENS
17996 MO 13, Reeds Spring
(417) 272-6666
Located on MO 13 in Branson West, Wedgewood Gardens is a family-owned and family-operated assisted-living facility. It is state licensed for 46 residents. The facility opened in 1996 and features one- and two-bedroom living areas. All meals are provided, along with laundry and housekeeping services. Bird-watchers can spend their days enjoying the aviary or reading a book on the birds of Missouri from the facility's library. In addition to a 150-gallon aquarium, the facility boasts a central living room with a fireplace. The husband-and-wife owners, Marty and Bill Kenny, a registered nurse and a licensed administrator, respectively, are both on hand to answer questions and provide information.

TRANSPORTATION

OATS TRANSPORTATION SERVICE
3259 East Sunshine St., Suite L, Springfield
(417) 887-9272, (800) 770-6287
OATS Transportation Service provides daily bus service to folks in the tri-lakes area. You may call the Springfield number to arrange a ride. Please give at least two days' advance notice. Once a month, the OATS bus makes a trip from Branson to Springfield and back. The cost is $6 round-trip, and you may ask to be picked up at your home. If you are traveling to Springfield for a doctor's appointment, they ask for a donation of $4. A round-trip in Taney County is $2, and a round-trip in Branson is $1.50.

EDUCATIONAL OPPORTUNITIES

GIBSON TECHNICAL CENTER
MO 13 South, Reeds Spring
(417) 272-3410
www.wolves.k12.mo.us
Gibson Technical Center offers a number of

community education classes of interest to senior citizens. These classes are not part of the center's regular degree program. (For more information on the degree program, see the Education and Child Care chapter.) The community classes, which average less than $100, are offered in the spring, summer, and fall and last from one to eight weeks. You can take classes in computers and computer software programs, cake decorating, sign language, floral arranging, accounting, welding, and auto body repair. If you are interested in learning about a particular subject, or would be interested in teaching a class, call the center and let them know. They try to tailor their course offerings to demand.

 Much of the theater workforce is made up of retired residents. They hold jobs such as ushers, ticket takers, gift shop clerks, and concessions clerks. Many retirees say one of the benefits of working at a theater is getting to know the stars who perform there.

EMPLOYMENT

MISSOURI CAREER CENTER
2720 Shepherd of the Hills Expressway, Suite B
(417) 334-4156
www.missouricareersource.com
This statewide network of Missouri Career Centers provides valuable workforce services: personalized career-assistance services from trained workforce specialists for job seekers; assistance from business representatives and access to other valuable business services for businesses. To find contact information and directions to the Career Center nearest you, visit the Web site or call (888) 728 JOBS (5627).

Money magazine has ranked Branson as one of its 20 top retirement towns.

RECREATION

DOGWOOD LANES
2126 MO 76 East
(417) 336-2695
Dogwood Lanes bowling alley offers a senior citizens mixed bowling league for those interested in competing in ABC and WIBC tournaments. The league travels throughout Missouri, Illinois, and Iowa. If no openings currently exist for the league, you may still sign up to be an alternate. (For more information on bowling alleys, see the Recreation and the Outdoors chapter.)

SPECIAL-INTEREST ACTIVITIES

BRANSON TOPS 468
St. Paul's Lutheran Church
221 Malone St.
(417) 336-4662
The Branson TOPS (Take Off Pounds Sensibly) group meets each Friday at 8 a.m. at St. Paul's Lutheran Church, just across from Skaggs Community Health Center. The group's philosophy is based on a combination of moral support and sound nutrition practices. The dues are $20 per year plus $2 per month. Guest speakers from area health-care facilities drop in from time to time.

INTERNATIONAL ROSE O'NEILL CLUB
www.irocf.org
The world headquarters for the International Rose O'Neill Club is located where else but in Branson, where Rose O'Neill, creator of the famous Kewpie doll, once lived. The club has affiliate chapters in many states and Japan. Each year members gather for Kewpiesta, one of the area's most extravagant festivals (see the Annual Events chapter). All stops were pulled out in 2009, the 100th anniversary of the Kewpie. Many of the club's members also belong to the Bonniebrook Historical Society. While the International Rose O'Neill Club is primarily concerned with the study of O'Neill's various works of art, the historical society helps raise money for Bonniebrook Park (485 Rose O'Neill Rd., Walnut Shade). For information on the historical society, call (417) 561-1509.

KIMBERLING AMATEUR RADIO CLUB
American Legion Table Rock Post 637
52 Lake Rd., Kimberling City
(417) 739-2888

With more than 200 members from across the globe, the Kimberling Amateur Radio Club does its duty to spread the word about Ozark Mountain Country. Ham radio buffs know the club by its call letters, KOEI. The first Saturday of each month, the club gives FCC license exams at its regular meeting spot, the American Legion building next to Harter House. The cost to take the exam is $6.35. If you want to enjoy their breakfast buffet beforehand, bring another $4. Members range in age from 8 to 90. (More are closer to 90 than 8.) Not only do these people like to talk, they like to pitch in to help their community. Each year the Kimberling Amateur Radio Club helps organize the Kimberling City Christmas parade. Occasionally they put on a garage sale to help pay for repeater equipment.

LIBRARIES

FORSYTH LIBRARY
162 Main St., Forsyth
(417) 546-5257
www.forsythmolibrary.org

With the exception of one librarian, the Forsyth Library is run entirely by volunteers. From time to time the library hosts guest speakers and special workshops for seniors. The Friends of the Library club operates the Markdown Thriftshop, which is located next to the library just across from the courthouse.

KIMBERLING AREA LIBRARY
52 Lake Rd., Kimberling City
(417) 739-2525
www.kalib.org

With just 22,000 volumes, the Kimberling Area Library may not have as many books as some of the other libraries in the area, but it has much to offer in the way of services. If you want to learn more about computers or the Internet, the library can set you up with a facilitator for $1 an hour. A special tax-consulting workshop is held each year for seniors, and the Investment Club meets at the library to discuss stocks, bonds, and other money-making opportunities. Literacy tutors offer free help to area adults so they too can enjoy the escapades of the Play Readers Club, which gathers regularly at the library. The volunteer staff is available to help you find information and phone numbers for area senior citizen services. The Friends of the Library club raises money to help buy new books and brings in guest speakers each month.

LYONS MEMORIAL LIBRARY
College of the Ozarks, Point Lookout
(417) 334-6411, ext. 3411
www.cofo.edu

Just southwest of the chapel on the campus of College of the Ozarks, the library features a variety of books on religion, history, and education. Missouri and Boone County (Arkansas) residents may obtain a library card by showing proof of residency or a driver's license.

STONE COUNTY LIBRARY
106 East Fifth St., Galena
(417) 357-6410
www.stonecountylibrary.org

The Stone County Library, which sits on the south side of the square in Galena, is a great resource for local history and books on Missouri. Funded by county tax revenue, the library has 55,000 books and a large selection of books on tape, as well as access to the Internet.

TANEYHILLS COMMUNITY LIBRARY
200 South Fourth St.
(417) 334-1418
www.bransoncommunitylibrary.org

This privately funded library is home to nearly 48,000 books, and with the help of the Taneyhills Library Club, that number is climbing. The Taneyhills Thrift Shop is located in the lower level of the library and contains clothing, housewares, and other used merchandise. Volunteers from the Taneyhills Library Club operate the shop and help out upstairs as well. You can find a good selection of reference books at this library as well as books on tape.

VOLUNTEER OPPORTUNITIES

BRANSON SENIOR CENTER
201 Compton
(417) 335-4801
Volunteers are always needed to help deliver Meal on Wheel to to seniors in the Branson and Hollister area and to help out in the Branson Senior Center.

RSVP
627 North Glenstone Ave.
Springfield
(417) 862-3586
www.ccozarks.org
The Retired Senior Volunteer Program (RSVP) coordinates the efforts of some 800 seniors age 55 and older in a variety of programs throughout the Ozarks. In Taney County, volunteers oversee the Source Water Mentor Program to make sure homes and businesses have clean well water. In Springfield, seniors help students in the public schools, assist with functions at the Juanita K. Hammons Center for the Performing Arts, assist the staff at area hospitals, and help run many of the area's visitor information centers. RSVP volunteers present programs and serve as guides and staff at the Springfield Conservation Center and the Wonders of Wildlife Museum. Volunteers also give lectures to area clubs and organizations. If you have extra time on your hands and want to find out more about RSVP, request a copy of their newsletter.

SKAGGS COMMUNITY HEALTH CENTER
US Bus. 65 North and Skaggs Road
(417) 335-7140
www.skaggs.net
The Skaggs Community Health Center Auxiliary provides more than 180 volunteers known as Pink Ladies (although some of the volunteers are men). The volunteers staff the hospital's six information desks, operate the Forget-Me-Not Gift Shop and the Pink Door Thrift Shop in Hollister, and help out at various community wellness events. In one recent year, the auxiliary gave 33,837 volunteer hours to the hospital. If you would like to get involved, call the Community Relations Department at the number above.

FRATERNAL ORGANIZATIONS

Each Wednesday the *Branson Tri-Lakes Daily News* prints an area clubs page that lists the meeting dates and times for the following organizations. You may also request a copy of the Branson/Lakes Area Chamber of Commerce's Community Guide by calling (417) 334-4136. The guide lists information about groups such as the Branson-Hollister Rotary Club, Daughters of the American Revolution, Forsyth Masonic Lodge, Knights of Columbus Council #6470, Lake Taneycomo Elks Lodge #2597, Masonic Lodge #587, Sertoma Club, and the Salvation Army.

HEALTH CARE

Branson has consistently been rated in surveys and publications as a good area for retirees (see the Retirement chapter). Its clean environment, fresh air, and clean water, as well as entertainment options, rate high with families and those looking for a place to settle in for their golden years. These individuals are also interested in health-care facilities and hospitals and their continued growth. In fact, the two large area hospitals, Cox Health Systems and St. John's Health System, with 7,600 and 6,900 employees, are the top two Springfield-area employers. Such growth will continue, as it is expected the populations of Greene County and Springfield, with the ancillary counties of Webster, Christian, Stone, and Taney, will increase 25 percent by 2010.

Branson has its own nonprofit hospital, Skaggs Community Heath Center, and Branson is only minutes from the large hospital facilities in Springfield. Because Branson is also a tourist area, we have some special health-care issues and problems.

With its 105 beds, Skaggs Community Health Center and its $23 million, five-story outpatient medical facility is a hospital unusual in size and quality for a community with Branson's deceptively small population. Each year some 25,000 people find themselves in the Skaggs emergency room, a number that is average for a hospital three times the size. The eight million tourists who visit Branson each year bring with them their heart conditions. They are involved in fender benders or worse. They fall and break bones or catch themselves on their own fishing hooks. They get their backs out of whack playing too hard. Children get into poison ivy or end up with scrapes and cuts or broken bones in their pursuit of fun on the family vacation. In fact, about 40 percent of the ER patients in our local hospital are tourists.

Branson's emergency-room care received good marks in the Missouri Department of Health's report in the *Show Me Buyer's Guide: Hospital Emergency Services,* a statewide survey of 128 hospitals. The Skaggs emergency facilities were praised because among the hospital's emergency service personnel, 80 percent of the full-time physicians are board certified. All of the registered nurses have completed advanced cardiac life support training. Specialized medical practitioners are on call. The medical director and all of the nursing staff have specialized pediatric training. Because of the large number of retirees in the area who demand high-quality medical services, Branson has a higher than average number of specialized medical practitioners for a town its size.

In October 1999, an Iowa tourist became the first Branson visitor saved by the Branson Fire Department's new automatic external heart defibrillator. Branson, as a tourism magnet, is a natural location for such equipment because of its high resident population of retirees and because it gets a lot of older visitors. In fact, of 147 people who died of cardiac arrest in Taney County the year before, 48 were tourists. So Branson has become "heart friendly." The Branson school district bought five defibrillators, one for each building and one for the football facility. And Ozark Mountain Bank offered interest-free loans for the first 100 businesses that bought defibrillators, which cost $1,500 to $3,000 each. The demand for heart health care necessitated the remodeling of a portion of the new hospital so that cardiac surgery can be performed. Heart surgeries are now performed by new cardiac physicians under the guidance of Ralph J. Damiano Jr. MD, chief of cardiac surgery at Barnes-Jewish Hospital and the John M. Shoenberg Professor of Surgery at Washington University School of Medicine.

A growing number of patients and a long waiting list have pushed Ozarks hospitals to add magnetic resonance imaging machines to their facilities. Skaggs Community Health Center, as well as Cox Health Systems and St. John's Health System, have added MRIs to their facilities. Both St. John's and Cox have clinics just north of Skaggs Community Health Center, giving Branson its own "medical mile."

If you are on vacation, Branson is as good an area to get sick or have a medical emergency as any. We don't encourage you to do so, and we hope our visitors have a safe and healthful vacation. But if you don't, we have the facilities to take care of you.

We've included information about the general state of health care in the Branson area, what to do in case you're involved in an accident, and a list of emergency numbers. We've even provided medical information for your pets.

COMMUNITY HEALTH RESOURCES

TANEY COUNTY HEALTH DEPARTMENT
15479 US 160, Forsyth
(417) 546-4725, (888) 707-4725

320 Rinehart Rd.
(417) 334-4544, (888) 294-9530
www.taneycohealth.org

The Taney County Health Department, in cooperation with the Division of Health of Missouri, has both Branson and Forsyth offices and plays a vital role in promoting the general health of the people of Taney County. Its services are offered on a sliding-fee scale or are free of charge. It provides a general immunization clinic and annual flu clinics; family planning (annual physical and pap test and a year's supply of birth control);

a breast and cervical cancer control project; a women's wellness program; a WIC (Women, Infants, and Children) program for supplemental nutrition and education for pregnant/postpartum women and for children up to the age of five; prenatal services (including pregnancy testing); blood pressure screenings; a communicable disease program (tests for HIV, STDs, and TB); a preventative hepatitis A program; and a rabies control program (with annual rabies vaccination clinics). Some of the programs and offerings are specifically for seniors, and all programs are open to seniors (see the Retirement chapter). You may obtain a list of the department's programs and a descriptive brochure by writing the Taney County Health Department, P.O. Box 369, Forsyth, MO 65653 or calling either the Branson or Forsyth office at the numbers listed above.

HOSPITALS AND INSTITUTES

COX MEDICAL CENTER NORTH
1423 North Jefferson Ave., Springfield
(417) 269-3000

COX MEDICAL CENTER SOUTH
3801 South National Ave., Springfield
(417) 269-6000
www.coxnet.org

Cox Health Systems is a three-hospital system in southwestern Missouri, with the two Springfield hospitals of most interest to those living in the Branson area. Cox North is a 274-bed community hospital in north Springfield; Cox South is a 562-bed tertiary-care facility in south Springfield. The third, Cox-Monett Hospital, is a 78-bed hospital in Monett. The Springfield south facility is the newest of the three. Other Cox facilities include 50 regional clinics throughout the Ozarks; Primrose Place Health Care Center; Oxford HealthCare, a home health agency; Home Parenteral Services, a home infusion-therapy agency; and Burrell Behavioral Health, which offers behavioral health services in 19 locations in southwestern Missouri.

The Cox System evolved from the Burge Deaconess Hospital, which opened in Springfield on Thanksgiving Day in 1906 in a modest frame

Emergency Numbers

For emergency service (fire, police, etc.) in Taney or Stone County, you can simply dial 911. For nonemergencies dial the numbers listed below.

Branson Fire Department:
(417) 334-3300
Branson Police Department:
(417) 334-3300
Forsyth Fire Department:
(417) 546-3074
Forsyth Police Department:
(417) 546-3731
Hollister Fire Department:
(417) 334-8902
Hollister Police Department:
417) 334-6565
Kimberling City Fire Department (Stone County): (417) 272-1510
Kimberling City Police Department (Stone County):
(417) 739-2400
Reeds Spring Fire Department (Stone County): (417) 272-1510
Reeds Spring Police Department (Stone County): (417) 272-3107
Rockaway Beach Police Department: (417) 561-4424
Taney County Ambulance District:
(417) 335-5312

duplex. Cox has provided medical care for Springfield and area residents for a century. Today Cox Systems provides medical care for an 18-county primary service area in southwestern Missouri.

DOCTORS HOSPITAL, SPRINGFIELD
2828 North National Ave., Springfield
(417) 837-4000
www.dhos.net
Doctors Hospital specializes in geriatric and psychiatric care. It has about a 15 percent share of the Springfield market. Doctors Hospital is able to provide approximately 80 percent of all health-care service needs, and they refer patients requiring more extensive treatment to facilities that deliver specialty care. The Springfield facility has a twenty-four-hour emergency room, an obstetrics unit and ward, an intensive-care unit, and other general hospital services. It also features a women's care facility, outpatient/ambulatory facility, an occupational health center, and an extended-hours clinic.

ST. JOHN'S REGIONAL HEALTH CENTER
1235 East Cherokee St.
(417) 885-2000
www.stjohns.com
Founded in 1891 by three members of the Sisters of Mercy, St. John's became Springfield's first hospital to serve the growing town of 22,000. Housed in a small brick home, the new hospital had four patient rooms. Its stretcher was an old door. Today the hospital includes a 1,016-bed medical facility, 375 physicians, and home-care services for southwestern Missouri and northern Arkansas, and has recently been under a multi-million-dollar face-lift and expansion. They have hospitals in Aurora, Lebanon, St. Francis, Cassville, and Berryville, Arkansas, in addition to the main hospital in Springfield. St. John's provides expertise in 40 medical specialties as well as services in general areas such as pediatrics, mental health, nutrition, pregnancy, intensive care, heart disease, and many others. The hospital is active in educational programs and offers support groups and outpatient services. St. John's will provide a services and information packet if you call the number above. You can access an online version of the hospital's publication Healthy People by going to the Web site listed above.

SKAGGS COMMUNITY HEALTH CENTER
251 Skaggs Rd.
(417) 335-7000
www.skaggs.net
Skaggs is a 132-bed community-owned and supported health-care facility recognized by Medi-

269

care as a sole community provider. Close to 130 medical doctors are on staff, with specialties in cardiology, gynecology, internal medicine, nephrology, neurology, oncology, ophthalmology, orthopedic surgery, pathology, pediatrics, plastic and reconstructive surgery, pulmonary medicine, and urology, among others. Skaggs provides 24-hour emergency care at its Level III Trauma Center with a physician always on duty.

Skaggs offers other services to meet the health needs of the Branson community. Skaggs Professional Home Care offers skilled home health-care services to residents of Taney and Stone Counties. The Skilled Nursing Unit cares for people who need continued recuperative care after the acute phase of hospitalization.

Skaggs operates satellite clinics in Stone and Taney Counties that are staffed by physicians specializing in family medicine, infectious disease, internal medicine, obstetrics/gynecology, pediatrics, and urology. They are Branson Family Medicine Clinic, Branson Neurology and Pain Center, Skaggs Family Health Clinic, Skaggs Internal Medicine Clinic, Skaggs OB/GYN Care, Skaggs Pediatric Care, and Tri-Lakes Urology, all located in Branson; Branson West Medical Care and Rehab Services in Branson West; Crane Medical Care in Crane; Forsyth Medical Care in Forsyth; and Skaggs Medical West in Kimberling City.

Skaggs Health Center has been adding services since its opening in 1950 to meet the growing and diverse medical needs of tri-lakes-area residents and visitors. A $23 million, five-story outpatient medical facility opened in 2000. The 112,000-square-foot building houses a lab, radiology service, cardiac rehabilitation services, and other testing facilities. At the same time, because of the growth of the permanent population and tourism, approval was gained to increase the number of beds in the critical care unit from 8 to 14.

The hospital's helicopter service can airlift patients to Springfield and other facilities when necessary.

ASSISTED-LIVING AND RETIREMENT COMMUNITIES

CULPEPPER PLACE AT BRANSON MEADOWS ASSISTED LIVING
5351 Gretna Rd.
(417) 334-3336
www.culpepperplace.net
This $2.9 million, 36,848-square-foot facility has 45 one- and two-bedroom with kitchenette rental units that provide independent living, with options including meal service, activities, and a staff nurse. It was completed in spring 2002. An observation deck offers telescopes to enjoy the panoramic view of the Branson hills. There are walking paths, three common areas, and an exercise room and beauty shop. The facility is within walking distance of the Branson Meadows Mall.

OAKS RETIREMENT COMMUNITY
127 Hamlet Rd.
(417) 239-1112
www.oaksretirement.com
The Oaks, a modern retirement community that opened in 1999, boasts of "a country-club lifestyle with small-town charm." The Oaks is a community unto itself, with card clubs, college classes, dancing, dining, church services, and other social opportunities all within walking distance. The 48 units range from comfortable efficiency apartments to spacious two-bedroom suites, all with fully equipped, modern kitchens. Most offer patios or balconies. Residents can exercise in the fitness center, have breakfast in the Creamery Cafe, go online in the Computer Center, or entertain friends in the Terrace Room, a private dining area. It is located close to the Branson Junior High School and Skaggs Community Health Care. It has a commanding view of Branson Landing and Lake Taneycomo.

QUICK MEDICAL, DENTAL, CHIROPRACTIC, AND EYE-CARE HELP

If you need some general medical attention and

What to Do in Case of an Accident

Accidents do happen, and in an area in which you have lots of people not familiar with the roads and gawking at the various sights, straining to read road signs, and trying to ignore the fighting children in the backseat, you have more accidents than usual. If you're involved in a traffic accident while in Branson, here is what the Branson Police Department suggests you do.

If it is a minor accident in which no one is hurt and the road is blocked, first move the vehicles so traffic is not blocked. Dial the local police department, (417) 334-3300 (not 911), and report the accident to the authorities. While waiting for an officer, exchange driver information: name, address, phone, insurance company and vehicle information, and identification. Since insurance companies rely on the officer's report, it is important that such a report is filed with basic information about the accident.

If there are witnesses to the accident, ask them if they are willing to stay at the scene until the investigating officer arrives. If they can't, get their names, addresses, and phone numbers so that they can be called by your insurance company for accident verification.

If someone is injured in the accident, dial 911 for emergency services. Do not move the vehicles until the investigating officer arrives and directs their removal. Obtain all the information listed above.

If the accident occurs on private property—such as the parking lot of a theater or restaurant—call 911 and have the officer deliver a private-property accident report in which the parties involved exchange basic information: name, address, phone, vehicle information, insurance company, etc.

---

are a tourist or newcomer, it is rather difficult to obtain an appointment unless you have a personal physician in the area. It's expensive to go to the local hospital emergency room for a problem that is not major or life-threatening, and it ties up facilities for someone who may need help more desperately. The area has some clinics at which you can obtain general, on-the-spot attention for nonemergencies or fill a prescription.

Visitors may experience various types of medical emergencies: a tooth chipped or knocked out in a fall, glasses broken in a fender-bender accident, a dislocated shoulder from too much casting for Taneycomo trout, or a crown that comes loose in some irresistible taffy. Whatever the problem is that can't wait until you get back

home, Branson has some medical professionals who are willing to go the extra mile and work you in so your vacation won't be spoiled. A visitor who had a crown pop loose at breakfast once got it fixed by 9 a.m.—and picked up two free tickets to a local music show the dentist couldn't make that evening. Happenings like that maintain Branson's reputation for hospitality and provide the best type of public relations there is: word-of-mouth recommendations.

Dental Care

KEITH WALL, DDS
221 College St.
(417) 334-5999
Dr. Keith Wall advertises, "When you don't know

Health Services and Organizations at a Glance

Special Needs and Services, Support Groups, Substance Abuse, and Counseling

Alcoholics Anonymous, 1031 East Battlefield Rd., Springfield, (417) 823-7125

Center for Addictions, Cox Medical Center North, 1423 North Jefferson Ave., Springfield, (417) 269-3269 or (417) 269-2273

Lakes Country Rehabilitation Center, 11016 East MO 76, (417) 272-0065

Larry Simmering Recovery Center, 360 Rhinehart Rd., (417) 335-5946

Ozarks National Council on Alcoholism and Drugs, 25 St. Louis St., Springfield, (417) 831-4167

Crisis Intervention

Family Violence Center, (417) 837-7700 (office); (417) 864-7233 (hot line)

Women's Crisis Center of Taney County, (417) 561-5105 (office); (417) 561-5084 (24-hour crisis hot line)

Family-Planning Services

LAPS (Living Alternatives Pregnancy Services), 833 Lakeshore Dr., (417) 336-5483

Planned Parenthood, 626 East Battlefield Rd., Springfield, 417) 883-5899, www.plannedparenthood.org

Springfield Healthcare Center, 1837 East Cherry St., Springfield, (417) 831-7298

Other Assistance and Organizations

AIDS Project of the Ozarks, 1901 East Bennett St., Suite D, Springfield, (417) 881-1900 or (800) 743-5767, www.aidsprojectoftheozarks.org

American Red Cross, (417) 832-9500

---

who to call, call us!" If you're in the area and have an emergency dental problem, it could be some very good advice. As you turn west off US Business 65 in downtown Branson, Dr. Wall's practice is 1 block west on College Street.

NICKOLAS C. YIANNIOS, DDS, PC
920 MO 86
(417) 334-2131
Dr. Nickolas C. Yiannios, D.D.S., P.C., accepts emergency dental patients at his practice on MO 86 at Ridgedale. Dr. Yiannios is open evenings for appointments.

Chiropractic Care
BRANSON CHIROPRACTIC CENTER
120 East Price St.
(417) 334-4441
Dr. James Thress's practice, located at the corner of Price and Sycamore Streets in Branson, only blocks from the Branson City Campgrounds, treats emergency chiropractic patients. Clinic hours are Monday through Friday, 8 a.m. to noon and 1 to 5 p.m.

EXTRA CARE CHIROPRACTIC
136 Spring Creek Rd.
(417) 334-5330
www.extracarechiro.com
This center provides chiropractic care for walk-in patients. It's located just off Fall Creek Road in Branson.

Walk-in Clinics

BRANSON FAMILY MEDICINE CLINIC
545 Branson Landing Blvd.
(417) 335-7022
www.skaggs.net
A skinned knee or a broken leg and every minor medical emergency is handled by this clinic at the local hospital, Skaggs Health Care Center, open 8 a.m. to 8 p.m. Monday through Friday. The clinic is closed 11:45 a.m. to 2 p.m. Tuesday.

BRANSON ST. JOHN'S URGENT CARE
1940 MO 165, Suite 10
(417) 337-5000
www.stjohns.com
Quick medical help is available at this walk-in clinic operated by Springfield's St. John's Hospital. It's in Corporate View near Pointe Royale and the Welk Resort. The clinic is open from 9 a.m. to 7 p.m. seven days a week.

BRANSON WEST MEDICAL CARE
18452 MO 13
(417) 272-8911
www.skaggs.net
Located in Branson West, this facility is open from 8 a.m. to 6 p.m. Monday through Friday, with walk-ins accepted 4:30 to 5:30 p.m. Monday through Thursday and 9 to 11:30 a.m. Saturday.

BRIDGES WALK-IN CLINIC
256 MO Y, Forsyth
(417) 546-4200
Here's family medical practice taken to new dimensions. Husband-and-wife doctors Leonard and Rachelle Bridges provide medical care in this extended-hours clinic in Forsyth. Hours are from 9 a.m. to 7 p.m. Monday through Friday and 1 to 5 p.m. Sunday.

HOLLISTER ST. JOHN'S MEDICAL CENTER
151 Birch St., Hollister
(417) 336-4355
www.stjohns.com
This family-practice clinic, affiliated with St. John's Hospital in Springfield, is located along US 65 just south of the intersection with US Business 65. Walk-ins are welcome Monday through Friday from 8 a.m. to noon and 1 to 5 p.m., but call ahead if possible.

SKAGGS MEDICAL WEST
11863 MO 13, Kimberling City
(417) 739-2520
www.skaggs.net
Located in the shopping center near the MO 13 bridge, Skaggs Medical West sees walk-in patients from 3:30 to 5:30 p.m. Monday through Friday and 9 to 11:30 a.m. Saturday.

SKAGGS SOUTHSIDE FAMILY CLINIC
590 Birch St., Suite 1-C, Hollister
(417) 239-3400
www.skaggs.net
This facility accepts patients Monday through Thursday from 8 a.m. to noon and 1 to 5 p.m., and Friday 8 a.m. to noon. It is conveniently located just off US 65 South, near the Southtowne Shopping Center.

Eye Care

OZARKS FAMILY VISION CENTRE
1000 James Epps Rd.
(417) 334-7291

14974 US 160, Forsyth
(417) 546-4464
www.ozarksfamilyvision.com
Sore eyes, pollen reactions, eye injuries, broken glasses or frames, and lost contact lenses are eye emergencies that can be handled by Ozarks Family Vision Centre, opposite Skaggs Community Health Center in Branson. They can mend frames,

usually provide a temporary contact lens, or just reassure you with an eye examination after an accident so that your vacation can be worry free.

PHARMACIES

The yellow pages of the phone book will direct you to any number of local pharmacies that can handle your medical prescriptions during their regular hours. Currently there is no 24-hour pharmacy in the immediate Branson area. A pharmacy at Walgreens in Springfield, at Campbell Avenue and Battlefield Road South, is open 24 hours. The Walgreens in Branson at 210 MO 165 South near its junction with 76 Country Boulevard has the longest operating hours: Monday through Friday 8 a.m. to 9 p.m.; Saturday and Sunday 9 a.m. to 5 p.m. You can call them at (417) 339-3996.

MENTAL HEALTH SERVICES

The organizations listed below provide services to help individuals achieve, maintain, and improve their emotional well-being. These services include psychological evaluation and testing, sexual and substance abuse counseling, divorce mediation, bereavement counseling, referral assistance, and educational programs and workshops. They also have counseling for veterans, individuals, families, groups, and married couples. For assistance get in touch with Burrell Behavioral Health, 155 Corporate Place, (417) 334-7575; Center for Self Control at Skaggs Community Health Center, 221 Skaggs Rd., (417) 882-9734; Family Life Center, 714 South National Ave., Springfield, (417) 864-6088; Family Therapy of the Ozarks, Inc., 200 East College St. in Branson Town Center, (417) 335-3633 or (888) 449-2229; and Forest Counseling Center, 398 MO BB, Hollister, (417) 334-2502.

HOSPICE SERVICES

Branson is blessed with several facilities offering alternatives in case of life-limiting illness. Counseling services for the patient and family are helpful. Some points you may want to consider when selecting a hospice: Ask if the institution is Medicare/Medicaid certified and if it accepts private insurance. Check to see if it has a 24-hour emergency service line. Inquire as to whether the hospice has membership in national certifying organizations and what types of licenses it holds.

COMMUNITY HOSPICES OF AMERICA
1756 Bee Creek Rd., Suite G
(417) 335-2004
Community Hospices of America is a Medicare- and Medicaid-certified hospice facility that serves the counties of Stone, Taney, Barry, and Ozark. It focuses on the special needs of the patient and family, helping meet physical, emotional, and spiritual concerns of those diagnosed with a terminal illness and with a life expectancy of six months or less.

It has a staff of 22 medically trained personnel as well as 48 volunteers who assist with errands and other housekeeping chores. A full-time chaplain is on staff to counsel patients and family members. It offers hospice care free of charge. Additional services are provided for those who use private insurance or the Medicare/Medicaid hospice benefit.

SEASONS HOSPICE
1831 W. Melville, Springfield
(417) 890-5533
www.seasonshospice.com
A nonprofit faith based hospice serving all surrounding counties. They believe that Hospice treats the person, not the disease; focuses on family and friends, not just the individual; and emphasizes the quality of life, not the duration.

SKAGGS PROFESSIONAL HOSPICE
Skaggs Community Health Center
611 South Sixth St.
(417) 348-8580
A team of health-care professionals, social workers, chaplains, and trained volunteers provides ongoing support for the terminally ill patient and family in the home setting. A complete range of hospice services is available to the patient on a 24-hour basis. A service of Skaggs Community

Health Center, it is the only not-for-profit hospice organization operating locally and is Medicare and Medicaid certified.

VETERINARY AND PET CARE SERVICES

Bransonites love their animals, and it does seem like we have a high animal population, both wild and domestic. Area farmers often need the services of veterinarians for cattle and horses and other farm animals. Many retirees keep pets. Tourists who travel with pets sometimes need a doctor for their dog or cat. There are several area veterinarians at the service of Fido when he's on vacation, and you'll find pet grooming and pet boarding in the yellow pages of the local phone directory.

BRANSON VETERINARY HOSPITAL
220 Branson Hills Parkway
(417) 337-9777
Dr. Jeffrey O'Dell takes veterinary emergencies during his regular hours, 7:30 a.m. to 6 p.m. Monday through Friday. The practice is located just off US 65, north of Branson at the Bee Creek/Branson Hills Parkway exit.

EDUCATION AND CHILD CARE

Travel in the Ozarks prior to graded roads and paved highways was difficult and slow even in the best of weather, but area residents and the U.S. Postal Service took it in stride. How is this for service that neither rain nor sleet nor gloom of night (and we could add bad roads) affects? Teacher Lizzie Johnson, who lived at Forsyth and taught school at Reuter, a distance of 14 miles, wrote home on a one-cent postcard, postmarked November 12, 1908: "I would like to come home Saturday, but don't think I can get a horse. I thought if papa would send old Prince by the mail carrier Friday, I could come home Saturday and return Sunday, then he could lead the horse back home on Monday." (Quoted in Elmo Ingentron, *The Land of Taney,* The Ozarks Mountaineer Press, 1974.)

EDUCATION

Settlers arriving in the Ozarks did their best early on to establish schools for the widely scattered homesteads. Students would often walk miles through the woods to attend "subscription school" financed by the parents of a community, who paid $1 or $2 a month per child to the teacher. Prior to the Civil War, these schools provided the only means of education, other than homeschooling. Not until the decade after the war were feeble attempts made to establish public schools, as the White River valley and Missouri-Arkansas border area was virtually a no-man's-land because of marauding bands of guerrillas and bushwhackers. Whether subscription or public, these rural schools, with a single teacher whose education frequently was only a few grades above the oldest students', provided the basics and usually encompassed grades one through eight, with students ranging in age from 5 to 20. The master provided readin', 'ritin', and 'rithmetic, taught to the tune of the hickory stick. These early pedagogues knew how to make quill pens from feathers and ink from oak galls or pokeberries with the necessary preservatives to deter fermentation. Paper was scarce, and some students shared a common slate whose surface could be spit on and rubbed clean with the sleeve. Probably the new knowledge of pathogenic organisms and how they were transmitted caused the slate, as well as the common dipper and drinking cup used by everyone in school, to disappear shortly after the turn of the last century.

Books were as rare as paper and usually were donated or loaned. Later schools made use of *McGuffey's Eclectic Spelling Books* and *Readers* (now used as a theme for a local restaurant's menus) and *Barnes' Brief History of the United States,* as well as *Steel's Hygienic Physiology.* As school districts were formed by act of state legislature, under the direction of an elected county superintendent of schools, they were often named for the locale or community nearby. Some had picturesque names (sometimes a nickname) such as Three Johns, Box, Iron Sides (because the building was sheeted with tin to prevent it from burning when fires were set in the woods to kill ticks and chiggers), Brown Branch, Hogdanger (in Ozark County, so named for the free-range hogs that slept under the school), Possom Trot, Gobler's Knob, Lone Pilgrim, Loafer's Glory, and in Douglas County the school whose name every scholar aspired to: Neverfail. In 1890, 26 districts operated schools in the county, and by 1914 the number had grown to 75. Most schoolhouses were made of logs, but the county already had two frame schoolhouses in 1892. In 1869, there were 1,145 pupils enumerated, but the enrollment was only 300. A growth in school-age population and an increased interest in schooling caused enrollment to rise, and the county schools reached their maximum of 3,687 students in 1904. Social and economic conditions pushed many rural families to migrate to larger cities and other states. As the rural population declined, especially during the Depression and the years following, and as school districts with their one-room schools were consolidated, the county superintendents went by the wayside. Taney County's last one was elected in 1967. Today, just Kirbyville, Taneyville, and Mark Twain School near Protem retain systems that encompass only grades kindergarten through eight. Because students frequently were called upon for work at home, especially during planting and harvesting times, education was often haphazard and sporadic. Organized high schools simply didn't exist or were too far for students to attend. Distances were often great, but even if not, transportation over trails and roads wasn't easy. Little is known about the first schoolhouse in Branson, but the April 1907 school election saw voters approving bonds in the amount of $1,000, by a vote of 14 to 5, to construct a new school building. The town grew rapidly after the coming of the railroad, and by the school term of 1925–26, Branson was maintaining a first-class high school. There was a general interest in education at the turn of the 20th century. In 1908 the Presbyterian Church formed the School of the Ozarks in Forsyth as a private boarding school to provide an education for poor but deserving students, grades one through high school. The school was unique in that its students worked to pay for their room, board, and tuition.

As better roads developed, public high schools began providing free public education to many area students, but the School of the Ozarks existed as a private high school until 1967. It capitalized on the growing need for higher education by adding a junior college in 1958, then a college (1965), but still kept to the philosophy and practice of having students work to pay for their education.

Now the Taney County area has three major public school districts—Branson, Hollister, and Forsyth—and two smaller ones—Bradleyville and Blue Eye—plus three districts that have grade schools only. Branson and Hollister public high schools are across the river from each other, a carryover from the days when the White River would get so high that there would be no crossings. It was practical to have schools on each side of the river, but with bridges across the river and the building of Table Rock Dam to control flooding, it made sense to consolidate the two schools. Town rivalries, however, persisted and prevented consolidation. The rapid growth of both communities provided equally rapid growth for the schools, and the area's population can easily support two high schools in such close proximity.

Branson has always been the wealthier of the two school districts. Hollister patrons have frequently had to vote themselves higher taxes than Branson because so much of the district's land was not taxable as it is owned by College of the Ozarks. Bradleyville, likewise, has had higher school taxes because much of the district falls within the federal Mark Twain Forest.

The public school districts in our neck of the woods generally have as high or higher standards than the state sets. District scores on assessment tests overall meet and often exceed state averages. School board elections in Taney County are often hot contests and result in voter turnout as high as presidential campaigns. The Branson boom in the 1990s resulted in a large influx of school-age children, and area schools were caught unaware. The result was a shortage of classrooms and frequently crowded classes. Citizens rose to the occasion, however, and voted to tax themselves to build new schools. Even outlying schools, such as those in Omaha, Arkansas; Taneyville; Spokane; Reeds Spring; and Blue Eye, experienced rapid and unexpected enrollment. In the past decade, several private schools have been founded.

Another phenomenon schools have experienced as the result of the interest in Branson is student mobility. A student may be in school for only several months and then move, but another moves in as a replacement. For example, Taneyville school district lost 38 students in a semester but gained 40 new ones. In the quiet pre-boom days, it was likely that those children who entered the first grade would be in the graduating class 12 years later, with no or few new faces added or lost along the way. The people who work in Branson's service industry are likely to move on to greener, or at least different, pastures, which causes a certain student instability in schools.

Because of the large number of people who work in service industry jobs on The Strip, which are often seasonal, many of the area's students meet standards for free or reduced-cost school lunches. At some schools, as much as 60 percent of the students receive free or reduced-cost lunches.

The start of school varies a little, depending upon how many snow days each district builds in, but most schools start early in September before Labor Day, and some start as early as August 20. The school year is usually done by June 1. Though the area doesn't get that much snow, when it does snow or we experience an ice storm, school is often cancelled. Buses simply can't navigate the area's hilly and twisting back roads. Such weather frequently results in no spring or Easter vacation (those days being used as snow days), an extended school year, or Saturday classes—and sometimes all three.

In Missouri, children must turn five by July 31 to enroll in kindergarten that fall. Registration and testing/screening begin in the spring for most schools. The Missouri Department of Health and Family Services requires students enrolling in public school to be current with vaccinations for diphtheria, tetanus, polio, whooping cough, measles, mumps, rubella, and hepatitis. Kindergarten screening includes ear, eye, and speech exams. At the screening, the student's Social Security number and state birth certificate must be presented.

The Missouri Safe Schools Act of 1996 requires of all enrolling students, including transfer students, a notarized form that provides a variety of information, including proof of residency and the enrolling student's law enforcement record. Parents planning to enroll children in school should contact the school superintendent's office in the district where they'll be living or the headmaster of the private school. Each district decides what credits to accept from transfer students. Parents or guardians will need to request that records or transcripts be forwarded to a student's new school.

PUBLIC SCHOOLS

BLUE EYE R-V PUBLIC SCHOOL
658 MO EE, Blue Eye
(417) 779-5331
www.blueeye.k12.mo.us

The Blue Eye School District, home of the Bulldogs, takes in 98 square miles in southeastern Stone County on the Missouri-Arkansas border. It has an enrollment of more than 700. It consists of three schools: an elementary school, middle school, and high school. The elementary school has 235 students (grades kindergarten through five) and 23 certified teachers, including specialists in special education, art, music, library, and remedial reading. The middle school has 192 students (grades six through eight) and 27 certified teachers. The high school has 276 students (grades 9 through 12) and 20 certified teachers. The school is fully accredited by the Department of Elementary and Secondary Education. The assessed valuation of the district is $84 million. The school, like many in the area, has had growth due to the Branson boom, mostly confined to the elementary level, but not as much as Branson and Hollister. Growth is steady and is expected to continue.

BRADLEYVILLE PUBLIC SCHOOL
16474 MO 125
(417) 796-2288

Bradleyville R-I School in the eastern part of Taney County encompasses a district of 137 square miles. Much of the district is in the Mark Twain National Forest. Total enrollment is 240 students, with 98 students in grades kindergarten through 6 and 145 in grades 7 through 12. Assessed valuation is about $7.4 million. The district has not been affected much by the Branson boom except that it provided employment for a large number of people already living in the district. The school suffered a major disaster several years ago when a building collapsed, but generous support from district patrons and fund-raising by Branson theaters, along with federal monies, helped build a new building in 1996. The school received a technology grant several years ago and added several networked computers with access to the Internet. All the classrooms and offices are connected through the networks, and the library has a computer lab for students to conduct online research.

BRANSON PUBLIC SCHOOL

400 Cedar Ridge Dr.
(417) 334-6541
www.branson.k12.mo.us

The Branson School District, home of the Buccaneers, is the largest school district in the area, with 111.47 square miles and an enrollment of 4,066. The district has an assessed valuation of $623,931,523.

Current facilities include three campuses. Three buildings, housing grades pre-k through four, are situated on the Cedar Ridge campus. Grades 2 through 4 recently expanded to the former intermediate building, while grades 5 and 6 are enjoying the new facilities on Buchanan Road, just west of the high school. Grades seven and eight are located in the former high school building on US 65 North at the Bee Creek Road junction. The high school, grades 9 through 12, moved in the spring of 2002 into a new facility located on Buchanan Road, just off US 65 north of Branson. The district office for special services, the social worker, classrooms for the alternative high school, and classrooms for early childhood special education are housed in the former Kindergarten Center Building in downtown Branson on Sixth Street.

Most of the buildings of the school system are new, but even the older ones are well maintained and clean. The high school makes an attractive impression with the large, colorful, and appropriate-themed wall murals done by art department teachers and students. The Branson School District has 313 certified instructors as well as numerous counselors, speech therapists, librarians, and a testing coordinator. The school is accredited by the Missouri State Department of Education under the Missouri School Improvement Program Standards, the highest accreditation awarded by the department. The primary elementary was named one of eight Blue Ribbon elementary schools in the state. Exact percentages vary from year to year, but 60 to 70 percent of the high school's graduates seek post–high school education, and students on all levels score consistently above the norms on standardized achievement tests.

Contacts for the individual schools are:

BRANSON PRE K-1

402 Cedar Ridge Dr.
(417) 336-1887

BRANSON PRIMARY ELEMENTARY

(grades 2-4)
308 Cedar Ridge Dr.
(417) 334-5137

BRANSON INTERMEDIATE (GRADES 5 AND 6)

766 Buchanan Rd.
(417) 332-3201

BRANSON JUNIOR HIGH SCHOOL

(grades 7 and 8)
263 Buccaneer Blvd.
(417) 334-3087

BRANSON HIGH SCHOOL

(grades 9 through 12)
935 Buchanan Rd.
(417) 334-6511

SPECIAL SERVICES DISTRICT OFFICE

300 South Sixth St.
(417) 334-5131

FORSYTH PUBLIC SCHOOL
178 Panther Rd., Forsyth
(417) 546-6384

Forsyth Public School, home of the Panthers, is located in the county seat of Taney County and draws students from a 132-square-mile district. It has a central campus but separate buildings for elementary, middle, and high school. It has an enrollment of 1,108 plus 73 tuition-paying students from Taneyville and Mark Twain schools. Its assessed valuation is $71.5 million. The high school offers a dual diploma education (general track and college prep) and requires 25 credits for graduation but 28 credits for the college prep diploma. It offers more than 100 classes for credit. The school also offers adult education classes from time to time in response to community survey needs, and it has a GED program and an early school program for preschoolers. All classrooms and the library have Internet access, and all teachers and students have e-mail access. The school also has a U.S. Marine Corps ROTC program. It has 106 teachers, one-third with advanced degrees. The school prides itself on its student/teacher ratio, with an average of 18 to 1. More than 90 percent of the classes have the state's desirable teacher-to-student ratio, and all classes meet the required ratio average. The school experienced a great jump in enrollment during the Branson boom, increasing from 800 to 1,000 students in two years, but enrollment has been stable for the last several years. The student mobility rate is high, with about a 33 percent turnover each year. There is a Boys & Girls Club near the campus that provides activities after school and serves the community as a latchkey program.

GIBSON TECHNICAL CENTER
386 West Highway 76, Reeds Spring
(417) 272-3241
www.wolves.k12.mo.us

Gibson Technical Center, in Stone County, provides education in technology to area high-school and adult students. High-school students attend from 11 schools: Blue Eye, Bradleyville, Branson, Chadwick, Forsyth, Galena, Hollister, Hurley, Reeds Spring, Sparta, and Spokane. Tuition is paid by their home district. Adult students are expected to pay their own tuition; however, financial aid programs are available for assistance. The center offers programs in auto collision technology, automotive technology, building maintenance, business technology, construction technology, creative arts, culinary arts, computer technology, health technology careers, practical nursing, printing technology, small engines and marine technology, and welding technology. In addition, the center offers a variety of short-term classes and seminars to serve the needs of the community; such class offerings are of interest to the large number of retirees in the area. Classes are offered in the fall, spring, and summer.

The center is accredited by the Missouri State Board of Education, and the practical-nursing program is accredited by the Missouri State Board of Nursing.

HOLLISTER R-V PUBLIC SCHOOLS
1798 MO BB, Hollister
(417) 334-6119
www.hollister.k12.mo.us

The 1,312 students who attend the Hollister schools, home of the Tigers, live in a 71-square-mile area within Taney County. The district opened its new $10 million high school in 2005. The assessed valuation of the district is more than $158 million. The school is fully accredited under the new Missouri School Improvement Program Standards, the highest classification standards established by the Department of Elementary and Secondary Education. The school tries to maintain a teacher-pupil ratio that allows for maximum individualized instruction. Approximately one-third of the faculty have advanced degrees. The elementary facility houses 523 students, including 68 preschoolers. A latchkey program is offered at the elementary school immediately after school for students who have working parents; call (417) 334-5112 for details. The middle school (grades five and six) has 200 students, while the junior high has 181 students. Students are exposed to the traditional subjects of math, science, language arts, reading, health, social studies, and physical education but can also take word study, keyboarding, art, and music.

Extracurricular activities include art club, basketball, environmental club, chess club, Model UN, and quiz bowls. The high school has 405 students. More than 90 units of credit are offered, from which a student must select 24 for graduation.

The Hollister District has obtained three technology grants. As a result, networked computers have been placed in the middle-school core-subjects classrooms, the high-school computer labs, and most of the elementary classrooms. The district is participating in MOREnet, a state-sponsored program that allows access to the Internet and e-mail services for teachers.

KIRBYVILLE PUBLIC SCHOOL
4278 MO 76 East
(417) 334-2757

Kirbyville School, located 2 miles east of Branson, encompasses grades kindergarten through eight. A new middle school is 1.5 miles east. Students grades 9 through 12 may elect to attend high school in Branson or Hollister. Growth has been so great that there are plans to add a high school. Grades K through five occupy the existing school building. A preschool program was added in 1999. In spite of the student increase as a result of the Branson boom, the school has an impressive student-teacher ratio of 12 to 1. Total enrollment is 335. More than 90 percent of district patrons attend parent-teacher conferences. The assessed valuation is $34 million The district is classified as accredited, the highest classification given by the Missouri State Department of Elementary and Secondary Education.

MARK TWAIN SCHOOL
377707 US 160, Reuter
(417) 785-4323

Mark Twain School, located in the extreme southeastern corner of Taney County, is a small school, kindergarten through eight, that retains some of the best characteristics of the area's old one-room schools. The area seems isolated because

it has not had the road improvements that other parts of the county have experienced. This is because so much of the district is in the Mark Twain National Forest, and there is no bridge over Lake Bull Shoals to the south. The school even takes in some Arkansas students on the north side of Lake Bull Shoals. The Branson boom has had little effect on its enrollment, nor is student mobility a problem. Its enrollment is 69. The school is fully accredited, and with seven full-time and five part-time teachers it has one of the lowest student-to-teacher ratios in the county, nine to one. The district has an assessed valuation of $5.9 million. The school recently received a computer grant and has a computer lab with Internet access. High school students in the district may elect to attend Forsyth, Bradleyville, or Lutie School in Ozark County.

REEDS SPRING PUBLIC SCHOOL
MO 13
(417) 272-8171
www.wolves.k12.mo.us

The Reeds Spring School in Stone County, home of the Wolves, has been one of the area's schools most impacted by the Branson boom. The growth of Silver Dollar City, with the development of immediate area motels and restaurants in Branson West and Kimberling City, resulted in a population explosion for the district. For many people who work at the theme park or on the west side of Branson, Reeds Spring became the logical place to live. The school's district is 188 square miles, with a total enrollment of 2,191 in grades kindergarten through 12. There are 1,183 students in elementary school, 346 in the middle school, and 662 in the high school. From 1990 to 1997 Reeds Spring was the fastest-growing school district in the state. The growth mandated construction of a new high school, which opened in 1997. Existing buildings were renovated for the intermediate and middle school populations. Though the mid-1990s Branson boom has tapered off, the school district is still playing catch-up. Reed Spring opened a new elementary school in 2003. The district has a property valuation of $318. The district is classified as accredited, the highest classification given by the Missouri State Department of Elementary and Secondary Education. A unique feature of the Reeds Spring district is the Tri-Lakes Telecommunications Community Resource Center (TCRC), a partnership between Reeds Spring and Skaggs Community Health Center of Branson and the University of Missouri Extension Service. The center provides programming, professional training, and economic development training for the surrounding four-county area. It is a long-distance learning center, with an interactive video classroom, a multipurpose computer lab classroom, a training classroom, a multimedia production suite, and a public-access area for local residents to get on the Internet.

The center offers both credit and noncredit classes from the University of Missouri and other institutions, as well as continuing education in a variety of fields. It also provides special training for area businesses as needed or requested.

SPOKANE R-VII PUBLIC SCHOOL
1130 Spokane Rd., Spokane
(417) 443-3502
Spokane is a small school in Christian County north of Branson. Like most of the communities in the immediate Branson area, it has had some fallout from the Branson boom. There has been movement into the community, as it is about halfway between Branson and Springfield. Many of its residents work in one town or the other. In 2009 Spokane had an enrollment of 765, with a student-to-teacher ratio of 18 to 1. But like many schools, it has been hard-pressed to keep up with the unexpected growth. The school has had to build additions to both the middle school and the elementary school. In 2009 the district had an assessed valuation of $51.9 million. It received Missouri's A-plus rating in 2002. Undoubtedly the district will continue to grow as more people perceive it as an ideal location in which to live, a short commute to either Branson or Springfield.

TANEYVILLE R-II PUBLIC SCHOOL
302 Myrtle St., Taneyville
(417) 546-5803
Taneyville, named after U.S. Supreme Court Justice Roger Brooke Taney (as was the county), is a small village 18 miles east of Branson on MO 76. This largely farming community has been justly proud of its small K–8 school. Graduates attend either Forsyth or Bradleyville high schools. Agriculture is the largest industry in the district, but many parents commute daily to jobs in Forsyth, Branson, or even Springfield. Like many communities in the eastern part of the county, Taneyville has not enjoyed the wealth of the Branson boom, but it has had to contend with some of the fallout problems. The district has experienced an average growth of 3.3 percent a year since 1991. More than 60 percent of its students qualify for free or reduced-price school meals. It has had a high mobility rate, with some students living in the district only a few months then moving, but enrollment stays constant because of new students moving in. In 2009 its enrollment was 230, with 30 teachers and a student-teacher ratio of 14 to 1. Its assessed valuation was just under $10 million, and the tax levy was $4.26. Teacher turnover rate is low, and parental involvement in school activities is good. About 90 percent of the parents attend parent-teacher conferences, with the other 10 percent contacted by phone. The area will continue to attract residents and grow since the cost of land and housing is considerably less than in Branson.

PRIVATE SCHOOLS

RIVERVIEW BIBLE BAPTIST CHRISTIAN SCHOOL
13901 US 160, Forsyth
(417) 546-4580
Founded in 1982, Riverview Bible Baptist Christian School offers a program for grades kindergarten through 12. It uses the Accelerated Christian Education (A.C.E.) curriculum. Sports programs include basketball (boys) and volleyball (girls). Riverview is a member of the American

Association of Christian Schools and the Missouri Association of Christian Schools. In 2009 it had an enrollment of 70. Students enjoy a teacher to student ratio of 17 to 1, and tuition can be paid annually or monthly.

TRINITY CHRISTIAN ACADEMY
119 Myrtle St., Hollister
(417) 334-7084
www.tcaeagles.net
This private school advertises a biblically integrated college prep program within a Christ-centered environment. It has a K–12 curriculum and a preschool enrichment program for three- to five-year-olds. It prides itself on an intensive K–6 phonics program, as well as computer and foreign language (Spanish) instruction for grades 1 through 12. Sports include basketball, volleyball, track, and cheerleading. Trinity is a member of the International Christian Accrediting Association, North Central Association, and a member of the Oral Roberts University Education Fellowship. In 2005 it had an enrollment of 195, with a nine-to-one student-teacher ratio. Tuition is $3,015 per year, payable over nine months. Trinity Christian Academy also offers day-care and preschool services for children from infancy to age 5, starting at $355 per month.

HOMESCHOOLING

Newcomers to Branson and Missouri should be aware that Missouri has one of the most liberal homeschooling laws in the nation. According to Missouri law, any parent may educate a child at home. The parent does not have to have a teaching certificate or meet any education requirements. The parent must provide 1,000 hours of instruction during the school year, with at least 600 hours in the basics (reading, language arts, mathematics, social studies, and science). At least 400 of the 600 hours must be taught in the home location. There is no registering of homeschooling intentions. The statute says the parent may notify the superintendent of schools or the recorder of county deeds in the county where the parents reside, but it is not mandatory. Parents who homeschool a child must maintain certain records: a plan book or diary indicating the subjects taught and the activities engaged in, a portfolio with examples of the student's work, and a record of evaluation. An information packet and guide about Missouri's homeschooling law can be obtained from Families for Home Education, P.O. Box 742, Grandview, MO 64030.

HIGHER EDUCATION

Only in the past three or four decades has there been a great need for higher education in the immediate Branson area, and it has only been recently that enough people have lived here to support a college. Those who were inclined went to the University of Missouri or some other college out of the area. Only Springfield's Missouri State was within easy distance. As the need increased, College of the Ozarks filled the gap somewhat by becoming first a junior college, then a four-year college in 1965. However, with its mission of accepting only those who couldn't easily pay for a college education and by not broadening its mission to include a growing multitude of part-time, working, married, and continuing-education students, a need developed for higher-education alternatives. Several colleges opened branches in the area after the Branson boom, and Ozarks Technical College was established to provide for the area's growing need for technical education. And, of course, Springfield's colleges have expanded rapidly to meet the needs of a changing, growing area. Springfield has always been far enough away from Branson that students feel they are getting away, yet it is close enough that parents aren't unduly concerned about their offspring. Most students who attend Springfield colleges become residents of the town, but with the improvements on US 65 between Branson and Springfield, a growing number elect to work and live in Branson and attend class in Springfield.

COLLEGE OF THE OZARKS
P.O. Box 17
Point Lookout
(417) 334-6411, (800) 222-0525
www.cofo.edu

College of the Ozarks is the only college in the immediate Branson area. Founded in 1906 at Forsyth as the School of the Ozarks by the Reverend James Forsythe, a Presbyterian minister, the college evolved from the original Forsyth boarding grade school and high school. Now located 2 miles south of Branson on US 65 at Point Lookout, on a high bluff overlooking Lake Taneycomo, the beautiful 1,000-acre campus with its manicured grounds makes an impression on visitors. Its president, Dr. Jerry Davis, has said "image is everything," and the campus and the fact that students work to pay for their tuition make the college attractive to donors. Recent speakers on the campus—Oliver North, Ralph Reed, William Bennett, Gerald Ford, Dan Quayle, Margaret Thatcher, and Elizabeth Dole—indicate the intent, bent, and balance of its philosophy. Enrollment is capped at 1,500, and the college's endowment of more than $240.1 million makes it one of the wealthiest colleges in the nation. It has 88 full-time faculty, and more than 40 percent hold terminal degrees. Fifty percent of entering freshmen have an ACT score of 20 or above. The college offers both bachelor of arts and bachelor of sciences degrees.

Because students pay as they learn with their work, the college has been listed several times in national publications as a best-value school and a college at which students have low debt loads upon graduation. After the epithet "Hard Work U" was used in a *Wall Street Journal* article about the college, the college adopted it as an unofficial motto. Notable alumni include ABC news reporter Erin Hayes, Missouri state senator Doyle Childers, actor and director Jerry Tracy, and opera singer Meredith Mizell.

A special commitment of College of the Ozarks is to serve the youth of the Ozarks region. The founding charter commits the college to serving "especially those found worthy but who are without sufficient means to procure such training." This commitment is reflected in the policy that 90 percent of each entering class is limited to students whose families would have a difficult time financing a college education. The remaining 10 percent are primarily children of alumni or employees, athletic scholarship recipients, and a few international students. The college guarantees to meet the cost of education for the full-time students; that is, all costs of the educational program (instruction, operating costs, etc.), a figure estimated at about $10,000. The college requires that all students apply for any state and federal grants using Free Application for Federal Student Aid (FAFSA). The student's combined state and federal grant money, plus wages from work at an assigned campus job, pays for tuition. Students work 15 hours a week during the academic year plus two 40-hour weeks when school is not in session. Jobs include everything from A to Z: from airport work to zoology. In between are positions at the dairy, greenhouse, and academic offices. Room and board and incidental fees ($2,650 per year) as well as book costs (about $500 per year) are generally paid by the student, but room-and-board scholarships allow students to meet that cost by working 12- to 40-hour weeks during the summer.

Although primarily a residential college, College of the Ozarks admits a limited number of commuting students from the surrounding area. Part-time commuters (11 hours or less) pay $250 per credit hour toward the cost of education, with the remaining costs met by various grants and the institutional scholarship. The college does not allow students to obtain

i You can sit at a student desk in a one-room rural Ozark school at College of the Ozarks. Star School was moved from Flat Creek in Barry County and restored in the late 1970s. It serves as an excellent example of turn-of-the-20th-century school architecture.

principal-delayed federal loans. However, private educational loans are available to credit-worthy students at approximately 8.5 percent interest. The minimum loan is $1,000, the maximum is $7,500, and repayment begins immediately after the loan is obtained.

The 1,500 students, most of whom work a second job on The Strip in addition to their campus work assignment, are an important addition to the area's employment scene. The bright-eyed and eager young man or woman who serves you your dinner, takes your ticket, parks your car, or dips your ice cream for your after-show snack might very well be a local college student.

COLUMBIA COLLEGE, OZARK BRANCH
741 North 20th St., Ozark
(417) 581-0367, (800) 928-8843
www.ccis.edu

Located in the Diamond Center at the US 65 and MO 14 junction in Ozark, this extended-studies branch of Columbia College offers an array of night classes for those who work full-time and still want to work toward that college degree. The branch opened in 1997 to serve those who need classes offered during evenings and in short sessions. The main campus, located in Columbia, dates from 1851 as the Christian Female College, the first four-year women's college chartered by a state legislature west of the Mississippi River. In 1970 the college changed both its name and student population, becoming Columbia College, a coeducational, four-year liberal-arts institution.

Although it retains a covenant with the Christian Church (Disciples of Christ), Columbia College is a nonsectarian institution. It awards more than $14 million annually in federal, state, and institutional funds for need-based and merit-based scholarships, grants, and loans. The Extended Studies Division at Ozark offers relevant degree programs, convenient scheduling, and affordable tuition at $150 per credit hour in 2009. Classes are offered in eight-week sessions in the evenings and on weekends. Class size at the Ozark branch is small, often fewer than 10, so students get lots of individual attention.

SPRINGFIELD COLLEGES

The state's third-largest city spills over from Greene County into Christian County to the south, and the city's south side is the area that has shown most of the growth. When Ozark, Nixa, and surrounding towns are included, this metropolis has a population of almost 300,000. Springfield is home to nine institutions of higher learning, including three Bible colleges (Evangel University of the Assemblies of God, Baptist Bible College, and Central Bible College) and two for-profit technical/career colleges (Springfield College and Vatterott College). The high ratio of students to general population makes for a city with a plethora of fast-food restaurants as well as an active and interesting nightlife scene, mostly centered in the downtown area. The increasingly easy access between Branson and Springfield makes for mobile students who partake of the advantages of both a major metropolitan area and a national tourist playground.

i **If you're on the campus of the College of the Ozarks, visit Williams Memorial Chapel. The impressive neo-Gothic structure was built by student labor, from quarrying the stone and laying it, to the oak paneling and furniture.**

DRURY UNIVERSITY
900 North Benton Ave.
(417) 873-7879, (800) 922-2274
www.drury.edu

The oldest of Springfield's colleges, Drury was founded in 1873. Its 88-acre campus is situated in the elegant, old part of the city. The college has an enrollment of 1,550 and offers both bachelor's and master's degrees. President Todd Parnell, 16th president, Drury alumnus, and adjunct professor, has taken the reins from former president John Moore, who had done much to reaffirm the college's excellent academic reputation after a decade and a half during which the school lived on its past reputation. It has an undergraduate faculty of 108, of which 98 percent have terminal degrees. Drury has an endowment of just over $100 million, and students paid tuition and fees of $17,900, plus room and board of $6,934, in 2009. The college has one of the highest academic standards in the state, and no student who has an ACT score below 25 is accepted. Notable alumni of Drury include John Morris, founder and president of Bass Pro Shops, Inc.; Tom Whitlock, Academy Award winner; and Betty Dukert, producer of *Meet the Press*. The college often features nationally known guest speakers, poets, and writers.

EVANGEL UNIVERSITY
1111 North Glenstone Ave.
(417) 865-2815, (800) 382-6435
www.evangel.edu
Evangel University is the four-year arts and sciences college of the Assemblies of God, whose international headquarters is in Springfield. Founded in 1955, it is situated on Springfield's north side on a 60-acre campus. It offers both bachelor of arts and bachelor of science degrees, with master's degree programs in education, psychology and guidance and counseling. The college has an enrollment of 1,800. Its students come from 50 states and territories and 12 other countries. Students pay tuition of $7,525 per semester. Faculty consists of 90 full-time and 50 part-time instructors. Evangel has recently been on a building binge, and since it is relatively young to begin with, its campus structures present a clean, modern appearance.

i The Ozarks have made their contribution to the world of theater. John Goodman and Kathleen Turner are MSU alums. Actors Brad Pitt, Robert Cummings, Don Johnson, and Tess Harper are from the area, as is Pulitzer Prize–winning playwright Lanford Wilson.

MISSOURI STATE UNIVERSITY
901 South National Ave.
(417) 836-5000
www.missouristate.edu
Missouri State University (formerly Southwest Missouri State University) founded in 1905, is the state's second-largest university, and though it offers both bachelor's and master's degrees, its focus is on undergraduate education. It is a public, coed university supported by the state, but it has an endowment of $28 million. The university has been the fastest-growing campus in the last decade, and it has an enrollment of 19,489, with an additional 1,834 at the West Plains campus. Since it has a large number of applicants, MSU has been able to raise the standards for admission, with an ACT average of 23.4. It has a faculty of 718. Tuition in spring 2009 was $3,128 per semester for residents and $5,768 for nonresidents. Notable alumni include David Glass, retired CEO of Wal-Mart; actors John Goodman, Tess Harper, and Kathleen Turner; and developer John Q. Hammons. The university figures prominently in the area's cultural events. The Juanita K. Hammons Center, the home of the Springfield Symphony Orchestra, frequently features cultural events and touring Broadway productions. Individual academic departments often host speakers or programs.

The university's summer Tent Theater offers a repertory bill each year that has become famous. The campus is also home to KSMU, the area's NPR station, with satellite rebroadcast towers in Branson, Joplin, Mountain Grove, Sarcoxie, Neosho, and West Plains. The campus also hosts the PBS affiliate KOZK.

OZARK TECHNICAL COLLEGE
933 East Central
(417) 895-7000
www.otc.edu
Founded in 1990 to provide technical education for area students, the OTC district encompasses eight counties in the immediate Springfield area, including Stone and Christian Counties. It pro-

vides high school technical programs, customized training, continuing education, adult basic education, and college credit courses leading to an associate degree. The college, with its motto of "Learn a Living," has met with enthusiastic success and growth. Its enrollment has jumped from 1,198 in 1991, its first semester, to 10,249 in 2009. That growth has made it the third-largest community college in Missouri and the second-largest higher education institution in Springfield. Its main campus is at the corner of Chestnut Expressway and National Avenue. As one of the fastest-growing colleges in the nation, OTC has added campuses in Lebanon, Waynesville, Ozark, and Branson. The college offers an associate of applied science degree, one-year certificates in a variety of technical programs, and a two-year associate of arts degree. It has a full-time faculty of 140, with an additional 400 continuing-education instructors and part-time faculty. Tuition is $78 per credit hour for in-district residents, $108 for out-of-district residents, and $140.50 for out-of-state students. Financial aid by federal Pell Grants and guaranteed student loans are available, as well as other scholarship and financial aid packages.

VATTEROTT COLLEGE
3850 South Campbell
(417) 831-8116
www.vatterott-college.edu
All Vatterott College programs are based on a successful formula of specialized, technology-focused, hands-on training in the fastest-growing industries. The college was founded in 1969 and now serves nearly 9,000 students per year at 16 Midwestern campuses. Vatterott College's hands-on training method of instruction equips students with the specific skills that are desired by local employers. All courses are geared to the student's field of study. Classes are available in both morning and evening schedules.

WEBSTER UNIVERSITY
321 West Battlefield Ave.
(417) 883-0200
www.webster.edu/ozarks
From its home campus in St. Louis, Webster University reaches out to encompass a network of more than 70 campuses through the United States, Europe, Bermuda, and Asia. It is accredited by the North Central Association of Colleges and Schools, including all of its undergraduate and graduate levels at all locations where the university offers programs. Webster University opened Its Springfield campus in 1998 to offer the greater Springfield area seven master's degree programs in convenient one-night-a-week formats with a nine-week term. Webster was welcomed with twice the number of anticipated enrollment, and enrollment has grown significantly over the years. The graduate degrees offered are: master of business administration, human resources management, human resources development, health services management, management, computer resources information management, and business.

i **Education isn't just for the young. Branson and the Ozarks offer a number of Elderhostels, weeklong educational programs for those who are older than 55. It's a great way to see and learn about the area and its culture and history. Learn more by calling (877) 426-8056 or visiting www .elderhostel.org.**

Child Care
Beyond the beautiful scenery, the shows and attractions, and the lights of The Strip, Branson is known for being a boomtown. The tremendous influx of people during the Branson boom resulted in an increased demand for child care. Since so many of the jobs in the area are seasonal and often pay minimum wage or slightly higher, many families depend on two paychecks. Such families need child care.

For an area as kid-friendly as Branson (see the Kidstuff chapter), surprisingly few alternatives to traditional child care exist.

Traditionally, couples didn't need child care. They had relatives and older siblings to take care of children in emergency situations. And children in the Ozarks were expected to take care of themselves after they got a bit older. Women didn't usually work outside the home, and if they did, they were frowned upon. Times have changed. Now most women in the area work outside the home, and the need for child care has increased, but alternatives haven't. And attitudes have been slow to change. Several years ago, just down the road from Branson in Berryville, Arkansas, a pastor of a Baptist church closed the church's day-care center, saying that it "only encouraged women to work outside the home merely to be able to buy microwaves and bigger TVs." It was a controversial (and not a very popular) decision.

Working women and dual-income families in the area worry about finding adequate child care. Most can't afford a full-time nanny or au pair, and if they can, they probably won't be able to find one here. Most can't depend on relatives, either. People moving into the area don't have relatives here, nor do they have contacts. Newcomers should immediately establish a network by asking their employers and fellow workers for

i **If you need a list of day-care providers, call (800) 743-8497, the Child Care Resource and Referral Project of the Council of Churches of the Ozarks. They will take into account your needs and requests, then provide you with some options and a list of various day-care providers. But be warned: most providers will put you on a waiting list.**

recommendations. Another source is churches. Many churches, recognizing the need for child and day care, have built child-care facilities and operate day-care centers, so check your church or call churches in the community. Be warned, many church facilities have waiting lists. Also be aware of Missouri's standards when it comes to child care. Applications for being a day-care provider are available to anyone. An array of types of facilities exists: day-care homes, unlicensed (with four children or fewer); day-care homes, licensed (up to 10 children); group homes, licensed (10 to 20 children); and day-care centers, licensed (21 or more kids). Related children, even second and third cousins of the provider, are not included in this count. Then there is a category of church-operated day-care centers, which are license-exempt, but many make the extra effort to become licensed. Private schools also can be unlicensed child-care providers. Licensed facilities have annual inspections and must meet certain safety and sanitation standards, and their enrollment numbers are controlled. Unlicensed facilities have no monitoring. The lack of adequate care results in thousands of providers that each care for a single child. What we call babysitting is probably the biggest underground institution in the area. You can find excellent single-child providers, but it is up to you to do any checking of facilities and evaluating of competence. It is probably best that any day-care provider you choose be licensed. The facility will meet certain minimum standards, and it will be checked and inspected every so often by officials.

MEDIA

Since the tri-lakes area is not exactly a major population center, the news on any given day might include a report from a city council meeting, the score from last night's high school football game, or a story about a local charity fund-raiser. Since life is pretty laid-back in the Ozarks, so is the news. If you want to find out what is going on in the national or international scene, you can tune into CNN on one of the local cable stations. Most motels have cable TV, and most residents are either on cable or satellite. If you like that feel of paper, you can pick up a copy of the *Kansas City Star* newspaper, which is sold in stands at area motels and gas stations. The *Springfield News-Leader* also runs Associated Press articles of national and international significance. The three major area television stations, KYTV, KOLR, and KSPR in Springfield, focus on events primarily in southwestern Missouri and north-central Arkansas.

Those in the business of providing information to tri-lakes area visitors know that when you come here to relax you're probably less concerned about foreign trade policies than you are with finding the best new restaurant or the hottest new music show. The Branson Tri-Lakes Daily News usually contains one or two pages of entertainment stories each day, including interviews with the stars, announcements for new shows, and show reviews. There are a number of other publications too numerous to list here, which are printed weekly or monthly, that give more specific information on the shows, restaurants, lodging facilities, and special events. Most of these free publications can be found at any one of the area visitor information centers.

As you drive into Ozark Mountain Country you can begin to pick up many of the radio stations listed here, starting about 100 miles away. Expect when you get into the hills to have FM stations fade out at times, and as you go into a valley you can expect the same from mobile phones. Surprisingly enough, the music mix for an area of this size is quite varied. Most locals prefer country music, but since radio stations want to attract visitor listeners, too, everyone gets a nice variety of formats from which to choose.

Publications

Though the tri-lakes area offers only three newspapers, the *Branson Tri-Lakes Daily News,* the *Branson Daily Independent,* and the *Springfield News-Leader,* you can find a number of good tourist magazines at any tourist information center, especially the Branson/Lakes Area Chamber of Commerce (located on MO 248 at US 65). Each year the chamber publishes *Slip Away,* a comprehensive guide to area music shows, attractions, lodging, restaurants, and the lakes. You can request a free copy of *Slip Away* by calling (417) 334-4136, or stop by their visitor center and pick up a copy for a small charge.

BEST READ GUIDE/BRANSON
116 Wintergreen Rd.
(417) 336-7323
www.joplinglobeonline.com/branson_new
If you're looking for a detailed show schedule or coupons for motels, restaurants, attractions, or shows, grab a free copy of *Best Read Guide.* This pocket-size guide prints four times a year and contains feature stories on the music shows, shopping locations, and special events in Branson.

BRANSON DAILY INDEPENDENT
704 Veterans Blvd.
(417) 334-2285

The *Branson Daily Independent* is published Sunday, Wednesday, and Friday by Ozark Mountain Newspapers, which also publishes the *Taney County Times* and the *Stone County Gazette*. The *BDI* focuses on Branson and Taney County issues and has earned an early reputation of being a maverick and addressing community issues with little concern about offending the local powers that be. It is distributed free at many locations around town.

BRANSON TRI-LAKES DAILY NEWS
200 Industrial Park Dr., Hollister
(417) 334-3161, (800) 490-8020
www.bransondailynews.com
In the early '90s the weekly *Branson Beacon* became the *Branson Tri-Lakes Daily News*. It's not really a daily, since it publishes Wednesdays and Saturdays.

Each Wednesday the newspaper prints a local calendar of events covering area organizations and their meeting dates and times. The newspaper's primary focus is local topics, including government, the courts, schools, and, of course, entertainment. Each issue features a section on religion, business, education, or lifestyles, rotating throughout the week. Local columnists generally steer away from controversial topics, and editorials rarely take unpopular positions on community issues.

In addition to the newspaper, Tri-Lakes Newspapers, Inc. publishes the monthly *Ozark Mountain Visitor* tabloid, which is distributed locally in racks. The free publication includes feature stories on the music shows, restaurants, and attractions. The *Branson Tri-Lakes Daily News* office is located 2 miles south of Branson in the Hollister Industrial Park. The average Sunday circulation for the paper is around 12,500. The paper is distributed in racks and to subscribers through the mail.

THE NEW BRANSON'S REVIEW MAGAZINE
P.O. Box 328, Branson, MO 65615
(417) 334-6627
www.bransonsreview.com
This magazine focuses on the entertainment scene in Branson. Printed five times a year, the publication has a loyal subscriber base and is geared toward letting folks who live out of the area know the inside scoop on changes in the music show business. Each issue's cover story profiles an area entertainer or special event. There's also a calendar of events and a section on fun and exciting things for children to do in Branson. You can pick up a copy of the magazine at many of the area's retail stores.

THE OZARKS MOUNTAINEER
Editorial: 815 Lee St., Branson, MO 65616
(281) 516-2822, (866) 784-9444
www.ozarksmountaineer.com
If you really want to learn about the lifestyle of the Ozarker and the infinite variety of what the Ozarks has to offer both visitors and residents, get a copy of *The Ozarks Mountaineer* magazine. This bimonthly publication has focused on significant topics past and present for over half a century. A pool of local freelance writers and the subscribers provides colorful stories on early life in the Ozarks, the land, arts, and cultural events. The magazine has music and book reviews and a calendar of events that covers both Missouri and Arkansas. You can find a copy in retail shops throughout the tri-lakes area, or you may subscribe.

SHEPHERD OF THE HILLS GAZETTE
5586 MO 76 West
(417) 334-4191
www.shepherdgazette.com
This free tourist guide is published four times each year and features timely articles on entertainment in Branson. It also contains a show listing, an area map, and feature stories on outdoor activities in the Ozarks. Writer Linda Burlingame keeps on top of the entertainment scene in Branson, and you can read her informative articles when you visit the Web site. You can find the *Shepherd of the Hills Gazette* in racks, or you may subscribe for just $10 per year or an Internet version for free.

SPRINGFIELD NEWS-LEADER
651 Boonville, Springfield
(417) 836-1100
www.news-leader.com

This daily newspaper, owned by Gannett River States Publishing Corp., is the area's largest source for local, national, and international news. The Friday edition contains a special tabloid insert called *Weekend* that includes information on area entertainment and cultural events, including the music show scene in Branson. While the *Springfield News-Leader* does devote most of its coverage to hard news and focuses primarily on the Springfield area, it also covers events in Branson. The Sunday edition, with a circulation of approximately 102,000, features a section called *Life and Times*, with feature articles on interesting people, events, and places. The newspaper offers home delivery to subscribers in the Branson area and can be picked up in local racks.

SUNNY DAY GUIDE
(417) 336-6932
www.sunnydayguide.com

This free pocketbook-size guide is filled with coupons, maps, a calendar of events, ads, and articles of interest to the Branson visitor. You can find copies at the Branson/Lakes Area Chamber of Commerce, motels, and many ticket and brochure outlets. Visit the Web site for a Branson calendar of events and a listing of theaters and shows.

TANEY COUNTY TIMES
253 Main St., Forsyth
(417) 546-3305 (home office)

Published each Wednesday, the *Taney County Times*, owned by Ozark Mountain Newspapers, focuses on county government, schools, churches, family news, and what's happening in the Taney County communities of Bradleyville, Kirbyville, and Taneyville, to name just a few. The staff sometimes profiles interesting people or past events in Taney County, and the feature articles cut right to the heart of what life around

here past and present is really like. You can pick up a copy of this newspaper in racks, or you may subscribe.

TRAVELHOST AND HAPPY CAMPER
208 East College St., Suite 402
(417) 334-5297
www.travelhost.com

Happy Camper is published by *TRAVELHOST* and both feature lots of advertising by the Branson entertainment and shopping industry, as well as articles about area entertainers, shows and venues, and shopping. It often has several pages of money-saving coupons. The free magazine can be found at area motels, the Branson/Lakes Area Chamber of Commerce, and ticket and brochure outlets around town. It's a great way to get information about Branson attractions that advertise, but remember there are many non-advertising entities of interest in Branson. Visit the Web site and you can read the Branson edition online.

Radio Stations

Locals have their favorite picks, and KRZK 106.3 FM, Branson's Hometown Radio, usually comes out on top in surveys. The *Steve and Janet Show* with Steve Willoughby and Janet Ellis will wake you up and have you asking, "What did she say?" Not because of anything off-color, but because together Steve and Janet make a wacky comedy duo. Another favorite talk show with a wide following is the *Woody & Janet Show* on KGBX (105.9) 5-9 a.m. iFavorite country music stations are KHOZ 102.9 FM in Harrison, Arkansas and KTTS 94.7 FM, out of Springfield, the area's largest country station. If you are looking for National Public Radio affiliates, dial 90.5 FM or 91.1 FM in Springfield. Missouri State University's KSMU saturates the Ozarks with "repeater stations" in West Plains, Mountain Grove, Branson-Point Lookout, Joplin, and Neosho.

Adult Standard
KOMC 100.1 FM
(417) 335-8255

Big Band
KTOZ 1060 AM
(417) 832-1060

Christian
KADI 99.5 FM (REPUBLIC, MO)
(417) 831-0995
www.kadi.com
(contemporary)

KLFC 88.1 FM (BRANSON)
(417) 334-5532
www.klfcradio.com
(contemporary)

KLFJ 1550 AM
(417) 831-5535
(easy listening, talk)

KWFC 89.1 FM (SPRINGFIELD)
(417) 869-0891
(southern gospel)

College Radio (Point Lookout)
KCOZ 91.7 FM
(417) 334-6411, ext. 4279
(jazz, blues, New Age, soft rock; College of Ozarks)

KSMS 90.5 FM (SPRINGFIELD)
(417) 836-5878
(National Public Radio, Missouri State University, Springfield)

KSMU 91.1 FM
(417) 836-5878
www.ksmu.org
(National Public Radio, classical, variety; Missouri State University, Springfield)

Contemporary
KGBX 105.9 FM (SPRINGFIELD)
(417) 890-5555
www.kgbx.com
(adult contemporary, talk)

Country
KGMY 100.5 FM
(417) 890-5555
(country hits)

KHOZ 102.9 FM
(417) 334-6750

KLTO 96.5 FM
(417) 862-9965

KRZK 106.3 FM (BRANSON)
202 Courtney St.
(417) 334-6003
www.hometowndailynews.com

KTTS 94.7 FM
(417) 577-7000

KTTS 1260 AM
(417) 577-7070

Easy Listening/Nostalgia
KOMC 100.1 FM (KIMBERLING CITY)
(417) 334-6003

KTXR 101.3 FM (SPRINGFIELD)
(417) 862-3751
www.radiospringfield.com

News
KWTO 560 AM (SPRINGFIELD)
(417) 862-5800
www.radiospringfield.com
(news, talk shows)

Oldies
KOSP 105.1 FM (WILLARD)
(417) 886-5677
www.star1051.fm

Rock
KTOZ 95.5 FM (PLEASANT HOPE)
(417) 377-7955
www.alice955.com
(alternative/'80s, '90s rock)

KXUS 97.3 FM (SPRINGFIELD)
(417) 890-5555
www.us97.com
(classic rock)

Television Stations

The major network affiliate stations covering Ozark Mountain Country are KYTV Channel 3, KSPR Channel 33, KOZK Channel 21, and KOLR Channel 10, based in nearby Springfield. These stations primarily focus on events in Springfield but occasionally cover significant events in the Branson area. Branson is served by Suddenlink Cable, which carries each station listed in this section. The only newscast originating from Branson is produced by the Vacation Channel. *Ozark Mountain Country Update* is taped weekly and features news about area events and entertainment.

RFD-TV
RFD-TV The Theatre
4080 West Hwy 76
(417) 332-2282
www.rfdtv.com

RFD-TV is not a station but a 24 hour television network dedicated to serving the needs and interests of rural America and agriculture. The corporate and national sales office is based in Omaha, Nebraska. The channel is produced and uplinked via satellite to all 50 states from NorthStar Studios, in Nashville, Tennessee and is carried locally by Suddenlink Cable, Channel 4. The network has the RFD-TV Theatre in Branson, from which some of its broadcast materials originates. If you take in a show that is being taped for broadcast, you might be able to go home and see yourself on TV!

CHANNEL 10, KOLR
2650 East Division, Springfield
(417) 862-1010
www.kolr.com

KOLR is the area's CBS affiliate and provides the most complete news and information on Branson. KOLR is broadcast on Suddenlink Cable channel 10.

CHANNEL 31, KWBM
(417) 336-0031
www.mytv31.com

With offices in Springfield, tower in Taneyville, and studios in Little Rock, Arkansas, this affiliate of Warner Brothers Network features syndicated information and entertainment programming. You can find the station on Suddenlink Cable channel 12.

CHANNEL 33, KSPR
999 W. Sunshine St., Springfield
(417) 831-1333
www.kspr.com

In 2006 the FCC license for KSPR was acquired by Perkin Media with the station run by KY3, Inc. and Schurz Communications. ABC affiliate KSPR airs daily local newscasts as well as standard ABC programming. KSPR is broadcast on Suddenlink Cable channel 8.

CHANNEL 3, KYTV
999 West Sunshine, Springfield
(417) 266-3000
www.ky3.com

The area's NBC affiliate, KYTV broadcasts local news programs at least four times each day. KYTV is broadcast on Cable channel 3.

CHANNEL 21, KOZK
901 South National, Springfield
(417) 836-3500
www.optv.org

This station broadcasts local and national programming provided by PBS. A good way to pick up some local history and cultures is to tune in to the popular *Ozarks Watch*. KOZK is broadcast on Suddenlink Cable channel 13.

CHANNEL 27, KDEB
3000 Cherry St., Springfield
(417) 862-2727
www.ozarksfirst.com

Home of Fox programming, this independent station carries a variety of reruns and cartoon action shows for children each weekday beginning at 2 p.m. KDEB is broadcast on Suddenlink-Cable channel 7.

THE VACATION CHANNEL
225 Violyn St.
(417) 334-1200
www.tvcbranson.com

The Vacation Channel is an excellent source of information for the new visitor. Locally produced programming is designed to familiarize you with the roads, music shows, restaurants, lodging, and special events. You can tune into their local news program, which runs a number of times each day or the local weather reports. The Vacation Channel is broadcast on Suddenlink Cable channel 6.

Cable Television

MEDIACOM
1533 S Enterprise Ave., Springfield
(417) 875-5500, (800) 234-2157
www.mediacomtoday.com

Mediacom services Springfield and a number of small towns in the area.

SUDDENLINK CABLE
310 Walnut Extension
(417) 339-2200, (877) 869-7897
www.suddenlink.com

Suddenlink serves the Branson, Indian Point, Venice on the Lake, and F Highway areas along with Compton Ridge, Rockaway Beach, and Merriam Woods.

WORSHIP

Long before the area surrounding Branson was called Ozark Mountain Country, it was known as Shepherd of the Hills country. Many tourists who visited these parts in the early 1900s came here as a result of the writings of a young preacher named Harold Bell Wright, who, with publication of his enormously famous novel, *The Shepherd of the Hills,* some say single-handedly started the tourist trade here.

When Wright came to these parts in 1896, he did not come to preach, or even to write, but to restore his health. Yet he became both a preacher and a writer. The God-fearing people he befriended and the peaceful inspiration of the hills led to the writing of his tale.

Today Branson and Ozark Mountain Country are still influenced by Wright's story and by the same kind of religious climate he encountered a century ago. Many of the shows on The Strip include an "obligatory" gospel or religious number, because organizers believe that's what visitors expect and want. Some visitors, undoubtedly, will find the prevalent right-wing Christianity and apparent seamless merging of politics and religion offensive, and the area and some shows have come under recent criticism for the "one-way" attitudes that prevail.

In the days of schoolhouse services and traveling preachers, the church often served as the center of social activity in any given community. It was more the rule than the exception for people of varied denominational beliefs to all worship under one roof.

While the Sunday service was the tie that bound them together, parishioners could turn any wedding, funeral, pie supper, birthday, or holiday into a religious gathering. In the absence of a religious leader, the elders would gather up the younger folks to sing hymns and tell Bible stories.

In Dr. Robert Gilmore's book, *Ozark Baptizings, Hangings and Other Diversions,* he tells of the struggle many smaller area churches encountered in their quest for regular visits from traveling preachers. Many of the preachers did not request or expect payment for their services

since they routinely held other jobs; however, they were more apt to show up if the promise of a hearty meal was part of the deal.

One of the highlights of religious life was the camp meeting, a weeklong, sometimes even monthlong, revival full of all the spectacle of a Branson music show. Folks from miles around would gather in a tent, a shed, a brush arbor, or even outside to sing, sermonize, repent, and convert lost souls. Today some of the local theaters offer special musical services reminiscent of old-fashioned revivals.

While the method of worship has changed in the tri-lakes area over the decades, the makeup of denominational faiths really hasn't. Protestant churches, primarily Baptist, Methodist, Assembly of God, Pentecostal, and Church of Christ, encompass the majority of faiths. However, Branson has one Roman Catholic church and one Mormon church, and Rogersville is home to the nearest Jewish synagogue. A number of nondenominational churches can also be found in the area.

Most area churches welcome out-of-town visitors, but you might want to call first to con-

ℹ️ Springfield is home of the world headquarters for the Assemblies of God, 1445 Boonville Ave., Springfield, MO 65802-1894, (417) 862-2781.

firm the worship times. The Branson/Lakes Area Chamber of Commerce, (417) 334-4136, prints an annual community guide with a listing of area churches including their phone numbers.

The area's only Christian conference center, Stonecroft Conference Center, (417) 334-2404, 590 Windmill Rd., Hollister, hosts 12 weeks of Bible conferences each year. Each week you can hear a different speaker and musical guest. Stonecroft has 68 rooms, a 240-seat dining room, and an auditorium that seats up to 450 people. In addition to programs for adults, teens can attend Bible study programs during the summer. You can obtain information about and directions to Stonecroft Ministries by logging on to www .stonecroft.org or calling (800) 766-1337.

We even have a national religious show which originates in the area. *The Jim Bakker Show* (180 Grace Chapel Rd., Blue Eye, MO 65611) tapes every weekday at noon at Morningside Church, at nearby Blue Eye. Visitors are welcome. You can attend church and the show on vacation, then go home and see yourself on the later broadcast. Visit www.jimbakkershow.com for information. Revival Fires Ministries, based in Branson West, (417) 338-2422, holds gatherings at the Grand Palace and packs in more than 20,000 people over the course of the three-day events. Dozens of speakers, performers, and religious leaders come to the gatherings. For more information on Revival Fires Ministries, call the above number or visit www.revivalfires.org.

i A number of Branson theaters have been bought by church groups or for church groups and thus pulled off the tax rolls over the past several years to become mega-churches or conference centers. These include the old Mel Tillis Theatre (now the Tri-Lakes Center), The Yellow Ribbon Theatre, the Barbara Fairchild Theatre (now the Skyline Baptist Church), the Remington Theatre, and the White House Theatre.

i In Eureka Springs, Arkansas, you'll want to see Thorncrown Chapel, an architectural masterpiece made entirely of glass and pine. The chapel welcomes visitors to stop in and look around. (See the Day Trips chapter for more information.)

Musical Worship Services

In the last few years, a number of Branson theaters have begun offering free Sunday-morning worship services. Since many of the music shows are closed on Sunday, theater owners decided to bring in ministers and special musical guests to provide a unique service to visitors. Most of the services go heavy on the music and light on the preaching, with some exceptions. All of the following services are free. A donation may be requested.

The Grand Old Gospel Hour at Dick Clark's American Bandstand Theater, (417) 337-8888, is hosted by Sam Stauffer, who delivers a 30-minute sermon preceded by 45 minutes of music performed by a different area entertainer each week. Services begin at 10 a.m. For more information log onto their Web site at www.gospelhour.org.

You can usually find fliers advertising musical worship services at various shows and at ticket and brochure outlets.

INDEX

ABOUT THE AUTHOR

Fred Pfister is a native Ozarker (read REAL "hill-billy") who was born and raised on the old Emmett Kelly farm (Weary Willie of circus clown fame) in Houston in Texas County. He brags that it's the biggest town (2,000 population) in the biggest county (in area) in Missouri—as big as the entire state of Rhode Island. He was delivered by a neighbor because the doctor got there late, who took only a piece of apple pie in payment for "checking things out" after the fact, one of the cheapest deliveries on record.

He is a retired English professor who writes and edits. He spends time writing; teaching special classes; and speaking on Missouri place names, folklore, and other language and litera-ture topics. He also portrays poet Walt Whitman in a Chautauqua presentation, the reason for the "gray beard look" he wears.

He has a degree from The School of the Ozarks (where he was in the college's first graduating class and where he taught for 26 years). He worked his way through college as a radio announcer and as an actor in the college's local Beacon Hill summer stock theater. He has an M.A. from the University of Arkansas and a doctorate from the Univer-sity of Mississippi. He's the author of various scholarly articles and poetry and author of *The Littlest Baby: A Handbook for Parents of Premature Children*, published by Prentice-Hall. Currently, he is editor of the *Ozarks Mountaineer*, a magazine "more timeless than timely" and dedicated to

covering the Ozarks' history, culture, and folklore with articles about Ozarkers by Ozarkers.

Fred is active in Branson's community life. He is a member and past president of the Bran-son Arts Council. He is membership chair of the Ozarks Writers League, and a past president, and he has served on the Missouri Ethics Commission. Hobbies include reading, writing poetry, garden-ing, canoeing Ozark streams, and beekeeping.

He lives only a block off Branson's strip and almost in spittin' distance of Lake Taneycomo with his wife Faye, a potter and retired art teacher from the Hollister Public Schools. His daughter Falecia, the former pound and a half preemie, also lives in Branson. Sharing the wooded acre-age in Branson with wife Faye are the "backyard bees," over a half million strong.

Travel Like a Pro

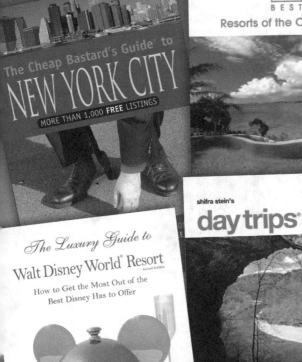